BOOKS BY ALLAN NEVINS
PUBLISHED BY CHARLES SCRIBNER'S SONS

THE DIARY OF JOHN QUINCY ADAMS (*edited by Allan Nevins*)
THE ORDEAL OF THE UNION
ORDEAL OF THE UNION (*two volumes*)
THE EMERGENCE OF LINCOLN (*two volumes*)
THE WAR FOR THE UNION: THE IMPROVISED WAR, 1861–1862
THE WAR FOR THE UNION: WAR BECOMES REVOLUTION, 1862–1863
A CENTURY OF CARTOONS (*in collaboration with Frank Weitenkampf*)
THIS IS ENGLAND TODAY
JOHN D. ROCKEFELLER, THE HEROIC AGE OF AMERICAN ENTERPRISE, 1940
STUDY IN POWER: JOHN D. ROCKEFELLER, INDUSTRIALIST AND PHILANTHROPIST, 1953
FORD: THE TIMES, THE MAN, THE COMPANY
   A History of Henry Ford, The Ford Motor Company, and The Automotive
   Industry, 1863–1915 (*with Frank Ernest Hill*)
FORD: EXPANSION AND CHALLENGE: 1915–1933 (*with Frank Ernest Hill*)
JOHN D. ROCKEFELLER
One Volume Condensation by William Greenleaf of STUDY IN POWER

PUBLISHED ELSEWHERE

ILLINOIS (*Oxford Series on American Universities*)
THE AMERICAN STATES DURING AND AFTER THE REVOLUTION
THE EVENING POST, A CENTURY OF JOURNALISM
AMERICAN SOCIAL HISTORY RECORDED BY BRITISH TRAVELLERS
THE EMERGENCE OF MODERN AMERICA, 1865–1877
GROVER CLEVELAND, A STUDY IN COURAGE
HAMILTON FISH, THE INNER HISTORY OF THE GRANT ADMINISTRATION
ABRAM S. HEWITT, WITH SOME ACCOUNT OF PETER COOPER
THE GATEWAY TO HISTORY
FRÉMONT, PATHMAKER OF THE WEST
THE WORLD OF ELI WHITNEY (*with Jeannette Mirsky*)
AMERICA, THE STORY OF A FREE PEOPLE (*with H. S. Commager*)
THE STATESMANSHIP OF THE CIVIL WAR
THE UNITED STATES IN A CHAOTIC WORLD

AS EDITOR

LETTERS OF GROVER CLEVELAND
SELECT WRITINGS OF ABRAM S. HEWITT
THE DIARY OF PHILIP HONE
THE DIARY OF JAMES K. POLK
DIARY OF GEORGE TEMPLETON STRONG (*with M. H. Thomas*)
LETTERS AND JOURNALS OF BRAND WHITLOCK
FRÉMONT'S NARRATIVES OF EXPLORATION
THE HERITAGE OF AMERICA (*with H. S. Commager*)
THE LEATHERSTOCKING SAGA
THE STRATEGY OF PEACE *by John F. Kennedy*

HERBERT H. LEHMAN

and His Era

Herbert H. Lehman and His Era

by

ALLAN NEVINS

CHARLES SCRIBNER'S SONS

New York

A-3.62[V]

PRINTED IN THE UNITED STATES OF AMERICA

Library of Congress Catalog Card Number 63-8464

Contents

Preface

My preparation for writing this book began, indirectly and remotely, many years ago when as an editorial worker on the *New York World* I watched the scene in Albany with curious interest. The spectacle presented by the annual legislative session was by no means wholly edifying. Each house was usually controlled by a small group of iron-fisted leaders who kept what was euphemistically called debate under tight control. Each chamber also held a large proportion of members who expected to make a living out of politics. Although some men of fine character and ability sat in the legislature, the general intellectual level was no higher than in most state capitals. The level of independence was probably lower, for economic interests were especially powerful in New York, and the want of a direct primary system made it harder for independent men to get a start. Legislation moved in the first months of each session with tortoise speed; then in the final week an appalling spate of bills broke through the barriers. The fact that various bills created neat local benefits or fat perquisites helped the leaders, some of them bosslets taking orders from the bosses, to maintain discipline in the ranks. Altogether, legislative Albany had its seamy aspect.

Fortunately, the governor's mansion between the two world wars was occupied by three men, Alfred E. Smith, Franklin D. Roosevelt, and Herbert H. Lehman, who lifted themselves and New York to a proud eminence in the nation. Differing sharply in traits and gifts, they all displayed a resourceful, courageous, and constructive leadership. The work they did has in part been fully described. Already the career and personality of Al Smith have been carefully depicted by Henry Pringle, Oscar Handlin, Emily Smith Warner, Robert Moses, and others. An array of scholarly and penetrating volumes has done justice to FDR's New York years; the books of E. K. Lindley, Bernard Bellush, Frank Freidel, Arthur M. Schlesinger, Jr., Alfred B. Rollins, Jr., and MacGregor Burns. The record written by Herbert H. Lehman, who like his predecessors went on to larger affairs, has alone been neglected. This, no doubt, is because he is still active; and though history and biography nowadays crowd closer on the heels of events than formerly, most writers are fearful that, as Lord Bacon put it, in thus crowding forward they may get kicked in the teeth.

Though valuing perspective, and insisting upon absolute independence of judgment, I feel that in this instance the advantages of a close contemporaneity outweigh the disadvantages. I have tried to write an objective biography. My narrative is always sympathetic, usually approbatory, and often admiring, for Mr. Lehman's character and achievement demand such attitudes. Yet I have tried to obtain facts and interpretations from his opponents no less than from his friends, and have candidly set down conclusions adverse to him when they seem warranted. It has been an incalculable advantage to have the help of Mr. Lehman, who is as much given to honest self-criticism as any man, in elucidating certain situations. It has been of immense advantage also to be able to talk or correspond with a long roster of men and women who, as supporters or opponents, knew him well; some of whom vanished even while I worked. The difficulties of the task have seldom lain in the circumstance that I worked with recent materials upon a figure still busy and influential. They have lain primarily in the fact that the career here chronicled has covered six full decades of public activity, and has reached into highly diverse departments of business, state affairs, national concerns, international labors, and philanthropy. I would have liked to dwell in more detail on many an event or episode, but considerations of space forbade.

Despite all the compressions of the book, despite all the shortcomings of the author, readers, I hope, will feel the exciting character of the many-sided career here narrated, and catch some inspiration from the selfless idealism which animated the man here drawn.

Allan Nevins

THE HUNTINGTON LIBRARY

Chapter I

WHEN
COTTON SEEMED KING

Usually the little boys ate their breakfast together in the front basement of the house, looking up into Sixty-second Street; but one autumn morning in 1886 found them rather excitedly devouring their oatmeal in the large family dining room on the first floor. "Babette," their father had said, "Herbert begins his new school today. . . . I'll take him over with Irving before nine. Let them eat upstairs this morning." And their mother, feeling that it was a memorable day, had seated them with their elder brothers and sisters.

Herbert, now eight, was stocky, active, and intensely interested in everything: in his brother Arthur's necktie and his sister Hattie's dress, the glimpse of carriages passing the Fifth Avenue corner sixty feet away, the platters brought up on the dumbwaiter, and the imperious way in which his mother managed the meal—she sometimes spoke sharply to the servants, who adored her. Irving, now ten, a slender boy tall for his years, was gravely reflective. The household rule was that breakfast should be served at seven-thirty, and though the large family (seven children together when all were at home) was sometimes noisy, the mother saw that they ate with orderly speed. Her quick ear caught the noise of wheels stopping outside before anybody else did.

"That's McGrath's man with the cart," she said. "Now, Mayer, don't take the boys off through the park or you'll make them late. Get them over to Dr. Sachs's in good time." Although on taking the reins her husband looked longingly at the Central Park drives, he obediently whisked the boys around to Dr. Julius Sachs's School for Boys on Fifty-ninth Street near Sixth Avenue. Irving had entered two years earlier, but Herbert had finished his initial training at a primary school in the neighborhood only the previous spring.

The youngsters were obviously glad to be together. The disparity in years meant little, for Herbert's active habits and adventurous spirit made him seem as mature as Irving.

The house they left was plainly that of a well-to-do, even wealthy, family. Still new looking, it was larger than most brownstone-front houses about it. In fact, it almost filled the 25 by 100-foot lot on which it was built, and it rose five stories. The sedate businessman who drove his boys to school, full-bearded, a little bald, and keen-eyed, just past his middle fifties, was patently Jewish, like many residents of that part of the city. He looked prosaic enough, and from the Sachs School hurried downtown to a prosaic brokerage in cotton and other commodities. Yet this first generation immigrant had seen his full share of struggle and vicissitude. Sometimes when such old friends as the railroad builder Henry Villard or the Cabinet member Hilary A. Herbert called, his sons heard fragments of the story.

• I •

No student of Southern history needs to be told that from early colonial days Jewish families of intellect, culture, and character enriched the life of the section. Particularly in Charleston, Savannah, Richmond, Mobile, and New Orleans, their piety, industry, zeal for education, and philanthropy were notable. In ante-bellum New Orleans the Jews, numerous enough to organize three synagogues, were an active force in commerce, finance, music, and journalism; and Judah P. Benjamin (of British West Indian birth) won eminence at the bar and a seat in the Senate. From Florida the railroad pro-moter David Levy Yulee entered the Senate in 1845 and became a champion of Southern rights. Philip Phillips of Charleston and Mobile also went into politics and was elected to the House. In Wilmington the Jewish congrega-tion was strong enough to lead the battle for religious toleration in North Carolina. The Mordecai family became prominent in Richmond, the Sartorius family in Mississippi, and the Hersberg family in Georgia. Estimates of the number of Jews who joined the Confederate forces have run as high as ten thousand.[1]

In 1848 an eighteen-year-old youth from Bavaria arrived in Montgomery, Alabama, as part of the steady trickle of Jews from Germany to the South. This was Mayer Lehman, from the village of Rimpar, just outside Würzburg, where his family had owned land and traded in cattle. He was taking no leap into the dark. His elder brother Henry had arrived in the United States four years earlier, accumulated a little capital by peddling, and settled in Montgomery to open a shop on Commerce Street. Doing well, he had attracted another brother, Emanuel, in 1847, and both had written to Mayer. The business sign of H. Lehman thus became first Lehman & Brother and then Henry Lehman & Brothers. Within a few years the original shop was given up in favor of a two-story structure at 17 Court Square, with a view of the courthouse and principal auction block for slaves.[2]

Montgomery, in the hopeful days at the close of the Mexican War, seemed as pleasant a place of residence as any in the South. A town of about 5,000 whites and 2,000 slaves, it had lately been made the State capital, and welcomed its first legislative session in December, 1847. All about it lay the black belt of Alabama, so called from its rich dark soil, occupied by large plantations and populated by far more Negroes than whites. The state was thoroughly rural, only ten places in 1850 having as many as a thousand people, but it was reckoned rich. Montgomery, lying near its center, had fairly good communications. Below the red bluff on which the town was built flowed the Alabama River, with steamboat connections to Mobile; a railroad to West Point, Georgia, about ninety miles distant, carried its first trains in the spring of 1851; and mail coaches ran in all directions.

The town had concerts, theaters, billiard halls, and churches. Its people amused themselves with barbecues and picnics, and flocked to political rallies where the best Southern orators—William L. Yancey, Robert Toombs, John Slidell—might be heard. Practically everybody read the *Advertiser* or *Journal*. Montgomery was proud to call itself a city of flowers. The dooryards and gardens, defined by Cherokee rose hedges, were bright with yellow jasmine, foxgloves, woodbine, hollyhocks, pinks, and azalea; flowering trees —chinaberry, crepe myrtle, and dogwood—abounded; wisteria climbed the walls. Some of the houses, built of timber grown in the primeval forests, were handsome pieces of architecture, with hand-carved mantels and paneled stairs.[3]

Above all, Montgomery was a center of the cotton and planting trade. Wagons and boats laden with heavy bales kept its warehouses busy, and stores dispersed miscellaneous shipments of goods among the planters, farmers, and villagers for fifty miles around. It was the opportunities in this trade which the Lehman brothers had seized.

While first listed as "grocers" in the city directory, they were really dealers in cotton, keeping a general store as an adjunct. They paid hard money advanced by New York or Liverpool banks and brokers for cotton or bartered goods for it. Their stock included not only groceries but dry goods, china, glassware, tools, bagging, and seeds. Early in the 1850s Emanuel was making annual trips to New York to replenish his shelves and talk with cotton manufacturers and exporters, and Henry went to New Orleans on similar errands.

Though Alabama had built a cotton mill in Madison County early in the 1850s, the major markets were in New England and Great Britain. Throughout the 1850s—even in the panic year 1857—the State remained generally prosperous. Its population climbed from 300,000 in 1830 to nearly a million on the eve of the Civil War. Though planters recognized the problems of the vicious one-crop system and rapid soil depletion under careless slave tillage, cotton as yet seemed truly king. Montgomery held an annual State Fair beginning in 1856 which attracted thousands to see the exhibits of farm implements, livestock, and fruits. Earnest efforts were made to persuade farmers and planters to grow their own corn, hay, pork, and wheat. But the invariable reply was that the high price of cotton made any other crop uneconomic —and the value of slaves rose with it.

Only once in the 1850s did the average cotton price sink as low as ten cents a pound (in 1851–52), and during the later years of the decade it reached thirteen and fourteen cents. The crop of 1859 almost doubled that of 1849, but still the demand appeared insatiable. Montgomery County was one of the richest cotton-growing spots on the globe and also one of the counties in which slave population was densest, with an average of ten slaves to the household in 1860. The Alabama River became crowded with cargo-carrying steamboats. In addition to regular packet vessels like the *Orline St. John*, which left Mobile late every Monday to reach Montgomery on Wednesday and immediately loaded for the return, many stern-wheelers plied the river irregularly. One diarist lists thirty-three boats reaching Wetumpka, the head of navigation above Montgomery, during a single January.

While most of the cotton was shipped to New Orleans, some of it paid the higher freight charges to Charleston, which was reputed to offer better prices. When Frederick Law Olmsted traveled down the Alabama in 1854, he noted that the boat stopped at almost every bluff and landing to take or discharge freight and that the river had a total of two hundred landings. Laden with 1,900 bales, his steamboat finally sank so low that ripples washed over its decks. Flatboats were also numerous on all the Alabama rivers, and choruses of steamboat roustabouts and flatboat hands often floated from the wharves up to Court Square.[4]

Every farm or plantation needed pork, sugar, molasses, coffee, and oatmeal to feed its slaves; linsey or cotton homespun, denims, and heavy brogans to clothe them; kersey blankets, kettles, and tinware. Every planter needed hoes, axes, plows, scrapes, harness, cotton gins, and presses. Although Montgomery had a few factories by 1860—a furniture shop, a flour mill, a carriage maker, some workshops in copper and iron—their total output came to only $300,000 that year, and they really did nothing to satisfy the region. Mayer Lehman had no sooner settled in Montgomery than he found heavy duties laid on his shoulders, and they steadily increased. He had to help Henry and Emanuel take care of the store, order invoices of goods, correspond with cotton brokers in New York, Liverpool, and Manchester, talk with planters, and keep books. When one of his brothers went out of town, Mayer stepped into the vacant place. He identified himself, naturally, with the sentiment of the South.

In 1856 his responsibilities were suddenly doubled. Henry, founder of the firm, had always feared yellow fever, which sometimes ravaged the district. When an epidemic began that summer, the younger brothers urged him to go to New Orleans as a safer center. There fever seized him, and on November 17, he died, leaving a widow, the much-beloved "Aunt Rosa," and four children.[5]

Emanuel and Mayer, aged twenty-nine and twenty-six respectively, now had to carry on the firm alone just as great changes were overtaking the cotton trade. New York was becoming the principal trading center. It was there that New England mills made payments for cotton in four-month drafts, and British buyers in sixty-day sterling notes. Emanuel, a man of conservative temper, had always done most of the wholesale buying and selling; Mayer, more buoyant and sociable, had kept in close touch with planters and farmers, was a keen judge of cotton, and managed the store with enterprise. No partners were ever more closely united. They never had separate salary accounts or thought of dividing the profits; instead, each took out of the business just what his family needed and put the rest back into expansion. But just before the war their paths did diverge.

• II •

In 1858 Lehman Brothers established their first New York office at 119 Liberty Street, and Emanuel took charge, making the metropolis his home. The following spring he married Pauline Sondheim, daughter of Louis Sondheim of New York. Mayer himself had recently married. In his trips to New Orleans he had seen much of a family named Goldsmith, probably also of Bavarian origin, and had fallen in love with one of their cousins, Babette Newgass, who had come from Würzburg. In 1858 he and Babette were married in the Goldsmiths' house. They at once returned to Montgomery, where they took up residence in a house roomy enough to permit the clerks in the general store to come in—after a general custom of the time—for meals. This was no great hardship to the young wife, for they had household slaves.

In this house the first four children, Sigmund, Hattie (for Harriet), Settie (for Lisette), and Benjamin (who died in infancy) were born. Thus Mayer kept pace with Emanuel, who soon had four children in his New York house.[6] The two brothers maintained a close correspondence and paid each other occasional visits until the war shut off intercourse.

Mayer and Babette always testified that they enjoyed Montgomery life during the last years before the war. The population had risen to 9,000, or nearly half as many people as in Mobile. As a substantial merchant, staunch Democrat, and loyal Alabamian, Mayer knew a succession of governors and Senators, with the leading legislators. He even knew Jefferson Davis. "My mother used to tell us," Herbert Lehman later recalled, "that they entered into the social life very well." Like the heads of such other cotton brokerage firms as Gilmer & Co. and John G. Murphy & Co., the Lehmans were an integral part of the socioeconomic structure of the Deep South. Mayer was often seen at the Exchange Hotel, one of the best in the cotton kingdom, at the imposing Commercial Hall, and at newspaper offices.

The little city by 1860 was gaining touches of distinction. The capitol on Goat Hill, with its long view of Market Street, lifted a glistening white dome almost a hundred feet above well-kept lawns. Some residences were good examples of the Greek Revival style: the three-story Lomax House with white pillars, built by the brother of a governor, for example, and the Teague House, with a columned portico from which a Union general was later to read the Emancipation Proclamation to a crowd of Negroes. The Lehmans were often guests in the massive brick mansion of Percy Gerald, who had made a fortune in the California gold rush. They of course attended not the fashionable St. John's Episcopal Church but their own humble synagogue.

Some Jewish merchants in the South, like some Yankee merchants, had a reputation for driving close bargains. One anecdote suggests that the Lehmans had a different temper. An old resident of Montgomery recalled long afterward that just before the war they contracted with a builder to erect a new cotton warehouse. Because of unforeseen difficulties, the man found himself unable to complete it except at ruinous loss. When he explained this, Lehman Brothers asked him to furnish an estimate of the cost of finishing the work, and after scrutinizing it closely, said they would pay him the extra sum required. "But," asked one of the brothers, "will this leave you any profit?" "No," responded the contractor, "the payment will just get me out unscathed." "Do your work well," crisply remarked the brother, "and we shall pay you an additional sum as profit. You shall not work for us for nothing." [7]

From the time of his marriage, Mayer kept a close connection with New Orleans and its Jewish population. His wife, Babette, who spoke English with little accent whereas he always kept a Teutonic pronunciation, had many friends there, for she had been a vivacious, attractive, strong-minded young woman. She had interesting connections besides the Goldsmiths. One sister, coming to America, married Isais W. Hellman, who founded the first bank in Los Angeles, later became president of the Wells Fargo Nevada Bank in San Francisco, and played a great part in the development of California finance. A brother, Benjamin Newgass, who later settled in London and became a British subject, possessed some delightful traits. "He was the most speculative man I have ever known," his nephew Herbert recalled later; "he made and lost several fortunes. Whenever he saw anything cheap, he could not resist it. A lace store in Venice, for example, might be for sale at a bargain. He took possession, though he had no idea what he would do with it." [8] The Lehmans made frequent trips to New Orleans in the stormy Buchanan years for business, pleasure, or both.

The outbreak of the Civil War was a staggering blow to Lehman Brothers, who practically closed their New York office and put the Montgomery business on a restricted basis. However, it did not sunder the two brothers, for both were Southern sympathizers. Emanuel succeeded in getting to England and was employed there by the Confederate Government in efforts to sell its bonds; these failing, he returned to live quietly in New York. Mayer bought, stored, and when possible shipped through the blockade such cotton as was available.

The Confederate Government at first embargoed all cotton exports. Later it took measures to destroy stores that might fall into Union hands and encouraged farmers and planters to grow food crops instead. Business stringencies meanwhile forced a widespread consolidation of firms. In 1862 John Wesley Durr, principal partner in a Montgomery firm which owned the well-known "Alabama Warehouse," joined Mayer in a new concern called Lehman, Durr & Co., which thereafter controlled two large warehouses. An advertisement the following April shows that, in unison with four other houses, it was forced by the ruinous wartime inflation to raise its charges for storing, shipping, delivering, and reweighing cotton.[9] This Lehman-Durr partnership was destined to outlast the war.

Mayer Lehman threw himself with ardor into the Confederate cause. In 1864 the Alabama legislature, harrowed by reports that soldiers were freezing and starving in Northern prisons, directed the governor to supply them with clothing, blankets, provisions, and money and authorized the expenditure of $500,000 or the sale of cotton or other Southern commodities for the purpose. Governor T. H. Watts decided on shipping the cotton. He appointed Mayer Lehman, the best available expert on cotton, to go to Richmond to negotiate the transfer.

"He is a business man of established character and one of the best Southern patriots," the governor wrote Jefferson Davis on December 14, 1864. "He is a foreigner, but has been here fifteen years and is thoroughly identified with us." [10] Lehman assured Davis that he had money in hand and was ready to go to the prison camps immediately. But Grant refused to pass him through the Union lines, declaring that the Confederate authorities could transact such business only through regular commissioners for prisoner exchange. Meanwhile, the Confederacy made arrangements with Washington to ship 1,000 bales at once, and another 1,500 conditionally later, for the benefit of prisoners in general, Alabama having the right to participate if she desired. But the Federal Government placed insuperable obstacles before the transfer of cotton.

Mayer Lehman showed persistence and wrote Grant in January, 1865, outlining his objects and suggesting that Mobile Bay would be the best point for transshipment of the cotton. His mission had no political or military character, he explained, and he would submit to any regulations laid down. "We well know that a gallant soldier must feel for the condition of those brave men who by the fortunes of war are held as prisoners; exposed to the rigors of a climate to which they are not accustomed, the severities of which are augmented by the privations necessarily attendant upon their condition. We make this request with confidence, assured that your sympathies for the unfortunate brave will lead you to do all in your power to promote the benevolent design. . . ." But after waiting in Richmond through a cold January, Mayer and a Protestant clergyman, who was assisting him, had to return to Montgomery confessing that they could do nothing. The Union authorities, in order to hasten the end of the war, refused to exchange more prisoners, and Secretary Stanton took no interest in alleviating their lot.[11]

· III ·

These were bitter years for honest and patriotic Southern businessmen. Mayer could only accept his losses, live on his savings, and wait for better days. When the Northern forces approached, his main warehouse was burned, but whether by Union or Confederate hands is uncertain. At last, on April 12, 1865, James Grant Wilson, with 14,000 men, chiefly cavalry, entered the city.

Mayer's family doubtless shared the general apprehension as this force rode in from the west. But the troops behaved well; they were astonished by the untouched wealth of the district, which still abounded in forage and provisions, and were pleased that they met no resistance. The mayor and several citizens hastily met them with a flag of truce and surrendered unconditionally. Thereupon the cavalry staged a triumphal entry. Wilson's five brigades rode through the city in columns of platoons, flags flying, bands playing, spurs and swords jingling, and with them came batteries, ambulances, and a wagon train. Not a man of the 12,000 left the ranks, and not a word was uttered to offend the people. Men and women, aware that the war was ending, witnessed the spectacle from doors and windows in melancholy silence. When some officers hoisted the Union flag over the State House, regiment after regiment in passing it gave voice to their exultation in cheers that made the city ring. "It was a great day for the Cavalry Corps," writes Wilson.[12]

With peace restored, Lehman, Durr & Co. reconstituted their business. Cotton reached unprecedented levels; in midwinter of 1865–66 it sold in New Orleans for fifty cents a pound, and it seemed safe to predict a price of twenty-five cents for the ensuing crop year.[13] Nearly everybody with capital, including many Northerners, rushed into planting. The Negroes, protected in their contracts by the Freedmen's Bureau, became sharecroppers. Montgomery had fared better than its sister cities and so recovered faster. Mobile had been half-devastated, for a Confederate ammunition storehouse had exploded shortly after the close of hostilities, killing four or five hundred people, leveling twenty blocks, and starting a conflagration which devoured a great deal of property. In Selma, about fifty miles west of Montgomery on the Alabama, many houses and shops, along with Confederate government buildings—arsenal, foundry, rolling mills, and warehouses—had been destroyed by Union forces. Although in Montgomery the capitol was shabby and dilapidated, the houses were unpainted, the wharves were in ruins, and much of the Montgomery & West Point line had been ripped up, the city was mainly intact, and railroad and river facilities were soon restored.[14]

Traders as enterprising and industrious as the two Lehmans could not fail to prosper in the postwar boom. By the summer of 1865 Lehman, Durr & Co. was again doing a brisk business on Court Square, and late that year or early in 1866 Emanuel Lehman resumed his activities at 176 Fulton Street in New York, the name Lehman Brothers reappearing in the city directory.

Cotton growing and the cotton trade were shifting westward. The Atlantic States became less important; Mississippi, Louisiana, and western Alabama produced more than half the national crop, and Texas and Arkansas grew increasing quantities. As New Orleans became much the most important entrepôt, in 1866 Lehman Brothers opened an office there. They put in charge of it Benjamin Newgass, the before-noted brother of Mayer's wife, a young man of twenty-six who had his share of the family vivacity and assertiveness.[15] He found a fertile field to till; New Orleans in 1866 handled nearly a third of all the cotton shipped from American ports and that summer had stocks in the storehouses four times those of its nearest rival, Mobile. Lehman, Durr & Co. still sold groceries, seeds, implements, and general goods at retail, but such trade tended to wither away while cotton absorbed the energies of the firm.

Family tradition pictures ante-bellum Alabama as an ideal place of residence, but the Alabama of Reconstruction, half-ruined, disorderly, full of sectional resentments and race hatreds, was uncomfortable. The emancipation of 450,000 slaves had thrown a heavy burden upon the state. Federal decrees excluded the most intelligent and forceful men from government positions. The almost complete failure of food crops in 1865 because of drought and labor shortages resulted in such distress that the provisional governor, Louis B. Parsons of Iowa, estimated a quarter of a million people would have to be furnished relief. He recorded the tragic fact that the state had sent 122,000 of its sons to war, of whom 35,000 would never return and an equal number had been made cripples or invalids. "Our fields are laid waste," he wrote, "our towns and cities, our railroads and bridges, our schools and colleges, many of our private dwellings and public edifices, are in ruins." During 1866, with another unfavorable season and short crop, the destitution in Alabama, among whites and blacks, exceeded that in any other state.[16]

Though the Lehman business did well enough, social and political conditions grew steadily worse. After a short period of military rule under arrogant John Pope, the carpetbaggers and scalawags took control of the state. "Life became almost unendurable," wrote one of the Lehmans' neighbors in Montgomery, Mary Powell. "No woman was safe on the streets. The native white man was subject to insult, attack, and robbery. He could obtain no justice from Negro or half-Negro juries. Intimidation of whites was attempted by arson. . . . Excessive taxation led to countless tax sales and to the breaking up of homes."[17] Mayer Lehman and his family suffered with the others.

He would have remained had his affairs demanded it, but the call of business came from New York. Though Lehman Brothers was still primarily a cotton firm, Emanuel had become interested in other commodities. His activities carried the house to larger quarters, first at 109 Fulton Street and later to 133–135 Pearl Street, just off Hanover Square, the center of cotton trading. Mayer saw that New York needed two men, while Durr could look after affairs in Montgomery and Newgass those in New Orleans. In 1868 Mayer joined his older brother in New York.

The next decade witnessed fairly continuous growth, so that Lehman Brothers became one of the more important commodity brokerages in New York. While Mayer devoted himself to cotton, Emanuel bought and sold petroleum, coffee, sugar, and one or two other staples. From affluence they rose to great wealth. They had reached that stage, still taking from the business the money they needed and no more, without any separate accounting, when on March 28, 1878, Mayer's eighth and last child was born and named Herbert, in honor of the father's friend Hilary A. Herbert. By that date Mayer was forty-eight, Emanuel fifty-one. Older sons of the partners were growing up with the expectation of joining the house: Sigmund and Arthur Lehman from Mayer's side and Philip Lehman from Emanuel's.

The two founders of the house were known in downtown New York by their well-accented individuality. In temperament they differed sharply, Emanuel being as cautious as Mayer was bold. Intimates used to say that in studying the situation Emanuel would remark, "It is a good time to sell," while, conning the same evidence, Mayer would announce, "It is a good time to buy." Others put the difference this way: "Mayer makes the money and Emanuel conserves it." They were alike in acumen, kindliness, and generosity, traits so marked that friends called them "the Cheeryble Brothers." They were alike, too, in their readiness to participate in civic enterprises and philanthropy. What an associate said of Emanuel at his death might equally have been said of Mayer: "He was a big-souled, kindhearted man, who combined with a grand character all the virtues." Various stories were told of their openhanded assistance to others.

Both bright-eyed, full-bearded, and slightly bald in later life, they had a close resemblance; but photographs show the optimistic Mayer with a gay bow tie, the conservative Emanuel with a sober cravat. As Herbert reached school age, he grew used to seeing them much together. They lived not far apart, kept all family festivals together, and shared a long list of institutional interests. Proud of their Jewish heritage and faith, they were loyal adherents of Temple Emanu-El, worshipping there every Friday night. They took the same keen interest in the Hebrew Sheltering House Association and in the Home for Crippled Children; while Emanuel gave labor, thought, and money with special generosity to the Hebrew Benevolent and Orphan Asylum and Mayer to the Mount Sinai Hospital, of which he was a director.

In fact, there was hardly an important Jewish benevolence in which they were not concerned. Herbert as a child heard them talk over these institutions with as much fervor as they bestowed upon the affairs of the New York Cotton Exchange, which both had helped to organize in 1871.

The brothers spoke English with a guttural accent and preserved from Old World Jewry some customs and tastes which marked them as first generation immigrants. They were patriotic, but their roots did not yet run deep into American soil. The urchin of eight who attended classes in Dr. Sachs's school that autumn of 1886, and who rushed yelling into Central Park with his playmates at recess time to clamber over the rocks, was a native-born American, beginning an education which would make him American through and through.

Chapter II

CONTRAST
OF TWO BROTHERS

NEW YORK in the 1880s and early 1890s, when Herbert Lehman was a boy, retained many of the attributes of a small city. Brooklyn had not been annexed, the Bronx had not been developed, and upper Manhattan was largely empty. Traffic did not jam the streets, and no skyscrapers pierced the upper atmosphere. Areas even in the middle of town had the appearance of a neighborhood. It was a good place for well-guarded youngsters, and Dr. Sachs's School for Boys, decidedly Jewish, aristocratic—the boys came to class in smart suits and starched stand-up collars—and austere, was a good school for Herbert and Irving Lehman.

The two brothers were inseparable; where Irving went Herbert went also, their differences in taste and temperament erasing the gap of years and bringing them closer. While Irving, gentle and studious, found the self-assertive Herbert just the champion he sometimes needed, Herbert found in Irving's reflective mind an intellectual stimulus he needed still more. One family story has a symbolic value. When they were well-grown youths, some emergency forced them to dress in haste for dinner. They hurriedly pulled on their suits, only to find, when they reached their destination, that the tall, thin Irving and short, plump Herbert had gotten into each other's clothes; but they laughingly made the best of the situation. Once, much earlier, when Irving went for a vacation trip, Herbert at the train gate in Grand Central suddenly found himself in tears. Friends meant a good deal to the boys, and they were devoted to their parents, especially the diminutive, imperious mother, but they never lost their David and Jonathan attachment.[1]

Herbert was the quintessential boy, fond of the outdoors, all kinds of games, talk, banter, exertion, and a good deal of scuffling. When he was not busy with classes and playmates he was following college and professional sports with enthusiasm. The lads at the Sachs School carried on hot feuds with two neighboring institutions, Public School 54 and a Catholic parochial school called La Salle Institute. After a snowfall in winter the pupils would race for occupancy of a summerhouse in Central Park near Sixtieth Street, perched on a hill so steep that the garrison could usually fight off assailants charging up the slope. The snowballs were packed hard and sometimes contained a rock.

Spring and fall the boys played fearlessly on the streets. Automobiles were unknown, electric trolleys had not been installed, and only the carriages or drays, and the horsecars on Madison Avenue, had to be dodged. The Sachs School had some small athletic activities in which Herbert fervently enlisted. His specialty was the mile walk, and in an interscholastic meet he won a medal of which he was inordinately proud. "At one point the course ran behind a large billboard," he later recalled. "When we got to that billboard we all sprinted a little."

When seven or eight, Herbert caught his first bass in the Delaware River somewhere near Port Jervis. This was a memorable thrill, and he continued to fish on river and seashore. He was hardly older when he began playing tennis, very badly—as he played most games—but with passion. Sometimes he played with Irving, sometimes with other boys; no matter with whom, he took his inevitable defeat with a cheerful grin. Irving and he were recipients, early in the 1890s, of one of the first safety bicycles seen in the city. The old high-wheeled machines had been dangerous, but now the boys could take turns in going all over town without risk. A little later both had bicycles and ranged farther afield. In summers on the Jersey coast a bevy of young people, thirty or forty strong, would sometimes set off early in the morning to pedal to a place called Pleasure Bay, where, tired but hungry, they ate breakfast. (As a matter of course, Herbert and Irving had dogs, too, from early boyhood; the breed did not matter so long as the dogs made good companions.)

As Herbert rose in his teens to become president of the athletic association at the Sachs School, his interest in sports deepened. A. A. Stagg was now teaching football elevens a fast-moving mass attack, and Walter Camp was devising new tactical uses for guards and tackle. For some reason Herbert became a fervent partisan of Yale, familiarized himself with the special qualities of the Yale ends and quarterbacks, and joined frenzied rooters on trains to New Haven. At the Yale-Harvard game in 1893 he became so excited that, leaping to his feet on the bleachers, he fell through to the ground below. With hardly less fervor he attended baseball games. Cigarette companies in the 1890s enclosed in their packages pictures of leading professional players, which boys traded with each other, and at one time Herbert had almost a complete collection. In spring he played baseball on vacant lots and used to come home from games so tired and grimy that his parents worried about him. He had a mischievous streak, but being at bottom a conscientious, sensitive boy, he realized that his strict mother regarded him as a bit wayward.

Irving was the favorite of his parents; they both had great respect for learning, and Irving's quiet studiousness, which with his keenness of mind made him a remarkable scholar, impressed them. He seemed marked out from the beginning for some great intellectual career. Always reading and thinking, he astonished his teachers by unexpected bits of lore and original ideas. One of his special interests was Jewish history and thought, for he took pride in his heritage. His parents had called him Irving as a substitute for Isaac, the name of his maternal grandfather, but he used to say stoutly: "I am Irving Isaac Isidor Lehman!" Another interest was law and especially legal history. He followed the press accounts of important cases, talked with attorneys who were friends of the family, and was mightily impressed by one such friend, Edward Douglass White, later Chief Justice of the United States. Before he left Dr. Sachs's School it was evident that he planned to become a lawyer and that he would become an expounder and interpreter of the law rather than a trial attorney. With his deepset dark eyes, long thoughtful face, and rather heavy features—broad forehead, large nose, strong mouth and chin— he looked the future judge.

Their father did a great deal to confirm Herbert's outdoor tastes, for he loved the country himself. Fond of driving, he kept a good team at Mc-Grath's livery stable between Fifty-ninth and Sixtieth on Park Avenue, near their house. Most mornings he would have his T-cart brought to the door soon after eight and would take one of the sons on a spin through Central Park. On Sundays and holidays they might drive much farther. Herbert early learned the attractions of the dirt and tanbark course on Jerome Avenue leading to the Jerome Park Race Track. Many people had sleighs in that preautomobile age and eagerly awaited the first snowfall; each winter the owner of McGowan's Inn in Central Park near Ninety-sixth Street offered a magnum of champagne to the first New Yorker to drive his own sleigh behind his own horses to the hotel.

In summer the family usually rented a house in the Irvington-Tarrytown area of Westchester, which the father specially liked. But during Herbert's boyhood they spent several summers on the Jersey coast near Elberon, a more attractive shore area than the crowded strip from Asbury Park to Manasquan below. Elberon, a center of large estates, laid claims to elegance, though it had a sporty quality, too, for some well-known gambling houses catered to rich Philadelphians and New Yorkers. Inland lay the Monmouth Racetrack, and the first horse race Herbert saw was a match there to which his father took him when he was about ten. But it was the woods, fields, and beaches of the Shrewsbury River and Sandy Hook area that most delighted the boy in the Elberon years, just as the wooded Hudson Valley gave opportunities for rambles and play when the family went to Westchester.

He saw a true wilderness when he began visiting the large hunting and fishing preserve in the Adirondacks called Kildare. This had originally been the property of a club of sportsmen which included members of the Vanderbilt family and which induced the New York Central to build a spur from its Albany-Montreal line to the clubhouse. It was bought jointly by Herbert's brother Sigmund and Jules Ehrich, who had married Herbert's cousin Evelyn, the daughter of Emanuel Lehman; Ehrich being the owner of a department store on Fourteenth Street but much more interested in camping, hunting, and fishing than in his business. He and Sigmund converted the primitive clubhouse into a woods lodge, at first rather rough but later comfortable.

Several thousand acres of primeval forest were comprehended in the preserve, full of wild animals from porcupines to bears, alive in summer with birds, and threaded in part by trails and riding paths. Portages connected a chain of lakes, and the cottage looked out on a long stretch of water which afforded fishing, boating, and rather chilly bathing. It was a boy's paradise. Early in the 1890s Herbert and Irving began going there for a month in summer, sleeping in a tent even when the nights grew cold, whooping, splashing, firing at marks, dragging trout out of the coves, and enjoying themselves thoroughly. Sigmund and Jules gave them nature lessons; three girl cousins, among others, lent companionship; and Mrs. Ehrich, whom Herbert later described as "one of the kindest, sweetest, gentlest women I have ever known," made an indulgent matriarch. The debt the boys owed Kildare for health, fun, and education in woodcraft was beyond computation; it did more than anything else to keep them from becoming citified.[2]

Life was by no means all play, however, in these years. It embraced more discipline in home life, school, and community undertakings than most growing boys receive.

· I ·

Physically, the Lehman home had the characteristic Victorian ungainliness of the period, with some rugged features that were doubtless good for the boys' character. Herbert's and Irving's room at the back of the third floor (counting the basement as one floor) was at first very hot in summer and very cold in winter, for the fourth story did not project over it; but later an additional room was built overhead. A large front sitting room on this floor held what Herbert later recalled as "the ugliest green furniture I have ever seen." The fourth floor had two large and two small bedrooms, a bath, and a book room; the fifth floor a large front sewing room, a family bedroom, a bath, and three maids' rooms—the maids got plenty of exercise climbing flights of stairs. The bathrooms, after the fashion of brownstones, lacked direct outside ventilation. Down below, on the second or street floor, was the most attractive room of the house, a long parlor furnished with late Victorian pieces, upholstered in light gold satin so as to produce a bright effect. A broad bay window let in the sunlight. Here, too, was a library, which the boys—usually excluded from the parlor—made their favorite room. The basement floor had a front room for the children's breakfast and lunch and a kitchen, pantry, and laundry.

In short, it was a characteristic Manhattan house of the Brownstone Era, though larger and better kept than most of the habitations stretching in solemn rows across town. The image of its long stairs, airless central rooms, and gloomy furniture (Herbert always recalled the stiff walnut chairs and the sofas in green-and-black brocade) seems depressing. Actually the Lehmans liked their house, which the children remembered as cheerful, roomy, and comfortable. Doubtless it was the servants who felt its hard-favored aspects.

Mayer Lehman made a careful but indulgent father. He did not forbid the boys to smoke. Instead, he offered each of them $1,000 if he refrained until twenty-one, a reward which nobody earned. When punishment had to be administered he turned the duty over to Babette, who never flinched. She could be extremely stern to children and servants alike, though she never passed the bounds of justice. "I used to writhe sometimes with the scolding my mother gave a delinquent maid," Herbert recalled; "but I don't think anybody ever left my mother—they always stayed with her." She scolded the boys just as severely. Mayer seldom needed scolding, but she advised him constantly and with such practical keenness that he never took an important business step without consulting her.

Both parents being religious—the father had attended a sectarian school in Bavaria and read Hebrew fluently—they of course enforced attendance at Sunday School. Herbert was not a particularly good pupil, but he tried hard. Each year the rabbi gave a silver medal to the boy who made the highest marks before being confirmed. As Herbert's confirmation approached, the rabbi remarked to Mayer Lehman: "Your son and Nathan Stern are making the same excellent record, and are running neck and neck. We have decided, in the circumstances, that this year we should give two medals, one to each." This aroused Mayer's indignation, for he suspected the officers of the congregation had been influenced by his business and philanthropic standing. "Oh, no, rabbi," he protested, "I have watched the two boys, and Nathan is the better scholar. He deserves the medal without any diminution of the honor. I cannot allow Herbert to accept a medal." It was a just decision—but Herbert would have liked the medal.

The Mayer Lehmans had a wide acquaintance, including such men of distinction as the before-mentioned Hilary A. Herbert and Edward Douglass White. Hilary Herbert was not only attorney for the firm in Montgomery but in time a close friend. Leaving the Confederate army with the rank of colonel, he had opened a law office in Montgomery some half-dozen years later and gained a successful place at the bar. He entered Congress at the close of Reconstruction to sit in the House for eight years, giving special attention to the puny navy and helping re-create it with adequate appropriations. Cleveland in 1893 rewarded him with the Secretaryship of the Navy. A scholarly man, he found time to write some skillful defenses of the Southern position in race relations. It is doubtful if Irving learned much about the law from him—Hilary Herbert had spent just four months in study before admission to the bar—but he could talk entertainingly about his cases and his share in Fredericksburg, Antietam, Gettysburg, and the Wilderness. He was an enthusiast for the business development of the South, and applauded Mayer Lehman's growing investments in mines, mills, and railroads in the section.

As for White, a younger man, he was a more gracious and courtly Southerner, whose tremendous bulk gave him an imposing presence but who was quick of gesture and of mind. He had enjoyed unusual cultural advantages, for his father was a wealthy planter-lawyer who had sat ten years in Congress and gave him a good education in Jesuit institutions. Though he served in the Louisiana legislature, and briefly on the supreme bench of that state, he was best known as a corporation attorney. The New Orleans firm of Lehman, Newgass & Co., later Lehman, Stern, was one of his clients. Like Hilary A. Herbert, he approved the part which Lehman Brothers took in developing the South. White's visits to the Lehman home were by no means entirely on legal affairs. He had money, he ultimately married a woman of wealth, and he put their joint fortune in the hands of the firm. Moreover, he liked Mayer and Babette as much as they liked him. He probably never visited New York, at least until his elevation to the Supreme

Court by Cleveland in 1894, without depositing his bulky frame in one of the golden chairs of the Lehman parlor. Herbert always recalled him as simple, gay, talkative, and full of kindly courtesy: "We children and young people liked him very much."

Henry Villard was a friend; he, too, had come from Bavaria, where his father Heinrich Hilgard (Henry changed the surname), had been chief justice. As he lived at Dobbs Ferry during their Westchester summers the Lehmans saw something of him. The elder Hermann Hagedorn was another friend, for he was in the cotton business. Their next door neighbor, General Joseph Dickinson, a handsome Civil War veteran with white sideburns, occasionally called. As a Democrat, Mayer knew some leaders of the conservative or Cleveland wing of the party. But to say much of such acquaintances would be misleading. The immediate circle of the household was a family circle, tightly maintained after the Jewish tradition, and the circle next beyond it was a Jewish circle.

Throughout the years to the end of the century the families of Emanuel and Mayer always kept the Day of Atonement, Passover, Hanukkah, and New Year's (when they exchanged gifts) together. The Passover dinner or Seder was particularly important. Mayer would read the service and responses, and the children would join in chanting the hymns. To the youngsters the tongue seemed amusingly outlandish. "My brothers Arthur and Irving, respectively five and two years older than I, would break out into fits of laughter," Herbert later recalled. "Invariably we would be sent from the table." Later, of course, Herbert learned to love the Seder service and understand its interest and beauty. Emanuel lived on Forty-sixth Street, a few doors east of Fifth Avenue, only a short walk from Mayer's house. In time, marriage of Mayer's son Sigmund to Emanuel's daughter Harriet sealed the unity of the two households.

Everywhere in that part of Manhattan were scattered Jewish households, many of which looked to Temple Emanu-El as their religious citadel. Its rabbi, the learned Gustav Gottheil, was a towering figure in moral and spiritual influence. Born and educated in Prussia, he had served in the Berlin Reform Synagogue before he was called to a thirteen-year pastorate in Manchester. Exposure to the best English liberal thought had helped prepare him for an assistantship to Samuel Adler, who had become rabbi of Emanu-El shortly before the Civil War. Eighteen months after arriving, Gottheil in 1874 was chosen head of the congregation, over which he was destined to preside for almost a quarter century. Even the orthodox Jews of the city, who at first disliked his heterodox ideas, were charmed by his geniality, generosity, and in later years his Zionist leanings.[3]

The country had no churchman of greater erudition and breadth than this open-minded man, who often occupied Protestant pulpits, helped found the New York State Conference of Religion, graced the memorial services for Henry Ward Beecher and Phillips Brooks, and was one of the editors of a *Book of Common Worship* issued in 1900. He studied anti-Semitism objectively, combating it with as much wit and tact as fearlessness. One of his remarks was much quoted: "In ancient times, the Jews refused to eat with publicans and sinners; in modern times, publicans and sinners refuse to eat with Jews." Though Mayer Lehman had once been orthodox, he came to prefer Dr. Gottheil's teachings. As Rabbi de Sola Pool has written, the man's combination of Jewish, English, and German culture was peculiarly useful in giving the reform faith a shape adapted to America. What President Taft said of Oscar Straus could be said of him: "He is a great Jew, and the best Christian of us all."

A striking number of the Jewish families of mid-town Manhattan had histories akin to that of the Lehmans. They had come from Germany to America before the Civil War, had accumulated capital in some small center, often in the South, had removed to New York during or just after the conflict, and had emerged from retail trade into manufacturing, finance, or wholesale merchandising. Their general identity of experience enhanced their sense of religious solidarity.

The Straus family, originating in Rhenish Bavaria, had settled in Georgia in 1852, where Lazarus Straus became a merchant. His oldest son, Isidor, served the Confederacy as loyally as Mayer Lehman, first as a buyer of war supplies in Europe and later in Liverpool as a dealer in Confederate bonds. After the war the father and son formed a wholesale crockery firm in New York which led them into partial and eventually complete ownership of Macy's great department store. All of the sons became prominent in political life. Isidor made a useful member of Congress, supporting Grover Cleveland's policies. A younger brother, Nathan, was in time named by popular vote the man who had done most for Greater New York during its first quarter century. Oscar, who was still younger, after practicing law long enough to master its principles and to become a friend of two distinguished men, Simon Sterne and Joseph H. Choate, developed a keen interest in civic affairs. He was secretary of a reform group organized to reëlect William R. Grace as mayor, and threw all his energies into the battle in 1884 to put Cleveland in the White House.[4]

When Herbert Lehman was a boy he undoubtedly heard of Straus's services as minister to Turkey. He must also have read the fervent public letter which Henry Ward Beecher sent President Cleveland arguing in favor of the selection. "It is because he is a Jew," wrote Beecher, "that I would urge his appointment as a fit recognition of this remarkable people, who are becoming large contributors to American prosperity, and whose intelligence, morality, and large liberality in all public measures for the welfare of society deserve and should receive from the hands of the government some such recognition."

The eight sons of David Seligman similarly came from Bavaria, three settling in the United States by 1840. They established a mercantile house in Selma, Alabama, with branches at Eutaw, Clinton, and Greensboro in that state. Joseph Seligman derived enough capital from the Greensboro store to open the importing business in New York in 1848 and at the outbreak of the Civil War founded the banking firm of J. & W. Seligman, which did signal service in helping finance the Union effort. A. P. Loveman planted a business in Florence, Alabama, before coming to New York.[5] Isaac and Louis Stern migrated with their parents from Hesse-Cassel in 1843 and lived in Albany before establishing their dry goods business in New York in 1867.

We might run through a long additional list, including such famous names as the Guggenheims, Schiffs, and Lewisohns. These families, marked by character and intellectual power, were all public-spirited and all philanthropic. Bringing artistic tastes and respect for learning from the Old World, they contributed massively to the cultural wealth of the city. They invariably sent their children to college. To Columbia came, among others, Isaac Newton Seligman, reformer, philanthropist, and promoter of musical organizations; Sam A. Lewisohn, founder of one of New York's great art collections; Irving Lehman; and (at Barnard) such women as Mildred Straus and Helen Goodhart. Because it was near at hand, was conspicuously liberal, and had a succession of presidents widely acquainted in the Jewish community, Columbia was in fact a favorite institution. Oscar Straus had successfully competed there with Brander Matthews for the place of class poet.

Most members of this Jewish elite were highly cultivated. They helped support musical societies, libraries, and art galleries. While they seldom knew Yiddish, they had at least a smattering of Hebrew and were usually proficient in German. They read and traveled widely, took a keen interest in ideas, and gained from their rabbis some concern with advanced religious thought and social reform. Of course they were clannish, for the heads of these families, meeting at Temple Emanu-El or other synagogues and sitting on the same boards for hospitals, orphanages, and other charitable agencies, felt a close bond. Their young people intermarried. Nevertheless they remained clearly-cut individualists. Peggy Guggenheim wrote of her grandfather, James Seligman: "Most of his children were peculiar." Wishing to preserve the best traditions of their Jewish-American community, they wished still more to be good Americans.

The younger generation to which Herbert belonged, children and grand-children of the immigrants, felt themselves completely American. Those who clung to the ancient Jewish faith usually accepted it in a new garb. The re-formed ritual had evolved naturally under the pressures which early Jewish immigrants faced in America and the influence of American Protestantism. A Jewish peddler found it difficult to adhere to some ancient modes of wor-ship. The Jewish owner of a general store in Peoria or Jewish manager of a cotton firm in Montgomery, for example, was handicapped if he kept his doors closed on Friday evening and all Saturday, the day farmers flocked into town. The storekeeper's wife would not see neighboring women enter-ing the Presbyterian church on their husbands' arms without asking why women and men were separated in the synagogues. Children who grew up ignorant of Hebrew and bashful about foreign ways objected to the religious shawl, a reminiscence of the old desert garb, and wanted the prayers trans-lated into English. The organ of the Methodists around the corner seemed useful. Inspiring young rabbis arose who were imbued with the ideas of the German Enlightenment and English Unitarianism; such rabbis as Isaac M. Wise and David Einhorn.

Herbert Lehman later recalled that although his father doubtless followed the ancient faith precisely when he came to America, "by the time I knew him he was no longer orthodox. . . . I don't think he paid very much atten-tion to or was particularly affected by ritual." In this, like others of Dr. Gottheil's congregation, he followed the path which Rabbi Wise had first clearly defined.

Wise, "infected by the American fever," as he put it, had come from Bohemia in 1846 and was immediately chosen rabbi of the Albany congrega-tion. He was disturbed by what seemed to him the chaotic condition of Judaism and grieved by the gap between the orthodox faith and the Ameri-can way of life. With characteristic foresight he set to work on a modern-ized prayer book and a new ritual, *Minhag America*, to replace the old Sephardic (Spanish) and Ashkenazic (German) rituals. He proposed a na-tional federation of synagogues and drew up a plan for a seminary to train rabbis in the new approach to the old faith. His appeal for congregational federation, "To the Ministers and Other Israelites," appeared in 1848. When a majority of the Albany congregation refused to follow him, he became head of a Cincinnati congregation in 1854 and there founded the *American Israelite* as chief organ of the reform movement. An unquenchable flame burned in Wise, still young even in his eightieth year.[6]

In the warmth of that flame and its counterpart in the breast of Dr. Gottheil, who went even further on the road of change, Herbert Lehman absorbed his religious convictions. The *Minhag America* omitted all prayers for a return to Palestine, for the rebuilding of the Temple, for a revival of the system of sacrifice, and for the restoration of the Davidic dynasty. Shortly before Herbert's birth Wise had inaugurated in Cincinnati the Hebrew Union College under his own presidency, to assure such congregations as Temple Emanu-El, hitherto served by foreign-born ministers, of an American-trained rabbinate. When Herbert was seven, Reform Judaism adopted the Pittsburgh Platform. It thereby committed itself to the doctrine that Judaism was "a progressive religion, ever striving to be in accord with the postulates of reason" and able to conform to the advances of knowledge. Such advances made for the rejection of those Mosaic laws badly adapted to the views and habits of modern civilization and the abandonment of any nationalist character or aim for Judaism.

"We consider ourselves," ran the platform, "no longer a nation, but a religious community, and therefore expect neither a return to Palestine, nor sacrificial worship under the sons of Aaron, nor the restoration of any of the laws concerning the Jewish state." [7]

Of the three Jewish denominations, the orthodox, the conservative, and the reformed, Herbert, who incidentally was a friend of Isaac M. Wise's son Jonah, belonged to the last. This meant that he received a religious training not widely divergent from that of American Unitarians; the English sermons, the music, and the prayers were much the same. It meant that he was not a Zionist, though he could sympathize with the emotion behind Zionist aspirations. Separated from Protestants in his rejection of the New Testament, he nevertheless approximated the views of followers of Theodore Parker, William Ellery Channing, or even Horace Bushnell. Youths in the Jewish Reform synagogue were taught, within the framework of acceptance of God, the free exercise of reason, the importance of strict morality, and the value of benevolence; dogma and ritual being given but secondary emphasis.

But Herbert always minimized the ritualistic divisions in his ancestral faith; to him, Judaism was integral. As a youth, and throughout life, he felt that the fields of agreement far outweighed the small and sometimes superficial differences. In time he became a member of synagogues conducted under the rituals of the three groups. "All that I require of a Jew," he used to say, "is that he follow the basic laws, precepts, and traditions of our faith. It makes no difference to me whether a man goes to a reform, orthodox, or conservative synagogue." Great strides were made during his career toward unity in fundamental philosophy, Talmudic studies, and philanthropic effort.

· II ·

The Lehman home had a stock of the English and American classics, among which Herbert foraged with an eye to action and adventure. "In my boyhood days," he later wrote an enquirer, "I particularly enjoyed the works of Thackeray, Scott, and Cooper." To this list should be added some novels of Dickens and George Eliot. He specially liked *Ivanhoe*, *The Mill on the Floss*, and *David Copperfield*. At an earlier age, he took delight in Marryat's sea stories, G. A. Henty's solid historical tales, and Horatio Alger's yarns. Although he realized that Alger's books followed the formula of the poor ragged boy who rose to be president of the bank while the banker's proud but dissolute son went to jail, whenever a new title came out he could hardly wait for it. His young friend Lewis Einstein, later a diplomat of note, had Alger for a tutor, and Herbert was devoured with envy. Part of the winter of 1888, when a transient illness led his parents to keep him at home, gave him the longest uninterrupted period for reading in his life. Irving, who had more austerely intellectual tastes, read studiously in harder books, and was prepared to debate about them.

Among periodicals Herbert was addicted to the *Youth's Companion*. This interesting weekly sometimes offered prizes for contributions by boys and girls, and to him any challenge of the kind was irresistible. At nine or ten he wrote a story and without showing it to anybody mailed it in. In due course a letter of rejection arrived, softened by some words of praise. His brother, Sigmund, already a young man, read it. "I'm sorry they didn't take the story —I thought it was good," he said. "But *I* am going to give you a prize." He handed Herbert a dollar, a bit of kindness the boy never forgot.

The boys were not encouraged to attend the theater and forbidden to enter Tony Pastor's variety house on Fourteenth Street, near Tammany Hall. Irving and Herbert nevertheless stole in once in a while, without harm, for the tone was low only by prim Victorian standards. They could have watched some important performers there: Nat Goodwin, Francis Wilson, May Irwin, Marie Lloyd, Lillian Russell. Elsewhere Herbert saw *Shenandoah* when it caught the popular taste. He thrilled to the scene which showed the Army of the Shenandoah recoiling in defeat at Cedar Creek, with Sheridan spurring his foam-flecked steed on the Valley pike fifteen miles away and finally, amid a storm of huzzas, arriving to rally the Sixth Corps and defeat

Longstreet. It was just the play a boy was bound to find enthralling. So were *Uncle Tom's Cabin* and melodramas of the *East Lynne* type.

As he grew older he became close to Jerome Koehler, whose family knew the impresario Maurice Grau, famous not only as the first business manager of the Metropolitan Opera but as the associate of Henry E. Abbey in managing the Abbey Theatre, which opened in 1893. The youngsters got free tickets for the appearances of renowned actors and actresses. They thus saw Richard Mansfield, Stuart Robson, Lawrence Barrett, Ada Rehan, and even Ellen Terry. Several plays made a tremendous impression on Herbert, so that all his life he recalled the power of Joseph Jefferson in *Rip Van Winkle* and *The Rivals* and of Henry Irving in the Erckmann-Chatrian drama built on the murder of a Jewish peddler, *The Bells*. Characteristically, he felt challenged to attempt some acting himself, and when he got to college, did so.

The Sachs School, responsible for the formal side of Herbert's education from the lower grades through its "Collegiate Institute" or high school, derived both faults and merits from the strong personality of its founder and head. The merits were of a rugged type. Julius Sachs, a native of Maryland who graduated from Columbia shortly after the war, studied in four German universities, and then, in a deliberate effort to improve the level of instruction in the United States, opened his school in 1871. He attained his goal, for by its example and the training it gave to future teachers, it had a salutary effect on scholastic standards. The keynotes of its work were Teutonic system and thoroughness, both needed in the United States of the period. Pupils were drilled to realize they would profit in direct ratio to the labor and thought which they gave to their tasks, and they were never indulged in indolence or carelessness.

Sachs himself, a handsome man of marked physical and intellectual vigor, set an example of unremitting industry. He taught classes, helped manage various professional and learned societies, published articles on classical literature and pedagogy, and took part in reform movements in politics. Always he enforced stern labor. "When you graduated, you really knew something," testified Herbert later.

He was nevertheless altogether too much like Dickens's Mr. Gradgrind. His aims, as Herbert and others divined, were too purely intellectual, too little moral or imaginative; he lacked the inspiring quality of Arnold of Rugby or Peabody of Groton. Quick-tempered and razor-tongued, he kept the boys in terror of his wrath, particularly as he tweaked their ears sharply for poor work. Hans Zinsser tells us that he detested the school and put off the hour for dragging himself inside its doors until he was often tardy. Years afterward, Lehman placed the responsibility for his bad penmanship on Sachs. If boys broke the rules, the doctor kept them after school to copy out some maxim several hundred times. Herbert was thus frequently corrected, and being in a hurry to get out to play, got into the habit of writing with more haste than finish. "Ever since then, I have written extremely fast but with complete illegibility," he has recalled. A Latin teacher named Weiberzahl was also a martinet, while the teacher of German was a Prussian of rasping severity. It is not strange that the boys looked about for a ray of sunshine. The drawing teacher, Mrs. France, was popular because she had a pretty daughter. "All of us kids worshipped the daughter. She was the only young thing around the place." [8]

From the English teacher, Frank Erwin, and the French teacher, Jean Pierre Auguste Porret, Herbert learned without severity or drudgery. Still more did he learn from his schoolmates. One boy he specially admired was Paul J. Sachs, a short, fat lad just his own age, later to become noted as professor of fine arts at Harvard. Another was Zinsser, who gained renown both in medicine and authorship. George S. Hellman, son of one of Seligman's daughters, wrote verse even in his school days and in time became noted as poet, author of an excellent biography of Washington Irving, and director of important enterprises in art.

Herbert needed the comradeship which these lads and his brother gave him. Beneath his lively, extroverted qualities, his eagerness to undertake activities, his good nature in defeat, lay a sensitive and worrisome nature. He was so earnest in his work that his fingers were always ink-stained. He was also so fearful that he could not live up to the lofty standards set by his parents, and so certain he could never match Irving's achievements, that he was often depressed. Dr. Sachs, who held himself as rigidly aloof from the boys as the head of a Prussian gymnasium, gave him no sense of friendship: "We all felt frightened of Dr. Sachs; I would never have thought of asking his advice." Though Frank Erwin, a warmhearted man much interested in social problems, came closer to bridging the gap, it was the boys who made the school pleasant.

While still a small boy, Herbert had the benefit of foreign travel. In 1884 his parents took him to Europe on the Cunard liner *Servia*, for his father, who admired the British generally, felt a special trust in British seamanship and always used Cunard ships. The vigilance of the white-whiskered captain impressed the boy. The ship was lighted by oil lamps, and every night the captain watchfully traversed the passageways to make sure the wicks were low enough to avoid danger of fire. In 1887 the family made a second European trip. They were in London to see Queen Victoria's Golden Jubilee, and Herbert always remembered the throngs that filled the streets, and the parades.

On these journeys they visited Herbert's aunt in Liverpool, his uncle in London, and his grandmother and two aunts in Würzburg. During the first visit Aunt Hanschen did him a service he never forgot. Like other boys of six, he wore curls, of which adornment he had become ashamed. Hanschen, a forceful woman, decided he was too old for them, and as soon as his parents left to drink the waters at Carlsbad, took him to the barber. The removal of his thick black curls was one of the happiest moments of his life; but his mother cried heartily on her return, and after her death, he found a well-tied box labeled, "Herbert's curls."

On these and later journeys Herbert imbibed some views of his elders respecting European affairs. His father disliked Germany, partly for its restrictions on the Jews and widespread anti-Semitism. Once in Würzburg— this must have been in 1887—Herbert had a provoking experience. He and one of his sisters, a pretty, spirited girl to whom he was devoted, walking down one of the principal avenues, encountered three Prussian officers, who marched straight forward. They crowded the young girl into the gutter. "I was mad enough to fight the whole German army," he said later. It is significant that although he learned to speak German fairly well, he quickly forgot it. German had been the language of Emanu-El until the early 1880s, but with few exceptions, the Jews of central Manhattan had no love for Germany.

Some American journeys widened Herbert's knowledge of his own country. His father took him to White Sulphur Springs when the guests and atmosphere there were still strongly Southern. They went repeatedly to Saratoga, whose waters Mayer Lehman thought more beneficial than Carlsbad's, staying in the United States Hotel. The neighboring Grand Union had been the scene of one of the first noteworthy manifestations of anti-Semitism in the country. In 1877 Judge Henry Hilton, who controlled it as well as the A. T. Stewart department store in New York, excluded Joseph Seligman and his family on racial grounds. Not only had Seligman performed unforgettable financial service for the Union during the war; he was a friend of President Grant, who had offered to make him Secretary of the Treasury. The episode evoked from Henry Ward Beecher a long-remembered eulogy of the Hebrew people. Before the echoes of the controversy died away, Hilton's store went bankrupt, passing into the hands of John Wanamaker.[9] When Mayer and his sons visited Saratoga, both hotels were open to Jews and Gentiles alike.

· III ·

In 1892 Irving Lehman began his studies in Columbia College, still on Madison Avenue at 50th Street, only a short walk from the family home, but soon to remove uptown to Morningside Heights. His interest in the law, his studiousness and thoughtfulness, had deepened. Herbert instead looked forward to a career in engineering, which his father fancied, or at any rate to pursuits suiting his active temper. An excursion early in the nineties gave him a new comprehension of the work to be done in his own city.

Frank Erwin was determined that the affluent boys of the Sachs School should realize how much poverty, illiteracy, and misery lay at their doors among what Jacob Riis called the submerged tenth. One day he took Herbert's class of 1895, neat in dark suits, polished high shoes, starched collars, and bowler hats, downtown on the Third Avenue elevated. Dismounting at the Bowery, they were soon in the heart of the so-called Great Ghetto of the Lower East Side, surrounded by squalor. All about rose tenements crowded with immigrants who could not afford to pay decent rentals. Their sharp features, rough dress, and foreign speech, Yiddish, Polish, or Russian, as they clustered about pushcarts loaded with food, clothing, or oddments, struck a chill to Herbert's heart. Though in a real sense these were his people, they were a world away from the comfortable brownstone houses, bright parlors, and hotels, theaters, and exclusive schools amid which he had been reared. His impressions were those set down by another sensitive young Jewish observer of a slightly later day: [10]

> I shall never forget how depressed my heart became as I trudged through those littered streets, with the rows of pushcarts lining the sidewalks and the center of the thoroughfare, the ill-smelling merchandise, and the deafening noise. . . . So this was America, I kept thinking. This was the boasted American freedom and opportunity—the freedom for respectable citizens to sell cabbages from hideous carts, the opportunity to live in those monstrous, dirty caves that shut out the sunshine.

Erwin led the boys through Livingston, Hester, Madison, and other slum streets. He visited the "lung block" which Jacob Riis had graphically described in *How the Other Half Lives*, a spot where thousands of people were crowded into one tenement block with no sewer connections, no recreation space, and so many windowless, airless rooms that the tuberculosis rate was horrifying. "I was shocked," Herbert has recalled. "I'm sure I couldn't have described my feelings to anybody. How much direct effect it had on my later thinking I don't know, but probably a good deal." His own father, after all, had begun life as an impoverished immigrant; his family kept the same devotion to the Torah, the same Jewish holidays, the same ancient loyalties, as these newcomers from Warsaw and Kiev. While the ritual and atmosphere of the dignified Temple Emanu-El were quite different from those in one of the little orthodox Shuln on Henry Street or Canal Street, both looked back to the teachings of Moses and Isaiah. After that visit in his twelfth year, he kept continuously in touch with the Lower East Side. He read some of Riis's exposures of slum hardships; and he soon found an institutional connection there—the Henry Street Settlement.

Just when his family became acquainted with Lillian Wald it would be hard to say; doubtless early in the 1890s. She grew up in prosperous German-Jewish surroundings in Rochester (though born in Cincinnati) and became interested in nursing. Several years after she graduated from the New York Hospital Training School for Nurses in 1891, the Women's Medical College of the city asked her to organize a course of instruction which would help the Lower East Side families to care for themselves. Persuading a fellow-nurse named Mary M. Brewster to join her, she went down to the slum district to live, obtained financial help from Mrs. Solomon Loeb, Jacob H. Schiff, and others, and set to work. Her sunny, sensible personality quickly brought her the affection of the hard-pressed families among whom she worked, nursing the ill, teaching diet and sanitation, and lending sympathy and counsel. As her staff of nurses grew she rented quarters in 1895 at 265 Henry Street, where she was to remain nearly forty years.[11]

When Herbert began going to the Nurses' Settlement, he found the house pulsing with vitality. He saw classes to instruct immigrant mothers and daughters in home nursing, cooking, and sewing in full swing; boys' and girls' clubs holding noisy meetings to plan recreation; and little groups presenting programs in music, dramatics, and art. With the people there tugging at his sleeve for help, he caught the inspiration and vigor of Miss Wald. She "radiated," as friends said.

Something of a gulf had to be crossed, for two different cultures were not easily reconciled. The new Jewish immigrants from Eastern Europe looked back to an immediate past far darker than that of their Central European brethren. Their lot in the Old World, long bleak, had taken a sharp turn for the worse in 1882. In that year Alexander III of Russia put into effect the first of a series of repressive acts forbidding them to acquire land and fixing a quota of ten and then three percent for them in secondary schools and universities. Finally, the government in 1890 ordered them en masse into the long-established "pale" of the western provinces, where they were confined in towns under strict surveillance. Many found life intolerable. Pogroms, sometimes organized by government officers, broke out among the more ignorant and prejudiced Russian people in 1881–82, again ten years later, and then again after 1903, the mobs giving themselves up to arson, plundering, and sometimes massacre. In the single year 1891 more than 75,000 Jews left Russia and Poland, great numbers pouring into the United States.[12]

Unlike their German-Jewish predecessors, they found the nation fully industrialized and to a great extent had to take factory jobs. Some successful German-Jewish mercantile firms, like the clothing house of Hart, Schaffner & Marx in Chicago, and the department stores of Macy, of Stern, and of Oppenheim & Collins in New York, also recruited employees from the East European influx. Sweatshops became a prominent element in the industrial scene; and as Jewish workers rebelled against exploitation, angry strikes ushered in a period of conflict in which Russian-Jewish operatives were aligned against the German-Jewish employers, East Sider against Uptowner.[13]

When census-takers in 1900 inquired into the occupations of 143,337 Russian immigrants, practically all Jewish, in the largest cities, they found three-fifths of them employed in manufacturing and construction, one-fifth in trade, and nearly one-tenth in domestic and personal service. Only 2.6 percent were as yet in the professions. By that date, as Ellis Rivkin points out, "the Jews whose roots were in the German phase of immigration had achieved a durable position in American life. Most of them had by this time firmly established themselves as very respectable middleclass entrepreneurs: retailers, wholesalers, private bankers, and manufacturers. As a consequence, they enjoyed the prestige that attended such entrepreneurship. It is not surprising, therefore, that they felt themselves more threatened by the vast hordes of Jews from Eastern Europe than did the non-Jews." [14]

One group was wealthy, cultivated, and in general conservative, its culture that of western Europe; the other and far more numerous body was poor, largely ill-educated though thirsty for knowledge, and possessed of Slavic attitudes. They had a common tie in the Jewish religion, but it was weakened by the resentment which some of the later immigrants felt over the secession of many of the earlier comers into Reformed Judaism. While they had common memories of persecution, those of East Europeans were more immediate and bitter; and while in time they shared a common drift toward Zionism, it was strongest among the East European Jews. Eventually the sense of Jewish solidarity triumphed over all obstacles, but the obstacles were sharp and irritating.

Although the statement of one Jewish historian that the Teutonic groups saw in the Russians and Poles "a frightening apparition" seems exaggerated, at the turn of the century the uptown and downtown Jews of New York were unquestionably as different from each other as the Irish Catholics and Anglo-American Protestants of the same city. Another Jewish historian, Moses Rischin, writes that to uptowners "nothing in the newcomers seemed worthy of approval." Yiddish was denounced as a piggish jargon; immigrant dress, ceremonials, and rabbinical divorces were attacked as alien; and the downtowners' trade unions were especially distasteful to uptowner employers. German Jews, resenting union activities or their rivals' business competition, seized on the fact that the names of many Russian Jews ended in "ki" and called the later immigrants "kikes." The uptown-downtown gulf separated employers from employees, classes from masses, and "desirables" from "undesirables." [15] Still, Dr. Rischin adds that uptowners of means spared no effort to assist downtowners in need, priding themselves on the maxim: "The uptown mansion never forgets the downtown tenement in its distress." Along with charitable associations like the United Hebrew Charities, such educational organizations as the Hebrew Free School Association, the YMHA, the Aguilar Free Library Society, and the Educational Alliance did much to bridge the gap between old and new.

Doubtless it was well that the newer immigrants kept much of their special spirit, and they had ample means to do so. The East European synagogues had no need for an English sermon, for the second as well as the first generation knew Yiddish. The tightly knit community of East Europeans gained more than it lost by adherence to the spirit and letter of the Talmud, for this strengthened their main traditions. Naturally, their harsh experiences in Poland and Russia, their stark poverty in the East Side slums, and their exposure to the polemic writings of the Yiddish press, gave many of them a radical outlook. If they left the synagogue it was to become complete heretics and free-thinkers, and they often combined with agnosticism a Socialist view of politics. The orthodox rabbinate naturally regarded their old forms of worship as a citadel against this radicalism. While the German Jew, with his ingrained West European culture, took easily to Anglo-American ideas and traditions, the East Europeans retained many of the Slavic traditions.

And what numbers the new immigrants marshaled! The United States in 1880 had 270 synagogues, most of them Reformed. But between 1880 and 1914 more than 600 new congregations were formed in New York City alone, nearly all Orthodox. In every year, 1904–08 inclusive, and again in 1913 and 1914, the East European Jewish immigration exceeded 100,000.

Everything about the newcomers had an intensity unknown to the old order. "Their poverty was more desperate than German-Jewish poverty, their piety more intense than German-Jewish piety, their radicalism more extreme than German-Jewish radicalism." Nearly as much as the old-stock Americans, German-Jews were taken aback by the intensive drill which the synagogue schools of the East Side gave to ghetto children, for these schools reproduced the work of the chedarim of Russia and Poland with little change.

"Children of a very tender age" (wrote one observer in 1905) "are admitted to these schools, and some ambitious parents send their offspring to a cheder even before they have attended a public school. The methods of instruction are as antiquated as one could imagine. The first years are devoted to teaching the art of reading, then translations, and finally the study of the Talmud. The drill is continuous and wearing. Specimens of children who attend these chedarim are not at all creditable as models of physical development. The cheder-bred youth has his earmarks, of which he is unable to rid himself even when fully grown. The schoolrooms are unsanitary and often a menace to health, but from the opposition of the patrons of these schools [to change], one would gather that just these features, the incessant drill, the long hours, the lack of ventilation, the crowdedness, are essential." Intense intellectualism, intense devotion to a special culture, and intense ambition were their natural product.

In the long run, one of the strongest ties between the old and new migration lay in the intellectual verve they shared. They were alike in their avid desire for knowledge, their appreciation of art, and their interest in concert rooms and theater. More and more frequently the poor East Sider found his way into the same university class as the grandson of the Rhenish or Bavarian merchant. Simeon Strunsky, born in Vitebsk, Russia, was in Columbia College while Irving Lehman studied in the Columbia Law School, the two young men matching each other in brilliance. Though Herbert never saw a performance by one of the five Yiddish theaters busy at the end of the century, he knew that talented actors and actresses—Boris Tomashefsky, Jacob P. Adler, Bertha Kalisch, Mrs. Sarah Adler—presented lively dramatizations of life in the "old country" and of the trials, aspirations, and achievements of newcomers in America. Though he never read the Yiddish press, he was well aware of the power of editors like Abraham Cahan of the *Daily Forward*, and knew that Cahan's *Yekl* and *The Rise of David Levinsky* were among the best immigrant novels written on American soil. The two branches of the Jewish stock drew slowly closer.

The huge population of East European Jews was to prove one of the most fertile seedbeds of talent the country has known. From it were to spring many of the best poets, novelists, critics, musicians, architects, painters, and scholars of the twentieth century. It was obviously important in another re-

spect. The great voting population of the Lower East Side, pressing steadily
outward (the Yiddish-speaking element being highly mobile) was soon to
form a special political body; for though Jews seldom voted as Jews, they did
vote with a pervasive intelligence, liberalism, and faith in ethnic democracy.
This political body was to prove vital to Herbert Lehman's career. It and
his inherited means, which after 1910 made it a matter of indifference
whether he followed a gainful pursuit or not, gave him full command of his
time, and allowed liberal contributions to party chests, were two corner-
stones of his political success.

· IV ·

In 1895 Irving Lehman completed his junior year at Columbia, where
President Seth Low was already planning the removal uptown. It was still a
college, the name "University" lying just ahead. That same June, Herbert
ended his studies in the Sachs School and prepared to enter college himself.
Though their paths were now to lie apart, their mutual devotion was un-
changed. The meditative Irving was fully resolved on the bar; the energetic
Herbert thought he was destined for an engineer's instruments and blue-
prints.

The family was beginning to break apart. All three daughters were married—Hattie to Philip Goodhart, Settie to Morris Fatman, and Clara to
Richard Limburg; and the Goodharts had a boy named Arthur who would in
time become the first American head of an Oxford college. The two oldest
sons, Sigmund and Arthur, were in the business. The father, Mayer, remained busy as ever, working hard at the office, but sparing time for the
affairs of the Montefiore Home for Chronic Invalids, the Hebrew Infant
Asylum, of which he was a director, and above all, the Mount Sinai Hospital,
where as board member he conscientiously walked the wards and kept a
vigilant eye on nurses and doctors. He and the mother, the strict, high-
spirited little Babette, were confident that Irving had a distinguished career
before him. They hoped that the robust, stirring Herbert would at least give
a good account of himself.

Chapter III

FROM COLLEGE
TO COUNTINGHOUSE

Early in 1895 a cloud which only one man had the wit to perceive hung over Herbert's head. It was the threat that he would enter an unsuitable career chosen to meet Mayer Lehman's idea of family symmetry, preparing for it by more years spent comfortably at home and close to old friends; years of acquiescence instead of initiative. Mayer had planned that two elder sons should go into the business, Irving should be a lawyer, and that Herbert should follow engineering. "I didn't argue with my father at all," Herbert later remarked. No youth living cared less for science, mathematics, or physics, and few knew less about them. However, he took his examinations for the Columbia School of Mines and to everybody's astonishment passed them.

At this point his teacher Frank Erwin intervened. Erwin took a personal interest in Herbert, knew the difference between a practical, resourceful businessman and a precise technologist and realized that the boy needed independence. He took the trouble to call on the Lehmans and spoke his mind: "If you send Herbert to the School of Mines you will spoil a capable business executive to make a poor engineer." The boy, he argued, should select his own business avenue. And when Mayer asked advice, Erwin had a ready answer: "I would send him to a good small college, for example, the one I attended, Williams." He explained that Herbert was not an intellectual and needed all-round training; and the parents agreed to the change.[1]

That autumn found Herbert under the reddening leaves of Williams, which he had not even considered until Erwin spoke. The time-mellowed college of William Cullen Bryant and James A. Garfield was a little institution of four hundred students, meager funds, limited faculty, and conservative outlook. Standing partly in the 18th and partly in the 19th century, it possessed a fine mossy classical tradition. Greek had just been struck from the list of required subjects (May, 1894), but most entrants still presented it. All freshmen pursued a rigidly required set of courses, but thereafter students might choose from a gradually widening number of electives. Life was simple. The $1,000 a year which Herbert's father allowed him seemed princely; it enabled him to pay tuition, dormitory rent, and board at $4 a week, and have a substantial sum left over. The student body was drawn almost wholly from prosperous old Anglo-Saxon families, and many of them had been trained at rather exclusive academies.[2] Two other graduates of the Sachs School, one named Kaufman and the other Mosenthal, entered Williams at the same time. Their arrival excited some consternation, and during the first week a thoughtless lad at the boardinghouse table made some slighting remark about the Jews. But when Herbert flared up resentfully and doubled his fists, the critic withdrew his aspersions, and they became good friends.

Nevertheless, the newcomer faced an ordeal. He was in a very strange place, a rural New England village; he was surrounded by strange young men, some suspicious if not half-hostile; he had to adjust himself to strange ideas and traditions. It is plain that he felt a sense of insecurity. One evidence of maladjustment was the self-assertive way in which he struck out to join nearly every organization he could. He was not much of an actor, but he competed for a place in the dramatic club. He played the cello badly but sought a place in the college orchestra. Without literary talent, he submitted material to the student newspaper and literary monthly. Lacking any special gifts of brawn, speed, or agility—he weighed 125 pounds on admission and barely reached five feet seven—he toiled perseveringly in athletics. He was ambitious to join the debating team.

All this might look like aggressiveness. But Herbert was a boy of such transparent honesty and goodwill, without a shred of guile or crumb of malice, that his ready grin, good sportsmanship, and—at that point—real humility, made friends even among rivals. This was the easier because at first he got nowhere. For most of the winter he remained a lonely outsider, suffering from homesickness and feeling isolated and rejected. He had many melancholy hours, all the bluer because everybody else seemed happy. Then toward spring a single incident completely changed his outlook.

"On the track team was a man named Harry Patterson," he relates, "whose father was a highly respected judge of the Supreme Court in New York. This boy was a senior and I was a freshman. He was captain of the track team, one of the big men on the campus, and looked about a million miles above me. I remember I jogged two miles a day; I was out for distance running. As I came into the dressing room in the gym Patterson hit me on the back and said: 'Freshman, you're not going to make the track team this year, but I do want you to know I admire your spirit, and I'm glad to have you on the squad!' Well, the biggest sum of money wouldn't have meant as much to me as the encouragement I took from that speech. It did everything for my morale."

The Big Man of the college had hailed the freshman as comrade and equal! At last, Herbert felt that he was inside the gates.

The freshman year had been gray enough, but the sophomore year offered a warmer atmosphere. Returning to the Williamstown hills as the Bryan-McKinley campaign raged, he continued his efforts to make a mark in some organization. Proof that his persistency was noted and his sportsmanship admired began to crop out. The second spring brought him an unexpected triumph. Time came to choose an assistant track team manager under the rule that the sophomore class should present three nominees and the whole college should then elect one. Three nominees were duly brought forward, capable young fellows; a boy later killed in the First World War, another who became prominent in the Corning Glass Company, and Herbert. When the whole college body met, Herbert took second place on the initial ballot, moved up on the next, and won a majority on the third. That not only made him assistant manager but automatically ensured him the managership at the end of his junior year.

In his later years he was on the debating team, acted parts in Cap and Bells productions, and joined the board of the literary monthly. He was also made acting manager of the football team.

Clearly, it was an energetic youth of versatile tastes and more interest in practical affairs than books who thus identified himself with the social life of the college. Although he would not have said so, he wanted to be an all-round man. At the same time, he was gentle and relaxed rather than sharply competitive, and never laughed better than when the joke was on himself. Despite the debating team, dramatic society, and literary monthly, he remained primarily an outdoors boy, with athletics his really passionate interest. As such he became a favorite of the director of the gymnasium, Charles F. Seeley. Williams and Amherst were old-time rivals, and their football and baseball matches generated much undergraduate excitement. Herbert, as hot a partisan as anybody, never forgot such encounters as one historic baseball game on Decoration Day, 1896. The team and its supporters streamed over the hilly roads to Amherst. They had a crack pitcher in Theodore Lewis, later president of the University of New Hampshire, but Amherst brought forward his superior in a Negro pitcher named James F. Gregory. Herbert cheered louder than anyone until, in the twelfth or thirteenth inning, Amherst won by a squeeze play. As the sad youths rode back to Williamstown, he was the most dejected of all.

The college had its special occasions: Chip Day, when students removed the debris that collected about the buildings during the winter; Gravel Day, when they cleaned up the muddy footpaths; the Cane Contest, the Burial of Euclid, and Class Day. One day, however, stood out above all others. Once a year fifteen or twenty men were elected from the junior class to the honorary Gargoyle Society. Doubtless it, like the Hasty Pudding Society at Harvard, and Skull and Bones at Yale, was more of a bane than a blessing, for it caused much heartburning; still, there it was. As the junior class perched on the fence in front of the laboratories, the senior members would appear, walk down the row, take the chosen neophytes by the hand, and lead them into their select circle.[3]

Of course Herbert aspired to be a Gargoyle; he aspired to everything. He awaited the critical moment with palpitation. It was creditable to him and the society that he was chosen—he was the first Jewish member.

The bustling youngster never tried to make high grades and never got them. Marks of B and C studded his record, with a solitary A for oratory; once he was conditioned in physiology, and he flunked analytical geometry. Nevertheless, some facts and ideas from the abler members of the faculty lodged in his mind. The president, Franklin Carter, a tall, slender man with long side whiskers and stately bearing, seemed a cold fish, and certainly held himself aloof from the boys. But he was anxious that Williams should preserve its old-time piety, intellectualism, and democracy and in his chapel talks (chapel being compulsory) laid emphasis on these traits. The dean, Warner Fite, was a psychologist of German training who, though hardly thirty, struck many students as already fossilized and who was more of a scholar than a humanist. One teacher of English and French literature was the brilliant Frank Jewett Mather, who later gained distinction at Princeton as a critic. The professor of chemistry, Leverett Mears, had a large reputation in his field and a robust personality that gave him a wide influence among the students. Leverett W. Spring taught rhetoric with skill, and Richard A. Rice was an experienced professor in "American history, literature, and eloquence." The tradition of Mark Hopkins and the log remained dominant, with capacity in instruction valued far above research. All the teachers worked hard, and some were overburdened.[4]

Personality counted in such a college. O. M. Fernald, professor of Greek, insisted on drill, discipline, and thoroughness. Cyrus M. Dodd, who had known William Cullen Bryant, taught mathematics, but loved literature, and was said to read the works of Walter Scott once a year. The professor of astronomy, Truman H. Safford, was a prodigy who solved intricate mathematical problems intuitively. Once a student propounded the query, "I was born at such and such an hour, minute, and second of a certain day; how old was I in seconds at the same time today?" Safford cocked his head on one side, strode up and down the room, and gave the answer. "No," said the boy, "I computed the number myself, and it is so and so." Safford cocked his head again, took several more turns across the room, and then exclaimed: "Ah, you forgot the leap years!"

Herbert learned quite as much outside the classrooms, however, as inside: lessons of persistence, good nature, tact, and leadership. He joined a chess club and helped edit a volume of stories of undergraduate life, *Williams Sketches*. He was finally elected president of the New England Intercollegiate Association, which managed track contests, and he played an active part therein. Once at an evening gathering of managers he drank so much "sherry-flip"—sherry with a raw egg in it—that he made himself desperately sick. He jested in verse about Carter's sideburns:

> And long may Prexy's whiskeriness
> The gentle zephyrs woo.

Once he let unruly companions drag him into a demonstration of which he was later ashamed. "Dean Fite was really a nice man, but as disciplinarian he became quite unpopular," he related. (Herbert received his full share of cards asking him to call at the office.) "The boys made their feelings known on a number of occasions. We had a ceremony every March 17th called the Shirt Tail Parade, which supposedly marked the cessation of hostilities between freshmen and sophomore classes. They always had a big bonfire around which all the members of the two classes gathered, and after a final tussle, which got pretty rough, they made peace. Then all joined hands and marched around the fire. On this particular night somebody suggested, 'Let's go up to Fite's house and show the way we feel about him.' Of course everybody agreed, and in the end the whole college went up, upperclassmen as well as freshmen and sophomores. We crowded under his windows and became most insulting to the poor man. It's something I've always regretted, and it taught me how a crowd can be carried away by mass emotions. Dean Fite left at the end of that year."

When Herbert graduated from Williams in June, 1899, he could feel that an understanding of its spirit, an appreciation of its traditions, was the principal acquisition that he had made in his four undergraduate years. Here was an institution founded by the brave provincial colonel who fell in the

Mayer Lehman, the father of Herbert H. Lehman, about 1867
Photo Leonhard Kuhn, Würzburg

The Mayer Lehman Family at Tarrytown, about 1886

First row, left to right: Herbert H. Lehman, Irving Lehman; *second row, seated, left to right:* Sister Hattie, Mrs. Philip J. Goodhart, with daughter Helen (later Mrs. Frank Altschul) on lap, Mayer Lehman with grandson Howard L. Goodhart on lap, Babette Lehman with grandson Allan Lehman on lap, sister Settie (Mrs.

Morris Fatman) with daughter Margaret (later Mrs. Werner Josten) on lap; *top row, left to right:* Philip J. Goodhart, sister-in-law Harriet (Mrs. S. M. Lehman), Sigmund M. Lehman, sister Clara (later Mrs. Richard Limburg), brother-in-law Morris Fatman, brother Arthur Lehman.

Photographer unknown, probably by local photographer

Above: Herbert H. Lehman
and his brother Irving
Lehman, in 1884, when the
former was six and the latter
eight years old

Photo Thomas, New York City

Right: Herbert H. Lehman in
1899, the year of his graduation from Williams College

Photo Pach Brothers

defeat of the French at Ticonderoga, Ephraim Williams; nursed to strength by frugal, God-fearing Congregational teachers; seat of the Haystack Meeting in 1806, which marked the effective beginning of foreign mission work by Americans; lifted to eminence by President Mark Hopkins, one of the great teachers and administrators of his time; and alma mater of famous men —Bryant, William Lowndes Yancey, John J. Ingalls, David Dudley Field, Garfield, Bliss Perry. It had long kept its door open to poor boys. "Until the day of my graduation," wrote one, "I never had an article of woolen clothing which was not spun and woven and made upon the farm from the wool of our own sheep, and I never wore a boot or shoe that was not made from the hides of our own herd, slaughtered on our own farm." It had graduated many a minister as eloquent as Orville Dewey, many a public servant as useful as David A. Wells, and many an educator as powerful as the John Bascom who remade the University of Wisconsin or the Samuel Chapman Armstrong who founded Hampton Institute. Surrounded by its august memories, and seeing its distinguished alumni come back to lecture, Herbert caught something of Mark Hopkins's passion for three great goals: intellectual power, refined taste, and moral excellence.

His devotion to Williams was never to flag. In time he was given an honorary doctorate of laws; he furnished money for a dormitory called Lehman Hall and for a professorship; he contributed to current needs. Some thirty years after he left the college, an unprecedented event occurred. All other candidates for the post of alumni trustee withdrew, asking that he be elected unanimously, and the college notified him that he had been chosen by acclamation for a five-year term.

· I ·

On graduation in the spring of 1899 the young man unhesitatingly entered business. The family still owned interests in some cotton mills, and his father had been a friend of J. Spencer Turner, head of a New York textile firm of importance. It was one of the largest manufacturers and jobbers of cotton canvases, denims, and duck; that is, coarse strong fabrics used for summer clothing, tarpaulins, tents, bags, and other sturdy purposes. The offices were at 86 Worth Street, in an old building within a block of the structure that the famous dry goods firm of H. B. Claflin & Company had used as a store. Lehman, living at home, began at five dollars weekly. This did not suffice for his needs, but it gave him pride, and from his first pay envelope he took a crisp two-dollar bill, which he framed as a lifelong memento. All kinds of unimportant jobs were given him as training, and he soon became a fairly proficient salesman of duck: duck for trousers, duck for heavy belting in mills, duck for everything.

His father's sudden death on June 21, 1897, of an intestinal obstruction that physicians of the next generation could easily have cured, had been a heavy shock. It had called forth many tributes from business and charitable organizations, some of which went beyond formal panegyric to express real feeling. Kindliness, manliness, and courtesy were the qualities on which his friends most dwelt. The Cotton Exchange closed for his funeral, his fellow directors in the Hamilton Bank, the N. K. Fairbank Company, the International and Mortgage Bank of Mexico, and other concerns voted appropriate resolutions, and all his many charitable organizations drew up tributes. The family continued to occupy the house at 5 East Sixty-second Street until 1902, when Herbert's mother sold it, and she and he removed to 175 West Fifty-eighth Street, "the Spanish Flats." The circle remained as closely knit as ever, for her children in the city made it a rule to call at least once a day, usually in late afternoon. The spirited little woman was as much the matriarch as ever. Herbert always remembered how, when Rector's Restaurant became famous, she demanded to be taken to it and ate a larger meal than he did.

In those presubway days Herbert took the Sixth Avenue El downtown to work. At noon he lunched with friends at Bustanoby's Restaurant, then in its infancy and a small place. In the evening he often walked all the way uptown with his old schoolmate working in the neighborhood, Jerome Koehler. They would stop at the Hoffman House on Thirtieth Street for a glass of beer, or at Huyler's farther along for an ice-cream soda, and forge on home. Another friend was Larry Arnstein, of a California family, who shared Herbert's interest in East Side slum work and talked with him about such books as Jacob Riis's *How the Other Half Lives* and *The Ten Years' War;* we shall hear of Arnstein later.[5]

Herbert found his activities congenial. Though he always said later that he had not been a success in drumming up trade, his likable personality made him a favorite with certain customers, who specially asked for him at Spencer Turner's. One was Myron C. Taylor, an upstate New Yorker a few years older than he with a law degree from Cornell. Taylor's father for years held the contract for supplying mail bags to the government and used Spencer Turner's canvas. The two young men became fast friends. Altogether, Herbert showed a flair for business. Before the end of 1906—that is, at 28— he had become vice-president and treasurer of the Turner Company.

"Whatever knowledge I have had of business came much more from my ten years' experience in a merchandising house than from the investment banking business," he has recorded. The firm being of medium size, he had to master every aspect of its activities; to solve problems of management, credit, hiring and discharging employees, public relations, and all the rest. One of his first assignments was to visit a small cotton mill in North Carolina and work two or three months to familiarize himself with factory methods. He learned the merits of different looms, became able to identify at sight the various weights and counts of cloth, and knew how to appraise the best market outlets—though he was never an expert manufacturer.

Worth Street was (and is) a great metropolitan center of the textile industry. Scattered about on Leonard Street, Thomas Street, West Broadway, and neighboring thoroughfares were cotton firms that Lehman came to know well. Large commission houses like Wellington, Sears & Company and Dearing, Milliken and Company did an important business. The Cone interests in North Carolina, with large mills, maintained an export corporation in New York. Stevens & Company, headed by John Peter Stevens, whose son Robert in time became Secretary of the Army, was active. One young executive whom Herbert Lehman came to know well was Leon Lowenstein, associated with his father in Morris Lowenstein & Sons, then a modest house but one destined to grow to tremendous size, with a completely integrated array of cotton textile and rayon factories, bleaching plants, and printing mills, served by its own large sales organization.

To young Lehman the revolution which overtook the cotton textile industry in the first dozen years of the century was a fascinating process. Until 1900 manufacturing and selling had been divided among a large number of companies, some of them extensive and prosperous. Now the day of great combinations of mills was dawning. At the same time, the rise of powerful department stores and chain stores, able to buy directly from the mills, was destroying the middlemen's business that firms like H. B. Claflin's had conducted. Most striking of all was the geographical shift of the industry from New England to the South, a shift which Lehman appreciated the more because of his Southern background.

At the beginning of the century most of the giant textile mills were still in Lawrence, Lowell, Pawtucket, Providence, and other Yankee cities, or just across the line in upper New York. But by 1910 the gravitation to the Carolinas, Georgia, and Alabama had made impressive progress. The more obvious reasons for it lay in proximity to raw cotton, the low wages of Southern mill hands, and occasional advantages of preferential tax and freight rates.

An equally important if less prominent factor, however, was the rise of shrewd and dynamic management in the South. The older Northern mills had passed largely under absentee ownership. The able New Englanders who had made them famous—Amos A. Lawrence, Francis C. Lowell, Nathan Appleton, William Sprague—had long since died; their children had gone West or to Europe; and these heirs refused to plow enough of the profits back into the business to keep the mills abreast of new competition. They failed to buy the best automatic machinery, to develop waterpower, and to hire enterprising salesmen. The principal Cohoes mills offered a classic example of the power of one generation to dissipate the wealth which the previous generation had amassed. The founder established his factory solidly, made a large fortune, and died while his business still flourished. The daughters then married foreigners who neglected the works, spent all the profits, and let the company become too feeble to compete with its rivals.[6]

Lehman took an informed interest in the mechanization of the industry, for soon after he joined the Turner Company he acquired an interest in a concern near Boston which made new automatic looms of remarkable power. This was the Stafford Company headed by one of Lehman's oldest and closest friends, S. R. Fuller, Jr. The firm was then struggling against an older and well-entrenched manufacturer of automatic machinery called the Draper Company. Having large financial resources, the Draper firm could give longer credits and better service than the Stafford group. Nevertheless, Herbert and a brother who joined him maintained the struggle until they got their factory squarely on its feet, when they sold it to Draper.

Another department of the industry which specially interested Lehman was the export trade. The Turner Company tried to sell a large part of its denims, coarse shirts, canvases, and yarns in China and the Middle East. It found, however, that competition with Great Britain and Japan was difficult, for the textile manufacturers of these countries paid assiduous court to foreign lands. Other American houses gave Spencer Turner no cooperation; they were too independent, ignorant, or indifferent to study alien tastes. British and Japanese firms would pack their goods for the Asiatic markets in carefully labeled packages holding just the sizes demanded; they would fill orders for forty-eight yard pieces; they would take infinite pains with patterns, colors, and textures. American manufacturers, meanwhile, were contemptuous of foreign specifications except when a domestic slump put them in dire need of the overseas market. This spasmodic alternation of inattention and frenzied interest did much to explain why nearly all American industry was weaker in export trade than Germany, Britain, and Japan.

Altogether, with his lively temperament, his interest in people and processes, and his taste for active participation in affairs, Lehman found the combination of manufacturing and marketing more congenial than engineering, banking, or the law would have been. A bit awkward, decidedly quiet, and the soul of courtesy, he was not what people called a hustler, but his unvarying geniality, good humor, and unselfishness made friends everywhere. As a salesman he became familiar with a wide range of customers: the buyers who wanted eight-ounce duck for summer skirts, buyers who wanted awnings, buyers who wanted "drier-canvas" for conveyers of wood pulp in paper mills. He learned to cope with the unpredictable variations of business: slumps in demand, the easing or tightening of credit, the effects of good and poor cotton crops. His business associates, including his boss, J. Spencer Turner, were likable men. Turner, a gentleman of taste who lived with a delightful wife and three sons in an old-fashioned brownstone house on Brooklyn Heights, sometimes asked Lehman to a meal. After his death, the company remained prosperous. In 1906, however, it merged with most of the other canvas and denim manufacturers in the country under the name of the Mount Vernon–Woodberry Cotton Duck Company, the Turner organization becoming the sales component. Lehman agreed to remain for three years and found the new relationship nearly as pleasant as the old.

· II ·

During these early years of the century Lehman's social life, though healthfully active, was simple. He had numerous companions of his own age, Gentile and Jewish, men and women, business and professional people. The automobile was still a rarity; most amusements were inexpensive; drinking in his circle was unknown; and young men worked too hard to keep late hours.

His ambitious associates were rising in the world. Eugene Meyer, several years older, who had come to New York from California and Yale, was head of his own banking firm; Paul Sachs, after leaving college, joined Goldman, Sachs & Company, his career as head of the Fogg Art Museum all before him; Sam A. Lewisohn, whose sister Adele married Lehman's brother, had entered his family's banking house; and Hans Zinsser was well embarked upon medicine. Isaac Untermyer and Samuel Untermyer had gone into the law—both much senior to Herbert. Irving Lehman, leaving Columbia with his LL.B. in 1898, had started as a law clerk in the office of Marshall, Moran, Williams, & McVicker but had not remained in that humble station long. His brilliant mind—with his rich connections helping—made him a partner in 1901, the year he married Sissie Straus. Before the end of 1906 the firm had become Worcester, Williams & Lehman, and he was recognized as one of the abler young scholars at the New York Bar.

Three years later he became a justice of the Supreme Court of the State. On grounds of merit a better selection could not easily have been made. But such posts were then political plums, and he later explained his swift rise frankly. "I was a very young lawyer, in practice only a short time; I was deaf; and I was Jewish. None of these helped. But I was married to Nathan Straus's daughter, and Mr. Straus was a dear friend of Al Smith, and Smith knew the governor of New York. So I became a judge." Party gifts did help smooth his way, for Irving and his father-in-law both gave substantial sums. At a public dinner Irving once spoke so frankly about owing his early place on the bench to Straus's campaign contributions—"Oh, I guess he gave $25,000 or $50,000 that year"—that Robert Moses heard Chief Judge Crane cut in: "Please, Lehman, leave a little mystery about the way we reach our high stations!"

Herbert's zest for outdoor pursuits was still keen. He spent some summer vacations in the Catskills, where one of his uncles owned a place on the East Branch of the Scoharie, near the area where the Fleischmann family had developed a resort village bearing their name. He knew several of the children of this energetic trio of brothers, one the founder of the Fleischmann Yeast Company, one a distiller, and one owner of a popular bakery and restaurant near Grace Church. They and their two sisters owned five or six hundred acres, with a grid of roads and paths, a large swimming pool, and a riding academy. "If you were friends of the Fleischmanns you were all right; if you weren't you didn't have much of a time"—and he had been a friend since his teens. A good many young people lived in cottages scattered over the resort. The village had one train daily, which arrived at dusk, and a favorite evening diversion was to troop to the station to see whom it brought and then to Miller's drug store for an ice-cream soda.

At Kildare he continued to spend occasional weeks in Adirondack woods nearly as wild as in Uncas's day. He, his cousins, and their friends swam, rode, fished, and picnicked. They also, as he relates, played practical jokes on each other. "Isaac Untermyer was very proud of his marksmanship, and we were much amused by his pride. Behind his back we used to make fun of it, because we didn't think he was nearly as good as he supposed he was. One day we brought a stuffed deer down from the clubhouse to the banks of Kettle Creek, and rigged it up so that we could move the head. We put this deer into a thicket about a hundred feet from the road. He arrived at the station very early in the morning and drove up, and when he got to this place about two miles from the clubhouse somebody pointed out this deer. He jumped from the carriage with his repeating rifle, put it to his shoulder, and started to pump. He shot and shot, the deer kept standing, and he got madder and madder and more embarrassed."

An Adirondack episode cured Herbert of all interest in hunting. He drove one afternoon to the Kildare station to pick up some provisions, taking two girl cousins with him. As they returned dusk came on. When they passed some open fields below the Kildare forest they suddenly saw on a hill, outlined against the sky, a deer. In the gloom it appeared a large animal, and the driver exclaimed: "That's a fine buck!" Lehman leaped from the carriage, seized his rifle, and took aim. He was notoriously a wretched marksman, and the animal was fully 200 yards away, but with one of the few accurate shots of his life he brought it down. They all ran over to examine the quarry— and it was a beautiful fawn! He was so sore-hearted that he never aimed at an animal or bird again; clay pigeons he would shoot, but nothing else.

Of fishing he was fonder than ever, losing few opportunities to cast a hook into water. One summer he was able to go to Canada with his eldest brother and a cousin to try for salmon in the Tobique River. He found strenuous exercise but little luck until one morning he came close to a great feat. Going out with an Indian guide to paddle the boat, to his astonishment he hooked a monster fish. The rule was to play the salmon a while, then bring it to shore, and continue playing it till it could be netted. But he was totally inexperienced, did not know how much faith to place in his line, and could not get the salmon within reach of his guide. A good fisherman could have made the catch within half an hour, but Lehman bungled it, his excited yells bringing onlookers until everybody within miles seemed watching. After an hour and forty-two minutes he had the salmon at the shore, so exhausted it was nearly dead. The Indian lifted the gaff and struck at its side; but in his eagerness he struck over the line instead of under it, cutting the leader. With a flip of the tail the fish swam away. Lehman leaped into the water for a despairing grab, but he was too late.

Shortly before leaving Williams in 1899, he had joined one of the earliest Westchester golf associations, the Century Country Club, which laid out a nine-hole course on the Sound. Mosquitoes proved such an affliction that the club removed first to White Plains and then to Purchase. Lehman used to plod over its 18-hole course in 100 to 105 strokes, the quality of his game neither rising nor falling. After college he bought a Mercedes car and drove about adventurously. He kept up his tennis, too, with enthusiasm but without improvement, giving spectators plenty of amusement.

An old family investment in Everglades land meanwhile furnished opportunity for several interesting Florida trips. His father had bought a participation in the Southern States Land & Timber Company, which, with an eye to the timber values, acquired two million watery acres in the area. The charges for taxes, assessments, canal-building, and swamp drainage, however, steadily destroyed any prospect of a profit. Shareholders had the rueful experience, after paying out a great deal more than they expected ever to get back, of listening to the sarcastic comments of friends on the colossal fortunes they were making as owners of two million Florida acres, bought at 22.5 cents an acre. When Lehman visited the district between Lake Okeechobee and the Atlantic in 1905–06, the primitive wilderness of the swampy country made a lasting impression on him. The roads were rough, the jungles thorny, the waterways infested by alligators, moccasins, and cottonmouths. Palm Beach was a mere hamlet. Although Miami had been given railway connections by Henry M. Flagler ten years earlier, its real development had not begun, and Miami Beach had not yet been founded. To get to a fishing hamlet on the eastern side of Okeechobee, Lehman had to jounce twenty-five miles in a strong-wheeled cart, and then to cross to the western shore he had to hire a gasoline launch.

Here, as in the textile business, he learned some lessons in practical economics. The deep rich soil of the Everglades district, once drained, would obviously lend itself to an extensive agricultural development, and before long did support flourishing farm communities. But this was only after science had come to the aid of the settlers. The soil was so deficient in certain chemicals and excessively rich in others that not until analysts prescribed an expert treatment could the farmers grow successful crops. When the Southern States Company experimented with sugar, its cane grew luxuriantly, but it proved all stalk and foliage, with little sugar content. Scientific research eventually made sugar production profitable. When the company introduced cattle its managers found that the area was full of ticks which spread the lethal Texas fever among them. Again the scientists prescribed, and the Rockefeller Foundation popularized the correct remedy, tanks of cattle-dip disinfectant through which the livestock was driven, so that Florida soon boasted some of the greatest cattle ranches of the country. Citrus fruit had long been grown with profit in central Florida, and the help of expert pomologists carried the industry into the southern part of the state. To the end, however, the history of the Southern States Company remained one of wretched returns.[7]

· III ·

In 1908, after finishing his promised term with the Mount Vernon–Woodberry Company, Herbert joined Lehman Brothers as a partner. Control of that firm was now in the hands of the second generation. Emanuel, retiring soon after Mayer's death, had died on January 10, 1907. The business had then been carried on by Philip, Sigmund, Arthur, and Meyer H. Lehman, under whom it rapidly expanded and altered its character. Taking advantage of the booming industrial activity of the decade 1898–1907, when the United States advanced to world primacy in many areas of manufacture and trade, the house invaded new fields. Sigmund, who had always said that he would retire at fifty, did so in 1908. As it was still the rule that all partners should be members of the family, Herbert was enlisted to close the gap.

When he began entering the large door at 16 William Street, where the Farmer's Loan & Trust Building sheltered the firm, the financial community had almost completely recovered from the recent panic. The next five years were to witness a renewal of the economic boom and to give Herbert opportunity to play an active part in a complete transformation of the house.

Under its founders Lehman Brothers had been mainly occupied with trading in such basic commodities as sugar, grain, cotton, petroleum, and coffee. Gradually, however, the firm had undertaken large ventures in financing. For some years it had represented Alabama in the North, selling state bonds, paying interest due, and helping supervise contracts. Always interested in the development of the South, the Lehmans had helped finance railroads, iron companies, textile mills, and land and timber companies there. In the New York area they had helped organize several large banks and trust companies: the Queens County Bank on Long Island (1873), the Mercantile Bank (1880), the Trust Company of America (1899), and the Mutual Alliance Trust Company (1902). Beginning about 1890, they had shared in the formation of important gas, ferry, and traction companies in and about New York, this work being of special interest to Emanuel.[8]

Now, in the years between Theodore Roosevelt's accession to power and the First World War, the country was manufacturing consumer goods on a new scale. Living standards were rising, leisure was growing, and new commodities from breakfast foods to Model T cars, and from refrigerators to phonographs, were being popularized. Mail-order houses, like Montgomery, Ward and Sears, Roebuck, and chains of retail stores, like Woolworth's and Kresge's, were covering the nation. An active investment-banking house had to take an alert interest in this broad new sector of the national economy. Down to 1906, very little of the public money-market was open to entrepreneurs in the mass-merchandising field. But in that year Lehman Brothers adventurously joined with Goldman, Sachs in selling the public some $10,-000,000 worth of preferred stock in Sears, Roebuck, along with a considerable amount of common stock. Similar offerings followed. This type of enterprise culminated during the prewar period in the underwriting of security issues for the Studebaker Corporation (1911) and the F. W. Woolworth Company (1912).

The inspiration of the Sears, Roebuck flotation came largely from Philip

Lehman. Julius Rosenwald of Springfield, Illinois—a brilliant man of German-Jewish stock, born in a house just across the street from Lincoln's—had become vice-president and treasurer of Sears, Roebuck in 1895, at the age of thirty-three, and held that office until fifteen years later he became president. Though he was anxious to enlarge the activities of his firm, for some time he never thought of going to a large investment banker for money. Then he discussed with Philip Lehman and Henry Goldman his desire to borrow $5,000,000 privately. They suggested a sale of stock instead and he agreed. The public subscribed eagerly, and no investor ever had reason to regret his purchase.

The Lehman partners showed equal enterprise in assisting other great distributors of merchandise. They began supplying capital to the Underwood Corporation in 1910 and the Continental Can Company in 1913. Then the launching of the Studebaker Corporation in the latter year was an undertaking which required great boldness and scored a memorable success. The name Studebaker had originally represented a family-owned manufactory in South Bend, Indiana. In 1908 the corporation made arrangements with the Everitt-Metzer-Flanders Company, manufacturers of automobiles in Michigan, which gave it exclusive marketing rights for what were to be called the Studebaker-E-M-F cars, and shortly afterward it became sole owners of the business. At the same time, in response to the wave of consolidations sweeping the automobile business, it acquired the Wayne Automobile Company and the Northern Automobile Company of Detroit. By 1910, in fact, it had absorbed the properties of seven different makers of cars, steel, and automobile parts. That year it earned profits of more than $1,600,000 upon the sale of nearly $14,000,000 worth of cars.[9]

Money was clearly needed for expansion. Under the leadership of a son-in-law of J. M. Studebaker named Frederick S. Fish, a new Studebaker Corporation was formed early in 1911 to take over the assets of the combination. Philip Lehman and Henry Goldman helped to create it and to market 175,000 shares of seven percent preferred stock and 3,000,000 shares of common stock. The conservative nature of the financing is evidenced by the fact that the $13,500,000 worth of preferred stock was issued for only 57 percent of the net tangible assets, giving it an original book value of $175.50 a share, while the common stock had a book value of $36.49. The new corporation did well from the outset. More than a thousand sales agencies handled the 22,500 cars manufactured in 1911 and the 28,500 manufactured in 1912. Net profits in the former year ran above $1,650,000 and in the latter above $2,-300,000.

The close personal friendship of Philip Lehman and Henry Goldman made the cooperation of the two houses congenial. Both men were conservative in outlook and methods. Lehman Brothers made it a rule, for example, never to advertise in magazines, trade journals, official programs, or any media except the daily press, and then only in connection with specific securities. Goldman, Sachs had a similar reputation for caution, dignity, and gilt-edged solidity. In their homes as in their offices Philip and Henry felt a congenial harmony of tastes.

Year by year Lehman Brothers prospered. Of course, the house made its share of mistakes. Herbert found that although it never owned any large body of securities in its corporate capacity, for its business was to sell them to customers, it did have a ledger which listed certain holdings. Soon after he became a partner he examined it. One page recorded ownership of three hundred $1,000 bonds of the Chicago & Alton, then regarded as a veritable Gibraltar of security and strength. Other pages carried entries for one thousand shares of Bethlehem Steel, which was esteemed a cat-and-dog stock, and a block of Electric Boat Company stock, also deemed highly speculative. During the war, Bethlehem, with large British and American contracts, shot up to about $500 a share, and Electric Boat, with heavy orders for submarines, rose spectacularly, while the "prime" Chicago & Alton dropped into a gulf. But conservatism usually paid.

If the cotton duck business had been interesting, the varied and large-scale undertakings of Lehman Brothers were still more absorbing. While they meant hard work, and the mastery of forbidding masses of detail, they were full of instruction upon the economic growth of the fast-advancing nation. To this story we shall return. But Lehman's absorption in business was temporarily interrupted by his marriage on April 28, 1910, to Edith Altschul, and then for a longer period by the outbreak of the European War.

· IV ·

The marriage was very much a love match. Edith Altschul, a tall, slender, blonde girl of twenty, carried herself with Western independence, for she had begun life in California. Her father Charles was English-born of American parents, obtaining American citizenship through them. He had been educated partly in German schools but for much the same reasons as Mayer Lehman always loved England and hated Germany; in fact, he devoted years of effort to the promotion of better relations between Britain and America. Migrating to California as a young man, he had married there and taken a place in the London-Paris-American Bank of San Francisco. Later he returned East to become head of the New York branch of Lazard Frères.

Edith, who was ten or eleven at the time and unhappy over the move, had attended Dr. Sachs's School for Girls two years and then Dr. Jacobi's School, finishing her formal education in private classes in history and literature taught by Louis K. Anspacher, the poet and dramatist. Perhaps her best training, however, was informal. Since her father's business took him frequently to Europe the family traveled widely, and as he loved art and music —he was a passionate Wagnerian—she went to galleries, concerts, and operas in every capital from Vienna to Paris and London.

Herbert and Edith first met in 1908, while she was laying plans to enter the nursing school at Mount Sinai Hospital, and they became engaged in February, 1910. The Altschuls had lived on the West Side in Manhattan, on 80th and then 86th Street near Central Park, and the two had moved in much the same social circle. When Herbert first became interested, he was known as a debonair young bachelor who drove a sporty Mercedes, attended many parties, loved children—he gave much time to nephews and nieces—played games badly, was devoted to his mother, and took a hand in social work. The Larry Arnstein already mentioned, a relative of Edith's, spoke earnestly about him one day.[10]

"It is time you were getting married, Edith," he said. "You ought to look around; in particular, I wish you would look at Herbert Lehman. He is a solid young man. We used to read and discuss Jacob Riis and Charles Booth together. He goes to the Henry Street Settlement to be useful. There is good stuff in him. He was not born in a tuxedo!"

"I was much amused by this," Edith later commented. "Here Herbert Lehman was already quite attentive. When we were apart we corresponded. And out of a blue sky Larry Arnstein suggested that I give him favorable consideration!"

For his part, said a friend, "he was madly in love." [11] And he realized that Edith had qualities that he lacked. She was a better judge of people. In many matters he was often naïve; she was shrewd. He remembered names badly; she seldom forgot them. Where he was clumsy she was tactfully adroit. For example, they agreed they should be married by their friend Rabbi Judah L. Magnes. They went to pay a courtesy call on him several days before the wedding, and Herbert enjoined on his fiancée: "Now if he asks us to tea, we must not accept, for we ought to get away early for an evening engagement." The call was pleasant and they lingered longer than they should. As they shook hands on departure, Herbert blurted out: "I am sorry we cannot stay to tea, for we are really much pressed." Astonishment overspread the rabbi's face, for he had never thought of asking them to tea! But Edith quickly covered their confusion.

For their honeymoon they went to Europe—the gay prewar Europe that was so different from the half-wrecked continent of a few years later. Then they took an apartment at 88 Central Park West, a part of town she always thought intrinsically preferable to the fashionable eastern side. However, they soon decided on a country residence and removed to the rural area of Westchester called Purchase, just northwest of White Plains; thereafter spending the summers and most weekends at their new home and the winters in a hotel, first the Gotham and then the Ambassador. Herbert taught his wife to play tennis, at which she soon bested him.

Purchase has a township history dating back beyond Anne Hutchinson's days. What attracted the Lehmans to it was its completely open character, its fine views from a plateau overlooking the Sound, and its proximity to Herbert's country club. Soon after marriage they found a house which they would have bought at once but for the exorbitant price. Lehman made what he thought a fair bid and asked the owner to decide at once, for he wished to make the property a gift to his wife on her birthday in 1911. Finally he delivered an ultimatum: "I won't change my price, but you must make your decision before midnight tomorrow." The owner still delayed. Then, the Lehmans found another place just across the road which since Revolutionary days had been in the hands of the Burling family who gave their name to Burling Slip in Manhattan. The owner had cultivated it as a farm, and the well-kept fields, unspoiled woods, and distant prospect of the Sound made it beautiful. At first Lehman thought he would remodel the century-old house, but his architect warned him it would be cheaper and more satisfactory to erect a new dwelling; and this he did.

After their marriage, almost by accident, the Lehmans as a pastime took up the breeding of boxer dogs and for some years were the leading American specialists. This was the easier because they were childless. The stocky, spirited dog had been developed principally in Germany, and was almost unknown in the United States when Irving Lehman acquired an inferior specimen. The Lehmans made a pet of it, appreciated its intelligence and affection, and resolved to produce more worthy types. In 1912 they imported a pair from Switzerland for breeding purposes, established a kennel at their new house, and soon had the first American champion, with which they won prizes all over the East. The kennel grew until at one time between 75 and 100 dogs made the air resound. Of course, when election as Lieutenant-Governor finally called Lehman to Albany, his interest in the establishment diminished. Nevertheless, he and Mrs. Lehman kept breeding boxers until about 1938, when they disposed of the few remaining dogs. One reason for giving the kennel up was that they almost monopolized the prizes;

another was that they refused to accept the general practice of cropping the ears of the dogs. They never permitted any such mutilation, and Lehman was pleased when it was later forbidden by state law.

After 1942 even intermittent residence at "Meadowfarm," as they called the Purchase place, ceased. But it was not until 1954 that they sold the farm to a neighbor, the noted book-collector Carl Pforzheimer, who later donated it to Westchester County as a health center.

Not until after marriage did Lehman begin to take a keen interest in politics. He had gathered from Alabama traditions, the family friendship for Hilary A. Herbert (after whom he was named) and Chief Justice White, and from his father's strong convictions a set of Democratic opinions. "One of my earliest recollections of my father," he tells us, "was in 1884. In those days, of course, they had those old-style torchlight processions, and my father marched in the Cleveland procession carrying one of the tallow torches. . . . He was wearing a new coat which he had just bought, and when he came home the coat was covered with tallow. My mother was not too pleased about it." [12] The rise of Woodrow Wilson found him an enthusiastic adherent of that impressive leader. When the National Convention of 1912 met in Baltimore he did not attend, but he was so anxious over the result that, as the struggle between Champ Clark and Wilson reached its climax, he went down to his office at night to get the news hot over the telegraph ticker. He argued fiercely with Republican friends that fall. Before he could find time for much political activity, however, the war carried him outside the state.

Chapter IV

WORLD WAR AND
AFTERMATH

To THE New York business community the murder of Archduke Francis Ferdinand at Sarajevo seemed a meaningless episode and was soon half-forgotten. But Lehman, who had repeatedly visited Germany and Austria and followed Continental European politics with interest, at once anticipated that the Central Powers might use the crime as an occasion for provoking war. With horror he watched the reckless activities of Count Berchtold in pressing his ultimatum, the excited responses of Belgrade, Berlin, and St. Petersburg, the mobilizations, and the stumble of Europe into the abyss; but he was less astonished than those about him.

From the outset his feelings were strongly aroused on the side of the Allies. Family antipathy to Germany counted in this, but his devotion to democratic principles and Anglo-American ideas of law and civil liberties, with detestation of militarism and autocracy, weighed a good deal more. Since he believed that two irreconcilable ideologies were in conflict, Wilson's plea for neutrality in thought and act simply irritated him. Convinced that the victory of imperial Germany would menace the future of the United States, he quickly grew impatient with Administration policy, and as the war became more desperate, felt incensed that the government did nothing to help Britain and France. He shared the bellicose attitudes of Theodore Roosevelt. When the *Lusitania* was sunk in May, 1915, he thought the United States should declare war on Germany at once. From the standpoint of our subsequent knowledge his position was naïve, for he exaggerated both Allied virtue and German villainy. But from the same standpoint his and Theodore Roosevelt's impetuosity was more sensible than it seemed at the time; American intervention in 1915, before Europe was exhausted and animosities grew incurable, might have ended the war on a healthier basis than that of 1918.

Disgusted though he was with Wilson's waiting policy and the phrase "too proud to fight," Lehman was ardently in favor of the President's reëlection in 1916. He approved of Wilson's domestic program and believed him a man of larger mind and vision than Hughes, whose stiff personality repelled him. (Years later, spending several days with Hughes in Jasper Park, Canada, he came to know him as a warmhearted, companionable man, a lively story-teller, and a penetrating commentator on events.) On election night the Lehmans went to the Democratic headquarters in a midtown hotel to hear the returns. By midnight, as state after state in the East and Middle West declared for Hughes, a sodden melancholy had settled upon the crowd. Nearly everybody admitted defeat. The only person present who remained hopeful was Irving Lehman, now on the bench but a strong partisan, who kept stubbornly maintaining: "No, I won't concede. Let's wait until the returns come from the Pacific and Mountain States."

By five in the morning Democrats saw that the election would hinge on California, where Wilson seemed to have a narrow margin of 4,000 or 5,000 votes. Their fears mounted that the Republican leaders then in power in California might steal the election. Money was needed instantly to hire guards over the ballot boxes, and nobody knew where to find it. Happily, Lehman recalled his uncle in San Francisco, I. W. Hellman, head of the Wells Fargo Nevada National Bank.[1] He telegraphed asking that $5,000 be placed immediately to the credit of the Democrats, and although Hellman was a Republican, the money was ready as soon as the bank opened. Guards were forthwith posted over the ballot boxes. Lehman never knew whether they were needed, but he did know that for years afterward Wilson men on the Coast were loud in their gratitude. The party carried the State by 3,773 votes, and Wilson rode to his inauguration in 1917 to the strains of bands playing, "I Love You, California."

Foreseeing and advocating American entry into the war, Lehman felt it his duty to begin drilling. Months before the Germans announced their renewal of unrestricted submarine warfare, he began going over to Governor's Island with a knot of like-minded men who wanted some kind of training. Every afternoon found them on the little ferry. Having no arms, they used broomsticks for rifles and a wooden box to mark the supposed position of a 155 mm. gun, but they learned the rudiments of tactics. His brothers Arthur and Irving and indeed the whole family felt as he did; his nephew Arthur Goodhart made a vain attempt to enlist in the British army.

"I am a fighter," Lehman often said in later life. He was at any rate always a man of action. Immediately on the outbreak of war he asked for admission to the officers' training camp at Plattsburg, was accepted, and passed the physical tests. But he was never called, because—as he learned

The Williams Dramatic Club "Cap and Bells," 1899; Herbert H. Lehman at far right
Unidentified college photographer

Herbert H. Lehman and Edith Altschul in March, 1910, at the time of their engagement

Family snapshot

Herbert H. Lehman on horseback at Augusta, Georgia, 1917

Family snapshot

later—the law provided that an officer of thirty-nine had to be commissioned as major, and the Plattsburg authorities correctly thought that the brief training they gave would not justify such a rank. Chafing with impatience, he asked for any other assignment the army could give him. As none turned up, he went to Washington, applied at the Navy Department, and found a position in the Bureau of Supplies and Accounts—the equivalent of a Quartermaster's Bureau—helping direct textiles procurement. As the main business office of the Navy, this soon became one of the busiest commercial centers in the United States; it was responsible for feeding, clothing, and paying the entire personnel of the Navy and supplying the fast-growing roster of naval vessels with all their stores and equipment.

The slender peacetime organization which had sufficed to care for 300 ships and 55,000 men had suddenly to look after 1,100 vessels and 300,000 men. Total naval expenditures had not exceeded $19,000,000 a year; money was soon pouring out at the rate of $30,000,000 a day. The initial strain, confusion, and delay were enormous. Lehman at first tried to reject the label of textile expert which his superiors pinned on him; but the supply services were run on such an improvised basis in those hectic days that he soon found himself in charge of buying all the woolen materials used in uniforms, underwear, caps, haversacks, and blankets. "I don't know how I got by," he mused later, "but I did." His immediate superior was Rear Admiral Samuel Mc-Gowan, one of the ablest administrators in Washington; really abler, in Lehman's opinion, than General Goethals, whom he later had opportunity to study closely.[2]

In his naval purchasing Lehman saw something of Secretary Josephus Daniels and a good deal more of Assistant Secretary Franklin D. Roosevelt. Approaching Daniels with some prejudice created by the Secretary's immovable hostility to the use of liquor on warships, Lehman soon changed his mind. Despite certain North Carolina eccentricities, Daniels was shrewd, tolerant, and well informed, an efficient naval head; and his order against intoxicants was sound, for tipsy officers could not handle the modern naval machines. But to a dynamic businessman he was incurably cautious, and Lehman formed a greater liking for the dashing Roosevelt. Here was an administrator of imagination and boldness, qualities then much needed. It was refreshing to see him cut through red tape.

Large purchases had to be approved at the top, and occasionally Mc-Gowan would ask Lehman to take a contract upstairs and get it signed. The sequel was illuminating. Daniels would scrutinize it vigilantly and then doubtfully remark: "Well, leave it with me, and I'll study it." But Roosevelt would genially inquire: "Are these papers all right?" As soon as Lehman replied,

"They are, sir," FDR would dash his name on the proper line. In the unprepared state of the Navy name-dashing was imperative. Daniels assented to it, for he regarded FDR as his protégé and took pride in developing the talents of the young man.

"I can't overemphasize the degree of unpreparedness that existed in all the services," Lehman has said. A firm named Bannerman's had flourished in New York City since Civil War days, dealing in second-hand materials and surplus stocks, with a great warehouse on a Hudson River island near West Point called Bannerman's Island. "We used to go up there," Lehman recalled, "and pick up almost anything and everything they had." Despite the pressure for rapid action, however, he made determined efforts to keep prices and profits within bounds. The American Woolen Company headed by the aggressive W. M. Wood had to be watched with care. Seeing a chance in the nation's urgent need, Wood set unreasonable prices on cloth for uniforms, and despite Lehman's protest, stuck to them. Fortunately, Congress had authorized a system which permitted the Navy, if bids seemed exorbitant, to reject them, order an accounting officer to the supplier's factory, make a searching inquiry into cost data, and determine the fair rate. Under this "Navy Order" the government thereupon requisitioned the material at cost plus ten percent. Losing patience with Wood, Lehman threatened him with a "Navy Order"—and his charges came down instantly.[3]

After about four months with the Navy Department, on September 10, 1917, Lehman received his army commission, but not for field service. He was assigned to the General Staff Corps as a captain in a division of the War Department Ordnance Bureau, continuing to work in the dingy old State, War, and Navy Building at much the same tasks as before—placing contracts for textile supplies, allocating raw materials, and conferring with manufacturers on contracts.[4]

His first superior was Colonel John R. Simpson and his second General Hugh Johnson. He always remembered "Old Ironpants" as an explosively able man but a stickler for discipline. One specially hot day in 1918, as he was busy in a building just across from State, War, and Navy, he loosened the choker of his uniform and strolled into the hall for a breath of air. He ran almost into the arms of Johnson. The general glared, halted him, and ejaculated: "Major, don't you know you're out of uniform?" Lehman swallowed hard: "Yes, sir." Johnson went on: "Don't you know that the General Staff Corps must set the tone for the entire army? And here you come into the hall out of uniform, with a wilted collar, and your blouse open!" He launched into a dressing-down Lehman never forgot.

An encounter with General Peyton C. March, the Chief of Staff, was much pleasanter. Lehman emerged from the old building one evening. "I came down those steps," he recalls, "carrying a briefcase in one hand, and three or four books under the other arm, and smoking a big black cigar. As I came down I looked up and saw an officer. He looked fourteen feet tall to me. Four stars! I realized that this was General March, Chief of Staff, and here I was so laden down I couldn't salute, with this cigar in my mouth." Lehman halted in acute mortification, which touched March's sense of humor. "He looked at me and then he broke into a broad grin. He said, 'As you were, Major,' and I walked past him."

In the spring of 1918 a new division was organized in the General Staff Corps under the Overman Act, which permitted the President to reorganize or consolidate any parts of the government to meet war needs. Lehman was transferred on July 27 to this new Purchase, Storage, and Traffic Division, as chief of the Methods Section of the Purchase Branch. After the Armistice, in December, 1918, he became head of the Purchase Branch, and on January 21, 1919, was appointed Assistant Director of the entire Purchase, Storage, and Traffic Division.[5]

This division, with General George W. Goethals as head, had been charged with an immense complex of war activities. In Secretary Baker's words, it supervised "the various requirements, procurement, production, storage, issue, transportation, finance, and accounting, and sales activities connected with the supply of the Army." As the armies grew the buying of supplies became a colossal task. During 1918, for example, the government had to procure fifty million yards of Melton cloth for overcoats and eight million blankets. In the fiscal year 1917–18 some 16,000 contracts were placed for materials valued at about five billion dollars. Goethals, who had a marvelous grasp of detail, mastered this work as he had mastered the construction of the Panama Canal, becoming in General March's estimation one of the greatest supply men of history. Some of the credit for his achievement in supplying five million men and moving them to wartime stations should, however, go to subordinates like Lehman.

In Washington the Lehmans lived at the old Shoreham Hotel at Fifteenth and N, just across from the Cosmos Club, then occupying what had once been Dolly Madison's house, and five minutes' walk from the State, War, and Navy Building. Social life was limited, but he enjoyed lunching at the hotel, which had been for a generation past the liveliest noonday center in Washington, always full of diplomats and high civil, military, and naval officers.

The friends Lehman had made in the Navy Department, with newer associates in the War Department, were young and congenial; some of them, like Franklin D. Roosevelt, had families of small children. Of one intimate in the Navy Department, a brilliant young man named John M. Hancock who hailed from North Dakota, we shall have more to say. Simple suppers were frequent, and in good weather a dozen couples with their youngsters would hold impromptu picnics. Though the Lehmans went to White House receptions, they had no real acquaintance with President Wilson, and they knew Secretary Newton D. Baker, Assistant Secretary Benedict Crowell, Barney Baruch of the War Industries Board, and other eminent figures only through official relationships. Wartime Washington had little time for anything but hard work. Mrs. Lehman threw herself into relief activities, and Lehman often stayed at his desk far into the night.

As the troops went overseas he burned to follow them and made urgent requests for foreign service. Whenever a friend got overseas orders he would say: "Now if you see a chance to put in a good word for calling me to France, I hope you'll do it." Two opportunities flickered before him and then disappeared. When the Army organized its first chemical warfare work, headquarters proposed to make him Chemical Warfare Officer of one division of the Fourth Army which was then being organized. "I was as well qualified to become a chemical officer as to develop a sputnik!" Lehman later commented. Goethals refused to let him go, saying he was indispensable. A proposal to make him assistant to a high staff officer abroad, which would have carried promotion beyond the grade of lieutenant colonel, was vetoed on the same grounds. He continued his work in army purchasing, storage, and transportation until the Armistice.

Thereupon President Wilson appointed him to the Board of Contract Adjustment hurriedly created as soon as peace became certain. Its duties were urgent. Surplus supplies and cancellation of war orders constituted problems of the utmost magnitude. The wholesale destructions of war made large-scale consumption a tremendous problem as long as hostilities continued; then suddenly the problem of glut was equally formidable. The War Department, for example, had worried continuously over the difficulties of getting enough blankets. As soon as the armistice was signed, it had on hand a four years' supply of blankets for 1,000,000 men in the United States and 2,400,000 overseas! Stock of marching shoes had seemed dangerously low so long as armies were active in the field. But the moment the Germans signed the armistice, the army was again embarrassed by a four-year supply of shoes for 3,400,000 soldiers at home and abroad. On November 1, 1918, the Clothing and Equipage Division in the War Department had on hand reserve stocks valued at well over $800,000,000, and more than 30,000 War Department contracts were in various stages of completion. Most of them had to be terminated abruptly, with equitable payment for work done and goods delivered.

The board, which consisted originally of three members, had to conduct hearings and reach prompt decisions. At the outset its judgments were final, but when complaint arose, in January, 1919, a War Claims Board was created to handle appeals from it and other agencies. This whole matter of contract adjustment in the various branches of government became so complicated that it would be wearisome to recite the enactments bearing on the subject and the changes in the structure of adjudication. It is sufficient to say that the War Claims Board was the highest tribunal and that Lehman was elevated to it January 28, 1919, eventually attaining the rank of full colonel. By November, the War Department had settled roughly 22,600 contracts and agreements on a basis that saved the government colossal sums.

Lehman would gladly have remained in government work. For two and a half years he had performed increasingly difficult tasks with satisfaction and a steady rise in rank. He felt that he had contributed something to victory, and he liked the sense of positive accomplishment. He had developed his power of decision. Men later recalled him as young-looking for his years, his face still unlined, his general aspect serene and even complacent; but he carried his short figure erectly, he had a brisk air, and his brown eyes snapped under heavy black eyebrows—a dark line accentuating his wide forehead. In college days he had parted his heavy black hair in the middle; now it was thinning too much to be parted. Once his lips had been heavy; now they closed in a firm line. He no longer worried inordinately, for he felt himself a link in a chain of command; only he wanted more scope. When Benedict Crowell resigned as Assistant Secretary of War, he asked Baker for the vacant place. But the Secretary had promised it to another. And soon afterward he saw that the hour was unpropitious, for clouds were thickening about Woodrow Wilson's administration. The star of the Democratic Party was sinking, not to rise again for twelve humiliating years— when Lehman's political fortunes would rise with it.

In 1919 he resigned, quitting office June 2, and with Mrs. Lehman and their infant son Peter went west to spend three months in California. Peter was the first of three babies, two boys and a girl, whom he and his wife adopted. Fond of children as they were, they had been terribly grieved by the want of any of their own; but first Peter, and later John and Hilda, supplied the lack. After California, the spring of 1920 found him at his familiar post in Lehman Brothers, and that summer he and his family were again in Purchase. Though his business responsibilities were more exacting than ever, they allowed him to undertake, in a short time, some important public labors.

His war work had a personal epilogue. Late in the spring of 1919, when busiest with claims, he had learned that Secretary Baker intended to award him the Distinguished Service Medal. His mother was critically ill with cancer at the house of his brother Irving in Rye on the Sound. When he hastened to tell her, she was delighted. Thereafter, on each new visit she inquired: "When is the medal coming through?" He would reply, "I really don't know, but before long. Don't worry about it." Her inquiries nevertheless continued, and as she was sinking, he felt relieved when in late August he received word to present himself to Baker for the medal. "I hurried back to New York," he tells us; "my mother by that time was obviously dying. I went right up to Rye to see her, about five or six in the evening, and I gave her the medal. It gave her great pleasure. She said, 'Leave it with me. I want to show it to the children.'" He did so, and the next day she died.

· I ·

The brief depression shortly after the war gave way to a decade of uneven prosperity, culminating in the bull-market excesses of the Coolidge-Hoover days. During this period Lehman Brothers regarded themselves as possessing, over and above their reputation for rocklike soundness and conservatism, two peculiar distinctions.

One was their leadership in financing and advising the largest companies in the distributive industry of the country. This leadership they were destined to keep, so that in 1950 the firm could declare: "Of today's twenty largest retailing enterprises, Lehman Brothers has been or is presently regarded as investment broker for more than half." The house has had a peculiarly close connection with the development of the department store in the United States. It played a principal role in finding capital for the creation of Federated Department Stores, Allied Department Stores, and Interstate Department Stores, and it acted as financial agent for R. H. Macy & Company, Gimbel Brothers, and other famous establishments.

Widening the path which they had opened by financing the F. W. Woolworth Company in 1912, the partners also acted as investment bankers for S. H. Kress & Company, the W. T. Grant Company, and other chain stores. The list of connections with food-store groups, tobacco companies, household supply concerns, and building-materials firms could be greatly extended. Obviously, Lehman Brothers' abandonment of the commodity industries they had originally served, and their transfer of attention to the distributive businesses, was connected with cardinal new trends in American life: the urbanization of the country, the rise in standards of living, and the demand for a broad new range of consumer goods.

The second distinction which the partners claimed lay in the skill with which they cured sick companies and their acumen in strengthening weak businesses. A striking example of this can be found in the history of the Jewel Tea Company, one of the fastest growing chain store systems of the early years of the century. The parent concern had been founded in 1899 with a capital of $700 to market groceries by delivery wagon, and it rented its first store in Chicago two years later. By 1910 the company was one of the principal distributors of tea, coffee, spices, and other specialties in the nation, manufacturing its own baking powder as part of a million-dollar business. Six years later, as Herbert Lehman was about to leave for Washington, the company was reincorporated with a capital of $16,000,000, Lehman Brothers distributing both the common stock and the seven percent preferred. For the continued well-being of the company the Lehmans felt a special concern.[6]

For a short time the sky was roseate for Jewel Tea. It rapidly brought its list of stores up to 1,645, built the world's largest coffee-roasting plant in Hoboken, N.J., and established distributing centers in New Orleans and San Francisco. When America entered the war, however, some serious perils appeared. The government commandeered the Hoboken facilities, many salesmen joined the army, congestion made rail shipments difficult, and costs rose alarmingly. The company seemed to be slipping toward disaster. In 1919 it lost nearly $1,850,000 on sales of $16,500,000 and the next year about $2,185,000 on sales of $17,500,000. It had exhausted its surplus, ceased paying dividends, and owed debts of almost $3,000,000. A program of rescue was imperative.

This program Lehman Brothers supplied. At Herbert's instance his friend John M. Hancock, the former naval purchasing chief, joined the Lehman staff and before the end of 1919 became vice-president of Jewel Tea. He and his associates enforced a sharp retrenchment; they reduced inventories, shut down unprofitable stores, closed the San Francisco and New Orleans plants, and abolished many of the wagon-delivery routes. Lehman Brothers persuaded the company to fund its indebtedness by issuing gold notes aggregating $3,500,000. A new spirit pervaded the whole organization, with a greater regard for economy and hard work. In 1921 net profits slightly exceeded $320,000. The next two years witnessed a solid recovery; in 1922 the company emerged from debt, and by 1925 it reduced the arrears on the preferred stock and resumed dividends on the common. Hancock secured the adoption of a profit-sharing plan in the belief that it would improve working morale and provide an incentive for superior accomplishment. About the same time that he was made a partner in Lehman Brothers he became president of Jewel Tea (1924), then as solidly based as any business of the kind in the country.[7]

Other instances of the regeneration of a tottering company could be given. Meanwhile Lehman Brothers escaped any real infection by the fever for overseas investments that seized many American banking houses after the war. The firm sold a few issues of foreign securities, but never with enthusiasm, and it steered clear of the more dubious bond issues of Latin America and weak European governments. It did finance several substantial groups of department stores in Germany, largely controlled by Jewish interests. Later, of course, Hitler took them over. Incidental to its foreign operations, the house at one time had about $100,000 in Reich money deposited in a German bank. When inflation swept over the Reich, this dwindled to a tiny sum. Finally the bank ceased sending statements to New York, and the firm wrote to inquire why. The reply was conclusive: "The stamp that we must put on a letter to you costs more than the whole account is now worth."

Visiting some relatives in Germany after the war, Lehman saw for himself the widespread destruction wrought by inflation. One incident clung to his memory. Two spinster friends of his aunt kept a rather pathetic shop in a town near Würzburg, selling handbags, laces, and other feminine appurtenances. One afternoon Lehman bought three beaded bags for 200,000 marks each, worth at the time perhaps $10 in all, and carried them home. Early next morning the two rang his doorbell. "We deeply regret asking you a favor," they said. "We never had to do anything of the kind before. But the mark depreciated overnight so badly that today we cannot replace those bags we sold you for less than 600,000 marks apiece." Even as Lehman paid the difference, he knew that inflation was wiping out the additional margin.

Herbert was pleased by one fundamental change in the structure of Lehman Brothers during the Twenties—a change which he thought overdue and strongly promoted. He had always been critical of the policy pursued in keeping the firm a tight family organization; from 1850 onward, nobody had been admitted who did not bear the name of Lehman. He felt certain that unless new blood was brought in, with new outlook and new ideas, the vigor of the house would decline. This was one of the reasons which led him to press for the admission of John Hancock, an energetic, imaginative, and liberal man with a broad experience gained in the war. Philip Lehman,

Emanuel's son, who had been the guiding hand since the beginning of the century, became progressively less active after 1925. After Hancock was made a partner in 1924 other new talents were enlisted. One was Monroe C. Gutman, an honors graduate of Harvard and a man versed in securities valuation, who became a partner in 1927; a second was Paul Mazur, another Harvard graduate added the same year, with experience in retail trade and the ability to write such lucid books as *American Prosperity* and *New Roads to Prosperity* (1928–31); and still another was William J. Hammerslough, an expert in investment banking. The leaders of the firm after Philip's recession were Arthur Lehman and Philip's son Robert, a Yale graduate with an informed interest in art.

Hancock was an especially striking figure. He was a large man—"ponderous," as one associate recalls him.[8] Tall, burly, and restless, he found an outlet for his energy in sport: he hunted, fished, rode, played tennis and golf, and loved to go after big game in the Canadian Rockies. A strong gust of the Dakota prairies came into the office with this big, direct, and dynamic man. In the days of the War Industries Board he had been close to Barney Baruch, who admired and valued him. Living in Scarsdale, he took a keen interest in township and county affairs until the death of his son in an automobile accident had a shattering effect upon him. But all the partners possessed special gifts. Mazur, for example, whom Lehman had met in Washington, was one of the ablest living students of the economics of distribution.[9]

The connection between Lehman Brothers and Goldman, Sachs, long so close, gradually dissolved in circumstances so painful that both groups felt the rupture keenly. For one factor, the comradeship of Philip Lehman and Henry Goldman was shattered by the war. Some New York Jews hated Czarist Russia, with its record of pogroms and persecution, so intensely that they hoped for a German victory. Henry Goldman, who had been educated in Germany, was one of them. Philip Lehman was heart and soul on the Allied side. The association became more and more uncomfortable until a partial severance resulted. Eventually Henry Goldman was forced out of Goldman, Sachs, and the newer members of both houses saw diminishing reason for continuing the connection. When the war ended, a bright executive of Southern birth, Waddill Catchings, long associated with the iron and steel industry, joined Goldman, Sachs. He had ability and vision, and soon attracted national attention by throwing into a series of books written in collaboration with William T. Foster an exuberant view of the economic future of the country. But he lacked balance, some of the Lehman partners thought him too ambitious, aggressive, and buoyant, and their distrust contributed to the divergence of paths. They liked much better his assistant Sidney Weinberg, who was destined to a spacious career in finance.

Three phases, one of the Lehman partners has said, might be distinguished in this connection with Goldman, Sachs. The first, from 1906 or so to 1915, was of cordial and fruitful collaboration; the second, down to 1925, was of growing strain; and the third ended in the bull-market days of 1928–29 in total alienation. Feelings became ruffled on both sides and heat was generated. But this did not affect Herbert Lehman very directly or importantly.

Despite its reputation for conservatism, the Lehman partnership often showed a pioneering courage. At the time it marketed the Sears, Roebuck securities, for example, the character of the mail-order business, a Western institution, was but dimly understood by investors on the Atlantic Coast. The firm underwrote the Studebaker offering when the automobile industry was still in its early youth and much overcrowded and when the low-priced car on which Studebaker relied seemed a gamble—for the Model T was but four or five years old.[10] The capital requirements of Fruehauf Trailers were also supplied by Lehman Brothers when motor freight-haulage was still an experimental element in the economy. The house had the courage to lend its support to the American Export Lines, though ever since Civil War days the ocean shipping business had seemed speculative. It helped underwrite the C.I.T. Financial Corporation when that credit agency was a pathbreaker in organizing the installment-buying of consumer goods. As early as 1929, moreover, it was helping the Aviation Corporation, the first large integrated company in the new aviation industry, to get on its feet.

During these years Herbert Lehman completed his education in business and finance; years of tough, anxious work and far from the happiest of his life. For the sensitive task of selling securities to the public he had little skill and less taste and so devoted himself to larger matters. When Lehman Brothers helped finance Federated Department Stores, for example, they had to make an exhaustive study of the business, past, present, and future. When they assisted the B. F. Goodrich Company to find new capital in 1920, and the American Metal Company to do the same two years later, they had to be ready with shrewd suggestions for improving the activities of these concerns. Since the house as yet had no Industrial Department, Herbert and his associates had to do much of this work singlehanded.

By 1928 he had studied the statements and books of a long array of companies which had come to the firm for assistance. He had traveled widely around the country inspecting the factories or stores of these companies and had talked with their directors and managers. He read financial and industrial journals and attended meetings of businessmen and economists. In time, as his expertness made him a valuable adviser, he was elected a director of numerous companies—Studebaker, Van Raalte, Pierce Oil, Spear & Company, Empire Fuel & Gas, Franklin Simon, Coal & Iron National Bank, and so on.[11] His partner Hancock became director of more than twenty corporations. One of Lehman's last important undertakings before the stock market crash of October 24, 1929, was to act as intermediary, along with Samuel D. Leidesdorf, in the sale of the great Newark department store of Bamberger Brothers to Macy's. Louis Bamberger, a bachelor, and his sister and brother-in-law, Mrs. and Mr. Felix Fuld, who were childless, were growing old; they had large philanthropic plans in view, for they had long shown a fine public spirit. The transfer of title to Percy Straus and others controlling Macy's was one of the largest transactions of the time in the department store field, involving something like $25,000,000.

Out of this sale, incidentally, came the creation of the Institute for Advanced Study at Princeton, with Abraham Flexner as planner and first head; and Louis Bamberger, who had a warm friendship with Lehman, asked him to become one of the original board of trustees.

All this work, involving a minute attention to numerous businesses, and the mastery of a mass of detail on manufacturing, marketing, company administration, public relations, and general economic problems, was an onerous burden.[12] Lehman was not unhappy in it, but since his Washington experience he could not be very happy either. "He liked the excitement of putting through a big deal," recalls a partner. "He liked the process of negotiating a complicated arrangement. But he was not heart and soul a businessman. Why, once he had spent months of close labor on the preliminaries of a large business agreement, requiring the sale of both common and preferred stock. Then, when the last details had been perfected in a day-long conference, the casual remark of a bystander infected the principal with some irrational doubt, and he begged for a drastic modification, the omission of the common stock issue. Herbert did not even expostulate. Despite his months of toil, he instantly assented: 'Certainly,' he said, 'we shall drop both common and preferred if you prefer.'"[13] That is, he was ready to take a large and generous view of any transaction. Most of all, however, he felt the call of public affairs. He was not much interested in making money, and business problems seemed to him in general duller than professional or civic problems. In time, he gladly purged his mind of much that he had learned.

Yet the experience had its value when he became governor of the greatest industrial state in a period of dire economic distress. He knew less of the ways of politics and politicians than most men elected to high office, but he did know how big enterprises were run, he could face powerful business interests with a fearlessness born of familiarity, and he had a sense of the importance of budgets, balance sheets, and solvency that many found refreshing against the background of lavish New Deal spending.

· II ·

Most observers would have pronounced this hardworking businessman, forty-five years old in 1923, for all his alertness and sociability, a limited person; genial, likable, and intelligent, but with a restricted sense of values and uninspired mind. He apparently differed from ten thousand other businessmen only in his lambent geniality, generosity of temper, and exceptional interest in sports. The quintessential boy had grown into a man's man, robust, energetic—and seemingly a bit narrow. Those who took this view, however, did not see one side of his interests and activities. The businessman who does not lift himself above self-interest is narrow indeed. Fortunately, by inner impulse and outer pressure, Lehman had been propelled into philanthropic activities broad in range and poignant in appeal.

The crushing impact of war in 1914 had exposed European Jews to even harsher perils than other peoples in the war-torn regions. Over wide areas they had always been too poverty-stricken to meet a crisis; despised socially, fettered politically, and crippled economically. As the Germans smashed through Belgium, as the Austrians overran Serbia, and Russian troops swarmed into Galicia, multitudes were rendered homeless and starving. About 600,000 Jews who lived in Germany, 2,500,000 in Austria-Hungary, and 7,000,000 in the Russian "pale" were cut off. Every American synagogue resounded with prayers for them. A group which numbered Julius Rosenwald, Cyrus Sulzberger, Louis Marshall, and Arthur and Herbert Lehman, but which was led above all by Jacob H. Schiff and his son-in-law Felix Warburg, brought into existence the Jewish Joint Distribution Committee, one of the greatest of all the relief organizations which Americans created to succor the destitute masses of Europe. Dr. Julius Goldman was chosen director; large sums were collected; and amid the frost and snows of the war's first winter, its agents clambered through the ruins distributing food, clothing, medicines, and funds.

A truly heroic effort! This Joint Distribution Committee represented much the largest cooperative enterprise and the most unselfish suppression of old animosities and jealousies in the history of New World Jews. Before the war they had splintered their foreign relief work among numerous small agencies, some of them active both at home and abroad. Each of the three

major denominations, orthodox, conservative, and reform, had in general carried on its many charities separately, and each had done a good deal of
glowering at the other two. The powerful body of Jewish Socialists, enlisting a majority of proletarian workers, rejected any partnership with economic groups further to the right. During the first war emergency the
American Jewish Committee, of which Schiff and Marshall were leading
members, stood foremost in answering appeals from abroad. Beside it rose a
Central Relief Committee founded by the orthodox congregations and a
People's Relief Committee established by labor groups. The weak Provisional
Zionist Committee also took a hand. With Eastern Europe a seething arena of
war, the armies trampling back and forth over the home communities of
millions of Jews, such a division of energies was madness.

Schiff was approaching seventy; a friend of Woodrow Wilson and many
other leaders, whose abilities, wealth, long experience in banking and railroad promotion, and benefactions made him the foremost figure among the
Jewish people. Felix Warburg, a cultivated, tireless humanitarian, possessed
a gift for organization. It was a tribute to their character and influence that
all eyes turned to them. To bring the different agencies together in the Joint
Committee required imagination and tact as well as patience, but their masterful leadership overcame all schisms and jealousies.

As the squabbling and name-calling died away before the international
tragedy, the "Joint" (as Jews called it) swiftly enlarged its scope, efficiency,
and money-raising zeal. Herbert Lehman, one of the youngest of the organizers, was as active as anybody. As an officer he soon occupied a central position. At first money was raised in relatively small amounts, but by the end of
1915, when something over $1,500,000 had been collected, it became clear
that a really titanic effort was needed. Mass meetings were held throughout
the country, President Wilson proclaimed January 27, 1916, Jewish Relief
Day, and the financial objectives were steadily pushed higher. In 1917 the
goal of the annual drive was fixed at $10,000,000—a sum that many thought
impossible, until Julius Rosenwald electrified his people and set an example
in generosity to all Americans by giving one million on condition that others
raise the remaining nine. The mark was soon surpassed. Many pledges represented great sacrifice, the Jewish laborers, for example, promising to give one
dollar out of every twenty they earned.[14]

His proved business capacity marked Lehman for hard labor. He helped
fix community quotas, he managed drives, he addressed meetings. After a
rally at Carnegie Hall just before Christmas in 1916, he announced that Jews
of the city would give more than $3,000,000 to the national total of $10,000,-
000 for the ensuing year. "The enthusiasm kindled at the meeting continued

to burn yesterday," reported the *New York Times* of December 23. "Mr. Lehman and his assistants were busy all day and late into the night in the treasurer's office at 20 Exchange Place, opening letters and listing contributions. Each mail brought checks, cash, and pledges, and it would be several days, it was said, before a complete list of contributors would be ready."

Altogether, in the First World War, the JDC collected $16,584,000 from the Jewish people of America; and the work done by Schiff, Warburg, Rabbi Judah Magnes, who later became the first president of the Hebrew University in Jerusalem, and Julius Rosenwald was not forgotten when later crises demanded far larger efforts.[15]

The first crisis quickly came, for the wartime ordeal proved only the prologue to a deeper tragedy for Old World Jews. The armistice ushered in two of the blackest years in Hebraic history. Turmoil, civil conflict, and penury enveloped Europe, darkening into chaos and starvation east of the Vistula. While the whole continent was cold and hungry, the lands in which Communism struggled with Western civilization were racked by famine and pillage. The Central and Russian Empires were overthrown, boundary lines were changed, and amid revolutionary struggles, great populations were forcibly shifted. In the newly emerged nations popular hatred of the Jews ran strong. Because their political emancipation had been delayed, and their social and economic progress retarded, they had often remained an alien element, distrusted by the patriots who strove for a homogeneous state. In Rumania, Hungary, Poland, the new Baltic nations, and the Ukraine, where anti-Semitism had always been a powerful undercurrent, it now bubbled to the surface.

The ancient hostility in Rumania became more intense when the country found itself required to absorb the large Jewish populations of Transylvania and Bukovina, taken from Austria-Hungary, and of Bessarabia, taken from Russia. The clauses in the Versailles Treaty which guaranteed equal civil and political rights to all minorities simply made many Rumanians more fiercely anti-Jewish. Meanwhile, in Hungary a systematic and merciless persecution grew out of the civil strife which tore the country apart. An embittered radical faction assailed the Jews as a body of greedy bourgeois reactionaries; an implacable conservative faction indicted them as revolutionists. Both Count Karolyi's liberal government, which failed to prevent anti-Semitic riots, and the subsequent Communist regime of Bela Kun, a Jew whose "Lenin Boys" perpetrated terrible outrages, proved catastrophic for Hungarian Jewry.

Worst of all was the situation in Poland and the Ukraine. The *London Times* reported that anti-Jewish disorders occurred in 110 Polish villages and towns during the single month of the armistice. Savage pogroms took place in the Ukraine just after the war, costing, according to a later estimate, the lives of 200,000 people.[16] Throughout most of 1918–19, after the treaty of Brest-Litovsk, the Ukrainian Republic was a field of angry conflict among its own nationalists, the Bolshevists, Denikin's counterrevolutionary troops, and guerrilla bands. In this bloody hurly-burly many Jews were massacred, the nationalist forces under Petlura staging especially violent pogroms.

During this period the United States carried out a colossal work, magnificently organized by Herbert Hoover, in feeding Russia and her stricken areas, restoring communications, stamping out typhus, and succoring children. Congress early in 1919 appropriated a hundred millions for provisioning the Continent, and Washington made large loans to various nations for relief. Hoover's distinguished lieutenants in practical benevolence, Vernon L. Kellogg, Alonzo E. Taylor, William N. Haskell, and others moved busily over stricken areas of Eastern Europe to direct the undertaking. Supply trains more than once ran through hostile battle lines firing at each other. In March, 1921, Hoover's American Relief Administration, which by that time was a private body, concluded a great drive which raised almost $30,000,000 —primarily to save the children. Of this sum $10,000,000 was allotted to the Red Cross to spend, $2,200,000 to the JDC, and nearly $800,000 to the Friends' Service Committee. Millions of children were saved.

One mountain range of trouble was surmounted in these years, however, only to bring a new Alp within view. In the summer of 1921 the novelist Maxim Gorky appealed to Hoover and the American people to help meet a stupendous famine developing in the Ukraine and the Volga Valley; the sequel in part of callous Soviet efforts to collectivize the peasants. Kellogg and ex-Governor Goodrich of Indiana reported that fifteen to twenty million people were in dire peril. Again American relief agencies set to work, and again they brought starvation under control.

In this proud chapter of American history the JDC wrote only a fraction of the story, but it was a creditable fraction. In 1919–20 it raised roughly $27,000,000 by its own efforts, a work in which Lehman was prominent. With the approval of Secretary of State Lansing, it sent agents into Eastern Europe. Four of its men arrived in Esthonia in the spring of 1920, and though one was murdered, the others reached an agreement with the Soviet Government which permitted Jewish organizations to send relief to their coreligionists on a systematic basis.[17] Their work was soon merged into the activities of the Hoover organization, of which Walter L. Brown was made European director. All the principal American relief bodies at this point joined hands under the aegis of the European Relief Council. Colonel William N. Haskell was put in charge in Russia, and an astute Jew, Dr. Joseph A. Rosen, set to work with him.

· III ·

As the immediate postwar demand for relief subsided, the necessity for reconstruction took a paramount place; and this gave Lehman a larger role. At first, of course, the line between relief and rehabilitation was often hazy. In general, however, it can be said that during the years 1922–25 the JDC was able to devote itself primarily to rebuilding. It organized separate agencies to occupy special spheres of action in Eastern Europe, and its rule was not only to give help, but to train people in self-help. While furnishing the means of rehabilitation, it created bodies which would take over the job and go on with it.

Five subcommittees of the JDC dealt with as many distinct spheres. One concerned itself with refugees; a difficult problem, for every renewal of anti-Semitic outbreaks meant a new wave of fugitives, and Congress in 1921 slammed the door shut with the three percent quota law and pressed it tighter in 1924. Nevertheless, the JDC slowly aided stranded refugees to find havens in Canada, Latin America, and Palestine. A second subcommittee under Dr. Cyrus Adler undertook the reorganization of schools and other cultural centers destroyed by the war. Within a few years it had restored and was helping maintain almost 1,800 educational institutions in Europe, meanwhile giving special aids to writers, rabbis, artists, and musicians. Simultaneously, a medical and sanitary subcommittee under Bernard Flexner was conducting a war against disease and its parents; against lice and typhus, against malnutrition, against polluted water, against bad air and tuberculosis, against vermin. It also subsidized and reorganized medical schools. A fourth subcommittee devoted itself to child care, giving special attention to the 60,000 Jewish orphans in Eastern Europe outside Russia. All kinds of services for children, from summer camps to workshops, received aid.

The fifth subcommittee, with the most far-reaching functions of all, as was shown by its appropriation of $5,000,000, undertook the economic rehabilitation of Jewish communities from the Baltic to the Black Sea. Lehman was its chairman. He first had surveys of the situation made in Poland, the Baltic States, Hungary, and other areas, the object being to determine just how to breathe new life into the half-dead Jewish economy. The rebuilding of houses and shops obviously had cardinal importance; so did the restoration of trade and technical schools. But emphasis was also given the revival of those interesting cells in the economy of the East European Jews, the credit cooperatives and loan societies. These loan agencies had spread their network throughout much of Eastern Europe, and were especially strong in Poland. For many decades they had pooled the resources of each Jewish community for the common good, but the war had wiped them out. Now Lehman, Rosen, and their helpers, notably Paul Baerwald and James N. Rosenberg, with an initial grant of $250,000 from the JDC and the approval of the national authorities, began placing the *kassas* on their feet.[18]

Lehman and Rosenberg tried to establish a new economic front which the Jewish communities of Eastern Europe, forbidden to own land, had never been able to open—agriculture. They believed that large numbers of people might be persuaded to take up farming. The JDC bought scores and in time hundreds of tractors and sent over mechanics to teach farmers to operate them; it distributed livestock—3,000 horses, 1,000 cows, 50 stallions, and 50 bulls. It established seed stations to make it possible to sow nearly 3,000,000 acres of land with superior, not inferior, seed. More than thirty cooperative cheese factories were set in operation. Rosen, an expert who had written authoritative books on grain, was anxious to get the Jewish farmers to substitute corn for wheat, barley, oats, or rye, for in the Ukraine corn could be planted much later in the spring than the smaller grains and would be safer from both frost and drought. He knew just where Illinois corn would flourish, and where Dakota corn was needed, and succeeded in getting 2,700,000 acres planted in 1922.

By 1924 Colonel Lehman, as the press called him, was vice-chairman of the JDC as well as head of the economic reconstruction work. We need not rehearse the statistics of money spent, food packages distributed, seed sown, loan banks organized, and hospitals rehabilitated. It is necessary only to say that Dr. Rosen's program, the first large-scale effort at crop diversification in Russia, and one of the most imaginative works ever carried out by any relief organization, had large permanent results and that Lehman's attempts to stimulate self-help scored a distinct success. In view of political pressures, it had to succeed, for the Soviet authorities wanted the Americans to finish and get out. We should add that all the many American agencies working in Eastern Europe threw increasing emphasis upon the revival of prewar societies and institutions and received increasing assistance in this from local and national authorities.[19]

Lehman profited from his association with many Jewish and Gentile leaders of whom he might otherwise have seen little. His fellow workers on the reconstruction subcommittee included Louis Marshall, Morris L. Ernst, George W. Naumburg, and Bernard Flexner, to name but a few. Of the men in the American Relief Administration he got to know Hoover, and officers of the Red Cross, the YMCA, the Rockefeller Foundation, the Federal Council of Churches of Christ, and the Friends' Service Committee. He learned more than he had ever expected to know about the peoples, politics, and ideas of Eastern Europe, about agriculture, housing, and medical work, and about modes of business in that wide area. Incidentally, he had to familiarize himself with the newest techniques in fund-raising and in that essential element of money-collecting, publicity. Himself giving substantial sums, he learned the truth of Rockefeller's maxim that a good cause requires a good beggar.

Out of the JDC work, in part, grew several more enduring enterprises for the assistance of Old World Jewry. One was the "Agro-Joint," begun with an appropriation of $400,000 by the JDC in 1924 as an experiment in settling many hundreds of Jewish families on farms—Dr. Rosen supplying the direction and James N. Rosenberg much of the inspiration. The object was to see what could be done in "restratifying" Jews; that is, diversifying their occupations and status. Government restrictions had long shut them out of all but trading and money-lending occupations. Now the plan was to revive the love of the land shown in the ancient history of Palestine and make them proficient small manufacturers. Money came from varied sources. Within a few years the response was so enthusiastic that the rechanneling of a substantial part of the Jewish folk of Eastern Europe into directly productive callings proved a brilliant success.

For this work greater funds and better organization were required, and in 1928 the American Society for Jewish Farm Settlements, with Rosenberg as chairman and Lehman, Felix Warburg, Julius Rosenwald, and Louis Marshall among the leaders, undertook financial responsibility. Up to that time the Agro-Joint had spent nearly $6,000,000; the Society at once raised another $8,000,000 in subscriptions payable over the next eight years, Julius Rosenwald alone giving $5,000,000. The Soviet Government promised to match the dollars with double appropriations and to help in other ways. Another enduring enterprise was the "ORT," or Organization for Rehabilitation Through Training, which established technical and vocational schools for Jewish communities not only in Russia but in other parts of the Old World.

Even in the hard years of the Great Depression the Agro-Joint made progress, until it had settled about 250,000 people on three million acres in the Ukraine and Crimea. As these colonies took root they began absorbing new members without outside help and raised their own funds for irrigation, water supply, electrification, and buildings. Their farm schools gave short courses for adults as well as regular courses for youths. Among artisans, meanwhile, the Agro-Joint encouraged cooperative workshops which not only produced goods but taught unskilled workers useful trades. Crowning proof of the success of the whole program came in 1937–38, when heads of the Agro-Joint turned all its activities—farm colonies, *kassas*, trade schools, medical services, cooperative shops—over to the people involved and to the Soviet Government and its services.[20]

It had accomplished a memorable work, this Agro-Joint, transforming a large part of Russian Jewry from an oppressed ghetto population, living largely by bargain and barter, into a body of self-reliant workers in their own fields and factories. It had helped solve the problem of the "declassed" Jew, or *lishentzy*, who had been without recognized political or social rights. Herbert Hoover credited it with one of the most striking feats of "human engineering," to use his term, in all history. And then, alas, Hitler smashed all its fruits.

No great attention was paid by the general public to all this activity. Larger problems absorbed their attention. Americans took Jewish relief work for granted and paid little notice to its details. If asked about it, they would have said: "Oh yes, we know the Methodists, the Lutherans, the Quakers, the Catholics have all done good relief work; the Jews have had a special problem, and have therefore raised money with special zeal." The fact was that the terrible crisis faced by the Jews demanded not only a special zeal but unusual foresight and planning capacity. The men and women who gave so generously received a return in self-satisfaction and in heartfelt gratitude, but still more in inspiration; for the eagerness of Jewish people in war-ravaged lands to re-create their ancient spiritual values at the same time that they restored their economic foundations was inspiring to sensitive Americans.

"If anything has made me feel the value of Jewish spirituality," Lehman told a Relief Conference in Albany in 1928, "it is my connection with the cultural and religious activities of the Joint Distribution Committee. When you know of hundreds of thousands of men and women who preferred to have money used for the development of their religious life rather than for terribly needed food, clothing, and shelter; when you see these people making tremendous sacrifices to maintain their synagogues and religious schools, and bring up their children in their ancient creed, you realize why the Jewish people and faith have indomitably survived the storms of several thousand years." [21]

The ten years of labor that Lehman gave to Jewish relief and rehabilitation abroad interested him decidedly more than his concurrent business activities. They helped mature and broaden him; they substituted for the cheerful, sociable young man satisfied with finance, family, friends, and sports an earnest, hardworking social servant concerned with world affairs and absorbed in the plans of important men and organizations. He had always been naturally conscientious—by spells; now he was immersed in conscientious activities. Fortunately, he still kept his quick grin over a joke, a mishap, or one of his own mistakes. His friends sometimes thought that he lacked a sense of proportion. They complained that all problems, big and small, appeared of the same magnitude to him; but while there was truth in this, the fault was a product of his conscientiousness.

A day was to come when he would embody no small part of the public conscience of his era. His relief work had a direct practical benefit which he could not comprehend at the time. It was the best possible training for the larger responsibilities which, in the wake of a still more calamitous war, he was to confront when he became first director of UNRRA. But its indirect value in fortifying his optimism and tolerance, in teaching him patience, and in deepening his faith in the power of constructive work to conquer human calamities was of far greater value.

Chapter V

FROM SULZER
TO ALFRED E. SMITH

Lᴇʜᴍᴀɴ always credited Lillian Wald with a large part in introducing him to social problems and hence to public affairs. Meeting her late in the 1890s, probably through some member of the Jacob H. Schiff family, who helped support her work, he became an admirer of her keen-minded, placidly busy benevolence when he was a junior or a senior at Williams. As we have noted, her Nurses' Settlement on Henry Street had already flowered into a variety of social activities. She had formed classes in cooking, clothes-making, and nursing, and was providing games, dances, excursions, and other recreations for young people. Boys' and girls' clubs took form. The first boys' club (the Heroes), headed by Elsie Nathan (later Mrs. Leo Arnstein), delighted Lehman, and before he had been out of college many months, Miss Wald asked him to organize a second group of about fifteen who dubbed themselves the Patriots Club. These youngsters, aged twelve to fourteen, were drawn from Henry, Grant, Livingston, Delancey, and surrounding streets. "I quickly became much interested," Lehman recalls, "and formed a great affection for these boys, some of whom turned out very well."

He ran the club for three or four years, leading formal discussions and then taking the boys to an ice cream parlor for refreshments and chatter. Some of the boys asked him home to meet their parents. They had the self-assertiveness natural in street urchins. Once, after he had talked a great deal about democracy, the time came to elect a new president. It was a much-coveted dignity, and as he had emphasized the importance of fair elections, secrecy ruled. "Every boy could vote for whomever he wanted. When we counted the ballots, the thirteen boys present had cast thirteen different votes! Each boy had voted for himself." In summer Lehman sometimes visited the camp for Henry Street boys on one of the Croton Lakes. As his club members grew up, however, and he became busy with other affairs, he dropped the work.

He retained two permanent benefits, a friendship with Miss Wald and a realistic understanding of slum problems. Miss Wald's combination of gentleness and power fascinated him. A quiet, restrained woman, never importuning acquaintances for aid, and never showing the least peremptoriness with subordinates, she was remarkably successful in gaining support from a wide circle of friends and commanding the loyalty of co-workers. With all the vision, humanitarian sympathy, and administrative energy of Jane Addams, though never the literary talent or national influence, she had a sweeter personality. The people of the Henry Street area adored her. In the social settlement movement as first transplanted from England she stands beside Stanton Coit, Miss Addams, and Robert A. Woods, but in New York she was a unique figure. Until her death in Westport, Connecticut, in 1940, Herbert and Edith Lehman often called on her, for she was concerned about all kinds of reform causes; better schools and housing, better parks and playgrounds, stronger trade unions, shorter working hours, abolition of child labor, and decent government.

Anyone in her circle met political leaders of the city. "She had great influence," as Lehman noted. Not only members of John Purroy Mitchel's idealistic administration but hard-bitten sachems of Tammany Hall consulted her, and knowing that she was an effective crusader, gave weight to her desires. Among her friends Lehman found such reformers as George McAneny, Leonard Wallstein, and Henry Bruere, the salt of the city, and young lions like Al Smith and Robert Wagner, who soon moved into a larger political scene.

Social reform was gaining impetus. The Triangle Fire of March 25, 1911, in which 146 people, mostly women and girls, lost their lives, shocked New York into appreciation of the urgency of a war upon bad building codes, inhuman factory conditions, and lax or corrupt municipal administration. The death of these burned or mangled garment workers fired a tremendous surge of public wrath and reformative zeal in both the city and state. The owners of the Triangle Shirt-Waist Company, charged with responsibility for the tragedy, employed as attorney Max Steuer, who later served a long list of notorious clients, including Frank Warder, the thieving superintendent of banks in the state, A. J. Vitale, removed from the bench for his relations with the gambler Rothstein, and Harry Daugherty, Harding's Attorney General. He gained the nickname in legal circles of *Geltschwessel*, or goldsweater. If it could be proved that representatives of the Triangle Company had ordered the locking of exits in violation of law, the owners would face conviction for manslaughter; but Steuer's adroit handling of the case contributed to the acquittal of the men. Deeply disturbed, city and state set about a general house-cleaning—and they had much to clean up. The metropolis suddenly realized that for all its wealth, all its boasts of luxury and power, many of its people were toiling twelve hours daily in dangerous surroundings for a pitiful wage and living in slums as squalid as those of Naples and Warsaw. Lehman was one of the men who determined to do something about this.

Immediately on leaving Williams he had joined the Grover Cleveland Osceola Democratic Club in the Fifteenth Assembly District and become a member of Tammany Hall. These were the days of Boss Richard Croker, to whom Lehman and the silk-stocking section of the city in which he lived were intensely hostile; but he thought he could best work for betterment within the organization. Croker had in due course retired and been succeeded by Charles F. Murphy, a leader of cold-blooded ruthlessness but greater personal honesty and fitful regard for political decency. In the Osceola Club Lehman was associated with highly reputable men, for its president was Thomas Rush, a good lawyer and liberal Democrat who later became head of the National Democratic Club. The Osceola Club gave the young businessman his first lessons in practical politics. In fact, there he suffered his first defeat, for, running for vice-president on a Rush-Lehman ticket, he was soundly beaten. He kept active, and helped give Osceola a standing not far below that of the Manhattan Club, so that in 1910 he was chosen a delegate to the Democratic State Convention. He had hoped to cast an independent ballot, but when the roll of counties was called he heard Boss Murphy stand up with a stentorian edict: "New York County casts all its votes for John A. Dix."

Now in 1911 he aligned himself behind the local reformers in the metropolis who were shortly to bring the John Purroy Mitchel administration to power. He was anxious to see a similar reform movement in the state, where Dix proved an inefficient governor, wretchedly subservient to the Tammany machine. Neither city nor state had been well governed since the days of T. R. in Albany and Seth Low in City Hall. His hope of change shaped his first real venture into politics, which proved a disillusioning experience.

· I ·

In 1912, with progressivism and reform in the ascendancy everywhere, the forces of righteousness promised to sweep New York State. Dix had so bitterly disappointed honest citizens that the opposition to his renomination seemed irresistible. The Democratic Presidential nominee, Woodrow Wil-

son, who was calling for free and unbossed conventions everywhere, was opposed to him. It seemed certain that if they selected an able reform candidate,
the Democrats could carry the state, for the Progressive schism had divided
the opposition, the regular Republican nominee for governor, Job E. Hedges,
facing the implacable hostility of the Bull Moose men under Oscar S. Straus.

But whom should the Democrats choose? Most eyes turned to Congressman William Sulzer. As he had grown up on the Lower East Side, and during his continuous service in the House since 1895 had championed the rights
of its people, he would hold the Jewish Democrats against Straus. He was
one of the more respectable members of Tammany Hall, a fact which might
blunt the enmity of that powerful body; yet as he was decidedly liberal in
his views, he might also attract the reform element in the party. He seemed
able, honest, and high-minded. Lehman, with many other independent citizens—Henry Morgenthau, Sr., Abram I. Elkus, and Jacob H. Schiff among
prominent Jews—thought him much the best choice.[1]

At the convention in Syracuse on October 3, 1912, where Boss Murphy
reluctantly told the delegates to vote as they pleased, Sulzer was nominated
on a platform promising direct primaries for state officers and a program of
advanced social and industrial legislation. Liberals rejoiced. Wilson praised
him as "a man whose reputation for integrity and independence is unques-
tioned, a man of high principle"; Bryan extolled him as a champion of the
people; and State Senator Franklin D. Roosevelt withdrew his anti-Tammany
faction, the "Empire State Democracy," from the field to support him. The
Times and *World* urged voters to fall in behind him. Like others, Lehman believed there were three good reasons for making Sulzer governor. His nomination had been a severe blow to Tammany; he had been an eloquent defender of oppressed minorities, and had vehemently denounced pogroms and
the Czarist abuse of the Jews; and with Wilson standing for President, earnest support of the whole Democratic ticket was clearly desirable.

During the campaign the nominee emphasized his antagonism to bossism.
He kept reiterating that William Sulzer was his own master, that he would
fearlessly serve the public will, and that he would put on the lawbooks the
reforms long overdue. With some fellow contributors, Lehman defrayed the
cost of publishing a volume of Sulzer's speeches; and in September he provided $5,000 in cash.[2] "I gave him the $5,000 unconditionally," said Lehman
later. "I knew he was a man of straitened circumstances. I did not care what
he did with the money, whether he paid his rent, or bought himself clothes,
or paid for his office or any other expenses." On election day Sulzer soared
to victory with nearly 650,000 votes, far above the 444,000 cast for Hedges
and the 393,000 for Straus.

Trustful citizens waited for a valiant advance. However, veteran political observers were cynical, predicting a stage encounter between Sulzer and Murphy of the paper shield and tin sword variety, to be followed by an all too practical agreement.

For a time Sulzer seemed likely to justify the allegiance which idealists and reformers gave him. "The hour has struck and the task of administrative reform is mine," he claimed in his inaugural. His first message to the legislature proposed replacing the state nominating conventions by direct primaries and called for the enactment of minimum wage, workmen's compensation, and child labor laws, objectives dear to all liberal minds. He delighted enemies of corruption by appointing a Committee of Inquiry into the administrative departments, with John H. Carlisle of Watertown, a veteran critic of Tammany, in charge. When it began to expose waste and graft, the governor summarily dismissed the superintendent of highways and disciplined other machine men.

He pressed bills for the public development of waterpower on the St. Lawrence, state supervision of the New York Stock Exchange, and the regulation of tenement house labor; and when they passed he signed them amid resounding applause. But then came the final test. When on April 10 he tardily brought forward his direct primary measure with a special message, he became the center of a battle which showed just how much of his character was steel, how much brass, and how much clay.

The sequel was in fact one of the tragic dramas of New York history. Machine Democrats had already introduced their own milk-and-water primary bill, which made a few trifling alterations in the existing system, but left the boss-controlled convention substantially intact. With Senator George A. Blauvelt in charge, it had been debated for weeks before Governor Sulzer threw down the gage before Murphy with his own measure for complete abolition of the convention. To Sulzer's defiance Murphy made equally defiant reply. The Tammany legislators and their allies in both parties upstate, with words of scorn and contumely, passed the Blauvelt bill by impressive majorities. Sulzer immediately vetoed the "fraud." The legislature repassed it, and the governor, vetoing it again, appealed directly to the people. On May 8 he called the legislature, which had adjourned, into a special session beginning June 16 and prepared to make a speaking tour of the state.[3]

Many reformers disapproved both of the governor's measures, which they believed went too far, and his methods. They thought that the state convention, which could be traced back to Jacksonian days and which had brought forward such true statesmen as Samuel J. Tilden, Grover Cleveland, and Charles E. Hughes, might continue to be a valuable agency for drafting party platforms and choosing leaders; all that was needed was a purification of its membership. Sulzer's use of intimidation, cajolery, and punitive action in an attempt to carry his bill bore too close a resemblance to Tammany's own methods, and opponents who called him "a political Tamerlane" seemed near the truth. Nevertheless, most independents and liberal Democrats stood by him, and so did many Republicans. Supporters in New York City formed a Direct Primary Campaign Committee of 100 to rally citizens to his side. Its leaders included Charles S. Whitman, John Purroy Mitchel, Ralph Pulitzer, Vincent Astor, William Randolph Hearst, George W. Perkins, Henry Morgenthau, Sr., who was chief fund raiser, and Herbert H. Lehman, the treasurer.

The governor swung through upstate cities with a series of belligerent speeches. When he opened a visit to the metropolis on May 28, the Committee of 100 arranged meetings for him all over the city. An enthusiastic gathering in Cooper Union on June 14 listened to fiery arraignments of Murphy and boss-politics by Oscar S. Straus, Hearst, and Bainbridge Colby. Next day Sulzer presided in the Executive Chamber at Albany over a conference which laid plans for giving bossism its Waterloo. But as the special session began the Tammany tiger remained rampant, and many Republicans who had grown up under Tom Platt's tutelage stood battling beside it. Practical politicians were determined to save the *ancien régime*. At the public hearings on Sulzer's bill Franklin D. Roosevelt, among others, stirringly assailed the machines and extolled reform. Unperturbed, the legislature overwhelmingly rejected the measure.

By this time perceptive men like Lehman realized that Bill Sulzer was three quarters demagogue and at best one quarter statesman, a man attached to reform less because his heart was in it than because he hoped it would carry him into the White House. But they did not know that he was a cheat and thief. Just before adjourning, the legislature had created an investigating committee dominated by Murphy's henchmen. It lost no time in boring into the governor's personal finances. The election laws required candidates for governor to report all contributions received between nomination and election day. Sulzer had reported the trifling sum of $5,460 from 68 contributors, omitting substantial checks from Jacob H. Schiff, Abram I. Elkus, Henry Morgenthau, Sr., Herbert H. Lehman, and William F. McCombs. The committee proved that between September 1 and the end of the year he had deposited about $24,400 in his bank and that in the latter half of October he had bought $11,800 worth of Big Four railroad stock, with other securities. The champion of unselfish, honest public service stood exposed as greedy and dishonest. Amid the jeers of politicians and wails of liberals he was impeached and removed.

All the idealists whom Sulzer had betrayed had to confess in sackcloth and ashes their misjudgment. Lehman looked even more naïve than most of them. Sulzer's impeachment trial of course took place before the Senate in Albany, where Bob Wagner, rising in influence, and Jim Foley, later surrogate, the son-in-law of Boss Murphy, were leaders. Lehman's testimony was frank, disarmingly honest, and a bit amusing. The senators grinned at his recital of gifts. As he came down from the stand a Republican senator plucked his sleeve. "You really gave Bill Sulzer $5,000 with no strings whatever?" he demanded. "Yes," said Lehman. "Well," said the politician, "you're just the kind of man the Republican Party needs!" [4]

Yet the reform battle was not wholly lost. When Sulzer returned to the East Side from Albany, an immense crowd cheered him as a martyr. If intelligent men were disgusted by his corruption, they were angered by Murphy's arrogant brutality. The boss broke him because he could not bend him. Lehman, who came to know Murphy fairly well, credited him with an intelligence far above Boss Kelly's and a personal honesty far above Boss Croker's. But Murphy here showed himself a mean and vengeful despot and so committed his worst blunder. In the mayoralty election of 1913, a fusion of reform groups carried John Purroy Mitchel to a victory which stunned Tammany. Murphy lost the board of aldermen, the board of estimate, and practically every county and judicial post. In Buffalo and Albany local Democratic machines were smashed. One of Mayor Mitchel's first acts was to begin an investigation of Tammany corruption in the city services.

· II ·

The Carlisle Committee which Sulzer had appointed to investigate the departments made one recommendation in 1913 which gave Lehman an opportunity. It proposed that a group of experts study the banking laws and lay before the next legislature a comprehensive statute which would eliminate incongruities, ambiguities, and obsolete clauses, abolish abuses, and thus provide a model system for other states. The superintendent of banking, who concurred, duly appointed a committee of thirteen under A. Barton Hepburn, president of the Chase Bank, and named Lehman one of the members. To serve with Hepburn, a financial authority of international renown, was a high privilege. Four subcommittees were soon at work. One dealt with general banking, one with trust companies, and one with the law of bankruptcy and liquidation. The fourth, which was Lehman's, was assigned the consideration of private banking, investment companies, and loan companies, his associates including the financial expert Professor Joseph F. Johnston of New York University, Louis Stern of the great department store on 42nd Street, and others.

Lehman looked with awe upon the chairman, a man of imposing presence who had been famous ever since the "Hepburn Report" of 1879 upon rail-road-rate discriminations had hewed out a solid foundation stone for Federal regulation of interstate commerce. At this very time Hepburn was exerting a healthful influence upon plans for the new Federal Reserve System. A big-game hunter, a philanthropist, a friend of statesmen and bankers from Tokyo to London, his suavity and cultivation charmed all associates. But Lehman of course worked much more closely with Johnston, Stern, and others on the subcommittee, analyzing the activities of ten mortgage, loan, and investment companies, twice as many personal loan associations, and more than a hundred private banks.

The result of the committee's work was a new statute filling about four hundred printed pages, which completely codified and revised the state's banking law. For one feature, it facilitated the entrance of state banks into the Federal Reserve System and made other urgent adjustments to the new order created by the Glass-Owen Act. A variety of fresh safeguards for the public were provided. Savings banks, for example, were required to build up reserve funds and forbidden to pay any dividends until this reserve amply protected all depositors. Personal loan companies, which had been formed all over the state to protect necessitous borrowers from loan sharks, were encouraged in their work and permitted to loan money on doubtful securities, charging more than the old legal rate for the service. Depositors in private banks plainly needed greater protection; the failure of one banking firm, Henry Siegel & Company, while the legislation was being considered, emphasized that fact. Governor Martin F. Glynn immediately sent the legislature a special message urging that all such institutions be brought under supervision of the banking department, whose powers were otherwise enlarged. State banks and trust companies were given broader authority in extending short-term credit than the national banks in the Federal Reserve System possessed.

Altogether, this Act of 1914 was a sweeping renovation of the banking code which benefited rural and urban areas alike. When the governor signed it on April 16, its authors felt that it brought the financial institutions of New York, far and away the most important state, into a greatly improved position. This satisfaction lasted only until 1929.

Lehman's part in the committee's work related chiefly to the protection of small depositors and borrowers. He helped formulate plans for a Land Bank to lend money to farmers, something the national government did not get around to for two more years; and he assisted in devising precautions to avert such disasters as the recent failure of the Union Bank in Brooklyn, a savings institution, which had ruined many small depositors. In thus giving time to the needs of humble people, he unconsciously strengthened his social and economic liberalism. His work on banking legislation fitted into the pattern of his activities at the Henry Street Settlement and his labors for the Joint Distribution Committee. He was not a theorist but very decidedly a practical man. Although this was a period of voluminous writing upon socio-political problems, no evidence exists that he paid much attention to the books of Henry George, John Spargo, Robert Hunter, Seebohm Rown-tree, J. A. Hobson, and their like. His deepening sense of social responsibility was founded upon his natural kindliness, tolerance, and sense of justice, rather than any pondered ideology of society or government.

His wartime activities, of course, had shut him off completely from politics. When Alfred E. Smith was first elected governor in 1918 Lehman was too busy in Washington to pay much attention. When Smith was defeated in 1920 by Nathan Miller, and reëlected in 1922, Herbert was intent on the Leh-man Brothers' undertakings and his charitable and civic work. He first heard Smith make a speech in 1922 to the League of Women Voters on the power resources of the St. Lawrence; a speech which converted him to public power development. After that they met on various social or political oc-casions. They had common friends in Judge Joseph M. Proskauer and his wife and in Mrs. Belle Moskowitz, a social worker widely known as the governor's adviser. Finding occasional opportunity for talks, by 1924 they were friends.

The rise of the Ku Klux Klan after the war angered Lehman. With no il-lusions about the difficulty of ejecting Coolidge from the White House, he resolved to throw himself behind Smith for the Democratic nomination in 1924. He knew that the "dry" conservative South and other rural areas, tinged by Klan prejudices, would control many delegates at the national convention in New York and bitterly oppose Smith. If there was to be a fight, he meant to get into it. He began assisting the groups aligned behind the governor in New York, Massachusetts, and other states. But weeks be-fore the convention he was plunged into work for government and not party.

· III ·

Early in June, 1924, when Lehman was at his Westchester place one Saturday morning, the governor telephoned him.

"We have a threat of a serious garment workers' strike on our hands," he said, "and I want to avoid it. I'm appointing a mediation commission to go into the dispute and use its best energies to settle it. I'd like to have you on the commission."

Lehman knew little about the garment industry, though he had some familiarity with the evils of the New York sweatshops. But it was on other grounds that he expostulated with Smith.

"Look, Governor," he said, "the trouble with this is that I want to be very active in preconvention organization and later on in the convention itself."

"Oh, don't worry about that," Smith said. "We hope this row will be over before the convention. Anyway, you can get into the convention fight. Either the dispute will be straightened out quickly or it will run into a long strike."

Lehman therefore took a seat on the commission, which was headed by George Gordon Battle, a prominent New York lawyer of Southern birth and liberal views, and comprised Arthur D. Wolf, vice-president of the Chatham & Phoenix Bank, Lindsay Rogers, professor of political science in Columbia University, and Bernard L. Shientag, attorney. They opened public hearings on June 17, with William Klein as principal counsel for the employers and the persuasive Morris Hillquit as attorney for the International Ladies Garment Workers' Union. Lehman had previously seen something of Hillquit, a Russian-born Jew who had grown to maturity on the East Side and was nearing the end of a stormy career.[5] When Lehman graduated from Williams, Hillquit was organizing the Socialist forces which ran Debs for President in 1900; while Lehman was busy with the Spencer Turner Company, Hillquit was preaching cohesive action to the helpless men and women who made women's suits and cloaks, men's shirts and trousers; while Lehman was in the War Department, in 1917, Hillquit was polling more than a fifth of the vote of New York as Socialist candidate for mayor. By 1924 he held an international eminence among moderate leftists of the United States, as brilliant a figure as Ramsay MacDonald, Jean Jaurès, and Wilhelm Liebknecht abroad. Now he helped enlighten Lehman upon a situation of fascinating interest.

Behind the International Ladies Garment Workers' Union, organized in 1900 as the first great national organization in the clothing industry, lay an heroic story. Since the later years of the nineteenth century, a group of leaders had been struggling to organize the metropolitan clothing workers, next to agricultural laborers the most impoverished and defenseless toilers in the nation; masses of Russian Jews, with smaller bodies of Italians, Poles, Portuguese, and Greeks, all new immigrants, all bewildered, and all more or less ignorant of the English tongue and American ways. They were savagely exploited and cheated, often by their own folk. When Ray Stannard Baker printed an article on their hard lot he put at its head a few lines by Morris Rosenfeld: [6]

> I work, work, work without end,
> Why and for whom I know not,
> I care not, I ask not,
> I am a machine.

Many of them, toiling in littered, airless shops and tenement rooms, literally worked themselves to death. "I shall never forget," writes Baker, "my first visit to these workshops, the crowded homes in slum tenements, the swarming, half-clad children—and the heat, the noise, the obscene poverty." [7] A local union federation, the United Hebrew Trades, lent a hand to the movement, and so did the Yiddish daily, the *Forward*. [8]

Between its foundation and the First World War, the ILGWU struggled desperately for life and strength. One angry strike after another marked its growth. After a severe culminating conflict, a body of negotiators which included Hillquit and Louis D. Brandeis in 1910 secured the adoption of a "perpetual protocol of peace" between employers and workers, marked by a happy liberality of terms. The union spread to other cities in the United States and Canada, and when the war ended seemed in substantial control of the industry. In New York, however, powerful disruptive forces were undermining the position of the workers, forces which found their strength in the difficulty of policing nonunion shops. Lehman soon learned that a body of the larger garment manufacturers belonging to the so-called Industrial Council favored the union and tried loyally to foster it; but a more numerous array of small employers outside the Council, many of them transient occupants of some loft, ignored the union, paid cut-rate wages, and worked their hands for long hours in unsanitary premises. America had lagged far behind England and Germany in the regulation of working conditions in the garment trades.

Some four hundred jobbers, a group who had become powerful in New York during and just after the war, encouraged the rise of the "outside" manufacturers of low standards. They furnished materials and patterns to a multitude of "social shops"; that is, shops started by an enterprising worker or foreman who, after saving a few hundred dollars, rented some rooms, assembled a staff of relatives or friends, often newly arrived, and put them to work usually at wretched wages amid repulsive surroundings. Early in the 1920s the number of small firms competing fiercely for orders rose above a thousand, and the jobbers tossed orders to these subcontractors as a man might toss bones to a pack of hungry curs. [9]

Even in a small industry this cutthroat sweating of labor would have been deplorable. But New York garment manufacture was one of the largest metropolitan industries in the world, with an estimated production in 1924 of $370,000,000 worth of goods. Three-fourths of the industry fell into this diseased condition, with the workers not merely maltreated but on the edge of beggary—for at any moment a hard-pressed shop might fail and throw its hands on the street. The petty employer had only a razor-edge margin.

"He hires a little room with five or six machines and starts up," testified one union witness. "The chances are that just in the middle of the season, perhaps he comes to the end of his rope and has to give up. With what results? Not only do we not get our wages paid, but also a group of employees is left there in the midst of the season, outside of the actual work for the industry." That is, all the seasonal contracts having been let, they were stranded —often penniless. In the old days practically all the work had been done in large "inside" shops, which made patterns, bought materials, and cut and finished the garment under one roof. The new fragmentation played havoc with the ILGWU, for few but the "inside" shops had provided conditions favorable to unionization or were careful to observe protocol requirements.[10]

To replace disorder and irresponsibility with well-enforced rules protecting wages and working conditions had been the object of the ILGWU in threatening the strike. It wished to compel both "inside" and "outside" manufacturers to recognize and deal with it. Its strategic plan was to use the jobbers' association, which had achieved such rapid domination of the industry, as its agent in extending union standards throughout the industry. It demanded that members of the association agree to deal only in garments bearing the union label and to do business with five times as many "stable manufacturers" running union shops as their own numbers. They should give these stable manufacturers preference in the apportioning of contracts, refuse to allot any work at all to shops with fewer than fourteen sewing machines, and guarantee prices which would cover the minimum labor costs of the shops. The ILGWU further asked for the establishment of an unemployment insurance fund to which manufacturers, jobbers, and union should all contribute.[11]

In this effort the union leaders felt a sense of desperation, for all the gains they had made since the beginning of the century seemed in peril. Under the cutthroat competition in the industry, every year hundreds of the small garment-making shops were forced out of business; two out of five in 1923–24. When the next season began they were replaced by equally dismal concerns struggling desperately for life. Workers whose former employers had gone bankrupt had to join in a wild scramble for new places. Frequently they were compelled to take jobs on the old sweatshop level. The petty "outside" manufacturers were not inhumane; they were simply caught in a situation in which they had to enforce inhumane terms to survive. Small wonder that

Lehman and associates in the Al Smith Campaign of 1928
Left to right, front row: Herbert H. Lehman, John J. Raskob, Major General
William Haskell (Commanding General of the New York State National Guard),
Frank Hague, John J. McCooey, and William Kenny

Wide World Photos

Herbert H. Lehman at Warm Springs, Georgia, November, 1928
Left to right: Maurice Bloch, Minority Leader in the Assembly, Franklin D. Roosevelt, Herbert H. Lehman, Samuel I. Rosenman, Bernard Downing, Minority Leader in the Senate, and William Bray, Chairman of the New York State Democratic Committee.

Photo Warm Springs Foundation

many workers had turned toward Communism—and small wonder that the devoted, honest-minded president of the ILGWU, Benjamin Schlesinger, struggling against mortal illness as well as industrial chaos, seemed to Lehman sometimes bitterly irascible and unreasonable.

· IV ·

The governor's advisory commission, first at City Hall and then at the state labor department building in the city, spent nearly ten days, June 17–25, 1924, listening to vehement arguments of union leaders, big manufacturers, little manufacturers, and jobbers. The jobbers were the target of attacks by all three other elements. "Can their alleged stranglehold be removed?" inquired Lehman. "Yes, make the jobber directly responsible for labor," replied William Klein. But the jobbers wildly maintained that they could never do all the policing of industry themselves or meet demands which included the preferential shop (union members to be hired first), the spreading of work in slack seasons, and a sharp limitation of the right to discharge, with a five-day forty-hour week. The problems indeed seemed almost insoluble.

However, the commission did avert the strike by proposing a compromise course. Its preliminary report, laid before Smith soon after the hearings ended, forcibly supported the ILGWU demand for union shops throughout the industry and labor's contention that jobbers should be made responsible for proper shop conditions among submanufacturers. But it called only for a sanitary label, not a union label, in each garment. While the union proposal for an unemployment fund was accepted, the suggested contribution of the jobbers was sharply reduced, and the demand for a forty-hour week was passed over. A number of intricate questions, such as the union proposal for a limitation in the number of shops, were set aside for further study. They and certain more technical problems of the industry would be examined by experts, who would report back to the commission. All concerned accepted the report, and in midsummer the employers and union leaders concluded agreements based on its findings. Morris Hillquit and the union organ *Justice* were much pleased.[12]

But the implementation of the report demanded continued labor by Lehman, for the establishment of order and prosperity would have been a difficult process under the best circumstances, and new forces of disorder had to be combated. He and his associates saw to it that some of their proposals were carried out: a joint board of sanitary control established a label department under Dr. Henry Moskowitz, and a committee on unemployment insurance began work under Arthur D. Wolf. The ILGWU, by mass demonstrations and picketing, brought many of the nonunion employees within its ranks. Meanwhile, the committee of experts began a study of the means of preventing the multiplication of small shops, of the nature and control of unemployment, of the possibility of raising wage scales while limiting labor costs, and of other problems; Lehman and Shientag lending a hand when possible. With their findings digested, the governor's advisory commission made its final report on May 20, 1926.[13]

This report, accepting the ILGWU contention that the jobbers must play the decisive role in a reform of the bad contracting system, and must stop farming out the production of garments to a multiplicity of small shops which ground the faces of their workers while performing slipshod work, centered its attention on the regulation of submanufacturers by joint union-jobber effort. The two antagonistic bodies must join hands to put reason into the industry. Lehman, Rogers, and Shientag proposed that the jobbers' association and ILGWU should agree on standards of wages, hours, working conditions, and workmanship; that at stated intervals each jobber should make contracts with a limited number of subcontractors meeting these standards; that he should divide the business equitably among these shops; and that he should give nobody else work unless all were too busy to handle it. The "outside" shops would thus be brought up to a level approaching that of the "inside" establishments. That these were sound principles nobody could doubt.

Alas for the fate of this final report! The goal of order, decency, and stability was not reached until 1933; for when the advisory commission submitted its findings, the industry was falling under the control of a left wing which the Communists had thoroughly infiltrated. This wing had always regarded any friendly agreement with employers as a vicious form of class collaboration, a treason to the proletariat. Although ILGWU leaders were willing to use the report as a basis for negotiations, intransigent leftists carried the day for rejection. Two of the three employer groups, the "inside" manufacturers and the submanufacturers, were also ready to accept it, but the jobbers maintained a stony hostility. The upshot was that the controlling union board, dominated by Communists, announced on July 1, 1926, an industry-wide strike, not troubling to hold a referendum. To support this strike during the next half-year they expended not only $3,500,000 of the workers' money, but $800,000 that the employers had deposited in securities with the union as a guaranty of the observance of collective agreements.

A long agony ensued. Finally the strike failed, and the union had to sign an agreement with the "inside" manufacturers on terms much less favorable than those proposed by the governor's advisory commission. Its leadership was immediately reorganized, and, weakened in numbers and practically bankrupt, it was freed from Communist control—though Communist elements in the needle trades continued to make trouble. David Dubinsky, who had been vice-president of the ILGWU since 1922, took charge of the restoration, first as secretary-treasurer, later as president. This remarkable man, a graduate of the Siberian exile system and the cloak-cutter's table, had an ability and integrity which matched his social vision. When he came to Lehman, Felix Warburg, and a few others to ask a loan of $25,000 apiece to put the union on its feet, he met a ready response.[14]

Lehman provided $50,000 all told. "I had no idea when I made the loan that I'd ever see the money again," he said later. "I thought it was gone. Thanks to David Dubinsky, every cent of it was paid back."

Lehman had abstracted a great deal of time from business and the JDC for the work of the commission. Although his labors seemed for a time cast away on the rocks of left-wing factionalism, the final result was to show that his group had not labored in vain, for their ideas helped achieve the triumph of constructive arrangements. Meanwhile he had profited from his long hours of talk with manufacturers, jobbers, and union organizers, his visits to shops, and his study of statistics and expert analyses. He had learned all about one of the giant industries of the city and state. He had deepened his understanding of the hard lot of the immigrant poor and their capacity to rise whenever capably led; his sympathy with trade unionism had grown, and in Hillquit, Dubinsky, Benjamin Schlesinger, and others he had found staunch new friends. He had gained at first hand a keen appreciation of the importance of the work of expert, impartial investigators in a complex situation involving capital, management, and labor. In short, his pragmatic education had been carried a step forward.

In all his public labors, it should be said, he relied upon two invaluable advisers, his brother Irving and his wife Edith, and never failed to consult both. Irving had not only a philosophic mind, which saw further into some questions than Herbert did, but sound practical judgment; Edith possessed faculties, as we have said, which he lacked—an ability to remember names, unfailing tact, and social *savoir-faire* as well as intuitive sagacity. Their aid enabled him to shoulder burdens he could not have carried alone.

· V ·

While thus occupied, he had taken a small part in the tragic Democratic Convention of 1924. Smith's friends, in planning New York hospitality, sought out prominent citizens to look after each state delegation. They persuaded Lehman to be host to the Massachusetts group. He called on them, entertained them, and argued the merits of Smith's candidacy—no hard task, for most of them supported Smith already. As a delegate, he watched with chagrin the long deadlock between Smith and McAdoo until on the 100th ballot McAdoo released his delegates, and on the 104th John W. Davis won a prize which was then not worth having. This was the first convention broadcast by radio, and what the nation heard of the bickering and prejudice disgusted it almost as much as it did Lehman. The fine appeals of Newton D. Baker for the League and against the Klan alone stirred him.

That fall he threw himself into Smith's campaign for a third term as governor. As vice-president of the National Democratic Club and treasurer of the Citizens' Committee for Governor Smith, he was in a position to exercise some influence. He spoke repeatedly to explain Smith's fine administrative record and total freedom from group bias. "Just as he has never allowed politics to affect his duty to all the people," said Lehman, "he has never shown either favoritism or prejudice because of race, religion, or social condition." [15]

Smith's reëlection over Theodore Roosevelt, Jr., at the very time that Davis went down in crushing defeat, strengthened Lehman's hopes for the man and the party.

Two years later, in 1926, he became chairman of the Citizens' Committee for the Reëlection of Governor Smith. The Republican nominee, Ogden L. Mills, was a man of character and ability who was sure to run far ahead upstate, and Lehman's task was to rally the independent voters behind Smith. He temporarily withdrew from business to throw himself into the last six weeks of what became a harshly abusive struggle.

Faced by a governor who could point to an impressive list of liberal achievements, "Oggie" Mills searched for some vulnerable point in his record. He charged waste, Tammany Hall domination, complicity in border rum-running, Socialism, and hostility to business—all without effect. Finally he found what seemed a weak spot, in which William Randolph Hearst would help him push his spear home: the Smith administration had permitted the sale of contaminated milk (pure milk was a favorite Hearst cause)! Mills's adherents took samples from grocery cans, found a percentage of foreign matter, and filled the air with ululations. The babies of New York were being killed by unclean milk; Al Smith was abetting the sellers of the foul stuff; he was shielding Tammany officeholders who blinked at the crime! When Lehman denied that the state had been negligent about inspection and showed that the governor was not responsible for carelessness in local groceries, Mills renewed his attack.

"We have an issue," he said, "which Herbert H. Lehman will find it hard to ignore or Smith to laugh away. I consider it such an issue that I am very much tempted to have my car attached to a milk train with which to tour the state."[16]

Mills's double-barreled charge, that unhealthy milk was being sold in New York City and that Governor Smith had been afraid of offending Tammany by dismissing state officials who permitted the sale, was untrue in both parts. Lehman and others quickly proved that the milk was sanitary when it reached the stores and that the governor was protecting no unfit officials. Hearst's headlines in the *New York American* fell flat. At a half-dozen other points Lehman was Smith's enthusiastic champion. When Mills talked of "influence," he showed that all the governor's acts and appointments had demonstrated unflinching independence. When Mills spoke of loose financial administration, he proved that Republican figures grossly exaggerated the public debt and halved the true cash surplus. When Mills applied the epithet "Socialist" to Smith's measures, Lehman retorted: "If this is Socialism, I thank God for it and am proud to be arrayed under its banner."

Lehman had predicted a plurality for Smith of more than 400,000. The governor's actual margin of 257,000 was impressive enough, and helped carry Robert Wagner into the senate against James W. Wadsworth. Such a demonstration of popularity made Smith's nomination for President in 1928 almost inevitable. Anxious to improve his organization and assuage party rancors, Smith realized that he could not afford to make a Tammany regular the chairman of the Democratic State Committee, a place which Lieutenant-Governor Edwin Corning was ready to vacate. He offered Lehman the post. This gave offense to Tammany, for although Lehman was a member, he had repeatedly shown hostility to its leaders. Indeed, Tammany was already so much irritated by Smith's friendship with Judge Proskauer and Abram I. Elkus, and his selection of the aggressively independent Robert Moses as secretary of state, that Lehman's appointment would have seemed the last straw.

Reluctant to take the place, but anxious also to please Smith, Lehman hesitated until one evening he attended a concert at Carnegie Hall. In leaving, he found himself jostling the Democratic national committeewoman, Elizabeth Marbury, an old friend whose judgment he respected. Looking down, for she was a head taller, she spoke decisively:

"Young man, I understand that you're thinking of taking the chairmanship of the State Committee. Let me give you a piece of advice. Don't take it. All you're going to get out of it is a kick in the pants."

Lehman left Corning in the post.

· VI ·

New York City was perennially in financial trouble and under John F. Hylan and Jimmy Walker kept slipping deeper into the morass. George Olvany, who had become Tammany boss when Murphy died in 1924 (getting a splendid funeral in St. Patrick's Cathedral while 60,000 people jammed Fifth Avenue to view his hearse), was partly responsible for the maladministration. Though he was the first college graduate to head the Hall, Olvany was a weak, colorless man who manipulated city contracts, condoned graft on condemnation payments, and exercised no control whatever over his district leaders. He perhaps made corruption more polite, but he made it duller; he disgusted Lehman. By 1926, when annual expenditures exceeded half a billion, and the debt almost equaled that of all the states combined, a constructive study of the situation was desperately needed. Mayor Walker appointed a City Committee on Plan and Survey under Judge Morgan J. O'Brien. Of its eight subcommittees, that on budget, finance, and revenue was organized near the close of the year under Lehman's chairmanship. The members included the economist E. R. A. Seligman, the bankers Charles H. Sabin, Walter E. Frew, and Otto H. Kahn, the municipal reformer Richard S. Childs, and Judge Bernard Shientag. An able Columbia group—Luther Gulick, Howard Lee McBain, Robert Murray Haig, Lindsay Rogers, Joseph McGoldrick—was enlisted to analyze the financial administration and fiscal structure of the city. Professor Rogers later remembered the generosity with which Lehman, paying costs from his own pocket, fixed his compensation at a well-earned $1,000 a month.

At that period the board of estimate had sole responsibility for preparing city budgets. The board of aldermen, a generally corrupt and incompetent group, could do nothing but reduce or eliminate cuts and the mayor nothing but veto these changes. Frequently the aldermen delayed approval of the budget to reach an "understanding," fat with favors for district leaders, with the city commissioners who were waiting for departmental appropriations. Many of the fifty-eight aldermen had no experience in budgets outside of the saloons they had run, and one observer thought that not more than five could read intelligently the annual report upon the use of tax money. When Ruth Pratt became alderwoman in 1926, she was appalled by the ignorance of her associates, but one of them bade her not to fret: "They have a lot of experts to go over this budget, so we needn't bother about it."

Clearly, this diffusion of financial irresponsibility should be ended, and Lehman's subcommittee pointed out a better road. The mayor and not the board of estimate, it declared in a report laid before Mayor Jimmy Walker on June 5, 1928, should be responsible for preparation of the budget and should present it as *his* document. To assist him a department of the budget should be created, its director to be his appointee and subject to his removal. This department should schedule all expenditures, prepare the tax program for current income, and submit an additional program for outlays financed by borrowing. Thus the director would stand second in power only to the mayor himself. The completed budget would be submitted to the board of estimate, which would be vested with an enlarged authority over the city's operating expenses, including the numbers, grades, and pay of employees. So far as possible, New York City should be run on a pay-as-you-go basis.

In time, the main reforms thus proposed were put into effect. The city in 1933 created a Budget Bureau, and the new city charter which was adopted in 1937 embodied some of the more important of the other recommendations. The central feature of the reforms was the centralization of responsibility for the budget in the mayor and budget director, whose schedules could not be exceeded; the board of estimate and city council having powers of review and excision, but not of initiation. The new charter included a pay-as-you-go plan on important types of improvements, such as buildings, sewers, and communications systems. Lehman's subcommittee had urged that the heavy bonded debt of the city be reduced, and the charter provided that an increasing percentage of the cost of improvements should be paid without issuing corporate stock or bonds.

The long-smoldering quarrel between New York City and Albany over the division of taxes collected in the metropolis, a dispute which Lehman later had to face as governor, received due attention. Real-estate taxes provided about four-fifths of the city's revenues in 1928, while the state also took large revenues from city realty. The subcommittee suggested that Albany should abandon its own real-estate tax, leaving that source entirely to the city, and recoup itself by a gasoline tax, a tax on unincorporated businesses, and other special levies. It was a fair proposal, but it could not immediately be followed. In fact, most of the committee recommendations took time and some of them a great deal of it. The press was cordial in praise of the full report, the *New York Times* terming it "masterful." Unfortunately, the financial maladies of the metropolis were deep-seated and in the great depression just ahead were to demand desperate surgical action.

Nothing did more to center public attention on Lehman than this financial survey; nothing did so much to make him a logical choice for office. Before he finished with it new opportunities beckoned him to a complete abandonment of business for public affairs.

Chapter VI

THE RISE OF
FRANKLIN D. ROOSEVELT

THE chief uncertainty of the men who in 1927 were trying to promote Al Smith from governorship to Presidency lay in the question whether his old-time Tammany affiliations, hostility to prohibition, and Roman Catholicism still estranged the West and South. Three close friends, Joseph Proskauer, Robert Moses, and Mrs. Moskowitz, together with some professional politicians, decided early this year that they should get some prominent party men to tour these sections, combining exploration with missionary work. Lehman helped discuss the matter. As he was planning to go West during the summer, he was asked to take responsibility for the Rocky Mountain States, sounding out politicians and arguing Smith's preëminent merits. He assented and traveled through all the states from Idaho and Montana down to New Mexico and Arizona, pausing longest in Colorado.

"I met with a very friendly reception almost everywhere I went," he reported. Most Democratic politicians and editors were cordial to Smith's candidacy. Though Denver reputedly had a good many Klan members, they kept out of sight and comparatively few Westerners supported Smith's rival, Senator Tom Walsh of Montana, a Catholic "dry." In the end, Smith received solid Mountain States support in the convention.

That winter the Smith organization asked Lehman to carry his work into California. Talking with Senator James Phelan and the state and national committeemen, he found Los Angeles lukewarm but San Francisco enthusiastic, and Smith ultimately commanded the entire California delegation. On his return home Lehman continued raising money, for the preconvention struggle took a good deal. "I don't know why," he subsequently remarked, "but I suppose we all felt that whatever was judiciously spent before the convention might be educational enough to pay returns in the campaign."

Those who joined him in large gifts included William Kenny, a contractor who was reputed to have made $36,000,000 in business, and John J. Raskob, identified with the Du Pont interests.

State after state, the South alone reluctant and grumbling, fell into line behind the governor. Though other men aspired to the nomination—Cordell Hull, James A. Reed, Walter F. George—by June in 1928 Smith's lead was decisive.

The governor's nomination was so certain, in fact, that Lehman knew the convention to be held in Houston that month would prove comparatively dull. He correctly anticipated that Texas would be torrid; and he felt relieved when Mrs. Lehman made an initial decision to stay at home in cool Westchester. However, when he reached St. Louis on a special train which ran through the Mountain States to gather up delegates, he was paged for a telephone call, and hurried to the booth to hear her announce that she was starting West that very hour. "Meet me in Houston," she commanded. She loved Democratic conventions, had attended all of them since her marriage, and suddenly found this one irresistible.

The gathering long haunted men's memories for its fearful heat. The tortured delegates, herded into a great tentlike building open on three sides to the oven winds, saw the thermometer climb above 100° day after day. Sideshow diversions offered a little relief; one exuberant Texan, for example, gave the party a herd of forty-eight donkeys, promptly increased by the birth of a forty-ninth. Claude G. Bowers opened the proceedings with a keynote blast reminiscent of the spellbinding oratory of Henry Clay's day. Meanwhile, as evidence of the bull-market boom which was then hypnotizing the country, some moneyed men put on a display of affluence that startled people who thought Democrats were by definition poor. On the sidings lay Raskob's private car, Nicholas Brady's private car, Kenny's private car, and others, while multimillionaire oil barons unleashed droves of costly foreign automobiles. Yet the spirit of the gathering was vibrant with liberalism.

Franklin D. Roosevelt signalized his partial recovery and his reëmergence as one of the party chieftains by his long-remembered speech nominating Al Smith as the "happy warrior." Everybody knew how he had conquered his illness. "A wonderful impression!" testified Lehman. "To see him standing there so strikingly handsome—to hear him speaking in that beautiful voice—to think of the gallant struggle he had made against his ailment—it was thrilling." With unfeigned enthusiasm the delegates rallied behind Smith as their champion against Hoover, who had just been nominated in Kansas City. Joseph T. Robinson of Arkansas, after a touching appeal to his fellow Southerners to display religious tolerance, was named for Vice-President. "We went back home with high hopes," records Lehman.

• I •

High hopes and deep feelings—for Lehman's emotions were more fervently enlisted in this campaign than in almost any other in his life. He had formed a warm affection for Al Smith and a conviction of his genius for government; he was disgusted by the isolationism, corruption, and big-business favoritism that had seamed the Harding-Coolidge record; and he felt scant confidence in Hoover. The battle that summer and fall meant to him all that Woodrow Wilson's battle had meant in 1912.

For the first time he held a central position in a Democratic national campaign, for, as chairman of the finance committee, he was a member of the inner executive group of the national committee. His associates included National Chairman Raskob and James W. Gerard, Jouett Shouse, Pat Harrison of Mississippi, Peter Gerry of Rhode Island, Mrs. Roosevelt, Mrs. Moskowitz, Bruce Kramer of Montana, and an astute New York politician, John Delaney. Out-of-town members moved to New York, for the work at headquarters, 1776 Broadway, was incessant and arduous. Though Hoover kept his own appeals on an elevated plane, the struggle soon dropped into a phase of great bitterness, and a stream of loyal visitors from the South and West reported alarming ebullitions of prejudice and misrepresentation.

Governor Smith, as Lehman felt, had almost three strikes against him at the outset. For one, the prohibition issue alienated many voters, as prohibition was the law of the land, and feeling against its abuses had not yet crystallized. For another, many voters believed that Smith was essentially a state leader, who knew little about national affairs and still less about international problems. Finally, his Catholicism, immigrant background, and connection with Tammany gave many good citizens a conviction that he was somehow alien to the traditional, well-established forces of American life; if many Iowans and Texans thought a New York City man a little the outlander, a Catholic from the East Side was a complete foreigner. While all three sources of opposition were serious, the religious question was the most important. In dealing with them all, the task was to erase prejudice and substitute for a distorted stereotype an impression of Smith's real ability, generosity, and sturdy Americanism.

This required money, which it was Lehman's special task to raise and which as usual the Democrats found it hard to get. Though business was enjoying unexampled if precarious prosperity, most businessmen poured their largess into the Republican coffers. Jesse H. Jones, licking the wounds he had sustained in an unsuccessful effort to be nominated for Vice-President, congratulated Lehman on succeeding to Jones's old finance chairmanship—and then pledged for the battle the trifling sum of $25,000.[1] Large gifts from a few enthusiasts of the Kenny-Raskob type had to be supplemented by small checks from many people. The concourse of visitors to headquarters included numerous lukewarm Democrats. For their benefit leaders plastered the walls of one room, the "chamber of horrors," with hundreds of cartoons, editorials, and news items assailing Smith in vicious language; and Lehman found that when he led a caller into this arcanum of bigotry the man often emerged with a white-hot desire to write a check. While the "drys" were angrily aroused and sometimes shrilly fanatical, they were far less unfair than the Protestants who could not get St. Bartholomew's and Bloody Mary out of their minds.

Just how best to dispel the objections to Smith was a difficult question. Lehman was realist enough to see that the nomination had involved the party in certain liabilities that went beyond mere prejudice. It was true, for one fact, that with all his brilliant insight, swift grasp of public questions, and mastery of the problems of the Empire State, Smith had sharp limitations of experience and outlook. He was a townsman, he never understood rural or village life, and his sympathy for the farmer was an exterior sympathy. When later on Governor Roosevelt toured New York State, he loved to get off the main roads, visit numerous hamlets and small towns, and talk with country-folk as one farmer to another; but Smith's tours had usually been from one city to another.

Moreover, while Smith was an internationalist, he was as unfamiliar with foreign nations and international problems as Coolidge had been. He had never gone abroad, he had read little on international affairs, and the Irish-Americans of his milieu had fought Wilson and the League at a time when Hoover was one of Wilson's most effective supporters. For that matter, Smith knew little about the United States west of the Alleghenies. His autobiography, *Up to Now*, shows his wonderment over some of the areas he visited on this campaign; the Wyoming-Colorado country, for example, moved him to exclaim upon the "waste and barren condition of the land." [2]

Nor were the apprehensions of people on the religious question wholly irrational. It was as fatuous to say that the Catholic hierarchy never interfered improperly in public affairs in New York or Massachusetts as to say that Protestant leaders never interfered in Virginia or Georgia. New Yorkers remembered the police disruption of a perfectly legal meeting in Carnegie Hall to hear Margaret Sanger, on orders traced to Archbishop Hayes, and

Bostonians knew of sharp Catholic pressures against civil liberties. It was on the basis of justifiable apprehensions that Charles C. Marshall had addressed an open letter to Smith in *The Atlantic* of April, 1927. This was something more than the "fool article" that Franklin D. Roosevelt called it. In a courteous argument, Marshall, an Episcopalian, a retired attorney, and a student of church law, asked the governor if the canons of his church were not at variance with the Constitution and laws. He quoted Pius IX as declaring that in the event church law conflicted with state law, the church must prevail; and he cited the assertion of Leo XIII that the state could not hold all sects in equal favor, whereas the American Constitution forbade it to do anything else.

Smith had replied with one of the ablest of all his papers, a communication in which Chaplain Francis P. Duffy of the 165th Infantry helped him to interpret technical questions and to cite refuting authorities. As released to the press on April 17, it was warmly applauded by all fair-minded people. During his service in elective positions since 1903, Smith said, he had never known an instance of conflict between his official duties and religious belief, and if they ever did collide, he would hold state interests paramount. He pointed out how energetically he had always supported the public schools and the State Department of Education. Of particular importance, in view of the current troubles of the church in Mexico, and some hotheaded Catholic demands for action, was his repudiation of the idea of American intervention in any foreign land in support of any sect.[3]

Smith made two long tours, one into the West and Southwest and one through the upper South. Then, after a trip through New England, he closed his appeal with speeches in Philadelphia, Brooklyn, and Madison Square Garden. Lehman, with special opportunity to study the governor at close range and measure his virtues and shortcomings, saw much to enhance his admiration and affection. Al made mistakes. He had blundered at the notification ceremonies in Albany by boring delegates with a long recital of his achievements as governor. Later he erred in choosing Raskob, a Catholic, an officer of General Motors, a close friend of the du Ponts, and a man of colossal wealth, as campaign manager. Yet not only his quick apprehension of complex questions but his elevation of purpose and firmness of conviction were impressive.

At his best Smith was as convincing a speaker as New York had known since Theodore Roosevelt, with a warmth and charm that T.R. had not possessed. He had cultivated an informal mode of discourse that plain people liked. Depending on his agile mind and amazing memory, he did not prepare carefully. He could dictate an address at two in the afternoon, get the text at five, and after reading it twice over, rise at eight and deliver it almost verbatim. More frequently, he would write one or two words on each sheet of a stack of papers and with these in hand speak with fluent vigor, carrying his hearers with him. He could be superb in these hastily organized efforts, sometimes rising, like Lloyd George, to sudden eloquence.

Great crowds turned out to hear Smith, moved in New York by appreciation of his record but elsewhere by a combination of esteem and curiosity. As William Allen White put it, out West Smith was supposed by many to have horns and a tail. His eager reception gave him the illusion that he would probably be elected. In Denver, Minneapolis, and Chicago the cheering throngs, the bands playing "East Side, West Side," and the optimistic assurances of politicians delighted him. On some stretches hundreds of people would board the train at each stop to shake hands while they rode to the next station. Lehman could have told him that all this meant little, for ever since the Bryan-Taft campaign in 1908 Lehman had distrusted crowds. That year he had dined with Nathan Straus, an influential man in Democratic circles, and joined his host and others in hurrying down to an evening rally in Madison Square Garden which Bryan was to address. The crowd was so dense that they never got within four blocks of the Garden, and its enthusiasm deluded some people into believing that Bryan would easily carry the state. Yet in point of fact he lost even that historic Democratic stronghold, New York City.

A sensitive man, Smith hesitated to use blunt language in answering religious prejudice. All his supporters believed that he should carry his attacks on the Klan and ignorant critics into enemy territory, and he yielded to their wishes. But where should he speak? His final decision was Oklahoma City, and Lehman relates the disappointing sequel:

> Well, the Saturday night before he was starting on this trip I was up in Albany, staying overnight at the governor's mansion. Two or three other people were with me. We sat upstairs in the great central hall with bright red walls, one of the ugliest rooms I've ever seen, until late in the evening, having a drink and discussing the outlook for this trip. Smith said to me, "Would you be interested in hearing my speech for Oklahoma City?"
>
> We all knew this was a very important speech. I said, "Yes, I would be very much interested."
>
> So he got up, and without any notes at all, as was his habit, strode from one end of the room to the other, giving this speech. It was a beautiful speech; wonderful, I thought. When he got through he said to me, "Have you any criticisms? Any changes?"
>
> I said: "No, I haven't any criticism. My only suggestion is that

you don't change a word of that speech. I think it's a knockout, a wonderful speech."

I came back to New York so impressed that I said to my wife—for this was in the early days of radio, when not everybody had a set, and people used to hold radio parties: "Now this will be a marvelous speech. I know just what he is going to say. Let's invite a lot of friends over to listen to it. I'm sure we'll make many converts."

So we did. And then he gave a completely different speech, in which he largely dodged the religious issue. It was a poor speech. I was almost in tears, because I had expected so much, and in place of a superb performance we had a poor one.

Later I learned that in Oklahoma City he met an extremely hostile audience, which depressed him. They burned crosses in his face. The hall was crammed to the doors, with people standing in the aisles, and they all wore a look of stony enmity. He, more than most political leaders, was a man who responded quickly to the mood of an audience. If it was cordial, he let himself go, but if it was hostile he felt frozen. The local committee could not be accused of poor planning, for we had almost no friends out in Oklahoma at that time; religion and prohibition made it chilly or malevolent.

In his autobiography Smith dwells upon the defiant forthrightness of his speeches, but on this critical occasion he was not his usual determined self.[4]

· II ·

In the full sweep of the national campaign, Lehman had to drop it early in October for state affairs. By a dramatic turn of events the party nominated him for lieutenant-governor and Franklin D. Roosevelt for governor. Ten days earlier he would have deemed either nomination highly improbable.

The New York Democrats were in an unhappy predicament in 1928. They had only one man of great political strength available for the governorship—a reformer, an upstate Protestant, a neutral on prohibition—and he was at Warm Springs, Georgia, recovering from his malady. They faced a strong Republican nominee, the Jewish attorney general, Albert Ottinger, just completing four aggressive years of battle against crooks and profiteers. The various alternatives to FDR mentioned—Robert Wagner, George R. Lunn, John H. Finley—commanded no enthusiasm. Many in the metropolis spoke of Lehman, but he knew he would not suit upstate leaders and rejected the idea: "I told them that I would be a poor candidate, and I didn't want it." At an early date he publicly suggested Roosevelt. This was at an outdoors meeting at his Purchase farm which Mrs. Roosevelt attended. Turning to her in his speech, he remarked, "I certainly hope that your husband is going to be the next governor"—and the crowd applauded. But was he available?

As the convention approached, the party chiefs, though well aware that a ticket naming Roosevelt for governor, Lehman for lieutenant governor, and Dr. Royal S. Copeland for Senator would be powerful, remained confused. They feared they could not get these men. So the situation stood when on October 1 delegates flocked to Rochester.

Lehman, Smith, and Wagner, who all attended, agreed that Roosevelt was their one hope. But Roosevelt, cannily remaining in Warm Springs, did not wish to run. He felt that another two years' treatment was necessary to his recovery, that he must see his financial commitments for the establishment of a therapeutic center at Warm Springs fully met, and that 1928 was not a Democratic year anyway. Louis M. Howe, his political adviser, shared his conviction that the hour had not struck for him to step into the political hurly-burly.

When the leaders asked Mrs. Roosevelt to exert her influence, she had emphatically refused. "It is a question for my husband to decide," she said; "it is too important for any intervention of mine; I shall offer no advice, and whatever he decides will be satisfactory to me." She, too, was at heart against acceptance. If she spoke to Roosevelt by telephone on the subject, the leaders never knew it.

Smith had talked with him at length from Milwaukee and got a firm no, reinforced by a telegram of refusal. But the matter was so important that the leaders, huddled in the Hotel Seneca on the 1st, resolved to try again.

Roosevelt was plainly trying to dodge his pursuers. When the four worried men, Smith, Raskob, Lehman, Wagner, got through to the Warm Springs cottage they were told he was out, and new calls met the same answer. Late in the afternoon on October 2, a final desperate call elicited the information that he had left for a political meeting at Manchester twenty miles away. They reached the hall only to be told that he was on the jammed top floor, speaking, and could not come to the telephone. Smith, Raskob, and Lehman waited. They telephoned the hall again and found that he had left for Warm Springs. Finally, about midnight, they got him on the wire. He said that he couldn't run, that he wouldn't if he could, and that the imperative duty of putting Warm Springs on a sound financial basis—for he had invested $200,-000 in it—would make acceptance a breach of faith.

In short, they met a complete refusal. But this they simply could not take. The convention had been in session all day waiting for Roosevelt's assent, and would expect it on the morrow. As they conferred, Smith told Lehman that his agreement to serve as lieutenant governor, taking as much burden as possible off the governor's shoulders, might be a decisive consideration. Then, at two in the morning, they telephoned once more. Smith made an eloquent personal plea.

"You've got to run," he told Roosevelt, in effect. "The interests of both the national ticket and New York demand it. I know your health is a very important consideration; I can sympathize with your feeling on that. But you won't have to do too much here. You know the job of governor isn't impossibly difficult, and we'll give you Herbert Lehman as lieutenant governor, so that you can go away for as long a time as you like."

When Smith ended his argument, Roosevelt asked that Lehman come to the telephone and put him a pointblank question. "Will you run as lieutenant governor?" he asked. And Lehman replied, "Yes." At this point Raskob seized the telephone. "Frank," he said, "don't worry about your financial obligations at Warm Springs. I'll take care of them." *

The plea by Smith and the assurances by Lehman and Raskob turned the scales. "Well," said Roosevelt, "I guess that in view of this very strong appeal that has been made, I'll accept the nomination." He did it, Lehman thought, with a heavy heart.

That morning the announcement that he would stand for the governorship electrified the convention. Nominated by Mayor Jimmy Walker of New York, he was chosen by acclamation. Lehman's nomination immediately followed. Henry Morgenthau, Sr., forthwith telephoned Mrs. Lehman to announce: "Have you heard what they have done to your husband? They have named him for lieutenant governor!"—a statement that took her utterly aback.

But at the time this step did not seem the crossing of the Rubicon in Lehman's career that it later proved. He expected to serve only two years and return quietly to business, as most lieutenant governors had done. Under the circumstances, his decision had been inescapable. He still hoped that by some miracle Smith might achieve the Presidency; he knew that Roosevelt might enable the national ticket to carry New York; and he was anxious that the state should continue under liberal leadership. Ottinger, if elected, would adopt conservative policies on water power and social legislation.

Roosevelt at once came to New York to begin a tireless four-weeks' campaign, in which Louis Howe reluctantly assisted him. Betting on a Democratic victory in the state shifted from even money to six to five. He organized a caravan of automobiles, with an extra bus for newspapermen, and multi-

* According to E. K. Lindley's version (*Franklin D. Roosevelt: A Career in Progressive Democracy*, Indianapolis, 1931), Raskob had already told FDR: "Damn the Foundation; we'll take care of it!" Raskob did give more than $100,000 in the next three years.

graphing equipment to make copies of his speeches. With this he rolled from town to town, village to village, making ten or twelve stops a day. Calling himself "an upstate farmer too," he was cordially greeted everywhere, and his attractive personality and resonant voice, as he spoke frankly on state issues, made a host of friends. His fine physical vigor dispelled the ugly rumors about his bad health. Meanwhile, in the metropolis Frederic R. Coudert, James W. Gerard, Jesse I. Straus, and others formed a Citizens for Roosevelt and Lehman Committee which provided speakers and printed circulars. Large sums were raised there with surprising ease. Lillian Wald made a personal appeal for Lehman, praising his interest in the poor.*

By mid-October Lehman had given up hope that Smith could win the nation, but he remained confident that Roosevelt would carry the state. "In all my later elections," he said, "I ran scared. But this time I thought Roosevelt was so strong I was bound to be successful." Early on election night he and Mrs. Lehman went downtown to hear the returns at the 69th Regiment Armory. The local leaders had filled the place with seats for 6,000 or 7,000 people, for some of them shared Smith's anticipation of victory. But discouragement was so general that only a small crowd, at most a thousand, huddled in the huge barnlike place. Each news dispatch thrown on the screen was worse than its predecessor. By eight o'clock everybody knew that Hoover was sweeping the country, and the watchers gradually ebbed away. Al Smith sat in the gloom with seeming imperturbability, waiting for an answer to the great remaining question—whether he would carry New York. By the time that late returns made defeat in his own state certain, he too had gone; gone to the Biltmore Hotel to break the news to his family. He then knew the substantial facts of the debacle: that he would fall short of 90 electoral votes while Hoover took 447 and would receive a popular vote of only about 15,000,000 while his rival obtained 21,400,000. The brave career that had begun in the Fulton Fish Market was ended.

But the state ticket had a happier fate. As returns came in victory veered first one way, then another. Finally, at four in the morning it appeared that Roosevelt had been narrowly victorious, but that Lehman would lose, for, though he stood slightly ahead, the 1,500 election districts that remained to

---

* One amusing episode of the 1928 campaign always stuck in Lehman's memory. Mrs. Moskowitz, whose usefulness to Smith as a counsellor was equaled only by that of Mrs. Simkhovich, Joseph Proskauer, and Robert Moses, was still a beautiful woman but had grown very stout. During the battle a Democratic meeting was held at the Sherry-Netherlands. An elevator car full of party leaders stuck between the 22nd and 23rd floors. By great exertion it was brought up to the point where a small aperture opened on the 23rd floor. Everybody crawled out—but it took a terrific tussle to pull Mrs. Moskowitz through.

be counted were supposedly all upstate and hence Republican. He and his wife reached home tired out. Mrs. Lehman took an envelope and wrote a message for the three children, who were very young: "Don't wake us. Daddy has been beaten, but he doesn't feel badly." They were still sleeping when at eleven her brother, Frank Altschul, telephoned to congratulate him! It turned out that a third of the tardy election districts were in New York City, and they wiped out all the adverse majorities above the Bronx.

For several days the Republicans seemed inclined to dispute the election. Roosevelt had received 2,130,193 votes against 2,104,629 cast for Ottinger, a majority of little over 25,000. Lehman's margin was still closer, only 14,039. Governor Smith telegraphed the sheriff in every county to impound the ballot boxes. But after nearly a fortnight, the Republicans conceded that Roosevelt and Lehman had won.

Certain sequels of the crushing national defeat were depressing. The Democratic Party was slow in picking itself up from the dust. It had to face a financial deficit of $1,400,000, which meant that the leaders would have to raise not less than $1,600,000 to render it solvent and pay running expenses for the next four years. During the campaign Raskob, Kenny, and Lehman had guaranteed the repayment of sums borrowed from the banks. After its close twenty-two men signed an agreement to contribute amounts which would reduce the deficit to approximately half a million, Lehman being one of four men who gave $150,000 each. Gifts came in so slowly, however, and expenses remained so high, that the summer of 1932, with another national campaign opening, found the national committee still $559,000 in debt.[5]

Lehman was meanwhile a grieved spectator of another sequel, the growing breach between Al Smith and Roosevelt. This had complex origins, one of which was doubtless Smith's natural feeling that fate had dealt him an unfair blow in depriving him of victory in his beloved state while giving it to FDR. His sensitivity rose when Roosevelt passed over some members of the old leadership to appoint new men to high office. Robert Moses, for example, had expected to be continued as secretary of state, and the selection of another man was a shock both to him and to Smith. Roosevelt held more advanced views on social and economic legislation than Al Smith entertained, and this fact contributed to the misunderstanding.

Each man thought that he had done the other a favor in the recent battle; and while Smith felt he was entitled to see the ship held on its old course, Roosevelt felt that he had a right to put it on a changed tack. Then, also, Smith's wife and daughter Emily helped turn the "happy warrior" into an unhappily jealous man. They hinted that FDR was assuming a superior social status, and they brooded over the affronts to their faith. They believed that by his valiant battle in 1928 Smith had earned the right to stand again in 1932 if he wished to do so; and while Al at first indicated that he would not run again, when Hoover began to lose ground because of the depression he changed his mind. FDR of course took a different view of the Party's future. As we now know, Roosevelt had never felt sure that Al Smith was a sufficiently strong man to furnish the leadership that the country, after eight years of Harding and Coolidge, so badly needed; he felt that *he* was the man who could and should take charge. Altogether, the growing breach seemed to Lehman tragically sad.*

As the year 1928 ended, the Lehmans changed their residence to the De Witt Clinton Hotel in Albany, leaving the children in New York to continue school. The outgoing lieutenant governor, Corning, assured Lehman that the task of presiding over the senate would not be formidable. He might feel awkward for a week or two but would soon swing into the routine. "Perhaps once or twice in the session some strange technicality may come up, when the simplest and in fact only thing to do is to lean down and ask the clerk what is the proper ruling." New Year's Eve found all the new crew in the capital ready to be sworn in.

As his secretary, Lehman took to Albany an experienced newspaperman, Joseph Canavan, who had been night city editor of the *World* and knew government and politics thoroughly. During Smith's campaign for the presidency he had been one of the Democratic publicity men and had attracted general attention by his talents. Joe was to do such efficient work that when Lehman became governor he retained him. Few positions in the state government are more important than that of the governor's secretary, who screens visitors and mail, keeps in touch with men, current opinion, and events, and offers expert inside advice on political questions. Of Canavan, who met all requirements, we shall say more.

• III •

Lehman was expected to be a fully active partner of Governor Roosevelt, and he met the expectation. The lieutenant governor's powers had normally been slight, and most holders of the office had been figureheads. But Roose-

---

* Lehman said later of FDR: "I think he was sensitive to any implication that he was not in fact the governor of the state. I think it was on that account, more than any other, that he decided to put in people of his own choosing, who he felt would be exclusively loyal to him. I certainly do not think he did it with the idea of hurting Smith. He remained very fond of Smith, even though he had sometimes great reason for a different attitude. But he made up his mind he was going to be governor, and he *was* the governor."

velt was determined to make full use of Lehman's experience and abilities, and the two men gave the office new meaning. During his first year FDR spent considerable periods in Warm Springs pursuing recovery. Though some people supposed he was neglecting his duties, this was not true; he worked hard and efficiently, keeping in close touch with all state business. Of course, whenever he left New York Lehman became acting-governor, with full power to meet any emergency, and even when he was in the state Lehman relieved him of many physically taxing duties of travel and inspection. Roosevelt had a happy skill in deputing work to others, and his chief deputy was Lehman.

Something of an informal "brains trust" arose in Albany, as it did later in Washington. Samuel I. Rosenman was one of its central figures; he had been bill-drafting commissioner 1926–28, and was special counsel to Roosevelt 1929–32. Robert H. Jackson, later a justice of the Supreme Court, was an important adviser in politics and law, and Joseph Chamberlain of Columbia University, courtly, tactful, and learned, was invaluable in matters of social legislation. These men worked with Barney Dowling, Democratic leader in the senate, which the party controlled, and Maurice Bloch, the intelligent young party leader in the Republican assembly.

The partnership with FDR was congenial and at times exhilarating to Lehman. His friendship with the governor was never clouded for a moment, and his esteem for the man steadily grew. "He was indefatigable," recalls Lehman. "He always was in good humor. Fortunately he had a characteristic which few of us possess: he never took his troubles to bed with him. When he closed his desk, which was not until pretty late, he was through for the day unless some emergency arose. Many problems do arise during the evening in the life of a governor. But he didn't worry about them, and so far as I could tell, he didn't worry about his decisions. I was never able to master this detachment; I always took my problems to bed with me, and I always worried until I saw how my decisions turned out." Lehman adds: "I've always been deeply grateful that I wasn't elected governor in 1928, when they were looking around for somebody of standing, because I'm sure I would not then have made a good governor. I've always felt that a great part of the contribution I may have made in the state was largely due to the training that I had under him for four years."

Roosevelt not only had complete confidence in Lehman's ability and judgment but foresaw that he might well succeed to the governorship— something that few previous lieutenant governors had done. Lehman himself had no such anticipation but felt bound by his promise to lift any burdens he could from FDR's shoulders. He not only resigned from Lehman

Brothers but severed all active business association, keeping no advisory connection. He asked his former partners to refrain from making bids on the state bond issues thrown open for competitive offers, for he wished no loophole open for misconstruction. Whenever he was required to act on a public question, he made sure that he had no stock in any company whose interests might be affected. Later as governor, he followed the same practice. When the legislature required all cars to be equipped with nonshatterable glass, for example, he instantly sold his shares in a company which was manufacturing the material. He made his office a busy full-time position, though by long custom its holder had always devoted most of his energies to business or a profession; and in so doing, as the *New York World* commented, he "lifted a routine job out of routine mediocrity and made it a vital and helpful agency of the State."

In presiding over the upper house he met no difficulties, though he was often taken aback by the partisanship of the Republican majority. Once his effort to modify it nearly got him into trouble. The board of regents of the University of the State of New York was elected by the two chambers in joint session. This meant that as the legislature was uniformly Republican, the board was almost solidly of that party. But in 1930 a vacancy permitted the Democrats to bring up a candidate of exceptional stature, who gathered strong popular support. Lehman was presiding when Barney Dowling, the Democratic leader, presented the choice and was grieved to see that he did it badly. He fidgeted as he saw the man's chances being wrecked. Finally he seized a sheet, wrote on it, "Please point out more vigorously the iniquity of having, year after year, a representation of twelve Republicans and one Democrat," folded it, and called a page. "Tony, take this down to the leader," he said, thinking the boy would carry it to Dowling. Instead, Tony made a beeline toward the hawklike Republican leader, John Knight. Lehman almost stood up at his chair to shout, "Tony, come back!" while the boy kept straight on to Knight, who scanned the paper closely. The lieutenant governor, who is supposed to preside without partisanship and refrain from influencing debate, apprehended a sharp rebuke. But Knight merely looked up at him and grinned.

His main fields of usefulness were three: assistance to Roosevelt in meeting those financial and budget problems in which his business experience gave him special competence; the improvement of administrative agencies, and of the state's humanitarian institutions in particular; and the settlement of emergency difficulties. Within a short time he had unexpected crises in labor and in the prison system on his hands.

Like other New Yorkers, he was dismayed when on July 2, 1929, the

ILGWU called a new strike of the cloakmakers. The garment industry had by no means shaken itself free from the evil conditions against which he had helped it struggle. The once-powerful union, as we have noted, was left bankrupt and almost prostrate by the temporary Communist ascendancy, and many workers had been forced back into sweatshop conditions.[6] Hearings in 1928 on the plight of nonunion employees had disclosed a situation so miserable that the next spring, as Roosevelt and Lehman were coping with their first legislative session, representatives of labor, employers, and the public established a Joint Control Commission to enforce union standards.[7] But this committee soon proved ineffective; and the main object of the strike now begun was to eradicate the remaining shops of bad labor conditions.

While this object was sound, the strikes might do great harm to all the sound elements in the industry if continued long. Governor Roosevelt immediately asked the ILGWU and the employers' associations to meet him, Lehman, and Raymond V. Ingersoll, the "impartial chairman" mediating small disputes in the business, in an effort to compose all differences. "Surely," he wrote, "none of you wishes a repetition of the long and disastrous strike of three years ago in which an entire season was lost. . . . More complete organization and stabilization is the great need." After the meeting on July 5, the governor appointed Lehman chairman of a board of conciliation, and by intensive work it settled the strike on the 18th. Both the employers and workers made concessions, the most important of which was an agreement by manufacturers to allow the union to send its agents into shops operating under the impartial chairman plan in order to check on union membership; for this gave hope that a stronger union could help stop the depression of standards which hurt employees, and the cutthroat competition which injured employers.[8]

It remained necessary to find a substitute for the weak Joint Control Commission, and in August, 1929, Lehman, then acting-governor, asked George W. Alger to serve as chairman of a state commission on industrial standards in the cloak and suit industry which took its place. It successfully instituted a continuous investigation of the recalcitrant "outside" shops, with reports which helped the union bring some of them inside the employers' associations and widen the sphere of decent working conditions. Serious troubles, to be sure, continued. Workers continued to toil for low wages in crowded, unwholesome shops, petty businesses still struggled desperately for survival only to go under at last, and suspicions and antagonisms yet pervaded the industry.

Finally, early in 1930, Governor Roosevelt invited Benjamin Schlesinger, president of the ILGWU, and the heads of three manufacturers' associations, to meet him and Lehman in the executive chamber to facilitate some con-structive action in one of the state's greatest industries. This meeting (February 7, 1930) found Schlesinger in an angry mood. He declared that only one-tenth of the garment manufacturing was done in the great modern buildings on Seventh Avenue and Broadway, the remainder being carried on in sweatshops of the Lower East Side, Harlem, and Brooklyn. "It is not only against the actual sweatshops wherein our workers are exploited that our union is waging the fight, but against the so-called aristocrats in the Garment Center Capitol Building and other buildings . . . which foster them. Our unions will not rest and our workers will not give up their fight until both of these elements are eliminated from the industry."

This program would clearly take time, and a full restoration of the garment industry to comparative health was in fact not reached until the New Deal put a great new labor code on the statute books. Meanwhile, Lehman had to help another sick industry of the state, the millinery business, whose 15,000 workers suffered from much the same disorder and instability as the garment workers.

• IV •

On December 11 of his first year, while Roosevelt was absent in Chicago, an Albany newspaperman startled Lehman about dawn—it was a bitterly cold day—with a telephone message that a riot had broken out in the Auburn penitentiary. This grim structure dated back to 1816, and discontent had long festered within its walls. Now a gang of long-term convicts, all desperate criminals, had killed the chief keeper, who was second in control, wounded one or two guards, and were holding eight guards as hostages on the third floor. They had also seized the warden of the prison, a former brigadier general in the National Guard, and threatened to break out upon the town. Lehman was aghast. He hurried to the capitol, which he found in high excitement, reporters swarming the corridors, and telephoned the commissioner of correction and superintendent of the state police to meet him at once.

They learned that a relatively small number of men had been involved in the rioting but that several hundred prisoners were parading around the yard in uncontrollable frenzy, apparently ready to join any revolt that promised success. By telephone Lehman instructed the second head keeper at Auburn to take charge and to summon the rioters to surrender; and though the rebels were barricaded, they received the message. He also ordered the commander of the State Police at the Oneida Barracks to send troopers instantly to Auburn and mobilized the National Guard units at Syracuse and Geneva.

An additional supply of tear gas and a considerable police force were summoned from Syracuse.

All this took time, and before his measures had been fully carried out he had to deal with the weak-kneed brigadier held as hostage. This officer sent out an urgent appeal for acquiescence in the rioters' demand that they be released from prison with a promise of transportation and safe conduct elsewhere. His suggestion of surrender was preposterous, and Lehman at once responded that no compromise could be considered. Nevertheless, the brigadier repeated his request. Moreover, he got support from the mayor of Auburn. Fearful of the effect of the riot on his community, this flustered official telephoned that the situation had tragic possibilities and asked Lehman to consider two alternatives. He could issue pardons to the rioters insuring their safe egress from prison and then rearrest them on new charges; or he could give them immunity for the current revolt and agree, if they would now behave, not to punish them for what they had already done—including the murder of the head keeper.

"Impossible," was Lehman's curt answer. "As long as I am here there will be no compromise, no matter what the circumstances or what the result may be." Much as he felt the horror of further loss of life, he believed the warden and captured guards would have to take their chances just as soldiers did in battle. To double-rivet his rejection of any compromise, he telephoned the head of the State Police to instruct the captain at Oneida Barracks that the authorities could not yield an inch. The decision was agonizing, for it might cost good men their lives.

It was imperative for the authorities to move rapidly, for some 500 convicts in the industrial shop, and as many more in the corridors, though nonparticipants as yet in the riot, were milling about restively. Moreover, midwinter darkness would begin at five, and a large body of convicts loose at night would present the gravest danger. Before noon Lehman had word that National Guardsmen from Rochester, Syracuse, and Geneva were reaching Auburn and that tear gas bombs were at hand. He directed the commanders of the militia and state troopers to make a determined effort, as soon as they felt they had sufficient force, to rescue the warden and keepers. "About four o'clock," he has recorded, "I received word that a successful attack with tear bombs had been made, and that the warden and keepers had been released, although several of them were wounded. There were no casualties on the part of the attacking forces."

This done, Lehman directed the armed forces to enter the prison premises and return the convicts to their cells. By six in the evening he learned with intense relief that the troopers and militia had disarmed all of the rioters and that all other inmates were in their cells or about to be returned thither. Roosevelt reached Buffalo from the West early in the evening, and Lehman, talking with him by telephone, was able to assure him that the situation was in hand. As a precaution, he had sent a small body of troopers to Dannemora, where Clinton Prison, New York's "Siberia," had already seen a violent outbreak.

Samuel Lewisohn, with other leaders in prison reform, lost no time in pointing out that under a proper administration of justice such episodes would not occur—that the riot was symptomatic of failure in public policy toward offenders or in prison government; and Lewisohn sent a number of letters to the lieutenant governor, an old friend. Lehman was sympathetic. But he warned Lewisohn that, admirable as some of his proposals were, he would find progress slow; "because, after all, the care of prisons and prisoners does not seem to appeal to the people in the same way as that of other unfortunates in our community."

One other incident of the time had an interest so melodramatic that Lehman often recounted it to friends. A man had been convicted of murder and sentenced to death, and his conviction had been confirmed by the Court of Appeals. He was to go to the electric chair at 11 P.M. on January 22, 1930. At five in the afternoon that day, Lehman, who was in New York City, had a visit from the man's lawyers who said they possessed new evidence that would justify a reprieve for further investigation. Lehman was impressed by the presentation of this evidence. But he said he had no authority in the matter; a reprieve must come from the governor. He would get hold of Roosevelt, who was out speaking somewhere, as soon as possible, and urge him to hear the story.

About six he finally reached Roosevelt by telephone and made his suggestion. The governor said: "Well, I'm terribly sorry, but I can't possibly talk to these men now. I have a number of people waiting to talk to me, and I simply must attend to them. I'm making an important speech on agriculture downtown at the Hotel Edison tonight. Tell the attorneys that I will see them there. If they are on hand at seven o'clock I will talk to them before I go in to the dinner." At seven Lehman and the lawyers were pacing the hotel lobby. But the governor, impeded by a heavy snow that was falling, was late in arriving. The dinner was half over, and the farm leaders tugged at his arms. He said: "You must wait. I'll cut my speech short. There will be plenty of time to confer with you afterward and get the facts."

The rest of the dinner of the State Agricultural Society seemed to Lehman endless. When Roosevelt rose to speak it was past nine—and the man would die at eleven. His discourse, for agriculture always fascinated him, dragged on and on. Finally at ten-fifteen he finished his speech and went into a private room, to which Lehman hurriedly brought the frantic attorneys. Roosevelt heard them and examined the papers.

The storm had thickened until a veritable blizzard was raging. Roosevelt determined that he must intervene. "Well," he said, "I'm going to reprieve the man for a sufficient period to let us look into this. I'll call the warden right away and tell him of the reprieve." But the blizzard had felled telephone wires, and he could not get through to Sing Sing. They tried alternative lines, enlisting the help of the State Police. Finally, at ten-fifty-five, they reached the warden. The man was saved by five minutes!—for in the end he was given a new trial and acquitted.

As a result of this hairbreadth escape from tragedy, Lehman later, when governor, issued an order that no matter what the circumstances, no man was to be executed until the warden at ten minutes before eleven had communicated with the governor and secured his confirmation of the sentence. He adds, "I made a hard and fast rule that I never would accept any invitations to go out on execution night. And I made a further rule that I never would have a drink that evening. My mind had to be clear, because I had a number of cases in which petitions were presented to me for the purpose of getting a reprieve, some of them justified, most of them not."

It was Lehman's practice, as governor, on the night of an electrocution, to arrange for a motion picture on the top floor of the executive mansion. "On these nights the time passed very slowly, believe me." One evening it turned out that the picture was *The Last Long Mile*, a story of a man's tragic descent, downfall, and execution; and they all came out of the room badly shaken. Lehman never believed in capital punishment as a penalty for crime and regarded its utility as a deterrent as debatable. On the whole, he would have approved of the abolition of the death penalty. A long prison sentence, he thought would be a greater punishment and would offer opportunity in some instances for reformation.[9]

· V ·

Two groups of state institutions had badly deteriorated by the time Roosevelt was elected, and every passing month made their conditions more scandalous: the prisons, and the state hospitals. Roosevelt's physical condition making it impossible for him to visit them, he relied upon Lehman, and to some extent Mrs. Roosevelt, for inspection. In obtaining appropriations for remedial work, Lehman was also the governor's principal liaison agent with legislative leaders.

The Auburn riot, with the worse outbreak at Dannemora that same month, had riveted public attention upon the atrocious congestion, bad food, and other abuses inside the prisons. It was in Auburn that Thomas Mott Osborne, while chairman of a state commission on prison reform in 1913, had spent the voluntary term as inmate which he described in his book *Within Prison Walls*. Later Osborne applied his theories of prisoner self-government at Sing Sing, where he was warden 1914–15. Though by this time he was dead, his contentions that prisons should educate, not punish, had found wide acceptance. A report by Roosevelt's special investigator brought out the fact that Auburn was grossly overcrowded, with 1,550 men in quarters for 1,280; that it was dark, unsanitary, smelly, and under excessively harsh discipline; and that the prisoners were fed on twenty-one cents a day. Both it and Sing Sing had large cell blocks with no toilet facilities except buckets. It was evident that the whole prison system was almost medievally unenlightened. Roosevelt, Lehman, and R. F. C. Kieb, commissioner of corrections, called not merely for more space and better equipment but for adoption of the latest ideas of crime prevention and an attempt at the reform of criminals through educational work and the use of scientific probation methods.

The improvement which they undertook required both money and time; particularly time, for men could not be moved from an old cell block until a new one was completed. But they began a work which Lehman was later to continue as governor. To the good modern penitentiary recently built at Great Meadows others were added at Attica and near Lake George. Believing that many prisoners were not actually dangerous, and might be trusted to behave without harsh restraints—they could be given a good deal of liberty in farm prisons or workshops without bars or high walls—Roosevelt and Lehman proposed the opening of semisecurity penitentiaries, accompanied by reforms in parole procedure. In the past, the prison commissioners, serving as a parole board, had met just once a month at each prison. Lehman insisted that they should be replaced with officers expert in penology and psychology. He explained these ideas in numerous speeches. Before long, two semisecurity prisons were put in operation, and a large new boys' reformatory was also built, offering much better vocational training than the old Elmira reformatory. The semisecurity experiment worked out well, though a few prisoners abused their liberty.

"We have evolved a definite and clear prison policy," wrote Roosevelt early in 1931. A new parole law, which Lehman, with the aid of Senator Caleb H. Baumes, carried through the legislature, provided for a board of three skilled and properly compensated appointees of the governor, giving full time to the work. The overcrowding of prisons had been lessened though by no means wholly ended.[10]

State hospitals for mental patients were as grossly overcrowded and understaffed as the prisons. They presented fire hazards, lacked medical appliances, and were usually so jammed that the officers used recreation rooms as dormitories and placed cots in the corridors. Roosevelt had his wife accompany him to some institutions, and while he sat in the car, for he could not walk the long corridors, she made a thorough inspection. But much the largest part of the investigations fell to Lehman. He took pains to see that his visits were fully covered by newspaper correspondents, for he wanted good descriptive writing. What he found when he inspected Central Islip State Hospital in May, 1929, was typical. Calling the place a "disgrace," for one ward with a capacity of 646 patients held 1,058, he reported: "I saw in the wards row after row of from 35 to 40 beds placed one immediately next the other, without an inch of space between. The patient could enter or leave only by climbing over the other beds or the foot of his bed."

When Lehman took the reporters to mental hospitals in Syracuse, Buffalo, Binghamton, and five or six other places, they again published telling articles, which did not exaggerate the deplorable state of the institutions because exaggeration would have been difficult. Besides overcrowding, understaffing, want of proper appliances, and poor arrangement, they presented fire hazards. Brutality on the part of guards was not unknown. Lehman records that after seeing the Hudson Valley Hospital at Poughkeepsie, "I was just sick. I was sick for a week afterward." His reports laid a foundation on which Roosevelt and he acted in 1929–30 in persuading legislative leaders to draft plans for improving the hospitals. Considerations of mere humanity, they declared, required 6,000 new beds in 1931 and 6,000 more in 1932. Roosevelt threatened to call a special session to place a fifty-million-dollar bond issue before the voters, and when the Republican leaders recoiled, he told them he would drop the call only if they agreed to appropriate money in the next legislative session. Lehman, persistent and businesslike, worked so effectively that, in November, 1931, he could report that facilities would be duly provided for the first 6,000 patients. As the *World* said, his teamwork with the Republicans had been a public service of high importance.[11]

In enlarging hospital facilities, Roosevelt and Lehman deliberately followed the second-best plan of building additions to old structures instead of erecting entirely new institutions. Economy counseled this; it was cheaper, when a thousand new beds were needed, to add a new wing to an old structure than to establish another hospital, for the grounds, heating and lighting system, sewage facilities, and other necessities were ready at hand. More-over, whenever a new mental institution was discussed the community in view was sure to object indignantly. For example, Roosevelt and Lehman decided to build an asylum, the Pilgrim Hospital, well out on Long Island. They encountered vehement opposition, much of it inspired by the Catholic Church, which had a girls' school several miles from the proposed site. After long delay, the hospital went up, and not a single untoward incident occurred. When later the state rejected a proposal to enlarge this institution, the community protested vociferously, for it had taken so much business profit from the hospital that it hoped to see it doubled in size! [12]

Roosevelt was often accused of extravagance, but a letter of this period to Lehman lends no support to the idea. "I notice," he wrote from Warm Springs on November 28, 1930, "that they have eliminated $50,000 for the building of a morgue. While I have never had much experience in the building of morgues, I regard the expenditure of that amount of money for that particular purpose as absolutely criminal. I know that you or I could build a perfectly good morgue for $10,000. By the same token I notice that they have added a railroad shelter at Pilgrim Hospital to cost $10,000. You could build a complete suburban railroad station for that sum and I know perfectly well that any good trolley company or railroad company could build a watertight, airtight, architectural gem of a railroad shelter for not more than $3,000 or $4,000." [13]

The number of mental patients in the state rose toward the hundred-thousand mark while Lehman was lieutenant governor and passed it while he was governor. Although he was happy to see the hospitals enlarged, he could not help feeling that some patients were improperly admitted. Many were senile men and women whose families refused to care for them. Some-times the reasons were valid—inadequate income, limited house-room, a realization that the mentally ill needed expert psychiatric treatment; but too many families seemed to Lehman to take a callous attitude toward their elders.

Lehman found other fields for usefulness. Banking in New York, as in other states, was becoming shaky. In the first weeks of 1929 people in the metropolis were alarmed by the sudden death of the rather wild Italian promoter of the City Trust Company, Francesco M. Ferrari. Rumors devel-oped which threatened a run on the bank. It soon appeared that these rumors were well grounded, for auditors representing the Giannini interests found evidence of forgeries, fictitious credits, and a general cooking of the accounts. The state superintendent of banks, Frank Warder, was to be supplanted by Roosevelt's new appointee, Joseph A. Broderick, on June 1; and careful bankers, who had distrusted Warder, pinned great faith to Broderick's capacity. In February Warder closed the City Trust and secretly prepared to leave for Europe. On April 22 he suddenly resigned, and the press broadcast the news that he had asked for a passport. Roosevelt was then at Warm Springs.

Much shocked, Lehman saw that he must prevent Warder's departure. Invoking the Moreland Act, which empowered the governor to inquire into any branch of the state government, he appointed Robert Moses to head an investigation into the relations between the banking department and the City Trust. Moses, able, honest, and irascible, had quarreled with Roosevelt in the affairs of the Taconic Park and earned his dislike. Had Lehman asked his advice, the governor would have vetoed the choice; but taking full responsibility—after all, he was a banker—Lehman did not telephone Warm Springs in advance. He explained to Roosevelt later that not only was Moses keen and courageous, but his familiarity with the state government would enable him to work efficiently with the new banking superintendent and other officers. The choice, in fact, proved decidedly useful to Roosevelt, for it disarmed suspicious Republicans and gave assurance of a thorough report. Moses unhesitatingly criticized Smith's appointment of Warder, censured Smith's nephew for leaving the banking department to become one of the City Trust attorneys appearing before that body, and helped uncover evidence which convicted Warder of accepting a $10,000 bribe, so that he soon landed in Sing Sing. Unfortunately, Roosevelt shouldered aside Moses's wise recommendations for a new formulation of the banking laws.

Meanwhile Lehman, much distressed over the hardships of depositors in the City Trust, took a leading part in the organization of a new company, the Mutual Trust, to assume its assets and liabilities, and himself gave financial guarantees which eventually cost him a large sum. He also tried to save the County Trust Company, which was greatly overextended, and whose head committed suicide; but in this he was unsuccessful.[14]

Far more serious was the failure of the Bank of United States in December, 1930, bringing grievous loss to 450,000 depositors in New York City, many of them needy people of immigrant origin. Some early intimations of this memorable crash had greatly worried Lehman, who hoped that the house might survive if its frozen assets were thawed out and urged the banking superintendent to improve its liquidity. By that date frozen assets were a nationwide worry of bankers. Superintendent Broderick, with the aid of the governor of the Federal Reserve Bank and other financial leaders, did his best, but met grave difficulties. Many financiers of the city disliked the Bank of United States. With reason, they thought it had no right to such a name;

they were jealous of its rapid rise and disapproved its unconventional and daring methods; and some of them possibly felt a prejudice because practically all its officers and main stockholders were Jewish. It was sometimes called "The Pantspressers' Bank"!

On the afternoon of December 10, Lehman was notified that a meeting of bankers would be held that evening to consider rescue measures. Roosevelt being in Warm Springs, he was acting-governor. He at once informed Broderick, then in New York City, that he would come down and join George Harrison of the Federal Reserve and others at the bankers' conclave. His supposition, from what he heard, was that while many of the bank's assets were tightly frozen, it was really solvent. When he reached his Park Avenue apartment about 8 P.M., Broderick informed him that arrangements for the rescue were well in hand, his presence was not needed, and that it would be inadvisable to attend. Several times in the course of the meeting Broderick telephoned again to say that all seemed going well. Soon after midnight, however, Lehman was dismayed by a new and alarming message; the bankers had scented some irregularities in the management, they balked at advancing the large funds necessary, and the gathering was a failure. Imploring Broderick to keep the group in session, Lehman caught a taxicab downtown. When he arrived, however, more than half the bankers had gone, and the remainder were obdurate.

"I made the strongest possible plea," Lehman records, "not to let the bank fail. I pointed out the effect that its closing, with very large deposits mainly from small people, would have on the entire business situation and expressed the belief that the bank was solvent. I was unsuccessful, but never in all my life have I fought harder to save others." [11] Next day the bank closed. Two of its principal officers, Bernard K. Marcus, president of the bank, and Saul Singer, were convicted of misappropriation of funds and sent to prison. But the event showed that Lehman was substantially right, for even after the tremendous costs of liquidation were paid, the bank finally returned to its depositors more than ninety percent of their money. The episode left him bitterly resentful. He always believed that the fall of the institution had a marked effect in sapping general confidence in the banking system.

Since Lehman had invested a million dollars in the rescue of City Trust depositors, largely Italians, by the Mutual Trust, some of the depositors in the Bank of United States, who were largely Jewish, asked why he had not come to their assistance also. But this institution would have required a sum of money quite beyond his means, and its affairs were in such posture that financial aid alone could not have saved it.

· VI ·

During 1929 and 1930 Lehman was immensely impressed by Roosevelt's energy, grasp, and strategic resourcefulness. Al Smith as governor had efficiently reorganized the executive machinery of the state, initiated important social reforms, and given New York a sound business administration. Roosevelt showed greater social vision and thrust, a special skill in appealing to the plain man whether farmer or urban dweller, and striking ability to outmaneuver Republican leaders of the legislature. In a long battle with the chairmen of the finance committees of the two houses, he finally vindicated his special powers over the state budget. He was ceaselessly busy; though we have mentioned occasions when he was absent from the state, he spent most of his time there and even when away gave hard study to its problems. Not only did he have a hundred ideas, on tax relief, on old-age insurance, on state development of St. Lawrence water power, on farm betterment, on schools, but he knew how to drive them home to the public consciousness.

In the fall of 1929 the stock market crash suddenly opened what proved a great chasm in the nation's history. On September 3 the market began to turn down; on October 21 came the first heavy drop; and on October 23 the panic became headlong. The whole climate of politics as of business and of social life changed. Few men saw immediately what a far-reaching change was taking place, and Lehman was not one of that few. But thereafter all issues and prospects appeared in a darker light.

He had borne a helpful hand in Roosevelt's constructive program of 1929, realizing that his moderate temper and reputation for business sagacity might be particularly helpful in winning legislative support. He assisted the governor in introducing a new plan of getting bills into the hopper. Up to this time they had nearly always been prepared and introduced by members of the assembly or senate. But Roosevelt was so intensely concerned with certain social reforms, and the onset of the Great Depression in 1930 demanded so much emergency legislation, that he adopted the expedient of getting many bills prepared in his own office. He then asked members to introduce them. Everyone knew they were the governor's bills. The plan saved so much time, effort, and friction that when Roosevelt went to Washington he carried it with him, and when Lehman became governor he used it. "I liked the system, I was used to it, and it worked well," he commented.

Roosevelt fought hard, like Smith before him, for the ownership and development by the state of its water power resources, with an invigoration of the control exercised by the public service commission. His social program embraced sharp limitations upon injunctions in industrial disputes, the requirement of a true 8-hour day and 48-hour week for women and children, and minimum wage legislation for women. After getting an expert study of old-age security, he compelled in 1930 the passage of an old-age pension law. He labored—often against stubborn opposition by what he called "the unprogressive, shortsighted Republican legislative majority"—for better roads, the reform of election laws, the improvement of local government, and the reduction of rural taxation. He asked for safeguards on banking that would prevent speculators from squandering the funds of hundreds of small depositors and for court changes that would end the costliness and delay of judicial processes. Some of these goals were left for his successor to attain.

"Opponents of reform," Roosevelt wrote later, "have rushed forward on nearly every occasion to urge that the slightest departure from laissez faire would cause business and industry to leave the state and go elsewhere." *

---

* Roosevelt, like Lehman, also took an interest in measures to replace the sordid slums of New York City by model housing; and Lehman, in conjunction with Aaron Rabinowitz, carried out a memorable pioneering step. The three men, Rabinowitz relates, were sitting one day in Roosevelt's inner executive office in Albany and talking about housing possibilities. Knowing that Rabinowitz was a director of the Amalgamated Housing Cooperative, Roosevelt asked him: "How are you getting along?" "Slowly, slowly," replied Rabinowitz. "Everybody I try to enlist is doubtful." The founder and head of a large firm of real estate developers, he had become connected with various construction and reality-management concerns, and was president since 1920 of the Pershing Square Building Corporation. He described the doubters, adding: "I'll prove that model housing will pay. I'm going to build one example of it myself to show that it can be done."

"Good," said Roosevelt. And turning to Lehman, he demanded: "Herbie, why don't you join him?" Lehman never hesitated. "I will," he responded. Rabinowitz was taken aback. "Do you realize what you are letting yourself in for?" he asked Lehman. "We'll have to put in $250,000 apiece, or maybe $1,000,000 in all. And maybe we'll never get a cent back." "I'll risk it," said Lehman.

They bought a solid block of ground on Grand Street, where the factory of the R. G. Hoe Company had stood, employed architects Springsteen and Goldhammer, and planned a handsome seven-story brick and steel apartment house. The cost of ground and building came to a great deal more than a million; according to Rabinowitz, about $1,500,000. They were ready to invest approximately half of the money themselves, and went to the Bowery Savings Bank for the rest. The loan was obtained with difficulty. Henry Bruere, the head, wished to grant it unhesitatingly, but the directors insisted on a careful investigation. Finally they caught the enthusiasm of the venturers and made the loan to the limited dividend corporation which Rabinowitz and Lehman, with the support of the Amalgamated Clothing Workers of America, organized.

The architects, men of vision, planned the tenement around a great central court, with trees, grass, and flowers, and designed bright, attractive rooms. It became a distinction to get an apartment. They were sold at $500 per room, with upkeep rental, and complete credit was given buyers who had no ready cash. To assist applicants, Lehman and Rabinowitz established a $350,000 loan fund. No purchaser ever defaulted. The tenants kept the premises in spotless condition, and the house is still a model of its kind.

Beginning early in 1930, Roosevelt and Lehman had to meet an ever-grimmer advance of depression, unemployment, and poverty. The formulation of plans for the local relief of distress was then well under way. On March 29, 1930, Roosevelt announced the appointment of a Committee on the Stabilization of Industry, which made its report that fall, and in November he and his advisers took steps to initiate fresh public works to provide jobs that winter. Much of the labor fell on Lehman; for, leaving the state in November, 1930 to get a much-needed vacation after the election, Roosevelt deposited the task of unemployment relief for the moment in Lehman's lap.

"I ask you," he wrote on the 17th, "to act as a committee of one to survey and speed up as far as possible all of the public works of the State." Lehman no sooner got the letter than he conferred with Col. Frederick S. Greene and other department heads to learn if highway building, canal improvement, park development, and other activities could not be pressed forward in ways that would offer needy men jobs. As a result, he announced on November 20 that he would recommend to the governor a request for emergency appropriations by the next legislature, so that public construction might be given a fresh start with greater promptness. He also summoned representatives of the principal railroad companies to two meetings to persuade them to advance the work of eliminating grade crossings; and Vice-President C. C. Paulding of the New York Central submitted figures showing that his road would place contracts totaling about $21,000,000 before the end of 1931.

The situation steadily worsened during the winter of 1930–31. Reports came from all parts of the state of helplessness, destitution, and despair. A body of "hunger marchers" under Communist leadership had to be driven from the assembly chamber in March. Frances Perkins made public a harrowing report of the pitiful situation of unskilled women workers. By June William Green of the A.F. of L. estimated that 5,300,000 had lost employment in the nation, a number still rising, and Norman Thomas was calling for a five-billion-dollar Federal loan to be applied to unemployment relief. The regular term of the legislature did little to meet the crisis, rejecting one after another of the governor's proposals. With a desperate winter looming ahead, Roosevelt on August 21 called the two houses in special session and recommended a $20,000,000 relief program, financed by a rise in income taxes. After a brief but bitter struggle, the essentials of the governor's plan passed; the Republicans reluctantly assenting to the twenty millions and the creation of a Temporary Emergency Relief Administration (TERA) to administer aid to the workless.[12]

Meanwhile, the second election of Roosevelt and Lehman had come and gone. At the beginning of 1930, while Roosevelt was ready to run and the party anxious to have him, Lehman was reluctant, feeling it his duty in the anxious economic situation to go back to his firm. In May Roosevelt wrote him a persuasive letter. You have good reason, he admitted, for declining. "Nevertheless, you and I both have the same kind of sense of obligation about going through with a task once undertaken, and, frankly, the only reason either of us would run again is that sense of obligation to a great many million people." [13] Amid general enthusiasm, they were renominated. The Republican nominees, Charles H. Tuttle for governor and C. H. Baumes for lieutenant governor, were not impressive. Tuttle's stand for repeal of prohibition was certain to lose him votes upstate without cutting into the general "wet" support for Roosevelt; and Baumes was best known for his inhuman law prescribing life terms for fourth offenders. The Democratic executive committee, including Farley, Louis Howe, and Rosenman, had little difficulty in raising money.

This was plainly a Democratic year. The record of Roosevelt and Lehman, the discontent with Hoover, the depression unrest, the feeling that nation and state needed men of imagination and strength, put an irresistible tide in motion. The only difficulty was Tammany. Making frantic efforts to cloak the corruption in Jimmy Walker's administration of the city and avoid a state investigation, it embarrassed the governor. One woman active in philanthropic work wrote: "Securing votes for Herbert Lehman is a cinch; not so easy for Roosevelt on account of the supposed Tammany situation." [15]

But even Jim Farley's exuberant predictions were outstripped by the election day landslide. Roosevelt swept to victory with a plurality of 725,000, while Lehman, carrying the metropolis with a plurality of 607,000, ran 50,000 votes in advance of him, leading the entire Democratic ticket.

Chapter VII

HELM OF THE STATE

As the elections of 1932 approached, a nasty storm in New York threatened shipwreck to the Democratic Party and the political future of Roosevelt and Lehman. The storm centered in the old, old situation, revelations of Tammany corruption in the city and county governments that scandalized voters from Long Island to Buffalo and arrested attention all over the country. This was bad enough. But what made matters really difficult was the fact that the exposures had given Boss John F. Curry and most of Tammany's district leaders a furious antagonism toward reformers—especially Democratic reformers.

Striking party changes had taken place during the previous decade. The death of Boss Murphy had been a catastrophe to Tammany, for though he made bad blunders—the Sulzer impeachment the worst—he maintained outward decency and ruled his district lieutenants with iron fist. His successor, the big, horse-faced, solemn Olvany, had tried to impress the city with an image of a New Tammany in white robes with a golden harp. Unfortunately, this ponderous dullard had failed to maintain discipline. The dapper Mr. Curry took his place in 1928 amid general relief, which faded when members of the Hall discovered (as Milton Mackaye writes in *The Tin Box Parade*) that while Olvany was merely dull, Curry was stupid. The best that could be said of these two men was that they were anxious to keep such graft as pier fees polite and well perfumed.

Additional perfume was meanwhile contributed by their mayor, Jimmy Walker, who was a combination of P. T. Barnum and Fernando Wood, or as Robert Moses put it, a mélange of Beau Brummell and a guttersnipe; and who made the gaudiest showman in the city's history. He loved the theatrical world, night-clubbing, receptions, gay jaunts to the Kentucky Derby or Europe, orchestras playing the song he had composed, "Will

You Love Me in December as You Do in May?," and riotous parties; loved everything, in fact, but work. The city read one morning how he was off on some such trip as that to Sacramento in a private car (never paid for) to plead for Tom Mooney; a few days later it read of some such civic welcome as that to the Queen of Rumania, with platoons of troops, naval men, police, and a throbbing Department of Sanitation band, as the official welcomers under Grover Whalen, in frock coats, striped trousers, and silk hats, bent over their shiny canes in deep salaams. Everybody got a civic welcome, from Lord Allenby to the Channel swimmer Gertrude Ederle.

Important political changes overtook the boroughs. In Brooklyn, John McCooey was now at the apogee of his power, but aging fast. This one-time shipyards worker had taken control of the Kings County machine in 1909, at a time when Brooklyn Democrats still flaunted their independence of Tammany with the slogan: "The Tiger Shall Not Cross Brooklyn Bridge." But with McCooey to help, the tiger was soon trotting across the bridge, purring loudly, and looking for prey; for the boss made a series of astute bargains with the Hall. One newspaperman described McCooey's rise as "the triumphal progress of a jellyfish"—a jellyfish who always absorbed a *quid pro quo*. By using jobs, jobs, and more jobs, McCooey built up a tremendous organization under his personal dictatorship, until he had 125,000 more enrolled Democrats than Tammany had. His method of dealing with potential troublemakers was to choke them with butter, or as Milton Mackaye put it, "he drowned them in maple syrup." One evidence of his genial tolerance was his willingness to give Hymie Shorenstein of Brownsville a large fiefdom in that heavily Jewish part of Kings County. Shorenstein, calling his political supporters "mine poys," was a benevolent man who, talking in a Weber and Fields dialect, sent ample food baskets at Christmas to Christians and at Passover to Jews. He had a Sam Goldwyn or Henry Ford idea of the value of the many jokes about him, and his influence was tremendous.

In the Bronx, though the population was more heavily Jewish than Irish, Edward J. Flynn had risen to power in the 1920s, a man of solid abilities whom Al Smith liked and pushed forward and for whom Lehman formed a marked attachment. Strikingly handsome and impeccably groomed, he had exquisite manners and a very real cultivation. He was a graduate of Fordham College and the Fordham Law School; he collected etchings and owned a Whistler; well-read and widely traveled, he was a good conversationalist. He and his wife rode well and were often seen together on the bridle paths. In politics he was industrious, systematic, and meticulously honest. When the Bronx polled a heavy vote for Roosevelt for governor in 1928, FDR gladly made him secretary of state; the first time that a Democratic governor had ever conferred high office on a county boss.

Flynn gave the Bronx a reputation for political independence, intelligence, and integrity. It was "the good borough," even "a capital of civilized political thought." Disliking Curry, he was loyal to Roosevelt when other county bosses, like McCooey, adhered to Smith. He liked to bring forward promising young men, such as Joseph V. McKee, who had earned his way to a doctorate of laws at Fordham and taught English literature in De Witt Clinton High School.

The Tammany tiger crouched and snarled in 1932, as Mayor Walker, Sheriff Thomas M. Farley of New York County, and a huddle of city magistrates were accused of contemptible crimes. Jimmy Walker was the pet and hope of the Hall, the sheriff was one of its chief fuglemen, and the magistrates' courts were among its traditional strongholds. The state investigations under Samuel Seabury, a pompously intelligent judge whom the Republicans had once nominated for governor, reached their climax in the spring of 1932. He proved the crass dishonesty of the sheriff, whom Roosevelt removed, and the greed of some political hacks sitting as magistrates, one of whom had paid a Tammany district leader $10,000 for his place. He also exposed the flabbiness of the district attorney, a friend of Boss Curry's who completely failed to track down offenders. When Seabury gave Walker's acts an implacable scrutiny, it became plain that whether the mayor was a rascal or simply a debonair playboy, he had let corruption flourish and had a good many personal secrets to conceal. In March Rabbi Stephen S. Wise of the Free Synagogue and the Rev. Dr. John Haynes Holmes of the Community Church challenged the governor to remove him for misfeasance and incompetence.[1]

The situation placed Franklin D. Roosevelt in an unhappy dilemma. If he showed unrelenting severity toward Walker, an embittered Tammany might throw the city and even the state against him in any future election. If he betrayed any softness, the South and West, traditional haters of Tammany, would scorn him as a coward. Roosevelt, now intensely ambitious to be elected President, vacillated for an inexcusable period; he was stalling. The press, the reformers, the Republicans, watched his predicament with sardonic interest. Even Lehman, who sympathized with his general attitude, had critical moments. Finally, the movement of events, with the newspapers in full cry, left him no alternative. Seabury formally slapped his charges against Walker on the governor's desk three weeks before the Democratic Convention. Roosevelt forwarded the fifteen counts to the mayor for a reply; and Walker thereupon postponed his response until after the convention was over. This left Roosevelt in the happy position of an executive who had the situation well in hand, and who could be expected to meet the final test. Though Tammany fumed and prepared to fight him in the national convention, it was not as mortally offended as if he had ousted the mayor; while most Democrats beyond the Hudson and reformers in the metropolis were satisfied that justice had been done.

· I ·

Wrathful as they were over what they regarded as Roosevelt's and Lehman's complicity with their enemies, the Tammany leaders nevertheless realized that it would be folly to indulge in an open rupture. Al Smith, with his long-felt dislike and contempt for Curry, would be quick to denounce any attempt to knife the party tickets that fall. Hearst made it clear that his newspapers would do the same. When the Democratic Convention opened in Chicago, the Hall helped to rally most of the city bosses against Roosevelt: the Kelly-Nash men of Chicago, Frank Hague of Jersey City, Pendergast of Kansas City, and others. After they went down in defeat, as Farley, Flynn, Louis Howe, and their allies carried the governor to victory, Curry realized that any disloyalty to Roosevelt and Garner would be fatal to him and his organization.

But Tammany was determined not to accept Lehman for governor if it could get anybody else; it knew that Albany was much closer than Washington and that he would take a more grimly uncompromising attitude than Roosevelt toward political crooks, chiselers, and racketeers.

Of Lehman's vigilance and industry this year no reader of the press had any doubt. Beginning with the early state primaries, Roosevelt was more and more occupied with his campaign, relying on "Herbie" to do all he could to lighten the governor's load. Lehman made two summer tours of state institutions and resumed his inspections in September. He sat on boards for Roosevelt, attended tiresome conferences, and made dutiful speeches on state problems. He pressed the relief measures in the legislature, advocated large programs of public works, urged the repeal of the Eighteenth Amendment, and opposed the placing of bankers on the new state banking board. In short, he was what Roosevelt often called him, "the other governor." Should he be nominated for governor? Everybody knew that he had a wider knowledge of state business than any other available man, that he possessed more political strength, and that Roosevelt was anxious to have him nominated.

Though early in the year he had been reluctant to run—for his former firm had difficult problems to meet, his own finances had suffered in the depression, and four years in Albany seemed enough—he saw after the Chicago convention that his candidacy was almost a necessity. He could do something to wipe away the stains on the Democratic shield, offset Tammany desertions by bringing Jewish and independent voters to his side, and emphasize the value of experienced businessmen in government in a time of economic crisis. (He had written a much-publicized article in *The Atlantic* the previous fall on business and politics.[2]) John Boyd Thatcher, Jr., mayor of Albany, the other Democratic possibility, would look weak if pitted against the expected Republican nominee, W. J. ("Wild Bill") Donovan of Buffalo. But Curry in New York, the O'Connell brothers in Albany, and other bosses were ready to waylay him on the convention floor.

An incident early in the year accentuated Curry's hostility. During the session the boss called at Lehman's office just off the senate chamber for a chat. They talked about Roosevelt's prospects. Finally, Curry remarked: "You know, I'm going to put up your name as district delegate to the Chicago convention." Lehman was astounded. "District delegate?" he asked. "Yes," replied Curry.

Said Lehman: "Save yourself the trouble, for I will not go as a district delegate. I've been lieutenant governor for four years. I've done a pretty good job. And if I go to Chicago, I'm going as a delegate-at-large."

Curry did not like such independence, nor Boss McCooey, nor their upstate allies. It underlined the fact that Lehman would neither accept suggestions from the machine leaders nor ladle patronage to them. Curry in part blamed him for what he called the "crucification" of the Hall. But most of all he opposed Lehman because he wanted to go back to the days when governors knew their duty to the organization. He maintained his hostility while in July Cattaraugus County instructed its delegates for Lehman and in August Livingston, Cayuga, Putnam, and Wyoming counties followed. He maintained it while Smith and Roosevelt reiterated their support of Lehman, the *New York Times* threw its weight behind him, and the *Tribune* warned the Republicans that if Lehman were named, only a man of the highest capacity could hope to defeat him.[3] Curry was stupidly obstinate, and Walker's resignation on September 1, after a series of hearings before Roosevelt which exposed all his peccant incompetence, increased the boss's stubbornness.

Yet when Adolph S. Ochs, chief owner of the *Times*, wrote Roosevelt expressing a fear that Lehman would somehow be sidetracked, the governor was reassuring. "Only an utter madness on the part of a handful of people who would rather commit suicide than give in will prevent his nomination and election," he assured Ochs. He seemed right; as the liberals, the Al Smith and Roosevelt men, and papers like the *Times* exerted their strength, Curry was forced to retreat. Jewish areas demanded the lieutenant governor in no uncertain voice. Several local leaders issued an ultimatum: Lehman's nomination, or wholesale desertion of the party. Governor Smith and Robert Moses were standing with a knot of machine men in the principal Democratic clubhouse in Brooklyn one day when Hyman Shorenstein bustled in. Hymie, a self-made man, was reputedly so illiterate that when he was made county recorder of Kings, people said he rode to work holding his newspaper upside down, but he was shrewd and honorable. He listened angrily as some petty politicians voiced their prejudices. Then he strode to a French window and uttered one pregnant half-sentence in his inimitable English. "If Lehman is not nominated," he declared, "the shades in the clubhouse"—and he slowly and solemnly lowered the shade to the floor. The gesture terrified the men who saw it.

At the last moment Curry, McCooey, and their allies attempted by a sudden maneuver to cheat Lehman into accepting removal from the state scene. They were aware that a score of civic organizations, business organizations, and philanthropic bodies were demanding the lieutenant governor. Moreover, Curry knew that Roosevelt would reach Albany the day the convention met there and make a speech. "I told him," FDR wrote Felix Frankfurter September 14, "that the subject of my address will depend largely on the decision he makes during the next three weeks!" [4] Only a sharp trick would serve.

When the convention opened on October 3 the bosses yet cloaked their position in mystery. The alignment of delegates remained uncertain. As the day wore on, Farley and Flynn tried to elicit promises that Curry and McCooey would accept Lehman but without success. Four o'clock came with no word; six o'clock and still no decision. At that hour Roosevelt telephoned Lehman. "I've learned they're meeting up in John Curry's room at the De Witt Clinton," he said. "They know now that they can't put over Thatcher, and they have a new scheme. It's to nominate Senator Wagner for governor, and you for the Senate. They're discussing it now. If I were in your place, I'd go up and have a talk with them."

Lehman knew that if he telephoned the room and asked to speak to Curry or Wagner he would be told they could not be reached. He therefore had Mrs. Lehman ask Wagner to come to the telephone. She had a bombshell ready: "Herbert is standing next to me and understands that you're all meeting up there, and he's coming up right now to talk to you."

A minute later Lehman and his secretary, Joe Canavan, knocked at the door. They marched into the room to find fifteen or twenty politicians, all in Tammany or close to it and all hostile or frigid. Not a single real friend was in the suite. Lehman's defiant gaze swept Curry, Dan O'Connell of Albany, Kelley of Syracuse, Murphy of Troy, McCooey, and others. He saw Daniel Cohalan, the man whom Woodrow Wilson in 1919 had refused to permit on the same platform with himself. Wagner, liberal but pliable, was present, and the criminal lawyer Max Steuer, of razor mind and unscrupulous temper. All wanted the loaves and fishes of politics.

"I understand," began Lehman, "that you gentlemen have discussed the nomination." O'Connell and Steuer barked defiantly, "Yes, we have."

"More than that," said Steuer, "We have it sewed up. You are going to be nominated for the senate and Bob Wagner here for governor."

"Well," responded Lehman, "that won't suit me at all. I have stated that I expect to be nominated for governor, and I will not take a nomination to the senate."

"What can you do about it?" demanded Steuer. "We nominate for the senate before the governorship. If you are nominated, what are you going to do about it?"

"I'll get up and decline," declared Lehman. "And I can assure you that I will nonetheless have my name presented for the governorship."

This struck consternation in the group. For a moment, not a word was spoken.

"Now, gentlemen," concluded Lehman, "I've had my say. If you nominate me for the senate, I'm not going to accept. Then when nominations for governor are called for, my name will go before the convention." The group knew that Franklin D. Roosevelt would place it there. "Come along, Joe," Lehman said to Canavan, and they walked out. He boiled with anger as they returned to his rooms, and as they entered, he stalked up to his wife, shook his finger under her nose, and declared: "I want you to make me one promise. Keep me a little vindictive!"

He had no idea what the upshot would be. But he was not astonished when a half hour before the evening session began Curry telephoned him with a morose announcement: "You win." [5]

It was now certain, as delegates and spectators crammed themselves into the huge Albany armory, that Lehman would be chosen for governor and Wagner for Senator. Suspense transferred itself to the question how Al Smith and Roosevelt would greet each other, for Smith was so hurt and jealous that, according to current gossip, he pronounced Roosevelt unfit for the White House. To a great blare of bands the two men met on the platform, one to nominate Lehman, the other to second him. As they clasped hands, the roar of the multitude drowned out their words. James A. Farley, standing beside them, heard Smith say with real fervor, "Hello, Frank, I'm glad to see you," and Roosevelt respond with equal feeling, "Hello, Al, I'm glad to see you too—and that's from the heart." A newspaper reporter invented a more memorable version of Smith's greeting: "Hello, you old potato." Lehman was named almost by acclamation.

"McCooey forced to yield," ran headlines. And the *Times* published an editorial headed, "The Fall of the House of Curry."

The ensuing campaign was spirited, for "Wild Bill" Donovan of Buffalo, with his brilliant record in the First World War, made a doughty opponent. The principal issues threshed out concerned public utilities, prohibition, labor, agriculture, and economy in government. While Donovan argued that Lehman's financial policies were "ruinous," Lehman retorted that Donovan was tied to the utility interests and lacked social imagination. Supporters of prohibition denounced Lehman as "wet," and Lehman derided Donovan as a "semi-dry." Roosevelt and Al Smith took pains to stump for Lehman, Al declaring that Donovan's "wild" speeches proved him ignorant of state affairs. Both sides had active veterans' committees. Lehman also had a committee of one thousand lawyers, an independent citizens' committee in which Frank L. Polk was prominent, and groups of social workers, including nurses who reflected Lillian Wald's influence. When Hoover spoke for Donovan, Owen D. Young and Felix M. Warburg answered him. The Depositors' Protective Association of the City Trust testified to their gratitude. It was a lively battle, but its outcome was always certain.

On election day Lehman polled 2,659,519 votes, Donovan 1,812,080, and Louis Waldman, the Socialist candidate, 102,950. Lehman's plurality was unprecedented. He snatched a brief vacation and then, as Roosevelt went to Warm Springs to lay plans for his Presidency, became acting-governor. They confronted a fast-developing crisis, but while Roosevelt had four months before taking power, Lehman had only two. Roosevelt had also the advantage of a Congress with large Democratic majorities, while Lehman would face the familiar New York situation, a Democratic senate and Republican assembly. Happily, he would have two experienced legislators, John J. Dunnigan in the upper and Irwin Steingut in the lower chamber.

· II ·

A few minutes before five on New Year's Eve in 1932, Lehman's family, office force, and household staff gathered in the largest room of his apartment at 820 Park Avenue for a private ceremony of oath-taking. Judge Irving Lehman of the Court of Appeals, a head taller than the governor-elect, swore him in as his brother Arthur Lehman, Mrs. Lehman, and the children, Peter, John, and Hilda Jane, looked on. William Bray was then sworn in as lieutenant governor. It was a somber occasion, for Lehman's sister Clara had just died, and her funeral was to be held at Temple Emanu-El. Then on January 2 the official inauguration took place in the assembly chamber. To the crowd jamming the hall Al Smith and Franklin D. Roosevelt spoke, the latter declaring that his object would be "to maintain a government of definite action founded on liberal thought." In his inaugural address the new governor pledged himself to care for the unemployed, needy, and helpless, and to broaden the sphere of government for social ends.

Lehman had been taking what steps he could to heal dissensions within the party. He would need all the support he could get to continue the march of progressive legislation. With Curry it was hopeless to try to reach an agreement, and Boss McCooey was nearly as intractable. He was very smooth, very arbitrary, and totally disinclined to take advice from anybody. Though Lehman never had any break with him or any acrimonious encounters, they lived in different worlds.

Upstate New York had only one powerful Democratic leadership, that of Dan O'Connell and his younger brother Ed in Albany, who had done much to change the political complexion of their city and county. In the old days of Tom Platt and his successor William Barnes, Albany had been reckoned a Republican fortress. By astute strategy, taking advantage of shifting currents of population, the O'Connells between 1925 and 1940 converted it into one of the staunchest Democratic fiefdoms in the state. The brothers had supported Thatcher for the nomination. Both, but especially Dan, were rough, self-centered, and rigidly conservative. They took no interest in social measures, were hostile to the Big New Deal in Washington and the Little New Deal in the state, and remained isolationists in foreign affairs. Again Lehman avoided any open quarrel with them, as with upstate bosses like Kelley in Syracuse and Zimmerman in Buffalo, but he found the gulf between his ideas and theirs unbridgeable.

The strongest leader on whom the new governor could count was Flynn of the Bronx. An efficient secretary of state under Roosevelt, he filled the post with equal vigor under Lehman. As the Bronx had a large Jewish vote, he would have felt it expedient in any circumstances to take a friendly attitude, but his loyalty was spontaneous and genuine. He made few political suggestions, for he thought his chief should make all his own decisions. In the background Farley, who was soon called to Washington as Postmaster Gen-

eral, gave as much support as he could. Tammany was in fact soon conducting an offensive against the combined Flynn-Farley forces in the city.

The immediate prospects of the state, as Lehman settled before the
papers on his desk, were appalling. The depression had paralyzed the
energies of the country. In Albany the treasury deficit was estimated at
$114,000,000 for the current fiscal year, and actually proved to be $106,-
000,000. Because the state could not constitutionally fund its deficit, as
the nation could, drastic measures would be required to meet every penny
of it. Unemployment had become horrifying; at least a quarter of the whole
working population of the state were out of work. The Temporary Economic Relief Administration (TERA) estimated that 1,750,000 were idle
on January 1, 1933, and reported that it had aided 410,000 familes the previous year, with destitution steadily increasing. During February, 1933, in
fact, 325,000 familes or about 1,250,000 individuals had to be helped. Cities
and towns were breaking down under the financial strain of relief payments. Mortgage foreclosures, both on farms and urban dwellings, were so
numerous and cruel that the Albany mails were flooded with demands for
protection. All kinds of public services were being discontinued or limited.
Banks were shaking with weakness.

· III ·

The most imperative step was to fortify the credit of the state, and as
a matter of sheer necessity, Lehman reluctantly asked the legislature to levy
a one percent sales tax. He knew that it would fall on the poor as heavily
as the rich, but in the crisis he had no alternative. Fifteen states this year resorted to a sales tax, seven of them as an emergency measure.[6] For the same
reasons he asked for an addition of one percent to the income tax, levied
without allowance for personal exemptions. The sales tax proved so fertile
a source of revenue that many legislators wished to retain it; and although
Lehman was glad to discard both it and the extra income tax after one
year, when the financial pinch became severe in the later 1930s he sometimes had twinges of regret. The two temporary levies, however, served
their purpose of moderating the deficit.

Unemployment was a much more stubborn problem, which could be
met only by the united efforts of nation, state, and local governments. In
1932 the people had voted a bond issue of $30,000,000 for unemployment
relief. The governor suggested in his annual message that the state apply
to the Reconstruction Finance Corporation for loans to support self-liqui-
dating enterprises in public works and on January 19 announced that New

York was asking for $45,000,000. But this was of course only a beginning. An emergency public works committee which he appointed arrived in Washington in February to hear the glad news that the RFC was then considering a large allotment for the state. One Federal grant after another was approved. In May Congress passed the Federal Emergency Relief Act, and the Administration which it created, with Harry L. Hopkins in charge, supplanted the relief division of the RFC and other early agencies, New York and other states then obtaining help on a broader and more systematic plane. Meanwhile, Lehman had urged through the legislature a bill submitting a $60,000,000 bond issue to the voters in the fall, signing it April 10. It was overwhelmingly approved.

It was obvious that the terrible shock of the depression might have been cushioned if industry during the boom years had set aside unemployment reserves. It was obvious also that no reliance could be placed upon voluntary action for the creation of such reserves. Only a few advanced and highly prosperous employers of the country had thus acted to protect their workers. All the industrial states realized that they must pass legislation, a conclusion underlined by an Interstate Commission on Unemployment Insurance, representing six of the chief Eastern manufacturing states, which Governor Roosevelt had initiated. The same recommendation was made by public commissions in other states all the way to California. Industrial concerns naturally protested that, wallowing as they were in the trough of the depression, they could not afford the cost of starting a new insurance system. This, Lehman told the legislature early in April, was a valid contention, but the proper course was simply to pass a good bill with a provision that it should not go into effect until business recovered. He suggested that a certificate of recovery from the state industrial commissioner, endorsed by the governor, could fix the time. The legislature, however, influenced by reactionary outcries against anything like the much maligned English dole, did not act in 1933, nor in 1934.

Lehman maintained his pressure; Al Smith and a great array of economic experts and social workers supported him; and the enlightened part of the press took his side. In the spring of 1935 the legislature at last passed the Byrne-Killgrew bill for a state system of unemployment insurance. While it protected unemployed wage earners for only thirteen weeks in any year, it marked a beginning, and the governor signed it with an expression of profound satisfaction. "In my mind," he wrote, "it stands out as the most progressive and enlightened piece of social legislation enacted in this state in many decades. The people of the State of New York should feel proud that it is once again leading the nation in legislation which will increase the economic and moral security of its working people. . . ." *

· IV ·

Another emergency to be met in 1933 was the banking crisis. When Lehman took office the financial institutions of the whole country were shaking under the economic storm. Most of them were vulnerable, as the list of RFC loans published by the House of Representatives, against the protests of many banking organizations, showed, and few were really liquid. The increasing public nervousness, evinced in long lines of depositors withdrawing their money in order to hoard it, was forcing more and more of them to suspend. After the governor of Nevada had announced a short bank holiday in October, 1932, numerous cities and towns resorted to moratoria to forestall the summary closing of their banks. During February, Lehman clung to a fast-ebbing hope that he could avoid any interruption of bank activities. The institutions of the metropolis seemed generally sound and liquid, and benefited for a time through the transfer of large sums from the interior by people seeking a safer refuge for their money.

But in mid-February the imposition of a bank holiday in Michigan by the governor of that state gave the country a staggering shock, for it was clear that the Detroit banks were in no worse condition than those of most other great cities. State after state took action to shield is own banks; people began cramming gold into cupboards; and capital was soon in full flight to London and Paris.

Lehman knew that the Federal Government under Hoover was taking no effective action. While it waited, the banks of New York City not only

---

* Meanwhile in 1934 the voters had approved a $40,000,000 bond issue for relief of the unemployed; this was one third less than the previous year, for the governor had recommended that the state should pay a gradually increasing share of the costs out of current revenues. The Federal Government was bearing much of the expense, so that the share of the state during 1934 averaged about $4,000,000 a month. In the spring of 1935 Lehman proposed another bond issue of $55,000,000 to be submitted to voters that fall so that the money might be available during the year 1936. (*Public Papers of Governor Herbert H. Lehman*, 1935, pp. 140, 141.) Of this sum, $35,000,000 was to be used under the Wicks Act for local units for two-fifths of their relief expenditures. Another $20,000,000 of the bond issue was to be devoted to the construction of hospitals, prisons, highways, parkways, and the like—permanent improvements. In the executive budget for 1936, Lehman recommended that the legislature appropriate another ten millions from the general fund to relieve unemployment, and this was done. Before the legislature adjourned it was necessary to double this amount. *Public Papers of H. H. Lehman*, 1936, pp. 292–293.

ceased to receive deposits from the interior but lost large sums which were called back to banks in the states which had protective moratoria. The breakdown of the banking machinery of the nation was involving the metropolis. He conferred steadily with the superintendent of banking, Joseph Broderick, a man of courage and imagination who was as well fitted to cope with the crisis as anybody in the land. Broderick for his part was holding incessant conferences in Albany and New York with bankers and other financial leaders. The two men fought till the last against the closing of the Manufacturers' Trust Company, one of the events which precipitated the final catastrophe.

Lehman had intended to go to Washington for Roosevelt's inauguration. But on March 1 four states proclaimed full or partial moratoria, on March 2 six more followed, and on March 3 another seven joined the procession. He canceled his trip in order to meet on the night of March 3 with representatives of banks and the clearinghouse committee at his Park Avenue apartment. One amusing feature of the conference was that the governor, anxious to have learned counsel present, and knowing that his attorney general had gone to the inauguration, called Robert Moses into the circle. He supposed Moses to be a lawyer, whereas he was as ignorant of law as Lehman himself; "a good joke on me," said Lehman later.

When the conference began at ten in the evening, Lehman knew that the principal New York financiers were anxious to have him declare a banking holiday, as of his own initiative, to save the prestige of the clearinghouse banks and the Federal Reserve Bank of New York. They had asked Broderick to press him to take this step. He was determined not to declare a banking holiday except on receipt of a very strong joint request of the clearinghouse and Federal Reserve Bank heads themselves. Broderick had told the financiers so. It was in an atmosphere of high tension that the members of the conference gathered: Lehman, Broderick, Thomas W. Lamont and Russell Leffingwell of the Morgan firm, Gordon Rentschler of the National City Bank, George Harrison of the Federal Reserve, Frank Altschul, and others; an entire roomful of anxious men. At times the debate became stormy. Broderick later supplied the governor with a memorandum which partially summarized the sequel: [7]

[New York, Friday, March 3, 1933.] The conference lasted from 10 P.M. until 3:30 A.M. March 4. The whole situation was thoroughly discussed. As there was no prospect of any action by the Washington authorities, the governor was requested to declare a two-day holiday by the Clearing House Committee with the recommendation of the Federal Reserve Bank of New York. It was felt that this action was absolutely necessary in view of the rising feeling of uncertainty through the failure to check the tremendous cash withdrawals, not only in this State but throughout the country. As to the solvency of the New York institutions, there was no question, but the withdrawal demand had been concentrated in the large New York City institutions, and there appeared to be no other way to check the movement. . . . Illinois was prepared to declare a holiday in the event that the New York State governor took action.

Saturday, March 4.—The Governor agreed to declare a two-day holiday on March 4 and March 6, and the reasons for his action are best described in the following statement which he issued to the press at 4:20 A.M. on that morning: "The spread of hysteria and the restrictions imposed upon banking facilities of the country . . . have placed upon New York banks a burden so great that it has finally rendered drastic action imperative here."

As banks in Illinois and in Pennsylvania outside Pittsburgh similarly shut down, the three principal cities of the nation lost their bank facilities. When Roosevelt took office, financial institutions from the Atlantic to the Pacific were almost completely paralyzed, and he immediately proclaimed a banking holiday from March 6 to March 9 inclusive—a term later extended. But the skies soon partially cleared. The Secretary of the Treasury was empowered to reopen banks that proved their soundness, and in New York State by March 18 no fewer than 476 of those belonging to the Federal Reserve System, and about 575 of the 715 nonmember banks, were busy again. As public confidence returned, the new deposits which flooded in vastly exceeded the withdrawals.

Lehman had never previously known William H. Woodin, whom Roosevelt appointed Secretary of the Treasury, but now they met and during the crisis talked repeatedly on the telephone. One great bank which must remain unidentified stood on the ragged edge during the holiday. Of its solvency no question could exist, but it was not sufficiently liquid, for it had tremendous mortgage holdings on which it could not collect. By the 17th of March Lehman was convinced that it must reopen. It was one of the half-dozen largest banks in the country; it had a multitude of depositors and hundreds of millions in deposits; if it remained shut people would take fright and the panic might start all over again. "I was on the telephone literally for hours with Woodin," Lehman recalls, "and arguing with equal fervor to Roosevelt." The president of the bank came to his house in intense anguish, begging that every means be exhausted to get a favorable verdict. Finally, the Administration accepted the governor's advice, and the doors swung open.

"Within two years," Lehman records, "this man was one of FDR's main critics, denouncing him venomously. There were a good many instances of that." [8]

· V ·

One of the less exigent but important problems of 1933 was liquor legislation. When Lehman was inaugurated, it was clear that Congress would act swiftly to permit the sale of beer containing 3.26 percent alcohol and that later in the year the repeal of the prohibition amendment would become effective. He was convinced that serious trouble would arise if adequate controls over the sale of beer and spirits were not established before the "dry" regime ended. The old abuses of the days before prohibition would reappear and create a new wave of antisaloon agitation. All existing legislation on the subject had been swept away under Al Smith.

In his first annual message Lehman therefore recommended that the legislature authorize the appointment of a small commission to report within six weeks on a licensing machinery for the liquor trade. This body, under a former lieutenant governor, T. F. Conway, with Samuel Rosenman as counsel, made a report in mid-February which helped clear the ground, but did nothing more. As soon as the Roosevelt Administration began, Congress put a bill for 3.2 beer upon passage to go into effect early in April. The control situation grew urgent.

Thus March saw Albany the scene of a grand shindy, a row which fascinated the press and horrified Washington observers. Was the same battle to take place in forty-seven other states? The Anti-Saloon League, the churches, the restaurant keepers, the beer interests, the whisky interests, police chiefs, and reformers all rushed into the mêlée. Bill after bill was introduced. Issue after issue was debated. Should liquor advertising be allowed? Sunday sales? Sales to minors? The governor had strong views of his own. He vividly remembered the evil days when local politicians had controlled the licensing of corner saloons, many of them owned by the big breweries, many more by aldermen and ward heelers; too often centers of gambling, prostitution, and confidence games. Everyone knew the story of the meeting of the New York board of aldermen that was interrupted by a man who rushed in shouting: "Alderman, your saloon is on fire!"—whereupon the entire body bolted for the doors. At the same time, the governor had long detested prohibition for the racketeering it bred and the disregard of law it taught the rising generation.

Lehman believed that licensing should be placed in the hands of a state board of unimpeachable vigilance and rectitude; its politics bipartisan, its members appointed by the governor from lists submitted by civic and professional bodies, and its employees subject to civil service rules. His bill embodying these views was presented by Senator Dunnigan on March 24. It provided for a bipartisan central control board of five to issue licenses and lay down regulations, the governor to appoint the chairman and to select the other four from rosters submitted by the State Bar Association, State Medical Society, State Chamber of Commerce, and State Federation of Labor—all nominations being subject to approval by the senate.

The battle instantly grew hotter. Protests came even from the Democratic side. Upstate legislators of both parties vehemently demanded that county boards be given control of liquor sales, for they feared that New York City would dominate the state board. The governor sent in a special message on March 29, but the uproar continued.

Finally, a compromise bill was hammered out by conferences in which Lehman met with Speaker Joe McGinnies, acting-president John Knight of the senate, the majority and minority leaders, and others. The gist of it was that county boards of two each (four in New York City), creation of which was now mandatory, were empowered to recommend approval or rejection of applications for licenses, the state board then to have the final word subject to court review. This was an interim arrangement good only until April 1, 1934, and at first applicable only to the sale of beer, but it set the pattern of the permanent control scheme which went into effect when prohibition ended in December, 1933.*

The legislature passed the compromise April 8, and Lehman signed the new law on the 10th. That same day, Edward P. Mulrooney, who had resigned the police commissionership in New York to accept the chairmanship of the state board, took his oath of office and set about regulating the sale of beer. Some 20,000 places—coffee shops, sandwich stands, lunchrooms—raised a wail of anguish as they lost the right to sell it. The question of permanent controls after the spring of 1934, covering hard liquor, remained. Lehman directed Mulrooney and his associates—John Sullivan of the State Federation of Labor; Edward Schoeneck, a former lieutenant governor; Mrs. Rumsey Shepherd, prominent in social work, and James P. Duffy, an attorney—to formulate regulations which would be "a model for the United

---

* The main differences over the bill respected (1) the mode of selecting the local control boards and (2) the powers to be conferred in them. Lehman originally favored a greater degree of state authority than Fearon, McGinnies, and other members of the legislature, defending local home rule, thought advisable. In the compromise worked out the governor made large concessions to local authority. *Public Papers*, 1933, pp. 476–479.

States and a victory for temperance." While they embarked on this work, the legislature in a late summer session passed a new bill for the permanent system. On November 10, Mulrooney published the regulations, and next day a thousand applications for licenses came in.

The governor thus helped steer the state between the rocks of a return to the old-style corner saloons with all their vicious features and the whirlpool of excessively rigid controls. If New York had set an example of laxity, other states would have drifted with it; as it was, only half a dozen went back to the "wide-open" system. The new regime worked well. No criminal could hold a license; no brewery could have a financial interest in any retail place except a garden attached to its premises. The word "tavern" began to supplant "saloon," and many owners cultivated the genial decorum of the British pub. Among the early rules were one forbidding women to sit at a bar, for example, and another stipulating that, while patrons of a restaurant might pay for meals with a check, they must pay for liquor in cash. A new epoch began, which, if not perfect, was better than the Bowery days under Croker or the scoff-law years under Volstead.

The Lehman household had always set its own example of moderation, making limited use of beer and wine and taking a very reserved attitude toward spirits. Between the passage of the Eighteenth Amendment and the day it became effective, Lehman had decided to lay in a small stock. "So I ordered a case of gin and a case of Scotch and a case of Bourbon; that was all. And I remember saying to my wife, 'Now, this is plenty. This will last us through our lifetime.' I put a few bottles of champagne aside to be used at the weddings of my children. But the moment prohibition became an actual fact, of course everybody was serving cocktails, and my cases of gin and whisky lasted about two minutes. I've always laughed at my naïve idea they would last me the rest of my life." As a state officer before repeal, he never served liquor at dinners.

Repeal came in and prohibition went out amid general rejoicing, for although nobody denied the evils of drunkenness, the racketeering and social license under prohibition had become intolerable. Moreover, repeal gave a stimulus to the economy. Some people estimated that the reopening of breweries and distilleries, the reappearance of bars, the increased patronage of restaurants and hotels, and the larger trucking business furnished employment in New York State to a hundred thousand people. In the midst of the first exhilaration, the state convention met in June, 1933, to approve the repeal amendment. The Lehmans held a large garden party at the mansion for the members, and they long remembered its jollity.

"I invited all of them," the governor recalled later, "and with them many prominent people of Albany and the surrounding country. There must have been five or six hundred. I couldn't serve liquor there, because after all the Eighteenth Amendment was still in force. Repeal hadn't received its thirty-six state votes. But I served beer. I had great kegs of beer which we broached, and everybody was happy—for at last we could serve an alcoholic beverage without concealment. Here was an occasion when we could all get out in the open in the garden and drink beer without apologies to anybody or to our own consciences. It made a great impression on me." The day was symbolic: the country took its freedom to drink beer as a token of the greater freedoms, social and economic, that the New Deal was throwing open.

Still another emergency of 1933 was presented by the passing squall long remembered as the "milk strike." New York, like other parts of the country, suffered from an overproduction of milk. Everywhere the disorderly marketing of the surplus resulted in price-cutting, a flare of resentment among hard-working dairymen, and violent disturbances. "Milk strikes" had occurred during 1932 in Illinois, Iowa, Nebraska, and Georgia, with trucks of milk blocked or overturned and angry dairy organizations on one side and marketing companies on the other appealing to governors and legislatures. The following year the violence spread to New York, where the situation was especially complicated. The Dairymen's League, with some 50,000 members, insisted on better prices; the principal distributors, Sheffield Farms and Borden's, protested they could not afford to pay another cent; small grocers in the metropolis and other cities demanded "loose" (that is, unbottled) milk, which truckmen furnished them at rock-bottom prices, until the New York City Board of Health stopped its sale on June 1, 1933; and general disorganization marked the industry.

Though as 1933 opened a joint legislative committee was taking testimony, and Senator P. A. Pitcher and other leaders, with Lehman's support, were hammering out a bill establishing a state board to fix milk prices, the rebellious dairymen were in no mood to wait. On March 14, more than 2,000 of them appeared in Albany to demand the price control law. While distributors fought the measure, and independent producers opened a war against the Dairymen's League, violence broke out on the roads. Dairymen of the Rochester area, acting as pickets in the early spring, dumped thousands of gallons and temporarily defied state troopers. Assisted by a special message from Lehman, the bill for a state board passed the legislature early in April, the governor signing it on the 10th. The board began its work at once, established a minimum price scale, later increased, and was soon estimating that its decrees would put $12,500,000 a year into the overalls of the state dairymen. But rural discontent persisted, and tempers got out of hand. During the summer grave disorders took place in Oneida, Herkimer, Chenango, Lewis, and other counties. Rifle shots were exchanged with police; eight state troopers were hurt, one gravely; and more milk was dumped.

Lehman's first duty in the emergency was to preserve order. He refused to call out the militia, declaring that the state troopers and sheriffs could handle the situation. He ordered the sheriffs of a dozen counties to appoint enough deputies to quell the disturbance. At the same time, sympathizing with the producers—he could never understand the wide spread between the rates paid dairymen and those charged consumers—he had to press for remedies. Gladly signing a bill for an inquiry by the state board into prices, he urged an independent audit of the distributors' books. In time, the board's work restored peace, and the New Deal legislation assisted producers of butter and cheese; but the economics of the dairy industry remained very murky.[9]

· VI ·

Throughout the difficult years 1933–34, the governor had to consider the problems not only of the state but of the municipalities—and above all, his own city. When he left Park Avenue to be inaugurated, he knew how deep was the financial slough in which New York was plunged. The new mayor there, completing the term of Jimmy Walker, was the stalwart, bungling John Patrick O'Brien, who faced a sea of difficulties bravely but clumsily. The metropolis was not quite as badly off as Chicago, which, as a result of failure to collect delinquent taxes, was temporarily unable to pay the schoolteachers. But it had been tardy in carrying out the reforms recommended by the Survey Committee in 1927; its colossal debt-service bill, which was more than its entire budget a quarter century earlier, seemed crushing in time of depression, and its current budget exceeded that of Chicago, Philadelphia, and Detroit combined. Relief expenditures, running to about $5,000,000 of city funds a month in 1932, were staggering.

"We became very fearful of the situation," Lehman said; by "we," meaning Roosevelt and himself. Mayor O'Brien was still more fearful, and their apprehension grew. Almost as soon as he took office he found O'Brien on his doorstep. The governor told him that the city must economize heroically. The mayor took the same view and, despite his intention to run for reëlection that fall, adopted measures that were certain to earn him unpopularity. He ordered departmental heads to cut $20,000,000 from the budget, slashed salaries, and opposed appropriations for new public works.

Municipal Court justices took a ten-percent cut. Still the city's predicament worsened, and in April and May the city was unable to meet even comparatively small debt maturities.

O'Brien, who even considered levying a tax on stock market transactions—an idea withdrawn when the Stock Exchange threatened moving to New Jersey—continued his anxious visits to Albany. One conference at the governor's mansion lasted most of the night while reporters waited. As summer came on with a default narrowly averted, both the governor and mayor were anxious to keep their meetings out of the press. Lehman, with some difficulty, had rented a summer place on Lake George within commuting distance, thinking that he, his family, and his secretaries could frequently use it. As matters turned out, he got there for just two nights—and one of them was devoted to a secret conference with O'Brien and other city officials. When the New York bankers agreed in June to extend all securities due during the summer until mid-December, they demanded guarantees of new city revenues and charged an interest rate of $5\frac{3}{4}$ percent.

By September 18 the city's position had become perilous in the extreme. Funds were needed to meet the October payrolls and were nowhere in sight. The city comptroller resigned, George McAneny taking his place. At this point Samuel Untermyer, as special adviser to the mayor, and Frank L. Polk, as representative of a bankers' committee, wrote Lehman asking for a conference. The governor agreed the same day, informal conversations having preceded their exchange of letters. It was understood that the bankers and city officers would, if possible, work out a comprehensive four-year plan to protect the city's credit and that the governor would lay it before a special legislative session. The discussions of governor, municipal heads, and bankers began immediately, on the 19th, and dragged through arduous days. Those participating included McAneny, Gordon H. Rentschler, Thomas W. Lamont, Jackson Reynolds, and at some meetings Winthrop Aldrich.*

To Lehman the terms laid down by the bankers seemed severe. But he had been a banker himself, and realized that they held great sums in New York City bonds, that they believed careful temporary supervision over expenditures and revenues essential for the protection of the city as well as themselves, and that when they looked back over the stupidity, waste, and corruption that had characterized the city administrations under Hylan and Walker, they felt they must be precise in their stipulations. Mayor O'Brien's

* Historical memorandum prepared for Lehman by President Gordon H. Rentschler of the National City Bank, December 18, 1939. Lehman Papers. The prominence of McAneny and Polk, important in the affairs of the city since the Mitchel Administration, emphasized the seriousness of the crisis.

goodwill and earnestness were plain to all, but it was also clear that he knew little about finance and not much more about administration; he had been a judge. On September 27, the banks and city officials arrived at an agreement on their four-year plan, 1934-37; the city promising among other things that it would encourage tax payments by a temporary reduction of penalties followed by a stiff increase, would budget a reserve partially offsetting tax delinquency, and would limit the tax burdens on real estate for purposes other than debt service.

Lehman had been anxious to avoid a second extra session in 1933—the first had lasted from July 26 to August 24—and had told the press that he would call one, with all its cost and inconvenience, only if a sharp necessity were demonstrated. The New York Board of Estimate now urgently requested it, and he agreed. On October 13, the city and bankers settled the final form of the legislation needed. The moment this was done, Lehman telegraphed legislative leaders to meet him next day, and when they arrived, asked pledges of their support for the proposed legislation—his object being to get a short session.[10]

Dunnigan and Irwin Steingut on the Democratic side agreed, but the Republican senate leader, George R. Fearon, tried to do a bit of horse trading. He would promise Republican support, he said, only if the Democrats would agree to pass a twice-defeated bill in the interests of Rochester and Monroe County. Dunnigan refused. Despite Lehman's pleas, Fearon stood firm. Nevertheless, Lehman called the legislature for the 18th, declaring that he would use every means at his command to obtain enactment of the city bills.

Any further delay would have been disastrous. The banks refused to advance $54,000,000, which was absolutely necessary to pay city bills up to December 1, unless the legislation passed. Part of this money had to be obtained by October 24, to meet city requirements. The state could furnish no more direct support, for it was already giving too much. In 1932 it had collected $256,600,000 in taxes and had distributed about $160,000,000 of this to communities; if it collected and divided larger sums, it would encourage wastefulness by removing local pressures for economy. The state was also doing its full share in local relief of the unemployed. In the first five months of 1933, while New York City was spending $13,612,000 in home and work relief, the state and Federal governments had given the metropolis more than $17,000,000 for the purpose, without counting the state public works projects. The people of the city awaited final action on the four-year plan with rising anxiety. A default on its obligations, and a deferment of desperately needed relief checks, would not only plunge the community into confusion but shake municipal credit throughout the nation.

Happily, the legislature came up to the mark. Meeting October 18, it heard the governor argue for action without delays or political entanglements and then swiftly passed the bill. Thus the city was saved on the very brink of bankruptcy.[11] But the members had no sooner gone home than attorneys for the banks gave the governor and public a new shock. Discovering a flaw in the legislation which they decided might affect the validity of city bonds, they sent word to Lehman that he should call another extra session to correct it—the third of 1933! This he was, of course, unwilling to do. Fortunately, the overanxious lawyers had second thoughts and finally worded their documents so as to avoid all difficulties.

Fortunately for the public, still more fortunately for Lehman! During the protracted negotiations of city and banks he had been troubled by mild appendicitis pains, but as it seemed imperative to keep on his feet, he had ignored the protest of doctors that he should enter a hospital. As soon as the legislature adjourned he hurried to Mt. Sinai for an operation. It was so successful that he seemed on the road to immediate recovery when suddenly a pulmonary embolism developed. For some time he was in great pain and real danger. By coincidence, his nephew and former business associate, Harold Lehman, had been brought into the same hospital a day after he entered, had been operated on for appendicitis, and had also developed an embolism.

When the nephew died, a fact that was kept from the governor for some weeks, a rumor ran about New York that the state had lost its head. After Lehman left the hospital, his brother Arthur sent him a stern reprimand: [12]

> I think you must definitely get yourself in a different frame of mind from the one that has hitherto prevailed. It is, of course, quite in order for you to be entirely conscientious as far as your duties go and it is this conscientiousness which no doubt has helped create the feeling of confidence which the people of the State have in you—I am afraid, however, that you have let your conscientiousness carry you to some extent off your feet and this has made you take rather a distorted view of the situation. As I look back upon the events of the day that you drove up to White Plains, I just cannot understand how a man of your common sense could possibly have undertaken that trip knowing that you had had an attack of appendicitis the night before. Nor can I guess why I did not just use physical force to prevent your taking that foolish drive. In retrospect, I can understand your insistence in

going through with the banking conference regardless of the effect upon you personally. The matter was of such importance that it is possible you were called upon to take a risk, but the reviewing of the parade at White Plains was of such little importance that you only took the trip in order to keep a promise. It is not for me to suggest that you only took the trip in order to keep a promise. It is not for me to suggest your future conduct but I think you must arrange that some of these "personal appearances," if I may call them such, be made by others even if the substitution has to be arranged for at the last minute. You cannot possibly—if you are to continue in public life—continue under the same strain as you have been under during the last year.

• VII •

In the three-cornered city election of the fall of 1933, Mayor O'Brien faced Ed Flynn's cultivated protégé, Joseph V. McKee, on an Independent Democratic ticket and Fiorello La Guardia as the Republican-Fusionist nominee. Lehman had no time to participate in the contest and, as he was in the hospital on election day, could not even vote. Had he cast his ballot, it would have been for McKee. He then knew La Guardia merely as a friend of labor, a war veteran of fine record, and an impetuous, noisy member of Congress. He felt a qualified admiration for him as a good man, but "very flamboyant and very aggressive." Later he acquired a proper esteem for La Guardia's absolute honesty of purpose, untiring energy, and skill in choosing able lieutenants. It seems too bad that he never once voted for New York's greatest mayor; and his failure to do so was one of the facts that laid him open to the charge of excessive partisanship that was sometimes brought against him.

The two men were nevertheless entirely different in temperament and method and were certain in various ways to clash. In fact, the first clash came as soon as the new mayor took office.

La Guardia knew that the finances of the city remained disorderly, the relief burden was still terrifying, and a program of systematic economies was of desperate importance. As soon as he was elected he began preparing a legislative bill to give him sweeping power to reduce city expenses. Under the Constitution, no special act relating to a town or city could be passed except with a message from the governor certifying to an emergency and by concurrent action of two thirds of each house. La Guardia, therefore, startled the governor by calling on him late in December, 1933, and telling him that as soon as the legislature organized, he would have his bill introduced and would expect an emergency message from Lehman. When Lehman received a copy of the bill and read it, he was thunderstruck.

He showed it to his best advisers, who agreed that it was totally unallowable. The mayor's bill would empower him to abolish any agency of government in the city, establish new agencies in their stead, and override all state laws affecting the city—in short, to tear the city charter to pieces. It was true that La Guardia felt he was faced by a desperate situation. The aldermen flatly refused to eliminate numerous unnecessary offices in which they or their friends had a vested interest. Even if they were forced to consent, their action would involve such long controversial hearings that much of the anticipated saving would be lost by lapse of time. Delays in other areas of government would cost the city its opportunity for Federal loans and grants. Nevertheless, it was not necessary to make La Guardia a petty Mussolini. He had at hand unused means, legal and orderly, to effect economies and carry out a salutary reorganization.

The legislature less than two years earlier had given the city administration exclusive power to fix all but a few specified salaries; so that if the mayor thought any department held unnecessary positions, he could simply leave the places vacant and omit them from the budget. If he wished to go further, the Board of Estimate, its majority sympathetic with his aims, could do a great deal in trimming and eliminating expense. La Guardia declared in a letter of January 4 to Lehman that his bill merely paralleled the Congressional legislation vesting President Roosevelt with great emergency powers.

In his reply, the governor easily controverted this position. "President Roosevelt was faced with a world crisis," he wrote. "The banks of this country were closed; panic and fear stalked through our cities; we were on the brink of a calamity unparalleled in the history of the world. The President at that time was leading an almost forlorn hope; heroic measures were essential." And, for that matter, La Guardia demanded a dictatorial freedom far exceeding the authority given to Roosevelt. Congress, in its principal emergency act, had provided that all executive orders issued under its clauses should be submitted to Congress if in session; that none should become effective for sixty days after such submission except by Congressional assent; and that if Congress adjourned, the sixty days must date from the opening of the next session.

Lehman granted La Guardia's request for a conference, but in doing so he reiterated that he would not consent to any demand for "such broad, unrestricted, dictatorial powers." Public opinion and the important civic organizations supported him, and the mayor gave way. When he came up to Albany on January 10th the meeting, as Lehman wrote Lillian Wald, proved constructive, for the peppery little mayor agreed to rewrite his bill to make it conform to democratic procedures.[13] That is, he agreed that the emergency powers would be granted not to him but to the Board of Estimate and could not be exercised without at least ten of its sixteen votes. He agreed that old departments could be abolished, new ones created, and other changes in charter functions made by the Board only after ten days' notice and a public hearing. He agreed, finally, that the municipal assembly would have power to repeal the emergency statute at any time before it expired in the autumn of 1934. In short, he gave up temporary mayoral dictatorship in favor of temporary enlargement of the powers of the Board of Estimate, subject to control by the aldermen.

Lehman submitted the revised bill to the legislature with an argument on the propriety of permitting the metropolis a wide latitude in home rule. But even with his support, even with the changes, even with the advocacy of powerful newspapers, such heavy opposition arose in the legislature that he almost despaired of getting it passed. Many legislators viewed La Guardia dubiously, some had friends who might suffer, and others disliked New-Dealism whether national, state, or municipal. Even Ed Flynn was an objector.

After an initial defeat, the bill was amended, and Lehman redoubled his efforts. "Governor Lehman Near Break with Party Bosses on the Economy Bill," ran a headline in the *Times*. Finally the bill carried in April, 1934, and he signed it. The mayor and his Board of Estimate supporters energetically cut dead wood out of the city activities. The aldermen, too much afraid of public feeling to interfere, burned with an anger which they expressed in 1934 by trying to slash essential health services. "Actually, they were not cutting hospitals," said the aldermanic whip later. "They were cutting La Guardia."

The ensuing years found Lehman and the Don Furioso mayor, despite occasional clashes, usually on good terms and sometimes active partners.

· VIII ·

Meanwhile, the Lehmans were adjusting themselves to the changed conditions of life in Albany, Spending their first month at a hotel, they dreaded moving into the executive mansion, a Victorian structure of gaunt outline, big porches, a central tower of four stories, and preposterous cornices, with an interior distinguished by dark woodwork, red-painted halls, endless stairs, and insufficient windows. Once they took the plunge, however, Mrs. Lehman soon transformed the place. She repainted walls and woodwork, installed comfortable furniture, and brightened the rooms with cheerful pictures and hangings. She was hampered by rules of economy, for her husband decided that, although the legislature annually appropriated $40,000 for repairs and improvements, in deference to the hard times and state poverty they must not spend a cent of it.* But as they made improvements at their own cost, their feelings altered.

"We became so attached to that house," records Lehman, "that we hated to move away from it. It was roomy, it was homelike, it had a lovely garden, and it boasted a greenhouse. FDR had put in a good swimming pool so that he could swim in warm water. That part of Albany was far from smart, for the people were all wage-earners and some of the houses had run down. But they were decent, friendly people and I enjoyed them very much. We had a feeling of warmth on the part of our neighbors which I liked."

Some delightful reminiscences of life in the mansion have been left us by Mrs. Charles Poletti, who with her husband (one of the governor's indispensable aides) presently came to live there, staying three years. That stay during the last six months included a baby complete with nurse and nursery on the third floor. Mrs. Poletti became an assistant hostess to Mrs. Lehman at all entertaining, which was kept within careful limits. Life in the mansion naturally revolved about and reflected official life in the capitol. Writes Mrs. Poletti:

> Usually the four of us had dinner together and the talk was chiefly "business": what had happened at the capitol during the day—what might or might not happen in the legislature next day. During the daytime, Mrs. Lehman and I each went our own way. If we both happened to be home for lunch, we lunched together. If either was there alone, we usually had a tray in our room. . . .
>
> Mrs. Lehman became my best friend and closest confidante. Together, we sat with our knitting in the front row of either the As-

---

* Mrs. Lehman once mentioned the need for new curtains—the old ones were in tatters—to the governor's counsel, Nat Sobel. He took the matter up with the Republican chairman of the ways and means committee, Abbot Moffat, and the two devised a scheme whereby a $500 appropriation for new curtains was hidden in the 2,000-page state budget in an appropriation for a dairy farm in Orange County. Unfortunately, Moffat's clerk found the "error" and restored it to the executive mansion section. Moffat and Sobel, in desperation, woke up the Albany printing firm's head at midnight and at an expense far exceeding the $500 had one special copy of the state budget printed for the Governor, omitting this item. But Lehman found it and refused to approve it, after all. Judge Edward Weinfeld to the author, April, 1962.

sembly or the Senate for hours upon end. During the inevitable long dull interludes (which occur in all legislative bodies) we turned out an endless stream of sweaters, baby blankets, socks, mittens, and scarves, and giggled quite a lot at our own comments on the people and events around us. Work stopped and our attention was fixed when a bill in which the Governor was interested (and whose background we well knew) was under discussion. . . .

Each year the party for which Mrs. Lehman did the most careful preparation and where everybody had the most fun (including the hostess) was on the evening when the legislative correspondents gave their annual dinner and show for all state politicos, and Mrs. Lehman invited the wives of all correspondents plus Albany newspaper women to the mansion. One year she invited everyone to go on a cruise. The ground floor of the big old house was made to look as much like a ship as possible. There was a gangplank, life-boats, life-savers. Mrs. Lehman herself made a very natty captain. I, as the purser, had an impressive little office, and the guests turned up in every manner of costume, from hula-hula girls to haughty dowagers. Another year, everyone was invited to attend a county fair. . . .

Another annual party that both Mrs. Lehman and the Governor dearly loved was the Christmas one they gave for all the children in the Catholic orphanage whose back windows faced on the garden at the rear of the mansion. From 50 to 75 little girls attended. There was usually a movie on the third floor; always cookies and cakes and ice-cream afterward. The climax of the afternoon came when Governor and Mrs. Lehman stood under a gigantic Christmas tree in the big drawing room and each child was called by name to receive an appropriate present for her age. Not only did Mrs. Lehman expend time and thought on each gift, but she personally helped to wrap each one. From the earliest days of my life in the mansion I heard about the fastidious perfection with which each gift bearing the Lehman name must be wrapped.

Mrs. Poletti recalls other details illustrating the genial atmosphere which enveloped life in the mansion. They include the passion of the governor for pâté de foie gras, preferably from Strasbourg; the weekly "at homes" to which residents and visitors in Albany were welcomed, and at which it was an honor to be asked to pour tea or coffee; and the duties assigned the eighteen servants in the mansion.

Lehman had a strong sense of the historic lineage of his office. To the governorship had come George Clinton, fresh from Revolutionary battlefields, to serve eighteen years in succession, capped by a subsequent triennial term. His nephew, De Witt Clinton, had used the office to drive forward the Erie Canal, strengthen a system of free schools, and promote other sound policies. From the post of governor Van Buren had gone to Washington

as Jackson's Secretary of State, winning the President's regard by his courtesies to Peggy Eaton. The rugged Silas Wright, servant of the plain people, had been head of the state when the nation plunged into the Mexican
conflict; and later Edwin D. Morgan had earned renown as one of Lincoln's
best lieutenants among the war governors. Horatio Seymour and John A.
Dix, with totally diverse ideas of their duty in the national crisis, had
played great roles, and Seymour had come close in 1868 to gaining the
White House.

Then the bachelor Samuel J. Tilden had been the first governor to
occupy the mansion; an astute reformer and party strategist, who in the
eyes of millions was rightfully chosen President and cheated of the place.
In rapid sequence Grover Cleveland and Theodore Roosevelt followed, two
strong governors and powerful Presidents; Levi P. Morton, former Vice-
President, had served a term; and early in the new century came Charles
E. Hughes, who also missed the highest American office by a hairbreadth
margin. No other state could boast such a succession of leaders of power
and principle, and no other could show such varied illustrations of the capacity of a democracy to produce men answerable to changing needs.

The homely old mansion was indubitably one of the historic houses of
America. This was so well appreciated by Herbert and Edith Lehman that
when, from time to time, some legislator proposed tearing the structure
down and erecting a handsome modern residence, they expressed their
opposition in vigorous terms. Their children would have been much less
reluctant to see a change. Once when the governor expatiated on the illus-
trious line of occupants, half-grown Peter Lehman spoke up mischievously:
"And don't forget Bill Sulzer was here too!" The roominess of the house
and gardens adapted them to entertaining, which became feasible as the
depression relaxed its grip. Distinguished guests came and went; by custom, certain state dinners and receptions had to be held; and Lehman liked
to get leaders of the two houses in for a meal followed by relaxed talk of
plans. Albany had a cultivated society all its own, led by such pleasant
people as William Gorham Rice and his wife, daughter of the diplomatist
John V. L. Pruyn. Despite the rigors of the period, life in the old town
on the Hudson had its genial interludes.

Before the end of Lehman's second year, it was clear that his governorship was entering a new phase, in which the emphasis would fall not on
emergencies but on solid reform and carefully wrought plans for promoting
welfare.

Chapter VIII

BATTLES FRONT AND REAR

THE first emergencies of his governorship surmounted, Lehman had time to look about him and consider his position. A hard-working governor who carried his troubles to bed with him, he sometimes woke up at night recalling the days when he had been a worried urchin in the house on Sixty-second Street, his fingers ink-stained, his knees and elbows bruised by rough games, his mind troubled by his lessons, by his strong competitive urge in sports and study, and above all by his dread that he could never live up to his parents' expectations. They seldom scolded, but he nevertheless felt their concern over his rough-and-tumble ways and their rigorous insistence on standards. Now he had succeeded two of the greatest governors New York had ever known, Smith and Roosevelt. As head of the chief industrial state of the Union, half-paralyzed with unemployment, want, and despair, he had to measure his strength against ceaseless critical tasks. Could he satisfy the expectations of his party and friends? Could he meet the needs of four-teen million people between Lake Erie and Long Island Sound? Could he write new pages of history comparable with those inscribed by Smith and Roosevelt?

Lehman clearly lacked the picturesque qualities of his predecessors. He had none of the dash, electric vitality, and breeziness of Roosevelt, and little of the humor, gusto, and crisp incisiveness found in Al Smith. The squire of Hyde Park and the son of the Fulton Fish Market possessed clear advantages over him in appealing to newspaper readers. But Lehman wasted no time lamenting his want of flamboyant traits, for he had advantages all his own. He had gained a broader training, by virtue of Williams College, Washington experience, business years, and service in Old World relief, than Smith. While he would have demurred to the statement that he showed a deeper sense of responsibility, a sterner conscientiousness, than FDR, it would have been true. And he was aware that his special Jewish

152

background, for piety, idealism, and intellectual seriousness, need fear comparison with no other background whatever. It gave him standing among discriminating people of the older stock as well as the immigrant elements.

His conscientiousness might have been a little overwhelming but for his ready grin, sociability, and modesty. He was as friendly as a terrier, as human as a schoolboy. Of another walking conscience who made a distinguished but frigid public servant, a New Yorker once exclaimed: "If the world were made up of Seth Lows, it would not be worth living in!" Nobody would have said that of Lehman. If he did not have much imagination, he had a kindling vision; if he lacked gaiety, he possessed sympathy. Duty to him was no abstraction but an instinct born of his warm interest in the plain people. Nevertheless, duty always came first. He broke off his connection with a Southern corporation because its treatment of labor pickets offended him. When his wife, called away from home, sent him some concert tickets, he telegraphed her that it was "execution night" and he did not wish to stir from his telephone. He was scrupulous about everything; if some decision of his might affect a company in which he owned stock, he whipped off a sale of the stock.

Judge John F. O'Brien died on Christmas Day in 1939. Had he lived six days longer a pension would have been payable to his wife and children. As both houses unanimously passed a bill giving them the pension, letters poured in on Lehman from Mrs. Roosevelt, Frank L. Polk, Judge Philip L. McCook, and other friends exhorting him to sign it. Though his heart was wrung, he vetoed the bill. "I cannot begin to tell you how sorry I am," he wrote the widow in explaining that his duty was imperative. "Every year there are many cases similar to John's. In the aggregate during the past fifteen years the number has become very large. In virtually every instance there are circumstances which, as in your case, work a real hardship to the beneficiaries." As these bills were alike in character, they should be treated alike; nobody should get a special favor. And, he added, he had never made a single exception. "I never felt worse about vetoing any bill," he wrote his brother Irving, "but I do not see how I could have done anything else." [1]

Upon Irving he continued to depend for advice only less than upon his wife, and he took great comfort in his brother's long sojourns in Albany. Originally elected a judge of the court of appeals, the highest New York tribunal, for the term 1924–38 (and later reëlected for fourteen years on the nomination of the Democratic, Republican, and American Labor Parties) Irving became a member of the Fort Orange Club. He was on the most brotherly terms with Judge Benjamin N. Cardozo, whom he succeeded as chief judge, and shared the views Cardozo expressed in *The Growth of Law.*

A man of immense dignity, who enforced strict decorum in the court,* Irving nevertheless possessed a sweet and gentle nature and gave Herbert unflagging companionship as well as a steady flow of ideas and legal lore. Though he lacked the literary flair to make his opinions fully effective, he had touches of profundity denied his more dynamic brother and a strong grasp of fundamental principles of government. As he had become very deaf, he wore an electrical device which could pick up the faintest whisper in a corner of the courtroom, so that in the midst of a solemn trial he would sometimes smile suddenly. When bored, he would snap off his hearing aid as abruptly as Herbert Spencer used to don his earmuffs. Though he never attained the stature of a Cardozo or Learned Hand, the judicial system of the country had no more conscientious officer. Such was his objectivity that it was often necessary to read through his whole opinion, perfectly balanced between pro and con, to learn his final judgment. To the governor he was confidante and mainstay.

So, too, was Ed Flynn, boss of the Bronx and secretary of state, who was as useful for his general ideas as for hardboiled political advice. He remained a versatile and thoughtful man, who helped modify the excessive seriousness that sometimes made Lehman too tense for his own good. The governor's secretary, Joe Canavan, was as shrewd, tough, and quick as Steve Early had been when Early served Roosevelt in Albany, and like Early, was particularly good at press relations. Intensely loyal to Lehman, he showed a rough and ready common sense.

Newspapermen and associates, who found Lehman was unwilling to talk about himself but always ready to discuss state problems, soon discovered that he had a well-defined philosophy of government. At its center was the idea of social justice, on which he laid down several principles. One was that social justice must never be confounded with charity; another that it is most effective and durable when achieved with gradual forethought; and a third that no fixed program can ever be adopted to win and preserve it, for "it is continually in flux." A broad estimate of the duties of the state in the promotion of public welfare had made progress since the beginning of the century. So had higher standards of business ethics and of the treatment

* Nathaniel Goldstein, attorney general under Dewey, once at a trial before the Court of Appeals began a political harangue, a Fourth-of-July speech. Chief Judge Lehman halted him: "Sir, do you have a legal argument? If not, I suggest that you leave that to the solicitor-general, and SIT DOWN." It was a well-justified if harsh rebuke; Goldstein sat down and never again appeared before Lehman. Judge Henry Epstein to the author, December 10, 1961. Irving Lehman's zealous championship of civil liberties found various illustrations, notably in his defense of the right of Jehovah's Witnesses' school children to refuse to salute the flag (People v. Sandstrom, 279 N.Y. 523). He preferred to be called a libertarian rather than a liberal.

of employees in industry. "No longer," said Lehman at the St. Bonaventure College commencement in 1934, "is group isolation possible in a well ordered body politic." The public also took a more liberal attitude, which he thoroughly approved, toward the spending of public money in stimulating the economy and correcting its inequalities.

Lehman insisted on the need for executive leadership in government and for unyielding pressure in behalf of reform. His conservative opponents clamored for a strict interpretation of the Constitution, for giving business a sense of security, for peace, quiet, and inaction. The record, he declared, proved them utterly wrong: [2]

> If Governor Theodore Roosevelt had not fought for his policies we would not have taxation of public franchises obtained by corporations from government. . . .
> If Governor Hughes had not fought courageously and energetically, against even the legislators of his own party, he would not have secured for the people of the State the regulation of public utilities or the supervision and regulation of insurance companies, the primary election reform, and the short ballot.
> If Governor Smith had not for years appealed directly to the people, we would not have our factory laws, limitation of working hours, and improvement of working conditions. We would not have secured reorganization of the State government, the development of our park system, or the creation of the executive budget. We would have lost completely the waterpower resources of this State to powerful private interests.
> If Franklin Roosevelt had not appealed directly to the people we would not in 1930 and 1931 have secured old age pensions or the administration of unemployment relief by the State.

He intended in the militant spirit of these governors, two Republicans and two Democrats, to conduct an untiring battle for the protection of wage earners, the assistance of the helpless, the curbing of privilege, and the general maintenance of social progress. His most important weapon would be a direct appeal to the people. But at this period he was much more a social-minded businessman than an idealist; all his ideas were pragmatic. His worrisome ways misled some men into thinking him timid; his business mentality misled others into thinking him a plodder. It was true that he was in some respects limited, but he would grow.

• I •

While in confronting the problems of the state Lehman received little help from the ultra conservative Lieutenant Governor Bray, who let his office lapse into its ancient desuetude, he had the assistance of a generally able set of department heads. At the outset he kept as many of Roosevelt's staff as possible. Three or four were men of striking personality and marked ability.

That irascible Virginian, Colonel Frederick Stuart Greene, was a graduate of VMI in civil engineering who after an active professional career had made a brave battle record in France. Then, entering the state's service under Al Smith, he remained under Lehman as superintendent of public works. The depression made the position one of unusual responsibility, and his high standards and readiness to fight for them made him the stormy petrel of the administration. His peppery temper bred enemies, but Lehman could say: "He was a great comfort to me." The strong J. A. Broderick was missed when he resigned as superintendent of banking at the end of 1934, but another good man, G. W. Egbert, succeeded him. The health commissioner, Thomas Parran, inherited from Roosevelt, stayed with Lehman until in 1936 he was called to Washington, where he soon achieved national reputation as Surgeon General.

Another inheritance from Roosevelt who became a pillar of strength was the commissioner of insurance, George S. Van Schaick, a Rochester attorney. He was a big, slow-spoken, slow-moving Dutchman of great sagacity, a delightful sense of humor, and downright speech. Some of the insurance companies, while actually sound, were technically in an insolvent condition, but Van Schaick's courage was unshaken; he cheerfully faced the possibility of a penitentiary sentence to keep them going—to the benefit of countless thousands of policy-holders.* Mark Graves, a veteran office-holder—he had been in Albany since Hughes's time—became commissioner of taxation and finance in 1933, another post made onerous by the depression. He was a short, alert man whose keen glance was set off by the pince-nez he always wore on a ribbon. If there was anything about state finance he did not know, his associates never discovered it; and he had worked closely with leading economists on the theory of taxation and budget management. Lehman paid him the highest possible tribute: "His estimates of revenues were almost never wrong."

* At an Albany reception Lehman pronounced "Schaick" to rhyme with shake. "Skoik, Governor, Skoik!" piped up Mrs. Van Schaick, for that was the correct pronunciation. When late in 1933 Max D. Steuer made an attack on Van Schaick, the governor came robustly to his defense. By his work in rehabilitating insurance and mortgage companies, Lehman said, Van Schaick with superb courage and judgment had helped substantially to salvage two billion dollars in the holdings of half a million people. Van Schaick asked for a Moreland Act inquiry, the governor appointed George W. Alger to perform it, and complete vindication followed. See *Knickerbocker Press*, December 13-18, 1933.

Two of Roosevelt's family quickly found larger opportunities in Washington. When Frances Perkins left her post as industrial commissioner to become Secretary of Labor, Lehman felt keenly the loss of her talents and long experience. "Would she were twins!" he exclaimed. A little later Henry Morgenthau, Jr., resigned as conservation commissioner to go into the Department of Agriculture, with the Treasury Department just ahead. Dean Carl E. Ladd of the State College of Agriculture in Cornell University became the governor's principal adviser on farm and dairy perplexities.

Expert advice on special problems could always be furnished by specialists, but sound general advice based on law was harder to find. Who had the necesary common sense, breadth, and book knowledge? He felt happy to obtain as his counsel the congenial, if highly impulsive, Charles Poletti, a former student of Felix Frankfurter's. This exuberant young man, a native of Vermont, a graduate of Harvard *summa cum laude* and the Harvard Law School, had gone into John W. Davis's office in New York. Later he became close to Robert Jackson when that rising attorney from western New York spent much time in Albany assisting Roosevelt with his speeches and messages, and he had also been active in the Roosevelt-Lehman campaign of 1932. When Jackson went to Washington he proposed Poletti for the post of Assistant Attorney General under Homer Cummings, who was quite ready to put him in charge of antitrust cases. But Lehman's first counsel, Sam Rosenman, had resigned to serve on the state supreme court, and Poletti rejected the Washington opportunity.

"To my surprise," Jackson wrote Lehman, "Charlie told me he could not accept. He had been with you, and said your needs were so imperative and your kindness to him so great that leaving you would amount to desertion." [3]

During the summer of 1933, when the milk strike and other emergencies left everybody worn and tired, Lehman invited Poletti to take up quarters in the executive mansion, where he helped brighten that barnlike house. Short, dark, very Italian-looking, full of quips, laughter, and little practical jokes, he was vivacity itself. In June, 1934, he married a bright young Vassar graduate, Jean Ellis.

Many of Lehman's labors in these years were, of course, administrative rather than creative, and tested his judgment, vigilance and efficiency rather than his constructive powers. Yet they presented facets of interest.

In appointments to office he followed several definite policies. He tried never to nominate a man who lacked substantial qualifications. When machine leaders like McCooey, Curry, and the O'Connells of Albany brought him names, he told them he would be glad to hear their recommendations, and preferred to appoint Democrats, but as the party had plenty of good men, he would not take a poor one. "It took me some little time to convince them that I meant what I said, but after the first year or two they grasped it." Ed Flynn and Jim Farley never made an unreasonable request—though he rejected some of their suggestions. They agreed with the bosses that he should choose more Democrats. But his rule was that, while he would gladly name a Democrat to succeed any Republican who died or resigned, all Republicans who had served efficiently to the expiration of their terms should be reappointed. On his first day in office he had a dispute with the O'Connells. A vacancy opened in the presiding justiceship of the appellate court of the upper Hudson division, and the Albany bosses wanted to put in a Democrat; but Lehman promoted the senior judge, a Republican.

In making judicial appointments he consistently submitted names to the bar associations with a request that they advise him of any objection. He never, however, permitted them to dictate appointments, as they would have liked to do. Nor was he so much influenced by prominence, professional distinction, and intellectual training as some other governors. He found that an experienced politician, close to the people and aware of their problems and desires, often did better than a luminary outside politics. Nevertheless, as the *New York Times* remarked late in 1934, he was a better defender of the state civil service system than Roosevelt had been. He vetoed one bill after another intended to breach its walls. "Some of his veto messages might have been written by Dorman B. Eaton or George William Curtis," said the *Times,* "so ringing has been his rebuke of the spoilsmen."

In preparing his detailed annual messages to the legislature, which went through a number of drafts with much laborious rewriting, Lehman needed the help of his best aides. The messages had to be ready on January 15th in the first year of the governorship and January 1st in succeeding years. During the fall he would preside over the initial meeting of a little group comprising Ed Flynn, Sam Rosenman, Charles Poletti, Robert Jackson, and Professor Joseph Chamberlain of Columbia University, as they decided what subjects to cover and what to say on them. Then members of the group pressed forward with the writing while he advised and revised. After the first year or two he called on various commissioners to furnish sections on their specialties—agriculture, penology, highways, and so on. "Be brief—condense!" he would order, but the sections invariably needed drastic pruning.

Compilation of the annual budget also meant protracted labor. Beginning late in October, the governor presided over budget hearings which, though open to public and press, were held primarily to enable heads of departments to justify their estimates for the coming year. The chairmen of the finance committees of the two houses, and leaders of both parties there, were asked to attend. "I wanted to bring them into the decisions as much as possible," said Lehman. During and after the hearings, Robert Murray Haig, the Columbia expert on taxation and finance, lent assistance; and then the budget director and commissioner of finance would whip the budget into final shape. Mark Graves, holding these two posts in succession, proved especially resourceful. In its final shape the budget represented weeks of toil extending into every detail.

This was in conformity with the constitutional requirement that not only every sum expended and every function performed but every position and specific expense be itemized. It would not do to write, "Secretarial costs of the governor's office, $65,000"; the budget had to specify: One secretary, $10,000; two assistant secretaries, $8,000 each; fourteen stenographers, $2,000 each; six attendants, $1,500 each. Every item in supplies, every item in travel costs, had to be entered with similar precision. The state functions being broad in scope, many officers had to be consulted. The state-supported branches of Cornell University, the heads of such institutions as Alfred University, the superintendents of each hospital and warden of each prison, had to appear at *their* public hearings. Altogether, his message and budget kept the governor engrossed from October till mid-January.

Never eloquent, never a gifted phrase-maker, Lehman labored over his speeches much harder than Smith or Roosevelt. He tried to confine his appearances pretty closely to public affairs; in fact, at the beginning of 1935 he announced he would make no speeches whatever except on state business—a rule he promptly broke.[4] Probably he spoke more frequently, and in more localities in the state, than any previous governor in New York's history and also used the radio with more assiduity.

Except on campaign tours, he wrote nearly all his speeches himself; aided, of course, by Joe Canavan and other secretaries and when expert treatment of a special subject was required, by department heads. For the feverish hurry and incessant platform appearance of campaigns the party heads and he would organize a panel of fifteen or twenty volunteer speech writers. He would depute two or three men to draft speeches on farm problems, two or three more speeches on public power, and others to deal with welfare legislation, foreign affairs, and other questions. Then, usually, he would rewrite their work drastically. Sometimes he got a speech worth using entire. More often he would take a section here, a bit there, and weld them together with material of his own. And sometimes he would graze disaster. "Once, up at Watertown," he recalls, "I was getting ready for an important speech next day in Syracuse. When I went over the draft prepared for me I found it was completely useless. Of course, I stayed up all night writing a new speech, which wasn't bad."

Every spring the flood of bills passed just before adjournment presented a frightening challenge. In 1936 he had about 600; in most years a thousand or more. A spate of advice, warning, and entreaty poured in along with them. To approve or veto them within the allotted month meant frenzied toil, especially as he worried over minor bills nearly as much as the major ones. In this work the sagacity of Sam Rosenman was especially valuable.

· II ·

In carrying his programs through the legislature, Lehman often had to face a double opposition: Tammany fitfully and capriciously, the Republican conservatives constantly and immutably. Since a few Tammany leaders were enlightened, and others were responsive to the hope of patronage, the Hall could sometimes be managed. But the hidebound, obdurate, and selfish opposition of the main Republican cohorts upstate, led by "the Black Horse Cavalry," never varied. They were partisans of the narrow Odell-Whitman tradition, holding the social views of the McKinley period with a standpat bigotry worthy of Aldrich and Joe Cannon. They had a fidelity to big corporate interests traceable back to Tom Platt and Chauncey M. Depew. It is true that in education and deportment the upstate Republicans stood on a level distinctly above that of New York City Democrats. Such leaders as Abbot Moffat and Thomas C. Desmond, university trained and broadly cultivated, would have graced any assemblage. They compared well with the metropolitan average. Robert Moses recalls once telling Al Smith: "Why, Governor, you have hardly more than three men in the assembly capable of explaining your more complicated measures!" Too many of the Hudson or Mohawk Valley conservatives, however, would have liked to keep the state just about where it had stood in 1885.

At times, as in the national election years 1936 and 1940, the obstructiveness of the Republicans became infuriating. The legislative majority clung to every point of party advantage. They locked up bills in committee, impeded them with dilatory motions, confused the voters with noisy obfuscations, and chanted "no" every roll call like trained choirboys. "They have the votes and they are simply proceeding on the theory that might makes right," Lehman wrote to Carolin Flexner on April 21, 1940. "I have never known a more distressing situation." Some of the legislative leaders would have delighted the caricaturists Daumier and Cruikshank. For example, one legislator, popping his head out of the Niagara–Hudson Corporation pocket, made Chester A. Arthur seem in some ways a wild radical. Assemblyman Louis Cuvillier, bald, hollow-eyed, and fidgety, spoke interminably on some points, and in speaking, as one reporter tells us, "rested his chin on his chest like a tired raven." [5] Several of the Tammany obstructionists were even more Dickensian. Senator McNaboe, then a very young man, had a vexed look comporting with his frequent outbursts of petulant speech. But appealing to public opinion by platform speeches, radio talks, press statements, and special messages to the legislature, Lehman gradually won ground.

His struggle to bring the powerful public utilities under control had specially dramatic values. Striking at the alliance between the Republican Party and the electric and gas industries, it hit sensitive pocket nerves, and brought the laissez-faire philosophy of the Republican majority into question. Success swayed in the balance until an unexpected piece of fortune decided the struggle.

Al Smith, when governor, had concentrated general attention on the development of the St. Lawrence water power by public instead of private agencies, and he did his work so effectively that he completely blocked a number of power grabs. Roosevelt had turned as governor to the issue of utility rates and regulation, to holding-company abuses, and to rural electrification. Before leaving Albany, he forced a reluctant legislature to appoint an investigating group to prepare information for a new public service commission law. Since the subject was really of national scope, these experts, who included Professor James C. Bonbright of Columbia and Frank P. Walsh, dealt in their report with the situation not in New York alone but throughout the country—in Illinois, in Wisconsin, in California, in the Muscle Shoals area, and in Pennsylvania. Books like William E. Mosher's *The Electric Utilities* meanwhile hammered at prevalent malpractices; so did the liberal weeklies led by the *New Republic* and leaders like Julius Henry Cohen, the shrewd counsel for the Port of New York Authority. The utilities struggled to maintain their position. In New York their forces were aggressively led by the Niagara–Hudson Company and a former Republican state chairman.

By skillful maneuvering, Governor Roosevelt had effected the creation in 1930 of a commission authorized to bring in a plan for state development of St. Lawrence power; and this commission early in 1931 declared emphatically for public development under a Power Authority authorized to negotiate with Washington over rights on the St. Lawrence and with the Niagara–Hudson Company over distribution of power. Roosevelt promptly established the Authority, with Frank P. Walsh as chairman. He meanwhile took steps to have the Public Service Commission review telephone rates. The great central problems of the financial methods of the utility companies, their organization, their rates, their lobbying, and their scope, however, remained undetermined. Various regulatory measures were proposed, but Roosevelt dismissed them contemptuously. He wrote in 1930: "Out of the whole lot there is only one bill with any teeth in it—the bill to control holding companies. The fight has only just begun." [6]

Lehman took up the fight with large additions of his own. Early in 1933 he urged the passage of a series of bills conforming with the recommendations of the Public Service Commission and the Power Authority. They would give the commission jurisdiction over all agreements between operating and holding companies, allow municipalities to appear in commission or court proceedings bearing on utility rates or services, and make the utilities liable for the costs of regulatory investigations.

Most important of all, Lehman proposed that municipalities be empowered to generate, purchase, or sell electrical energy, and to sell in adjacent territory when they offered low rates. More than fifty communities already owned and operated power plants. The Power Authority had just pointed out that Niagara–Hudson occupied a specially advantageous position in bidding for distribution of the enormous amount of energy to be produced on the St. Lawrence, and should be given public competition. The Public Service Commission had also just demonstrated that the public power plant of Jamestown offered what it called an "inspiring and encouraging example" of the potentialities of municipal ownership.

Nothing was accomplished in 1933, however, beyond allowing municipalities to appear in rate and service cases. This was an unpropitious year. The economic storm, the distressing problems of unemployment and relief, and the precarious situation of many banks and other corporations made legislators reluctant to seem to harass business. When counsel for Niagara–Hudson declared that the municipal ownership bill would enable Buffalo to "reach out and snatch Niagara Falls and use it to generate power at lower rates and sell it to other communities at higher rates," even the Democratic senate drew back. The program went over to the 1934 session.

Of course, Lehman then immediately reintroduced it in broader terms than before. With economic recovery under way, the climate of opinion had improved. On the national scene the exposure of the financial extravagances of Samuel Insull and other holding-company magnates had provoked a storm of wrath. Federal legislation for developing public power in the

Tennessee Valley and for the regulation of interstate power distribution was being put on the statue books. Lehman's new program covered not only the objects already noted but some others. It made gas companies and electric transmission companies clearly amenable to state regulation. It authorized the Public Service Commission to establish rates temporarily valid while court-ordered hearings were being held. It required utility companies to let contracts, above a certain figure, on the basis of competitive bidding, and prohibited them from lending money to the holding company above them. They were forbidden to use their funds for lobbying or any other political activity. But as before, the most controversial element in the governor's program was the wide authority given municipalities to build their own plants and distribute power.

Once more the utility companies, led by Niagara–Hudson, rushed to join battle with Lehman. At public hearings before legislative committees, a portentous collection of corporation officers, lawyers, and lobbyists assailed the twelve bills before the state. "They put on a show of opposition," Lehman wrote, "such as had never been seen in Albany." The program, they declared, would ruin—positively destroy—all privately owned utilities, wiping out the savings of widows, orphans, and thrifty men. An NRA code for the utilities industry was being drawn up; that, argued Floyd Carlisle of the Niagara–Hudson, was regulation enough. The Chamber of Commerce of the State of New York argued for the protection of private utility enterprise.[7]

Governor Lehman had to rally all his forces. The Hearst press joined hands with the *New York Times* behind his program, and Governor Pinchot of Pennsylvania, Mayor La Guardia, Norman Thomas, and most leading New Dealers applauded it. Farley used his influence with Manhattan and Brooklyn legislators. Aid came from an unexpected quarter when W. Kingsland Macy, the Republican state chairman, a Harvard-educated Republican who had gained wealth as a broker, and who delighted in fighting Tammany corruption and predatory special interests, telegraphed in January his complete support of the program. He had repeatedly charged Carlisle with an unhealthy control of the Republican organization. But the issue still hung in the balance—for upstate Republicans were firmly entrenched in the legislature—when Lehman had a decisive stroke of luck in the Thayer scandal.

On the national scene the Federal Trade Commission had been conducting a close investigation of the finances, propaganda, and management of the chief holding companies. At the height of the Albany contest it suddenly offered the New York legislature evidence of grave dereliction on the part of one of the most prominent senators, Warren T. Thayer of Rochester. It showed that while chairman of the public service committee of the senate, fighting reform and regulation, he had been a paid servant of one of the largest utilities, the Associated Gas & Electric Company. Lehman at once asked the legislature to investigate the relations between the public utilities and state officers. Macy, backed by Suffolk County and other Long Island areas, seconded the demand, for he wanted an inquiry into the "power lobby."

Though the senate squirmed out of a comprehensive investigation, it could not avoid voting an inquiry (April 4) into Thayer's relations with Associated Gas. This, beginning within a few days, showed that the senator had not only taken at least $21,600 from the company but had given its heads grossly improper assurances. He had promised that one regulatory bill "will never see the light of day," for if it got to the senate "it would be killed in committee." He amended another bill "to make it satisfactory to your people." He was glad to note at the end of the 1927 legislative session that "many detrimental bills . . . we were able to kill in committee." On June 10 Lehman called a special session of the senate. Next day Thayer resigned, but the senate nevertheless unanimously voted him guilty of official misconduct.[8]

All this, sending a wave of indignation across the state, so effectively broke the opposition that Lehman's program went through with a rush. The public was in no mood to accept evasions, and senators who would once have voted an emphatic "no" displayed a sudden sensitivity, refusing to answer the roll call on the ground of a possible conflict of interest. Macy's assistance remained invaluable. The governor signed two bills in one day and then nine in another, April 24th. Though the assembly defeated the remaining bill for competitive letting of utility contracts, he had won an almost complete victory. Members of the Black Horse Cavalry were left exceedingly sore. "We are voting under duress," complained Senator Joseph R. Hanley of Wyoming County. "This is a time of hysteria. I want to voice my resentment against being compelled to vote on these bills at this time."[9]

• III •

Almost equally dramatic, but less fortunate in outcome, was Lehman's struggle in 1935 to effect a fair reapportionment of the state's legislative and congressional membership. The census of 1930 had shown not only a gain of more than 2,200,000 people since 1920 but striking shifts in population. This year, as a result of the party sweep in the fall of 1934, both houses were in the hands of the Democrats for the only time in his gubernatorial service. If lines held firm, he could get a long overdue redistribution of assembly seats that would break the iron grip of the Republicans on that chamber. "If!"—for it would be difficult at best. While Congress could pass measures by a mere majority of any quorum, in each house in New York they had to receive a majority of the entire membership. The Democratic margin in the assembly was just one vote!—and this could easily be canceled by illness, accidental or deliberate nonattendance, or revolt.

Still, the hopes of Lehman and other Democrats ran high. They had an effective organization in Albany under the speaker Irwin Steingut, a keen-minded, liberal young attorney, and the experienced senate leader, J. J. Dunnigan. Ed Flynn and Farley exercised their usual influence. Though Tammany obtained some of the best committe chairmanships, new rules drafted by the leaders and announced by Steingut on January 19 gave the rules committee in the assembly enhanced powers in advancing important bills. Some of the many pending Democratic measures were highly popular; for example, a set of banking reforms drafted by retiring Superintendent Broderick and Henry Bruère, which Lehman took satisfaction in signing in February.

But from the moment Lehman urged reapportionment in his annual message, it was plain that John Curry and Tammany would oppose him. The population of Manhattan had fallen while that of Bronx, Queens, Nassau, and Westchester Counties had sharply risen. A fair reapportionment would reduce Manhattan, the Tammany stronghold, to six members in the senate and sixteen in the assembly. This was serious in itself, but far more serious in that it would jeopardize the long-established domination of the Hall over the Democratic organization in the state. Throughout January and February Tammany blocked any action. It was facing overdue internal changes by which Curry would step out and James J. Dooling take his place, but this shift would not take place until mid-April, and meanwhile Curry ruled. He rallied to his side two Negro assemblymen of Harlem, who declared reapportionment unfair to their race.[10]

The governor felt a glow of hope when the rules committee favorably reported his bill to the assembly on March 14, and Dooling took his stand with Lehman and the upstate and suburban Democrats. But Tammany maintained its blockade. To cloak its obstruction, Senator John L. Buckley and Assemblyman Louis A. Cuvillier brought in a bill calling for a constitutional convention the next year to deal with reapportionment. This simply played into the hands of the Republicans. Lehman was quick to denounce the maneuver, pointing out that a convention would cost a million dollars. He

delivered so hot an attack on the Tammany-Republican alliance that Cuvillier drafted a resolution of censure—which Steingut of course crushed. Then
as the legislature deadlocked on the convention, reapportionment died. A
just representation of the people, not to speak of long-term Democratic
party interests, had been sacrificed to Curry's monumental stupidity. For
as Lehman had foreseen, the Republicans no sooner got a governor of their
party, Thomas E. Dewey, than they carried out their own redistricting with
some truly hideous gerrymandering, to rivet their grip on the legislature.[11]

Few men heard of Curry's retirement with more pleasure than Lehman.
And the contest had a sequel of interest. While it raged, Horace M. Stone,
a Republican assemblyman from Marcellus in Onondaga County, had made
himself particularly offensive to the governor. He was a furious partisan
who, as Lehman put it, fought anything that came within forty miles of being liberal. He kept up a furious bombardment of mudballs—talked of im-
peaching the governor, called him an echo of FDR, and prophesied that if
he ever ran for office again the voters would trounce him. "Let him come
up to my district, and I'll show him who's master here!" This so incensed
Lehman that when next year Stone was renominated, he did invade the
district. Not only did he make speeches analyzing the man's reactionary
record, but he helped organize independent committees to oppose him. The
result was Stone's crushing defeat. Though this was the only time in Lehman's career when he deviated from his path to assail an opponent running
for a minor office, he felt that his course was justified.

Despite the failure of reapportionment, the 1935 session as a whole gave
him profound satisfaction. One of the most turbulent in the annals of the
state, it was also one of the most constructive. Each week had produced a
storm. Speaker Steingut early in April had used state troopers to prevent
members from leaving the assembly while important measures were being
voted on; he had threatened at times to eject noisy members. In the last
tempestuous sitting of nearly twenty-nine hours, riotous scenes attended the
passage of important bills. Yet some of these measures were carried by a
union of former antagonists. George Fearon, able Republican leader in the
senate, sponsored a county home rule amendment to the constitution which
received support from both parties and which Lehman gladly signed. Buckley, the enemy of reapportionment, brought forward another constitutional
amendment permitting counties to choose among several forms of government, which passed with bipartisan support and received Lehman's signa-
ture. The City Club lauded the session as one of the most useful in memory.[12]

The *New York Herald-Tribune*, under headlines "Legislature Ends in
Row After 28½ Hour Tumult," described some of the achievements. De-

spite a margin of only one vote in the house, Lehman had obtained a long list of important enactments, which included:

An unemployment insurance law.

A law raising the compulsory school age from fourteen to sixteen.

A law abolishing certain abuses by physicians in workmen's compensation cases.

A law providing jury trial in all labor injunction cases.

A law placing occupational diseases under the compensation statutes.

A law providing free milk for needy children.

A law ending suits for breach of promise and alienation of affections.

A law permitting Sunday performances of legitimate stage productions.

A law for giving the State Transit Commission full control over all transit lines in New York City.

A law requiring utility companies to file semiannual statements.

A proposed constitutional amendment increasing the governor's term from two to four years and assemblymen's terms to two years.

Though the *Herald-Tribune* ran an editorial, "Nothing to be Proud Of," this list belied it, and the news columns contained a significant sentence: "Not in years has so much legislation backed by the American Federation of Labor gone through Albany." George Meany, in fact, described the legislation as the most enlightened, humane, and progressive ever enacted in any state. Some of the legislation of 1935 requires more detailed notice, with a look ahead into 1936.

· IV ·

The most controversial and far-reaching of all the governor's programs in these years was that on welfare. Building on what Smith and Roosevelt had done, he went further than they; the principal reason being that the national government was enacting a series of welfare measures which required state cooperation.

He and his party had begun in 1933 with the passage of a minimum wage act for women. Never was a law more desperately needed. In the depths of the depression some industries were paying women and children starvation pittances of a few dollars a week; canneries, for example, 8 to 22 cents an hour. About a fourth of the women workers of Manhattan early in 1933 were getting an average of $8 weekly. Frances Perkins gave a conference arranged in the metropolis by the National Consumers League a heartrending picture of the situation.[13] Lehman in February appealed to the legislature to stop the exploitation of these helpless earners. A bill drawn by Senator Albert Wald creating agencies in the labor department with authority to put a floor under wages nevertheless encountered bitter resistance. Most Republican legislators assailed it, and even one group of women opposed it, on the ground that if their wages were pegged, desperate men would step in to seize their jobs. But with the support of Al Smith, a great array of civic and humanitarian agencies, and liberal people everywhere, the bill passed. Lehman had a telegram from President Roosevelt (April 11, 1933):

> Passage of the New York fair-wage law is a great forward step and I congratulate you and the people of the state on this enactment. I am calling the action taken by New York to the attention of the governors of other industrial states in the hope that they too will cooperate by similar enactments to end the lowering of wages which jeopardizes stability of industry and the welfare of the workers.

Almost simultaneously New York, at the governor's instance, moved to strengthen its workmen's compensation law to save injured employees from the all too real peril of falling into the talons of unscrupulous physicians, "ambulance chasers," and "clinics" which gave them wretched service with padded bills or which showed more interest in saving the employer money than in relieving the poor wage earner. A panel of ten distinguished physicians, appointed by the governor, looked into the matter. The result was an act which, making use of the readiness of medical organizations to police the conduct of their members, guaranteed injured workers real protection. The compensation of victims of occupational diseases was also greatly extended.[14]

Throughout the spring and summer of 1935 Congress, prodded by the Administration, had been debating the Wagner-Doughton social security bill. This took the epochal step of creating a comprehensive system of unemployment insurance and old-age insurance, with financial reserves built up by contributions of both workers and employers. The principle was fairly old in Great Britain and a few other countries, but the United States devised its own special plans. The bill also provided certain maternity and child-care services. Administration was lodged in a Social Security Board, of which Roosevelt appointed John G. Winant the first chairman. Standards of admission to the services and rates of benefits were to be determined by the various states, which would have to pass their own laws. Whether this was a wise arrangement may be doubted, for a standard national arrangement covering the whole Union would probably have been preferable; but it recognized the old American dislike of centralization.

Most states moved with satisfactory speed. They put the old-age insurance program into force at once and within two years made the unem-

Herbert H. Lehman and Shirley Temple at Mirador Hotel,
Palm Springs, California, November, 1936

Photo Mirador Hotel

Christmas Party at the Lehman apartment at 820 Park Avenue, probably 1936

Photo Tommy Weber

James A. Farley, Herbert H. Lehman, Franklin D. Roosevelt, and Fiorello La Guardia in 1936

Herbert H. Lehman being sworn in as Governor, December 31, 1936
Left to right: Peter G. Lehman, Hilda Jane Lehman, Chief Judge Irving Lehman,
Herbert H. Lehman, Mrs. Herbert H. Lehman, and John R. Lehman

Herbert H. Lehman at his first inauguration as Governor, January 2, 1933
Left to right: Franklin D. Roosevelt, Herbert H. Lehman, and Alfred E. Smith

ployment insurance system as well effective throughout the country. "There is no reason why everybody in the United States should not be covered," Roosevelt had said; "from the cradle to the grave they ought to be in a social insurance system." [15]

Already New York had an old-age pension act, passed in 1930, which applied to people of seventy and above, or about one person in seven. It had no unemployment insurance; Wisconsin alone had that. The busy legislative session of 1935 anticipated that, as Lehman told it, Congress would soon pass the comprehensive measure. It therefore, as he recommended, enacted laws authorizing the governor to accept on behalf of the state any Congressional aid for the aged and for dependent children. It also created a machinery for making immediate use of Federal payments for assisting the unemployed.

A commission on unemployment relief which Lehman had appointed with the attorney Allen Wardwell as head was reaching the conclusion that all state welfare agencies, including TERA, should be consolidated; and, in fact, there was general agreement that hand-to-mouth measures for relief should be discontinued in favor of a systematic, permanent plan. On February 14, 1935, Lehman signed a bill making provision for connecting TERA with the existing board of social welfare, and in April he approved an amendment to the labor law establishing an unemployment insurance fund. "The people of New York," he wrote, "should feel proud that it is once again leading the nation in legislation which will increase the economic and moral security of its working people." Indeed, after Wisconsin, New York was again in the van.

This was the basis on which the governor built when he sent the legislature of 1936 a comprehensive measure to meet eight different welfare objectives. In his annual message he outlined the provisions of the Wagner-Doughton Act as Congress and the President had finally completed it the previous August and asked for state participation in the activities it authorized. He also asked the legislature to place unemployment relief on a broad permanent basis, a recommendation which he underlined a few days later in sending it the final report of the Wardwell Commission. His general welfare bill included support of orphans; medical and surgical treatment of crippled youngsters; action to safeguard the health of mothers and children; local child-welfare services in rural areas particularly; enlarged public health activities; and the vocational rehabilitation of disabled persons.

All this would have lifted New York out of the social atmosphere of the days when the submerged third, in country and city, just stayed submerged; out of a callous tolerance of slums, soup lines, raggedness, and child-neglect disgraceful to the age. Lehman knew that many smug prosperous citizens would hold up their hands in horror at the anticipated costs. He was, therefore, at pains to point out that these costs would be slight; that, indeed, state cooperation in the new national scheme would yield benefits very nearly counterbalancing the costs of the whole welfare program. Under the Wagner–Doughton Act, once New York presented a plan of old-age assistance acceptable to the Winant board, the Federal government would repay half of all sums the state and its localities expended for the aged, up to $30 a month for each person. It would similarly reimburse the state for expenditures in other welfare categories.

All in all, wrote the governor, the best obtainable estimates indicated that New York under his program would have to pay in the next fiscal year only $4,000,000 in order to obtain $20,000,000 from the Federal treasury; and for this sum it would gain immeasurable benefits in social well-being. Where could they get the four millions? A twenty-percent increase in the taxes on liquor, he calculated, would yield even more. He ridiculed the objection that such an increase would revive bootlegging, for it would amount to just one cent on every thirty glasses of beer or a nickel on every quart of whisky or gin! And if the state accepted the age of sixty-five suggested in the Wagner-Doughton Act, pensions would begin flowing at once to about 110,000 New York citizens.

At first all went well. Wide distribution of the eight-point bill throughout the state with a request for suggestions helped to gain it public support. When the senate and assembly committee on public welfare and relief held a joint hearing, which many labor officials, social workers, and municipal officeholders attended, the speakers unanimously endorsed the bill. Not even the Colonel Blimps raised an objection. Thereupon the senate passed the measure by unanimous vote, George Fearon and other Republican leaders supporting it with enthusiasm. Nobody cried out over the expense, nobody beat his breast over Federal interference in state affairs, and nobody shouted "New Deal Dictatorship!" [16]

When the bill went to the assembly, however, now with a Republican majority dominated by Irving M. Ives, speaker and chairman of the rules committee, the prospects darkened. Ives, an able graduate of Hamilton College, had left banking to go into the insurance business upstate. He possessed some strong liberal attributes, had sponsored progressive legislation on labor and race problems, and had helped found the valuable Cornell University School of Industrial and Labor Relations. But he and other Republican leaders, including James J. Wadsworth of the famous Genesee Valley family, had views of their own, and brought in alternative legislation. This did not go as far as Lehman's program, for they declared that it was not necessary to go so far. Some of the more partisan Republicans doubtless smarted under the party defeat on the control of utilities; they detested the New Deal, and longed to strike a blow against it; and they hoped for victory in the imminent presidential election. Others, including Ives and Wadsworth, were sincere in believing a moderate approach wiser than the governor's sweeping measure. At any rate, they prepared to freeze Lehman's comprehensive bill in the rules committee.

Lehman sent the assembly a vigorous message on May 4, and in a fiery public address three days later he replied in detail to the objections marshalled by the opposition.[17] Still the measure remained locked up in the rules committee.

Twice supporters tried to force the administration bill out on the assembly floor, and twice they were defeated 74–71, every Democrat voting "aye," and all but three Republicans "no." On May 8, Wadsworth, as Republican spokesman, gave his party's reasons. He declared that the state was already supplying financial assistance in all of the areas covered by the Federal Social Security Program, and that this assistance was sufficiently adequate and flexible to meet the growing social service needs of the state. He furthermore argued that the minimum benefits in the existing state program were higher than those provided in the Federal Act, while the cost of the existing state program was considerably less than that anticipated under Governor Lehman's legislation. Unfortunately for him, in his speech he made some rash statements. "There is no such thing as social security in the world of ours today," he declared. He stigmatized President Roosevelt's legislation for the aged and blind, and for crippled children, as "just another New Deal boondoggle which originated in the minds of the New Deal's most confirmed theorists."

In still another message to the assembly on May 11, Lehman pointed out that his bill had no proper connection with party politics. "With all sincerity," he wrote, "I respectfully urge that New York State join the ranks of the thirty-three states which have already decided to cooperate with the Federal Social Security Act. . . . With all earnestness I again plead for its passage." But on the 13th he had to accept a third defeat for the effort to bring the measure out of committee.[18] Then, on the 14th, the assembly passed Wadsworth's old-age Assistance bill by a unanimous vote. It was fully in line with and integrated with the national program. However, Wadsworth, Ives, and their associates continued to fight the Democratic minority on the remainder of the Social Security Program.

Already the governor had eloquently told the people just who were

being defeated by this obstructive attitude. "First, and in the greatest degree hundreds and thousands of old men and women, mothers, dependent
children, crippled children, will lose. Their welfare is fundamentally affected." Taxpayers would also lose; they would forfeit the $15,000,000 or
$20,000,000 a year that the national government stood ready to pay the
State. The municipalities shouldering heavy relief payments would lose.
"And finally, all the people of the state would be losers. It is unquestionably
in the interest of all the citizens that the social services contemplated . . . .
be rendered to our needy and less privileged members. It is in the interest
of all that such citizens be given assistance, protection, and security. It is
in the interest of all to develop a stronger, healthier, and happier people."
He went out of his way to offer an unnecessary personal indictment of
Wadsworth, which the people of western New York justly resented, for
the Wadsworth family had given the State an able line of public servants.

When Lehman seconded the renomination of Roosevelt at the Philadelphia Convention late in June, he made the most of the opportunity that
Republican obstruction had given him. The performance of the party in
Albany, he said, was a ghastly revelation of its true character. Conservatism had trodden underfoot a vital measure for the protection of the poor
and afflicted in the greatest of the states. Would the voters let such a
policy dominate the government? Roosevelt's program represented the most
beneficent social movement of the era. "Are we to allow it to be . . . .
killed by the forces of merciless reaction?"

· V ·

The sweeping victories of Roosevelt and Lehman in the fall elections
in 1936 gave the governor a secure vantage point from which, delivering
his annual message in January, 1937, he could insist that his program be
made the first order of business. This time a bi-partisan alliance was effected. Lehman agreed to confer with Republican leaders. A broad social
security bill satisfactory to both sides was drafted, and it was adopted by
an overwhelming vote on February 10. Wadsworth voted against the program as a token of opposition to the welfare state philosophy upon which
it was being offered to the people, but his associates accepted it.

In short, whereas in 1936 Lehman and the Republican leadership in the
assembly had been willing to compromise only on the question of old-age
assistance, in 1937 both parties were ready to compromise on the total
Social Security Program. The governor had at first demanded everything
and got nothing. Now, he and his opponents were alike ready, under pres-

sure from the public, for concessions. Both Lehman and Wadsworth must be credited with complete sincerity. But, in a broad view, Lehman's position was correct, and Wadsworth's was proved by time to be untenable. Without Federal assistance, important health and welfare services for women, children, and the blind in New York would have been tragically restricted in their scope and development.

Meanwhile TERA, going out of existence, had concluded a truly monumental public service. For nearly six years it had cared for a huge body of semidestitute men, women, and children in the state, numbering at one time more than 2,200,000 and requiring the expenditure of more than a million dollars a day. The unstinted devotion of its staff was, as Lehman often said, worthy of all praise, and the state owed a special debt to the successive chairmen, Jesse I. Straus, Harry L. Hopkins, Alfred H. Schoelkopf, and Frederick I. Daniels, who had directed the work. Straus had shown an effective crusading determination to make sure that every penny of the relief dollar went promptly to those in need. Hopkins had served so astutely that he was a natural choice for the office of National Relief Administrator. Schoelkopf and Daniels had borne the burden during the difficult period of the organization, operation, and demobilization of the Civil Works Program in New York. The whole cost of relief had been staggering, but the money had been efficiently spent.

Lehman's correspondence shows how widely honest citizens differed upon relief work and welfare legislation. Social workers like Homer Folks were, of course, enthusiastic about the policies of the governor. This veteran head of the State Charities Aid Association felt certain that every step was not only needed but long overdue. He praised Lehman's aggressive plans unreservedly. "You are a master of the machinery and operation of every phase of the state government," he wrote just before Christmas in 1938; "you know every phase of public welfare, public health, and mental hygiene, as a public responsibility; and you have on all occasions demonstrated, not only by your words, but by your official acts, your very deep and genuine interest in the humanitarian work of the state." Yet other good men felt quite differently.

William T. Dewart, president of the *New York Sun*, for example, declined an invitation to one of the governor's official luncheons in 1937 with acrid words. Though he had supported Lehman in four elections, he now felt disillusioned. "As the head of a newspaper I have a duty to be frank. My opinions about budgets and the taxes that are imposed to pay for them have been given in the *Sun*. My advice . . . about the need of economy and the mistake of crippling business with new taxes might as well never have been given. And in the name of 'social justice,' which is the alias under which every new scheme of the trade union bosses parades, business has felt one shackle after another rivet its arms. The state and its agencies have followed the New Deal down the road of socialism and extravagance."

Much the same plaint came from the advertising executive Bruce Barton. He had never made much money, he wrote Lehman in 1937; he tried to live modestly; but now with a substantial income, "I am hard up for the first time in my life." He would have to dismiss his servants, or throw family dependents on relief, or move to Connecticut to escape the income taxes. Why was it that with industry improving, the relief rolls steadily grew larger? He suspected they were full of aliens. "Can you, as a business-man, see any hope for us taxpayers in New York?" This groan from one of the famous trio of Martin, Barton, and Fish was truly heartrending; and Lehman offered to talk with the ragged, ill-fed executive and explain to him just how complicated the matter was.

In sober truth, Lehman thought a great deal about expenditures, debts, and taxes, for he never shared FDR's insouciant attitude toward money. The fact that the state had to be kept clearly solvent and balance its books, or nearly that, every year, gave him deep concern. He had inherited a large deficit from Roosevelt, the consequence primarily of high relief spending at a time when tax receipts dropped by roughly one half. Throughout most of his service in Albany the position of the state treasury was perilous. A great number of expenses, notably those for education, health, debt service, and highways, simply could not be cut. Nor was borrowing easy, for the constitution forbade the selling of bonds to meet a deficit. Whenever the state ended the year in red ink, it had to carry the debit sum forward with some definite provision for wiping it out. Only in emergencies, or for permanent improvements, could the state turn to voters and ask their approval of a bond issue.

In 1938, Mrs. Lehman gave the governor, on his sixtieth birthday, a fine boxer dog. He was worrying, as usual, about monetary matters and spending many half-sleepless nights. It seemed appropriate to call the dog Budget. She had been bred, and in due course two fine puppies arrived. A group of newspapermen called with a solemn request. "As a special favor," they asked the governor, "we ask you to name one of the puppies Surplus, and the other one Deficit. We can watch closely to see which grows the larger." Lehman said yes, adding that he would keep Surplus well fed. Sure enough, Surplus grew the larger.

Chapter IX

MALICE DOMESTIC
AND FOREIGN LEVY

L<small>IKE</small> every other governor in the country in these years, Lehman sometimes had a feeling that his part of the circus was a side show while the
main performance under the big top was holding everybody's attention.
The first New Deal, with its emphasis on relief, recovery, and reform,
gave way to a second New Deal which lent primary attention to a compensated and competitive economy and strict enforcement of old laws
and standards. What went on at the state capitals—and in Albany, Harris-
burg, Columbus, Springfield, and Sacramento a great deal went on—often
seemed of minor import compared with the colorful mélée and wild uproar in Washington. The national Administration did call a tune, in welfare
legislation, business regulation, farm aid, public works, protection of organized labor, and the like to which the states danced. Yet the state governments not only performed countless administrative duties but sometimes
acted on their own initiative—nowhere more than in New York; and occasionally they led the way.

The sense of operating a side show did touch Lehman rather closely,
however, in the election of 1934. Voters from Maryland to Oregon went
to the polls that fall primarily to express their endorsement of Roosevelt's
policies and the change he had wrought. "To us," the head of the Farm
Bureau Federation told FDR, "you are the Andrew Jackson of the Twentieth Century," and labor, professional people, small businessmen, and most
minority groups would have echoed the statement. Yet the New York
side show that fall was peculiarly interesting.

Lehman's renomination and reëlection had seemed to most New Yorkers
a matter of course. He was reluctant to stand for a second term, and late in
the spring decided that he would refuse; he had served the state for six

years, he had achieved many of his objects, and he wanted a change. He notified FDR of the decision with a statement that much as he disliked to take a position in any way contrary to the President's wishes, he felt certain he was right. The pressure, however, proved too much. On August 7 he telegraphed Roosevelt that he would announce his candidacy next day, and got a relieved response: "You have made me very happy. I congratulate the people of our state on your unselfish decision." The short-lived Liberal Party of 1934, with Nathan Straus as chairman, made its first act a tender of unqualified support. Straus wrote: "You are an outstanding liberal Democrat who typifies the ideals to which the Liberal Party is dedicated and for which it was created."

The Republican candidate was Robert Moses, who had served in Al Smith's Democratic administration but with the support of Smith's Liberty League now stood up to be counted a Republican. Though extremely able, this Baron Haussmann of New York did not make a strong opponent, for his arrogant ways had raised up enemies in both parties, and he was politically maladroit. Roosevelt felt an intense dislike for him. Indeed, Roosevelt was much upset when Mayor La Guardia made Moses a member of the Triborough Bridge Authority, controlling a work for which Federal funds were essential.

In a disagreeable campaign, Moses made aggressive attacks on Lehman which lost rather than gained him votes—and this while holding two separate positions by favor of the governor. He attacked FDR. He attacked the patient Jim Farley. He attacked the insurance commissioner, George S. Van Schaick, in a peculiarly unfair way.* He attacked public works while himself helping direct one of the greatest, the triborough span. The President grew so irate that in the following March he wrote a letter to La Guardia, which Harold Ickes helped him make "quite savage," saying just what he thought of Moses. But the outcome of the campaign could easily have been prophesied in advance. In an irresistible flood of ballots people registered their enthusiasm for Roosevelt's work. Lehman, who had his share of public enthusiasm, overwhelmed his opponent by a vote of

---

* Van Schaick later wrote of this attack: "I felt outraged by it because it was a complete distortion of what had actually happened. I had gone to Moses's office at *his invitation* for lunch in the State Building and we had discussed the guaranteed mortgage matters. He was interested because his family had some certificated mortgages, and that conference and luncheon had been perfectly friendly and perfectly fine, but when Moses told the story it became an attack upon me. He told how I had come to his office to beg him to do something, while I had gone there for lunch at his own invitation! One feels outraged over such things." Mr. Van Schaick's Oral History Memoir, Columbia University. Moses's memory had betrayed him. Italics are Van Schaick's.

2,202,000 to 1,394,000. Felix Frankfurter added his voice to the "tumult of hosannas," writing: "No governor ever entered his second term more propitiously, with deeper confidence more unequivocally declared. . . ."[2]

Loss of the election was no misfortune for Moses, whose greatest years, in a variety of non-political posts, lay before him. As Lehman said, he was unmatchable in the planning and administration of parks, parkways, and recreational areas. "My real misfortune," Moses commented later, "was in being nominated!" It would have been a sad day for the state, however, had Lehman's tenure been interrupted.

· I ·

New issues were coming into state as well as national affairs, and one which riveted the horrified gaze of the country was organized crime. Its roots were various: the long tradition of violence in frontier America, the war, prohibition, the immigration of such criminal elements as the Italian Mafia, and the general rootlessness and restlessness of many young men. Perhaps the most prominent source was prohibition, for its repeal sealed off a field of corruption, intimidation, and wholesale lawlessness which had enabled thousands to build large fortunes and turned their energies into new channels. Desperately serious in Detroit and Chicago, organized crime was still more sinister in New York. Governor Lehman had to deal sternly with it.

The St. Valentine's Day massacre in Chicago in 1929 had given people some conception of the increasing ruthlessness of the gangster element. Crime at the beginning of the 1930s was a national industry estimated to cost 12,000 lives a year and to yield its practitioners between twelve and fifteen billions annually. It was in 1932 that Bruno Hauptmann kidnapped and killed Charles A. Lindbergh's infant son. That year found in full career the Dillinger gang of robbers, whose principal members were not hunted down until 1934, when John Dillinger himself was slain by Federal agents in Chicago. The kidnapping of Charles F. Urschel of Oklahoma City attracted wide attention, for the $200,000 ransom extorted was the highest ever paid until that time. Racketeering, which may be defined as the systematic extortion of money by the use of violence and intimidation, had taken a wide hold upon business in various cities and particularly New York. The New York "artichoke king," for example, a Sicilian named Castaldo, made a large fortune from his control of that single vegetable. Homicide was so frequent in some parts of the country that little attention was paid to it.

Lehman's first sharp realization that he would have to deal with crime came early in 1935. On March 3 that year, one Samuel Druckman was murdered late at night in a garage at 225 Moore Street, Brooklyn. He had been employed by his brother-in-law Meyer Luckman, who with Morris Luckman stored the cars used in their trucking business in the building. Though the murder attracted little attention, the police arrested Meyer Luckman, his nephew Harry Luckman, and a business associate. When the district attorney, William F. X. Geoghan, brought them before the grand jury of Kings County, however, this body failed to indict, and the prisoners were discharged—a fact which again escaped public attention. The governor was not sure later that he had heard of the case. But newspapermen who looked into it found it had a suspicious odor of gangster quarreling, police corruption, and grand jury inefficiency.[3]

Little by little, facts began to leak out. During the summer Lehman had a visit from Mayor La Guardia and Police Commissioner Valentine, who told him about the murder, efforts to bribe the police to cover it up, and the grand jury failure; in short, evidence of a grave miscarriage of justice. Autumn brought an election for district attorney in Kings, and Joseph McGoldrick, professor of government in Columbia University, was nominated against Geoghan. In October he took up the case and blew it wide open in the press. Crime in Brooklyn, he charged, was being protected by the police and covered up by the public prosecutor. As the murder became a *cause célèbre*, with Geoghan on the defensive, the governor saw that an investigation would have to be made. He decided, however, with McGoldrick's approval, to postpone it until after the election. When Geoghan was returned with a heavy majority, he took immediate action.

The ensuing developments shocked all New York. Lehman appointed a special grand jury to deal with the case, ordered an extraordinary trial term of the supreme court of Kings County, appointed Supreme Court Justice Erskine C. Rogers, a Republican of Hudson Falls, to preside over it, and named Hiram C. Todd, another Republican, as special prosecutor superseding Geoghan, to present all the evidence to the jury. The upshot was the trial and conviction of Meyer and Morris Luckman, with an accomplice, as murderers, and the presentation by the grand jury of formal charges against Geoghan which necessitated his arraignment before the governor.* Amid a press of other duties, Lehman had to listen to a long,

* Lehman issued his order for the special term of the supreme court December 10, 1935, and Todd was sworn in December 11. The Luckmans got sentences of twenty years to life. The governor's examination of Geoghan, who was represented by the noted attorney Lloyd Stryker, lasted from August 26 to September 14.

dull recital of testimony and arguments in late August and early September, 1936. Having fully weighed the evidence, he decided, with the concurrence of his principal legal advisers, including Dean Charles Burdick of the Cornell University Law School, that it did not justify Geoghan's removal. The man had been inefficient, had associated with raffish people, and had not maintained the dignity of his office, but that was all. The fact that the governor's powers of removal are so sweeping, and that he need not assign any reason for removing a mayor or other official, makes restraint in action a duty.

But in the course of the various proceedings New York learned facts that outraged decent citizens. It learned that the Luckman circle were gangsters who, by violence, political connections, and a corps of "fixers," had gained almost a monopoly of flour-trucking to Jewish bakeries. It learned that large bribes had been offered policemen and that a system for the corruption of justice flourished. It learned that suspects had been severely beaten in a police station, possibly to extort confessions, but more probably to impede justice. It learned of an alleged alliance beteen crime and the Democratic machine in Brooklyn. And meanwhile the whole subject had been opened in a larger way, for the Luckman case proved only a curtain raiser to the real drama.

• II •

The scene quickly shifted to Manhattan. In May, 1935, reports thickened concerning the prevalence of racketeering and gangsterism in New York County and the suspicious inability of the police and public prosecutors to cope with it. The district attorney was William Copeland Dodge, a man of breeding and education, but singularly lacking in energy. Suddenly the grand jury rebelled against his dilatory tactics, its foreman, Lee Thompson Smith, startling the city by a dramatic announcement: "We have labored under the most difficult handicaps. Every conceivable obstacle has been put in our path." Instead of taking prompt steps to satisfy the jury and public sentiment, Dodge continued to postpone action and make evasive statements. If the grand jury had any substantial evidence of wrongdoing, he said, he and his aides were at their disposal. This was absurd, for most jurors were morally certain that businessmen by hundreds were being bled by racketeers, that tens of thousands of poor people were being robbed by the cruel lottery called the numbers game, and that gangsters of the Waxey Gordon type (Waxey, whose true name was Irving Wexler, had recently been sent to the penitentiary) infested the city. But they had no means of tracking down criminals; it was Dodge's duty to put in hard shrewd work amassing evidence. As May passed, the angry exchanges between the jurymen and the public prosecutor seized general attention. The jury asked Dodge to call in a competent aide and suggested six names; Dodge, rejecting them, named a man whom the jury in turn rejected! Prominent citizens thereupon requested the governor to name a special prosecutor.

It was difficult for Lehman to intervene until formal application was made to him, with a valid assignment of reasons. A majority of jurors finally went into executive session, voted a statement complaining of crime and corruption, and accused Dodge of failure to perform his duty. This paper they laid before Judge Koenig, brother of the well-known Republican leader in Manhattan. The judge, making it clear he would not take sides between jury and prosecutor, refused to file the paper as a public document, for it brought in no indictment and could not even be termed a presentment, as it made no definite certification of charges. Indeed, the grand jury—a "runaway" jury, for its term had expired—was not even unanimous. Nevertheless, on June 10 the document reached Lehman.

By this time the press was full of the subject, the Citizens Union and City Affairs Committee were anxious for a real inquiry, and the Bar Association, which kept a close watch on grand juries, courts, and public prosecutors, was intently following developments. A massive public opinion was being created in support of a thorough investigation.

To some spectators Lehman seemed slow to move. Actually, he no sooner read the grand jury statement than he saw that an inquiry was indispensable. It might demonstrate that few real abuses existed, or it might uncover important evidence and make many criminal prosecutions feasible, but in any event, it must be held. He discussed various aspects of the situation with La Guardia, Dodge, Police Commissioner Valentine, and the state attorney general. "My survey, study and consideration," he wrote Dodge on June 24, "have led me to the definite conclusion that a concerted and vigorous drive should be made to curb and stamp out the various types of organized crime and vice existing within the county of New York." He might direct the attorney general to supersede Dodge, specifying the criminal activities to which the attorney general should devote himself. Alternatively, he could appoint a special prosecutor as assistant to Dodge, making his powers as broad as the situation demanded. The second course, which would leave Dodge and his staff responsible for routine law enforcement, was clearly preferable.

On the 24th he sent Dodge a request which was really an ultimatum:

he must appoint as special prosecutor one of four men, all eminent Republicans: Charles E. Hughes, Jr., George Z. Medalie, Thomas D. Thacher, and Charles H. Tuttle. The governor planned to convene a special trial term of the supreme court of New York county, with Justice Philip J. McCook, another prominent Republican, presiding. Clearly, he wanted no taint of partisanship about the proceeding. Omission of the name of Thomas E. Dewey, the brilliant young Chief Assistant United States Attorney, from the list of possible prosecutors, was a surprise upon which the press commented, for since taking office in 1931 at the age of twenty-eight, Dewey had made a spectacular record.

At once, unfortunately, the governor ran into difficulties. All four of the men he proposed to Dodge informed the newspapers that they could not accept. Lehman telegraphed a special appeal and arranged a conference with them at his New York apartment, but they remained immovable. "I felt," he records, "and my conviction was strengthened later, that these men had met, discussed the matter, and decided in unison to refuse the appointment and seek to force the appointment of Dewey." In refusing, they all urged the selection of Dewey, whom at that time the governor had never met. He had considered placing his name on the original list sent to Dodge but had decided he was too youthful and inexperienced. Now, after talking with the four distinguished attorneys, he felt that he had perhaps underestimated Dewey; for they assured him that the young man was extraordinarily able, had complete integrity, and would conduct a highly efficient investigation untainted by political considerations.

"Under these circumstances," declared Lehman in a press statement, "I am . . . recommending to District Attorney Dodge that he appoint as special prosecutor Mr. Thomas E. Dewey. . . . I am advised by those who know him best that he is well qualified by experience and ability to conduct a vigorous and independent investigation into racketeering, vice, and organized crime within the County of New York."

It should be emphasized that at no time did Lehman feel that Dodge was corrupt and that no accusations of dishonesty were ever leveled against him. The trouble was that he lacked vigor, had chosen a commonplace staff, and left the office largely to his assistants. It should also be noted that Tammany brought no pressure upon the governor to soft-pedal the inquiry. This was not because of any spasm of virtue in the Hall, which was unhappy over the independent probe, but because the politicians knew that any effort to swerve him from the path of duty would be futile. Early in June, Lehman and Dewey, in a long afternoon talk in Albany, agreed upon what the governor now called "a concerted drive against racketeering and organized crime"—for both men saw the work as a drive rather than an investigation. The costs would fall primarily upon New York City. The governor supported Dewey in asking for a large appropriation, $250,000, and although the Board of Estimate pared this, the funds remained ample. "He never came to me and said, 'I'm handicapped for lack of money,'" Lehman later recalled.

Convening an extraordinary term of the Supreme Court under Judge McCook, the governor directed him to empanel a special grand jury. He watched with approval as Dewey assembled a highly efficient corps of assistants and investigators and set to work on the fourteenth floor of the Woolworth Building, interviewing thousands of men for evidence. Police Commissioner Valentine made a swift census of all the known criminals in the town. In a radio speech at the end of July, 1935, Dewey told the city that he would not follow the hackneyed reform line of suppressing ordinary prostitution, lotteries, and gambling. He would aim at the racketeers who formed "trade associations" or similar gangster groups and extorted money from businessmen by breaking their windows, crippling their trucks, and ruining their goods with acid or stink bombs:

> There is today scarcely a business in New York which does not somehow pay its tribute to the underworld—a tribute levied by force and collected by fear. There is certainly not a family in New York which does not pay its share of tribute to the underworld every day it lives and with every meal it eats. . . . Every barrel of flour consumed in New York City pays its toll to racketeers, which goes right into the price of every loaf of bread. Every chicken shipped into the City of New York pays its tribute to the poultry racket, out of the pockets of the public. There are few vegetable or fish markets in the City of New York whose restaurants are not forced by sluggings, destruction of goods, threats, and stink bombs to pay heavy toll.[*]

Lehman appealed to all victimized people to come forward with assistance. "Those of us who have been racket-ridden or victims of exploitation, those of us who have knowledge of such conditions, must give their information. . . ." Yet with impressive unanimity, these frightened victims refused to break cover; they knew too well what retaliation might fall upon their heads. It was necessary for Dewey to issue subpoenas, and he soon had the corridors of the Woolworth Building crowded with hundreds of potential witnesses waiting to talk with his assistants. They included numerous labor union men. One union had been so terrorized that when its president was murdered in the presence of twenty-two witnesses, all twenty-

[*] Rupert Hughes, *Attorney for the People: The Story of T. E. Dewey* (Boston, 1940), pp. 65, 66.

two swore under examination that they had not seen the assassin and could not identify him.

Dewey's "rackets investigation," as it was popularly called, pressed with tremendous force and skill, proved a dazzling success. It included a drive against usurers and loan sharks, who were hauled into court in the fall of 1935 by the dozen. It covered the horrible little organization which shifted approximately two thousand prostitutes among several hundred houses in the city, collecting most of their nightly earnings. It peered into the garment industry, controlled by two men whom Dewey described as the principal industrial racketeers in the country: "Gurrah" (Jacob Shapiro), "a short, beetle-browed, bull-necked thug," and "Lepke" (Louis Buchalter), a well-dressed businessman living in an expensive apartment overlooking Central Park. Dewey tracked down the thugs, including Dutch Schultz, who extorted money from the city's restaurant keepers and the waiters' union; he arraigned in court the rascals who dominated the poultry industry, sending three large-scale robbers named Herbert, Diamondstone, and Frankel to the penitentiary; and he went to the bottom of the gangster shakedown of trucking unions.

All in all, Dewey richly earned the gold medal which the Hundred Year Association gave him in 1937 as the principal contributor of the year to the welfare of the city. He earned the popular applause represented by Rollin Kirby's cartoon in the *World-Telegram* after his attack upon the restaurants racket, showing him tendering a prison warden a big rat trap crammed with lawbreakers. He demonstrated the truth of his own assertion: "The law is bigger than money—but only if the law works hard enough."

For his success Lehman was as grateful as any other New Yorker. The governor fully appreciated Dewey's unsleeping energy and aggressiveness in attack, which struck fear to all malefactors. As Lehman scrutinized the methods by which Dewey sometimes attained his goals, however, he shared with other onlookers certain reservations. Though Dewey protested that he would entertain no political considerations or ambitions whatever in his work, this seemed increasingly dubious, for he gave Tammany men unrelenting attention. Moreover, stories became current in legal circles and among newspapermen that disturbed the governor: stories of witnesses obtained under promises of immunity, or of liberal expense allowances offered some men who cooperated with the investigation, and of other men prosecuted implacably although their guilt seemed debatable. While these stories were possibly mere rumors, they made Lehman apprehensive about the conformity of the drive to the old Anglo-American rule that it is better to let ten guilty men escape than to punish one innocent man. That Dewey and his aides had a flamboyant way of making their achievements known there could be no doubt whatever.

On one issue Lehman and Dewey came to an open breach. This was the question whether a convicted prisoner, serving a long term, should be enticed into giving evidence against an accused person by the prospect of a mitigation of his sentence. Lehman was rigidly insistent that no promise of pardon, commutation, or other form of leniency should ever be made a convict in order to obtain testimony against another man. "Just think of it," he often said. "When a man is in prison for life, or thirty years, he is under tremendous temptation to find any way out. When he gets on the witness stand, and sees that the prosecuting attorney is determined on convicting a prisoner, he is under strong temptation to deviate from the truth. And if the attorney didn't want a conviction, he would not call the prisoner to the stand." Use of such testimony was sometimes grossly unfair.

"I've always been afraid of that practice," said Lehman years later. "I'm afraid of it now. I know there have been many cases in which prisoners serving long sentences were given the impression, if not the definite promise, that if they would testify against the accused, liberal treatment would be obtained for them from the governor. In every such case, whenever it was put up to me to compensate a man for his testimony, and I gathered that such an indication had been given him, I refused to exercise clemency." He took pains, however, to support Dewey's proper work. When the exhausted special grand jury resigned June 30, 1936, he at once ordered two new juries of the same character empaneled for Dewey, continuing Judge McCook in office for one and appointing Supreme Court Justice Ferdinand Pecora for the other.

· III ·

Additional legislation to cope with crime was a glaring necessity. Dewey pressed one important law, later known by his name, which was a state adaptation of familiar Federal practice. As he said, crime had become so well organized and syndicated that a type of master malefactor had emerged who, like Lucky Luciano, left to his employees and assistants the scores of actual offenses which he ordered. For coordinating these crimes he could not be punished; each separate wrongdoer had to be tried separately by a separate court and jury. Under the so-called Dewey Act, related or like offenses could be joined in a single indictment and punished with an appropriate sentence. Major John A. Warner of the state police also spon-

"Yanked Out!"
As Rollin Kirby recorded the Druckman Case in the *New York World-Telegram* for December 7, 1935

Photo Allen Colbert Associates. Reprinted by permission of *New York World-Telegram and Sun*. [Copyright 1935, New York World-Telegram Corp.]

"Destroy that Handclasp!"
As Rollin Kirby recorded Governor Lehman's Crime Message in the *New York World-Telegram* of January 9, 1936

Photo Allen Colbert Associates. Reprinted by permission of *New York World-Telegram and Sun*. [Copyright 1936, New York World-Telegram Corp.]

sored a bill which the legislature passed in 1935, and which Lehman signed, creating a bureau of criminal investigation (promptly dubbed the "State Scotland Yard") in his organization.

This year 1935, with Dewey's drive moving inexorably forward, saw public concern over crime mounting higher than ever. It was the year not only of the conviction of Hauptmann for murdering the Lindbergh child but of the kidnapping of George Weyerhauser in Tacoma. An uproar over an alleged "crime wave" led Commissioner Valentine to order the police of New York City to redouble their efforts to control the criminal element. District Attorney Dodge, who had continued such a limp performance of his duties that public resentment became uncontrollable, was compelled to appoint an earnest attorney, Samuel Marcus, as assistant; but he promptly quarreled with him and amid charges and countercharges revoked the appointment. Gunmen repeatedly exchanged shots in the New York streets with each other and the police; murders and assaults took place in apartment hallways; and though Dewey and Valentine forced many gangsters to flee to Miami, the metropolis seemed acquiring a reputation nearly as bad as Chicago's. "Dutch Schultz" (Arthur Flegenheimer) was in the news most of the year. Indicted and twice tried for income tax evasion, he was acquitted by a jury that the judge angrily castigated. Then in October, while transacting business in a Newark saloon, he was cornered by gunmen who killed two of his aides and left him mortally wounded.

That autumn, just as another notorious gangster named Amberg and a partner were shot down by rival Brooklyn racketeers, Lehman convened in Albany a four-day conference of specialists on crime. With a cohort of reporters attending, some 900 delegates registered. Between the daily debates of five round tables, various prominent men delivered set speeches. Dewey lucidly expounded the racketeering evil, emphasizing the reluctance of the ordinary businessman to give information, and concluding: "It is obviously a prosecutor's job to make him talk. No policeman can possibly do it." Federal Judge John C. Knox advocated a freer discretion for state judges in commenting, after the English pattern, on the value of evidence and credibility of witnesses. Police Commissioner Valentine read a paper attacking the state parole system, a paper which, said Chairman Moore of the parole board, was all wrong—"for concentrated misinformation his address transcends anything I have listened to for some time." Joe Canavan, who had left the governor's employ to join the parole service, defended it in detail. Lehman himself made one suggestion showing impulsive bad judgment, a proposal for universal fingerprinting as a weapon against crime, which met with such a chorus of dissent that he quickly dropped it.[4]

At the end the judges, penologists, police chiefs, social workers, and psychologists heard the governor announce that his administration would formulate a broad program of action based on the million-word transcript of papers and discussions. He would name a committee to study the hundreds of suggestions made and sift from them a constructive program. In this committee work Poletti was active. The atmosphere was by no means wholly favorable. A strong tincture of hysteria had crept into the talk of "crime waves," the demand for keeping fourth-time offenders in prison for life, and general denunciation of softness with malefactors. But despite the fact that hysteria waves were more real than crime waves, something had to be done.

Lehman, his attorney general, and other advisers set to work upon a sweeping program of criminal enactments to which expert outsiders contributed. They brought before the session of 1936 the most comprehensive law enforcement legislation ever presented to any legislature. When it encountered heavy opposition from conservatives, the governor embarked on a state-wide educational effort: making public statements, writing argumentative messages, and using radio speeches. In the end, he carried a very mixed body of measures, some large, some small. Their effect in making crime a more perilous occupation was to be felt for decades.

One new law was the so-called Dewey Act, generally agreed to be sound. Other unexceptionable acts created a felony court in New York City and increased the state police by a hundred troopers. Local authorities were required to broadcast over the state news of any felony, if no arrest was made, within five hours of its commission. Prison wardens before releasing a convict had to give two days' notice to the community in which he had been arrested and the one in which he intended to live. The courts were empowered to inflict heavier punishments for crimes committed by armed offenders than those done by unarmed men, and it was made a felony to carry a concealed weapon without a license. Contradictory testimony in court was made presumptive evidence of perjury. Improved extradition laws, applicable both to criminals and to witnesses who had fled to other states, were passed. One new law provided more effective protection against abuses of bail bond. At the same time, the system of parole was broadened and liberalized. Altogether, a fairly long roster of commendable bills went through.[5]

It must nevertheless be said that Lehman lent his influence to a few proposals that were dubious or worse. A bill sponsored by Herbert Brownell, Jr., a New York lawyer who later became Attorney General under Eisenhower, called the Brownell Public Enemy Bill, aroused much protest. It forbade known criminals, under heavy penalty, to consort together, and a still abler attorney, Walter H. Pollak, assailed it as tyrannical—"it permits a prima facie case of guilt to be made out by showing that a person has a bad reputation." A bill introduced by John J. McNaboe requiring former convicts to report daily to the police came in for similar attack. "If that's American," ejaculated one legislator, "then I'm a Russian." Assemblyman John A. Byrnes of New York City declared that to pass some of the bills would be to throw the Bill of Rights out of the window, and Assemblyman Horace M. Stone of Onondaga supported him. "If anyone thinks you can wipe out the crime wave by taking the fundamental rights away from innocent people, he is all wrong." Organized labor vehemently opposed several restrictive bills.

As the session ended, Lehman congratulated the state on the enactment of thirty-nine laws strengthening the administration of justice but deplored the failure of half a dozen more. At least two of them, one establishing county police forces and one empowering a judge to comment on the failure of a defendant to take the stand and testify at his own trial, were no loss.[6]

· IV ·

Early in 1936, Lehman decided that in order to give more time to his family and business he would not run again. He told Roosevelt of his decision on a visit to the White House in February and confirmed the statement by a letter of March 17th. This greatly disturbed the President, who was worried about his chances of reëlection, and feared that Lehman's withdrawal might make New York a doubtful state. He asked Henry Morgenthau to bring pressure to bear from every possible source, writing: "He simply cannot be permitted to withdraw. You and I know what a mess would be caused by trying to find a successor, quite apart from the fact that the state and citizens need him as governor." When Lehman made a public announcement on May 20 that he thought eight years of service in Albany had earned him a respite from the cares and responsibilties of office, he received a flood of protest.

The fact was that nobody else was visible in either party who seemed capable of taking his place. It was also a fact that angry dissenters from the New Deal had arisen in such vocal numbers that Roosevelt could well be anxious to strengthen his lines in New York.

Some dissenters, like Lewis Douglas, Newton D. Baker, Albert Ritchie, Dean Acheson, and William Randolph Hearst, lived outside New York; some, like John W. Davis, were half New Yorkers; and some, like Al Smith, had considerable influence in the state. James P. Warburg published two pamphlets arraigning Roosevelt as more Socialist than Democrat, *Hell Bent for Election* and *Still Hell Bent*. Al Smith, his old-time associates Raskob and Jouett Shouse, and Herbert Hoover were the backbone of the American Liberty League, which, formed in 1934, had many wealthy patrons as it vehemently denounced the New Deal policies as next door to Karl Marx. Most of the press, including the *Times*, was against Roosevelt. The threat to the Administration and party for a time seemed portentous. A union of Liberty League forces and Republicans might make New York doubtful; it must be held at all costs.

Less than a fortnight after the Republicans nominated Alfred M. Landon for President, the Democratic convention met on June 19 in Philadelphia. Its enthusiasm was unmistakable, and so was its general dullness, for the nominations were certainties. Only two or three bright spots illuminated the dreary Sahara of the proceeding. One was Alben Barkley's colorful keynote address. One, the greatest of all, was the tremendous ovation for Roosevelt when he accepted his renomination in the "rendezvous with destiny" speech. And one was the spectacular half-hour demonstration for Lehman when he seconded Roosevelt's nomination; the delegates cheering and parading in a tribute that was mainly prearranged by Farley and others to influence the governor to run again, but was half-spontaneous. Though Lehman knew that it had been contrived, he found it heart-warming nevertheless. Amid the hurly-burly the New York delegation voted unanimously that he should head the state ticket.

Immediately afterward, on June 29, Roosevelt wrote from Hyde Park a persuasive letter. He spoke of "all the grand things you have done in these four years," adding: "And the more I look at it from every angle the more I'm convinced of the very great importance of your running—important to the social security of the whole nation in all that implies." [7] Next day Lehman announced that he would accept a nomination.

That autumn the governor could look back on a campaign which had moved so heavily in his favor that the election eve betting odds were five and a half to one. The Republicans had nominated William F. Bleakley, a judge of the supreme court, and a man of integrity and ability, who made economy and fiscal policy the central issues. He endorsed social security. The American Labor Party, the People's Party (right-wing Socialists), and the State Federation of Labor all supported the governor; and though Al Smith strongly attacked FDR, he refused to speak for Bleakley out of his old friendship for Lehman. Tammany Hall at first took a sullen attitude, but in midsummer J. J. Dooling, its head, fell ill, and was replaced for the time being by a triumvirate comprising Farley, Ed Flynn, and Frank V. Kelly, the Brooklyn leader, who threw their full weight behind both Roosevelt and Lehman. The governor spoke vigorously all over the state. He was delighted when he arrived in one town to meet a gala reception with a band lustily performing, "Onward, Christian Soldiers"!

Twice Roosevelt came to New York to speak. On one occasion Lehman met him at the Battery, and they drove through Brooklyn, Queens, the Bronx, and down Fifth Avenue. "I have never seen such warmth of demonstration and applause as he met that day," Lehman recalls. Even on Park Avenue he was cheered until he reached the Racquet and Tennis Club, where not a soul was to be seen—the place was a tomb. But in the dining room, where the help gathered, all the servants were hanging out of the windows, "yelling their heads off." On election day the Democratic nominees won by a heavy New York margin; Roosevelt by 3,293,000 against Landon's 2,181,-000 and Lehman by 2,970,500 against Bleakley's 2,450,000.

The American Liberty League had proved to be just what Farley termed it, a drum with a noisy tympanum covering but a total void. As for New York affairs, even a good Westchester judge made a feeble impression on voters familiar with Lehman's energetic accomplishments in constructive reform. Roosevelt had written him that the tribute of the Philadelphia delegates "shows what the other states think of your fine and successful leadership." This is doubtful, though he had certainly achieved national esteem; but since his victories in dealing with the public utilities, his success in carrying fair wage laws, unemployment insurance, old-age pensions, and legislation for the crippled and helpless, his broad program for dealing with crime, and his improvement of the state hospitals, no citizen of New York could be ignorant of what his leadership meant.*

• V •

Roosevelt's second inaugural struck a challenging note which Lehman applauded. "I see millions denied education, recreation, and the opportunity

---

* To this campaign belongs another of the many Hymie Shorenstein stories. One of Hymie's supporters, whom we may call Irving Cohen, was nominated for city magistrate. He became worried about his prospects, and several weeks before election day came to Hymie, complaining: "I don't see any advertisements in the Brooklyn *Eagle* saying, 'Vote for Irving Cohen.' I don't see any billboard posters saying, 'Vote for Irving Cohen.' You aren't doing anything for me, Hymie. I'm sure to be beaten!" To which Shorenstein replied: "Irving, you don't need to worry. Roosevelt is running. Lehman is running. You ever seen them big ferryboats come into the slip? Yes? Then you should know when it comes in, all the garbage comes in with it?"

to better their lot and the lot of their children," said the President. ". . . I see one-third of a nation ill-housed, ill-clad, ill-nourished." The governor sympathized with FDR in his resentment of the Supreme Court annulment of important Administration measures. Down to January, 1937, it had invalidated the AAA, the NRA, and all but two others out of eleven major enactments, the TVA and gold devaluation alone escaping. The age of the chief obstructionist justices—Van Devanter 77, McReynolds 75, Sutherland 74, Butler 70—raised the question whether convictions formed in one era could properly be applied in another. A struggle for power had to be resolved. Nevertheless, Lehman was startled when on February 5, as he struggled with the 1937 legislature, headlines announced FDR's famous proposal for reorganizing the judiciary.

Startled and offended; like countless other Democrats, he thought the plan highly objectionable. Irving Lehman refrained from discussing the subject with him, so that he made up his mind alone. He delayed writing the President because he expected opportunity for a talk in an imminent visit to the White House. But on February 26, when the visit had become impossible, he sent FDR a letter, saying in part:

> I share your disappointment that many important measures have been declared unconstitutional by a narrow and unconvincing vote of the Supreme Court. Unfortunately, however, I feel that the end which you desire to attain does not justify the means which you recommend. I do not believe that your plan will permanently correct the situation with which you have been confronted since a mere enlargement of the Court will not remove the possibility of narrow decisions in the future. I feel, too, that nothing should be done which is merely an attempt to meet an immediate situation at the expense of orderly and deliberate processes of government. From a governmental standpoint, whatever gain might be achieved through liberalizing the decisions of the Court would be far more than balanced by the loss of confidence which would result from the enactment of your proposals.

When asked later what he thought Roosevelt should have done, Lehman had a crisp reply. "I didn't want him to do anything. I wanted him to wait. I believed that in all probability vacancies were coming along which he could fill." After all, the fact that six judges were past seventy favored an early change. The governor's letter remained private; but while the President did not say so, he resented it. His Supreme Court Bill was giving covert Democratic antagonists of the New Deal an opportunity to come into the open against the Administration, and though he could blame only himself, he was irked when staunch friends took their stand beside his foes.

In the legislative session of 1937, facing the familiar spectacle of a Republican assembly and Democratic senate, Lehman had two special preoccupations. Early in January he urged the houses to pass a minimum wage law; and for the fifth successive year he asked them to ratify the child labor amendment to the Federal Constitution, which had been before the country since 1924 and had been accepted by twenty-four other states. In the tightening economic situation, children were again returning to the factories at pitiful wages. Political observers expected him to succeed in both enterprises. The assembly, however, showed its usual stubbornness. It was not until April 27 that he was able—using ten pens—to sign the Fischel-Steingut minimum wage act; and meanwhile, ratification of the child labor amendment had been blocked. With Nicholas Murray Butler, who on principle opposed the amendment, Lehman had an interesting exchange of letters. He also encountered opposition from shortsighted Catholic leaders who thought the amendment might limit parental rights. Early in March ratification, to his chagrin, failed, and his administration had to content itself with a state law, the Moffat Act, signed June 2.[8]

Meanwhile the Supreme Court Bill had been tossing in stormy waters. Republican opponents were joined by redoubtable Democratic senators: Tom Connally of Texas, Joseph O'Mahoney of Wyoming, Bennett Clark of Missouri, Carter Glass of Virginia, and Royal S. Copeland of New York. Two fighting progressives, Burton K. Wheeler and Hiram Johnson, took their stand against the bill. So, to Roosevelt's consternation, did George Norris, though he finally changed front. Ed Flynn was against it. Republican leaders, anxious not to convert the struggle into a party contest, stood silently watching the internecine Democratic war.

Chief Justice Hughes, at a well-timed moment, published a letter proving that the court had efficiently dispatched its work and arguing that enlargement would impair its efficiency—though if necessary, he declared, he would "preside over a convention." The court's decision of April 12 sustaining the Wagner Act weakened the argument for the bill, as did Justice Van Devanter's resignation the following month. When the Senate Judiciary Committee on May 18 voted ten to eight against the measure, with six Democrats opposing it, Roosevelt turned to a compromise plan.

A drastically altered measure, the Logan-Ashurst-Hatch bill, was introduced as July opened. Providing for the appointment of new justices at the rate of one yearly for each member passing seventy-five who failed to retire, it seemed to have a strong chance of success. Senator Joseph T. Robinson of Arkansas, whose lovable personality commanded the loyalty of many colleagues, toiled so indefatigably in the Washington heat for the President's cause that on July 14 he fell dead. The bill really died with him. On July 20 Vice-President Garner, after his own poll of Senatorial votes on the funeral train, bluntly told Roosevelt: "You are beat." [9] But the public did not know this, talk of a spirited resumption of the fight filled the press, and the outcome seemed doubtful. Lehman, intensely stirred by the battle, believed that as the governor of the greatest state he ought to raise his voice. Every other leader had spoken out. He had written Senator Wagner strongly urging him to vote against the bill but had withheld the plea. "Now, I thought that we were getting to the critical point, and unless I released the letter it would be useless for me to do anything." [10]

This letter, published on front pages July 20, just when everything on Capitol Hill seemed "at sixes and sevens," as Ickes put it, caused a commotion.* "I believe," Lehman wrote, "that the orderly and deliberate processes of government should not be sacrificed merely to meet an immediate situation." He went on to argue that from the standpoint of public interest, whatever immediate gain might be achieved by the proposed change would "be far more than offset by a loss of confidence in the independence of the courts and in governmental procedure." Some of Roosevelt's supporters were taken aback. Two of Lehman's old friends, Samuel Untermyer and David Dubinsky, sharply criticized the letter, and Governor George H. Earle of Pennsylvania and others denounced it. While Administration circles termed the intervention "gratuitous," Wagner contented himself with a noncommittal reply.

That the President was highly irritated there can be no question. Talking with Farley, he not only made a wry face but threw out some resentful remarks—Mrs. Lehman liked being first lady in Albany, and the governor was not working as hard as formerly. This coolness on Roosevelt's part lasted for some months. But the general reception was decidedly favorable. The press almost unanimously commended the letter, the *New York Herald-*

---

* Irving Lehman wrote him July 24 about the "excitement." Boston and New York sentiment alike had been highly favorable. "As I telegraphed to you I liked the tone of the letter very much. The end of the fight followed so quickly upon its publication that it seems to me impossible to estimate how great its influence was in bringing about the result. Personally I have little doubt that it had very considerable influence in at least hardening and perhaps in effecting the sudden collapse. . . . No one had a right to stand aside in what I regard as a very great crisis, if he could help materially in averting it. The way both sides received your letter shows clearly, I think, that its influence was great. I spoke to Benjamin N. Cardozo over the phone. He was greatly pleased—that is putting it very mildly." Lehman Papers.

Actually, that it had any influence on the decision is highly doubtful. It was too belated; the fate of the bill was already sealed, as Garner told FDR, when it appeared.

Tribune and *Washington Post* publishing strong editorials. Nicholas Murray Butler was delighted. When Anna Rosenberg lunched with the *New York Times* editors, Arthur Sulzberger was extravagant in his praise, and she reported that she had "never heard such enthusiasm from that group about anything"—the *Times* then being violently against Roosevelt.[11]

With the President's attempted "purge" of Senatorial opponents after the loss of his Supreme Court plan Lehman had no sympathy. He was confident that it deserved failure and would get it. A principle was involved: in nation and state alike, an executive had no right to try to punish legislators for an honest difference of opinion. He was not astonished when several nominees, like Walter George in Georgia and Millard Tydings in Maryland, seemed to gain rather than lose by Roosevelt's attacks. But meanwhile a great deal happened in New York.

While FDR's attitude toward Lehman remained uncertain, the gubernatorial campaign of 1938, which was certain to be close and hot, drew near. At first Lehman intended to refuse a renomination, for he was tired. This resolution was strengthened when a seat in the Senate came within his grasp through the sudden death of Royal S. Copeland in June, 1938. Peter Lehman that spring married Peggy Rosenbaum, daughter of a noted concert singer, Mme. Hulda Lashanska, and it was just after seeing them off to Hawaii for their honeymoon that the governor heard of the unexpected vacancy. "Mother and I thought the matter over very carefully before reaching a decision," he wrote Peter afterward, "and as you know I had definitely decided not to take the renomination this year as I wanted some relief from the tremendous strain and responsibility under which I have been working for the past many years." He had also long hoped for an ultimate Senatorial career.

It was clear that he could have Copeland's place for the asking. While the duties would be heavy, he would have fewer responsibilities and worries than as governor and would be comparatively free for the intervals when Congress was not sitting. His announcement that he would run for the Senate offended Roosevelt and others by its precipitancy, but seemed well received by the rank and file of the party.* Other men, including former

---

* The fact that Lehman declared his candidacy without consulting Democratic leaders gave offense both in New York and Washington. Ed Flynn in the Bronx and Frank Kelly in Brooklyn were decidedly irked, while FDR told Farley that the governor "should have come to us with his desires." Roosevelt's colored valet McDuffie remarked, "Mr. President, I noticed that the governor announced for the Senate before the other man had a chance to lie down"; a comment that FDR greatly enjoyed. *Jim Farley's Story*, 139, 140.

Congressman James Mead and Attorney General James J. Bennett, came out for the Democratic nomination for governor.

This was the situation in June and July. Then August brought a sweeping demand among Republicans for the nomination of Dewey as governor. It gained force when Justice Ferdinand Pecora, supported by many for the post, made a decision that month in the trial of James J. Hines for alleged racketeering, which aroused a storm of indignation. "Dewey Tidal Wave is Unstoppable," announced a *Herald-Tribune* headline. The conviction spread among Democrats that neither Bennett nor Mead could possibly defeat Dewey with all his well-won prestige. President Roosevelt would have supported Bennett reluctantly if at all, for he did not consider him a liberal; neither, for that matter, did Lehman nor Al Smith. Mead, though capable and progressive, had an uninspiring personality. Accepting the fact that the only man who could defeat Dewey was Lehman, party leaders began a concentrated campaign to make him change his mind.

Farley, Flynn, and other chieftains argued, pleaded, and cajoled. President Roosevelt abetted their draft-Lehman movement. The result was that the governor went to the late September convention in Rochester in an anxious frame of mind. Munich coincided with the gathering. Believing that a European war lay not far ahead, and that the United States would be drawn into it, he saw how useful he might be in the Senate. Yet he was fearful that if he stepped aside and let Dewey become governor, with a Republican majority in the legislature, much of the welfare legislation and the other progressive measures that Smith, Roosevelt, and he had put on the statute books would be repealed. As a matter of fact, Dewey could probably not have done this even if he had tried, but he could have made trouble, could have stopped all progress, and as head of the most important state could have weakened Roosevelt's position while the foreign situation grew more menacing. This fear was a specter that walked with Lehman and lay beside him in the watches of the night—for he still took his worries to bed with him.

He had more to worry about in that the coming election would be for a four-year term; this change in the constitution, for which Smith, Roosevelt, and he had labored, having at last been made.

He and his wife no sooner left the train in Rochester than they were invited to meet with party leaders that evening. Farley, Flynn, and other friends held the delusion that Mrs. Lehman was the impelling force in the governor's desire to move to Washington. The fact was that she was just as ready to go to the national capital as he was, and no more; she shared all his views, wishes, and decisions. The leaders argued with Lehman until midnight, but he refused to budge; next forenoon they met him again, and still he refused.

But when they saw him the second evening, they found him in a different mood. News had come from Saratoga that the Republican cohorts were gathering exultantly to nominate Dewey, wild with enthusiasm over a victory they thought within grasp and vocal with reactionary sentiments. Proofs of Dewey's popularity were rolling in from every part of the state. Lehman reluctantly turned to Farley and Flynn.

"Well," he said, "I feel so strongly that we must protect our social gains in this state that I am going to run again."

In accepting, he made one stipulation, that he must have a lieutenant governor who would work at his job and do something to lighten the governor's burdens. Bill Bray had never been more than a drag on the administration. As head of the Utica machine he had been an ally of Curry and Tammany Hall; a rooted conservative, he had opposed all New Deal measures; he was anxious to see somebody like Garner succeed Roosevelt in 1940. Lehman wanted Charles Poletti named in his stead. In the hurry of the convention he had no time to send for Bray and explain that he must have a working associate, and he neglected to write a letter. Naturally Bray felt hurt, and he and his central New York friends gave Lehman but lukewarm aid in the campaign.

The harsh struggle that filled September and October required the party to breast adverse currents. The court battle had done something to revive the Liberty League. What FDR called the fat-cat newspapers were berating the New Deal more wildly than ever. His program of legislation on wages and hours, agriculture, executive reorganization, and new agencies of TVA type had been postponed amid signs that the country was tiring of change and exertion. Early autumn brought an economic recession, with industrial activity, the stock market, and employment dropping to low levels; and nowhere was it worse felt than in New York. Some newspapers which realized that Lehman had reëntered the gubernatorial contest because of what the *Christian Science Monitor* termed his "prodigious sense of public stewardship" nevertheless regretted that he had not run for the Senate, where his championship of sound finance was needed. Fortunately the American Labor Party, the A.F. of L., the C.I.O., and other labor bodies all supported the governor.

Dewey by cleverly aggressive tactics threw Lehman on the defensive. He exploited the issue of Tammany corruption and used a charge that the governor had impeded legal proceedings against Albert Marinelli, county clerk in Manhattan, to dramatize his own accomplishments as racket buster.

He larded his speeches with references to the nefarious ways of Dutch Schultz, Waxey Gordon, Tootsie Herbert, and other racketeers. He tore into Ed Flynn, assailed the O'Connells and "the vicious mess of corruption in the very shadow of the capitol," and harshly criticized Lehman's management of the civil service and the budget. In response, Lehman attacked Dewey for dropping the office of district attorney after just seven months tenure to run for governor, his lack of a definite stand on utility regulation, and his total ignorance of state administration. Near the end of the battle La Guardia came out for Lehman, and Roosevelt devoted part of a fireside chat on the radio from Hyde Park to a plea for the governor and the two candidates for the Senate, Wagner and Mead.

Judge Edward Weinfeld and his wife were with the Lehmans that evening. As they sat at dinner Mrs. Lehman turned on the radio. When FDR's voice boomed out in the heartiest support of the governor, recalls Weinfeld, "he beamed like a small boy."

Some of Dewey's campaign speeches, like some of his courtroom procedures, had a hard, vituperative, and ruthless tone. But his hard-hitting energy did capture the imagination of voters. To his credit, he emphatically repudiated the religious prejudice that some men injected into the contest. The fact that Poletti had renounced Catholicism and adopted Protestantism was used against him by a few Catholic leaders, especially as the discarded Bray was a Catholic. In some upstate districts a "Vote American" slogan, really meaning "vote Gentile," gained currency. "Insofar as Onondaga County is concerned," wrote an indignant Syracuse citizen after the *Post-Standard* had published a vicious front-page article, "I know for certain that there was a very bad whispering campaign carried on. . . . In addition to that, there was put under every windshield wiper in every car that was on the street Monday night a very nasty circular containing the Benjamin Franklin lie that is used in reference to the Jews." Such tactics were in Dewey's mind when he said: "I condemn and despise any support based on racial or religious prejudice."

The returns on November 9 proved that Lehman was the only man who could have defeated Dewey. Out of 4,821,631 votes cast, Lehman received 1,971,307 Democratic and 419,979 American Labor Party votes. Dewey had just over 2,302,000 Republican votes and nearly 25,000 more from the Independent Progressive Party. Thus Lehman's plurality fell short of 65,000 votes. The tremendous appeal of Dewey in the light of his achievements against organized crime carried him far ahead of his ticket. Lehman ran proportionately as far behind, Poletti getting a plurality of nearly 230,000 votes and Wagner of nearly 440,000. Had Bennett made the race against Dewey, he would have been overwhelmed.

Everywhere this was an unhappy election for the Democrats. They lost 81 seats in the House, 8 in the Senate, and 11 governorships, including Michigan, Pennsylvania, Wisconsin, and Minnesota. Had New York been lost, the party skies would have seemed black indeed. Lehman had made the right decision in deciding to run again; nor did he later feel any reason to regret it. His four-year term, with his "little New Deal" legislation out of the way, enabled him to obtain a larger measure of Republican cooperation than ever before. Completely familiar with the duties of his office, possessing an able and industrious partner in Poletti, and with a host of friends from the ocean to the lakes, he found nearly all his tasks congenial. "Those four years," he said when they ended, "were the happiest of my governorship."

His friendship with Roosevelt was now completely restored—if restoration had been needed. The President had sent him a cordial letter late in 1937 congratulating him on Peter's engagement and discussing which portrait of himself should be hung in the executive chamber in Albany; his family, he wrote, liked that by the English painter Salisbury best. A little later the governor again congratulated him on his liberal policy with respect to the admission of European refugees, and was again thanked. It had seemed to Lehman when he announced his candidacy for the Senate that Roosevelt might well have sent an expression of good wishes. None had come, and in the meantime the press had teemed with articles asserting that since the Supreme Court letter the President was no longer friendly to Lehman. To clarify the situation, Lehman, on August 30, 1938, wrote expressing a certain amount of hurt that the White House had never contradicted these articles and saying that he would be glad to come down to Washington whenever invited. He added: "I hope you will feel that my public record entitles me to your support." Of course, Roosevelt's reply was cordiality itself.

· VI ·

The Albany session of 1938 had been pleasantly fruitful, for the Republicans showed a warmer interest in social legislation, and the governor, whom they had accused of dictatorial traits, met them in a more cooperative spirit. After recommending provision for low-rent housing in the state, Lehman compromised with assembly leaders on a workable plan. The legislature voted to lay before voters a constitutional amendment authorizing a $200,000,000 revolving fund, financed by a bond issue; and the governor took satisfaction in signing the legislation on April 7. This endeavor was destined to grow lustily. The legislature had enacted a law guaranteeing labor the right to organize and bargain collectively, New York's supplement to the Wagner Labor Act; and Lehman appointed a Catholic clergyman of wisdom and tact, John P. Boland of Buffalo, its first head.* He saw some recommendations for enlarging municipal home rule written into law, notably an authorization of planning boards in all towns. And he delighted in vetoing the McNaboe bill to bar radicals from public office, a bill condemned by the Civil Liberties Union.

The American people, however, could no longer devote themselves to cultivating their own garden. As the legislature sat in March, Hitler occupied Austria. As the Democrats were meeting in Rochester to nominate Lehman, Chamberlain and Hitler were holding their conference in Munich. While Roosevelt sent European leaders message after message affirming American hopes that a way of peace could be found, every day war drew nearer.

The time had come when the states as well as the nation had to divert their central energies to tasks of military preparation.

Lehman, believing with Washington that in time of peace the nation should prepare for war, had spoken repeatedly in the early 1930s for reasonable expenditures on armaments. After all, he had been a colonel, and he always liked to be called by that title. Observation taught him that preparation for the defense of national rights and liberties was not an invitation to war but a preventive of war. As an old Wilsonian internationalist he had deplored the blind isolationism of the 1920s and early 1930s. No record exists of any public statement on the neutrality legislation of 1935–36, but it is certain that he thought it shortsighted and foolish. He was horrified by Hitler's march into the Rhineland, his rearmament of Germany, the brutalities of the Nazi and Fascist dictatorships, their intervention in the Spanish Civil War, and Mussolini's savage conquest of Ethiopia. The events of 1937–38 in Europe convinced him that with another world war imminent, the United States should be ready for an almost inevitable involvement.

By that time, he had become militant in his utterances. He sent a meeting

---

* The labor relations board, with three members, proved effective from the outset, and remained so. One of the original members, who became the second chairman, was Paul Herzog, an old friend of Lehman's; later he became chairman of the National Labor Relations Board, then assistant dean of the Harvard Graduate School of Business Administration, and later still head of the Arbitration Association. The board devoted itself to intrastate affairs, settling labor problems in hotels, department stores, and other local businesses. At the same time, the legislature created a board of mediation for labor disputes, of which Lehman made William H. Davis the head.

in Madison Square Garden early in 1937 a call for the defense of freedom. In many parts of the world, he wrote, the enemies of democracy were triumphant. They had established regimes not to guarantee liberty and justice but to destroy them. "The spirits of Washington and Jefferson, the spirits of the men who conceived the ideals of America, who fought to attain them, who embodied them in our institutions, are calling to us: 'On Guard!' With a united voice, Americans who have received and cherished these ideals, regardless of creed, race, and national origin, must give back the answer: 'We are here!' " On the short-lived Munich agreement, which Roosevelt and most Americans greeted at the time with relief, he passed no judgment. But a few days earlier he had spoken to the American Legion Convention in New York City with the same moral indignation that infused Roosevelt's "quarantine speech" the next month—though he made no specific proposal for action. At the spectacle of the harsh suppression of freedom abroad, he said, "America gasps in horror. . . . Almost overnight the work of centuries has been undone."

Midnight darkness was closing in on the Jews of Central and Eastern Europe, and their agony of course specially touched Lehman. It had been his practice to circulate a special message among his coreligionists at the Jewish New Year each September. In 1938 he wrote under deep emotion. For thousands of years, he declared, the Shofar had summoned all Jews to prayer and meditation. "Never before, perhaps, have we needed courage and strength so urgently." Under the dictatorships, Jews were being ruthlessly robbed, jailed, and murdered. One faint ray of light had lately appeared, for Washington had invited the governments of the world to meet in conference to seek a means by which Jewish refugees might find homes in free countries. This ray, however, quickly dimmed. The United States, like other nations, kept its gates barred, its immigration laws forbidding refugees entry except in limited numbers and under onerous conditions. The Dominican Republic and certain British dominions and colonies would admit some; but how arrange for their transportation and settlement?

First in dozens, then in scores, then in hundreds, Jews of Central Europe appealed to the Jewish governor of New York. The Lehman family had established a trust fund to assist relatives abroad, placing Mrs. Richard Bernhard, a niece of the governor, in charge. They furnished money for emigration and posted guaranties, as the law required, that the entrants would not become public charges. At the same time Lehman gave affidavits and financial aid to a large number of nonrelated refugees who were helped by various organizations. A letter the governor sent Mrs. Bernhard in the late summer of 1939 indicates the line he had to draw. He wrote:

I have taken note of the very long list of people who have written asking for help but to whom you felt we could not give assistance because their relationship could not be proved, or because they were too old, or undesirable for emigration. While many of these cases are undoubtedly worthy or very pathetic, I think you will have to maintain the position you have already taken. . . . I think that we have assumed all the responsibility that we dare to undertake, and those people who are not related or not connected will have to be helped through general funds. The list for whom we have already issued affidavits is really a staggering one, and I believe we now must simply permit those who wish to emigrate to work through usual channels. I hate to take this position because I know of the urgency of the situation. I think, however, that these people who have written us are in no different position from the thousands of people who need assistance and must be helped, if at all, through general funds.

"If at all"—and this on the eve of a war in which millions of Jews would be wiped out! American immigration laws, which as Lehman said later it was impossible to change materially, raised impassable barriers. The funds of philanthropic organizations were limited. In an era of depression, unemployment, and apprehension most doors throughout the harried world were as nearly closed as our own. Zionists rejected the idea of Kenya, and the Palestinian Arabs, who had their own rights to protect, rejected the Zionist solution.

Although Lehman was under great pressure to join the Zionist ranks, he steadfastly refused. The Zionists wished to create a state—they had a political motivation; but he, and most American Jews at this time, thought it the part of wisdom to create simply a refuge, a home. Such men as Rabbi Stephen S. Wise, the Hungarian-born founder of the Free Synagogue in New York, an ardent co-worker with the governor in the labor movement, social reform, and the protection of civil liberties, tried assiduously to convert him. Lehman was deeply impressed by Wise's magnetic personality, vision, and kindling eloquence; he was impressed by the fervor of other Zionists, like Ben Fleischmann of the Joint Distribution Committee; he noted how generously British and French Jews, the Rothschilds being especially prominent, had given money for Palestinian settlement. "But I explained," he said, "that while I was deeply sympathetic with the idea of building up Palestine economically, socially, and spiritually, I did not want to align myself with any political group doing it." He never contributed to the Zionist coffers.[12] And the question now swiftly became academic: war would place all the persecuted minorities and all the liberal elements, in lands dominated by the Nazis and Fascists, within an iron cage, locked and triple-guarded.

"Look Out! He's Not As Meek As He Looks"
As Rollin Kirby recorded Governor Lehman's Social Security Program in the
New York World-Telegram of May 8, 1936

Photo Allen Colbert Associates. Reprinted by permission of *New York World-Telegram
and Sun.* [Copyright 1936, New York World-Telegram Corp.]

"That's Tellin' Em, Dan!"
As Rollin Kirby recorded Judge Dan Cohalan's stand in the *New York World-Telegram* of May 19, 1936

War in Europe was at hand. The legislative session of 1939 had but fairly buckled down to work when Hitler tore up his Munich agreement in the face of Britain and France by occupying all Czechoslovakia, and Mussolini followed his example by seizing Albania. Lehman and the other leaders in Albany—Poletti, Senators Hanley and Dunnigan, Speaker Heck, and Assemblymen Steingut and Ives—realized that they must set aside old concerns and old party antagonisms and do what they could to ready the state for the imminent storm.

Chapter X

INTO WAR

I AM looking forward to the next two years with full faith that under your leadership our State will maintain those high standards of social justice and progress that have kept it in the forefront of the nation." So ran Roosevelt's telegram to Lehman on January 2, 1939. The President forgot that the term was four years instead of two. He also forgot, or did not wish to say, that the international convulsion which was already racking the world could quickly erase any program of social progress from the agenda of government. As a matter of fact, men were then only eight months from the explosion of war in Europe, and a greater value than social justice was now at stake—the liberty of the world.

The governor might have been able to press more strenuously in the legislative session of 1939 for social reform but for the perverse quarrel which the two houses stirred up over finances. Early in the session he presented a budget of approximately $415,000,000, simultaneously recommending a set of taxes to meet the deficit of about $60,000,000 which it would create. All would have been well had the legislature come up to the mark. As usual, however, the assembly kicked over the traces. The able Abbot Moffat and other party leaders reclassified the itemized appropriations of the budget into large groups, determined the costs for each group according to Lehman's figures, and then slashed three-fourths of these groups. Their aggregate cuts came to about $26,000,000. At the same time they adopted their own scheme of taxation, based upon cigarettes, liquor, and the extension of the state income tax to Federal employees. The legislature was trying to take complete control of the budget, which under statutes achieved by Alfred E. Smith was an executive responsibility.

The result was a state-wide uproar. The governor declared the Republican plan an unwise and unconstitutional breach of a great principle; for the executive budget had saved the state uncounted millions. He had the support of public school teachers, for the Moffat scheme cut state aid to schools by $9,710,000. He was supported by farmers and other citizens requiring better roads, for Moffat had reduced the capital outlay on highways and parkways by more than $10,000,000. While hospital heads protested against a cut of $1,564,000 in the expenditures for mental hygiene, civil service employees objected still more vehemently to pay reductions. Various civic organizations upheld the executive principle. Attorney General Bennett and Solicitor General Henry Epstein declared that the constitution prohibited such mangling of the budget by lump-sum action and forbade the legislature to alter it except by dealing with individual items. But Lehman and the two houses remained at loggerheads, and the governor finally let the principal act become law without his signature, for this was the only way in which a constitutional question could be presented for judicial decision.

At once the dispute went into the courts, with the whole state anxiously awaiting their action. First the Appellate Division of the Supreme Court upheld the position of the governor. Then on June 21 the Court of Appeals unanimously ruled that the legislature had no constitutional power to reduce appropriations by groups instead of items, though it did validate the main reductions in public school aid and the highway appropriations. As this decision left the state without appropriations for the departments, Lehman had to call an emergency special session, which reënacted the budget in constitutional form. Most of the cuts stood, but Lehman and Bennett had been vindicated in their stand on principle.[1]

The unfortunate fact was that the dispute had impeded public business and disrupted what had at first promised to be a harmonious session. The most striking pieces of new legislation that passed were a response to the riots that had occurred in Harlem in 1937. A legislative commission on the condition of the urban Negro population made its report in February, analyzing widespread discriminations against the half million colored people of New York. The maladies of the situation, it declared, could not be met until Negro income was raised. "Bad housing, juvenile delinquency, high mortality rates, and attendant evils will continue as long as vast areas of possible and preferred employment are barred to a large percentage of the population." The fourteen bills recommended by the commission had Lehman's energetic backing, but only a fraction of them passed. Public opinion would have to be aroused before the full program—including a Fair Employment Practices Act passed under Governor Dewey—could be put on the statute books. In speech after speech, the governor tried to enlighten citizens on the subject, and was delighted to sign the two Feigenbaum Acts that penalized discrimination in its more flagrant forms.

• I •

Meanwhile, in June, 1939, King George VI and the Queen arrived from Great Britain, entering the state on June 7 at Niagara Falls, going at once to Washington and returning to New York City on the 10th. The Lehmans greeted them at the Battery along with Mayor La Guardia and his wife, escorted them to the World's Fair and Columbia University, and then drove with them to Hyde Park, attending the luncheon picnic given there next day by the Roosevelts. Their visit, as Lehman wrote one of his English relatives, was not only a complete success but unexpectedly enjoyable. "Edith and I, like all the others, were greatly attracted to them. They appeared to us to be simple, kindly, gracious, and thoroughly human." He was able to tell them that as a boy of nine, he had seen Queen Victoria's Golden Jubilee. "I think the crowds here last Saturday fully matched anything that I saw in London." In July he went for a vacation to Jasper Park Lodge, where Chief Justice Hughes, staying at one of the cottages, gave him good company. Hughes told him that Irving Lehman would certainly be the next Chief Judge of the Court of Appeals, for he had heard that the Republicans as well as Democrats would nominate him.

While still at Jasper, Lehman was ruffled by an unexpected and unreasonable attack that La Guardia suddenly made on his brother and the court. It nonplused him. "I cannot fathom La Guardia's motives," he wrote Irving. "I know that he has taken every opportunity of slamming the courts, but he certainly has nothing against you. The papers mention the possibility that his action might have been inspired by a feud with me. If any feud exists it is news to me." They had worked together throughout the legislative session, the governor vetoing every bill affecting the city of New York that La Guardia asked him to disapprove and signing every bill but one which he wished made law. Perhaps, he surmised, La Guardia was trying to force his hand on a pending Supreme Court appointment.[2]

The hotheaded, impulsive little mayor, who often lost his temper and lashed out at anyone who displeased him—calling his opponents bums, punks, and reptiles—constantly did inexplicable acts. Lehman admired his courage, idealism, fighting energy, and skill in staffing the city administration with able men. At the same time, he disliked La Guardia's way of going off at half-cock, his abusiveness, and his autocratic temper. The mayor, who once gave a subordinate named Paul Kerr hell for intemperate language, now called the Court of Appeals "a bunch of murderers." This because it refused to permit the city to repair substandard tenements and send the bills to the owners! His outburst quickly faded from the news. But Lehman remembered it when a graver explosion came from him two years later.

Irving did receive the nomination for Chief Judge this autumn, and was sworn in on the last day of the year after a series of congratulatory dinners. For the first time in the history of any state two brothers headed two coordinate branches of the government, the executive and judicial. "I am very proud of him," the governor said of Irving, and this was an understatement. Still leading a quiet, studious life, devoted to books and art, he remained the governor's closest adviser, always in reach at his home in New York just off upper Fifth Avenue or in Albany. Lehman had written FDR early in 1939 asking the President to consider Irving for the Supreme Court, but Roosevelt had replied that geographical considerations made the appointment impossible; now he had a post of equal dignity and opportunity.[3]

When September brought the thunderclap of Hitler's invasion of Poland, and the British and French declarations of war, Lehman immediately appealed to the leaders of both houses to meet with him for planning state action in the crisis. They could discuss the important social and fiscal matters that might come before the next session and agree, he hoped, upon the financial measures that had just provoked so much acrimony. "I propose a truce on politics," he wrote. The appeal was received in good spirit. But with a presidential election at hand, politics could not be postponed. Harmonious plans were made for various measures in the next session, and an agreement was reached on fiscal questions. The governor's budget for 1940–41 was only slightly cut, and since national defense expenditures were swelling employment and revenues, no new taxes were needed. Political passions, however, soon ran about as high as ever.

The state was now to count for less and less, with national needs and authority paramount in the world crisis. Defense more and more absorbed public attention. Nevertheless, Lehman in the session of 1940 had the cooperation of the legislature in the passage of some important new acts. The laws regulating industrial homework, including child labor, were strengthened. The estate tax was stiffened. Large additions were made to the coverage of the civil service system. Experimentation in county government was encouraged. He vainly tried to get the legislature to provide for stricter prosecution of local corruption but failed. After vetoing in 1938 a measure which sanctioned public bus service for private and parochial schools, because it clearly violated the constitutional separation of church and state—an act which cost him Catholic votes that autumn—he had taken satisfaction the next year in signing a revised bill which placed free transportation on the basis of a contribution to the health and welfare of children. Many people doubted if the revision really met the objection in principle, but it satisfied his conscience. And he carried some final parts of his program for fuller control of public utilities.

Lehman worked better with the legislature, in part, because he had become better acquainted with the leaders, though he was never on really familiar terms with them—familiarity was not in his nature. Legislators often debated the question whether he had a sense of humor. Of course he had, but it was significant the question was raised. He almost never went out to public restaurants in Albany; never was seen in a bar; never cracked a joke in his speeches, and almost never elsewhere.

One night some leaders lingered in the Ten Eyck bar until two in the morning, growing mellower and mellower. John J. Dunnigan, after many potations, demanded: "I wonder if the governor has ever made a night of it?" Weaving his way to a telephone, he routed Lehman out of bed. "Some of the boys are having a very good time down here," he said. "Why don't you come down and join us?" The governor was affable. "It is somewhat late," he apologized. "I must ask to be excused. Please just give my regards to all present." Late next morning Dunnigan, sober again, recalled the episode with embarrassed contrition. He must hurry over and apologize, he decided. Entering the office of the governor's counsel, he explained his errand. "Don't bother," said the counsel. "No apology necessary. The governor came in this morning all smiles and said to me, 'Nat, the nicest thing in the world happened to me last night!'—and told me the whole story." [4]

All the while, the European war gripped men's minds, and before France fell in June, 1940, Lehman saw that it made a third term for Roosevelt almost imperative.

• II •

The President early that year had given him the benefit of a graceful gesture. Complimenting him on the close of a trying session—"you have handled things beautifully"—he suggested a Washington visit to talk over various matters, adding confidentially, "I had hoped that Jim [Farley] would initiate the idea of the New York delegates to the coming convention casting a vote for you. It would have been a decent thing to do for the leader of the Democratic Party in the state . . . for eight years its thoroughly successful and able governor. Not a word has come from Jim—so I mentioned it to Eddie Flynn, who has been spending the weekend, and Flynn thinks it not only wise but the right thing to do in every way." This suggestion never bore fruit. Political events made it impossible.

Farley had been one of the men—Cordell Hull, Garner, Harry Hopkins, Paul V. McNutt, and Henry A. Wallace were others—full of hope at the beginning of 1940 that he might be nominated as Roosevelt's successor. But Hitler's swift conquest of Denmark, Norway, Belgium, and Holland swept away such dreams. As Winston Churchill notified the President that "the small countries are simply smashed up, one by one, like matchwood," and as the British and French armies were pressed back against Dunkerque, Roosevelt devoted Sunday evening, May 26, to a radio speech to the nation. The country must not give way to panic or fear, he said, and must guard its hard-won social gains, but it would have to strengthen its factories, modernize its weapons, and fill up its arsenals. He took steps to expedite the shipment of military supplies to Britain. Speaking at Charlottesville on June 10, the day that Mussolini declared war on reeling France, he declared: "The hand that held the dagger has struck it into the back of its neighbor." He went on to define national policy:

"In our American unity, we will pursue two obvious and simultaneous causes: we will extend to the opponents of force the material resources of this nation, and at the same time we will harness and speed up the use of these resources in order that we ourselves . . . may have equipment and training equal to the task of any emergency. . . . Signs and signals call for speed—full speed ahead."

The popular demand for Roosevelt's retention of the helm swiftly over-bore the traditional antipathy of Americans for a third term. California, Texas, and other states elected delegations supporting his renomination. Although the President himself said nothing about his intentions, Ickes, Robert Jackson, William O. Douglas, and James F. Byrnes gave all their energies to the movement to draft him. They had the aid of seasoned Democratic leaders all over the land. Ed Flynn tells us: "The persons in the forefront in support of the president's ambition for a third term were largely drawn from the political machines of the country." [5] He might have added that they included many of the best governors and Senators. Lehman was emphatically with them.

A fortnight after a roaring Republican convention nominated Wendell Willkie for President, the Democratic gathering opened July 15 in Chicago. Though Garner and Farley were so rebellious that they presented the threat of an adverse coalition, nearly everybody else agreed that Roosevelt must be chosen again. He announced on the 16th, through Alben W. Barkley, that he wished to make it clear that the delegates were free to vote for any candidate they pleased. But an instant roar swept the hall: "We Want Roosevelt!" As a wild demonstration got under way, it swiftly changed to

"Everybody Wants Roosevelt!" and "The World Wants Roosevelt!" [6] On the first ballot next day he was nominated by an overwhelming vote: Roosevelt 946, Farley 72, Garner 61. The only remaining question that furnished any suspense was the Vice-Presidency, a prize which McNutt, Farley, Henry Wallace, Speaker William B. Bankhead, and Jesse Jones of Texas were all eager to seize.

Lehman as chairman of the New York delegation watched the vice-presidential drama unfold. It had been customary for the presidential candidate to suggest his preference in this matter or even dictate the choice. Nearly everybody now took it for granted that Roosevelt would identify a man acceptable to all, whose nomination by acclaim would follow. In that belief about half of the New York delegation trooped aboard a special train and went home; why wait? This left Lehman with only a little more than fifty delegates to answer to their names if a roll call were demanded. And as this happened the vice-presidential nomination suddenly became highly controversial.

Roosevelt had at first hoped to persuade Cordell Hull to accept second place on the ticket. When he failed, he waited too long to let Harry Hopkins and others know that for undisclosed reasons he had decided upon Henry A. Wallace. The news, falling belatedly on the convention, stunned many leaders. Wallace, they declared, was an impractical Westerner, a mystic who had written foolish letters about Rosicrucianism, and a naïve believer in the greatness and goodness of the Russian government. Moreover, he was a former Republican. Many of the delegates, including some who had voted unwillingly for Roosevelt, flew into open rebellion. The rejected vice-presidential aspirants were of course sore and mutinous.

Paul V. McNutt's supporters had packed the galleries, and kept vociferating, "We want McNutt! We want McNutt!" until their hero took the platform and withdrew his name. This left Speaker Bankhead the principal rival of Wallace. He was an able Bourbon of the Deep South, who represented reaction as clearly as Wallace represented an idealistic liberalism. Roosevelt, following the convention proceedings by radio and wire, was so incensed over the possibility that the Alabamian might share the ticket with him that he talked to White House associates of rejecting the nomination.

Of course most spectators expected New York to cast its 96 votes solidly for Wallace as Roosevelt's selection.

"Well, I knew that if I merely cast the 96 votes for Wallace I would be challenged," records Lehman.[7] "So although I was importuned to cast the entire vote for Wallace, I paused. Jim Farley told me, 'If you try to cast the entire New York delegation, I will challenge you and ask a roll call.' So I took

the position, which was not only wise but right, that I was going to poll the
delegation and vote just those who were ready to answer to their names. I did
so. The major part of the delegation voted for Wallace, but some were for
Farley and some for McNutt." Jeers and catcalls from the galleries greeted
every mention of Wallace's name, but on the first ballot he was chosen by a
vote of 627—a narrow margin of 76 over the 551 necessary for nomination.
So high did feeling run that although Wallace was in Chicago, he stayed
away from the convention lest—it was said—the galleries make some hostile
demonstration if he appeared.

· III ·

In the ensuing campaign, with the redoubtable Ed Flynn in charge as
national chairman, Lehman of course took part with contributions, public
statements, and speeches. The current of popular feeling at first seemed to
flow toward the picturesque and dynamic Wendell Willkie, but by early
autumn it turned strongly to the President.

In this redirection of sentiment, international events held the governing
rule. As Hitler consolidated his grip upon France and the Battle of Britain
loomed just ahead, American emotions were powerfully engaged. It was
plain to all that unless the British defenses held fast, the United States itself
might soon be in the direst peril, for the Nazis would find ruthless means of
directing the armaments of all Europe against America. The speeches of the
great English leader reverberated across the world. "Upon this battle,"
Winston Churchill told the House of Commons in June, "depends the survival
of Christian civilization." If Britain wins, he continued, all Europe will yet
be freed. "But if we fail then the whole world, including the United States,
including all that we have known and cared for, will sink into the abyss of a
new Dark Age, made more sinister, and perhaps more protracted, by the
lights of perverted science. Let us therefore brace ourselves to our duties,
and so bear ourselves that, if the British Empire and Commonwealth last for
a thousand years, men will say, 'This was their finest hour.' "

Millions of Americans read this immortal burst of eloquence with the
most poignant feeling; millions felt that the United States should be throwing her weight into the balance. No one was more powerfully wrought upon
by the world crisis than Herbert Lehman. In the First World War he had
thought the United States should intervene long before it did, and so he felt
now. Though it was hardly possible for the governor of New York to preach
intervention in public speeches, he did so to his friends. Wendell Willkie
made his abhorrence of Fascism and Nazism emphatically clear. Neverthe-

less, Roosevelt's advantages of experience, world-wide acquaintance with forces and leaders, and political dexterity were so manifest that he was plainly the man for the crisis. And in August came a great decision which did much to consolidate national feeling.

Early that month Hitler, his armies and air force ready for operation Sea Lion, loosed first hundreds, then a thousand, and finally nearly two thousand bombers and fighters upon England. Children were evacuated from cities to country, multitudes huddled in the London underground, and firemen fought the flames while Spitfires battled the invaders overhead. Meanwhile, Germans by air and water struck at British sea power. Earlier in the year, on May 15, Churchill had asked Roosevelt for forty or fifty old destroyers and several hundred aircraft. Now he renewed his request in the most urgent terms. The next months would be vital, he wrote; within ten days the Nazis had sunk or crippled eleven British destroyers, and the situation might grow worse—"this is a thing to do *now*."

In grim reality the position of Britain remained perilous throughout August and well into September. While the Royal Air Force had much the better of the aerial combat, its margin of strength was narrow. A massive attack on London September 7 with 1,273 bombers and fighters fired the dockside area and blocked the railways to the south. The Germans assembled barges, transports, tugs, and motorboats at their Channel ports for a tremendous invasion effort, fixed first for September 11th and then the 27th.

Roosevelt, anxious to furnish the destroyers and other aid, was temporarily deterred by the threats of the isolationists, led by the *Chicago Tribune*, the America First organization under General Robert Wood, and such politicians as House Republican Leader Joseph Martin and Senator David I. Walsh. He at first saw no way to send such help except with the approval of Congress, and he knew it might hold up a bill for months. But in mid-August a better road was pointed out. He could exchange destroyers, by simple executive action, for long leases of bases on British territory stretching from Newfoundland to Trinidad. Soon after Roosevelt reached this decision Lehman, as he relates, talked with the President: [8]

> FDR asked me to come down from Albany to visit him at Hyde Park. After lunch he took me to a quiet spot and said, "I want you to know that I'm going to announce that I'm turning over fifty of these destroyers to the British. What do you think of it?"
> I said, "Well, it will make me very happy if you do it, because you know how strongly I feel that we should give every possible help to the British and French. But I think it's only fair to tell you, since you've asked me about it, that I think you'll get your head knocked off."
> He said, "Well, I think you're right, but I'm going to do it any-

how because I'm sure it's the proper thing to do and a necessary thing to do."

As Roosevelt put the draft agreement into shape, he had said to his secretary Grace Tully: "Congress is going to raise hell about this." The isolationists in Washington, cheered on by the America Firsters, Anglophobes, and virulent anti-New Dealers, did stir up as much of a rumpus as they could. But Willkie approved of the exchange, and the massive sentiment of the country rallied behind the President. The step was decisive. Once it was taken, military aid flowed in a deepening stream to Great Britain. The victory of the Royal Air Force, the energetic steps of Churchill to defend Suez and Egypt, and the wholehearted participation of Canada in the war all had their effect on Americans. So did the brutal—and unsuccessful—Italian invasion of Greece. It was not long before Lehman, visiting Boston in Senator Walsh's own bailiwick, had the pleasure of seeing a large British cruiser being rapidly repaired in the navy yard there.

One of the most important of Lehman's campaign speeches was made late in August at Niagara Falls to the A.F. of L. national convention, a body which contained many isolationists and pacifists and which had traditionally opposed compulsory military service. At the time one of Roosevelt's cardinal defense measures, the Burke-Wadsworth bill for drafting 900,000 men between twenty-one and thirty-six to undergo training for a year, was making dubious progress through Congress. Some observers feared that the A.F. of L. would adopt resolutions condemning it. Before he went on the platform Lehman had a talk with General Hugh Drum and Julius Ochs Adler of the *New York Times*, who encouraged him to strengthen his text. He made a fighting plea for the draft bill which impressed even opponents. Adler later wrote him that he had bearded the lion in his den—and the lion refrained from any roar against conscription. Elsewhere he spoke again and again for all possible aid to the Allies. At that time Lehman's son Peter was taking flying lessons at Roosevelt Field on Long Island, and his son John was a second lieutenant in the Fourth Armored Division at Pine Camp, N.Y.

The bitterness of the final phases of the election struggle in 1940 alarmed Lehman. The isolationists, mainly on Willkie's side, and the interventionists, mainly on Roosevelt's, attacked each other venomously. For himself, he liked and admired Willkie, though he thought the reëlection of Roosevelt essential as a symbol of militant democracy, declaring: "Nothing that could happen in the United States could give Hitler, Mussolini, Stalin, and the government of Japan more satisfaction than the defeat of the man who typifies to the whole world the kind of free, humane government which dictators despise—Franklin D. Roosevelt." Business was so largely with Willkie, and labor so generally with FDR, that class lines made an unpleasant appearance in the contest. When Willkie appeared in parades many workers shouted opprobrious terms at him or ostentatiously turned their backs. Some newspapers—as usual the press was strongly Republican—used outrageous cartoons and headlines. German-Americans, the Italian-Americans with whom the stab-in-the-back phrase rankled, and Irish-Americans all nursed their special hates. Willkie himself began attacking Roosevelt as a warmonger, and this finally brought the President into the campaign with a series of bellicose October speeches. "I am fighting mad," he told Ickes, and he threw barbed taunts not only at Willkie but at Hoover, Taft, the newspaper editors, and the immortal congressional trio, Martin, Barton, and Fish.

Roosevelt's decisive victory by 449 electoral votes to 82, and a popular vote of 27,243,466 against Willkie's 22,304,755, did not erase the bitterness. He had most of the masses with him, but some among the classes were vindictive. Various Republican newspapers had worked themselves into a frenzy. They continued to denounce the third term as a grave breach of national tradition, the New Deal as a surrender to Socialism, and Roosevelt as a reckless despot intent on war.

Immediately after the election Lehman therefore urged Roosevelt to try to improve national unity. The main body of Willkie's supporters could be brought into line "if they are shown, as I know you can show them, that you are the chief protector of our capitalist system, that you have not wanted and do not want autocratic powers, and that you are determined to bring all classes together in harmony." Certain more sinister forces behind Willkie— he meant the America Firsters and German–American Bund—would remain intransigent. They might maneuver Willkie into becoming the spearhead of some movement which, as the country came to the brink of war, would threaten its solidarity. The governor wondered if FDR might not invite Willkie to discuss with him the best means of ensuring national union against foreign enemies. Even if he rejected a conference the gesture might be useful, while if he accepted it the way would lie open for a continued association of the two leaders, "which I think would be at this time of the utmost value." [9]

No such immediate conference took place. Willkie returned to the practice of law. But early in 1941, while the blitz raged, he visited England at the request of the President, and the next year went to Russia, the Near East, and China as Roosevelt's special representative. While it was not possible for him to take important office under Roosevelt without sacrificing his position as Republican leader, feeling between them was cordial and everybody knew it. Roosevelt, who had long believed that a party division between liberals and conservatives would be more logical and effective than the Republican-Democratic alignment, had hopes in 1944 that he could persuade Willkie to join him in arranging a general political reorganization. But on October 8 that year a heart attack carried Willkie away.

• IV •

Lehman had a strong defense program ready for the 1941 legislature, but once more politics blocked his way. A. L. Moffat in the assembly charged him with "intense emotional alarm," and as chairman of the ways and means committee again made himself the police dog of the treasury. He sliced some $1,270,000 from the governor's budget provision for defense and at the same time added some $1,700,000 in state aid for local highways and county fairs. With the world burning up, subsidies for local fairs! Lehman indulged in one of his rare explosions. Were Roosevelt, Willkie, Hull, and Stimson also showing "emotional alarm"? Was Congress acting hysterically when it appropriated thirty billions for defense, put a draft act into effect, and placed one and a half million men under arms? "I would rather do too much than too little." In a new request for defense funds he rebuked the Republican majority which, by a strict party vote, had slammed the door in his face: [10]

> I asked your Honorable Bodies for money to guard the armories. It was refused.
> I asked for money for military guards to safeguard vital reservoirs and dams. It was refused.
> I asked for money to cover the pay of New York guardsmen if they had to be called for active duty. The amount appropriated was reduced to an almost negligible sum.
> I asked for a contingent fund. . . . This request too was refused . . .
> No money has been provided for an expanded program of vocational training or for the many things which the state may be asked by the Federal Government to undertake in National defense.
> In a word . . . the entire defense program, which has been built up so laboriously—and only after frequent consultation with the legislative leaders—is now in serious jeopardy.

Governor Lehman had ordered the compilation of an inventory of the industrial resources of the state, so that the general government in requisitioning materials or placing contracts would know just where to turn. The state planning council and the joint legislative committee on industrial and labor conditions duly produced a directory of more than nine hundred pages. This Domesday Book for New York, something no other state had completed, was ready at the beginning of 1941, with full details on every usable plant, classified by industry, by counties, and by cities. At the same time, the planning council made a list of idle manufacturers so that those who thought of new or enlarged facilities could consult the data thus collected.

Under fairly adequate existing legislation, he completed the organization of an emergency force termed the State Guard, to be called to the colors whenever the National Guard was ordered into Federal service. This was a body of ten thousand men and two thousand officers divided into twenty regiments and five brigades, three in metropolitan New York and two up-state. Steps were taken to establish special training centers for men who would be needed in the aircraft and munitions industries. The fire departments and police forces of all the large cities were placed in close liaison, and communications established that in the event of an enemy attack they could quickly be mobilized to assist each other.[11]

And in view of the rapid expansion of the Federal defense effort, Lehman on August 1, 1940, appointed a State Council of National Defense to help direct preparations for war and advise him on all points where state and national cooperation was desirable. Selecting each of the ten appointive members from some social or economic group, he named Poletti as general coordinator. This proved an invaluable body. It was the Defense Council, for example, which advised railroads, power companies, factories, and municipalities on the action they should take to protect their properties from sabotage and which gave the signal late in 1941 for practice blackouts in the various cities. A similar council had existed in the First World War.

The responsibilities of Lehman and his associates in preparation for war included acceleration of the production of defense materials, the provision of vocational training for 50,000 employees in defense industries, the administration of selective service, and the coordination of health, nursing, and medical activities. All these labors involved a huge amount of detailed effort. The state was blanketed during 1941 with air raid observation posts, classes were formed everywhere to teach people the best method of combating incendiary bombs, surveys were made of housing to enable communities to meet any sudden influx of defense workers, and a special committee worked out a plan for the evacuation of schoolchildren from New York City on the lines followed in London. Nothing was neglected.[12]

In the huge national effort 1940–41 to prepare for conflict, New York unquestionably acted with special promptness and efficiency, setting an example which guided other states.

One problem in the prewar months was presented by the indefatigable, invaluable, and effervescent mayor of New York City. When Lehman heard that President Roosevelt was considering the appointment of La Guardia as Federal Director of Civilian Defense, he took it for granted that he would resign as mayor. To be head of the nation's greatest city was a full-time job. To direct civil defense, which meant protection of the country against sabotage, rioting, raids by land, sea, and air, and maintenance of morale also seemed a full-time job. The governor thought that La Guardia was best left just where he was and wrote Roosevelt so; another capable man could be found for the Federal post. But when Roosevelt persisted, Lehman supposed that the president of the city council would step into City Hall, and was aghast when it appeared that La Guardia meant to hold both offices.

The annual conference of governors, held in New York at this moment, showed that other executives shared his view. All the members felt that the country was in a dangerous situation, and most of them believed war lay just ahead. They were nervously discussing plans parallel with those of New York. All along the northeastern seaboard, in particular, preparations for possible attack were under way. Lehman had made such arrangements that if bombs fell on Poughkeepsie, for example, all the fire engines and fire-fighters of the Hudson Valley from Albany to Manhattan would converge on the area; and Massachusetts, Pennsylvania, and other states were taking similar steps. The conference had its executive committee call on La Guardia.

"I remember going out and meeting with him in a clubhouse near the World's Fair, which was then in progress," states Lehman. "One of the committee was Harold Stassen, governor of Minnesota at the time. Another was Herbert O'Connor of Maryland. There were five of us in all. We asked him what his intentions were. While he didn't give us any definite promises, he certainly led me to believe that he would give up one job or the other, that he would not attempt to hold both. I remember protesting with the other governors." Lehman had to adjust himself to the opposite decision. Speaking to a conference of mayors in Albany on June 10, 1941, he announced that he had held a long conference with La Guardia, and had pledged him the fullest cooperation.

"Mayor La Guardia and I are in full agreement," he said, "that the machinery which we have already set up in this state through our state and local defense councils should be used to the fullest extent in carrying out the responsibilities that will come from the Federal authorities." [13]

On Sunday, December 7, 1941, the Lehmans, who had been staying in New York City, left for Albany by early morning train to help open an exhibition arranged by Bundles for Britain—an organization of which Mrs. Lehman was head—in the Albany Art Museum. They reached Albany early in the afternoon to find the city quiet. But one of his secretaries greeted them at the train with an incoherent report that the Japanese had attacked Pearl Harbor and been repulsed—that was all. Taking the news in their stride, the Lehmans went over to the opening of the exhibition. Then, arriving about four or five at the executive mansion, he learned some of the facts: the surprise, the catastrophic damage to the fleet, the loss of life.

For the next few hours he labored frantically. He feared riotous demonstrations against peaceable German-Americans and Japanese-Americans. Sitting at the telephone for several hours he talked with mayors and police chiefs of all the larger cities, warning them to take precautions to protect life and property. This done, he began using the telephone to warn communities of possible incendiarism and efforts to blow up factories. He doubled the guards at Croton, Kensico, other important reservoirs, and all the armories. The night passed without incident, but next day came new alarms. He recalls:

> I remember being in my office in the capitol quite early Monday morning, and I got a report—for we kept the adjutant-general's office open and the head of the National Guard was constantly in touch with me—that enemy planes had been sighted 500 miles from New York. I knew that I couldn't possibly get down to New York City in time to do any good there, and by staying in Albany I could direct affairs. I decided I would remain until we could see the situation a little more clearly. The next report came in that the planes were 250 miles from New York. I took it perfectly for granted that we were going to have an attack. Everybody else thought so. Then in a little while we got news that it was a mistake, they were not enemy planes at all; they were our own reconnoitering planes. But it was a very ticklish morning.

A series of war measures followed. The legislature, which sat for three and a half months beginning January 7, 1942, passed bill after bill recommended by the governor. In place of the existing defense councils it created a state war council and local war councils, with broad powers for civilian defense and blackout enforcement. It established a stronger mechanism for the care and feeding of people in bombed areas and for mutual aid among communities by the pooling of water, fuel, fire-fighting resources, and police. It voted an act for the closer guarding of shipyards, piers, and war production facilities. To conserve tires, cars, and gasoline it placed a forty-mile speed limit on the highway.

The governor had continued, despite his refusal to join the Zionist movement, to watch sympathetically the movement of refugees into Palestine. Between 1933 and 1940 about a quarter of a million Jews from Central and Eastern Europe had found homes there. Though the war of course sealed na-

Herbert H. Lehman at the Democratic National Convention of 1936
At Lehman's right is Senator Robert F. Wagner.

Wide World Photos

Governor and Mrs. Lehman at the Christening of the New York Central's
Empire State Express, December, 1941

New York Daily News

Governor Lehman with his pet boxer dog, Budget, in the garden of Executive
Mansion, Albany, about 1938.

Family snapshot

Herbert H. Lehman and his son Lieutenant Peter Lehman, in England, 1943

tional boundaries and closed the seas, still a thin stream filtered in. As Lehman said, they hoped not only to escape oppression but to revive their ancient cultural and spiritual life. The summer of 1942 found the British building a powerful army east of El Alamein in Egypt, armed in part with American bombers and tanks. Zionist groups in the United States wished to see a separate Jewish army organized in Palestine. To this Lehman was strongly opposed. The Middle East was under a threat which demanded unity among its defenders, he told a rally held in Madison Square Garden by the American Jewish Congress and others on July 21, 1942. He was confident that the Jews of Palestine would reject the idea of a separate force: [14]

> But the thousands of brave, strong young Jews of Palestine who have built up their land for the benefit of all—Christian, Jew, and Mohammedan alike—should be given the opportunity of defending their homes and the products of their bitter toil. They have long shown their courage and strength. By their sacrifices they have long given evidence of their devotion to the ideals of freedom and justice. They should be permitted to fight side by side with their British and American friends in behalf of our common cause. . . .

Of course they were so permitted, and history records the good account they gave of themselves, helping to hold the lines before Cairo and sharing the entry into Tobruk.

· V ·

The last of the constructive state measures near to Lehman's heart were now being written into law or otherwise put into effect. The work of eliminating railway grade crossings on important highways was being completed. Some funds were left over, and he gave his support to a constitutional amendment transferring $60,000,000 of grade crossing bonds to highway and parkway purposes. Adopted the second time in 1941, it was approved by the people that fall. He signed on May 22, 1942, a bill authorizing the construction of a superhighway or thruway from the west bank of the Hudson at the New Jersey line to the Buffalo area and Pennsylvania boundary beyond. This had to be made effective by repeated legislative appropriations. He made a successful effort to bring about the abolition of those pernicious bodies called blue-ribbon juries. Operating in New York City and Westchester, these bodies were hand-picked to be *convicting* juries, care being taken to exclude all persons who did not take the most rigorous attitudes toward suspected criminals. "To say the very least," declared Lehman, "such a practice is inexcusable."

In the fall of 1941 his patience with La Guardia was finally stretched to the breaking point. The sudden death of Morris Tremaine of Buffalo created a vacancy in the office of state comptroller. To fill it Lehman on October 17 appointed Jeremiah O'Leary, who for two years had been commissioner of standards and purchase, a well-trained, industrious official. The question arose whether O'Leary should fill out Tremaine's term or a special election be held; the Court of Appeals decided he might hold on. "It didn't mean a damn thing to me," Lehman recalls, "and I don't think it meant anything to anybody in the Democratic Party." But immediately following the decision La Guardia, who was running for reëlection as mayor, delivered an abusive tirade against court and governor. Lehman was supporting his Democratic opponent, Judge William O'Dwyer, largely on the ground he assigned in a speech in the Bronx:

"I state from my long experience as chief executive and from my knowledge of the needs of civilian defense that no man can at the same time successfully carry on the unusually heavy duties of mayor of New York City and United States Director of Civilian Defense."

La Guardia's outburst was couched in his own special billingsgate. Referring to the Court of Appeals, he said that Lehman and Ed Flynn "caused the opinion of their own attorney general to be kicked out of the window by the court"—an accusation that the judges corruptly took orders. And speaking of Lehman he declared: "You have heard of goniffs stealing from goniffs. Well, you are hearing now of double-crossers double-crossing double-crossers"—an accusation that the governor was a thief and hypocrite.[15]

Seldom if ever in his public career was Lehman so incensed as by these insults. The gratuitous attack on the highest tribunal of the state, headed by his brother, stung him to the heart. He issued a statement that throbbed with anger:

> The mayor, not only in this campaign, but for a long time since in his capacity as chief executive of the city, has abused and vilified everyone who opposed or criticized him. "Thief," "double-crosser," "crook," "bum" are among the milder of the mayor's epithets. The people of the city have heard a lot of the mayor's abuse and a few even seek to excuse it on the ground that it is merely an eccentricity. But now the mayor has reached a new low. The mayor's practice of abusing his opponents in both private and public life is not an eccentricity but a deliberate technique to intimidate those who oppose him. Unfortunately, to some extent these tactics have succeeded. . . .
> But I cannot be intimidated. I have treated the mayor with the utmost consideration and courtesy. It is my intention to continue that

course. But I do not intend now or at any other time to stand for abuse and misrepresentation. The mayor's tactics are . . . inexcusable in a high public official. New Yorkers are sick and tired of Mr. La Guardia's unbridled tongue.

The mayor accused me of taking orders from the so-called political bosses when the Democrats made their nomination for state comptroller. The mayor talks about dishonest deals and double-crossers. Every newspaper has published the true version, that it was I who urged the Democratic Party to nominate Mr. O'Leary. The mayor knows the facts. The leaders of his own party, the American Labor Party, have told him the facts. It is unfortunate when an intemperate tongue wilfully distorts the truth.

La Guardia issued no retraction. Instead, he made a new speech in which he repeated his charge, telling a mass meeting of the American Labor Party that "if the candidate doesn't deliver, then they can always find a court to kick him off." This fresh affront to the Court of Appeals drew from Lehman a slashing rejoinder: [16]

The insulting and vicious accusations cannot possibly be excused on the ground of a slip of the tongue. . . . They constitute a deliberate and unjustifiable attack on the highest court of the state and on the governor.

A governor who has been honored by the people of the State of New York with high office in six successive elections and who has served them for thirteen years with all his strength and ability, does not need any defense before the people.

The Court of Appeals needs no defense. The court, in the character and ability of its seven members, is second to none in the nation. No community on the face of the earth has been better served than New York State has been by its great Court of Appeals, whose Chief Judge, I am proud to say, is my brother Irving Lehman, who has served with great distinction on the bench for thirty-three years.

What is more vital than the personal insult to me is the shameless and scurrilous attack which Mayor La Guardia has dared to make on the highest court in our state. That is unforgivable.

Though La Guardia never publicly apologized, he later showed contrition for his upflare in various ways. The two men gradually resumed their friendly relations. Lehman always appreciated La Guardia's high public aims and admired the indefatigable energy and shrewd judgment he put into his administration. He even felt a certain indulgence for his hotheaded, irascible ways! That La Guardia's assault on the governor and court was deeply resented by the people of New York was perfectly clear. Though he was reëlected, it cost him many thousands of votes.

It was understood from the beginning of 1942 that Lehman would not again compete for the governorship. Not only did he feel that he had served the state long enough, but he was anxious to enter a wider sphere of national or international activity. Roosevelt, sympathizing with this purpose, assured him that when his term expired an important task would be awaiting him.

Thus nobody was astonished when in May Lehman made an emphatic announcement that he would not seek a fifth term. He made it, as he rue-fully confessed later, all too emphatic, for it was almost as strong as General W. T. Sherman's famous declaration. He instantly lost nearly all his in-fluence in state politics. Had he kept the door open to a possible renomina-tion he might have retained enough authority to make Charles Poletti his inheritor. As it was, the moment he left the stage Attorney General Bennett rushed to the footlights and declared himself an aspirant. Bennett had the support of Jim Farley, the prestige of four terms as attorney general, and the aid of an eager host of friends who had shared his disappointment when he was set aside in 1938. But his nomination by the state convention in Brooklyn split the party badly.

The convention, in fact, was a scene of discord. Another strong aspirant was James Mead. To Farley, the state Warwick, the contest between Ben-nett and Mead was a struggle for control of the New York delegation in the coming national convention of 1944, Bennett opposing, and Mead favoring Roosevelt's renomination for a fourth term. This consideration did not cross Lehman's mind. He was indeed surprised to see feeling run so high. "It was the only time, I think," he recalls, "that I was booed at a Democratic con-vention. I nominated Mead, and Wagner seconded him. FDR, Wagner, and I were all booed over there, for Brooklyn was the home of Bennett. That convention left a good many wounds." Mead had served for four hard-working years as Senator in Washington, thoroughly loyal to the President. Poletti's acceptance of the nomination for lieutenant governor astonished Lehman, for Poletti had supported Mead, but he made a strong candidate—stronger than Bennett.

In his contest with Dewey, who maintained all his old state-wide popu-larity, Bennett was doomed to defeat from the start. He was as colorless as Dewey was dynamic. He had wide support among veterans, among the more conservative labor men, and in Queens, but he aroused no enthusiasm among independents. When the American Labor Party opposed him and nominated a rival ticket, this hurt his chances badly. In the end he was over-whelmed, and it was to help induct Dewey into the governorship that Leh-man rode to the inaugural exercises in Albany just after New Year's in 1943.

As he did so, an arduous and adventurous new scene was opening before him.

Chapter XI

UNRRA: THE ORGANIZATION OF WORLD RELIEF

WHEN Lehman received a summons from Franklin D. Roosevelt to come to the White House on November 11, 1942, he knew that demands for the relief of general distress in parts of the war zone had suddenly become agonizing. Even as his train rolled into Washington, the Anglo-American armies were landing along the coasts of Morocco and Algeria, some of the troop convoys crossing direct from our Atlantic ports and some steaming from English harbors through the Bay of Biscay. Although American forces met bloody resistance from the Vichy French at Oran and Casablanca, and the British did heavy fighting in Algiers, they quickly consolidated their hold on the area and turned to meet its problems. The most urgent, of course, was a piteous demand from the population for food, clothing, and medicines. Lehman did not know what Roosevelt wanted of him; it might be anything. But he could guess that one possibility was a role in the management of relief activities abroad.[1]

From the beginning of their conquest of Europe the Germans had made their "New Order" a regime of ruthless economic exploitation. They had scattered "economic teams" throughout the occupied countries to discover, list, and confiscate machinery, stocks of metal, rubber, vehicles, foods, objects of art, and a great variety of manufactured goods, which they sent in trainload after trainload to the Reich or its captive factories and depots. Hans Frank in Poland, Artur Seyss-Inquart in Holland, Josef Terboven in Norway, and a variety of functionaries in France adopted a policy of greedy robbery. They squeezed every resource on which they could lay hands. Before long they were compelling helpless civilians and prisoners of war to serve as slave labor. Their policy of "Aryanization" meant the seizure of Jewish property and the wholesale deportation and extermination of Jewish groups. In the

First World War, Herbert Hoover had directed a magnificent work of relief behind the German lines in Belgium and some others areas; now nothing of the kind was possible. Reports of appalling hardship, want, and misery leaked out from the countries under the German heel.

Lehman was not astonished when Roosevelt told him that he was creating an Office of Foreign Relief and Rehabilitation Operations in the State Department. It was high time. Of this cumbrously-named agency (promptly styled OFRRO) he wished the governor to become head. Roosevelt let him know that OFRRO might not last long, as plans were already being made for a larger international relief organization; and he meant to keep Lehman in charge through all the changes ahead. The appointment had not been discussed with Secretary of State Hull, who first heard of it when the President, with the governor sitting beside him, telephoned an abrupt announcement: "I have just told Herbert Lehman that I want him to come down here and serve in the Department as director for foreign relief." It later became clear that this irritated Hull, who would have preferred Dean Acheson, Assistant Secretary of State, but he held his peace and the press announced the choice on November 21. Judge Rosenman correctly remarks that FDR thought it only poetic justice that, since the Jews had suffered so much from the Nazis, a Jew should be put in charge of relief in Nazi-dominated lands; but of course the President based his choice primarily on Lehman's well-known organizational ability.[2]

The scale and cruelty of the relief needs were steadily growing. Some miseries of the time were heart-rending. The German occupation of southern France in December, 1942, sealed the doom of a host of exiles trapped in Axis Europe. Clandestine exits were still open over the Pyrenees for the very hardiest, who escaped across the snowy passes into Spain at an average rate of a hundred a day. Some were Frenchmen intent on joining the Free French forces in North Africa, but a motley array of Dutch, Scandinavians, and Poles braved the perils to cross with them. The central problem, however, was the growth of hunger and disease all the way from the North Cape to Naples. While the extension of the Anglo-American lines in Africa brought hope to stricken peoples there, and especially to the millions of refugees scattered from Morocco around the Mediterranean to Syria, nearly all Europe remained in chains, with countless people in a desperate plight.

When Lehman left the White House he was pledged to take Federal office again; he was enlisting in his second war. But just what were his duties? He did not know. While he hoped that OFRRO might accomplish something, he realized that this purely American agency must soon be supplanted by an international organization, which would give him his best chance to serve humanity.

• I •

An earnest effort was under way, as Lehman knew, to bring this international organization into existence. Months before Pearl Harbor, in mid-1941, farsighted men had begun looking beyond the military liberation of Europe to plan for the social and economic revolution which must follow. Most of them were in London, seat of the principal governments in exile, and Winston Churchill and Sir Frederick Leith-Ross, Chief Economic Advisor to the British Government, were the pioneer leaders.

A far view indeed was then required to look to military victory and beyond, for the Nazis had continued to carry everything before them. Compelling the aid of Hungary, Rumania, and Bulgaria, they used the spring months of 1941 to conquer Yugoslavia and Greece. During a long battle summer their armies penetrated deep into Russia, besieging Leningrad, driving within sixty miles of Moscow, and battering their way into Rostov. Though the British had repulsed the Italian effort to conquer Egypt from Libya, Rommel with mechanized German forces soon regained the initiative and again threatened Cairo. Only near the end of 1941 did the gloom lift slightly as the Russians stiffened their resistance, the British began an African offensive which threw Rommel back, and Pearl Harbor brought the United States into the war.

Yet while the hour was darkest, the British Government on July 11, 1941, informed Dean Acheson that it had appointed a ministerial committee under Leith-Ross to draw up a plan for the relief of Europe. Churchill's associates knew that the primary producers of food and textiles, the United States, Canada, Australia, New Zealand, India, and Argentina, had suffered from the loss of Old World markets and were piling up surpluses.[3] They knew that the Nazi-exploited territories were falling deeper into hunger and cold every month, for the Dutch, French, and other governments kept them reminded of the fact. Malnutrition was causing a sharp rise in child mortality and the general incidence of disease. Somehow, London felt, preparations should be made to pour overseas surpluses into the aching void in Europe, North Africa, and the Middle East. Indeed, if the eventual Allied advance were not accomplished by energetic measures for revictualing, reclothing, and rehousing needy peoples, victory might prove partial and precarious.

The month after Leith-Ross's appointment, Roosevelt and Churchill met at sea on the warship *Augusta* to sign the Atlantic Charter. Other nations, including Russia, associated themselves with the Anglo-American declaration, and a new world organization adumbrated itself in the smoky chaos of the time. On New Year's Day, 1942, it took firmer outline as a powerful coalition for both war and peace, for twenty-six countries agreed in Washington to form the United Nations. It was hoped this would afford a foundation for collective security, for aiding impoverished lands, and for the general economic and social betterment of mankind.

Against this background, the developing London plans for European relief looked stronger. They had made some progress before Pearl Harbor. That is, fifteen nations had met on September 24, 1941, in St. James's Palace under Anthony Eden as chairman, had formed an Inter-Allied Committee on Post-War Requirements under Leith-Ross, and had created a bureau to collect information and estimates for its work.[4] After Pearl Harbor, the United States placed a representative on the Committee. But the formation of the United Nations made it clear that a broad international organization geared to that body was needed, and the British Foreign Office sent some draft ideas to the State Department. Various people mulled over them. Finally, in June, 1942, discussions were transferred to Washington, partly in a vain hope that Russian and Chinese delegates might attend. Hard work began, with Dean Acheson leading, but Leith-Ross, Richard Law (son of Andrew Bonar Law), and Harry Hawkins of the State Department all making important contributions.

Out of these discussions, running through June, 1942, came the text of a scheme for a United Nations Relief and Rehabilitation Administration (UNRRA). This document, ready by the end of August and approved by Roosevelt and Hull, was submitted to the British, Russian, and Chinese governments. But since the war was going badly again, for the British had lost Tobruk and the Germans kept their positions deep in Russia, the leaders decided to defer the holding of an international conference to discuss the scheme. Thus matters stood when Lehman left Albany to become head of OFRRO, leaving Poletti as Governor.

• II •

"They were in a great hurry to have me come down," said Lehman later, for the North African needs were imperative. He made haste, but even when he was free to begin full-time work in Washington in December, 1942, he found that his powers remained shadowy. As OFRRO had been created by executive order and no statute defined its functions, he had to obtain a letter from the President fixing its sphere and authorizing him to resolve conflicts of authority with other agencies. He was to have direct access to the President and to report to Secretary Hull directly, not through formal channels. OFRRO policies were to be hammered out in consultation with other countries.

One basic policy, that OFRRO should not try to ship goods through the Allied blockade into Axis-held lands, was established without delay. It did not please Herbert Hoover, who had pushed relief supplies for Belgium through the blockade in the First World War and wished the feat performed again. Lehman, who admired his work and valued his advice, responded to a letter from Hoover by asking him to lunch.[5] With characteristic earnestness, Hoover declared that the Allies ought to ship food forthwith into Western Europe in the same way that three neutrals, Sweden, Turkey, and Switzerland, were shipping it into Greece. The governments-in-exile could pay the costs. In mid-January, 1943, Hoover published a report describing the sufferings of people in the occupied countries and arguing for this policy. But transport difficulties, food scarcities in Britain, and Allied sentiment made such action impossible even had Roosevelt and Churchill favored it—and they opposed it.

"Let Hitler bear his responsibilities to the full," Churchill had told the Commons on August 21, 1940, "and let the people of Europe who groan beneath his yoke aid in every way the coming of the day when that yoke will be broken. Meanwhile we can and we will arrange in advance for the speedy entry of food into any part of the enslaved area when this part has been wholly cleared of the German forces." [6]

The history of OFRRO was short. It was not until March 19, 1943, that Roosevelt sent Lehman the explanatory letter, and in September the agency was nominally combined with the Lend-Lease Administration and the Office of Economic Warfare to form the Foreign Economic Administration (FEA). Actually, it was merged into UNRRA rather than FEA; Lehman thought the idea of absorption into economic administration senseless, opposed it, and found a natural home for his slowly increasing staff in the United Nations relief organization. The important fact is that OFRRO lasted only about six months, and was essentially a pathbreaker for UNRRA. Still, it accomplished something.

In the first place, it encountered and partly conquered endless difficulties in pathbreaking. Lehman had to use it at once to help care for the destitute and homeless in North Africa and the Middle East and to try to get some supplies, transportation, and staff for his imminent tasks when Europe should be invaded—all at a time when shortages of food, clothing, ships, and capable men were paralyzing. He met frustrations on every hand. When he attempted to study in detail the relief requirements in the lands the Allies expected to conquer, he found this subject enveloped in gloom. He would have been glad to begin stockpiling materials for the day of victory, but the armed forces demanded all the materials in sight. When he searched for experienced aides, he found that the forces, war industries, and government offices had gobbled them all up. Even for the half-starved people of Morocco and Algeria, and the sad refugee camps of Egypt and Palestine, the wheat, the tents, and the capable aides he needed were unobtainable. Always a worrier, he had never worried so intensely as now. He had a feeling that he was tied hand and foot while multitudes perished. And all the while he had to fight the Battle of the Potomac—the battle for power.

"I found the responsibilities were there," he records,[7] "but the authority was sometimes very much lacking. There was a good deal of jealousy within the State Department, and between it and other Departments, which felt that a new man in a new bureau or division would limit their authority and opportunities for managing operations. While on the surface I had cooperation, actually I frequently did not have it; quite the opposite. This was partly due to the fact that everyone in Washington was fighting for power." The Board of Economic Warfare was fighting for power. The Lend-Lease Administration was fighting for power. The Combined Boards—that is, the Raw Materials Board, the Production and Resources Board, the Food Board, and the Shipping Adjustment Board, all Anglo-American or Anglo-Canadian-American—were fighting for power. The Army, Navy, and Air Force did not need power, for they had it, but they fought to maintain it.[8]

The military attitude was that a lion's share was not enough: "When in doubt, take everything." If the Army wanted 10,000 tons of a certain commodity, and the relief agencies wanted 1,000 tons, the Army did not take 9,000 and give UNRRA, the Red Cross, and the Friends' Service Committee 1,000; it took 10,000, and kept it.

Once Lehman went to plead with Admiral Leahy, Roosevelt's chief military adviser, able, arbitrary, and brusque. "I told him of our plight; people were dying for want of supplies. He turned on me and said: 'Now look here, young man, I want you to know just one thing. I've no doubt you need the supplies, and I'm very sorry that people are suffering. But I'm here to look after the Army, and I'm going to see that the Army gets everything they want. No use your coming and arguing with me any more, because that's my position, and I'm going to stick to it.' " Of course, Lehman knew that the one absolutely essential goal was victory in the field; everything must yield to that. On another occasion Lehman talked over the supply problem with the Secretary of the Navy. Frank Knox was outwardly full of sympathy; relief organizations, he said, must be helped; but he did little helping. Secretary Hull exuded sympathy even more strongly but lifted hardly a finger to make it effective.[9]

Meanwhile the attitude of the public, the press, and Congress remained difficult. While humanitarians and idealists warmly supported international relief, isolationists were frigid. Congressman Claire Hoffman of Michigan, for example, in November, 1942 demanded how Roosevelt could reconcile his statement that one third of the nation were ill-fed, ill-clad, and ill-housed with a program for making the United States the Santa Claus of the world, packing gift baskets with goods needed at home.

Yet OFRRO in its six months did get some nutriment to the starving, some hope to the despairing. By mid-May, 1943 all North Africa was in Allied hands, and much of the wretched population around the southern rim of the Mediterranean could be succored. OFRRO had hastened to send a representative to Eisenhower's area. It was almost impossible to get plane seats; finally one place appeared, and two effective men, William Hodson, long Welfare Commissioner in New York City, and Fred K. Hoehler, who had held the same position in the State of Illinois, drew straws to see who would get it. Hodson, elatedly, won—but he won a death seat, for the plane crashed! [10] Soon afterward, Hoehler arrived safely and took charge of the distribution of foodstuffs, medicines, clothing and garments. Simultaneously OFRRO assisted the great numbers of West European refugees in Spain, sent goods into Greece through Swiss and Swedish intermediaries, and took over much of the work the British were doing in managing immense camps in the western part of North Africa for Greek, Yugoslav, Polish, and other refugees. These camps were vexatious places, for Greeks, Poles, and above all the Yugoslavs had split into warring factions, ready to cut each others' throats.

OFRRO was supported in this work partly by the President's Emergency Fund and partly by the Lend-Lease Administration, which obtained food from the Agricultural Department, medical supplies through the War Department, and clothing and other goods from the procurement division of the Treasury, the army lending a hand. For the OFRRO period Lehman kept his staff small, avoided creating any procurement facilities of his own, and leaned heavily for counsel on experts in the Board of Economic Warfare and the Inter-Allied Committee on Post-War Requirements, Leith-Ross's body. He developed procedures for handling supplies. Meanwhile, he did his best to push the work of organizing UNRRA. With this end in view, he helped oversee the labors of twenty-four committees, who wrote a set of reports on all aspects of relief and rehabilitation and on the modes of administering the UNRRA machinery. A good deal of this huge mass of information was ultimately gathered into a volume entitled *Handbook, United States Delegation*, which, when issued in October, 1943, proved of practical value.

The jackals of isolationism and national selfishness prowling in the background had meanwhile to be tossed bones in the shape of arguments and reassurances. Lehman and his aides had to explain to Americans over and over again that they could help emaciated Arabs, Belgians, and Poles reach a goal of 2,000 calories a day—all too seldom, alas, attained—without imperiling their own food stocks. They had to make it plain that the United States expected other countries to bear their fair share of the relief burden and that Britain, the Dominions, and Sweden were eager to do so. They had to assure timid people that the armed forces were getting priority for everything they asked. Lehman made tactful speeches, like that in New York on January 9, 1943, in which he dismissed as rubbish the idea that the government would underwrite any "utopian system." The aims of OFRRO, he said, were strictly practical: to help the liberated nations help themselves and regain their health in a better world.

He assured a group of Congressmen that American resources would not be dissipated to the injury of the citizens. "We look upon the problem as demanding the highest degree of human compassion, yet as one which can be solved only by a businesslike approach." [11] A speech at Swarthmore similarly emphasized practical considerations.[12] Though he told a Senate subcommittee late in February that he thought the invasion of Europe would necessitate world expenditures of half a billion dollars to meet urgent relief needs, as yet the President and he asked for nothing.

· III ·

So much for the brief flight of OFRRO, an emergency body. What of UNRRA, all the while in gestation?

Discussions of the form and function of this world agency had continued in Washington and London during the winter of 1942–43, and the ensuing months, with Lehman's twenty-four committees lending a hand. In April, 1943, Lehman had crossed to England to learn more about Allied ideas of the organization, the problems ahead, and the best modes of action. After a difficult air journey, on which he was greeted by some shipwrecked American sailors at Horta and kept waiting for a time in Lisbon, he was met in England by Averell Harriman, FDR's personal representative in England,

Lieutenant General Frank M. Andrews, then commander of the American forces in Great Britain, and Ambassador Winant. He had the pleasure of seeing his son Peter, who was in the air force and whom General Andrews had brought to London for the purpose. Then he and his assistant, Hugh R. Jackson, began a series of conferences.[13] On every hand he met jealousies.

He found that the American army staffs in Europe had done almost no planning for civilian relief and that General Andrews was for placing all such work under the Combined Chiefs of Staff, with army men controlling it so long as military occupation lasted. Andrews' attitude was not astonishing, nor was the fact that the British military authorities held the same ideas about their preëmptive rights. "It appears to me," recorded Hugh Jackson, "that the British have about the same confusion as between military and civilian provisions of supply for this period as we do, but they will probably muddle through without too much difficulty."

Britain had its Battle of the Thames to match the Battle of the Potomac, and Lord Woolton's capable Ministry of Food was in the thick of it. It was feeding Britain austerely on an equitable rationing scheme which favored mothers and children, but it did so only by herculean efforts and kept an anxious eye on every pound of meat, cheese, or bread. Lehman saw a good deal of Woolton, a Liverpool businessman, who actually improved British health by extra milk, vitaminized bread, and improved cookery; a big man with a big head and brow, a great promontory of a nose, and a kindly look. His slogan was, "We not only cope, we care." Lehman liked him, if not all of his ideas. Woolton declared that the job of providing relief supplies should fall mainly on the shoulders of his own ministry or other supply agencies working through the Combined Boards; and that actual distribution in the occupied areas might be done by UNRRA, but only with substantial assistance from Woolton's organization.

It was clear, noted Jackson, that the Ministry of Food wished to play a leading role in the relief work. "I also felt that he (Woolton) was making a very strong play for the continuance and the expansion of the Combined Boards, and it is my personal hunch that the Ministry of Food is one of the leading agencies to which Jebb of the Foreign Office referred the day before as believing that an organization such as UNRRA was unnecessary, or at most should have limited functions."

Harriman, sitting with Lehman, General Andrews, Ambassador Winant, and others, sympathized with Woolton's desire to exercise a large control over the flow of British foodstuffs into relief channels. He expressed the opinion that British reserves should be built up to a much higher level by use of the regular British machinery, without separate stockpiling for civilian relief; and then the outflow of food should be controlled by the Combined Food Board, a purely Anglo-Canadian-American body. American military authorities were receiving a considerable part of their food supplies through British shipping, warehousing, and other arrangements.

Both Lehman and Leith-Ross were somewhat horrified by these narrow views. They were emphatically of the opinion that it would never do to leave the tasks of relief and reconstruction to three or four English-speaking lands. What was needed was a great and willing organization of forty-odd countries, joined in an effort not Anglo-American, but world-wide. The undertaking should be international, enthusiastic, and prompt, with a clear prior determination of relative responsibilities and with as much pooling of supplies as possible. It would be important, Lehman knew, to make sure of full foreign assistance, for Congress and the American taxpayer would never accept the idea that Uncle Sam should do more than his share. It was also important to cover the whole field: the rescue of small children by supplies of milk; warfare against disease; the rebuilding of villages and towns; the investment of capital in new or restored industries; the return of millions upon millions of refugees to their homes; the distribution of seeds, plants, and livestock to revive agriculture.

Leith-Ross agreed with all this, and had strong opinions of his own on getting some immediate relief to the populations inside the Nazi blockade. He wanted milk and vitamins shipped to children and expectant mothers in the Western democracies as soon as safeguards could be devised, for he knew that the Belgians, Dutch, and Norwegians in particular sorely needed such aids.[14]

A great deal was said in a blunt way by various Britons about difficulties that the relief and rehabilitation effort would face. Woolton was pessimistic over the general food situation, expressing doubt whether enough would be available in the immediate postwar period for both the fighting nations and rescued peoples. Sir Robert Sinclair emphasized the probable inadequacy of transport—which, in fact, worried everyone.

The chief expert on the problem of displaced persons was Sir Herbert Emerson, the capable Commissioner for Refugees for the League of Nations and Director of the International Governmental Committee on Refugees, a body which had grown out of the futile Evian Conference called by Roosevelt in 1938. Everyone agreed that UNRRA alone could take responsibility for the refugees, for the problem would tax all the capacities of world philanthropy, and a weaker body would be impotent. Emerson estimated, in fact, that the displaced persons in Western Europe, North Africa, and the Middle East numbered fully twenty millions, many of them sunk in wretchedness and malnutrition; and while the great majority would voluntarily return to their old homes, he believed that fully two millions would be helpless and need to find new havens.

Maynard Keynes lucidly stated still further difficulties. Countries which had been spared a costly war effort, like the occupied lands, Sweden, and Switzerland, would emerge from the conflict with substantial balances abroad. Great Britain, which had fought heavily from the outset and for a time alone, save for the Dominions, would have an international deficit. Some appropriate adjustment of costs would be requisite. Keynes also pointed out that if the nations pooled their resources for relief, it would be difficult to determine the time when normal trade relationships should be recommenced. He emphasized the fact that the United States and Britain had developed their supply machinery during the war on the basis of a simple allotment of responsibility to the Combined Boards, without trying to arrive at predetermined proportions; they had left it to the Boards to furnish the right kinds and quantities of supplies at the right time and place. This machinery he thought might well be maintained for the postwar period. If a raw materials pool were now created, said Keynes, Britain could put little into it beyond coal, wool, and cocoa.

The most important accomplishment of these London conversations was the hammering out of a set of general principles to guide UNRRA in the early stages of its work. Everybody agreed that in the first occupation of enemy territory the military forces must have full control. Supplies might come from Lend-Lease or the Combined Boards, but army approval would have to be given for procurement, and the theater commander must consent to distribution. This fact made it important for UNRRA and the military forces to begin some joint planning immediately and for an able UNRRA representative to be placed in London forthwith to deal with this joint action. Joint civilian-military stockpiling should also be initiated, so that UNRRA would have adequate reserves of food, clothing, medicines, and other commodities.

The talks assumed a dietary standard of about 2,000 calories a day, or somewhat more than civilian populations were getting under Nazi occupation. As each country was rescued and began receiving goods, it should be asked to pay for them. Obviously, Western Europe would be in a position to make this payment in sterling or dollars, while Eastern Europe could not; obviously, too, lands like France, Holland, and Norway could quickly organize distribution systems of their own, and would insist on their own governmental controls of distribution. In Eastern Europe the problem would be more complex, and some form of food ticket would have to be devised, to be exchanged for local currency. Free distribution, while necessary in many places, should be kept at a minimum—for overburdened Americans and Britons would react strongly against loose world-wide philanthropy.

Lehman was emphatic in stating that sacrifice must be general and equal. "He emphasized," runs Hugh Jackson's summary of a conference on April 15, 1943, with Eden, Woolton, Dalton, and others, "that our Congress would be much more ready to proceed with substantial appropriations if they were assured of similar action on the part of the British and other governments. He also stressed the importance of having the Allies understand that it would be physically impossible to meet many of their demands, while at the same time we should be careful not to discourage them too greatly."

The last important conference in London, held April 20, 1943, at Claridge's, was almost wholly devoted to an exchange of views between Lehman and Leith-Ross. They agreed that while such countries as Belgium could pay for most of the commodities needed, the chances of payment from a nation like Poland were small. Leith-Ross suggested that after a competent authority under UNRRA had assessed each country's resources, some nations should receive supplies free, others part-free, and others at normal prices. He did not agree with the British Treasury's view that countries should pay up to the limit of their resources; on the other hand, neither he nor Lehman believed that credits should be advanced in order to finance relief; for when that was done after the First World War friction ensued, and the amounts repaid were negligible. But nobody in London, any more than in Washington, could throw much light on the amount of relief probably needed or the probable amount of the gifts to be made. Men could only hope that, inasmuch as the armed forces of the United States and the British Commonwealth would each approach eight millions when the war ended and would be rapidly demobilized, the supplies accumulated would form a large initial reserve.

It had been assumed from the beginning of negotiations for UNRRA that, since an important part of its work would be directed from London, the European Regional Office (ERO) there would be an important center. Lehman and Leith-Ross agreed that a sizable organization would be needed, that it should direct field operations throughout Europe, but permit a great deal of national autonomy, and that while it would be predominantly English-speaking (for Continental personnel were needed in their own countries to carry on relief), it might make some use of experienced neutral relief workers, especially the Swiss and Swedes. The headquarters staff of ERO would have to be drawn from nationals of member governments. A Supplies Committee would have especially important functions in dealing

with the Combined Boards, handling gifts, and creating a system of priori-
ties. Finally, the two men discussed the question of general organization in
Washington and London.

"Sir F. Leith-Ross," writes Hugh Jackson, "said he felt it was undesirable
to have cut-and-dried plans or organization worked out in great detail; he
thought that adaptation according to the needs of the situation would have
to be a guiding principle. Mr. Lehman agreed that there would have to be
a great deal of adjustment to secure efficient working, but quoted his own
experience in the establishment of OFRRO in which it had been difficult
to scrap an organizational set-up once it was established. It was very difficult to keep the organization simple, and at the same time, avoid overlap-
ping and duplicating arising from a lack of clarity in defining the functions
and the principles of an organization." Lehman was certain that the Combined Boards would have to be continued after the war to supply control
and guidance in their various fields and that the Supplies Division of
UNRRA would have to collaborate with them.

On his return journey Lehman met with many inconveniences. His plane
took him to Lisbon, to Bolama in Portuguese Guinea, to Liberia, and to Natal
in Brazil. On May 1 he and his companions were at Trinidad, which they left
early in the morning, to reach Bermuda late that night. A conference on
refugees had just closed there, and the entire American contingent rode
with them on the plane to New York, which they reached on May 2, 1943.
Lehman gave reporters a glowing account of his visit to Britain, which had
included talks with the King, Queen, and Churchill. "The ground," he said,
"has been well prepared for intimate collaboration."

· IV ·

When, in June, Dean Acheson and his helpers completed a draft agreement for UNRRA to be laid before representatives of some two-score nations, a storm blew up in Congress. The State Department showed the draft
to majority and minority leaders of both houses and then published it
(June 11) to invite full discussion. But nobody had discussed it privately
with the House or Senate foreign committees, which felt irritated. Moreover, Hull made it clear that it would not be submitted to Congress but
made effective as an executive agreement. The Senate Foreign Relations
Committee was particularly jealous of its powers over foreign affairs, and
Arthur Vandenberg, till lately the very isolationist-minded leader of the
Republican minority, was a sentry always on the alert. Seizing his trumpet
to sound an alarm, he warned the nation that the Administration was get-

ting out of hand. It was pledging the total resources of the republic for whatever schemes of boundless world benevolence the crystal-gazers of the New Deal might project. If the Senate did not stop Roosevelt, Hopkins, and Lehman, they would give away the whole national wealth.

A Senate subcommittee at once began investigating this plot to destroy American solvency, and Tom Connally questioned Cordell Hull so severely that the wrathful Secretary refused to return to later hearings. The controversy not only provided newspaper headlines but gave the isolationists hope that they could force Vandenberg, who was veering toward international cooperation, back into camp and deal the Administration a stinging blow.[15] The *Washington Times-Herald*, owned by Mrs. Eleanor Patterson, denounced the relief plans as a wicked example of "world planning, world WPA-ing, and World Spending of U.S. Money."

At this point the State Department tactfully gave ground. Under-Secretary Acheson and Senator Vandenberg set to work on an agreement and, as men of moderation and skill, found the task easy. The text was changed to make it clear that no blank check was being drawn and that the agreement carried nothing but an authorization for appropriations, under which subsequent specific votes would be required for any grant of funds. Congress thus retained full opportunity to make final decisions, but the Administration still avoided the risky necessity of asking the Senate for a two-thirds vote. In the course of his labors, Vandenberg learned so much about the vast and piteous need of stricken peoples that he became a heartfelt advocate of all the purposes of UNRRA.[16]

After much preparatory work, the UNRRA compact was signed in a colorful ceremony in the White House on November 9, 1943. Representatives of forty-four nations, embracing four-fifths of the people of the world, gathered about a long table. President Roosevelt, seated in a high-backed chair, with the flags of the United Nations ranged along the wall, at his back, dominated the gathering. Conspicuous as an observer was Herbert H. Lehman. At high noon an aide began calling the roll of nations; as each delegate came forward he bowed and shook hands with the President and sat down beside him to sign the document; this done, he rose, shook hands again, and returned to his place. After the eighty-eight handshakes, Roosevelt from his chair addressed the nation by radio. The nations would learn to work together, he declared, by actually working together.

> The sufferings of the little men and women who have been ground under the Axis heel can be relieved only if we utilize the production of *all* the world to balance the want of *all* the world. In UNRRA we have devised a mechanism, based on the processes of true democ-

Herbert H. Lehman and Dean Acheson at the First Council Session of UNRRA, Atlantic City, November, 1943

UNRRA Photograph in the National Archives

Commander Robert G. A. Jackson, Senior Deputy Director General of UNRRA
(Now Sir Robert Jackson)

UNRRA Photograph in the National Archives

racy, which can go far toward accomplishment of such an objective in the days and months of desperate emergency which will follow the overthrow of the Axis.

The organization thus agreed upon, with the busy Dean Acheson its principal architect, was to be administered by a Director-General with executive powers, a Council as its policy-formulating body, and a Central Committee to make policy decisions of an emergency character. The Council would consist of forty-four men from forty-four member nations (later forty-seven each), the Central Committee of men named by the United States, Britain, China, and the Soviet Union. Various lesser committees were authorized, notably one on supplies and others for special regions. The Council was to choose its own chairman and elect the Director-General on his unanimous nomination by the Central Committee. Very fittingly, the Central Committee made Dean Acheson its first chairman and Lester B. Pearson of Canada its second. The British foreign and economic ministries were deeply involved, and Acheson had carefully consulted the ambassadors of Britain, the Soviet Union, and China in the work of organization.

The day after the White House meeting, a special train carried the delegates to Atlantic City for the first session of the Council, some 240 delegates and alternates attending. On the 11th, Lehman was nominated for Director-General and on motion of Dr. T. F. Chiang of China was elected. In his acceptance speech that evening he promised that he would act as representative of all the member governments, never accepting instructions from one power. Next day he began the staffing of an organization which, while continuing the relief work already begun all along the southern and eastern littoral of the Mediterranean, would be able to help meet the emergency wants of suffering peoples as soon as the Anglo-American forces invaded Sicily and Italy proper. We must say *help* meet it, for the armed forces would initially have to do much of the work, and the American and British Red Cross, with other voluntary organizations, would play important parts.[17]

Both the Washington and London offices, as we have said, would have to be given staffs mainly English-speaking, for citizens of Continental countries would be needed at home as soon as relief work started there. Capable people long remained hard to find. Nevertheless, an exceptionally able body of men were soon drawn into top positions. In Washington Sir Arthur Salter was appointed first Senior Deputy Director-General or executive head—a member of Parliament, prominent in the United Nations work, holder of an Oxford chair, author of important books on international affairs, and the recent head of a British shipping mission to the United States.

In Washington, Francis B. Sayre, who had been Assistant Secretary of State in charge of Trade Agreements, was the diplomatic adviser; Abraham H. Feller was general counsel; Roy F. Hendrickson, a former newspaperman who had held posts in the Interior and Agricultural Departments, was the initial Deputy Director-General for supply; Hugh R. Jackson was Deputy Director-General for regional liaison; and P. W. Kuo of China headed the secretariat. Other men were found to take charge of the divisions of finance and administration, health, displaced persons, and welfare. Mikhail A. Menshikov of Russia, later Soviet ambassador to the United States, was named Deputy Director-General for area studies and plans.

Salter accepted office on a temporary basis. A man of great ability, quick, resolute, and farsighted, he was essentially a planner and writer, while his post required an operational chief, a driving executive. "I don't think he was entirely sympathetic with his work," said Lehman later, "and he and I didn't see eye to eye on it." He resigned in October, 1944, and a re- markable Australian, Robert G. A. Jackson—"Jacko" to friends—succeeded him a few months later. Jackson was a commander in the British Navy who had been put in charge of Middle Eastern Supply Center, a man of grasp and personal force who soon became quite invaluable—and more than that, a close personal friend of Lehman's. Their friendship was to endure through- out the years and to be doubled in value when Jackson married Barbara Ward of the *London Economist,* who often visited the United States. Under a stipulation of the Foreign Office, Jackson was to be armed with Lehman's full authority both in the London office and in visiting UNRRA posts in other countries. Not the slightest misunderstanding ever clouded the relations of the American head and the Australian deputy head. An exact definition of the functions of the Washington headquarters and the London subhead- quarters (ERO) waited until early in 1945.

The Atlantic City meeting of the Council, November 10–December 1, 1943, ratified the basic principles of UNRRA operations in what Acheson called an unusual exhibition of international cooperation. Some members particularly promoted harmony: Acheson himself, Pearson of Canada, Walter Nash of New Zealand, Jean Monnet of France, Leith-Ross and Oliver Franks of Britain, and Francis B. Sayre of the United States. The basic principles were four. The organization was to help people to help themselves; it was not to expend its own resources for relief and rehabilita- tion in any area whose government was in a position to pay with foreign exchange; on the other hand, it was not to burden any government with a heavy foreign exchange debt; and finally, it was to distribute its aids so that all classes of the population, prosperous and poor, Christian, Moslem,

Jew, and Agnostic, radical and conservative, should have equitable shares of essential commodities—that is, it must not use relief as a political, religious, or class weapon. Unless special exception was made by the Council, it was to conduct its operations in United Nations territories alone, not in enemy territories. In these activities it must never impede the effective prosecution of the war. It might be added that the word "rehabilitation" in its title did not mean "reconstruction" and implied only transitional action to restart economic and social activities.

The most important decision of this first Council session, however, related to finances. Money had to be provided—and in large sums. Discussions in OFRRO had indicated that between two and three billion dollars would be needed for the first year's work, and these figures were soon accepted as targets. How should the funds be procured? Various ideas were threshed over by Lehman, Acheson, Richard Law, Keynes (who had visited Washington for the purpose), and Harry D. White of the Treasury Department. It was White who argued that contributions should be based on a fixed formula and that the fairest formula would be one percent of the annual national income of each member country whose territory had not been overrun. At Atlantic City Dean Acheson advocated this formula, and Great Britain and Canada strongly supported it. Though a few adverse voices were raised, the political and practical advantages of the plan were so plain that the delegates heartily adopted it.[18]

Under this plan the United States, with a national income then estimated at 135 billions, would contribute about $1,350,000,000 annually; the United Kingdom, with a national income of nearly 33 billions, would contribute $330,000,000; Canada, with a national income of 9 billions, would furnish about $90,000,000; and so on. These three countries alone would come near the two-billion-dollar mark. As the *London Economist* remarked, the academic concept of national income, an obscure term used by theorists, became for the first time in history a realistic instrument of statesmanship.

· V ·

In December, 1943, a year after he had left Albany for Washington, Lehman was able to settle into UNRRA headquarters in the triangular Walker–Johnson Building on Connecticut Avenue at Dupont Circle—quarters very ugly and very hot in summer, but usable. He could call staff meetings of deputy directors, start the machinery moving, and lay plans for early activities in Greece, Yugoslavia, and (after the Anglo-American armies cleared the ground) Italy.

Of all the undertakings of his life, this direction of a vast international effort for the rescue of perishing masses gave him the strongest feeling of devotion to a cause and the greatest satisfaction. He took pride in the fact that he was able to labor on a world-wide scene to help tens of millions; all his previous responsibilities seemed a preparation for this. He brought to his new duties a large experience in the tactful and efficient management of men. In one respect he was deficient. He had almost no flair for publicity, for his approach, as observers often noted, was that of a businessman, not a politician, evangelist, or public personality. He had no distinction as a speech-maker, writer, or diplomatist. He was even more a businessman in essential character than Hoover had been in the First World War. Lacking any gift for advertising himself or his organization, he had to depute that work to others.[19] He appealed to the mind, not the emotions; he liked to persuade by argument, not by use of dramatic contrivances. But his experience was guided by a powerful sense of order and method; it was given force by his intense compassion for struggling, suffering peoples; and it was saved from rashness by his prudence. His strong belief in justice, his conviction that the rich should share with the poor and the strong help the weak, were satisfied by the whole basis of UNRRA.

As he set to work above noisy Dupont Circle he could have paraphrased Churchill's words: "This is my happiest hour." But he did not anticipate what ordeals and frustrations lay just ahead.

Chapter XII

THE RACE
AGAINST HUMAN RUIN

Hurry! Hurry! Hurry!—this was the demand which, by the beginning of 1944, stared UNRRA administrators in the face. Every day that hunger, cold, and lack of medical care were prolonged was a day of death for hundreds, perhaps thousands. Yet after Lehman's improvised skeleton staff swung into full activity, he knew that effective relief must wait on the progress of the armies. Until the Allied forces overran most of Western Europe, little could be done for peoples all the way from Norway to Naples, and until the Soviet armies crashed into Germany, very little succor could be given Poland, Yugoslavia, or Hungary. The rate of military progress toward victory regulated the pace of international relief work.

That pace, in the global war in which Germany, Japan, and Fascist Italy had secured such enormous initial advantages, and in which such heavy problems of distance, industrial mobilization, and transport had to be conquered, seemed painfully slow. If 1943 could be called UNRRA's year of organization, 1944 was the year of effort and frustration. When Anglo-American forces took possession of all Sicily in August, 1943, the hopes of many had run high. That same month Roosevelt, Churchill, and the Combined Chiefs of Staff, meeting at Quebec, had determined to give the invasion of northern France priority and had fixed May 1, 1944 as the target date; but D-Day did not come until June.

The first representatives of UNRRA were busy in North Africa during the fall of 1943, and the first contribution of funds had come in December from the government of Iceland. But it was clear that stubborn fighting on all fronts lay ahead and that all relief workers must steel themselves for painful waiting. The year 1944 opened with a vote by Parliament (January 25) approving the first United Kingdom contribution of £80,000,000,

239

but it opened also with grim doubts about the war. Even after the landings in France, the Allies did not reach the borders of Germany until autumn.

· I ·

Lehman was to have the worst spring of his life that year. In March, while savage fighting went on in southern Italy, he flew to North Africa to inspect the work being done by UNRRA agents and negotiate an agreement with civil and military authorities in Cairo upon relief in the Balkans and Middle East. On March 19 he had mapped out a busy day in Algiers. He was to lunch at the British Embassy with Duff Cooper, British ambassador to the Free French, and to call afterwards on de Gaulle and General Giraud. In leaving the embassy he slipped on a small rug and fell heavily, breaking his leg at the knee. Taken to the hospital, he had his leg placed in a cast; and as his engagements were imperative, he was flown in that condition to Cairo.

It proved a risky flight. The pilot of his plane, Captain Thomas Akers, was little over halfway to Cairo when three engines of the four suddenly went dead. The plane dizzily dropped from 11,000 feet to 4,000. "I thought my last hour had come," Akers said later. Then, with equal suddenness, the engines restarted, and the flight proceeded. Of course Lehman knew nothing of what had happened. But as they approached Cairo in post-midnight darkness they were again in danger, for a sandstorm threatened to stop the engines again. In fact, theirs was the last plane to land safely that night.

Cairo was one of the most picturesque places on the globe, crowded with officers, troops from Australia, New Zealand, India, South Africa, and Britain, civil administrators, supply workers and displaced persons from three continents. It was the center of a huge network of British wartime interests extending throughout the areas washed by the Mediterranean, Red Sea, and Persian Gulf. Immense armed forces, more than half a million men, were deployed over these areas or passing through them. When the Germans menaced the Nile, Cairo had been full of toil, excitement, intrigue, and anxiety, with men working or worrying themselves to death. Now, while the Allied authorities watched the battlefronts in Italy, the guerrilla fighting in the Balkans, and the nearer antagonisms of Arabs, Greeks, and Jews, its tensions had somewhat relaxed, but it was still a tumultuous city.[1]

Lehman took up cramped quarters at the military hospital of Camp Buckstep, with an American army doctor attending him, until Ambassador Alexander C. Kirk offered him rooms in his house. Here, with the aid of

Hugh Jackson, he carried on a series of conferences with the Egyptian Government, the Allied Military Liaison Headquarters, and the British-organized Middle East Relief and Refugee Administration (MERRA). The Prime Minister, Nahas Pasha, the British Ambassador, Lord Moyne (a member of the Guinness family), and the head of MERRA, Sir William Matthews, all had to be seen. As Lehman could not move from his bed, everybody came to him for talks—Sir William, described by an associate as "only a shadow of his real self because of his long toils in the Cairo atmosphere," Lord Moyne, Sir Herbert Emerson, the expert on refugees, General Smith-Dorrien, Ambassador Kirk, and others. An instant impression was made by the before-mentioned Australian, Commander Robert Jackson, in charge of relief supplies for the whole Middle Eastern area, who was so keen that all the interests centered in Cairo wished to grab him away from the British Government service. Particularly interesting was a visit by agents of Marshal Tito.

"They came to beg for medicines," Lehman later recalled. "They knew that nobody could supply them with arms at that time in sufficient quantities to do them very much good. I promised to send medicines in; of course, the only way was to drop them in. They didn't have anaesthetics, they didn't have surgical instruments, they didn't have medical supplies of any kind. They had to operate under the most painful circumstances. After the emissaries got my promise, they boarded the plane again, flew to Yugoslavia, and dropped by parachute.

"One of them was a young captain whom I had known as a little boy; I had known his parents, grandparents, and great-grandparents. His grandfather was Isidor Straus, who went down with the *Titanic*. One uncle was Oscar Straus, Secretary of Commerce under the first Roosevelt, and another was Nathan Straus, head of Macy's and Abraham & Straus. This young Captain Richard Weil, Jr., whom the American army had loaned to the Yugoslavs, went back, landed safely, and survived the war."

In Egypt itself the most critical problem was presented by the various refugees, and especially the Greeks and Yugoslavs, who had split into political factions ready to cut each other's throats. Hugh Jackson, Sir William Matthews, and others, visiting their various camps to get the latest information, brought back reports to Lehman. It was clear that the camps, ten or a dozen in number, had been efficiently managed by the British. At Moses Wells, on the Red Sea about ninety miles from Cairo, a large body of Greeks were living in tents in the wide desert spaces, with well-appointed kitchens, dining halls, and hospital. Near El Shatt, a camp of about 12,000 Yugoslavs would have offered a greater problem if followers of Mikhailovitch had appeared in any numbers; but fortunately for harmony, practically all the men, a vigorous, energetic lot, wore the red star of Tito on their caps. Here a Briton named Langman was in charge.

UNRRA was anxious to take over this work, and under the arrangement which Lehman now hammered out in Cairo, the British handed over all the property and facilities of MERRA as a free gift. The military authorities, or Allied Military Liaison (AML), simultaneously signed an agreement for the participation of UNRRA in helping succor the civilian populations of Greece, Yugoslavia, and Albania during the period of military control, with Sir William Matthews as chief of the Balkan Mission in charge. Forthwith a steady trickle of American workers began to pour into Egypt, ready for entering the three countries as soon as they were reconquered from the Nazis. They came in excessive numbers, and as the waiting period proved long and they had little to do, their morale suffered. They quarreled with each other, with the Egyptians, and above all, with the British, for many Americans were specialists, whose outlook differed from the more general views taken by the Britons; Anglo-American animosities became greater in the Cairo section of UNRRA than anywhere else. Perhaps the frightful heat had a partial responsibility.

Lehman's return journey to America was arduous, and tragedy awaited him in New York. Leaving Cairo at dawn on April 7, 1944, in a big C-54, his leg still painful in a cast which sometimes seemed to weigh several tons, he alighted in Algiers that afternoon. One of his first callers was General Sir Maitland ("Jumbo") Wilson, whose huge bulk almost filled Lehman's bedroom. He wished not only to pay a courtesy visit but to arrange for keeping an UNRRA liaison officer at his headquarters in Algeria—which was done. As Churchill states in his history of World War II, Wilson controlled seven or eight separate missions which were working with the partisan forces throughout the Balkans, a mountainous belt extending 900 miles in one direction and 300 in another; Yugoslavia alone having 200,000 guerrilla fighters. After Wilson came Harold Glasser of the Treasury Department, fresh from Italy. His gloomy reports of hunger and distress gave a dark warning of trouble ahead. "You can be thankful," he said, "that limitations have been placed on your action in former enemy countries, for you could spend two billion dollars in Italy alone in a year's time if it were all liberated." He estimated that the food requirements in the peninsula could well cost a billion annually. The army, he thought, might feed people but would be unable to do much constructive work, and it was particularly ill-equipped to attempt the rehabilitation of agriculture.

After a short stop in Casablanca to talk with General Mark Clark and others, Lehman—giving up his early plans to visit London—flew back across the Atlantic. He reached New York on April 10 to meet a fearful shock. His wife greeted him at the airport with news their elder son had been killed in a flying accident. After training with the Royal Canadian Air Force and transferring to the American Air Corps, Peter had just been awarded the Distinguished Flying Cross. He had completed no fewer than fifty-eight flights over Germany. It was his hope to give his father the cross on March 28th as a birthday gift. The direct return to New York from Casablanca spoiled this plan, and on March 31, in a practice flight from his English base in a fast Thunderbolt plane, he crashed and died. Messages of sympathy poured in on the governor and his wife. The *New York Times* and other papers carried editorials, H. I. Phillips wrote a touching poem in his Sun Dial column in the *World-Telegram*, and the Republican State Committee in New York passed resolutions of condolence. Later the young widow received for Peter, who was buried in the American military cemetery near Cambridge, his D.F.C.

These months of March and April, 1944, were a season of trial for Lehman in more than his personal affairs. Stubborn Nazi resistance delayed the campaign in southern Italy, so that it was not until late in May that the British and other troops took Cassino and the Americans scored a satisfactory advance from the Anzio beachhead. Operation "Overlord," the invasion of France originally scheduled for May 1, had to be postponed for weeks after that date, and nobody was certain when it would occur. Losses of merchant ships had exceeded new construction until the very end of 1943, and shipping remained very tight throughout 1944.[2] Food was rationed severely in Britain, with increasing strictness in the United States, and even to some extent in Australia. Throughout the world the shortage of meats, fats, and sugar was acute. Naturally the Combined Food Board and Combined Shipping Adjustment Board were reluctant to make any concessions to UNRRA. Naturally, too, the military and naval authorities begrudged the use of men and resources of any object except winning the war.

The American army had been glad to see UNRRA go into the Middle East and Balkans and heartily approved of Lehman's Cairo Agreement; this was a British theater. But in areas of American or Anglo-American activity the attitude of most army leaders was, "Please keep out of our hair." To them it was the fighting that mattered; emergency relief could be conducted by the army or as in Sicily assigned to the Red Cross—and long-term relief could wait. During the "military period" the army and navy insisted upon complete responsibility for supply, and UNRRA was not expected to purchase, stockpile, or move any commodities for enemy or former enemy countries—save in isolated instances with full military agreement.

· II ·

Throughout 1944 Lehman and UNRRA had perforce to continue waiting on the armies in most areas. After the successful June invasion of Normandy, Paris was liberated on August 25. The next day Bulgaria withdrew from the war. By that time Soviet forces stood on the borders of East Prussia and were pressing the conquest of Rumania. Montgomery on September 3–4 took Antwerp, a port quickly made of the greatest value as an Allied supply base. While Allied troops penetrated to the Meuse, capturing the fortresses of Liége and Namur, Patton raced to Verdun and reached the Moselle. Then in September the American troops, outrunning their supplies and transportation facilities, slowed down. Eisenhower had rejected Montgomery's proposal that all the Allied reserves be thrown into a northern offensive that would drive through the Ruhr to Berlin, for he preferred to slug toward the Rhine on a broad front. A new offensive did carry his troops into Aachen on October 24, and they struggled forward until December brought a staggering German counterblow and the Battle of the Bulge.

Thus in France and the Low Countries the "military period" continued. So, too, in Greece and northern Italy any real peace was postponed until 1945. The numerous British agents operating in Greece during the spring and summer of 1944 encouraged guerrilla elements to blow up bridges, cut railroads, and otherwise harass the German occupiers. The little nation, however, was torn by factional quarrels involving the Communists, the Anti-Communists, and the royalist followers of King George. As the Allied and Russian advances gained force on all fronts, the likelihood of a German evacuation of Greece increased. But this would leave a power vacuum. There could never be a major Allied landing there for the simple reason, as Churchill writes, that all large Allied forces were needed elsewhere. Finally the German retreat did come in mid-October, 1944, and British paratroopers occupied Athens as the enemy withdrew. But even then the UNRRA agents who had waited impatiently in Cairo, nursing their zeal and bickering with each other, had little scope for activity.

The Greek brigade came back from Cairo, and M. Papandreou attempted to establish an orderly provisional government in which Communist elements were given due representation. The British planned to prepare the ground for free elections. But at once the Communists tried to seize power; the British had to intervene with armed force, and only after much hard fighting did they save Athens and the surrounding country. When a storm of angry criticism fell upon Churchill from British and American radicals, he stood firm. He saw far more clearly than most people (including FDR) that, as he put it, "Communism would be the peril civilization would have to face after the defeat of Naziism and Fascism." He was to be completely vindicated within little more than two years, when the Truman Administration, supported by overwhelming opinion, made the most strenuous exertions to save democracy in Greece. For UNRRA, meanwhile, the essential fact was that to the very end of 1944 fighting continued in the outskirts of Athens. Churchill, flying into the city at Christmas that year, had to stay on the cruiser *Ajax* in the harbor for safety. Well into 1945 deadly fighting went on.

In Italy, too, final victory was postponed until after 1944 with a resultant paralysis of most UNRRA effort. The Allies had entered Rome on June 4, and the Germans, with Mussolini's forces, were driven north until late in August General Alexander launched his attack on the Gothic Line. He met with encouraging success and drove the enemy back close to Bologna and Florence. But then Kesselring brought in reinforcements. Roosevelt wrote Churchill on October 16, 1944: "My Chiefs of Staff accept Wilson's estimate that we cannot now expect to destroy Kesselring's army this winter and that the terrain and weather conditions in the Po Valley will prevent any decisive advance this year." [3] Here again UNRRA was halted; outside southern Italy the fierce war effort kept relief checked and frozen. Italy, a former enemy country, got special treatment on political grounds.

It was hard luck that the British returned to Greece only to find it racked by civil war; hard luck that a decisive victory eluded the Allies in northern Italy. As war ruled, the tasks of peace had to wait. Yet something substantial was done.

• III •

By the end of 1944 a fairly effective organization had been built. Of money, meanwhile, there was no immediate lack. While the £80,000,000 voted by Parliament was the first great sum provided, Congress on March 28, 1944, authorized the one percent contribution of the United States, or $1,350,000,000, and in June made its first appropriation of $800,000,000, of which $450,000,000 was made immediately available. The Canadian Parliament also voted $77,000,000 in June. Pioneer workers began to appear here and there all over the regions reclaimed by the armies. Thus in July the first UNRRA observers arrived in Italy, in October an UNRRA mission opened an office in Paris, and on October 23 the first workers came to Greece.

But organization and money were of no use without two other essentials. The difficulty lay with supplies—never enough—and still more with transportation—practically none. Until they materialized, the starving millions of Europe, Africa, and Asia were in the position of Tantalus: food and drink stood just out of reach.

The public learned that the UNRRA Council in its initial meeting had bidden Lehman to "consider it one of his first and most important tasks to arrange for necessary allocations and procurement of supplies." [4] They knew that Canada, Britain, and the United States had effective government machinery for procurement. They read that in September, 1944, UNRRA placed a supply and recruiting mission in Australia. One of its heads was Lithgow Osborne, Lehman's former conservation commissioner and the son of Thomas Mott Osborne, the other Rolf Nugent. Three months later a similar procurement agency was opened in Rio de Janeiro.

The public also read that proper bases or standards for the distribution of supplies were carefully fixed by UNRRA. How many calories did people need in different countries? What was a proper ration of suits, dresses, and shoes? How could the medical needs of a nation be estimated? How measure the needs in livestock, seed, fertilizer, and farm machinery? An *ad hoc* committee of UNRRA experts concluded that each person in Europe ought to have 2,650 calories of food a day, with a supplementary ration for children and nursing mothers. Other experts decided that medical supplies should be calculated according to the number of hospital beds, doctors, clinics, and dispensaries in a given land. The British rationing standards for clothes were adopted as a basis for UNRRA distributions. They were presently found to be insufficient and were increased at the very time, as it happened, that the British distributions had to be reduced; so that UNRRA standards became higher than those in the United Kingdom, which got no aid and was furnishing substantial amounts of clothing to other countries.

Many people who knew all these facts wondered throughout 1944 why UNRRA did so little. The answer was that it had precious little in the way of supplies and still less in ships, trucks, and trains. The will, the methods, and the cash had been provided, but not the bread, the coal, the coats, the ocean cargo-carriers, or the trucks.

Always goods and facilities hovered just beyond reach. When the second Council session met in Montreal in September, 1944, Lehman sounded a hopeful note. "Now the emancipation marches swiftly," he told the members. "Now the practical work of relief is at hand." Announcing the completion of arrangements for pouring supplies into the liberated areas, he warned everybody that certain categories would be "seriously short." But they must do what they could and do it fast. "UNRRA is not a permanent institution and we do not foresee a long period over which we can perfect the Administration." [5] Roosevelt, a few weeks later, was equally hopeful. "This government," he wrote Lehman on the first anniversary of the East Room ceremony, "has endeavored in every way to support you and your staff to the fullest limits of our ability." The war strain on goods and carriage had made this difficult. "But we are determined that the sacrifices of the liberated peoples shall be rewarded, and that, to the extent we have it in our power to help, these people shall promptly receive the clothing, food, and other supplies which they need to start life over." [6] Yet the realities of success still fell far short of the hopes.

When Congress opened in December, 1944, Roosevelt included a report on UNRRA in his annual message and asked for additional support. Europe was threatened by famine and pestilence, he said; if assistance did not come soon whole peoples would slip into the abyss. Already UNRRA had allocated more than $353,000,000 of its original American appropriation of $450,000,000. "All the world owes a debt to the heroic peoples who fought the Nazis from the beginning." Hitler had told some of his generals on the last day of August that the Allies would soon break apart, for "all the coalitions of history have disintegrated sooner or later." One mode of keeping the United Nations together was to use the resources of the richer members to assist the prostrate.

• IV •

In the late fall of 1944, as the progress of the Allies slowed toward a halt, Lehman made a third trip to Europe. He wished to examine the situation, talk with the overseas staff, and do what he could to get the program started. This visit gave him and his associates a double shock. It brought a greater realization than ever of the urgency of their work, for misery had steadily increased, and the invasions had rendered the problem of displaced persons —DPs—more difficult. Prisoners and slave labor were escaping; refugees were turning homeward. In the second place, Lehman grasped for the first time the widespread misunderstanding of UNRRA's position, for nearly all Europeans grossly exaggerated its power to aid them before peace came. They ascribed its delays to inertia, callousness, red tape, stupidity, stinginess; to anything but the three real causes, short supplies, lack of transport, and the reluctance of the military to give up anything they might conceivably need in any conceivable futurity.

Arriving in London by air on the afternoon of November 13, 1944, Lehman was greeted at Claridge's by Leith-Ross, Ernest Brown, M.P., chairman of the European Council of UNRRA, other staff members, and two Foreign Office men. Without delay they began a brass tacks discussion. In two hours, writes Lehman, "I got a pretty good background of what was going on and what some of the difficulties are. We stayed together until six P.M., when Sir Arthur Salter came in. I had about an hour's talk with him and he brought me up to date about a number of matters." Then, with some disturbance by the explosion of robot bombs, he slept until it was time for breakfast and a new conference at the UNRRA offices in Portland Square. In these he was aided by his secretary, Harold E. Caustin, an Englishman who never volunteered much advice but who was marvelously efficient in carrying out any task assigned to him.

Some of the intelligence he heard included sharp criticism. For example, on November 16 he talked at the Foreign Office with Richard K. Law, the Parliamentary Under Secretary, Edward L. Hall-Patch, a high Treasury official, and Denny Marris, who had just returned from Egypt and Greece.

"They were quite critical," records Lehman, "about my handling of certain matters in Greece and in Cairo. They were also not pleased that we had proceeded to form a mission for Ethiopia without first discussing the matter with the Foreign Office." Ethiopia had been liberated by British forces in 1941, and British advisers, judges, and military men, using annual grants from London, were helping run the country. "They were also critical," he pursues, "of some of the provisions which we had inserted in the proposed draft of the agreement with Yugoslavia." Here, too, Maitland Wilson's activities had given Britain a special position. "Denny Marris was critical about some of our personnel. This worries me more than anything else, as his criticism may be perfectly justified. My judgment is that we have a run-of-the-mine personnel (in the Middle East and Balkans)."

When Lehman called next day on the likable French ambassador in London, M. René Massigli, he had a glimpse of the impracticable temper of the de Gaulle Government. He told the ambassador that although he did not wish to press help on France, UNRRA stood ready to do whatever it could, and might offer a useful hand in repatriating displaced persons and strengthening public health and welfare. The ambassador was frank. "He told me that he knew that France did not want help previously, but that was at a time when the government felt that it had to show the people and the world that it was capable of coping with its own problems. He adds that when a man is weak his pride frequently will not permit him to accept assistance. He needs to stand on his own feet. On the other hand, when a man is strong he will accept the cooperation and assistance of his friends. He thought that this would undoubtedly be the situation in France." And, to be sure, the French government, with Massigli as foreign minister, was soon accepting large shipments of blankets that UNRRA sent it. What de Gaulle called "the psychology of exile" was shaken off in favor of the "psychology of victory." [7]

A conference which Lehman and Leith-Ross held with Yugoslav representatives revealed a different sensitivity, the defensiveness of a little nation afraid of political interference. The Yugoslavs distrusted certain provisions in the draft agreement for UNRRA work in their country. "They were afraid that we would employ our goods as a political weapon against them; they felt that in view of the fact that we did not limit the number of observers we might deluge the country with great numbers; and objected to the fact that none of the proceeds for UNRRA goods sold for local currency would accrue to the government." Lehman had no trouble explaining that goods would be turned over to the Yugoslav government at the ports and so could not possibly be used in political activities; that only a few observers would be sent in to make sure of equitable distribution; and that the local currency gained would be used only for further relief. The Yugoslavs left well satisfied.

Their apprehensions, however, were typical of those in every needy country then and later. Would relief open the way to political pressure, as de Gaulle complained military aid had done? Would sales drain a country of money? On the first point all fears were baseless. UNRRA agents carried political impartiality even to an extreme; in Greece some of them objected to any discrimination between Communists and Anti-Communists. On the second point UNRRA held a position sound in theory but sometimes unhappy in practice. Governments without adequate revenues desperately needed the money from supplies sold; if it were used simply to buy more supplies, UNRRA relief would become a chain of buckets dipping funds from the nation's shallow reserves, and inflation would get out of hand. Lehman found Sir David Waley of the British Treasury, just back from Athens, emphatic on this head. He said that unless proceeds from the sale of UNRRA goods were applied to the expenses of the Greek government, bankruptcy must ensue. Lehman concluded that the policy would have to be changed. "It is clear that unless there is currency and fiscal stability for a country," he wrote, "there is very little chance of helping to rehabilitate it." [8]

On his visit to the cemetery in which his son Peter lay four miles from Cambridge, he found it admirably kept. Among the two or three thousand graves he was struck by the large number bearing the Star of David. In London he saw a grandson of Hymie Shorenstein, a stalwart young soldier; visited an eminent orthopedic surgeon, Dr. Watson-Jones, to have his lame knee treated; had his nephew Arthur Goodhart, Master of University College in Oxford, down for dinner; and enjoyed a long talk with his old friend Jan Masaryk.

Wherever he went, he heard of the dire necessities of Europe. The Norwegian Minister of Supply, Mr. Frihaggen, for example, expressed grave doubt that the military, in spite of their promises, would bring in sufficient supplies. "I share their view," commented Lehman. "The situation is serious since the northern part of Norway already has been liberated, and except for some supplies that have come in through Russia, no relief has been given." The prime minister of the Polish government-in-exile, Mikolajczyk, was even more depressed. He spoke with emotion of the terrible suffering in Poland. Lehman could only tell him that UNRRA was anxious to send all kinds of help, but could do nothing without Soviet cooperation and some shipping—both as distant as Arcturus. "He seemed very sad indeed," Lehman wrote—and two days later he resigned. Queen Wilhelmina of the Netherlands was likewise sad. She spoke, when Lehman called, of the bitter destitution in the part of her country that had thus far been liberated; a lack of food, blankets, clothing, medicines, fuel—in fact, almost everything. From one to two million people would have to be evacuated from the flooded areas to other parts of Holland; and nobody knew how much further damage the Germans would do in evacuating the country.

"I am becoming increasingly concerned over the situation of the Western European countries and the inadequacy of shipping and supplies," Lehman wrote. "The shipping situation is to me an extremely dangerous one." In public speeches and private talks he emphasized the vital importance of close military cooperation with UNRRA and the release of shipping space for its most exigent calls. "I shall continue to do so whenever I get a chance," [9] ran a diary note ten days after his arrival.

A luncheon with Anthony Eden at the Foreign Office on November 23 gave him one opportunity. It was Thanksgiving Day, and Eden, who was in much gayer spirits than when Lehman saw him on an earlier visit to Washington, had been at pains to provide a roast turkey. The governor, intent on his message, failed to notice the bird till his attention was called to it! He told Eden, Richard Law, and others that while some criticisms of UNRRA were valid, many were not. "I laid main stress on the inadequacy of shipping; it

would not do very much good to have supplies or a good organization unless we could deliver the groceries. Military needs were of course paramount—but the military must realize that other needs were paramount too."
He strongly urged a new survey of shipping to see if more of it could not be
made available for civilian uses but got no promises.

• V •

When Lehman went on to Paris and visited SHAEF,* then housed in the
Trianon Palace Hotel in Versailles, he was able to present his views to
Lieutenant General Bedell Smith, General Sir Humfrey Gale, the British
Quartermaster General, and other army chiefs. These men were specially
worried over the refugees that were clogging roads and towns and were
already a difficult problem in the invaded segment of Germany. The Twenty-
first Army Group had just requested UNRRA to furnish a hundred teams
of twelve men each for assembly centers in the British zone of northwest
Germany. These teams were originally asked to bring their own transport
and camp equipment. After much discussion, however, the military conceded that it should try to supply them with trucks and jeeps and that
UNRRA would do well to accept all the mobile canteens and welfare outfits
that had been offered it in Britain. The military also agreed to make such
army facilities as mess and billeting arrangements, use of PX stores, and
military postal services available to UNRRA staff.

The conference at SHAEF gave Lehman a little encouragement, especially for his work with refugees, though he was disturbed by a rather
grudging attitude. "I think," he wrote in his diary, "that several of the officers have special reservations with regard to UNRRA. I believe they feel
that UNRRA is merely another layer which may cause additional complications as far as their command is concerned. A great many of the officers appeared to be jealous of their prerogatives, and to not want to be put in a position of having to consult with civilians. I hope that feeling will disappear." [10]
The armed forces in their advance simply had to do something for the masses
of displaced persons they encountered, so it was plain they would welcome
UNRRA assistance. But it was by no means clear that they would economize
on their own supplies or transport for the benefit of the general civilian
population. That would not win the war!

Yet the blindest could see the cold, hunger, and despair that came to the
surface behind the advancing columns. France shivered even more miserably

* The Supreme Headquarters Allied Expeditionary Force had moved to the area immediately on the liberation of Paris.

than Britain. Lehman, who had almost frozen when he dined at Brooks's Club in London, now found the Hotel Meurice in Paris shabby, gloomy, and of Arctic frigidity. At discussions in the UNRRA offices at 67 Champs Elysées his numbed hands and feet made concentration difficult. "The only way that I could keep reasonably warm was to wear my heavy overcoat. Even then I shivered and everybody else seemed equally cold." [11] A call on a family friend, Mrs. Gustave Levy, who was cold, hungry, and almost penniless, impressed him with the woebegone state of ordinary folk. Jean Monnet told him when they dined together just how difficult the situation was. "They have depended on the military for supplies, and the shipping is unfortunately so tight that it is difficult to bring in any. The result is that raw materials, coal, and some other things of which France is desperately in need are not available." Lehman got the impression that many half-famished people were exhausting their stocks of food without any thought of the morrow.

The problem of the displaced persons, according to M. Henri Frénay, Commissioner for Prisoners, Deportees, and Refugees in the new de Gaulle government, was getting worse. On the day of the Normandy landing, nearly if not quite a quarter of a million DPs were asking aid in France, and the number had since risen, for the advancing troops uncovered one new pocket after another of these wretched people. Frénay did not believe that SHAEF was organized for so huge a task as the care of the ten to twenty million Allied prisoners and slave workers that the armies would find in Germany. He condemned the plan of the military leaders for separating prisoners of war from other displaced persons as both wrong and impracticable. He also deplored the fact that the military never gave up anything they might possibly need. Again and again he had asked a little aid, but the army had not delivered a single lorry, a single blanket.

Frénay believed that the Germans in their last-ditch resistance were deliberately pushing the wretched Russian and Polish people whom they held to the west, while they carried French nationals to the eastward. Their army commanders wished to get rid of the hordes of DPs who were clogging the lines of communication but desired to keep able-bodied Frenchmen out of Allied hands. By mid-December, 1944, about a hundred thousand new DPs had already poured into France, and he heard that the Nazis were proposing to send a quarter of a million Dutch prisoners and deportees there. How could the country care for them? The army had stony ears; and, demanded Frénay, "What is the use of UNRRA?"

When Lehman and Fred Hoehler suggested that tripartite talks might develop a plan under which the French Government would provide the shelter, SHAEF the transport and supplies, and UNRRA the supervisory personnel for displaced persons, Frénay shook his head. "The question is not one of making plans," he declared. "It is one of assuring supplies. Unless we solve the problem a catastrophe will result." They must go to the highest authority—General Eisenhower—for a decision. He should order appropriate sections of the armed forces to face the problem of human survival immediately and realistically. "If this is not done," exploded Frénay, "I shall resign from the government!"

Lehman recognized the force of this demand. Most military leaders concentrated so exclusively on winning the war, and showed such a stubborn dislike of consulting with civilians, that it might be unavoidable to appeal to Eisenhower. It might even be necessary to go higher and talk with Roosevelt and Churchill. But he thought it expedient to make a last effort to clear the question with the generals below Eisenhower before going to that harassed commander or to heads of state. He felt this even though he was not certain that he could make the generals understand. From the North Cape to Messina millions might feel like human icicles, but army headquarters were always well warmed; from the Severn to the Rhine millions might be hungry, but Lehman always found steaks in the officers' messes. How many army hospitals were overstocked with medicines when civilian doctors lacked drugs? How many officers had an extra jeep when emergency civilian services needed a car or truck? Nobody knew. What Lehman did know was that all government offices were bitterly cold—"one sits shivering in one's overcoat"—and that not a lift was running in Paris, and few if any in London, for lack of power.

At last, on November 29, the increasing strain brought what Hugh Jackson would have called a showdown. The French Minister of Reconstruction, Raoul Dautry, indignantly told Lehman that the Allied armies had provided German prisoners of war with excellent clothing but had given none at all to the French DPs. He wanted two or three thousand tons of tarred roofing to make damaged houses temporarily rainproof and at least a hundred tons of clothing a fortnight as a "gesture" for the DPs. Thereupon Lehman and Leith-Ross bearded Sir Humfrey Gale, chief administrative officer of SHAEF, at his headquarters in a well-appointed villa. He served them a typically generous officers' lunch. When Lehman mentioned the tarred roofing, he responded with a loud "No!" Damage to houses in England was far greater than in France, he said; most of the repair material was being manufactured in Britain, which was itself very short; why didn't the French organize their own manufacture, thus saving foreign exchange and sparing SHAEF a burden on its shipping? Leith-Ross mentioned the modest French request for some clothing and met another stone wall. Gale admitted that

SHAEF had some stocks on hand but declared roundly that France was in a good position to find its own clothing and that instead of begging imports the authorities should arrange for home collections. To this Leith-Ross rejoined that M. Dautry *had* made collections which supplied 150,000 DPs but needed far more, and was anxious to get even fifty tons a week to keep his machinery of distribution going.

"It looks to me," said Leith-Ross grimly, "as if the army command will monopolize transport until the pressure gets so strong that they will have to let up and give priority to civil supplies." "Yes," agreed Lehman, "the position in France is really serious. And the position of the ten million displaced persons in Germany, when we get to them, will be more serious still." At this Gale became more conciliatory. "I will speak to General Snowden or one of his assistants," he said, "and try to get the supply situation loosened up." [12]

Lehman had made a little progress, and some blankets were shortly found for the French and the refugees. But the two basic blockades that were immobilizing UNRRA, one in supplies and one in shipping, remained as formidable as ever. The director made a trip to the front late in November which convinced him that an appeal to Roosevelt and Churchill would really have to be made. It carried him through Nancy toward Strasbourg and the Rhine, where heavy fighting stopped him; and he then turned back through Metz and Verdun to Châlons-sur-Marne and Paris again.

The weather being wretchedly cold and rainy, Lehman took the precaution of wearing two suits of woolen underwear, woolen socks, a woolen shirt, and a woolen scarf, with a heavy overcoat, and a sheepskin coat to cover his knees. At Chaumont he found an UNRRA camp where about 2,000 DPs and refugees were housed in Pershing's former headquarters, a large French barracks. "The camp made a very bad impression on me," Lehman noted. "It was pretty unsanitary, cold, did not have sufficient blankets, and the crowd which consisted of a number of different nationalities was milling about aimlessly." The previous night nearly a thousand people had been dumped there without previous arrangement, so that many of them had to sleep in straw. While the camp was nominally operated by the French, most of the personnel as well as supplies came from the American army.

At Nancy, Lehman dined with General Patton, who was still under a cloud for striking a sick soldier, but elated by his military progress. "He told me," records Lehman, "that had he sufficient supplies, particularly gasoline, he could have gone right through Germany, as the Germans could not possibly have regrouped in time to stop him. He also told me he was starting a new offensive the following day and gave me some details of it." By Patton's special permission, Lehman was allowed to approach the front lines in a jeep. He and his escort, Lieutenant-Colonel Codman of Boston, passed grisly evidences of battle; countless ruined trucks, ambulances, and cars, many dead horses and cows, and at one point a German gun dismantled by a direct hit. Trucks carrying supplies and ammunition constantly passed them. A tank battle was under way, and Lehman wished to get within view. But although Patton's chief of staff assented, they soon met the divisional commander returning. "I cannot let you go any farther," he said. "The line is very fluid, and I cannot guarantee that some of the German tanks won't break through and capture you." Lehman turned back to the north and west.

At Verdun he found another transient camp for DPs, housing about 2,500 people of different nationalities. It was short of clothing and blankets, but the food and discipline were good. After an overnight stay he proceeded to a quite unique camp for DPs near Châlons.

"The camp houses about 3,500 Russians," he noted. "No other nationalities are represented there. It gave me a good example of Russian discipline and regimentation. Nominally it is run by the French with Russian assistance. Actually it is administered by a Russian petty officer aged twenty-four, with fifteen or twenty assistants. He is in charge of all the discipline and control of the inmates. I have never seen more strict regimentation even in an army camp. When we inspected the dormitories everyone stood at attention immediately the Russian officials entered the room. They did not speak unless they were spoken to. Each bed had been carefully made up, all blankets folded the same way; the rooms were clean and well ordered." The inmates, who included many mothers with young children, marched to their two good meals a day with military precision. No flag but the Russian banner appeared anywhere, and the men were forbidden to do any work that would keep them outside the camp at night—for the officers insisted on absolute control.

· VI ·

Lehman returned from this trip to find that popular skepticism concerning UNRRA and criticism of its officers still continually mounted. The liberated zones were being widened in France, Belgium, Holland, and Norway. Governments in these lands were struggling to establish themselves, shelter the wandering masses of refugees and prisoners, and make urgent provision of food, clothing, and sanitary supplies for their home populations. They confronted some desperate situations. They knew that the military were preoccupied with fighting and that the Combined Boards were busy helping the military; but meanwhile, people were dying. The minds of government officers, editors, and plain citizens naturally turned to UNRRA. They had helped create it, and they had heard much of its splendid possibilities. But what was it doing? When would it get off the ground?

The acid test of the organization lay just ahead in Greece and Italy, France and Holland. If Lehman could not get supplies and transport he might as well shut up shop and confess failure. On December 3, he summoned all the UNRRA helpers within reach to his Paris hotel for a three-hour conference. With rising apprehension he listened to querulous reports from Belgium, Holland, Luxembourg, and various French districts. "Again I was struck," he wrote in his diary, "by the misunderstanding as to what UNRRA's responsibilities were. I am afraid that this misunderstanding exists not only among governments and peoples, but among our own staff." For with destitution all about them, the staff were impatient too; why wasn't UNRRA hard at work? A proposal was being urged, with the support of some high officials in London and Paris, that UNRRA as a token of its willingness to help should pledge $10,000,000 to $20,000,000 immediately for each country, primarily in food, clothing, and welfare supplies for the use of wandering, homeless millions of DPs.

To such demands Lehman could only reply for the hundredth time: "We want desperately to get to work. But even if we had supplies, we would have no means of getting them into the needy areas of Western Europe unless the military ordered them forward. And the military declines." He could only explain once more that UNRRA had never expected to send much in the way of supplies to France or Holland, which were solvent countries determined to pay their own way. While fighting lasted there, civilian supplies were the responsibility of the military; when fighting ceased, that of the governments themselves. But confusion persisted. "I am afraid," ran a diary entry, "UNRRA is going to suffer very greatly in prestige on account of this misunderstanding in the minds of even well-informed people both in Europe and in the United States." [13]

Something decisive had to be done.

Crossing to London on December 4, the now almost desperate Director found that Hugh Jackson had just come in from Italy and Greece. What he had to report upon Italy, its northern zone still under the Nazi heel, boiled down to three facts. First, UNRRA needed from 15,000 to 20,000 tons of supplies a month to supplement army aides in Italy. Second, though the military were courteous, they professed themselves so hard pressed for shipping space that they could spare nothing from their own stocks and promise no ship allocations for the future. Third, UNRRA in these circumstances would be helpless; far from furnishing 20,000 tons of supplies monthly to Italy, it could not furnish an ounce. Simultaneously, Lehman heard angry expostulations from voices in London. A Czech who was helping direct welfare plans there, and who was harrowed by the distress of Czech DPs in France, called for emergency action; so did Arthur Rucker, of the British Ministry of Health, who knew about the dire need on the Continent; and so did Sir George Rendel of the British Foreign Office. Excitable men, even MPs, were saying that since UNRRA was virtually dead, something should be done with the corpse.

On December 7 Lehman broke through his natural reluctance and appealed to the highest civil authority against the military stone wall. He drafted an urgent personal cable to Roosevelt. In this he recalled that he had several times discussed the provision of adequate relief shipping with the President and that the UNRRA representatives in Italy had gained the approval of the Allied Commission and the Allied Forces Headquarters for their request that relief supplies be shipped to Italy in quantities rising from 5,000 tons in January to 25,000 tons in May, 1945. In presenting this program to the Combined Chiefs of Staff, Allied Forces Headquarters had requested an allotment of adequate shipping. But now, the director went on, none had been granted, and the Mediterranean naval authorities (SACMED) told him that no such program was feasible; at any rate, not until March. Lehman argued frankly with FDR:

"You will recall that the UNRRA program for Italy, which was most urgently recommended by yourself and Mr. Churchill, was clearly understood to be a supplementary program, and not a substitute for the basic program of civilian relief supplies which was to be carried on by the American and British Governments. Unless extra shipping is allotted . . . UNRRA will not be able to undertake this program of assistance to Italy, and in addition, the Administration will be placed in the invidious position of not being able to proceed with an undertaking which was highly publicized at the time of the Montreal Conference and supported by all forty-four nations. I respectfully but urgently request that you issue instructions alloting the additional tonnage which will be required for the movement of UNRRA supplies to Italy." [14]

While awaiting Roosevelt's reply, Lehman talked with Richard Law, who warmly approved of his appeal; with an American lieutenant-colonel, just back from Yugoslavia, who assured him that Tito was the strong man there and would control the nation's future; and with Marguerite Higgins of the *Herald-Tribune*, who might help publicize the bottleneck in shipping. Law gave him a piece of good news—the British Government would now detach

Commander Robert Jackson from his Middle Eastern duties to take a post of Senior Deputy with UNRRA. Then Lehman spoke on December 11 at Chatham House to about 350 members of Parliament and various executives of the British and other governments on UNRRA and its activities. His reception was cordial, but the questions put him were searching, for the House of Lords was about to hold a debate on the subject, and Lord Samuel and Lord Strabolgi wished to be prepared to defend the organization.

At last, on December 12, he received a cable from Roosevelt that gave him gleeful elation. It promised an immediate road out of his trouble. "The War Shipping Administration," ran Roosevelt's reply, "contemplates allocating shipping space directly to UNRRA in order to meet your January and February requirements for Italy." He added that the Administration was undertaking a broad review of the Anglo-American shipping position. "With this review as a basis, a decision will be made with regard to the shipping which can be provided from United States and British sources to cover the UNRRA program after February, 1945." [15] If the Shipping Administration met its promises, UNRRA could now launch its full Italian program. If Administration pressure brought about some general relaxation of the military grip upon food, clothing, fuel, and transport, so that while essential army needs were satisfied a modicum of relief came through for civil needs, UNRRA could strengthen its activities all over the map: in northwestern Europe, in Greece and the Balkans, in Egypt and the Middle East, and even in China.

· VII ·

The tide now turned, and UNRRA began fulfilling its mission with comprehensive vigor. In the last weeks of 1944 and the first part of 1945 the initial pages of a striking new history were written; stories heart-rending and heart-warming, stories of misery attacked too late and aid brought in the nick of time, stories of ignominious failure and heroic success. Slowly but steadily the record brightened.

An impressive tale slowly unrolled in Italy, a nation which as the year 1944 closed was still slashed in two by the sword. While the Allies held the poverty-stricken rural regions of the south and teeming cities of the center, Kesselring and Mussolini kept the main industrial centers and much of the fertile Po Valley. UNRRA had sent in an observer mission during the summer under Spurgeon M. Keeny, a former Rhodes scholar and YMCA administrator of shrewd capacity. This mission considered the best ways of using a small amount of money, for since Italy was technically and in part actually an enemy country, funds were at first restricted. However, at the beginning of November Keeny was sent to Rome as chief of the mission in Italy to begin negotiating an agreement with the new government there. And while waiting for the agreement to be completed, the mission went to work with $50,000,000, of which it spent roughly $36,000,000 on the supplementary feeding of mothers and children, $9,000,000 on medical supplies, and $5,000,-000 on refugees. A host of Italians, including children, were very hungry, and a great part of the refugees were in miserable camps, for countless homes had been destroyed.

Another tale began to unroll in Greece and the Balkans. After the German evacuation of Hellas, the Allied Military Liaison was responsible for planning relief and delivering supplies, but the British and Greek governments agreed that their land forces would use the services of UNRRA. Uneasy progress was made in distributing aid. Then when civil war began, the chief of the UNRRA mission decided that the neutrality of his organization was being prejudiced—for it was impossible to deliver relief to Communists or their sympathizers. As British troops made sure of the safety of Athens, most of the mission was temporarily evacuated to Cairo. Then the Varkizi Pact of mid-January, 1945, gave a respite to hostilities, and the welfare workers began to come back. Another agreement was signed with the Greek Government, and a new era began. Unhappily, distribution of the benefits of UNRRA was placed in government hands, an arrangement which —since many officers had a predilection for waste and some for graft and theft—was full of peril. The Greek story became still more complicated.

Meanwhile, no country lay in a more poignant situation than Poland, one of the worst ravaged lands Europe had ever seen. The tide of battle had swept across the country thrice; in 1939, in 1941, and in 1944. Warsaw was a vast rubble heap. Gydnia, Danzig, and Stettin had been thoroughly wrecked. People in the rural areas about these cities were living mainly in cellars and dugouts. In the provinces of Posen, Cracow, and Silesia factories had been robbed of their machinery and gutted, railway and highway bridges had been demolished, nearly three quarters of the standard gauge track of the country had been torn up, and the power stations had been wrecked. More than six million people in Poland had died, and another six millions had been herded into forced labor compounds or concentration camps. Seven hundred thousand people were crippled; disease had run riot. The Germans had tried systematically to exterminate the Jews, wipe out the intellectuals, and destroy the physicians, engineers, and scientists in order to cripple the country; and the Russians had abetted them. It was an almost prostrate land into which UNRRA in March, 1945, brought its first shipments through the Rumanian port of Constanza on the Black Sea.

But the record of struggle and accomplishment by UNRRA in the fifteen months between the beginning of 1945 and the spring of 1946, the last fifteen months of Lehman's administration, requires a full chapter to present its drama.

Chapter XIII

DAWN OVER THE SHAMBLES

Wɪᴛʜɪɴ thirty days in the spring of 1945 the face of the world was transformed. Victory came in a sudden flood tide, like a swollen river bursting at a blow its winter fetters of ice. Vienna fell to the Russians on April 13, a few hours after Franklin D. Roosevelt's death. American armies were then occupying the Ruhr and pushing into central Germany from their Rhine crossing near Mainz; the British and Canadians were driving from Holland through North Germany. On April 22 Marshal Zhukov's forces fought their way into the suburbs of Berlin. Mussolini was slain by his own people on the 28th, the Germans in Italy signed an unconditional surrender on the 29th, and Hitler committed suicide on the 30th. More than a million German troops surrendered to Marshal Montgomery on May 4, ending the war in the north and liberating Norway and Denmark. In the Far East Lord Mountbatten was completing the recapture of Burma, the final embers of Japanese resistance in the Philippines were being stamped out, and Americans were fighting to conquer Okinawa, the doorstep to Japan itself.

Hostilities ceased in Europe at 12:01 A.M. on May 9th. Peace had come —but in many areas it was the peace of the graveyard. Russia had lost twelve million people dead or seriously wounded, Germany seven millions, Britain almost a million. The lives of tens of millions from the Atlantic to the Urals were utterly ruined; they would never recover in body or mind or spirit. Economic activity had sunk to a blue flame on an exhausted bed of coals; European mills and factories were producing at barely one third the prewar level and farms at one half.

All the greenery and blossoms that spring could not begin to mask the far-stretching destruction of property. It might be one of the lesser calamities of the great tragedy, but it was nevertheless appalling. In France the War Damage Commission reported that out of ten million houses, 1,785,000 had been smashed or burnt; out of 500,000 railway cars, 300,000 were gone;

261

half the livestock of the nation had perished without replacement. It estimated that the conflict had cost France forty-five percent of her total
wealth. In forty-nine of the largest cities of Germany approximately two out
of every five dwellings had been ruined. About two thirds of Berlin, according to the United States Strategic Bombing Survey, was rubble. More
than three and a quarter million separate properties in Britain were listed
by the British War Damage Commission as destroyed or badly injured.
The Dutch Government computed that the war had cost Holland one-fifth
of its housing and that the nation's property losses were three times its entire
annual income. Yet far worse, relatively, was the situation in Greece, Yugoslavia, and Poland.

Eagerly as all Allied leaders had awaited the end of destruction and
beginning of reconstruction, nobody had watched for it more impatiently
than the heads of UNRRA, so long balked in labors of desperate necessity.
They had no illusions about the future. They knew that for multitudes help
would come too late, that delays would still dog their efforts, and that their
organization would in the end prove too short-lived to meet all its responsibilities. They were far from certain that the recent promises won from
Roosevelt and the War Shipping Administration would lead to an early
relaxation of the military grip on supplies, transport, and personnel. "UNRRA
was always at the bottom of the barrel," said Lehman later. "During the
war and the first months of peace, it was at the bottom of the barrel." Yet
many tasks had to be shouldered instantly and given every possible ounce of
effort. First among them was the rescue of the host of helpless European
captives and refugees.

The end of fighting turned these woeful folk loose—to wander where?
The slave workers, the war prisoners, the political deportees, the Jews and
others marked by the Nazis for extermination, were charges of the armies;
but this was a temporary and unsatisfactory arrangement. Their numbers
were prodigious.[1] Never before in history had such huge populations choked
the highways, riverways, and byroads as these caught up in the spasmodic
and irresistible movements of 1945. Never had the resources of army commanders, local and national governments, and philanthropic organizations
been so taxed.

The first great refugee surge of 1945 had been inward toward the heart
of Germany. As the Soviet armies swept westward, people of Teutonic
blood in the Baltic States, East Prussia, Poland, Hungary, and Czechoslovakia, with many of other origins, who feared the Russians, fled pell-mell
in advance. They dreaded the Slavs as the Goths and Gauls had dreaded
Attila's Huns. Some estimates of those who sought asylum among Germans

of the Fatherland exceeded ten millions. They brought trifling property, little clothing, and no food.

In the wake of this movement, another equal in proportions and marked by far greater exhaustion, misery, and want began. As the Anglo-American and Soviet armies closed upon the Nazi-dominated lands, they liberated prisoners of war, threw open the gates of concentration camps, and made the horrifying discovery of such abominations as Dachau and Auschwitz.[2] They freed immense numbers who had been put to forced labor. Only rough estimates can be made of the totals. According to one of the most authoritative statements, about 8,000,000 foreign workers had been brought into Germany during the war: two million Russians, two million French, one and a half million Poles, one million Dutch and Belgians, six hundred thousand Italians, and smaller numbers of Scandinavians, Balts, Czechs, Hungarians, and Rumanians. Most of them were burning to regain their homelands and ready to breast every political and physical obstacle.

The fate of the displaced Poles was particularly hard. The postwar chaos of their twice-overrun homeland delayed them, for the Government of National Unity was not installed in Warsaw until late in June, and the general devastation made resettlement painfully slow. The tremendous movement of Russian prisoners eastward from Germany also impeded the Polish flow. Then as the new government became dominated by Communists, and more and more subject to Soviet pressures, Poles who sympathized with the London government-in-exile grew reluctant to submit themselves to the new regime. A considerable number of both Poles and Yugoslavs had taken refuge in the Middle East. Some 27,000 of the Yugoslavs there were quickly transferred home, but it was impossible to find shipping for the Poles, who had to remain in the camps.

The primary goal of the military authorities and the various governmental agencies which first dealt with the refugees, and of UNRRA as it assisted them during the summer of 1945 and took a major role later, was repatriation. "Get them home"—this was the motto. Formidable as the task appeared, it proved less difficult than experts at first anticipated. Most of the displaced masses were only too eager to get home. The armies continued to provide such assembly centers as Lehman had visited late in 1944, and UNRRA continued to share with the American and British Red Cross, which Eisenhower had specially selected as executive agents, the administration of these places. Food, clothing, and medicine came from various sources, including UNRRA, but chiefly from the army, and all supplies were subject to military control. The first disorganized exodus from the Nazi yoke, as tens of thousands trudged the highways, foraging or begging sustenance,

gave way soon after victory to well-managed transfers with proper care
and transport. Large-scale hospital facilities had to be provided, for countless half-starved prisoners and slave-workers were tottering with weakness
—and some even hospitals could not save.³ A service of trucks, trains, air-
planes, and boats was devised. As the autumn of 1945 drew on, cold weather
and the overcrowding of reception quarters slowed the pace of the transfer.
Still, millions had been repatriated before snow fell in Germany.

· I ·

It was while this spectacular and agonized movement of displaced millions was in its first stages that Lehman dropped his duties in Washington
to go abroad. He had to acquaint himself with European problems at first
hand, consult generals and statesmen, advise the chief UNRRA missions in
the field, and attend a session of the Council—the governing body, now
representing forty-seven nations—which had been arranged for in London
in August. He left Washington on July 5, flying to Paris by way of Newfoundland and the Azores. By the evening of the 7th, he was in Rome, conferring with Sam Keeney and six or eight others of the Italian mission. Commander Robert Jackson—"Jacko"—already his most trusted lieutenant, was
on hand. "I was terribly hot and dirty," he records, "but the cordiality
of my welcome made up for that." ⁴

Into fifty days he crowded a great deal of business. In Italy he saw Crown
Prince Humbert, Prime Minister Feruccio Parri, the Pope, and Marshal
Alexander. UNRRA was then feeding between 150,000 and 200,000 children
in Rome and giving supplies to some 2,000 non-Italian refugees in that city.
He visited some of the institutions to which it was furnishing food and other
aids and found these visits a poignant experience. One brought him to the
Quirinal Palace, where perhaps fifty children were housed. "It was one
of the most affecting and heartbreaking experiences I have had," he wrote.
"Half of the children are totally blind. Others have lost one or more limbs.
Several of them have terribly lacerated faces. Most of the injuries were
sustained from land mines. The children have not yet accustomed themselves to their handicaps. The little blind tots groped around until they
found someone to cling to, and then they held my hand in a puzzled, frightened way. The sight was almost more than one could bear."

In Greece he again saw all the ruling figures: the prime minister, who
was an admiral of good intentions but no political training; the influential
British ambassador, Caccia, later to become ambassador to the United States;
and most impressive of all, the Regent, Archbishop Dameskinos, a man of

Herbert H. Lehman with the children of Athens, July, 1945

Children being fed at Comensoli School near Rome, July, 1945
UNRRA Photograph in the National Archives

Lincolnian height, great dignity, and obvious courage and decision. Lehman was deeply pained as he traveled about Greece by the harsh gap between rich and poor. In some luxurious houses he found the richest foods and wines; elsewhere poor men were glad to make a dinner of bread and an artichoke. Scenes of suffering were encountered everywhere. At a foundling hospital to which UNRRA sent supplies an emaciated child died before his eyes. When he went to Crete he saw an island harshly furrowed and ravaged by the Nazi occupation. "One old woman, well in the eighties, was brought to see me. She was almost unable to talk because of her emotion. She told me her only son had been seized by the Germans, who had sprinkled gasoline over him and burned him to death in her presence. I was told that this was only one of thousands of similar incidents. At one place overlooking a ravine we were told of six hundred patriots who were shot by the Germans and buried in three common graves."

In Belgrade he found a tense political situation. King Peter II had yielded his power to a regency which had shortly installed Marshal Tito as head of the government, exercising a virtual dictatorship which would be confirmed by elections in the fall. All political opposition and nearly all religious activities were being suppressed. Lehman, met at the airport by members of the government, was at once tendered a Cabinet dinner. He was treated with all possible courtesy, for the country badly needed UNRRA's help. But American and British diplomats were unhappy about their position, told him that their nationals were under constant surveillance, and expressed a belief that UNRRA supplies were being used in part for political purposes and in part to enable Yugoslavia to release similar goods to Russia. They had no proof of these allegations, which the head and several other members of the UNRRA mission rejected, maintaining that the distribution was substantially fair. Nevertheless, Lehman went to his interview with Marshal Tito in a critical frame of mind and let the Marshal know it. He wrote:

"Marshal Tito lives in a palace of Prince Paul, the former Regent, situated not very far from the palace of the former king on the outskirts of Belgrade. It is an attractive but not particularly homey house. There were a great many armed guards within and without the palace. I was told they were a guard of honor for me. Whether they were, or whether they were there in their capacity as guards for Marshal Tito, I do not know. I was immediately ushered into a salon where Marshal Tito received me, dressed in a well-fitting and rather imposing uniform. He is a man of about 53 or 54, has a very strong face, appears to be in excellent health, and is full of vitality. Refreshments were served shortly after my arrival. Marshal Tito of course spoke in his language, I in mine, and through an interpreter. Present were members of the press, a number of photographers, and several ministers of state and three or four of our top UNRRA people.

"Marshal Tito was very cordial and expressed himself as very grateful for the assistance which UNRRA has given. I immediately countered by saying that I appreciated his gratitude, but wished he would express it more publicly than had heretofore been the case. I pointed out that so far as the public was concerned in his country and elsewhere, all they had heard was requests for additional supplies, and they were not informed of what supplies UNRRA had already sent in. He expressed regret at this situation, and promised to make a public statement the following day. He made good his promise, and a public statement was cabled to the United States and other parts of the world."

The Marshal also assured Lehman that the government would funnel all the goods it received from UNRRA to the people without favor or prejudice and would give mission members the fullest freedom of movement. Next day the Cabinet met with the Director-General, so that one by one the Ministers of Food, Health, Transport, Welfare, and other departments could tell him what they needed—which came to "everything under the sun." Lehman had to explain that the organization could furnish goods for relief and rehabilitation, but none for reconstruction; that was strictly forbidden.

Mrs. Lehman met him in London, looking very rested after her sea voyage. "I was terribly happy to see her," he writes. Meeting then followed meeting at the Portland Place offices, where he saw old friends like Leith-Ross, Philip Noel-Baker, and Harold Caustin and talked with the delegates gathering for the Council session. The American group included two Congressmen, Stephen Pace of Georgia and Christian Herter of Massachusetts. Endless questions needed preliminary discussion. Did Italy really need as many tractors as she demanded? Why was the distribution of raw cotton and wool to European textile manufactures moving so slowly? How should the work of the Washington office and the London headquarters of European Relief Organization be better coordinated?—for Lehman was anxious to give complete operating responsibility in Europe to ERO. Would they be ready to take up work in China on the morrow of V-J Day, plainly near at hand? What should be done about the request of Russia for $700,000,000? In all the talks worries concerning the financial future of UNRRA constantly beset the leaders and their advisers.

"I met with Ambassador Winant, Will Clayton, and Commander Jackson," runs Lehman's entry for August 4. "Our main discussion concerned itself with the extra one-percent contribution from the United States, with the problem arising out of displaced persons, and with arrangements

for undertaking a comprehensive relief program in Italy and Austria. I outlined to Clayton and Winant our financial situation and pointed out that
without further funds in the amount of at least one percent from the chief
contributing countries, we not only would be unable to undertake additional responsibility, but could not carry out our existing programs much
beyond the early months of 1946. I asked how much it was estimated the
Italian program would cost, and was told it would require between four and
five hundred million dollars. . . . No authoritative estimate could be given
with regard to the Austrian operation, but the amount we talked of was
$100,000,000. There was also some talk of UNRRA undertaking work in
Formosa and Korea, the cost of which cannot be estimated." Lehman
thought it would be impossible to meet even half of the Soviet petition for
$700,000,000 to be spent in the areas ravaged by the Nazis.

When Lehman visited the Foreign Office to talk with Noel-Baker, Sir
George Rendel, and others, he found them anxious to hear of his observa-
tions in Italy, Greece, and Yugoslavia and much more friendly in attitude
than the previous December. In justice to them he had to say that the picture had greatly improved in the intervening seven months. "In 1944
UNRRA had barely started operations and was in a most embarrassing and
difficult position vis-à-vis the British Government in connection with fighting in Greece, and there is no doubt that the British officials were much
discouraged and very suspicious of what UNRRA might accomplish. Now,
however, the situation has completely changed. UNRRA is in full operation in a number of countries, and has shown that it really can do the job
for which it was created."

As he called the first Council meeting to order at 2:30 P.M. on August
7, the Director-General could feel that a similar warmth of confidence was
observable in delegates from other nations. This was the day when the
bomb fell at Hiroshima. The war in the East was ending; a new age was
opening. But more than one grim cloud was rising on the horizon. Lehman
struck a prophetic note when he wrote in his diary just before the meeting: "I imagine there will be a lineup of the USSR, Poland, Yugoslavia, and
Czechoslovakia on one side with most of the other nations on the other."
Though he was referring particularly to the issue of full control by each
government over its displaced persons, the statement had wide implications.

Lehman was able to report to the Council that despite the tendency of
the military authorities to continue monopolizing supplies and transport,
1,250,000 tons of UNRRA food, clothing, and other materials had been
shipped by June 30, 1945. He was able to state that in Europe only the
countries of the eastern and southern part of the continent now asked for

aid, as Belgium, Holland, France, and Norway were using their own resources.

Nevertheless, he reported, even apart from the new plea of the Soviet
Union, UNRRA did not have means enough for the minimum needs of the
prostrate lands. China would soon be making large requirements. At least
$1,500,000,000 would be needed, in addition to the sums already appropriated
by member governments, to bridge the gap until international trade could
be restored and other methods of financing assistance created. Nor was
money alone enough. The member governments, he declared, must accept
the implications of any further support of UNRRA. They would have to
make sacrifices of shipping space, trucks, tractors, food, machinery, raw
materials, and if they were not prepared to do this, they would do well to
make no pledge of support. Military relief had been reasonably large, for
the armed services had shipped nine million tons of what they called
civil affairs supplies to invaded European countries up to June 30. But it
was little compared with the great responsibilities UNRRA would now hope
to assume.

The Director-General's speech, with the reports of representatives of the
Combined Boards and Combined Chiefs of Staff on the contributions of
these bodies and on the expectations they now pinned upon UNRRA, infused
a new spirit of determination into the Council. Delegates realized that they
would have to do more to awaken their governments and peoples to the
tests that lay ahead. "Many," writes the official historian of the organization,[5]
"were persuaded that UNRRA to date had not received the support from
member states in supplies, services, and personnel which was needed to accomplish its end. It was evident that the work of UNRRA, the limitations
on what it was empowered to do, as well as its achievements in the midst
of insuperable difficulties, were not understood by the people of most countries." The session closed with renewed promises of support from member
countries, behind which lay a new realism. The delegates voted a recommendation that each uninvaded member nation should repeat its grant of
one percent of national income. To reassure nations which feared an in-
definite continuance of this heavy burden, the session agreed that UNRRA
should cease shipments of supplies at the end of 1946 and terminate its work
in March 1947. The Council added to the list of nations eligible for UNRRA
assistance Italy, Austria, Formosa, and Korea; and against heated Communist
opposition, it authorized the Administration to assist certain groups of displaced persons without prior approval by their former governments.

Some memorable personal experiences marked the Lehmans' stay in
England. They went to Cambridge to visit Peter's grave and found the air

force cemetery now carpeted with grass and flowers, while the rolling, well-wooded country about was clothed in all its late summer beauty. "I was much more comforted on this trip than on the previous one," Lehman recorded. "I know that Edith, too, was comforted by the beauty of the cemetery and by the care which it is receiving from the military authorities." Lehman called upon the Archbishop of Canterbury, who answered the doorbell at Lambeth Palace himself, in rather shabby garb—nearly everybody in Europe was shabby—and though well informed on UNRRA was plainly more interested in the spiritual than the material reconstruction of Europe. The Director-General called on Attlee. But the minister who impressed him most was the robust, outspoken, oaken-hearted Foreign Secretary, Ernest Bevin.

"I had met him on two previous occasions," notes Lehman. "I found him as keen and energetic as before. He is obviously a very strong man and does not mince words. I reminded him of a conversation which I had had with him two years ago in which he said he did not fear unemployment in England after the war, as they had much construction work ahead on the repair of damaged buildings and the erection of millions of new homes. In 1943 he said that two million people had married during the war and were seeking homes. He now raises that figure to three million. He impresses me as an infinitely stronger man than the Prime Minister. . . ." Attlee's, of course, was a quieter strength.

On V-J Day, while all London seemed celebrating in the streets, the Lehmans had tea with George VI and Queen Elizabeth at Buckingham Palace. The crowds milling about the palace were interested to learn what foreign potentate or war leader was arriving with a police escort, and showed puzzled chagrin when they could not identify the guests. Tea was ready in a private sitting room, with the two young princesses hungry for it. The King and Queen were chiefly interested in recalling the visit to the New York World's Fair in 1939 when the Lehmans had been guides; the Lehmans were chiefly interested in the two girls. "We both liked the young princesses immensely. They appeared to be simple, and just like two very sweet American girls. Princess Elizabeth told a really funny story and got a real kick out of doing it. She giggled and gesticulated and acted the part just as any other simple girl would have done. The meal itself was a regular English tea with lots of bread and butter and jam and cake. The King himself escorted us to the door. The whole party was as enjoyable as anything we have done for a long time."

The end of the war hastened Lehman's return to America, where new questions had to be settled at once. He and Mrs. Lehman returned on the

Queen Elizabeth with 12,000 soldiers, every inch of the boat occupied. Altogether, the ship carried 15,000 people. Many soldiers slept on deck, only two meals a day were served, and walking space was so limited that Lehman spent his waking hours meeting and talking with the veterans. They had no complaints, but "it is pathetic how eager they are to get home."

Getting into Washington as September opened, the most exigent of his tasks were those concerned with finance. UNRRA's operating income for the whole period of its life into the spring of 1947 was now estimated at $3,766,600,000. Actually, it turned out to be $3,872,749,021, but this was the expectation when Lehman stepped off his boat. It was none too much —indeed, it was too little. Of the sums obtained, three nations, the United States, Great Britain, and Canada, in the end furnished about 94 percent. If a minor contributor like Chile failed, the program was not impeded; if the United States or Britain delayed its appropriations, the whole vast undertaking was imperiled.[6] On Labor Day in 1945 Lehman knew it was of the utmost urgency that Congress pass the final appropriation under its first one-percent authorization and also enact its second authorization of one percent. To make sure of this, he had to rally public sentiment, to rebut hostile arguments, and to mobilize effective witnesses before the House and Senate Appropriations Committees.

Fortunately, he had many and able backers. The *New York Times* and the *Herald-Tribune*, the *Christian Science Monitor*, the *St. Louis Post-Dispatch*, and many other influential papers were with him. In the House three members could be counted upon to furnish eloquent leadership to the friends of UNRRA; Sol Bloom of New York, in whose constituency Columbia University fell, Helen Gahagan Douglas of California, and Emily Taft Douglas of Chicago, wife of Paul Douglas. Vandenberg was a pillar of strength in the Senate. Charles P. Taft, from his vantage point in the State Department, where he was now Director of Transport and Communications, was unfailingly helpful. Dean Acheson and Will Clayton, two men of the highest ability, gave resourceful assistance at every turn. President Truman, though never so earnestly enlisted in the cause as Roosevelt, saw the importance of carrying UNRRA through 1946. McKellar of Tennessee, the benign old chairman of the Senate Appropriations Committee, who invariably fell asleep in hearings, was friendly.

At the critical moment one powerful figure lent his strength to the wheel. Just at Thanksgiving Eisenhower, now back from Europe, was asked to testify. He was suffering from a heavy cold; his wife was seriously ill; but he willingly appeared, and his hearty endorsement of UNRRA was decisive.[7] On December 14, 1945, Congress passed the final appropriation under the first one-percent pledge, $550,000,000; four days later it passed the second one-percent authorization for $1,350,000,000. Great Britain had already led the way, announcing in November its second contribution of £75,000,000, or approximately $325,000,000, and Canada on December 22 voted a fresh Dominion contribution of $77,000,000. The Minister of Finance in Ottawa, J. L. Ilsley, eloquently expressed his faith in the role which mutual aid would play in relieving the vast suffering of the war and "helping by constructive measures truly to secure a just and enduring peace."

Lehman could celebrate New Year's with a profound sense of relief. The money available was not enough; China's original estimate of more than a billion as the sum she needed, Poland's original estimate of $946,000,000, and Russia's estimate of $700,000,000 would alone have almost exhausted the budget. Nearly all requests had to be scaled down. The China program finally cost about $670,000,000, the Poland program $478,000,000, and the programs for the Ukraine and Byelorussia $273,000,000.[8] Still, the continuance of a great work was now possible: the greatest international effort of a constructive character yet undertaken.

· II ·

The burden of the displaced persons in Europe was rapidly reduced to manageable, though still difficult, proportions. It became plain that for a hard core of well over a million people the status of refugees would not be transitory but of long duration. UNRRA late in 1945 took almost complete responsibility for them. It signed an agreement with the authorities of the British zone in Germany on November 27, and although similar agreements for the American and French zones waited nearly three months, it was really in charge there too, from the autumn.

Some six hundred thousand Poles had more or less firmly refused to place themselves under the new Warsaw government. A quarter of a million former Balts, mourning the extinction of Lithuania, Latvia, and Esthonia, had no intention of abandoning themselves to the mercies of the Soviet Union. Perhaps fifty thousand Ukrainians had learned to hate the name of Stalin as much as Hitler's. Not far from a hundred thousand Yugoslavs, watching with anguish the hard fate of Mikolajczyk, refused to accept Tito. Nearly all these stayed on in German, Austrian, and Italian assembly camps. Meanwhile, Jewish refugees presented a special problem. When the war ended, about a hundred thousand were found in Central Europe, and the total was soon swollen to twice that number by the infiltration of groups from eastern and southeastern Europe. All in all, this hard core of one to one and a quarter millions was a heavy burden to Central Europe and Italy, a cause of much dissension between East and West, and a difficult problem for all the benevolent agencies. Among these agencies UNRRA shouldered the chief responsibility until in the summer of 1947 the International Refugee Organization took over.

The great majority of the woebegone mass possessed ability and character, and though unwilling to live under a government offensive to them, were able to carry important contributions to any free land. It was sad that America, with its stony immigration laws, offered them so little haven. Some, to be sure, were old and sick, some were chronic misfits and malcontents, some had suffered so much that they thought they had a right to special treatment, and some were the debilitated, discouraged debris of war. All, however, deserved help.

A final augmentation of human distress began under certain bad terms, badly interpreted, laid down by the Potsdam Conference while Lehman was making his European trip. Poland, Czechoslovakia, and Hungary, actuated by old hatreds and new political appetites, expelled some three million Germans from their domains. The Russians had annexed the eastern area of prewar Poland, and the Poles occupied the eastern part of prewar Germany; in effect, Poland had been relocated several hundred miles west of its former position. The people thus roughly torn from their old homes east of the Oder and Neisse imposed a heavy strain on the meager resources of Germany, which had also to accept minorities thrust out of Rumania and Yugoslavia. Some 200,000 people from Poland and East Prussia were caught in Denmark for lack of quarters in Germany, and had to remain there two or three years. Of course more problems were to come. The movement of refugees from East Germany to West Germany over the next ten years, for example, was to reach a total of about one and a half million.

Under its agreements with zone authorities in Germany, UNRRA was responsible for administering the camps, supervising the voluntary agencies that worked in them, distributing such "amenities" as razor blades, recreational equipment, and educational supplies, and operating a Central Tracing Bureau. It was to maintain headquarters in each zone and district and to establish needed subordinate offices. To please the Slav nations, emphasis was laid upon the encouragement of repatriation and the removal of all obstacles possible. The Soviet authorities angrily contended that in making sure of the health, comfort, and mental well-being of displaced persons, the Western humanitarians would simply encourage them to stay where they were or to hunt asylum in the United States, the Dominions, and Latin

America. Further to placate Moscow, the Council at its spring meeting in 1946 decided to limit further care to six months.[9]

Whatever the paper limitations, practical aid to the refugees soon hummed all over Central Europe. By the end of 1945 UNRRA was in charge of 263 assembly centers in Germany, of four-fifths of the people in them, and of nearly three-fifths of the displaced persons in the country. In Austria its work, though of narrower scope, was important. Throughout Italy it exercised a partnership with the military authorities under the Supreme Allied Commander of the Mediterranean area. Its activities in the peninsula were somewhat different from those farther north. Fewer people flocked into the assembly camps, more than half the displaced persons choosing to live outside. UNRRA workers gave these scattered dependents goods from stocks supposedly kept replenished by the Italian Government but which really came from military sources or UNRRA stores, and then sometimes gave the needy cash. In the Middle East the UNRRA officers continued to maintain some camps and keep the refugees clothed and fed; and here it also paid the costs of their transportation home.

The camps represented an effort as picturesque as it was valiant. "The purely physical accommodation," writes the official historian, "varied from tents on Egyptian deserts to castles . . . in Germany." Sometimes the clean, airy tent was a habitation superior to the moldy and ill-furnished castle. The typical accommodation in Europe, however, was a brick or stone barracks of three or four stories, a one-story wooden barracks which had often seen previous use as a concentration camp or forced-labor center, or a loose group of dwelling houses. The large brick or stone barracks were usually best. Some were in or near cities—Munich, Salzburg, Milan. Some were in the country, though here it was harder to provide employment. Sometimes an entire village was requisitioned, sometimes an integral part of a city, sometimes houses scattered all over a town. In Cremona, Italy, a large school was converted into an assembly center. The inmates might tarry for months or even years or might be migrants stopping a day or a fortnight.

Crowding, discomfort, and friction were inseparable from refugee life. The standard allotment of sleeping space, as fixed by military or national authorities, was thirty square feet a person, the equivalent of a six-by-five cubicle. Though families were housed alone when feasible, frequently a couple had to share a single room with another couple or a single person, a sheet serving as partition. Stoves and utensils had to be placed next beds. Real privacy was seldom attainable. But in the European chaos comfort was not a primary consideration; shelter, heat, food, toilet facilities, and some room for recreation and education were the essentials. Most of the home population from Brest to Kharkov had a bare and meager life.

Education, in the fullest meaning of the word, was a cardinal goal. A former fellow officer wrote Commander Jackson early in 1946 that one camp that he had seen efficiently administered by a British corporal and two privates was then being run by eleven UNRRA men, each getting more pay than any predecessor. Why, he asked, was this necessary? The answer was that although three soldiers sufficed so long as care of the inmates was the sole consideration, more workers were needed to achieve true rehabilitation; that is, to heighten morale, create initiative, and provide varied training. UNRRA intended to refit its charges for return to the active world.

To this end it fostered camp self-government, which meant the election of a managing committee and a leader. It saw to the formation of police and fire departments, of a camp court, and of subcommittees to deal with special problems. Many displaced persons seemed at first constitutionally dirty. In the end, however, most large camps became so effectively self-administered that not even three soldiers would have been needed. The inmates were so eager for self-improvement that no stimulation was necessary. Wishing their children educated according to their own national traditions, they organized primary and secondary schools. UNRRA had to help provide tutors and texts but not to blow the flame of zeal. It formed a pool of teachers whom it shifted from camp to camp, mimeographed educational material, and spurred on voluntary agencies in furnishing blackboards, pencils, and paper.

Thanks to UNRRA, every camp in time had vocational training courses. The inmates themselves obtained materials from the military, the Red Cross, the YMCA, the Friends' Relief, the Jewish ORT, or UNRRA and took apprentices and trained them in carpentry, shoemaking, tailoring, and other crafts. More ambitious courses in engineering and technology required machines, technical books, and expert instructors; they were provided. In addition, UNRRA established some special training centers outside the camps which gave advanced work in fields of special national need. One of the most remarkable was in Flensburg, where Poles mastered the theory and practice of railroad transportation, and Balts took courses in marine engineering, navigation, and radio work. Graduates were in keen demand when they returned home. Special agricultural schools were also set in operation. Even two so-called "universities" for refugees were opened; one at Munich with UNRRA guidance and help and one at Hamburg with British assistance. Unhappily, the Munich school was discontinued because of allegations that it interfered with repatriation. Good schools of nursing were carried on.

Emphasizing self-help, UNRRA encouraged the refugees to form orchestras, theatrical groups, debating societies, and of course athletic teams. Artists in the camps painted pictures, wove lace, composed music, made pottery, and carved statuary. They built their own churches and synagogues and held ceremonial pageants.

• III •

It was not with the refugees, however, but with the settled populations of war-mutilated lands that by far the greater part of UNRRA's activity lay. Lehman's principal concern was with the relief and rehabilitation of half-paralyzed communities.

The European countries to be aided fell theoretically into two groups. One comprised nations automatically entitled to help because of enemy invasions and their inability to pay. The other comprised six lands included on grounds of compassionate policy: Italy, Austria, Hungary, Finland, Byelorussia, and the Ukraine. In practice, all nations were aided according to need with as much equality as could be attained. Some of the Yugoslavs, supported by their Soviet protectors, made vociferous complaints that the Greeks fared better than they. This was untrue, except insofar as the Greek need was more desperate. Some Italians and their British friends declared that Italy was unduly neglected, but this also was untrue.

Unremitting efforts were made to avoid political bias. Even after relations between Yugoslavia and the Western Allies gravely deteriorated, shipments to Yugoslav ports continued without slackening. Albania became a storm center when Enver Hoxha hampered the UNRRA work and brought false accusations of sabotage against mission officers; but the organization showed signal patience until finally the intrepid head of the mission, Peter C. Floud, forced Hoxha to apologize and retreat.

A great many men in all the Allied capitals worked themselves to exhaustion in the aftermath of the war, but few worked harder than Lehman in his offices on Connecticut Avenue. We cannot give a history of UNRRA's justification of its two R's, but we can indicate Lehman's part in the many-sided international effort. The routines of the ever more complex machine alone required the most vigilant attention. Depute responsibility as much as he might, he still had to scrutinize the procurement of supplies, the creation of transport, the hiring of personnel, and the rise and fall of the financial barometer. He had to evaluate new relief plans every day. He had to enlist and, if possible, guide the many voluntary agencies working with UNRRA, some thirty in Germany alone. He had to see that the claims of the organization to Lend-Lease resources and military surpluses were pugnaciously pressed. He had to deal with public relations, a task for which he was not temperamentally well fitted, for he lacked color and tended too much to think that performance spoke for itself without special advertising.

In all this he worried ceaselessly, and displayed his characteristic sensitivity to "the tormenting cant of criticism."

The primary public relations task was to transform suspicious, narrow, grudging American attitudes, an outgrowth in part of pure selfishness and in part of vestigial isolationism, into a civilized temper. Lehman had labored against this stinginess, this nationalism, from the beginning; in the postwar reaction he and others had to labor harder than ever. Because they could not get steaks and were rationed on butter, many people objected to sending sausage or oleomargarine abroad. When Lehman suggested that soap should be rationed to meet Europe's sanitary needs, many people rushed to the stores to buy excessive home supplies.

The *Chicago Tribune* months after fighting ended lamented that the United States was expected to do "nearly all" for the relief of the cold and hungry. The *Detroit Free Press* simultaneously proclaimed that however sympathetic Americans might be, they should not be expected to "give what we haven't got." An editorial in the *Jacksonville* (Florida) *Times* warned the nation: "America Should Not Sap Its Strength for Relief." As Iowa turned from her wheat harvest to her corn harvest, the *Council Bluffs Nonpareil* deplored the bad taste of Russia in asking help for the devastated Ukraine. Few people realized that one percent of national income hit Great Britain and the Dominions, which had been in the war since 1939, harder than the same levy hit the United States.

At a rally in Central Park on "I-am-an-American Day," May 20, 1945, Lehman had told the huge crowd that true Americanism embraced internationalism: "Are we going to allow starvation in Europe or prevent it? If necessary, are we willing to make a small sacrifice at home in order that millions abroad can regain their health and dignity?" He continued to speak and write in this vein. Meanwhile, he had to answer petty carping criticisms of UNRRA inspired mainly by selfishness.[10] The distribution of cigarettes to refugee camps, for example, fell under criticism. Of course, countless inmates craved tobacco just as much as soldiers did and found it a contribution to morale; for that matter, most of it came from voluntary organizations. When UNRRA shipped claret from Portuguese and other sources to France, various donkeys emitted indignant brays. They did not know that the best French claret is a compound of cheap and expensive wines and that the shipments helped to rehabilitate the French industry. Similarly, when in the postwar fuel crisis UNRRA shipped about four million tons of American coal abroad, critics hastened to point out that this was uneconomic. So it was; but it was a necessity if some Europeans were not to freeze.

It was hard in all lands for self-interested men to comprehend that as UNRRA was a broad international venture in the rescue of stricken peoples, its participants must forego nationalist greeds. While the war raged, with men dying under the bombs and some countries agonizing over the question of survival, an intense patriotism ruled. It was difficult for even the most enlightened to shake it off for the one-world idea. In the United States a good many even of the men espousing relief and rehabilitation, including Congressmen and generals, thought it should be a purely American function, as under Hoover in the First World War, so conducted as to augment American prestige and influence. In all countries Lehman and his staff had to resist men who wanted to bend UNRRA to national aims.

"Wild Bill" Donovan, head of the Office of Strategic Services, was for all his essential integrity one such man. He came to Lehman with what he thought a reasonable proposal. "You need able men in your organization," he said. "I have some. I will release a few to you on the understanding that while they do relief they will collect information and send it back to me. Such agents will be specially useful to OSS in the Balkans and Middle East." Lehman's blunt rejection of this scheme for planting spies in UNRRA puzzled Donovan. A British member of the UNRRA staff in Athens had the same attitude. This man was unexpectedly blown up in a jeep—and a large sum in gold was found on his body. He was obviously using money from some British agency to support antiradical activities in Greece. For an anxious fortnight Lehman feared that the episode would get press headlines and do grave harm in southeastern Europe, but determined effort kept it secret.

Much the heaviest threat to the international honesty of the organization came from Soviet officials. Mikhail A. Menshikov, the Deputy Director-General who managed the Bureau of Areas in the Washington office with rather ill-defined responsibilities and who was sent on an important investigative mission in 1945 to Poland, proved untrustworthy. He spied everywhere for Soviet objects. "It was Menshikov's habit," Lehman recalls, "to keep his ears open. Whenever he heard anything that affected Russia, or the relations of the Soviet Union with other countries, he slipped around to the Soviet Embassy in Washington. No matter how sternly we emphasized the rule of secrecy, he leaked all he knew." Some remedy had to be found. "Finally," adds Lehman, "I had to lay down a strict rule that no confidential information could be imparted to any deputy." Menshikov was thus effectually gagged. He did his best to fetter UNRRA work in Poland by restricting the original mission to thirty men, with no regional offices, but the brilliant Canadian who took charge there, Brigadier Charles M. Drury, soon broke through all impediments. It should be added that Menshikov was a gentleman, and that one highly placed American, who remains anonymous, writes that he "was easier to deal with and work with as an international official than most of the other Russians with whom we had contact."

In creating a sense of the high international purposes of UNRRA and of the rewards to be reaped by generosity, Lehman and his associates made real if interrupted and halting progress. Grumbling never ceased. "The United States is short of tractors," murmured the farm press, "yet UNRRA is shipping overseas the machines we need at home." Senator Bankhead of Alabama croaked that foreign nations were not entitled to half they asked. Representative Edwin A. Hall of New York introduced a bill to halt shipments of grain overseas until areas which lacked livestock and poultry feed were given all they wanted and Americans had assurances of full supplies of white bread. While such voices made it clear that UNRRA's life would not last much beyond 1946, Lehman did keep majority opinion on his side.

The rather specialized public relations task involved in dealing with the voluntary agencies in relief was refreshingly easy. Nearly all these agencies were as friendly as they were helpful, and some—the Red Cross, British and American, the YMCA and YWCA, the Jewish ORT and Joint Distribution Committee in particular—gave indispensable aid. The American Catholics worked in Poland through UNRRA very amicably and efficiently. The American Friends Service Committee, with Clarence E. Pickett as secretary, sent a number of capable workers into the field, who were reinforced by British Friends. At the outset Lehman, Leith-Ross, and others rather naïvely hoped that all these voluntary societies would merge themselves into UNRRA and wear its badges. Of course this was impossible; some of them had far too much pride and *esprit de corps*. When Lehman undertook to argue with Lady Mountbatten as head of the British YWCA he found her courteously immovable. Cooperation, however, was readily given and direction accepted. One or two organizations, such as Myron Taylor's American Relief in Italy, which he hoped for a time might do for the Italians what Hoover had done for the Belgians, neither helped nor hindered. "Taylor never interfered with us, and we never interfered with him," recalls Lehman. One or two other organizations were troublesome. On the whole, however, this was a happy story.

On a grander scale, public relations also comprehended UNRRA's dealings with the governments which furnished it its supplies. Lehman leaned heavily upon his diplomatic adviser, Francis B. Sayre—Woodrow Wilson's son-in-law and former high commissioner to the Philippines—who wrote a conscientious record in heading UNRRA missions for support and supplies to twenty-three countries. But UNRRA made its procurement arrangements in such a way as to avoid friction. It planned its program for collecting food, clothing, and other goods, in the main, so as to take advantage of seasonal surpluses, support an increased production of scanty wares, and initiate orders for industries that needed stimulation. It used first the Foreign Economic Administration for procurement and then, after FEA died in the fall of 1945, the State Department. Its bureau of supplies, under Roy F. Hendrickson, tactfully informed the contributing countries just when, where, and in what shape their gifts could best be delivered to receiving nations. Such matters as priority of shipment rested entirely with the donor governments.

Thus UNRRA obtained, first and last, more than twenty-four million long tons of supplies from thirty-one countries, without noticeable jealousies or bickering. It had its disappointments, as when South Africa failed to give a second round of aid because of a drought. The growing schism between East and West troubled it. Nevertheless, it set an example of international cooperation on an equitable, friendly, and courteous plane.*

· IV ·

Lehman found by the autumn of 1945 that the outlines of his task were fairly well defined. The four European countries in which UNRRA had to make its greatest exertions and expenditures were, in order, Poland, Italy, Yugoslavia, and Greece. (China was a separate responsibility of the first magnitude.) The two largest elements in supply and costs were first, food, and second, aids to industrial rehabilitation. Of the perennial problems of finance, personnel, and transport, all critical, the last became the most serious once the Anglo-American appropriations were assured late in 1945. After a fair amount of ocean shipping had been obtained, a "Battle of the Trucks" had to be waged for inland transport. The last great crisis which Lehman faced in the winter of 1945–46 was the "Battle for Breadstuffs."

The end of the war released manpower on a gigantic scale all over the world, so that the UNRRA staff could be rapidly expanded. By the spring of 1946 this staff in all countries and classes numbered about 12,000, and

* See the table of supplies furnished in Appendix II.

eventually it rose to 20,000. Every country in helping carry on the work used its own citizens. The shortage lay not in men, but in first-class experienced men. Advisers like Jean Monnet of France and Oliver Franks of England, Lester B. Pearson of Canada and Walter Nash of New Zealand, Alain DuParc of Belgium and Anders Frihagen of Norway, were rare enough and were usually too busy to do more than advise. Executives of the highest type found tempting opportunities of a permanent character too abundant in business and government to be much attracted by UNRRA, with the smell of death already on its garments. Lehman could only be thankful for Commander Jackson and Frederick Leith-Ross in London, and such invaluable aides as Hendrickson, Sayre, and Hugh Jackson (who supervised "regional liaison") in Washington. They had few if any counterparts on the continent. At the lowest levels, UNRRA administrators had to struggle with both incompetence and dishonesty in various receiving countries, and had limited power to deal with both.

Ocean carriage became fairly adequate by the end of 1945. Merchant fleets at the end of the war reverted to national governments, which contributed to a common pool under the United Maritime Authority such ships as were needed for combined operations. The chief limiting factor soon became the ruinous condition of many ports, with wrecked wharves and sunken ships. But clearance dealt with this, and shipments of UNRRA materials climbed: 2,126,000 long tons the third quarter of 1945; 4,034,000 the fourth quarter; 8,252,000 the first quarter of 1946; and 12,855,000 the second quarter. It was inland transport that for a time was the worst bottleneck.

"Trucks and other vehicles have been our most constant anxiety, and for them we have made our most vigorous efforts," Lehman told the Council in August, 1945. Noel-Baker made an eloquent exposition of their vital importance. "A lorry is a lorry, but it is more than that: it is the lifeblood of organized society; it is, to the people of Europe, government stability, the maintenance of adequate policing of law and order, the hope of a return to democratic institutions. Transport for the peoples of Europe is food, clothing, coal, raw materials, work for people who have been hungry, ragged, and unemployed."

By frenzied effort, UNRRA gathered about 6,000 trucks from America, Britain, Italy, and Iran and got them into Yugoslavia in the autumn of 1945. The United States Army at that time had hundreds of thousands of vehicles in Europe, and Lehman had asked Secretary of War Stimson to release 50,000 of them. But somehow they were hard to pry loose. General Brehon Somerville, testifying before a Senate committee to a great surplus of trucks abroad, had astounded Lehman by asking if he wanted any of them. "Do we want them?" exploded Lehman. "The trouble is we can't get them released. I've got a telegram from Yugoslavia telling that one hungry city, Sarajevo, has only three trucks to feed thousands of people. Why, some towns are starving while they're burning food just a few miles away."

The great truck movement this fall was one of the most spectacular episodes in UNRRA operations. Some 23,000 American, British, and Canadian vehicles were collected in England and shipped into Poland and Czechoslovakia. In the Mediterranean area thousands of surplus trucks were furnished by the British and American armies for the Balkans. The Ninth Canadian Armored Regiment drove 3,638 three-ton military trucks and trailers out of the Netherlands, in convoys of fifty, to Pilsen, Czechoslovakia, whence they were distributed. Each carried a hundred gallons of gasoline so that it could be put to immediate use. President Beneš attended a special ceremony of welcome, at which the Czech people threw their hats in the air as they cheered. Altogether, by the end of 1945 some 40,000 trucks from UNRRA were circulating the "lifeblood of organized society" over ravaged parts of Europe, and by the end of the first quarter of 1946 nearly 80,000 had been distributed. The "Battle of the Trucks" had been won.

Substantial shipments of food under UNRRA began in the second quarter of 1945—the victory quarter—but from the outset Lehman met great difficulty in obtaining proteins and fats. Nations that had been living on turnips, Brussels sprouts, and cornmeal, and that after the war were glad to get a little whale meat, longed for cheese, eggs, margarine, canned fish, and condensed milk. The United States could give UNRRA none. When Lehman asked for more than 4,000 tons of canned pork he got 175 tons. Of bread grains the United States and the Dominions had full supplies in 1944 and the first half of the following year, but Europe protested that man cannot live by bread grains alone.

Then the autumn of 1945 brought a somber discovery: even bread grains would be scarce. Deficiencies of fertilizer and manpower rendered the European harvest poor. Severe droughts struck Australia, New Zealand, South America, and South Africa; in fact, a wide belt around the Southern Hemisphere. Crops were poor in the lands rimming the Mediterranean. Andrew Cairns, the able but always gloomy and often quarrelsome head of the food division in Washington, wrote in midsummer of 1945 that "with the sole exception of wheat all foods are in acute short supply," and for wheat too the outlook was unpromising. A threat of imminent famine in most UNRRA-supplied countries developed late in the year. In India, where the monsoon rains failed, and in Japan, prostrated by defeat, the situation was grave. Lehman and his associates succeeded, during the last half of the year, in shipping nearly 92 percent of the grain needed by the recipient nations, but as 1946 opened they felt dire forebodings for the future.

Lehman translated his apprehensions into an appeal to Truman. Would he request a national economy program in cereals? The President responded by asking the country to observe a nine-point program. The extraction of flour from wheat should be raised to eighty percent of the berry; the use of wheat in manufacturing liquor should be stopped; less wheat should be fed to livestock—these were three of his demands. Meanwhile, Lehman insisted that the UNRRA Council face the realities of the situation. It was his duty, he wrote in mid-March, 1946, to inform them of some harsh facts. The organization was running far behind in its transfers of food. For the first quarter of the year it would ship only about half the bread grain requirements of hungry countries, a fifth of the rice requirements, and less than four percent of the needed fats. In April 60,000 tons of flour were promised from the United States and Canada; nothing more.

This Battle of the Breadstuffs was destined to endure throughout most of 1946. The food shortage remained serious; so serious that, as we shall see, it affected the fall elections in the United States. Nevertheless, a diversion of grain shipments from countries with relatively large stocks—from Great Britain to Poland, for example—and an exceptionally early European harvest, averted any calamity. The United States, with a record crop of more than a billion bushels of wheat and three billion bushels of corn, besides a large meat production, helped save the day; so did Canada and Australia. In the fall of 1945 Lehman and Cairns had executed a timely coup in buying more than $135,000,000 of surplus foods from the United States Army Quartermaster at reduced rates. They obtained huge quantities of meat, cheese, butter, sugar, and peanut butter, and along with them candy, jams, and canned fruit. Shipped in the spring of 1946 during the most critical period, this filled a gap.

In supplying needy millions with clothing and shoes, UNRRA found its activities following a pattern which was both embarrassing and hopeful. Speaking roughly, its work fell into something like this sequence:

First, Lehman and his associates in 1944 and the first half of 1945 found painful shortages and urgent demand in Europe; they could forward almost no supplies; and they sent out desperate appeals.

Second, large supplies flooded in during the second half of 1945 and the first half of 1946, with increasing means of shipment; so that Europe and other lands reached a point where they were getting as much poor clothing and deteriorated footwear as they wanted.

Third, Europe asked UNRRA to furnish raw materials—raw cotton, raw wool, cloth, hides, and leather—and stop sending worn garments and second-hand shoes, so that factories could be restarted to turn out new goods. In short, Europe wished to advance from relief to rehabilitation. Unhappily, UNRRA had a scarcity of unfinished materials and a surplus of second-rate worn uniforms, donated suits, and rebuilt army shoes. Even in early 1946 it had to tell its beneficiaries: "Despite your reluctance to accept finished clothing and footgear, you will have to do it; the administration has done its best to dispose of them, but in vain."

Had it not been for the human discomfort involved, Lehman might have found some incidents in this wry story diverting. His efforts in 1944 to wring supplies out of the Combined Production and Resources Board, representing the United States, Britain, and Canada, led to tense scenes and vehement letters. He got little but recommendations that he turn to other countries and the grant of what were called "hunting licenses." Then in 1945 sufficient allocations of clothing, cloth, and yarn were made by the three countries and Brazil to flood UNRRA. Shoes, meanwhile, offered a special problem. While running OFRRO, Lehman had obtained from the army the use of a factory at Buford, Georgia, to rebuild discarded shoes, and UNRRA took it over. Unfortunately, when two million pairs of shoes had been successfully rebuilt, the army repossessed the plant. In despair, for many Europeans were going barefoot in winter, Lehman looked about for alternatives. As the war came to an end, he found an opportunity to buy about one and a half million shoes from the army—used shoes. He joyously seized upon it. With all possible speed, UNRRA early in 1946 established factories in Italy, Poland, Greece, and Yugoslavia to rework the heavy footwear. Miscellaneous collections were hurried abroad, mostly unmated, were sorted out, and given careful repair. Soon a stream of 2,200 to 2,500 pairs a day, good for fifteen months' wear, was pouring from factories in the four countries.

In long-term results, of course, industrial rehabilitation was the most important work that UNRRA accomplished. As a businessman, Lehman felt special zest in seeing it grow. He and his associates had to keep within a strict line. "Any work temporary in character," as he has put it, "was relief or rehabilitation; any work of permanent character was reconstruction, and forbidden us." Still, the rehabilitation of roads, railways, canals, and ports, the reopening of mines, the restoration of public utilities, and the provision of machinery and equipment for restarting essential industries, led straight to the door of reconstruction. A locomotive might be called an aid to rehabilitation—but locomotives, of which UNRRA distributed more than 650, had a useful life of thirty to forty years.

The activities in agricultural rehabilitation throughout Poland, Czechoslovakia, the Ukraine, and twelve other countries threw up many of the problems with which Lehman had dealt years before when the Joint Distribution Committee was active in Eastern Europe. Transportation of livestock—for hundreds of thousands of horses, cattle, sheep, and swine were moved long distances to replenish needy areas—was more difficult than that of tractors, seeds, or fertilizers. One frantic message from Ulster pleaded for immediate facilities to take pigs to Poland; they "still get fatter and fatter . . . and if a ship is not soon produced they will be too big for the crates." The provision of public utilities likewise recalled to Lehman some of the perplexities he had confronted as governor. The largest projects in Europe were the procurement of steam-electric power stations in Byelorussia and the Ukraine, but UNRRA also rebuilt the gas plants in several countries and gave Athens and Belgrade greatly improved water systems. One irony in its history was that the Athens water arrangements, built to meet a terrible five-year drought, were finished just as heavy rains ended the emergency.

· V ·

The Cold War between the Soviet Union and the West was by 1946 giving Lehman the acutest anxiety. He was presiding over the most far-reaching and effective international effort of the time; and while he toiled to maintain its harmony the world was being rent asunder. In August, 1945, representatives of the United States, Britain, Canada, and Russia had agreed upon the expenditure of $250,000,000 by UNRRA for Byelorussia and the Ukraine. Supplies were flowing into these areas when Winston Churchill made his epochal speech at Fulton, Missouri, in March, 1946, describing and lamenting the Iron Curtain that divided the world. For that matter, relief was still flowing into Russia when a year later President Truman asked Congress to give military and economic aid to Greece and Turkey to repel the thrust of Communism. This meant that unilateral assistance, in one quarter of the globe, was taking the place of multilateral aid. It was plain to Lehman before Churchill spoke that a crisis was approaching.

From the beginning the Russian attitudes toward UNRRA had been a mixture of the provocative, the discourteous, and the suspicious. The Soviet Union took part in organizing UNRRA, kept a member on the Central Committee, and made a real effort to furnish some competent and experienced men for its staff. When the financial board of UNRRA wished to get information on Russia's ability to pay costs, however, along with that of other countries, it collided with a stone wall. Not one statistic was vouchsafed.

When UNRRA approached the civil zonal administrations in Germany for an agreement on terms of work, the American, British, and French authorities responded cordially; the Soviet representative declared that his government would not invite UNRRA to perform any activity. It was rigidly excluded from the Russian zone. Learning that the Russians wanted some aid in the Ukraine and elsewhere, Lehman midway in 1944 made an effort to get realistic estimates from the Soviet Embassy in Washington. When all his pleas failed, he made arrangements to go to Moscow to discuss requirements for the eastern European lands then being "liberated" by the Russians. On the very eve of his departure, after he had gone to bed, a knock came at his door. A Soviet official was there, shamefaced, to say that he must cancel his plans; the Russian government, without explanations, did not want him to come.

In dealing with Lehman, Gromyko was always gruff and always ready to explode with a "No." Russian representatives before UNRRA committees were almost invariably rude, and one man in particular was so boorish that Lehman would not admit him to his apartment. In details of UNRRA business the Russians were deliberately obstructive, attempting to embarrass the administration, for example, by incessant demands for audits of its operations. The Soviet Government never budged from its insistence that Russian war prisoners and refugees should be compelled by force, if necessary, to return to the Soviet Union; fortunately, the West never gave up its opposing stand. Not only did the Soviet demand for an allocation of $700,000,000 to Byelorussia and the Ukraine seem excessive to Lehman, as it did to Secretary Acheson and Will Clayton, but the manner in which it was presented was unnecessarily truculent.

The first weeks of 1946 thus found Lehman in a divided frame of mind. He was proud of what UNRRA, all its energies now released, was accomplishing in Europe and of its new undertakings in China, to which the initial shipments had been made in November. The international organization which he had done so much to create and guide at last promised to discharge its tremendous responsibilities. He was elated by the messages he received upon famine stayed, epidemics blocked, the naked clothed, and the unemployed given work and hope. But he knew that the tension between Russia and the West was raising American hostility to plans of global cooperation. He knew that President Truman shared this hostility. As a matter of fact, Truman told the Cabinet on April 23, 1945, that American agreements with the Soviet Union had been a one-way street, and the next month halted Lend-Lease allocations to Russia. Lehman's happiness over achievements won was mingled with profound discouragement over the future.

Chapter XIV

FINAL REWARDS
—AND FRUSTRATIONS

W<small>HAT</small> sort of Europe we should have had without UNRRA, I really do not know," Ernest Bevin told the House of Commons on January 14, 1948. "It is too horrible to contemplate. I think it would have been swept by epidemics."

Europe even with the benefit of broad international relief was bad enough. Its sorrows and destitutions are recorded by the countless photographs kept in UNRRA archives. A little girl in ragged clothes and tattered shoes sitting abandoned on a railway platform, her head on a roll of blankets, sound asleep; a row of orphaned children at a rough pine table gulping soup, some out of pans, some from plates, some from tin buckets; a family of five voraciously devouring what seems to be its first good meal in months—the father gaunt, hollow-eyed, and shirtless, the little boy and girl with cheeks distended by the food they have hastily seized, the mother radiant as she feeds the thin-armed baby; two white-haired women, bent but indomitable-looking, standing guard over the sack and box that contain everything they have in the world; a physician examining a waif whose protruding ribs make him look rather a skeleton than a child; officials with a portable typewriter placed on an oil drum listing a hillock of supplies—with one huge sack labeled "Use No Hooks," cartons cryptically inscribed "C. A. Medical," big meat boxes from Australia, and rice bags from Burma; Ukrainian farmers with broad grins driving off heavy tractors, each with a gang plow hitched behind; legless and armless men waiting for artificial limbs; ruins and graves —the endless ruins and graves.[1]

In the first half of 1946 the activities of UNRRA were rising toward their height. During most of the year it was the largest exporter in the world. Before the organization ended it was to deliver to seventeen nations more than 24,000,000 tons of supplies for relief and rehabilitation, of which about three quarters was to go forward during 1946. At long last its staff was becoming fairly adequate. Class one employees, men and women liable for service anywhere as distinguished from the class two personnel who served only in their own lands, were an army of mercy scattered all over the needy countries.[2] Able men had at last been released from government service. Indeed, it was touching to see how anxious were some countries, like New Zealand, Brazil, and Holland, to be represented among the fifty-four nations contributing men and how proud the polyglot workers were of their scarlet shoulder flashes with UNRRA lettered in white. They included experts in everything from bone surgery to fiscal analysis, from dietetics to steamship operation.

"Auntie UNRRA," as the Czechs called it, had taken courage from the second round of authorizations in its behalf, when late in 1945 the United States, Britain, and Canada, its main supports, pledged their full financial quotas. Supplies were coming in now from all over the globe: coal from South Africa, wheat and wool from Australia, jute from India, sugar from Cuba, fish from Iceland, beans from Peru, lorries from Britain, locomotives from America. Of course, UNRRA never had money enough. It had to cut its garments according to its cloth, which meant that it budgeted much of its work all too sparingly. Lehman and his aides calculated in the last weeks of 1945 that Poland still needed relief and rehabilitation costing $888,000,000; she got $477,927,000. They estimated that Greece needed $476,000,000; she got $347,162,000. While Lehman, Leith-Ross, and others were abused for not doing more, they could easily have dragged UNRRA into bankruptcy if they had spent according to hopes, or even firm expectations, instead of certainties.[3]

Still, wonders were being accomplished. UNRRA was conducting the largest international medical program in history, stopping epidemics in their tracks. Under the skillful direction of Dr. Wilbur A. Sawyer the health division restored medical and public health services across the face of Europe, arrested or prevented pestilences, and in country after country started sanitation on the way to full recovery.[4] It was soon to hand over its responsibilities to the World Health Organization. Meanwhile, UNRRA was distributing more clothing than any other agency on earth had ever distributed. During the spring of 1946 Lehman arranged another clothing collection in the United States, setting a goal of a hundred million garments. It still had a tragic burden of hard-core refugees, for even in Italy in mid-March, 1946, it was caring for almost 36,000 displaced persons in camps and more in homes.[5] It was getting factories into operation in some of the worst-ravaged lands. For example, the shipment of some 53,200 gross long tons of raw cotton and wool into the textile area of Poland during the first half of 1946 enabled the mills of Lodz and other towns to revive their operations. From military surplus depots in Britain and France it brought urgently needed trucks, bulldozers, and cranes into Western Russia to enable the ruined cities—Kiev, Minsk, Vitebsk, and others—to clear their debris and begin rebuilding. It met recurrent emergencies, such as a threat this spring of a great new yellow fever epidemic in China.

Churchill said of Europe as late as May 14, 1947: "It is a rubble heap, a charnel house, a breeding ground of pestilence and hate." UNRRA, struggling to stand quite above party, checked the hothouse growth of disorder, social discontent, and revolution in one area after another. To this fact objective historians later bore witness. In Poland, writes Nicholas Halasz, a Hungarian, in *The Shadow of Russia*, UNRRA's aid of nearly a half billion "made the difference between starvation, and muddling through the difficulties of a new beginning." In Yugoslavia, he asserts, "the country would have been on the verge of starvation without the magnificent help of UNRRA, which restored the prewar number of vehicles in less than a year, brought in locomotives, freight cars, tractors, even horses and mules, and set up schools to teach machine operation and repair." Picturing the chaotic state of Czech industries after the rough expulsion of 2,700,000 Germans, he adds: "The exceptionally generous help of UNRRA, with goods to the value of $260,000,000 in the two years after the war, made reorganization possible." [6] Czechoslovakia, in fact, was the first liberated country which, while still on the receiving list, began to make contributions of value. In the summer and autumn of 1946 she aided her hungry neighbors by substantial shipments of vegetables and fruits.

When the whistle of the first supply ship echoed over the crowded Shanghai harbor in November, 1945, the most spacious chapter in UNRRA history began. As that vessel landed its cargo, a desperate struggle was under way between the Nationalist government and the Communists for control of the areas of China which the Japanese had occupied. At first the advantage seemed to lie with the Nationalists under Chiang Kai-shek. Obtaining air and water transportation from the American forces, they occupied the key cities and best railways, confining the Communists to the interior and to Manchuria. During 1946 Ambassador Patrick J. Hurley and General George C. Marshall endeavored to arrange and maintain a peace between the two sides and effect a consolidation of the warring armies. Though at times they seemed on the verge of success, the truces they obtained were always brief and precarious. Down into 1947 the Nationalists kept the upper hand, even gaining control of part of Manchuria. But factional strife disrupted the government, inflation and corruption sapped the economy, the ill-disciplined armies began to disintegrate, and by the end of that year the stage was being set for the conquest of the whole country by Mao Tse-tung and his Communist forces.

The Second World War had left most of China sunk in misery. The weak transportation system was prostrated; the industrial centers had been bombed or looted; wide areas of fertile land were flooded; and millions of people were forced from their homes in headlong flight. Japanese methods of exploitation had been even more ruthlessly efficient than German methods. Many towns and villages simply disappeared from the map. The UNRRA workers, wrestling with general chaos, congested ports, official dishonesty, lack of efficient workers, and the smoldering civil war, often felt their task hopeless. Fortunately the first director, Benjamin H. Kizer, a Spokane attorney, who served from the fall of 1944 into the spring of 1946, proved one of the ablest of Lehman's lieutenants.

Before the work in China ended, more than 2,360,000 gross long tons of supplies had been landed there, at a cost of very nearly $518,000,000. Nowhere was famine more incessantly a threat. At one time in Hunan alone food was sent through 3,000 special nutrition stations to approximately two million children, and in one month direct relief was given to 800,000 destitute people in Kwangsi province. The desperate need for medical assistance may be deduced from the fact that in 1944 China had only one physician, on the average, to every 40,000 people, and the shortage was growing. Kizer established work programs which gave more than two million people employment in rebuilding roads and railway lines, constructing sanitation facilities and public utilities, and carrying out conservation projects.

By far the most spectacular UNRRA achievement was the restoration of the Yellow River, traditionally known as "China's Sorrow," to its proper channel. In 1938 Chinese leaders, desperately trying to delay the Japanese advance, had blown up the diversionary dam at Huayuank'ou which protected a great fertile area. They delayed the enemy, but at a fearful cost; tens of thousands of people were drowned, six millions or more were forced to abandon their homes and flee, and more than three million acres were flooded and rendered worthless. By a Herculean effort, using nearly 14,000 workers at one time, UNRRA engineers rebuilt the dikes along more than 400 miles of the turbulent stream and thus tamed the giant. The new dam was completed in March, 1947, well in advance of the late spring freshets. Heavy repairs were also made along the downstream dikes and levies, upon which 200,000 people altogether were employed.

All this was done amid the bloodshed and confusion of civil war, with the Communists in control of most of the territory surrounding the channel. The UNRRA executives and technologists, who had used an army of men and a great panoply of machinery to put 22,000,000 cubic meters of earth and rock into place, deserved great credit. But still greater homage, as the official historian George Woodbridge writes, must be paid to "the persistent effort, fortitude, and patience of the peasant workers throughout the area, who . . . provided amid the dangers of air attacks and ground fighting the unstinted labor required to restore the dikes to approximately their pre-war level." They were rewarded with seed and implements for their new farms.[7]

· I ·

While the war of sword and cannon had ended in Europe, a fiercer ideological warfare had begun. Russia had amassed great armies all along the eastern boundary of free Europe, for Stalin and Molotov feared the American monopoly of the atomic bomb, and believed that their only reply was to present a threat of the rapid conquest of Western Europe. Communist fifth columns had been formed in many lands and in some, notably Greece, had precipitated civil war. The Soviet pressure on Persia and Turkey had become starkly alarming. In the great belt from Cairo and Athens to Istanbul and Teheran, the British had sustained governments friendly to the West and had resisted Soviet penetration; but Britain's own economic and financial position was so precarious that American assistance would soon become indispensable.

Meanwhile, even while UNRRA reached new levels of usefulness in the spring of 1946, the threat of extinction grew imminent. It had been agreed under leadership of the American and British governments that the shipment of supplies to Europe should cease at the end of 1946 and to the Orient by the second quarter of 1947. Will Clayton, speaking for President Truman and Secretary Acheson, reëmphasized this decision in the spring of 1946. After the fearful strain of war, the Americans and British were tired of high taxes and short rations; many people argued that international trade was finding its old channels and reviving the nations after its old way; and they pointed to the strong new agencies—the Food and Agricultural Organization, the International Bank, the Economic and Social Council, the International Monetary Fund, the International Labor Office, UNESCO—which ought to take the place of UNRRA. The principal recipients of aid, from Italy to the Ukraine and China, earnestly desired a continuance of help, and some leaders predicted dire results if UNRRA were not continued, but these voices fell on deaf ears.

Controversy, bickering, and criticism continued to attend half the activities that Lehman directed. The Russians remained incessant troublemakers. N. I. Feonov, who had been Deputy Director-General of the Department of Supply in the European Regional Office (London), and was delegate to the Fourth Council meeting, complained with other Russian spokesmen that the repatriation of displaced Soviet citizens had slowed down, that the program of aid in Byelorussia and the Ukraine lacked promptness and scope, that there was too much friction between the Russian occupation troops in Austria and UNRRA agents, and that Lehman wanted too rigid an inspection of the work in Soviet-controlled lands. The Soviet press echoed these assertions. "The same controlled press," as former Prime Minister Stanislaw Mikolajczyk writes, "did everything in its power to ignore UNRRA aid, for any attention drawn to that aid might cause the people to know that the United States and Britain, whom they were being instructed to hate, were supplying most UNRRA supplies." Mikolajczyk adds that UNRRA aid was stupendous; its dollar value of $478,000,000 was five times as much as the government budget for the period and meant the equivalent of a dollar a day for every person in the country. "Without UNRRA and the unflagging determination of the Polish people to rebuild even a country dominated by a despotic alien rule, Poland would have perished. Yet when UNRRA was forced to suspend operations, the Red press of Poland charged the United States with attempting to 'make slaves of our people through starvation.' " [8]

On the Western side, conservative men made continuous charges that a maldistribution of relief in Yugoslavia, Hungary, and other areas was favoring the Red elements. The American ambassador to Yugoslavia, a personal representative whom Lehman sent there, some visiting members of Parliament, Mr. Randolph Churchill, and other investigators all denied these charges; but they worried the State Department so much that it asked Sir Humfrey Gale, a general of the highest integrity and ability, to make inquiries in Belgrade and send it facts to be used in placating restive members of Congress.

The food crisis in the early months of 1946 meanwhile aroused angry European complaints about the "feebleness" of the organization. The fact was, as Lehman pointed out, that the necessity of assuming difficult new responsibilities in the Ukraine, Byelorussia, Korea, and other places—responsibilities authorized by the Council in August, 1945—had imposed burdens on UNRRA far beyond those first contemplated. The work in Italy had dragged out beyond all anticipations. But querulous voices added some criticisms wholly devoid of foundation or excuse. Philip Noel-Baker later recalled that one highly placed official launched two charges. He alleged that in a certain European country much of the UNRRA supplies was wasted by bad handling in ports and warehouses, instancing a frightful loss of milk; unfortunately for him, inquiry proved that his figure was four times greater than the total quantity of milk sent that country. He also declared that in a certain warehouse codfish, stored above flour, had dripped upon it and ruined it. The fact was that the codfish was separated by three concrete floors from the flour and that neither the codfish nor flour belonged to UNRRA.[9]

Other complaints, for the most part ill-founded, arose among American army officers, newspapermen, and assorted observers. They alleged that the UNRRA workers numbered too many social workers and other do-gooders with more idealism than practicality; that the organization lacked tightness and discipline; and that its intelligence service was poor—Washington knew too little about what was being done in remote corners of the field. Some color of truth could be given these statements. While army officers stood aloof from civilian undertakings, and the best civilians in America and Britain wanted to go home at the war's end, social welfare people had been willing to serve—and they included a few zanies and more incompetents. In the postwar chaos no strong intelligence service could be established. The principle of abstention from politics sometimes played into the hands of Communists, who practiced ruthless politics nine-tenths of the time; for example, the return of displaced persons across the Russian boundary was often a return to the firing squad. With Europe full of stateless people, some abuse of UNRRA credentials as well as Western passports was inevitable. Lehman, Leith-Ross, R. G. A. Jackson, and their aides were doing their best with inadequate tools in an almost impossible situation.[10]

One episode early in 1946 gave Lehman an amount of vexation and anxiety out of all proportion to its real importance. UNRRA just after the war had been fortunate in obtaining the services of Lieutenant General Sir Frederick Morgan, recently Deputy Chief of Staff in SHAEF. He had played the principal role in drafting plans for the invasion of France—Operation Overlord—and had won the high regard of Eisenhower and other American leaders. Tall, spare, keen-minded, industrious, a veteran of the Indian service and the First World War, he was a fine type of British officer. From the beginning of October, 1945, he was UNRRA Chief of Displaced Persons Operations in Germany. In this capacity he capably brought the three earlier zone headquarters in the American, British, and French sectors under control of his central headquarters. It was of course his duty, under obligations assumed by UNRRA, to facilitate the return of displaced persons to their countries of origin; a matter on which Russian, Polish, and other national authorities were sensitive, particularly as some organizations of exiles discouraged any return. During the winter he became disturbed by evidence that·numerous Jewish refugees who had returned more or less peaceably to Poland and settled down there—it was hoped permanently—were suddenly reappearing in Germany to seek asylum in camps.

Morgan, as it later appeared, was devoid of any taint of racial or national prejudice. It was merely as an officer charged with reducing the huge refugee burden and getting displaced persons resettled, and much worried over his difficulties, that on January 2, 1946, he wandered into unnecessary trouble at a press conference at Frankfurt-am-Main. He made a well-reasoned plea for some permanent settlement of the refugee problem, UNRRA's work being merely temporary. Had he stopped there all would have been well. But in an ensuing question-and-answer period he declared that a clandestine Jewish group was sponsoring an unnecessary entry of Polish Jews into Western Germany and expressed his irritation. Just how much some reporters may have misquoted him it is impossible to say. What is certain is that American newspapers appeared with front-page stories to the effect that Morgan doubted the gravity of threatened pogroms in Poland, that he pronounced many of the refugees well clothed and ruddy-cheeked, and that he regarded part of the emigration as artificial. The implication was that Zionist elements, intent on the in-gathering of Jews into Palestine, were responsible.

These newspaper accounts fell harshly on the ears of Jewish citizens whose hearts had been wrung by the terrible sufferings of their people. Some journals probably did garble Morgan's statements and used misleading headlines. Quite apart from that, he lacked the imagination, and perhaps the knowledge, to understand that world Jewry was in a highly sensitive state of mind after the awful events of recent years. No evidence was available that American Zionists had fomented a movement of refugees, and their leaders denied any such activity. British government circles, when questioned, gave no credence to Morgan's suggestions that an organized plan had been made for an exodus. One American newspaperman, interviewing Polish Jews in Munich, reported that a Polish Zionist committee *was* instigating and financing at least part of such a movement, but nobody knew how important this was. If the committee existed, its work was probably similar to that of the United Lithuanian Relief Fund of America and the United Ukrainian American Relief Committee, whose interferences with the peaceable resettlement of refugees had been condemned by UNRRA and the

State Department. But all this was conjectural. What was plain was that Morgan had brought implied accusations against international Zionism which he could not support.

For a fortnight the episode created a deplorable pother. Various Jews blazed out in angry statements, the comedian Eddie Cantor having the deplorable taste to pay for a newspaper advertisement likening Morgan—a major figure in defeating the Nazis—to another Hitler. Some American Gentiles were irritated by their intemperance. The Arabs, fearful of being swept out of their lands, gave Morgan a support which he did not want. Altogether, the episode threatened real injury to UNRRA.

It was Lehman who suffered most from it. He had been utterly worn out by his labors and anxieties, and his doctor had insisted that he take a short midwinter vacation. With Mrs. Lehman, he had set out for California. Hardly had he arrived before he was recalled to Washington to deal with the situation. As he returned he could study Morgan's hasty explanation to the press. "I made reference not to the Jewish question as a whole," Morgan declared, "but to local symptoms which seem to me to be as unhealthy as is the lack of a general plan to bring an end to the fears and wanderings of these unfortunate people. It is to be regretted that my remarks were interpreted in some quarters as an attack on the motives of European Jewry in their present itinerant state. It seems probable that some Jews have been encouraged to leave their homes by promises from hopeful but unauthorized sources. Many other Jews may well have been driven from their homes in eastern Europe by threats and occasional violence." He went on to argue for a permanent solution. It was a pity he had not been equally brief and clear in his press conference.

Then the teapot tempest rapidly subsided. Lehman's fundamental instinct in such situations was to be judicially moderate. Moreover, the general was a man of very high standing; and some of the American criticism came ungraciously from a land that could far better have taken the refugee Jews than any other but closed its gates to them. Morgan's associates of various nationalities, including high American military men, expressed confidence that he would be exonerated. UNRRA officers in Germany testified to his strong leadership, and L. S. B. Shapiro of the North American Newspaper Alliance, who had been at the press conference, published a full and inoffensive version of it.

Lehman, therefore, at once invited Morgan to Washington for a talk, and the general accepted. On January 28 the two men began an entirely amicable two-day conference, immediately after which Lehman issued a statement confirming Morgan in his post. The general simultaneously gave the press a statement expressing regret over "certain of my words" which laid him open to suspicion, adding: "I reject utterly that I am anti-Semitic in outlook." Eisenhower, who was in some petty trouble himself at the moment, had greeted Morgan joyously: "Come on in, boy. . . . The great thing about being in the doghouse is the good company you meet there." *

The Morgan affair thus ended quietly enough. But it had ruined the director's projected vacation—and it was a vacation that he badly needed.

It should be said by way of postscript that the problem of the Jewish DPs remained bewilderingly complex and continued to breed violent antagonisms. Many of the Jews, understandably, were full of scorn and hatred for Europe and America; their hostility, as Herbert Agar writes, "was a passion, maybe a disease." Richard Crossman, M.P., saw a Jew tear up his emigration papers for America, saying he would never trust a Christian again. "Do not put your faith into Christian civilization," cried one of their camp newspapers. The American army neither understood nor liked them, and General George Patton was particularly hostile; he wanted them out of his sight. The Czechs forbade them to enter their country. The Russians distrusted them as potential "spies." Much was heard in the United States of one proposal by Earl Harrison of the Intergovernmental Committee on Refugees that the President should ask Britain to help clear the DP camps by letting 100,000 Jews into Palestine at once. Little was said of his other proposal that the United States should let an equivalent number enter its own borders. President Truman duly made the request of London but flatly refused to ask Congress to relax the immigration laws. The Jews in the camps in mid-1945 formed a federation of committees, which became the Central Committee of Liberated Jews, overwhelmingly Zionist, anxious to

---

* Morgan reviews the whole episode acridly in *Peace and War: A Soldier's Life* (London, 1961, Ch. X). He indicates that he remained convinced that Zionist agents (he does not say American Zionists) had indeed organized a migration of Jews from Poland into West Germany and down into Mediterranean ports, preparatory to their illegal transport into Palestine. He also alleges that military training was organized in camps of Jewish refugees, with instructors from the British and American armies. He lunched with Mr. Hoover in New York and reports that "his views on UNRRA and all its works could bear no sort of reproduction." It is hard not to give weight to the remark which Mayor La Guardia, as Lehman's successor, made in dispensing with Morgan's services: "You know, general, I believe you were the wrong man for this job from the start." Professional soldiers seldom fit such work. But it is also difficult not to wish that a rigorously thorough and impartial investigation may be made into Zionist activities in Eastern and Central Europe in these years. Jon and David Kimche in *The Secret Roads* (New York, 1955), Richard Crossman in *Palestine Mission* (New York, 1947), and Herbert Agar in his fine account of the JDC, or "Joint," *The Saving Remnant* (New York, 1960), furnish a strong prima-facie case for Morgan's assertions; but more light is needed.

work militantly with the Jewish Brigade of the British Eighth Army, and, as Agar writes, intent on "the planning of a vast conspiracy against the British government."

In the whole complicated problem it was all too easy for those who saw but one aspect of events to give expression to a special set of prejudices. What could safely be said was that the situation of the Jews of Central Europe was an indictment of all modern civilization.

· II ·

Lehman said later that when he celebrated his sixty-eighth birthday on March 28, 1946, he was "completely exhausted," for his burden had been "indescribably heavy" both in the Washington office and outside. His desk was never clear of some urgent problem. The world situation changed from hour to hour, and each change bred new responsibilities. He had found that bringing UNRRA into effective working operation, with no clear definition of its powers until after the war ended, and with a complex task of adjusting relations to forty-odd governments, the armies, the navies, and the economic administrations of the great powers, was a very different matter from acting as governor of New York. As he put it, he had possessed "ground rules" to guide him in Albany, while in Washington and London he had to master a catch-as-catch-can technique. Night after night he had tossed in anxiety.

Moreover, his journeys to Europe, the Middle East, and North Africa had taken a great deal out of him. "I never liked flying at all," he recalls. "I was either scared to death or bored to death." We have described his narrow escape when flying to Cairo, and he had experienced another close shave in flying out of Athens in July, 1945. One of the two engines of his plane went dead at an altitude of ten thousand feet, and his pilot had to make a forced landing in an 85-mile gale. "We took a bad shaking, and believe me, everyone was mighty glad to be on terra firma again," was all that he wrote at the time; but he had been under anxious tension for an hour. Abroad more than at home, the loss of his son Peter haunted him.

The incessant bombardment of criticism, moreover, inevitably depressed and worried him. Though he became partially inured to the obstruction and fault-finding of the Russians, it saddened him. When he appealed to the United Nations Assembly on February 7, 1946, for some prompt action to help him meet the food crisis and got nothing more useful than resolutions of sympathy, he felt that he had asked for bread and received a stone. He knew that Congress was growing more restive in dealing with all forms of

The signing of the agreement with Soviet representatives for relief and rehabilitation shipments to Byelorussia and the Ukraine, December 18, 1945. Starting with the fifth person from *the left* are: Deputy Director General Nicolai I. Feonov, Chief of the Department of Supply in London, Deputy Director General Michail A. Menshikov (who later became Soviet Ambassador to the United States), Senior Deputy Director General Robert G. A. Jackson, and Roy F. Hendrickson, Deputy Director General in Charge of Supplies. Between Menshikov and Jackson is Dr. P. W. Kuo, Deputy Director General, Secretariat.

UNRRA Photograph in the National Archives

Secretary of State Edward Stettinius with Polish Ambassador Jan Ciechanowski and Herbert H. Lehman

United Press International Newspictures

Herbert H. Lehman wishing a safe voyage to Captain J. C. McKenzie, Master of
the first ship with relief supplies for Poland and Czechoslovakia

United Press International Newspictures

foreign aid. Only a world crisis, in fact, could shake it out of its apathy. He also feared that President Truman would lack the comprehension and sympathy that Roosevelt had always displayed in dealing with UNRRA. FDR had assisted in bringing the organization to birth, had sent message after message of encouragement, and had intervened decisively to get transportation; Truman, in his abrupt termination of Lend-Lease on August 21, 1945, had shown a regrettable attitude toward foreign need. Both the American and British governments were disposed to hasten rather than retard the end of UNRRA.

The *New York Times* of December 17, 1945, had devoted a large part of its issue to a series of articles by some of its best writers on various phases of the organization's accomplishment. It gave them a banner headline: "Survey Shows UNRRA Vital to the Distressed of Europe." C. L. Sulzberger had penned the glowing lead article. Sam Pope Brewer dealt with the labors in Yugoslavia, Kathleen McLoughlin with the Polish problem in Germany, A. C. Sedgwick with the Greek record, John McCormack with the activities in Czechoslovakia, and Clifton Daniel with those in the Near East. This able group reached a set of impressive conclusions. In Yugoslavia three million people faced starvation if UNRRA help faltered; in Italy, UNRRA's plans for distributing $418,322,100 in aid were regarded as the key factor in the national economy for the coming year; in Poland, festering with disease, want, and social disorganization, the agency was practically the only source of outside aid; Germany still had 850,000 displaced persons swarming in her reception depots and camps.

This issue of the *Times* had struck a resounding blow for the cause Lehman was trying to press forward; but it was the only such blow. Why was there not another? When, early in March, 1946, Truman asked Herbert Hoover to survey the needs of Europe and Asia for food, Lehman had already determined to resign his post; but this action confirmed his resolution. Truman had not consulted the Director-General on the mission. It would cover areas which UNRRA had already expertly surveyed; it could turn up little new information—Hoover's tour proved to be rapid and superficial; and Lehman, recalling Hoover's long letter to him when he began work, was apprehensive that the former President would press for putting relief into strictly American hands. After all, Hoover had been pretty much an isolationist, standing for America First. A change of policy just as UNRRA was turning the corner with large war surpluses available would be most unfortunate.[11] The idea that national aims should take precedence over international humanitarianism repelled the head of UNRRA.

On March 12, 1946, Lehman resigned, declaring that his health required the step. The Fourth Council met in Atlantic City on March 15, when he presented his last report and final recommendations, continuing on duty until the end of the month. His departure was a heavy blow. Few had anticipated it, for nearly everybody had hoped and expected that he would lead the now powerful agency to the end. Some feared that his departure heralded the American rejection of an international partnership in relief in favor of a purely national approach. Mrs. Franklin D. Roosevelt, in her syndicated newspaper column, tartly expressed the view that Hoover had better stay home and leave the exploration of foreign needs to more international-minded men already overseas. The *New York Times* remarked that Lehman's resignation lent force to the hypothesis that Hoover's trip to the overseas countries which were asking for relief "might perhaps be a forerunner of a more direct United States approach to the whole problem of world relief instead of continuing to pursue the international method."

At a plenary meeting of the Council late in March Lehman had the embarrassment of listening to tributes, some of them perfunctory, more of them earnest, and two or three genuinely eloquent. They were later gathered with other speeches and letters, and his last full address to the Council, into a volume published by the Overbrook Press.[12] President Truman sent a handsome expression of praise; so did Ernest Bevin. For Canada W. L. Mackenzie King and Lester Pearson spoke and for New Zealand that warm-hearted friend Walter Nash. The Australian on whom Lehman leaned so heavily, Commander Jackson, contributed an epigrammatic sentence; he had seen a bit of fighting in the war but never a better fight than Lehman put up for the men, the money, and the materials to do his job. Carlos Romulo declared that UNRRA was a monument to two men, Franklin D. Roosevelt and Herbert H. Lehman. The most fervent words came from the Greek representative, K. Varvaressos, whose land had been saved in its last extremity: "UNRRA has alleviated more suffering and misery than any human institution has ever done before." But the truest statement was Noel-Baker's:

"The creation of this machine has been a fine technical achievement. It is a great example. . . . No tougher assignment was ever faced by any man. He has carried it through. But his greatest service of all has been his personal leadership of the men and women who have worked under his command. His greatest service has been the moral authority which he has established with the governments and the peoples of the world. His greatest service has been the sense of spiritual power which he has given to all his colleagues in the work."

President Truman chose as the new head of UNRRA Fiorello La Guardia, who, after three successive terms as mayor of New York, had refused in 1945 to run again and wished to move in a larger scene. He brought qualities all his own, some of them highly useful: a flair for publicity, a taste for frank, hard-hitting, explosive speech, a delight in controversy and even in a good fight. He threw himself into the Battle for Bread-stuffs with enormous energy. Nevertheless, it could be doubted if his heart was so much in pushing forward the work of UNRRA, especially in rehabilitation, as in preparing to bring it to a neat conclusion. He was anxious to succor immediate need, and his dynamic energy contributed to that end, but he never had the bright vision of international partnership which Lehman had cherished; his was always a very American view. He was to administer UNRRA only ten months and more and more with a view to its liquidation.

It was with a pang of sadness that Lehman watched the breakup of the organization which had done such invaluable work for humanity. He always felt that it should have continued in full vigor at least a year longer than it did; down into 1948. Many of his friends regretted that he had not stayed at the helm until the end. Perhaps it would have been better for him and for UNRRA had he done so. This was the only task in his life that he left with a sense that it was unfinished. But as UNRRA ended, a new and more powerful organization, under the aegis of the Marshall Plan, was to appear on the international scene.

Chapter XV

IN THE POSTWAR REACTION

LEHMAN returned to his comfortable two-floor apartment on Park Avenue in a more perplexed psychological state than he had ever before known. He felt bruised and smitten by the blows he had received, yet proud of the record he had made. Regretful over mistakes and shortcomings in the administration of UNRRA, he was hurt by the failure of many people, including some close friends, to perceive that his limited powers, the hurry of the emergency, and the clashing interests he faced had made shortcomings unavoidable. He was gravely troubled by the lurch into the Cold War, the resurgence of selfish nationalism, and the reawakening of surly party strife in America. It was painfully reminiscent of the smothering of American idealism in 1918–21 by Irish-American and German-American rancors, the League battle, and the corrupt normalcy of Harding. He was troubled, too, over his future, for he wished to remain in public service. His relations with Truman were merely those of distant mutual esteem—they hardly spoke the same political language. He had been mentioned early in the year for the Senate, a fact which consciously or subconsciously may have played a part in his decision to resign, but he knew how much some machine elements among the New York Democrats disliked him.

Every newspaper this spring of 1946 made it clear that the United States had entered upon a year of rising peril abroad and irresistible reaction at home. Truman correctly remarked that Congress and the people were determined to "get the boys home." As they were hurried back, American prestige and influence throughout the world as well as American troops passed through the discharge centers. Yet from the beginning of the year the Russians had been abetting Chinese Communists in the rapid conquest of Manchuria, stirring up trouble in China proper, and maintaining their partial grip upon Persia, where they coveted both the oil reserves and the northern province of Azerbaijan. The Soviet refusal to withdraw troops from Persia in accordance with a solemn pledge to the Teheran government and Great Britain drew from George Kennan, chargé in Moscow, a stiff note dated March 6, 1946. No reply was vouchsafed. The following July Russia proposed an arrangement for the Dardanelles which seemed to Truman "an open bid to obtain control of Turkey." Yet the American government was caught between wind and water, for public opinion had not crystallized behind any definite foreign policy. The electorate was confused, indifferent, and content with selfish and shortsighted aims.

Part of the sullen, irritable temper of Congress and the public came to the surface in the handling of price controls. The Office of Price Administration under Leon Henderson and Chester Bowles had toiled manfully to keep inflation in check. But Congressional conservatives assailed it as socialistic, and under pressure from business interests anxious for big profits they refused to continue it except by a radically bad measure. Truman vetoed the bill, so that price controls ended July 1. Thereupon Congress and everybody else saw prices shoot toward the skies. New control legislation was too feeble to count. When ceilings were placed on meat, livestock growers moved to break them by refusing to ship beef and pork to the packing houses. The ensuing shortages aroused the indignation of housewives and of men anxious to see beefsteak, roasts, or at least sausage on the dinner table. Strikes in the coal mines and on the railroads—which Truman briefly seized—increased the public exasperation. Many people concluded that the Democratic Administration was bungling its work.[1]

It was to the position of Jewish refugees and the situation in Palestine that Lehman first addressed himself on release from UNRRA. Administered by a British High Commissioner, with the assistance of Jewish, Arab, and British officials, Palestine was in continual and apparently incurable turmoil. The Arabs, fearing loss of the whole land, had refused to acquiesce in Sir Alan Cunningham's announcement on January 30, 1946, that the government would "provisionally" permit the entry of 1,500 Jews a month, a figure shortly raised to 2,000. The Zionists, demanding an open door for the Jewish refugees who constantly arrived in Mediterranean ports with the hope of getting into some of the many ships carrying on an illegal traffic, wanted entry for hundreds of thousands. They organized underground terrorist groups who wrecked trains, bombed buildings and planes, and killed British soldiers. The British government, with which the State Department tended to take sides, was fearful that large concessions to the Jews would drive the Arab world into the arms of Russia.

Naturally Lehman felt the greatest sympathy with his fellow Jews. He remained outside the Zionist camp. He wished to see the Jewish home promised by Balfour created in Palestine, but he wanted no Jewish state. He condemned the bombings and assassinations of the Irgun Zvai Leumi and the still worse outrages by the Stern Gang. Nevertheless, he thought that the mandatory power should enlarge the admission of refugees to permit at least a hundred thousand a year to enter.

He was heartened when, on March 26, an Anglo-American Committee reported a series of recommendations with which he heartily concurred. It asked for acceptance of the principle that Jew should not dominate Arab nor Arab dominate Jew in Palestine; for formation of a state which should equally guard the rights of Moslems, Jews, and Christians; for the admission of 100,000 Jews forthwith; and for special measures to raise the Arab standard of living and education. Unhappily, these proposals had little chance. While the Arabs were adamant against letting in 100,000 refugees, the Jewish underground showed by new terrorist outbreaks, killings, and the running ashore of more shiploads of immigrants that it was determined upon far larger numbers. On July 31, Herbert Morrison told the House of Commons that Britain would accept the committee recommendations as a basis of negotiation if assured that the United States would help carry them into effect. This seemed to Lehman to open a door of hope. He realized that Ernest Bevin had a point when he asked why America did not itself take a large body of Jewish refugees. But in the face of opposition by extremist Arabs and extremist Jews, and of obstruction by indifferent Americans and Britons, the committee recommendations died.

In repeated statements Lehman assailed the British policy of appeasing the Arabs. "It is not only indefensible, but unwise," he told a New York dinner. He was ready to accept a partition plan proposed by an Anglo-American group in July, which would have demarcated a narrow coastal strip with an arm including the Galilee area—about 1,500 square miles—to be under Jewish control. Such a plan, he declared, "has had and will continue to have my support," for it would give shelter to a substantial part of the refugees. In pleading for these brave, homeless folk, he rose to heights of eloquence. "I have visited many countries," he said, "and I have seen with my own eyes the indescribably pathetic plight of the pitiful remnant of Jews which survives in Europe—a million and a half out of six million. The physical hardships they have endured cannot be calmly retold. The spiritual torment they suffered cannot be fully pictured. And yet, they stand before us not as beggars, pleading for crumbs of charity. They stand before us with a stirring faith and will, . . . as brave men and women who are anxious to take their rightful place in the world." [2]

The day-long strike of sympathy for coreligionists in detention camps which the Palestine Jews held on July 17, 1946, had his approval. But he was horrified when, a few days later, the Irgun blew up a wing of the King David Hotel in Jerusalem, used for government offices, killing 91 persons, maiming 45, and leaving 29 missing. Many of the slain were girl typists. He instantly issued an expression of his anger: [3]

"As a Jew who has been deeply interested in Palestine for a great many years, I condemn with all my force the cowardly and criminal bombing of the King David Hotel in Jerusalem which has resulted in the death and injury of many people. It was a cruel and utterly inexcusable act of a group of lawless fanatics. It will meet with the condemnation and abhorrence of the great majority of the Jews all over the world. Right thinking people, whether they be of the Jewish Faith or not, wish Palestine opened up as a haven for the cruelly oppressed and tortured Jews of Europe. Acts of violence such as the destruction of the King David Hotel will inevitably undo much of the statesmanlike and constructive work that has been carried on for years by responsible organizations and individuals. We Jews have a just cause and our fight to gain large-scale immigration into Palestine has met with a sympathetic and helpful response all over the world. We will not win our fight however by criminal violence of fanatical methods. To pursue such methods will merely lead to loss of our own self-respect and the respect and sympathy of the world. The Jews of Palestine are a law-abiding people and the handful of criminal fanatics who engage in atrocities of this kind must be curbed and rendered impotent. . . ."

Amid rising social and political discontent, the fall campaigns of 1946 came on, with a governor, Senator, and Congressmen to be elected in New York. The Republicans renominated Thomas E. Dewey for the governorship and Irving M. Ives, former speaker and majority leader in the assembly, for the senatorial seat. During the summer, Democratic sentiment for Lehman as Senator had risen, and when the state convention met in Albany in September he was chosen without opposition. For governor the delegates selected James M. Mead, respectable, experienced, and uninspiring. It was evident that each ticket had one strong and one weak man. Dewey was better qualified than Mead for first place in the state, and Lehman was better equipped than Ives for the Senate.

Democratic politicians could see that the contest would be nip and tuck at best, with the odds favoring the Republicans. Yet Lehman was curiously overconfident. Three considerations seem to have produced his optimism. One was the memory of many past victories; one was a delusion that his recent overseas experience would be an asset; and one was a low opinion of his adversary. "I had long known Ives," he said later, "I did not think much of his capacity, and felt sure I would win."

There was as little Democratic unity this year as world unity. A long-festering quarrel had broken open in February when Harold L. Ickes resigned as head of the Interior Department, refusing to countenance Truman's appointment of Edwin Pauley, a California oil magnate, as Under Secretary of the Navy. Pauley, said Ickes, had submitted "the rawest proposition ever made to me" concerning some California lands. Though Ickes wished to quit March 31, Truman resentfully ousted him on February 15. Then just after Lehman's nomination, the National Citizens Political Action Committee, together with the National Committee of the Arts, Sciences, and Professions, held an anti-Dewey rally in New York, at which Henry Wallace agreed to speak. He descended upon the city with an address that he hoped would bulwark the idea of Soviet-American coexistence and cooperation. Unfortunately for everybody, he made it an egregious intrusion into the domain of Secretary of State Byrnes, who was then in Paris trying to negotiate with the utterly intractable Russians.

That evening of September 12, 1946, witnessed a drama in Madison Square Garden that delighted all Republicans. Wallace had shown his prepared text to Truman, but the President was apparently inattentive to his statement that while Russia had been ready to cooperate in world affairs, the American government had not met the Soviet leaders halfway.[4] This attack upon Secretary of State Byrnes was offensive enough. But the wildly cheering audience of labor men, Socialists, and left-wing intellectuals in Madison Square Garden carried Wallace off his feet, and he added a reckless extempore sentence. "I realize," he declared, "that the danger of war is much less from Communism than it is from Imperialism." He also dropped from his prepared address two statements that would have given it a measure of balance: one condemning the American Communists who obsequiously followed "every twist and turn in the Moscow party line" and one calling on the Russians to stop teaching that Communism must ultimately defeat capitalism.

This when Communist forces stood poised for attack in Germany, in Greece, in Turkey, in Persia—and were actually to launch a surprise attack in Korea within four years! The speech precipitated a storm of confusion and anger. Byrnes at once gave Truman an ultimatum—Wallace must go, or he would; Senator Vandenberg declared that while he wished to cooperate with the Administration, he could cooperate with only one Secretary of State at a time; and the press castigated Wallace for rash meddling and the

President for lack of vigilance. Truman had no choice but to oust the Secretary of Commerce. Wallace's exit restored confidence in the nation's foreign policy and satisfied the great body of the American people. It nevertheless left a boiling wake of controversy and recrimination, strongest of all in New York State. The Republican Party gleefully prepared to use the effective slogan it had invented: "Had enough?" The Democrats faced crippling internal dissension. Their candidates for public office could be brought up short with the demand: "Where do you stand—with Wallace or with Truman?" Whatever the answer, they would lose votes.

The situation was embarrassing for Lehman because his internationalist background and strong ties with the Western democracies made him an easy target for furious leftists and fellow travelers. He and Mead had accepted the nominations of the American Labor Party, which numbered active Communist elements and threw itself vigorously behind Wallace's position. As it had cast a half million votes for Roosevelt and Wagner in 1944, it was not to be regarded lightly. He also accepted the nomination of the Liberal Party (September 18), which stood with Byrnes and Truman and which had cast 330,000 votes two years earlier. This looked like carrying water on both shoulders. "It is time for him to erase all doubts," thundered the *Rochester Times* on September 21. "Mr. Lehman cannot risk false interpretations of an election result by failing or refusing to proclaim where he stands. He cannot risk ambiguity, either." Up and down the state the same demand came from other journals, including the always-friendly *New York Times*.

Yet Lehman unwisely chose to risk ambiguity. In part this was because he had a high personal regard for Wallace and some sympathy with his espousal of coexistence; much as Soviet policies offended him, he had stood for cooperation with Russia in UNRRA. He told the women's division of the National Citizens Political Action Committee on September 24 that a friendly understanding with Moscow was the immediate task of American statesmanship: "About the means to this end, men of good will may differ. About the end in itself, there is and can be no difference of opinion." Less defensibly, his neutralism was influenced by what party leaders thought sound political strategy. They declared that a flat repudiation of Wallace would fatally alienate the ALP. Then also, in such matters Lehman was invariably gentle; he did not like to "repudiate" any old associate. He maintained his costly indecision to the end.

The *Binghamton Press* a fortnight before election attacked his position crisply: "While it is said that Mr. Lehman in private supports Secretary Byrnes's foreign policy, Mr. Lehman, fearing loss of Communist and ultra-leftist support, has lacked the courage so far publicly to condemn Henry

Wallace's attacks on that policy." Even the *New York Times*, in endorsing him, deplored his failure to make a specific statement on Wallace's views. And in the end his position proved bad politics as well as limp policy. Many Democrats were so chilled that they stayed away from the polls—particularly Catholic Democrats who hated the Soviet hostility toward religion and up-state Protestant Democrats who disliked the part that radicals like Sidney Hillman, a Wallace supporter, played in party and national affairs. In a year of general reaction, prejudice of many kinds had come to the surface.

Other issues, however, played a more important part in the election than Wallace and foreign policy. Voters were tired of effort, sacrifices, meatless days, rising taxes, and government restrictions; the mood of 1920 had come back. Vote for Lehman and Mead? cried the *Potsdam Courier*. Why, of course!—"if you favor the New Deal regimentation of your every-day acts and needs, the continuation of the present bungling of national and international affairs by the present administration, and the reckless expendi-tures of your money by the inexperienced crowd of guessers and radicals that control the present administration." Before the voters floated a vision of chops, butter, and low-priced canned foods, not to mention abundant new cars, refrigerators, and radios, that would be theirs if the Republicans won. Once the call had been, "Vote yourself a farm!" Now it was "Vote yourself a steak!"

Just before election, seasoned politicians came to Lehman shaking their heads. "We shall vote for you," they said, "but our wives won't. They are tired of finding nothing in the markets." During the last weeks the Demo-crats committed the error of playing on too many chords; they used so many issues and appealed to so many special groups that they made a wild discord instead of harmony. They directed appeals to labor unions, to veterans, to farmers, and to sensitive nationality groups. Lehman strongly supported the St. Lawrence Seaway, popular in the northern counties but disliked by large New York City interests; Mead opposed the Seaway. Anti-Tammany men established an Independent Citizens' Committee for Lehman, and Tammany men condemned its activities. Rabbi Stephen S. Wise declared that he deeply resented attempts to move the Jews on any ground whatsoever to vote for or against either party; but Minority Leader Irwin Steingut intro-duced Lehman at a rally in Public School 232 with the inaccurate and de-plorable assertion that, if elected, he would be "the first Jew sent to the United States Senate." [5] Without such an appeal, the objectionable Republi-can slogan, "Vote American," would have carried less innuendo than it did.

Above all, Reaction dominated the election. One of its aspects was re-flected in an advertisement by the Republican National Committee in many newspapers: "Irving Ives has put his finger on the source of our industrial ills: *Too much Government.*" One came into the reminders that Lehman's last appeal as head of UNRRA had been for strong compulsory food controls in all important nations, including the United States. Still another was later identified by Warren Moscow: a determination by the Catholic Church to strike a blow against Communism and its supposed sympathizers even though this meant electing the Protestant Dewey over the Irish Catholic Mead. "Officially the Church made no moves, but the vote on election day indicated that Catholics had followed the line the party leaders had been told about." They wanted a turn to the right in foreign affairs. Finally, various causes which Lehman strongly supported in his speeches—a higher minimum wage, a national health program, fair employment legislation—were distasteful to people of conservative temper.

On election day the Democrats suffered reverses all over the country and in New York a stunning defeat. The Republicans took control of both houses of Congress and elected twenty-five governors. In New York, Dewey smothered Mead for the governorship. Lehman, running about 400,000 votes ahead of his ticket, nevertheless lost to Ives by 250,000. His plurality of 485,000 in New York City was less than half that given him in 1932. This defeat, his first and last at the polls, enabled Republicans to seat their first New York Senator since 1920.

But the full meaning of the election could not be grasped until men had time to appraise the Eightieth Congress, and particularly the Senate. People read the names of the new lawmakers with little comprehension. Just how much ability and character had Senator-elect J. Howard McGrath of Rhode Island? Herbert R. O'Connor of Maryland? William E. Jenner of Indiana? George W. Malone of Nevada? Joseph McCarthy of Wisconsin? How liberal, how farsighted, how statesmanlike would these new men prove? How much aid and comfort would they give to Homer E. Capehart, who had been elected in 1944, or William F. Knowland, chosen in 1946 to replace Hiram Johnson?

· I ·

Not only had 1946 been a year of frustrations for Lehman; it was a year in which loneliness sometimes assailed his heart. The UNRRA he had built was being cut down, and as he approached seventy, he was thwarted in his long-cherished desire to sit in the Senate. This was hard, but much harder were the bereavements he had confronted when he and Edith Lehman returned to 820 Park Avenue to live. Their boy Peter, in whom they had found such joy and hope, was in his Cambridge grave. Irving Lehman, whose counsel and affection meant so much to them, had died unexpectedly on September 22, 1945, at his Port Chester home. On a woodland walk he had slipped and broken his leg; an embolism had developed, and the tall, grave, kindly man was gone before his fellow judges of the Court of Appeals knew he was ill. To the end he had been Herbert's thoughtful, widely read, sagacious comrade and adviser. He had never ceased to think independently; he was not misled, for example, by Russian valor, but during the war had warned his brother that the Soviet leaders would pursue sinister policies. His place, like Peter's, could never be filled.

There were times when Lehman thought his active career was over. Honors and duties he had aplenty as the months passed in 1947 and 1948. He spoke and worked for Truman's reëlection, he gave assiduous labor to the Jewish Theological Seminary and his charities, he continued unflagging in support of the efforts of refugee Jews to build a home in Palestine, he did what he could for better government in city and state. But just as some friends thought he was coming to the end of the road, he found a fresh beginning. He was lucky after all to escape the Eightieth Congress; it was better to go into the Eighty-first.

The way opened unexpectedly and swiftly. Less than six months after Truman's second Administration began, Robert F. Wagner resigned his Senate seat (June 28, 1949) because of failing health. Dewey appointed John Foster Dulles in his place. A special election was necessary that fall. Immediately after Wagner's resignation, Lehman received a telephone call from his old friend Ed Flynn. You must take the nomination, Flynn declared. But Lehman, thinking of his age, promised only to think the matter over. While he pondered it, an episode occurred which seemed to take him out of the running.

He was vacationing at Lake Placid when he was startled to read in the *New York Times* of July 23 a letter by Cardinal Spellman assailing Mrs. Franklin D. Roosevelt for the stand she had taken in behalf of the Barden Bill in Congress, a bill extending Federal assistance to the public schools of the nation while withholding it from parochial schools. "The separation of church and state is extremely important to us who hold to the original traditions of our nation," Mrs. Roosevelt had written. The Cardinal had plainly lost his temper. Terming the bill "infamous," he denounced Mrs. Roosevelt in violent terms. He declared that she "could have acted only from misinformation or prejudice"; he accused her of repeatedly pleading "causes that are anti-Catholic"; he stated that her attitude precluded her from comprehending the issues; he asked how she could have seen young Catholics fighting overseas without being "purged of all prejudice"; and he closed by declaring that her "record of anti-Catholicism" was "unworthy of an American mother." Horrified, Lehman at once determined to reply. Though he believed that any reply would kill his chances for the Senate, he felt he *must* speak.

He was not actuated by his old, deeply affectionate, and much-prized friendship with Mrs. Roosevelt; he was actuated by a feeling of principle. He had stood close to the President's widow in her bereavement and ever since,* but it was her right to express her views on a fundamental constitutional issue which he wished to vindicate. His letter to the *Times*, strong but moderate in language, appeared the day after the Cardinal's outburst:

> I am deeply shocked at the attack of Cardinal Spellman on Mrs. Roosevelt. I strongly believe, as I have always believed, that in our American democracy every responsible citizen is entitled to express his or her views on public issues without being subjected to the accusation of being against any religion or any race.
>
> The issue is not whether one agrees or disagrees with Mrs. Roosevelt on this or any other public question. The issue is whether Americans are entitled freely to express their views on public questions without being vilified or accused of religious bias.
>
> Mrs. Roosevelt has been a public figure for twenty-five years. Her every act has been a matter of record. In that splendid record I do not know of a single act or word that would in the slightest degree indicate bias or prejudice against any religion or any race.
>
> Her whole life has been dedicated to a constant fight for tolerance and brotherhood of men as children of one God.
>
> She will, I am confident, retain the trust and the affection of all peoples irrespective of creed or race.

To his astonishment, he found that his letter did him no harm whatever. Not only Jewish and Protestant voters but a great body of Catholics came emphatically to his side. His desk was flooded with letters of approval. Consulting with leaders identified with all three faiths, he found them as earnest as he was for the rule that no person should be abused or penalized for stating an honest conviction. He decided to run for the Senate, and the State Committee—for in this off year no state convention was needed—placed him without hesitation on the ticket.

----

* Mrs. Roosevelt had written Mrs Lehman May 19, 1945: "Dear Edith: It was a comfort to me to think that Herbert was with us on that trip to Hyde Park and here at the White House on Saturday and again on Sunday. Since God in His infinite wisdom saw fit to take Franklin, I know you will share with me the relief that he did not suffer. You are among our oldest and best friends, and it is such friends that I now hope will continue to work for his ideals." Lehman Papers.

The campaign which followed was unexpectedly acrimonious; at least Lehman, always very thin-skinned in political battles, thought so. The Republicans nominated John Foster Dulles, so strong a candidate that the *New York Times* endorsed him and Walter Lippmann wrote a special column in his behalf. Many independent voters agreed with the *Times* and Lippmann that while Lehman would make a Senator of sterling liberalism and ability, Dulles's special knowledge of foreign affairs and fine history of cooperation with Truman and Acheson in conducting them would render him a still more valuable asset to the country. Arthur Sulzberger, a lifelong friend, wrote Lehman, referring to the *Times*'s editorial endorsement, and elicited a characteristic response—Lehman accepted the paper's position, but its reasons seemed to him weak! As a trained lawyer of clear mind and ready tongue, Dulles made his tours of the state effective. He was blunt in speech, and some of his utterances hurt Lehman's feelings.

But the political pendulum that had swung so far to the right in 1946, and had registered so uncertain a result two years later, was now swinging back toward the New Deal and Fair Deal positions. When Dulles accused his opponent of favoring the "welfare state," Lehman accepted the charge. The term was misleading, he said, but if it meant care for the helpless, policies favoring the whole people as distinguished from special interests, and humanely enlightened legislation, then he was an apostle of welfare. One misstep by Dulles proved costly to him. Speaking at Geneseo, he remarked that if his audience could look at the faces in a typical metropolitan crowd of Lehman's supporters, they would never hesitate in their Republican loyalty. This slur on the foreign-born of New York City and on the immigrant types of the whole state, though doubtless inadvertent, was widely resented. Many Catholics admired the courage of Lehman in standing up to the Cardinal. Many Jews admired the equal courage which he had shown in September, 1948, in denouncing the assassination of Count Bernadotte in Palestine, presumably by members of the Stern Gang.[6] This "cold-blooded murder," this "revolting outrage," he said, ought to be swiftly and severely punished.

He could speak out on such sensitive points because nobody ever doubted that his heart was with the demand of minority elements in America for equal treatment. In particular, no Jew who knows how fervent was his interest in Israel, how much both of labor and financial support he gave to Jewish institutions, ever doubted his loyalty to his race.

While the Truman Administration threw all its weight behind Lehman, Governor Dewey placed all his influence behind Dulles; indeed, to no small extent the contest was a test of Dewey's prestige. The struggle attracted national attention, most voters feeling it a pity that both men could not be elected. But as the campaign neared its end, its result was hardly in doubt. Lehman came out of New York City with a lead of 788,000. When all the ballots were tallied his vote was 2,582,438 against Dulles's 2,384,281. Both men had done well and could feel proud of their standing.

At seventy-one, Lehman was about to open a colorful new phase of his public activities.

Chapter XVI

ANGRY NEW SENATOR

L<small>EHMAN</small> arrived in the Senate with great advantages and disadvantages. He was a neophyte, who knew nothing at first hand of the rules and traditions of that august body; he was expected to say little and do less until his betters grew accustomed to his presence. They would tolerate him in the engine room of the ship, learning its machinery, but they wished him to keep off the promenade deck. Of course he was too wise and tactful to be intrusive. At the same time, he brought to his seat some distinctions which gave weight to his words and acts. He had been governor of New York for ten years; he had been a close friend of Roosevelt; he had headed a powerful international organization; he was the leading Jewish figure in public life. He was regarded with respect by tens of millions from coast to coast who had scarcely heard of half of his colleagues. Given his temperament, it was impossible for him to play the mouselike part of the ordinary freshman member.

The new Senator began his service at the opening of the second session of the Eighty-first Congress on January 3, 1950, his office heaped with flowers, and his desk piled with congratulatory messages from friends. "I felt a very real thrill as I took my chair," he told intimates. To reporters he gave the closest approach to an epigram he could muster: "I hope to make a little news, but as little noise as possible." [1] Press photographs showed him conferring with the Democratic floor leader Scott Lucas of Illinois, William Benton of Connecticut, and other party associates. Immediately afterward he announced that he would support Truman's international policies, a broadening of the Social Security Act, repeal or drastic amendment of the Taft–Hartley Act, and Federal rent-control legislation; but this was hardly news.[2]

At once Truman's message on the state of the Union fell into Congress with a sharp splash, its waves sending the Fair Deal Democrats to one side and the conservative Republicans and Dixiecrats to the other. The President's proposals—the Brannan farm control plan, repeal of the Taft–Hartley Act, compulsory health insurance, Federal aid to education, increased public housing, statehood for Alaska and Hawaii, fairer taxation—were not unexpected, but they brought his opponents to arms. An indignant chorus rose from such Republican stalwarts as Robert Taft of Ohio, Kenneth S. Wherry of Nebraska, William E. Jenner of Indiana, and Homer Ferguson of Michigan, deepened by such Dixiecrats as John C. Stennis of Mississippi and A. J. Ellender of Louisiana. This boded ill for the Truman program. Nominally the chamber stood 52 Democrats to 44 Republicans, but these figures meant nothing. A fairly solid phalanx of 35 conservative Republicans could be rallied on any major issue, augmented by about 15 Southern Democrats and two or three jellyfish Democrats from other parts of the country—the "60 percent Democrats." This gave the opposition a decisive majority. Lehman praised the program in conventional terms, saying that Congress must "press on with a broad program of social legislation." [3] While he did not wholly agree with the Administration's views on medicine and health, he espoused its civil rights policies, including an FEPC bill; and he stood behind the plans for reorganizing various Federal agencies which Truman offered in March, 1950—plans based largely on the wise recommendations of Herbert Hoover.

When Lehman entered the Senate he did not expect to do much aggressive in-fighting—at least for a while. He exaggerated the deliberative character of the body, thinking that it really hammered out many decisions by debate. He also exaggerated its decorum, its intelligence, and its fund of elevated public spirit; while he knew it had its demagogues and clowns, and that personal, local, and regional selfishness were common, he fancied that a few trumpet calls would lift most men above them. Naïveté entered into this attitude, but something more than naïveté, for he had seen how FDR *did* lift legislators by some trumpet calls. His experience of the Senate in 1950–52 disillusioned him—and out of disillusionment came an anger that edged his natural combativeness in matters of principle. [4] Like other Fair Deal Senators—Brien McMahon, Paul Douglas, Lister Hill—he believed sufficiently in Truman's chief measures to make earnest speeches, argue with colleagues, and appeal to the people at home. He wanted to see the party keep its reputation for liberalism bright and shining for the 1952 campaign, and he saw that the only language which Southern conservatives such as Tom Connally, Walter George, and James O. Eastland understood was the language of battle. If unbattled, they would run amuck.

His swift disillusionment sprang partly from the ruthless treatment given most of Truman's domestic program in 1950–51. Sierra walls could not have been flintier than the Republican-Dixiecrat coalition. The Fair Deal forces did win an extension of Social Security to about ten million people not previously covered, did pass a 1.5 billion dollar appropriation for slum clearance and low-cost public housing, and did carry out part of Truman's plan for reorganizing the executive branches; but that was about all. The two-party coalition halted dead most of the progressive measures. When the House passed an FEPC bill, for example, the Senate at once blocked it. The record might have been better if Senator Joseph R. McCarthy had not convulsed the chamber at the very outset by his sensational, confusing, and fraudulent charges of disloyalty in the State Department and if the Korean War had not broken out in June. While the second of these events assisted the Administration's international measures, the two in combination diverted Congress from the work of constructive home legislation. The scales were weighted against liberal advances, however, even without these fell occurrences.[5]

With Lehman's response to McCarthy and McCarthyism, which he found truly shattering, we shall later deal at length. The wide destructive swath which the Wisconsin cheater mowed through public affairs, the terrorism he brazenly created, profoundly distressed the fresh arrival from New York. It was a shock he had never anticipated. But he found other and broader causes for disillusionment and indignation.

· I ·

The largely futile debates of 1950–52 gave Lehman opportunity to acquaint himself with the rules and methods of the Senate, its members large, small, and minuscule, and its atmosphere, at a time when it had reached its postwar nadir. He was insatiably curious. Drew Pearson termed him "active as a bright-eyed puppy, exploring each new issue." In this exploration he was immensely helped by the staff which he organized under the tough-minded, Navy Commander Julius C. C. Edelstein, a well-experienced assistant who was to stay with him for the next twelve years. A resourceful if moody worker, Edelstein came to him in a somewhat curious manner. A Milwaukeean, he had been in the Navy for seven years, had been special adviser to the Secretary of State and the President of the Philippines, had worked for Ed Pauley and Admiral Leahy, and was writing a book on occupation policy. As he was about to leave Washington for Missouri one day in 1949 to assist Thomas C. Hennings, Jr., in his campaign for election to the Senate, Lehman telephoned him. They met at the Mayflower, and the upshot of their talk was that Lehman offered him the post of executive assistant. After some hesitation, and after consulting Benjamin V. Cohen and Oscar Chapman, Edelstein accepted. "Why did I hesitate?" he said later. "Well, I didn't know just how liberal Lehman was. I had been at sea so long!" He helped the Senator organize an office force which, including eight full-time research workers, was almost unrivaled for size and efficiency; and he himself became one of the most familiar and highly esteemed figures on Capitol Hill.*

Though Lehman had not expected to find the Senate another Mt. Olympus, he was distressed by the abundance of mediocrity and perversity in the body. And while he was not displeased by the rigidity of the Senate's rules, he was nonplused by the extent to which it was dominated by a small inner clique. It was not a club, as people had said in the 1880s, but it was a loose association with a self-appointed, highly exclusive, and grimly autocratic club at its heart. This inner agency was partly a managerial body, partly a deliberative group, and very decidedly a disciplinary tribunal. It was casual and clumsy in many of its operations, but it meant to rule and it did. The members were like-minded men who had gained power largely through the seniority rule (that is, by sheer lapse of time, which lifted shifty politicians enjoying secure seats above able leaders with precarious tenure) and who exercised that power mainly through their dictatorships over major committees. These were politely called working committees. In Truman's second administration they were far more commonly obstructive committees.

The most prominent of the committee chairmen was Patrick A. Mc-Carran, head of the Judiciary Committee, to which more than half of the

---

* Lehman's Washington staff came to number between twenty and thirty hard-working people, of whom Thomas V. Brunkard and Elizabeth M. Leonard in 1962 remained in charge of office work. The staff provided him with an invaluable fund of expert knowledge on pending legislation; indeed, he doubtless spent more time being briefed than any member. They also kept him in close rapport with the executive departments and bureaus, enabled him to remedy injustices in immigration cases without the introduction of special bills, and made possible the maintenance of close ties with the people of the State of New York. Fully half of the staff were paid out of his own resources. Some of the particularly effective helpers were: Mildred Akins, Herbert Beaser, Jack Carter, Ruth Chertkov, Elizabeth Donahue, Mathilda W. German, Stanley G. Karson, Robert Low, Mary Ellen McFerran, Richard Sachs, Emma M. Volta, William Welsh, and Frances Williams. Special mention should be made of Miss Carolin E. Flexner, of the distinguished Abraham Flexner-Simon Flexner family, who not only served Lehman as secretary for many years but advised and scolded him when she thought it necessary.

The Eightieth Congress was the first to operate under the Reorganization Act which created the post of administrative assistant, an extra aide given a salary of $10,000. Most Senators simply gave their old secretaries the new title and better pay; some appointed sons or other relatives. Lehman's staff was accounted the most efficient on the Hill, prepared with the best information on every subject, "whether it be barge traffic on Long Island Sound or the Chinese minority in Indonesia." Robert S. Allen and William V. Shannon, *The Truman Merry-Go-Round* (New York, 1950), 225ff.

important bills were consigned. Nearly two years older than Lehman, a graduate of the University of Nevada while McKinley still sat in the White House, a farmer, stock raiser, attorney, and judge, he had been elected to the Senate in the Democratic sweep of 1932 and twice reëlected. He had nearly the abilities and more than the sinister qualities of a Talleyrand. Representing but 170,000 people, or as many as a minor county of Pennsylvania or New York, he exercised more power than any colleague; and he exercised it in such a way as to become one of the few men Lehman ever positively detested. A friend of Lehman's remembers Paul Douglas pointing to him with the words: "There goes an evil man."

As rasping on Lehman's nerves as the undemocratic management of the Senate was its responsiveness to local and regional interests and the pressures of economic baronies. Of course he had seen plenty of special-interest pressures in Albany, where the readiness of legislators to abet grabbers and grafters had been about as unblushing, at times, as it was in Washington. Still, the senatorial habit of exalting state profit over national welfare, and the alacrity with which a few men supported measures which diverted money from the public into corporation pockets, offended and alarmed him. He never forgot the way in which Robert S. Kerr of Oklahoma, the wealthy owner of oil and gas properties, pressed a "ripper" bill, and other measures favorable to petroleum including one to liberate natural gas transmission from Federal control. Members were quick to denounce any bureau chief who accepted presents, peddled his personal influence, or used inside knowledge of executive decisions for his gain, but some of them were less sensitive about their own conduct.[6]

Certain of the abuses that Lehman noted possessed a long history. For many decades Senators had represented special economic constituencies, as Allison of Iowa represented Western railroads, Jones of Nevada spoke for mining interests, and Quay of Pennsylvania personified steel. In the days of Harding and Coolidge the inner clique that managed the Senate was the "conference" that George Wharton Pepper describes in his memoirs. Only Republican members in good standing were invited or cared to come, such a maverick as Borah usually being absent. Their decisions were not binding, but they nonetheless ruled the Senate with a rod of edged steel. The work of the chamber had always been to a great extent subterranean. So much of its energy had always been expended in blocking legislation which conservative groups or special interests disliked that, long before Lehman entered its doors, frustrated men had popularized a definition: "The Senate is the reason why desirable things don't happen."[7]

As it was not in Lehman's nature to accept frustrations tamely, especially after a lifetime in executive office, his anger sometimes boiled over. The historic role of the Senate as a check upon President and House interested him far less than its constructive potentialities. As he had intimated in saying that the country should press on with social legislation, he was anxous not to apply the brakes but to open the throttle. His conception of the Senate also emphasized its educational function. History as he had read it showed Webster, Clay, and Benton riveting the attention of the nation with their great lessons; it invested Seward, Lyman Trumbull, and John Sherman with the mantle of forceful national preceptors. He knew that the most grueling labor of legislation had to be performed in the committee rooms. Nevertheless, he never cured himself of the belief that true discussion ought to remain feasible and that fact, argument, and eloquence ought to change votes as they did when Gladstone and Disraeli spoke in Parliament and Carter Glass and Oscar Underwood argued in Congress. He meant to do what he could, braving impatience and ridicule, to restore some effective debate.

This, based on all the research that Julius Edelstein directed, meant incessant work. Though as governor he had looked toward a seat as partial respite from grinding daily pressures, he now discovered that senatorial leisure was available only between sessions and seldom then. "If I were to compare the actual work load of a governor with that of a senator," he wrote in the *New York Times Magazine* in the fall of 1950, "I would say that a Senator's job is the more strenuous. In Washington almost each day is a race against the time hand." [8] Committee meetings crowded thickly on each other, a score or more in a day, and each Senator might be on a dozen subcommittees. Sometimes Lehman found he was expected to attend two or three committee meetings simultaneously. He would race from one room to a second and then a third, finally hurrying back to the first, in a hectic effort to catch the critical moments of each. The Senate sessions began punctually at noon; not somewhere around that time, as in Albany, but on the dot. They lasted until six, seven, or later, and he soon found one debate on rent control running until four in the morning. All Senators were theoretically supposed to attend all sessions, and Lehman did, or nearly that.

Working time, meanwhile, was subject to such constant interruptions and encroachments that, as one member indignantly said, a Senator seemed expected to perform simultaneously the tasks of bellhop, college professor, and political leader. As bellhop he had to rise for every constituent who sent in his card. The caller might be paying his respects, asking for a public lecture, urging some pet measure, or expressing readiness to lay himself on the altar of patriotism by taking a well-paid office. As bellhop the Senator had also to answer a torrent of letters that often rose above a thousand a day. He had to lend a respectful ear to the numerous organizations—labor leaders, veterans, businessmen, farmers, welfare workers, and what not—which sent officers or lobbyists to his door. In his capacity as professor he had to watch the thousands of bills and resolutions that rained into the chamber. He and his research staff had to give thorough study to the most important, some of them several hundred pages in length. He had to write speeches as carefully as any professor wrote lectures, and last year's speeches could not be warmed over.

As political leader, finally, he had to keep in as close relations as possible with the White House, the executive departments, and the independent commissions. Though Lehman and Truman greatly respected each other, they were never congenially intimate. He had to bend a vigilant eye on political currents in his own state and lend a helping hand to its party leaders. He also found it both agreeable and wise to confer frequently with the best members of the House, whose cooperation on bills was sometimes essential. Important as it was to talk with Secretary of State Acheson, or Secretary of the Treasury Snyder, or Maurice Tobin in the Labor Department, it was equally important to establish harmonious relations with Speaker Sam Rayburn and such capable, hard-working Representatives as Carl Perkins of Kentucky, Andrew Jacobs of Indiana, Tom Steed of Oklahoma, Brooks Hays of Arkansas, John A. Blatnik and Eugene McCarthy of Minnesota, and Richard Bolling of Missouri.

He appreciated them all, as he appreciated Senator John F. Kennedy of Massachusetts, and those able and liberal representatives, Clifford Case of New Jersey, Mike Mansfield of Montana, and Henry Jackson of Washington, all of whom soon became Senate colleagues.

Meanwhile, Lehman tried to keep up with newspaper and magazine comment, a task in which his secretaries, pasting careful scrapbooks, collaborated. He would have liked a larger opportunity than he had to discuss pending measures with economists, sociologists, jurists, scientists, and other experts; he missed the kind of counsel that the Columbia University group, Robert Murray Haig, Joseph Chamberlain, Lindsay Rogers, Philip C. Jessup, and Luther Gulick, had given him in New York. But he did profit from the support and to some extent the counsel that a number of veteran journalists—Robert S. Allen, William S. White, Doris Fleeson, Walter Lippmann, Drew Pearson, Jonathan Daniels—lent him.

Lehman's conscientious shouldering of his responsibilities—at times too laboriously, too worriedly conscientious—was not made pleasanter by the spectacle of *dolce far niente* negligence practiced by a number of associates.

The I.T.&T. Club, "in Tuesday and out Thursday," with long weekends spent in private business, law, or politicking, was necessarily confined to Congressional members from the Eastern seaboard, but it numbered some flagrant absentees. That suave Democrat from the Bronx, Charles Buckley, was out of Washington so much of the time that the press dubbed him "the phantom Congressman." From the beginning of the Eighty-first Congress in June, 1949, to the end of the same month in 1950, a quarter of the Senators missed more than seventy-five votes each. Dennis Chavez of New Mexico, a delightful gentleman, but a hard-boiled professional politician whose long record was almost totally devoid of other accomplishment than the steady deglutition of political plums, led the roster by missing 161 votes. Sheridan Downey of California, about to make an unmourned exit from the national service, was a close second with 145 voting absences. James Eastland of Mississippi, who rivaled Ben Tillman and Theodore Bilbo in prejudiced demagogy, without the force of these men, was third with 136 misses. Pat McCarran of Nevada and Elmer Thomas of Oklahoma came close behind. Lehman, however, had missed only two votes since he came to the Senate.[9]

In one respect his burden as Senator was lighter than that as governor: he had fewer unescapable social duties. He could, in fact, entertain or be entertained just as little as he chose. He and his wife spent most evenings quietly in their apartment in the Wardman Park Hotel, reading, listening to the radio, or chatting. However, they soon formed part of a small circle which they found far more stimulating than anything that Albany had ever offered and that formed the happiest single feature of their new life.

His name was regularly bracketed by the press with members of this circle. For Paul Douglas of Illinois, with his wife Emily, the Lehmans developed a warm affection. Paul had been chosen to the Senate in the remarkable election of 1948 in which he had topped Truman's vote by almost 375,000, while Adlai E. Stevenson, running for governor, topped it by nearly 550,000. Emily had sat in the House. They had the same simple tastes as the Lehmans. Paul expressed Lehman's own view when he remarked, "I would be willing to hold late afternoon and evening committee meetings to escape the people who think a Senator's time ought to be taken up with cocktail parties." As the former University of Chicago professor, an expert economist, was far more scholarly than Lehman but less experienced politically, they could pool their talents with profit; and Mrs. Douglas had the same artistic tastes as Mrs. Lehman. Senator Brien McMahon and his wife Rosemary were another pair with whom the Lehmans formed a firm friendship. The son of an Irish immigrant, who worked his way through Yale and elbowed his way up until in 1944 he defeated the Republican Senator from

Connecticut, John Danaher, he showed grim fighting audacity, vision, and imagination. Indeed, in dealing with the problems of the new atomic age he manifested more discernment than Truman or most others. To him went most of the credit for the battle which wrested control of atomic power from the military forces and placed it in civilian hands. Unfortunately, his life was cut cruelly short.

With Hubert Humphrey and his wife Muriel, the Lehmans felt the same instant congeniality. They were young, energetic, and ebullient. Hubert, born in South Dakota, had come through the University of Minnesota with Eugene McCarthy, taught there and in the University of Louisiana, made a brilliant record as mayor of Minneapolis, and landed in the Senate at thirty-seven. Besides engaging personal traits, he had enviable gifts. He was eloquent —which Lehman was not; he was quick, clever, electric—which Lehman was not. He was as boldly outspoken for his convictions as Lehman, and he spoke a great deal. Other engaging members of the circle were the brilliant and combative Senator William Benton of Connecticut and his wife Helen.

In 1950–52 some newspapermen used the rather deplorable term "Big Four of the Fair Deal" in characterizing Douglas, McMahon, Humphrey, and Lehman; deplorable but indicative.[10] They might have included Benton. These men were much alike in their New Deal convictions, their courage, for they made the most unpalatable statements with reckless frankness, and their refusal to compromise on any points involving principle. In many respects they differed, but in these regards they were five peas—New England, New York, Middle Western—in a pod.*

A few other names complete the Lehmans' social circle in Washington. Wayne Morse of Oregon, though always unpredictable, held their warm esteem. So did Lister Hill of Alabama, a state with which Lehman had old ties. When in 1954 Morse helped elect Richard Neuberger from Oregon, the Lehmans made an immediate place for the talented young journalist-Senator and his wife Maurine. Henry M. Jackson of Washington, another liberal, they saw occasionally, and his colleague, the delightful Norwegian-American Warren Magnuson, a confirmed bachelor, astute politician, and champion of labor. For Estes Kefauver and Mike Monroney they felt a mounting regard. Socially, the group made Washington a friendlier place than the New Yorkers had expected it to be. Politically, the men in it exerted an influence out of proportion to their numbers. Again and again they were checkmated by the ruling coalition in the Senate, but not before they had

* Humphrey and McMahon, however, went further in compromise than Lehman and Douglas; and McMahon was a stern partisan, intent on Democratic advantage. White, *Citadel*, 119.

registered their views with a force that friendly newspapers like the *New York Times, Baltimore Sun, Washington Post,* and *St. Louis Post-Dispatch* carried to the nation.[11]

· II ·

In the late summer of 1950, just before Congress adjourned on September 23 to let members go home to fight the fall elections, one battle over civil liberties came to its climax. All spring and summer an atmosphere of alarm had enveloped the capital. For the most part it had been artificially fomented. The notion that Communist plots against the internal safety of the country were numerous and formidable had been propagated primarily to serve the objects of reactionary troublemakers. It could be played up to augment the influence of self-appointed champions of the public safety, defeat important social advances, whittle away hard-won gains under Roosevelt and Truman, and reawaken all the selfish prejudices of isolationism. Lehman, with his ingrained hatred of any encroachment on freedom of speech and action, and his detestation of phobias that would paralyze constructive action, was deeply aroused.

Just enough basis for uneasiness existed to make timid people credit the exaggerated outcries. On January 21 Alger Hiss, recently in responsible office, was found guilty of perjury following his denial that he had transferred State Department papers to Whitaker Chambers, a confessed Communist agent. In March, Judith Coplon, who had been employed in the Justice Department, and a Russian engineer named Gubitchev hired by the United Nations were convicted of conspiring to carry on espionage. Though the Federal Court of Appeals was soon to reverse Miss Coplon's conviction on technical grounds, it declared that her guilt was plain and recommended a retrial. In April Harry Bridges, a former Australian who had become head of the International Longshoremen's and Warehousemen's Union, was convicted of conspiracy and perjury in a case stemming from his denial during naturalization proceedings that he had ever been a Communist. That same month Klaus Fuchs, a German-born atomic scientist, confessed in England that he had given secret information on nuclear research to Russians, and was sentenced by a British court to fourteen years in jail, an immediate sequel being the FBI arrest of several Americans as collaborators of Fuchs. On August 1, 1950, the Federal Court of Appeals upheld the earlier conviction of eleven leaders of the American Communist Party for conspiracy.

These cases, keeping the newspapers full of headlines, created a general public conviction that fuller protective measures ought to be taken. The shock of Communist aggression in Korea greatly accentuated this sentiment. An outcry arose for precautions not merely against overt criminals like Hiss and Bridges but against people engaged in covert subversion: those who broke down national morale, nursed plots against the existing political and economic order, published semitreasonable matter, and made inflammatory speeches. Senator McCarran as head of the Judiciary Committee rushed to meet the alleged need, for the existing Committee on Un-American Activities had limited powers.[12]

He introduced in association with Representative Walter and ruthlessly pressed an antisubversive bill which was a revised version of the Mundt-Nixon bill passed by the House the year before. It provided for Federal registration of both Communist "action" and Communist "front" groups, with a plain labeling of their publications. It barred members of these groups from defense plants. It stiffened immigration and naturalization procedures so as to shut out of the country anybody who had ever been affiliated with any totalitarian organization. It punished conspiracy to advocate the overthrow of the United States government by ten years in prison and a $10,000 fine. Finally, it empowered the government to clap potential saboteurs, whether Communists or members of any other suspect body, into prison camps during any war emergency. All these undertakings involved highly dubious judgments, definitions, and police activities and carried the government into a twilight zone where legitimate protective action might easily become harsh repression.

Essentially, the question was whether the civil liberties which English-speaking lands had long regarded as vital necessities—free inquiry, free speech, free group protest, due court protection of individuals—were to be pronounced luxuries unsuitable for a time of peril. In the prevalent hysteria many people hastily said yes. Some states and cities were passing loosely drawn anti-Communist measures that did more harm than good. Loyalty oaths were being imposed on many groups of public employees. Impetuous regents came near disrupting the University of California by demanding an oath which various faculty members resisted as an attack on academic freedom. In the Senate the liberals, led by Lehman, Douglas, Humphrey, and McMahon, came forward to vindicate what they regarded as the basic liberties of the people.[13]

McCarran tried to override the opposition without letting it even raise its voice. Not only was he a thorough reactionary, a zealous servant of special interests, and a Red-hunter so prejudiced that he regarded most immigrants as potential Communists; he was a natural bully, whose arrogance surpassed that of Nelson W. Aldrich and Joe Cannon a generation earlier. Knowing that his nod could make or destroy half the bills before the Senate, he used his power to whip the willing and unwilling into line. Elected by some 35,000 votes, he defied Senators whose vote ran into millions. "He'd come into the chamber and lay down the law," Lehman recalls. "It didn't make any difference who had the floor. He'd just take it and insist on his legislation being taken up at his will, frequently out of turn. He paid no attention to the amenities or to fair play." Extremely able himself, he was advised at every turn by two well-informed henchmen whom he had gotten appointed to the Judiciary Committee staff, one as chief of research; they shaped his measures according to his wishes and at committee hearings sat next to him whispering suggestions.

Senator Kilgore, the ranking Democrat on the Judiciary Committee, introduced a substitute bill which sought to strengthen the nation's internal security without dangerous abridgement of its liberties. It was hoped to use this substitute bill to defeat or drastically amend McCarran's bill. The bill, when it reached the floor, had relatively little support and was decisively defeated. Then Senator Lucas, instead of pressing for an adequate new piece of legislation, accepted the McCarran bill by adding as a futile amendment the text of Kilgore's measure, which had already been defeated. Perhaps he heard from the American Legion, which year after year made him its judge advocate; perhaps he was intimidated by the *Chicago Tribune* and some downstate papers in Illinois; perhaps in part he was just showing his characteristic ineptness. At any rate, he did not even consult his associates. Lehman, cornering him in the cloakroom, denounced him to his face. But his sudden change of front confused the Democrats, so that even Humphrey and Douglas voted for the bill, thinking that it had been changed for the better. It went through with a mere handful of noes.

Thereupon Truman, strongly abetted by Lehman, moved into the battle with characteristic decision. He sent Congress a veto message declaring that the McCarran bill "would open the way to thought control" and would be so unworkable that it would aid rather than impede Communism. Paul Douglas had meanwhile, as he said, spent a sleepless night regretting his vote. When the motion to override the veto came up, he and Humphrey joined Lehman in opposition, but it was too late; the measure passed with ease. Senator Taft hailed the prospect that the Republicans might make it a winning issue in the 1950 elections. The American Communist Party at once refused to register with the Attorney General, and protracted litigation by other organizations was certain. In fact, the legislation proved so unworkable that even its advocates eventually regretted its passage.

The remainder of the Eighty-first Congress, ending on January 2, 1951, was almost barren of accomplishment outside the fields of defense and foreign aid. Most of its energies were poured into investigations.

President Truman's dismissal of General of the Army Douglas MacArthur, which Lehman emphatically approved, was followed by the general's memorable appearance before both houses on April 19, 1951 and by weeks of inconclusive debate on the Far Eastern policy of the Administration. Equally spectacular was the investigation of interstate crime by a Senate committee under Estes Kefauver of Tennessee. The nation, after watching on television MacArthur's dramatic return to its shores, viewed with horrified fascination the appearance there of some of the worst criminals of the land as they answered committee-room questions about their organized activities. The inquiry did much to stimulate states and cities to institute a stiffer law enforcement. Another investigation, conducted by Paul Douglas, explored the ethical standards of the Federal government. While Douglas' report censured the executive branch sternly for various laxities, it also gave Congress due admonition. Pat McCarran continued his exploration of subversive activities but happily refrained from offering any fresh legislation.[14]

Throughout 1951–52 the familiar coalition of conservative Republicans and Southern State-Rights Democrats continued to block the President's major proposals: the Brannan farm plan, national health insurance, civil rights legislation, and admission of Alaska and Hawaii. Robert Taft, the Republican leader in the Senate, who during the fall of 1951 became an avowed candidate for the presidential nomination, was a sharp-tongued opponent of "Socialist" measures and practices, and almost anything in the New Deal or Fair Deal category seemed to him "Socialistic." NATO was now an accomplished fact. But in foreign affairs Taft termed the Korean conflict "an utterly useless war," declared that the United Nations had been "an utter failure as a means of preventing aggression," and asserted that the country should build up powerful sea and air forces with as little use of ground troops overseas as possible. In short, he and Herbert Hoover, to Lehman's great disgust, were trying to commit the Republican organization to a surly "neo-isolationism"—to a retreat within a "Fortress America." [15]

Yet while the legislative machinery stood practically stalled, Lehman had opportunity during 1951–52 to express his opinion on a variety of public issues; and this expression was always emphatic and sometimes angrily combative. One of the questions on which he felt most strongly was finance. Congress in his view fell far short of its duty in taxation, for it should levy drastically on high wartime profits, reduce swollen fortunes, and balance the budget. He knew a great deal about finance, he knew how wealth was being piled up, and he was familiar with the expedients used by rich men and corporations to evade taxes. Knowing this, he boiled with indignation over the protection that senatorial conservatives gave all manner of vested interests.

Supporting Senator O'Mahoney's excess profits tax amendment to the revenue bill of 1950, he denounced the anti-Administration coalition that gave Truman only three billions in new levies when it should have given him four or five. His stand expressed his fundamental social philosophy: his belief that great accumulations should be taxed relentlessly to provide a higher general standard of living and furnish larger social and cultural amenities. On June 7, 1951, he said in terms that sounded rather like a ragged radical than a man of great fortune:

> While the reactionary elements in Congress slash away at funds for public health, public power, and public housing—under the guise of economy—they move very slowly, indeed, to tax the unprecedented profits of big business. In the second half of 1950, American corporations made an average of 17.5 percent profit, after taxes, on the investment of their stockholders. In one of the largest industries these profits, for the last quarter of 1950, after taxes, amounted to 25 percent. But no new taxes have yet been enacted to tap these profits, made possible by the defense effort.
>
> The reactionary elements demand a halt to expenditures for the security, health, and welfare of the people, but they raise no outcry against the current practice of exorbitant tax amortization; yet, by this means, $2,500,000,000 of tax waivers have been granted to twenty companies for the purpose of plant expansion in the last six months.

While he kept pressing for higher taxes, a balanced budget on a pay-as-you-go basis, and high levies on the bloated profits made possible by Korean War contracts, he continuously attacked excise taxes, which placed the greatest burden on those least able to pay. As the summer session of 1951 drew to a close, the debate became acrimonious. Lehman, Douglas, Humphrey, and others fought for a far stiffer bill than the one that Senator Walter George had reported out of the Finance Committee. The crowded galleries of the Senate were with them. On September 27, Senator George aroused Lehman's ire by suggesting that he and Humphrey were actuated by purely political motives in demanding soak-the-rich taxes. Lehman responded that they were battling for a principle, against men whose weak tax bill would leave the country in the next fiscal year with a deficit of ten or twelve billions. A heated exchange followed:

Mr. George.	Mr. President, may I remind the Senator—
Mr. Lehman.	The Senator from New York has not yielded. . . .

Mr. George.	Let us finish the bill or we will not raise anything during this current year.
Mr. Lehman.	The Senator from New York has not finished and does not yield.
The Presiding Officer.	Let the Senate be in order.
Mr. Lehman.	I say that I believe the bill, as it now stands, favors men of high incomes, corporations, and others, and discriminates against the man of small and moderate income.
Mr. George.	Mr. President, I resent that statement, and no man worthy of a seat in this Senate will make that statement. [Manifestations of disorder in the galleries.] . . .
Mr. Lehman.	If the Senator from New York and his colleagues were not convinced that we are fighting for an equitable bill, a bill that would come at least within hailing distance of a balanced budget, do you think for a moment that we would be standing on the floor of the Senate battling with all our hearts, with all our power, with all our might for the achievement of that end? As the Senator from Minnesota has said, to fight for higher taxes, for higher revenue, is an unpopular thing, not a popular thing. That is why we are justified in resenting the implication and the imputation that we are seeking . . . political advantage. . . . We are fighting for equity and fairness to all the people of the United States, rich and poor alike.

In the end Lehman, Humphrey, Douglas, Morse, and Green of Rhode Island voted against the Revenue Act of 1951. Benton, while declaring that he disapproved of many features, voted for it on the ground that the government must have the revenue it offered. Although the four Senators first named united in a statement that the bill was grossly inequitable and inadequate, this availed nothing to halt its passage 57 to 19.

Lehman was happy to take the unpopular side on still another issue in dealing with the St. Lawrence Seaway and its hydroelectric potentialities. Franklin D. Roosevelt had urged Congress in 1933 to join Canada in building the seaway; he and Truman had steadily continued advocating the measure; yet in nearly thirty years nothing had been done. Nobody had fought harder for the proposal than Lehman. As governor of New York he had consistently advocated the Seaway and had concurrently argued for the development of low-cost public power on the St. Lawrence and Niagara

Rivers. In 1936 he had helped inspire the New York Power Authority to begin a comprehensive engineering study of possibilities at Niagara, and two years later it had reported an ingenious plan for generating additional power by nighttime and off-season diversion of water, with use of cleverly designed canals, all this involving no harm whatever to scenic values.

He had got nowhere. Now Truman was getting nowhere. Canada was not only willing but eager to go ahead. It was plain that the Seaway would convert Cleveland, Detroit, Toledo, Chicago, Milwaukee, and Duluth into ports which ocean-going freighters and liners from all parts of the globe could reach by direct voyage. But the Atlantic seaboard cities, including New York, Albany, and Buffalo, had fought the combined Seaway and power project to a standstill.[16]

With Franklin D. Roosevelt, Jr. cooperating in the House, Lehman introduced a Niagara development bill, in May, 1950, authorizing the army engineers to construct the works involved in the development, Truman having meanwhile sent the Senate a fresh treaty negotiated with Canada. In 1951 Lehman and Roosevelt reintroduced the Niagara measure. As for the St. Lawrence Seaway, the Senator pointed out that over fifty years it would pay for itself; that its cost would be less than the $500,000,000 to be spent for the New York Thruway; and that it could be financed by revenue bonds without a penny of national appropriations. Yet it would benefit the whole 150,000,000 people of the country. When the opposition resorted to dishonest arguments he exploded angrily.

"This entire debate," he told the Senate on June 17, 1952, "has been carried on in a most disingenuous way, it seems to me. Statements have been made which have had absolutely no basis in fact. Two or three days ago one of our colleagues on the floor of the Senate threw up his hands in horror and said, 'The country cannot afford this project. It would cost the taxpayers one billion dollars.' Ten minutes later another Senator, not satisfied with the incorrect, inaccurate, and false statement with respect to a cost of one billion, raised the ante and said, 'This is going to cost the taxpayers two billion dollars.'" It was by such dishonest tactics that the Senate was induced to defeat action for the dual Seaway-power plan on June 18 by the close vote of 43 to 40.

And the tactics succeeded. The St. Lawrence Seaway had to wait until years later Canada galvanized the United States into action by making preparations to build the entire artery at her own cost and under her own exclusive control. Then, and then only, the United States acted.

In a period when one outrage after another roused Lehman's indignation —the McCarthy outrages always the foremost—a special strain was put on his temper by the so-called tidelands oil controversy. The highly misleading

term "tidelands oil" referred to oil or gas obtained by drilling on the continental shelf off the Gulf States and California, drilling that really took place
not in the tidelands (the strip between high and low tide) but in the marginal
sea. The true tidelands had always been recognized as property of the individual states, but the marginal sea beyond low-tide mark was presumably
under Federal control. In June, 1947, the Supreme Court in a historic decision ruled that the national government had "paramount rights and full
dominion" over this marginal area off the California coast, and it shortly
made the same affirmation respecting Gulf states. A violent clamor at once
came from public and private interests in California, Texas, Louisiana, and
Florida, states which had authorized offshore drilling on a large and profitable scale.

The states wanted the revenues obtainable. Oil men and oil corporations
protested that they could "develop" the resources more readily under state
control, but were in most instances really actuated by a conviction that they
could gain fatter privileges from pliable state authorities than from the
Federal Government. Efforts by the Interior Department to get Congress to
pass legislation for the wise management of this great national resource soon
broke down. Not only this, but Congress, swayed by the coarsest kind of
state and private pressures—for as much as forty billion dollars, according to
estimates by some geologists, was at stake—threatened to override the
Supreme Court and throw away the Federal patrimony by a quitclaim law.
It was this threat that incensed Lehman and his liberal-minded associates.[17]

The subject was brought to a sharp issue when, in 1951, Representative
Francis E. Walter of Pennsylvania introduced a quitclaim measure that surrendered everything. Walter only the previous year had raised a nice point
of ethics by collecting a $170,000 fee for representing Pennroad Corporation
stockholders in a $15,000,000 suit against the Pennsylvania Railroad, it being
generally believed that as ranking Democratic member of the House Judiciary Committee he had special influence with Federal attorneys and judges.
Two able and public-spirited members of the House, Mike Mansfield of
Montana and Clifford Case of New Jersey, forthwith moved into the lists
against Walter's bill. Even before the measure reached the Senate—while
Case, Mansfield, and others were attacking it in the House—Lehman sounded
the tocsin. He called on Congress to pass a measure which would guarantee
careful Federal management of the great resource and devote its proceeds
to one of the most urgent needs of the country.

"The House," said the *New York Times* on August 2, 1951, "ruled out
on a specious point of order Representative Mansfield's amendment or substitute bill providing for Federal management of the marginal sea, and dedi-
cating the revenue to be produced from it to a program of Federal aid to

UNRRA shipments arriving in China, 1946

UNRRA Photograph in the National Archives

Herbert H. Lehman on the steps of the Capitol
The New York Times

education. This would provide a wise and magnanimous resolution of the long controversy. It would make possible a prudent conservation of the submerged oil in the interest of national defense while at the same time furnishing the means to deal with an urgent national problem—the crisis in the country's public schools—in the interest of the whole American people. This proposal will be advanced again, under bipartisan sponsorship, when the Walter bill reaches the Senate. It cannot be ruled out there on an arbitrary point of order. And it should not be ruled out on any fictitious plea of States' Rights. In the Congress of the United States the nation's rights ought to be considered paramount."

The struggle, as Lehman predicted, soon raged hotly in the Senate. Spessard L. Holland of Florida and Kerr of Oklahoma led the battle of the oil interests. Said Paul Douglas: "When you strip away all the legal gobbledygook, the offshore oil issue comes down to this: Will the Congress take away forty billions of resources which belong to forty-eight States and give them to four States?" Senator O'Mahoney's bill for management of the marginal sea preserved the principle of Federal ownership asserted by Case and Mansfield in the House. Lehman was one of the sponsors of Lister Hill's amendment to hand over all the proceeds to the resuscitation and strengthening of the public school system of the nation. But the four states with special interests, all the oil corporations and oil millionaires who hoped for easy state franchises, the State Rights fanatics, and other groups fought with dogged determination against a solution that would benefit the whole land.

On April 2, 1952, Lehman—sick at heart—saw the Senate vote down the Lister Hill amendment 47 to 36. And the success of quitclaim legislation was swiftly assured. Eisenhower abruptly declared himself—some thought partly with an eye on the Texas delegation in the national convention and the Texas vote in the ensuing election—in favor of the title of the states. A new and still fiercer battle in 1953, after the Republican victory over Adlai Stevenson, reached its inevitable end in the abandonment of national claims.*

· III ·

Lehman had meanwhile met no difficulty in 1950 in obtaining reëlection. His victory over the weak aspirant nominated by the Republicans, Lieutenant Governor Joseph R. Hanley, was never in doubt in spite of the fact that this was anything but a Democratic year. Governor Dewey was running for a third term as governor, and Vincent R. Impellitteri, who had become acting mayor of New York when William O'Dwyer resigned to accept the ambas-

---

* See Appendix I for the letter which Lehman and other liberal Senators addressed to President Eisenhower on April 17, 1953, concerning tidelands oil.

sadorship to Mexico, ran on an independent ticket against the regular Democratic nominee in the metropolis, both coming through victoriously.

Only one pathetic incident gave interest to the Lehman-Hanley contest. Hanley had long served in the legislature; dependent primarily on his small salary, he had contracted large debts; and growing old, he found his eyesight in danger. He would have liked to run for governor, but that was impossible, for Dewey wanted to keep the place. He therefore took the senatorial nomination only after a conference with Dewey in which he was assured, as he believed, of arrangements for his complete financial security whether he won or lost. He wrote the able Republican leader, Kingsland Macy, a close friend, a letter describing these assurances. This letter got into Democratic hands and was published. It produced an impression damaging both to Hanley and to Dewey. Nor did Hanley improve his position when, visiting the Wall Street district during the campaign, he pointed out to his wife the building that housed Lehman Brothers and told reporters: "I was just curious to come down and see where the $50,000,000 is coming from that I am running against."

The opposition to Lehman tried to gain a little ground by bringing to public light a letter which he had written to Alger Hiss on August 6, 1948: "Just a line to tell you how much I sympathize with you in the difficult position in which you have unfortunately been placed. I want you to know that I have complete confidence in your loyalty." The letter had of course been written long before Hiss's indictment and trial and shortly after he had been made president of the Carnegie Endowment for International Peace on the recommendation of a committee comprising John W. Davis, John Foster Dulles, and Arthur Ballantine. It was written, moreover, when Hiss was categorically denying the charges made against him during his first appearance before the House Committee on Un-American Activities. Lehman had assumed that he was telling the truth, and believed that a man should be considered innocent until found guilty. The Senator explained this, and publication of the letter did him no visible harm.

The *New York Post*, the day after his explanation appeared, printed a brief characterization of Lehman. He was a unique figure in politics, it remarked. He never raised his voice above a monotone; he never staged any clever tableaux; he argued political issues in a dryly serious way. He would not even compromise his dignity by riding in an automobile cavalcade. "He is easily the quietest candidate in the country, making an election campaign almost an exercise in understatement. Yet he gets the votes!" [18]

It was true that he got the votes. On election day Dewey, despite the Hanley letter, was chosen for his third term; the Republicans also elected their candidates for attorney general and state comptroller; and the Democrats lost the mayoralty of New York City. Yet Lehman emerged with a plurality of about 265,000.

The ease of his victory, and his growing prestige as a national leader, led a number of good party men, as the presidential campaign of 1952 drew near, to suggest that New York should present him to the Democratic convention as its favorite son. Such a compliment would have gratified him, but he felt that his age, and perhaps to some extent also his religious faith, debarred him from accepting it. He believed also that W. Averell Harriman, now Mutual Security Director, would make a stronger candidate. While the objection of age was quite valid, that of religion was not. No American of sense would have objected to a candidate from a religious group always distinguished by idealism, intellectual power, and loyalty to basic civil liberties. Least of all would any sensible American have objected to Lehman. He should have accepted the proposed honor, simply as a gesture of the esteem due him. For, though Harriman was an eager aspirant, who took his chances very seriously, and made a spirited preconvention campaign, the outcome showed that his ambitions were hopeless.

Other men, including Estes Kefauver, Alben Barkley, and Senator Richard B. Russell, were in the field. At the Chicago gathering Adlai E. Stevenson, though honestly reluctant to run, was placed before the delegates and at once established a decisive margin of strength. Lehman, who headed the New York delegation, was ready to support Harriman to the bitter end. But after the second ballot, restlessness appeared among the Empire State Democrats. Jim Farley defiantly remarked: "I'll go along for one more ballot, and no more. Then I'll switch to Stevenson." That was the feeling of many others, and on the third ballot Stevenson, still averse to the race, was chosen with 617½ votes. At that time Lehman, who did not yet know Stevenson well, was himself unenthusiastic.

Serving on the platform committee at Chicago, he made a valiant but only partially successful fight for a civil rights plank. It was only after an all-night contest, with John McCormack standing by him, that he consented to a compromise. The campaign taught him a great deal as to Stevenson's high ideals and abilities, and he was charmed by the wit, soundness, and bonhomie of the man. But he was not astonished by the smashing defeat of the party in November. He prepared to return to a Senate in which the prospects for progressive action were dark indeed, for it would number 48 Republicans, 47 Democrats, and 1 Independent. And in that Senate Joe McCarthy was rampant.

Chapter XVII

McCARTHYISM:
A STILL ANGRIER SENATOR

I$_N$ THE last two years of the Truman Administrations the nation confronted difficulties of dismaying magnitude. At home it faced a rising debt,
sharply increased living costs, and an inflation which greedy interests found
too profitable to check. As the Congressional deadlock over Federal aid to
education persisted, as Southerners blocked even weak civil rights legislation, and as the Brannan farm plan was defeated, some of the best Fair Deal
hopes faded. Labor remained bitter over the Taft–Hartley Act. Abroad,
success in the West was counterbalanced by partial defeat in the Orient. By
heavy exertions the government had protected Turkey, rescued Greece, and
used the Marshall Plan to mobilize the regenerative energies of both America
and free Europe. It had given effective leadership in the defeat of the Berlin
blockade by the Anglo-American air lift, and in the formation of the North
Atlantic Treaty Organization. China, however, had passed completely under
Communist sway, Formosa was threatened, and finally aggression struck
Korea. From the summer of 1950 onward American boys were being
slaughtered, and American strength depleted, in the confusions of an unde-
clared but savage war.

In this situation proper management of the national ship required unity,
discipline, coolness, and plan. It did not get them. A mutineer was in the
crew. He adroitly fomented discontent, personal and factional vengeance,
and general convulsion. The most urgent problems of national survival and
progress were thrust aside by a largely fictitious problem of internal security.

It was fortunate that when Joseph R. McCarthy loosed his attacks upon
civil liberties, the efficient operation of the executive, and the mutual trust of
Americans, some men of courage rose in an uncompromising resistance. One
was President Truman. All his life, as he writes in his memoirs, he had fought

against prejudice, intolerance, and hatred, "and as I grew older I could never understand how people could forget the origins and blessings of their own freedom." [1] Another was Secretary of State Acheson, who met impassively a storm of abuse as intemperate as it was unfounded. A band of distinguished journalists, radio and television critics, jurists, and university teachers rallied to the defense of the nation's best traditions.[2] Yet the unhappy fact was that these fighters for principle were, after all, few—most liberals were apathetic or timid; they were tardy—they waited until McCarthy was driven at bay for one of his lesser offenses; and they were clumsy—they did not know how to reach the public sentiment that he misled.

The central contest against McCarthyism had to be waged in his own chamber. It was only on the Senate floor and in the Senate committee rooms that his power for harm could be struck down. First and last, the Senate did muster a valiant group to expose his lies, obfuscations, and chicanery and to counterattack: Hubert Humphrey, William Benton, George D. Aiken, Wayne Morse, Brien McMahon, Mike Mansfield, Irving Ives, Margaret Chase Smith, Millard E. Tydings, and two or three others, along with Lehman. Yet here too the fighters were too few, too tardy, and too clumsy to make the record of the Senate really creditable.

It was on February 9, 1950, but five weeks after Lehman entered Congress, that the then obscure Senator from Wisconsin raised his voice to accuse the State Department of harboring a small army of Communists. To the end of Truman's tenure and through Eisenhower's first two years he terrorized official Washington like a Malay swordsman. He put the nation in an uproar, crippled several important executive arms and injured others, diverted Congress from its paramount concerns to a discussion of his brazen personalities, encouraged sensationalism in the press and cruelty in departmental tribunals, and sullied the good name of the United States in every foreign land. It seems almost incredible that he held his reckless course for nearly four years, leaping from half-truth to outright lie, dodging every exposure by a cuttlefish-ink explosion into new headlines, and threatening even the highest officers of the land.[3]

As Lehman well knew, similar ebullitions of panic and hysteria had occurred in the nation's past. The emotional spasms behind the Alien and Sedition Acts, the Anti-Masonic furor, the Know-Nothing crusade, and finally the Ku Klux Klan of the 1920s, had proved how easily demagogues can sometimes excite fear and prejudice among volatile elements in the population. In this instance real grounds for uneasiness existed. Americans were honestly alarmed by the acts of Alger Hiss, the Rosenbergs, Klaus Fuchs, and Judith Coplon; they were horrified to learn how strong a grip Communist ideas had laid upon many young people in the depression of the 1930s; and they resented President Truman's hasty remark to a press conference that such investigations as that in the Hiss case were a "red herring" to divert attention from Republican failures. The world had entered a danger zone of unexampled grimness, as Albert Einstein pointed out early in 1950, warning that "annihilation of any life on earth has been brought within the range of technical possibilities." Even before McCarthy spoke Senator Homer Capehart had tried to arouse panic in Congress: "Fuchs and Acheson and Hiss and hydrogen bombs threatening outside and New Dealism eating away the vitals of the nation! In the name of Heaven, is this the best America can do?" [4]

The mixture of fear, prejudice, and partisanship in Capehart's bit of rant was characteristic of much general emotionalism. Behind McCarthy soon stood a motley array. They included die-hard isolationists, in revolt against all internationalist tendencies; men of frontier mentality who admired eye-gouging, groin-kicking tactics; Irish Catholics who admired Joe as a fighting Hibernian; oil and stock market millionaires who equated high taxes with treason; and others who disagreed with the whole direction taken by the nation under FDR and Truman.[5] Here stood some who had a semi-Fascist outlook and who later drifted into the John Birch Society. "To many Americans," said Fulton Lewis, Jr., "McCarthyism is Americanism." McCarthy's following also included, as Richard H. Rovere writes, "large numbers of regular Republicans who had coolly concluded that there was no longer any respectable way of unhorsing the Democrats, and that only McCarthy's wild and conscienceless politics could do the job." [6] A plentiful reinforcement came from the eccentrics and ignoramuses who always rally to a Father Coughlin or Huey Long.

What most distressed Lehman was not this wide and varied popular response to McCarthy but the large number of public men who, while clearly realizing that he was a dangerous brawler, still showed a timid submissiveness to his acts. They became neutralists when they saw him tossing his stink bombs and knifing Tydings and Benton. Lehman was particularly disgusted by the jellyfish Senators. These men knew that Joe would readily concoct some malignant lie about them, as he lied about Tydings and Benton, and that he would flee from his first lie only to take refuge in another even worse. The lies might even be as bad as his statement in the Senate about General George Marshall: "He would sell his grandmother for any advantage." They knew that McCarthy could raise such a cloud of smoke that many would accept the myth that some fire must lie beneath it. "Nearly all the Senators," said

Lehman later, "did not lift a finger for two or three years." When they did, it was on an issue not of the national interest but of senatorial dignity.[7]

It can be said, of course, that in the first phase of the McCarthy onslaught, 1950–52, before Republican control of the Senate gave him his heaviest battle-ax in the chairmanship of an investigatory committee, his opponents in the chamber could be excused for a slow comprehension of the threat he offered. To some he seemed simply another of the long line of blatherskite Senators, as irresponsible as Cole Blease or Tom Heflin, who would run a brief noisy course and be heard no more. To others his exploitation of the issue of subversives in government called for careful appraisal before action was taken. It was true that Harry Dexter White, Alger Hiss, Lauchlin Currie, and John Abt had held responsible posts in government, that the Martin Dies Committee, though never catching a single dangerous subversive, had turned up some unpleasant facts, and that Truman's own Attorney General had listed eighty-two subversive organizations. Still other Senators had the feeling, later voiced by President Eisenhower, that dignity forbade them to wrestle in the gutter with McCarthy. He was unquestionably in the gutter when he denounced the "idiocy" of Truman, the "deceit" of Acheson, and the "black infamy" of Marshall. These attitudes help explain the fact that even Paul Douglas, with the most cultivated mind and one of the stiffest backbones in the Senate, went through the last Truman years without approaching the problem of McCarthy.

Texas oil men and other business adventurers, as Richard Rovere remarks, liked the Senator's snarling wildcat truculence, and wrote generous checks for his campaign. As late as January, 1954, when the worst facts about him were available, the Gallup Poll showed that half the American people took a "generally favorable" view of him.[8]

· I ·

Lehman read with indignant incredulity the February statement with which McCarthy startled a body of innocent West Virginia clubwomen: "I have here in my hand a list of 205 that were known to the Secretary of State as being members of the Communist Party and who nevertheless are still working and shaping policy at the State Department." His indignation did not diminish when at Salt Lake City a few days later McCarthy watered down his State Department list to "fifty-seven card-carrying Communists." With other Senators, he was ready to call Joe to sharp account on February 20, 1950, when McCarthy was back to try to justify his charges. On that date the Wisconsin Senator announced that he was ready to document eighty-one instances of loyalty risks: Communists, sex deviates, fellow travelers, and other moral lepers. He waved papers.

For six hours that afternoon McCarthy was the center of an angry hullaballoo in the Senate.[9] Democratic leader Scott Lucas and two others, Brien McMahon and Lehman, faced him with demands for names, dates, and factual proof. McCarthy, who had covered two desks with documents which he pawed about aimlessly, responded with blind numbers—Case No. 3, Case No. 61, and so on—saying that Secretary Acheson had the names identified by the numbers. This was a characteristic piece of dust-throwing. It soon turned out that nearly half of the eighty-one were not in the State Department at all; they were in other departments, private employ, or places unknown. Of case No. 12, McCarthy said, "where he is as of today, I frankly do not know." Eventually it also turned out that McCarthy's list of eighty-one had been taken from State Department screening files relating to the discharge of excess employees in the postwar period, augmented by the names of some men who had left the department in 1948 or earlier. These files the House Appropriations Committee had investigated two years earlier, without result.[10]

In short, McCarthy had uncovered not only a mare's nest but a very stale and empty mare's nest at that.

Though Scott Lucas and McMahon were McCarthy's most pertinacious inquisitors, Lehman also thrust at the weak joints in his armor. Lucas interrupted McCarthy's singularly opaque exposition sixty-one times, McMahon thirty-four times, and Lehman thirteen times. When Lehman reminded him that he should submit all names and incriminating facts to the Secretary of State, Joe replied waspishly: "If the Senator will but sit down and let me make my report to the Senate, he will have all the information he wants. The Senator from Wisconsin does not need any advice on his duty as a Senator, in this respect." When Lehman demanded that he tell his story in clear language, McCarthy responded: "I am afraid if it is not clear to the Senator now, I shall never be able to make it clear to him, no matter how much further explanation I make." [11] As Lucas moved an adjournment, fog still enveloped the Senate chamber.

By immediately introducing a resolution for an investigation of the State Department by the Foreign Relations Committee, Lucas put a subcommittee under Tydings on McCarthy's trail. This was the more important because several Republican Senators, notably Carl Mundt of South Dakota, Herman Welker of Idaho, and Owen Brewster of Maine, had given McCarthy aid and comfort by assertions that the Truman Administration was soft on treason.

Tydings was an excellent choice; a man of education, experience, and probity, holding a place in the Senate's inner circle, and enjoying high public prestige. Lehman and Morse strengthened the investigation by an amendment requiring that before the committee lodged formal charges of disloyalty against any person, it must give him an open hearing.[12] The Tydings Committee, a large group which included McCarthy, set to work at once, and by mid-July, 1950, had accumulated about 2,500 pages of testimony and documentation. But it gathered no facts about Communism in the State Department, for neither McCarthy nor anybody else had facts to contribute. "I am not in a position to file any formal charges," McCarthy told the committee.

What Joe did offer was loose accusations. One target of his random arrows was Dorothy Kenyon, a respected graduate of Smith College, former city magistrate in New York, and member of the League of Nations Committee on the Legal Status of Women, who had no connection with the State Department. Another target was Harlow Shapley of Harvard, and still another Frederick L. Schuman of Williams College—both innocent of State Department ties and innocent of any impropriety whatever. Joe was shifting his ground. He shifted it so far that on March 30, speaking in the Senate, he assailed Owen Lattimore of Johns Hopkins University, one-time adviser to Chiang Kai-shek and companion of Henry Wallace on Wallace's tour of parts of Eastern Siberia and China in 1944; John S. Service, who had been a political officer on the staff of "Vinegar Joe" Stilwell in the Far East; and Philip Jessup of Columbia, ambassador-at-large to the United Nations.[13]

The advantages of speaking in the Senate were two. McCarthy was immune there from libel suits, and in its easy atmosphere, surrounded by political colleagues, he could more easily avoid pointed questions than in the committee room. It might seem possible to pin down his preposterous assertions, wrote one reporter, "but no, McCarthy is as hard to catch as a mist—a mist that carries lethal contagion."

Lehman was happy to place Miss Kenyon's conclusive defense in the *Congressional Record*. He was still happier to deliver a resounding defense of Jessup, who really needed no defense. But it was in dealing with the charge that Lattimore was "the top Russian espionage agent" in America, and "Alger Hiss's boss in the espionage ring in the State Department," that Lehman came into one of his sharpest personal collisions with McCarthy.

Brandishing one of his eternal and usually bogus sheets of paper, McCarthy described it as a photostat of a letter by Owen Lattimore to his superior in the Office of War Information, dated June 15, 1943, and marked "secret," which recommended that the OWI hire men loyal to the Communist cause in China. Senator Charles W. Tobey of New Hampshire demanded why McCarthy did not print it in the *Congressional Record*. Because, said McCarthy, a secret letter ought not to go into that public repository. The mystified Tobey then asked why, if it was so secret, McCarthy was revealing its contents on the Senate floor. Joe evaded this query by saying that if any Senator wished to read the entire letter, with accompanying affidavits respecting the unusual personal habits of certain persons, he would be glad to let him do so. This was too much for Lehman, who cut in sharply: [14]

"May the junior Senator from New York," he said, "ask the Senator from Wisconsin whether he has made available to the Subcommittee on Foreign Relations of the Senate the information and the facts contained in his charges, a part of which, and only a part, is submitted here today?" McCarthy could only say: "The answer is No."

Lehman instantly pointed out that if McCarthy placed the letter and his charge before the Tydings Committee, Lattimore could reply before that same body; by bringing his accusation in the Senate Joe shielded himself from both reply and libel action. "In the way the Senator from Wisconsin has chosen, an accused man has no chance to answer."

McCarthy grew red. He deplored crocodile tears, he said, for the traitors who had sold four hundred million Chinese into slavery. "I shall proceed, regardless of what the Senator from New York thinks or says, to develop these facts in detail before the American people." Then, retorted Lehman, if you are so anxious to take the charges to the people, why do you refuse Senator Tobey's request for the full text of Lattimore's letter?

Still redder, McCarthy bristled. Clutching a sheaf of papers in his hand and raising his voice, he asked Lehman to step over to his desk to examine part of a document whose full contents must in all propriety be kept secret. "Does the Senator care to step over?" he shouted.

Amid a burst of laughter from the galleries, and a bustle of excitement on the floor, Lehman crossed the aisle and faced McCarthy at arm's length. "May I see the letter?" he asked, extending his hand for it.

"The Senator may step to my desk and read the letter," McCarthy returned.

"The Senator invited me to come over and read the letter," rasped Lehman, now thoroughly incensed. "I am here to read the letter. Will the Senator from Wisconsin let me see the letter?"

"Does the Senator wish to come close enough to read it?"

Lehman was angrily immobile. He understood McCarthy's tactics. Joe would let him read two lines on the sheet and snatch it away, saying "That's enough!" and giving onlookers the impression that he held a genuinely damaging document. Actually the Lattimore letter he held was harmless. It contained nothing whatever injurious to the writer. "I would like to read the letter in my own way," Lehman said.

"Will the Senator come here and see it?"

"I want to read it in my own way."

McCarthy smote his desk, booming, "Will the Senator sit down?" And as Lehman appealed to Senator Elmer Thomas of Oklahoma, president pro tem, McCarthy vociferated, "I do not yield further at this time." He had invented shocking statements and attributed them to Lattimore, a fact which became clear when a true copy of the letter was published. Then he had brazened out his deception.[15] Fortunately, Lattimore, a mild-mannered little man with a sharp tongue, proved amply able to defend himself, though he had a good deal more to defend than was at first supposed.

The report of the Tydings Committee, or rather its Democratic majority, submitted to the Senate in July, 1950, denied any Communist infiltration into the State Department, asserted that the FBI was capable of discharging its responsibilities then and in the future, and rebuked McCarthy for unsubstantiated allegations. The idea of a "spy ring" in the Department it pronounced preposterous. The attacks upon Jessup were "completely unfounded and unjustified"; Lattimore was neither the "architect of our Far Eastern policy" nor a Russian spy; Service, though guilty of error in supplying classified information to the magazine *Amerasia*, was "an otherwise competent and loyal employee." Joe simply sharpened his knives for Tydings; and his colleague Jenner of Indiana denounced the Maryland Senator for "the most scandalous and brazen whitewash of treasonable conspiracy in our history."

The able majority report should have destroyed McCarthy, but partisanship prevented this. Henry Cabot Lodge of Massachusetts attacked it, and Bourke Hickenlooper of Iowa rejected it. McCarthy, terming it a green light for Communists, pressed on unscathed. Many Republicans thirsted to avenge the defeat of Dewey in 1948, and were ready to use any issue to gain victory in 1952. Later this year Senator Ives drew up a resolution asking for Acheson's resignation, chiefly on grounds of his Asiatic policy, and the Republican caucus in both houses endorsed it. Lehman felt outraged. Such a pronouncement was certain to dismay the Western democracies, he said in a special press release. "As for our enemies, the attack on Secretary Acheson and on American foreign policy has played directly into the hands of the

Communists, who have so long regarded the Secretary of State as the chief spokesman of . . . policies which block the Kremlin's aim to enslave the free world." [16]

· II ·

After the defeat of Tydings in the fall of 1950 by some of the most indecent methods ever used in an American election (and Scott Lucas went down at the same time), leadership of the forces against McCarthy passed to a member almost as new as Lehman and much younger, William Benton. Though McCarthy called him "a mental midget," he was one of the most brilliant men in the chamber. A Minnesotan by birth, educated at Carleton College and Yale, founder of the advertising firm of Benton & Bowles, he had been vice-president of the University of Chicago and in 1945–47 Assistant Secretary of State. He had entered the Senate on December 17, 1949. On August 6, 1951, exasperated by McCarthy's unchecked pillaging of the reputations of innocent men, he introduced a resolution for the Senator's impeachment. His boldness startled fellow Senators, for Connecticut was full of the same kind of voters who had responded in Maryland to McCarthy's attack on Tydings.

The resolution was supported by a bill of particulars, reciting that McCarthy had accepted $10,000 from the Lustron Corporation, makers of prefabricated housing, to influence housing legislation; that he had tried to hoax the Senate with charges of treason against General Marshall; that he had perjured himself before the Tydings Committee and had hired another man charged with perjury; that he had practiced fraud and deceit in the Maryland election; and so on. It was all true, but Senators handled the resolution like a cupful of red-hot rivets. Finally a subcommittee under Guy M. Gillette of Iowa reluctantly but firmly inquired into Benton's list of particulars.

McCarthy's instant attack on the Gillette Committee brought into public view the fact that a number of Republican Senators, including Margaret Chase Smith of Maine and Robert Hendrickson of New Jersey, were as much repelled by his methods as the Democrats. McCarthy chose a new target in the chief counsel of the Senate Rules Committee, the much-esteemed Darrell St. Claire. One member after another came to the rescue of St. Claire, and the jurisdiction of Gillette's subcommittee was upheld 60 to 0—McCarthy not voting. The debate had given Humphrey an opportunity to restate his views with emphasis, and Lehman spoke with equal vigor: [17]

> I have been shocked, as have many other members of this body
> and of the public, by attacks on individuals constituting character

assassination, by charges unfounded, ungrounded, unproved. In the past two years a policy of indicting by smear has been indulged in, and the victim has no opportunity whatsoever to defend himself. There has been a policy of trying to prove guilt by association, not only of persons, but of ideas. . . . I do not think this is a time for the Senate of the United States to pussyfoot on a matter of as tremendous importance as that which we are discussing. . . . We are still being beset by the prevalence of distrust, suspicion, and accusations of subversion, disloyalty, and treason without foundation and without justification.

The Gillette inquiry, dragging into 1952, gave McCarthy fresh opportunity for his methods of delay, evasion, and diversionary adventure. He instigated an inquiry into an absurd set of his own charges against Benton. In the end the proposed impeachment came to nothing, though it helped lay a groundwork for future action against McCarthy. Benton's action was premature and, however much justified, impossible to sustain by votes. Two other men succeeded Gillette as head of the Subcommittee on Privileges and Elections, to use its official name. After stumbling through a maze of McCarthy's financial records, in which the Lustron check for $10,000 was only part of mysteriously large bank deposits, the committeemen, never issuing a single subpoena, reached an inconclusive result. They merely asked, in their final report, whether McCarthy "used close associates and members of your family to secrete receipts, income, commodity and stock speculation, and other financial transactions for ulterior motives." Jenner, as eventual chairman, saw to it that even this hazy document became as rare as a First Folio.

As 1952 opened, Lehman pointed out in a speech to the Women's National Democratic Club in Washington that McCarthyism was certain to play a part in the national elections.[18] He reiterated the fact in a six-point list of issues which he drew up for the press a few days later. His final and most important point stated the necessity of "proving by our every act, as a government and as private citizens, that we know that the boundaries of civil rights and civil liberties can never be withdrawn, but must always be expanded if we are to remain a dynamic democracy." [19]

Much credit could be given Eisenhower in the 1952 campaign and later for his firm maintenance of an internationalist position and the main social gains of recent years. Unfortunately, Republican leadership in the campaign furnished McCarthyism renewed impetus and higher standing. Eisenhower himself, under party prodding, deleted from a Wisconsin speech some sentences of warm praise for his old chief, patron, and friend, General Marshall. He allowed McCarthy to travel on his campaign train. In the Chicago Convention, Chairman Walter Hallanan set off a wild demonstration by introducing McCarthy as a fighting marine who was being maligned for his work in "exposing the traitors in our government." (It is a well-verified fact that McCarthy never exposed a single governmental traitor.) No less a person than Henry Cabot Lodge issued a statement urging McCarthy's reëlection. "I would not have expected this from Senator Lodge," Lehman told the newspapers, "who joined with six other Senators only a short while ago in condemning the tactics of Senator McCarthy. The cause of civil liberties is not just another issue. It is a central issue of our national life. Taking sides with or against Senator McCarthy is a choice for or against the basic decencies of public life and the protection of our fundamental freedoms."

During the summer Lehman seized every opportunity to speak up. Just before election day he made a Western trip for Stevenson. He told an audience in Detroit on October 25 that McCarthy and his abettors were destroying confidence in the whole government just to drive the Democrats from power: "It is really burning the barn down on the pretext of chasing rats." [20] And he told a Chicago audience the following night that McCarthy used the trappings of Americanism to achieve the goals of totalitarianism—that its aims and those of the Communists had essential similarity. In the general Republican sweep, McCarthy was reëlected by a small vote, carrying Wisconsin 870,444 to 731,402, while Eisenhower carried it 979,444 to 622,175. Joe was in fact the bottom man on the party ticket, but he was back in the Senate for another six years.

Once Eisenhower was in the White House, and the Republicans held a sufficient majority to organize the Senate, McCarthy's power was ominously widened; for Senator Taft allowed him to become chairman of the Government Operations Committee and the Permanent Subcommittee on Investigations attached to it. More than ever he was able to disrupt orderly processes of administration and terrorize any agency he chose to single out. He soon created, indeed, a little government of his own. "I would like to notify the million Federal employes," he announced, "that it is their duty to give us the information they have about graft, corruption, Communism, and treason, and that there is no loyalty to a superior officer that can tower above their loyalty to their country." Every Federal worker was to become an informer! McCarthy's office, Room 402 Senate Office Building, would become a central repository for every dirty rumor, every unfounded suspicion, every piece of personal malice, and, what was worse, every government secret that busybodies could carry there. File clerks, troublemakers, and amateur Paul Prys were beating a trail to the office or pouring letters into its mail slot.

Under Acheson the State Department had resisted McCarthyism, but under John Foster Dulles it made perilous concessions. The Senator soon induced it to install his friend W. Scott McLeod as head of departmental personnel and security, passing on appointments and hunting for homosexuals and subversionists. The Department of Justice under Herbert Brownell, Jr., who had done much to manage Eisenhower's campaigns for nomination and election, made equally unfortunate concessions and permitted use of FBI files for partisan purposes. Early in 1954—little more than a year after Eisenhower took office—Walter Lippmann explained the surrender of high Administration officers, including Brownell, to McCarthyism, by their sense of political insecurity. "Their line is designed as protection against the exploitation by McCarthy of a political setback in November. If the election goes better than they now fear, they will still be in the saddle though considerably bedraggled in appearance. If the election goes badly, they hope—though almost certainly in vain—to make McCarthy share the blame and not to be able to raise hell at their expense."

One early symptom of Administration flabbiness in dealing with McCarthy was the adoption of a security program defined by Executive Order 10450, April 27, 1953, relevant to a determination of disloyalty; it laid down six categories of evidence, four of them clear and precise as to overt acts against national safety, two of them hazily disputable. In the following October, the White House announced that during the first four months of the program, 1,456 persons had been dropped from Federal service, 863 having been dismissed and 593 having resigned when told they were the subjects of unfavorable reports. All but five of the 1,456 had been inherited from the Truman Administrations. This Administration figure for persons dropped, which was later raised to 2,200, inspired a long and heated debate over the "numbers game." Eisenhower himself stated publicly that it was wrong to assume that a man dismissed as a security risk was a Communist—and many were of course dismissed for reasons unrelated to security. While Brownell, Postmaster General Arthur E. Summerfield, and others lumped all the persons dropped together as disloyalists, Democrats declared the figures a meaningless hoax.

Lehman proposed an amendment to the Hatch Act forbidding political activities by security officers like Scott McLeod and others who tossed about the 2,200 total. Of course this was blocked. He, like Humphrey, Douglas, Mansfield, and others, demanded that the Administration give a breakdown of the total which would make it comprehensible. Here too they made no progress. But he did meet some success in publicizing nationally such articles as that of James Reston in the *New York Times* of January 28, 1954, deploring government tactics which elevated the misfortune of drunkenness to the level of the crime of treason. He was delighted to put into the *Congressional Record* a column by Joseph and Stewart Alsop in the *Washington Post* summarizing the testimony which Scott McLeod himself gave upon the "purging" of the State Department. According to McLeod's reluctant evidence before a Congressional committee, he had been able in a year of effort to cause just 11 persons to be taken from the payroll, not as Communists or subversives, but for loyalty reasons. Of these 11 cases, 7 had been initiated under Acheson. Thus McLeod's personal score stood: Communists abolished, 0; suspected dangerous thinkers smoked out, 4. The Alsops added a telling paragraph on the kind of personal tragedies involved. They wrote:

"What McLeod regards as grounds for dismissal or suspension should also be noted in this connection. A woman employee in the State Department had a great wartime misfortune. She was floating, so to speak, in the stenographic pool of the Board of Economic Warfare, when Nathan Gregory Silvermaster sent down an order for a secretary for his office. There is no proof that her assignment from the stenographic pool in Silvermaster's office, where she worked only briefly, was anything but an accident of government routine. Yet on this ground she is now charged as a loyalty risk and suspended. Unlike others, she has chosen to fight the charge."

When early in his second year President Eisenhower nominated Charles E. Bohlen to be ambassador to Russia, people who knew the nominee's experience and ability were gratified. But haters of recent Democratic leaders responded angrily, for Bohlen, versed in the Russian language and ways, had accompanied FDR to the Yalta Conference in 1945 and had gone with Truman to the Potsdam Conference. Moreover, he was identified with the bipartisan approach to foreign affairs cultivated under both Presidents. The McCarthyites shotted their guns. Pat McCarran announced to the Senate on March 20, 1953, that on the basis of information from the FBI, Scott McLeod had been "unable to clear" Bohlen but had been "summarily overridden" by Secretary Dulles. The Secretary responded that this was not so— he had been cleared; and when Senators Taft and Sparkman examined a summary FBI file on Bohlen, they agreed that his record was of sterling merit. Still McCarthy and his group insisted that the man was too dangerous to confirm.

At this Lehman's ire became irrepressible. He rose for a wrathful extempore speech. "Mr. President, I had not expected to speak tonight," he cried, advancing down the aisle. "But as I listened to the debate this afternoon, all the indignation which has been building up within me during the past weeks and months came out. What is happening today is incredible! But it it only a part of what has been happening for many months. From the halls of Congress a poison has been spreading throughout our land." He pushed farther down the aisle, shaking his finger in McCarthy's face. "Mr. President, what has been attempted in the case of Mr. Bohlen is merely a pattern—the same pattern that has been followed against many other loyal, devoted, honest Americans. Some were assaulted because they stood for progressive government . . . some others because they were convenient victims who could not fight back . . . still others because they . . . had the courage to fight for civil rights and the civil liberties guaranteed by the Constitution." He and McCarthy seemed about to come to blows. Smear and attack, he declared, were used "to fill men with fear."

Taft showed something not unlike fear when he helped secure Bohlen's confirmation, 74 to 13, only with the understanding, as R. J. Donovan writes in his report on *Eisenhower: The Inside Story,* that there would be "no more Bohlens." [21]

Lehman submitted to the Senate proposals for fairer rules of procedure by its investigative committees. The Rules Committee failed to recommend action on these proposals. He continued to press his demands for greater fairness and strict obedience to the Constitution, however, particularly in the case of Corliss Lamont, a man whom he did not know and of whose opinions he largely disapproved. Lamont, called before McCarthy's Permanent Investigating Subcommittee in September, 1953, denied that he was ever a member of the Communist Party and then refused to answer questions about his private associations and writings, citing the First Amendment as justification. When McCarthy asked the Senate to haul up Dr. Lamont for contempt, Lehman and Langer of North Dakota delivered eloquent challenges of his subcommittee. "I say to the Senator from Wisconsin," vociferated Langer in the best tradition of Western radicalism, "that if ever I was fighting for an underdog in my life, I am fighting for him now." Both men upheld Lamont's right to challenge the jurisdiction of the subcommittee. The Senate overrode them and approved of the contempt resolution by a vote of 71 to 3. But long afterward, when the case was carried into the Federal District Court of Southern New York, Lehman had the satisfaction of reading Judge Weinfeld's decision (July 27, 1955), that the McCarthy Subcommittee *had* exceeded its authority and that Lamont could not be required to answer its questions.[22]

The importance of Lehman's struggle against McCarthyism lay not in any single dramatic episode, though angry exchanges between the two were numerous. One of the hottest affrays took place when McCarthy accused the New Yorker of an abuse of the franking privilege in scattering broadcast copies of his exposure entitled "Creeping McCarthyism." Several times onlookers feared that verbal blows would lead to physical blows, and Paul Douglas once put himself in a strategic position to intervene. "I moved up to protect Herbert," he said (he was seven or eight inches taller than Lehman and powerfully built). Nor did the weight of Lehman's participation lie in such salient displays of leadership as Millard Tydings gave in his rough overhaul of McCarthy's first lies, or William Benton presented in forcing McCarthy to bring a libel suit which he was later glad to drop like a hot potato, or as the reluctant Gillette offered in his investigation. Nobody knocked McCarthy out cold until he did it himself. Either of two men could probably have done it by one well-aimed blow, President Eisenhower and J. Edgar Hoover; but neither tried.

The importance of Lehman's work in undermining and discrediting McCarthy lay in another area. It lay in the promptness with which he sprang forward in 1950 to make McCarthy substantiate or retract his reckless assertions; in the skill with which he exposed some of McCarthy's specific falsehoods; in the courage and tenacity with which he defended the men that McCarthy pilloried—George Marshall, Charles Bohlen, Philip C. Jessup, John Carter Vincent, John Paton Davies; in his willingness to uphold Corliss Lamont's invocation of the First Amendment when even Douglas drew back; and above all, in the assiduity with which he kept up, month after month, year after year, his incessant drumfire upon McCarthy and McCarthyism.

This bombardment of exposure and attack never ceased, never slackened. The radio, television, the Senate floor, the dinners and meetings of a hundred organizations, the newspapers and magazines, all became vehicles for Lehman's artillery. If he was not heard in one quarter he tried another. His eloquence and vigor grew, and the impression he made steadily widened and deepened.

Down the months and years his denunciation continued. He told the Metropolitan Conference of Temple Brotherhoods at Temple Emanu-El on April 9, 1950, that the greatest enemy of the people was fear. "There is a growing danger that our leaders and our neighbors will be impeded in their judgments and their actions . . . by the fear of recrimination and reprisal by the hysterical headline-hunters of today." He told the Democratic National Committee at their Waldorf dinner on December 12, 1950, that national unity was a necessity in the new age of peril. "It cannot be achieved by insisting on the sacrifice of this official or that official on the public block of unjust and undeserved attack." He told the Columbia Broadcasting System audience on the Capitol Cloakroom Program October 5, 1951, that McCarthy's tactics were "abhorrent"; that they constituted "character assassination, which is indefensible"; and that "they are indictments by smear against which the victim has no chance to defend himself." He assured the annual convention of the American Federation of Labor in New York on September 18, 1952, that they should feel a special scorn for cheap politicians who excused the evil acts of the McCarthyites as products of an excess of zeal in a good cause. "These political cynics are not much better than the McCarthyites themselves."

Now and then he blew an encouraging note. "The plant of liberty is too deeply rooted in the soil of America," he said at the dinner of the Washington Committee for Brandeis University on June 17, 1953, "to be torn out by the present violence." His ten-point indictment of McCarthyism at the Jefferson–Jackson Day dinner in Milwaukee on June 20 that year attracted much attention. It was only necessary, however, he repeated, to conquer fear. "This fear has been whipped up by the unscrupulous elements in our country into a hysteria, into a panic on whose wings McCarthy and his followers hope to ride to national power." But he never slackened his attacks. At the dinner of the American Association for Jewish Education on December 12, 1953, he denounced the "unscrupulous sophistry . . . creeping over our land." When he received the John Dewey Award from the New York Teachers Guild on March 6, 1954, he repeated the same message. He issued a special press release hailing the condemnation of McCarthy by Bishop Shiel of the Roman Catholic Church (April 10, 1954), a condemnation of special bravery in view of widespread Catholic support of the Senator. His radio report of May 12, 1956, his speech on November 24, 1956, to the Anti-Defamation League Freedom Forum in Washington, and almost countless other public utterances bore an identical burden.

Little by little at first, then more tellingly and decisively, the bombardment blew great gaps in the defenses of McCarthyism.

• III •

It was plain by the spring of 1954 that in dealing with McCarthy there would be no Jack the Giant Killer; no single champion would strike him down and perhaps not even any group of champions. In the language of Wisconsin he continued to ride high, wide, and handsome. He somehow came unscathed through every storm he raised. When he denounced the appointment of President James B. Conant of Harvard as High Commissioner to Germany, and when he accused Secretary Dulles of "untrue statements," the Administration folded its arms. He assailed the United States Information Agency in the spring of 1953, asserting that its foreign libraries contained thirty to forty thousand books by Communists and fellow travelers; but when the head of the USIA, Robert Johnson, tried to get the President to intervene, the White House replied that Eisenhower was too solidly engaged for weeks ahead to make a speech. Some books were burned.

Nobody in the government took effective measures to check McCarthy when that same spring he sent two of the most ridiculous agents this country has ever spawned, Roy M. Cohn and G. David Schine, on a whirlwind eighteen-day tour of Western Europe, where they made the United States a laughing stock and did untold harm to its foreign service. Scores of useful members of that service were ready to resign in disgust. At least a hundred, states one authority, had their resignations written out and ready to mail when the pair turned home. Yet the State Department made no effort to defend its operations. It got rid of Theodore Kaghan, an officer attached to the High Commission for Germany, whose offense was apparently that he had once roomed with a Communist and had called Cohn and Schine "junketeering gumshoes"; it meekly dispensed with several other men. Lehman voiced such bitter anger over the Cohn-Schine antics that he had to carry on a searing correspondence with Cohn's father in New York. Nor did the White House or any department evince any resentment of the fact that by 1954 McCarthy was receiving a steady flow of clandestine information, some of it classified, from his own network of spies and stool pigeons within the government.

The President might have been Jack the Giant Killer, and a Theodore Roosevelt would joyously have seized that role. An Attorney General with the resolute traits of Edwin M. Stanton, Richard Olney, or Frank Murphy might have played the part or might at least have crippled McCarthyism. William Benton and Millard Tydings, trying to strike down McCarthy, failed completely; even when Benton prodded him into a $2,000,000 libel action, he wriggled out of a courtroom battle. Brien McMahon, Hubert Humphrey, and Herbert Lehman would each have gladly been Jack the Giant Killer, but found the task beyond their powers. The New York Senator did have one profound satisfaction in the spring of 1954, that of seeing the President order the departments to adopt the principles of fair action that Lehman had vainly urged upon the Senate. Eisenhower, to his great credit, on March 5 issued a memorandum to all members of the Cabinet on treatment of governmental personnel, in which he laid down three rules to govern the preservation of security. First, fairness, justice, and decency must characterize all personnel procedures, for "we cannot defeat Communism by destroying Americanism"; second, each superior must remember his obligation to protect his subordinates, through all legal and proper means, "against attacks of a character under which they might otherwise be help-less"; and third, no hope of political advantage and "no threat from any source" should lead anyone to forsake these principles. It was too bad that he had not issued this statement a year earlier and followed it up by fighting action.

However hopeless the task of giant-killing, Lehman never ceased fight-ing. On June 17, 1954, he offered a resolution for the removal of McCarthy from his committee chairmanships. This was on the ground that he had meddled unjustifiably in the affairs of the executive branch, including the State Department and the Department of the Army; that he had arrogated to himself law-enforcement powers beyond the scope of members of the Senate; that he had similarly arrogated to himself and his committee judicial functions beyond his lawful authority; that he had publicly invited a whole-sale violation of the Espionage Act and the executive order forbidding dis-closure of classified information; that he had intimidated and harassed of-ficials of the government, including honored soldiers; that he had sought to intimidate the press; and that he had persistently and repeatedly violated the civil liberties guaranteed under the bill of rights of the constitution.

This resolution of course proved nugatory. It failed, as Lehman later told the Senate, because the majority leadership in the Senate prejudged it and sidetracked it. The Republican policy committee voted unanimously to table it or any other resolution aimed at the heart of the problem, the right of McCarthy "to continue to exercise the power and authority which he has so tragically abused and perverted, to the shame of the Senate and the disrepute of Congress and our country." Yet the Democrats too were culpable. They had widely circulated the cynical argument that McCarthy was a purely Re-publican problem, and many had accepted it. Lehman's frontal attack on McCarthy's misdeeds, like a similar frontal attack made by Senator Ralph Flanders in his original resolution, thus failed. And McCarthy steadily grew more reckless, more arrogant. On May 30 he spoke of the evidence of trea-son that had been growing up "over the past twenty" (here he paused and deliberately amended his statement) "twenty-one years." The Roosevelt, Truman, and Eisenhower Administrations were all full of treason!

In the end no Jack the Giant Killer was needed; the giant slew himself by his own excesses. McCarthy early in 1954 began an attack on the Army, asserting that he had found evidence of dangerous espionage in the Signal Corps at Fort Monmouth, where a body of scientists were working on de-fense problems of the highest importance. He once more began flinging personal accusations about; Robert Stevens, Secretary of the Army, suspended the men accused; and McCarthy was emboldened to attack General Ralph Zwicker as "a disgrace to the uniform" and a shielder of Communist conspirators. As the Army-McCarthy hearings went on television, with a Boston attorney named Joseph N. Welch magnificently conducting the defense, the whole nation watched. The Senator's ruthlessness, his disrespect for truth, his bullying temper, his cruelty to helpless witnesses, became plain to the dullest observer. When he took the stand to justify his accusations, and was sharply questioned by Welch, he placed himself above the law by refusing to disclose the names of his informants. The climax was reached on a June day when he tried wantonly to ruin the career of a young member of Welch's law firm by blurting out the fact that he had once belonged to the Lawyers' Guild, supposedly a Communist front.

"Until this moment, Senator," said Welch with trembling voice, "I think I never really gauged your cruelty or your recklessness. . . . I like to think I am a gentle man, but your forgiveness will have to come from someone other than me."

When the Army-McCarthy hearings came to an end on June 17, two facts were plain: that the McCarthy subcommittee was dead forever and that disciplinary action would have to be taken against McCarthy himself. The Senate might well have adopted the Lehman resolution, dealing with the really substantive misdeeds of the Wisconsin member. It might have adopted the Flanders resolution, censuring him for his contempt of the Senate, contempt for truth, and "habitual contempt of people." Instead, with a deplorable abdication of its responsibilities to the nation, it chose to act on far narrower grounds for a lesser object. On August 2, it voted 75 to 12 to create a select committee to consider whether charges justified adoption of the motion: "*Resolved*, that the conduct of the Senator from Wisconsin, Mr. McCarthy, is unbecoming a member of the United States Senate, is contrary to Senatorial traditions, and tends to bring the Senate into disrepute." It was not the outrages upon the Constitution, the country, and the most ancient English-speaking principles that counted; it was the outrages upon senatorial decorum.

It was therefore with mingled relief and disappointment that Lehman on September 27, 1954, read the unanimous report of Chairman Arthur Watkins's committee recommending censure and that more than two months later he joined in the Senate's vote, 67 to 22, condemning McCarthy's conduct. He was gratified to know that McCarthyism was banished—he hoped forever—from the national legislature and that McCarthy himself was reduced to a pitiable figure, treated with general contempt, and in fact ostracised. He was disappointed that the great chamber of Webster and Clay, Benton and Seward, Morrill and La Follette, should have taken such partial, circuitous, and essentially undignified measures against a leader who had thrown the government into confusion, lowered the standards of parliamentary action, menaced the liberties of countless citizens, and sullied the fame of the republic throughout the world.

Chapter XVIII

THE LONELY INDEPENDENT

THE struggle against McCarthyism was by no means waged in isolation from other issues of the day. It was closely related to a dozen other battle-grounds of Lehman and the liberal group and particularly three: immigration, internal security, and civil rights.

Immigration has always been a sensitive subject to the polyglot city of New York, which from colonial days sheltered all nationalities and faiths with a closer approach to impartiality than any other part of the country. As late as 1960 about half the people in each borough except the least populous, Staten Island, were foreign-born or children of the foreign-born. In the whole city the first or second generation Americans of Italian origin exceeded 850,000, or half another Rome. Two other great cities could have been made up of first and second generation Americans from the Austro-German and Slavic lands. Even those of Hungarian origin aggregated more than a hundred thousand. Although Ireland had sent a host and Great Britain more than 175,000, the city as a whole was peopled by the "new immigration." [1] These people were proud of their backgrounds; they would never admit that a Greek, Czech, or Pole was not as worthy as a Scot, German, or Dane. Countless citizens had relatives or friends in the "old country" whom they would be glad to see in America.

When Lehman entered the Senate the American population was under-going profound changes. The nation by 1950 counted about 150,000,000 people; ten years later the total had leaped to 180,000,000. While the death rate fell by one third, the birth rate rose by approximately one half. Young people married earlier and had larger families. The baby boom was in most respects gratifying, although predictions of 300,000,000 people by the end of the century alarmed many who could look that far ahead. A "population explosion" was taking place all over the world and was especially portentous in impoverished lands of Latin America, Africa, and Asia. The United States, whose birth rate exceeded that of any important country of Europe, could better take care of its swelling millions than most nations, but even it could not afford a rabbitlike procreation. While population rose, it shifted. Negroes, whose rate of increase paralleled that of the whites, moved from South to North in great numbers, while the shift from rural to urban areas continued unabated.

As population rose so astonishingly, immigration from the Old World became static or declined. Of the three millions who entered the country between the war and 1960, a great part came from Puerto Rico, and Canada. The days when a huge concourse from eastern and southern Europe poured through Ellis Island were ended; the immigration law of 1924, with its national origins basis, had changed all that. By 1960 ninety-five percent of the American population was native-born, and the war had weakened ethnic ties with Europe.[2] The ordinary citizen of Indiana, Alabama, and Oregon was inclined to hold that the needs for population growth were being met from home sources, and that a lifting of immigration restrictions was unimportant. Of course New Yorkers, with their closer European ties and consciousness of the desire of many of their own folk to flee the poverty of Southern Italy or the oppression of Poland, took a different view. Of course, too, many people everywhere felt that the national origins clause was unjust, was insulting to whole stocks, and for the good of the country should be repealed. Nevertheless, the general situation, including a lessening of European pressures, bred a certain indifference and even apathy.

On a long list of national issues differences in sectional or state interest meant an honest difference in senatorial opinion. An Iowa member might sincerely believe that the principle for America defined by Tocqueville and John Bright, one language, one stock, and one ideal over three million square miles, advised caution in the modification of the national origins plan. Lehman felt strongly on the subject of civil rights for the Negro. But if his friends Lister Hill and J. W. Fulbright wished to hold their very useful seats in the Senate they had to make some concessions to the conservative sentiment of Alabama and Arkansas; and for that matter, they might honestly hold opinions on the Negro's capacities and privileges different from his. The question whether the Hell's Canyon water power in Idaho should be developed by the nation or the Idaho Power Company bore one aspect to Lehman, who since 1933 had combated private power interests in New York. It bore another aspect in Idaho, which liked the company, preferred private enterprise on principle, and believed that the national government already controlled far too large a proportion of Idaho's grazing lands, timber, and other natural resources. A Capehart might honestly fear what Eisenhower called "creeping Socialism" when he saw the Rural Electrification Admin-istration building power plants, partly tax free, with government funds borrowed at two percent a year.

It was through the clash of honest opinion that the government ad-vanced to just conclusions.

Lehman was as independent as George Norris and Robert M. La Fol-lette before him, as unflinching in utterance of his opinions; and like Norris and La Follette he suffered loneliness in consequence. He sometimes seemed intolerant to his opponents, as they appeared intolerant to him. He was not —he was really open-minded on most subjects; but for three reasons he seemed so. He was very much a New Yorker. Though, as we have seen, he had traveled much in the South on business, had married a Californian, and had spent many vacations in the Far West, still to most people west of the Alleghenies, his experience of their parts of the country seemed limited. He was also so completely an independent that he refused to admit the utility of compromise; principle was principle and must not be weakened by expediency. He knew the philosophy of compromise as expounded by Burke, Mill, John Morley and Woodrow Wilson, but on essentials its prac-tice was repugnant to him. FDR often compromised; Humphrey and Neu-berger sometimes thought three quarters of a loaf better than no bread; Paul Douglas might settle for seven-eighths of the loaf. Scott Lucas, discuss-ing the attitude of certain southern and western Senators toward Lehman and his liberalism, said to William Benton: "They loathe him."

Undoubtedly his vehemence of language made him seem more extreme than he was. It was as natural to him as a Texas drawl was to Sam Rayburn. He felt as intensely on great issues as Charles Sumner had felt and spoke as fierily. He brought not only passion but sensitivity (he was always thin-skinned) and a temperamental emotionalism to his speeches. He agonized over reverses and criticism as he rejoiced over successes. Moreover, he never lost his before-noted conviction that debate could and should alter the de-cisions of Congress. Out of this conviction sprang his tendency at times to put a higher value on the clear opinion of other Senators than on the un-certain opinion of the people. As an orator, he lacked the grace, eloquence, and literary brilliance that made John W. Davis and Adlai E. Stevenson, for example, such captivating speakers; but in compensation he put an intense conviction, a burning zeal, into his arguments. His anger, when he faced what he thought a moral issue, poured out like red-hot lava, in language which, like La Follette's, sacrificed eloquence to force.

The issues of immigration, internal security, and civil rights certainly had plain moral aspects, and were certainly not viewed with temperance by Lehman. He saw one side only—and in some instances it is a question whether there *was* more than one side.

• I •

On immigration he was in part the voice of his special group and environment. He was the son of an immigrant, the ablest political representative of a powerful minority group, the spokesman of the most cosmopolitan city on the globe. In part, he was also the voice of an old American principle: the principle that a free, open, and egalitarian society should give a free, open, and equal welcome to all stocks and faiths—to what Lincoln called the whole family of man. Not that he believed in unlimited immigration; before long he fixed a roof of 250,000 entrants a year over his proposed structure. But he did maintain that limited immigration should rest not on national pedigrees but on human worth and need, with sympathetic attention to the social strains of badly overcrowded lands.

More than two years before Lehman entered the Senate, Congress had turned its attention to immigration policy. One product of its labors was a law of 1948 providing that 205,000 refugees might be admitted by special dispensation before June 30, 1950, the number subsequently being raised to 341,000, while the time limit was extended to the end of 1951. Especially for the Eightieth Congress, this was commendable. But the outcome of an effort at a codification of all the existing legislation on immigration and naturalization, with new features, was less fortunate. A sweeping and intricate measure emerged in 1950, which Pat McCarran introduced in the Senate and Francis E. Walter in the House; twice modified, it took its final form early in 1952 —one of the most important and unfortunate bills of the time.

This legislation was framed and passed while the anti-Communist game was being played by politicians with unquenchable gusto; while many people associated immigrants with such highly untypical people as the Rosenbergs; while the anti-Semites, Russophobes, Germanophobes, and Anglophobes were in the ascendent; and while other forms of prejudice masqueraded as patriotism. It had to be passed while much of labor was hostile to immigration as likely to introduce undesirable competition, dilute standards of skill, and weaken fidelity to unions. It went through while many Protestants were apprehensive of too much Catholic immigration and many old-stock citizens of too many Jews. It found support in a lingering unhappy memory of the time in the First World War when unassimilated agglomerations of the foreign-born had given the country a real problem of hyphenates—residents of divided loyalty. McCarran and Walter seemed to personify these varied suspicions and antipathies.

The final McCarran-Walter bill as introduced on January 29, 1952, retained the national origins quota system based on the 1920 census and fixed the maximum permissible immigration at 154,000 a year. No quota left unused by one country could be credited to another. All refugees admitted under the recent legislation were to be charged against future quotas of the lands from which they came. By ingenious roundabout provisions, the British, French, and Dutch West Indies, and the countries of the Asia-Pacific Triangle (India, China, Japan), were limited to a hundred visas a year apiece. Inside each quota certain preferences were established; a first preference of one half each quota to persons whose high education, technical training, specialized experience, or exceptional ability would benefit the United States; a second preference to parents of American citizens, and a final preference to spouses and children of aliens admitted for permanent residence. Not only was any Communist or other subversive debarred but anyone who had joined the direct predecessor or successor of a totalitarian organization. In brief, the measure might better have been called an anti-immigration bill than an immigration bill. The apparent motivation of its harsh restrictions was a belief that any foreigner was dangerous, and its aim was to exclude from the country all but a thin trickle of old-stock folk.[3]

The bill also established some 700 separate grounds for the denial of a visa or entry papers and gave our consuls broad powers to clap the gates shut. Any consul who suspected that an alien might become dangerous after entry had the power of exclusion. Some surly provisions upon deportation and the revocation of citizenship papers added to the rigors of the measure.

This was altogether too much for the liberal group in the Senate to stomach. Under the leadership of Lehman and Humphrey, actively abetted by William Benton and Brien McMahon, they took emergency steps in 1951–52 to write their own omnibus bill on immigration and naturalization. Lehman's large staff under Julius C. C. Edelstein was particularly valuable in the research required. Paul Douglas and his brilliant legislative assistant Robert Wallace lent a hand. Everyone concerned long remembered the grueling toil continued through endless hours. They also remembered the sense of despair which attended the labor, for they knew that McCarran would use his Judiciary Committee to block them; but they took comfort in the approbation of many church, civic, and educational organizations. They could at least raise a standard.

In its perfected form, for it took improved shape in 1953, this Lehman-

Humphrey standard proposed policies to which intelligent men could well rally. It provided for total annual admissions equal to one-sixth of one percent of the population of the United States in the latest decennial census—that is, about 250,000 at first—discontinuing the free admission of natives of the western hemisphere. Quotas would be based not on national origins but more rational tests. They would include family unification, on which ground as many as 35 percent of the whole quota might be admitted; occupational skills; pleas for asylum from persecution; consideration of the needs of friendly overcrowded nations; and the special merit of persons not able to qualify under the first four listings. In place of the second-class citizenship which the McCarran-Walter bill gave naturalized aliens, who might be thrown out of the country on various doubtful grounds during the first ten years, the Lehman-Humphrey bill gave them secure status. And instead of placing arbitrary administrative action in visa and deportation cases above question, as the McCarran-Walter measure did, the Lehman-Humphrey bill made the board of immigration appeals a strong statutory body and called for a visa review in the State Department as well.

All in vain! McCarran marshaled a Senate majority of Cossack ruthlessness. When Lehman asked the Democratic policy committee and Senate Leader McFarland for public hearings on his bill, he was rebuffed. Senate debate on the McCarran measure began May 13, 1952, with its author in his usual arrogant mood. He declared that while his bill was being formulated more than 6,800 pages of testimony had been taken and that although none of the sponsors of the Lehman-Humphrey substitute had attended, every point embodied in their proposals had been brought up by some other person or organization and carefully considered. This was a flagrant misrepresentation. The fact was that no hearings at all had been held on the *final* McCarran bill. But when Lehman, Humphrey, Benton, Douglas, and McMahon tried to organize a thorough debate on the defects of the majority measure, most Senators deserted the hall. In vain did Lehman declare that he did not intend to talk to empty chairs. "We have a story to tell. We have logic, justice, fair play, and humanity on our side; and we are going to tell that story. I think we may be debating this bill for a long, long time." Though he had ample press support, debate was cut short.

On May 21, the Senate voted down the Lehman-Humphrey bill. Tobey, Chavez, Anderson, and Lodge were among those who supported it. A few days later the chamber adopted the McCarran bill by a voice vote, amid new expressions of disapproval by organs of liberal opinion. This offensive measure, said the *Washington Post*, was "unbecoming to the world's foremost democracy"; Congress, declared the *Boston Herald, New York Times,* and

St. Louis Post-Dispatch, had manifestly fallen short of a real effort to achieve generosity and equity.[4] When President Truman sent his expected veto in June, he indicted the measure as a callous defiance of the human needs of a sorrowful era. "Seldom has a bill exhibited the distrust evidenced here for citizens and aliens alike—at a time when we need unity at home and the confidence of friends abroad." The President proposed a bipartisan commission to reëxamine the entire problem, and Humphrey and Lehman immediately introduced a joint resolution for such a body. It was no surprise to observers that the bill was immediately repassed over Truman's veto 57 to 26 and went on the statute books.[5]

What was deplorable was that the country made so little protest and that this little was short-lived. Indifference was the prevailing mood. The main reasons, no doubt, lay in the age-old antipathy to foreigners for which the Greeks had a word and which the Communist peril had reawakened; in the lack of really strong emigration pressures abroad; and above all, the fact that American population was rising so fast from internal sources. This national apathy had dictated the contemptuous silence of McCarran and his followers under attack. As Lehman said, it was a source of disillusionment to him that its opponents offered not even the courtesy of a reply to their objections and questions.

A further exploration of details of immigration legislation while Lehman remained in the Senate would be otiose and unprofitable. Year after year, he introduced his own measures, first the Lehman-Humphrey and then the Lehman-Celler bill, but he effected no direct result. President Truman's commission on immigration and naturalization, appointed in September, 1952, sat in eleven cities, heard six hundred persons and organizations, and reported that the McCarran Act "injures our people at home, causes much resentment against us abroad, and impairs our position among the free nations"; but it, too, accomplished nothing. President Eisenhower in his campaign speeches of 1952 asked for a revision of the McCarran-Walter Act, but nothing was done. When just after taking office Eisenhower asked for the admission of 240,000 wartime refugees within the next two years, the impasse continued. McCarran took the legislation under his control and made the requirements so rigid that Senate liberals regarded the statute as a dead letter from the outset. At the beginning of June, 1954, forty-eight persons had been admitted; by April, 1955, about a thousand.

In 1954 Ellis Island closed down, and two years later the Hungarian revolt found the United States almost helpless to assist the great body of would-be refugees. All that Lehman could do was to continue speaking against the iniquities of the existing system. He kept on denouncing the national origins quota basis: [6]

> This system has been and continues to be a legislative sacred cow. Yet it is based on the same discredited racial theories from which Adolph Hitler developed the infamous Nuremberg laws. This system is based on the hypothesis that persons of Anglo-Saxon birth are superior to other nationalities and therefore better qualified to be admitted into the United States, and to become Americans. That system was frankly created to cut down on immigration from Italy and Poland and Greece and the rest of Southern and Eastern Europe. It is still so operating today. . . .
>
> I need not tell you gentlemen how utterly repugnant such a theory is to every concept we call American. It is the complete denial of Americanism. To defend ourselves against the evil implications of this concept, we recently fought a great war and expended billions of our wealth and sacrificed hundreds of thousands of American lives, including untold numbers whose names were not Smith, Brown, or Jones.

He continued to point out the contradictions, ambiguities, and arbitrary penalties contained in the McCarran-Walter Act: [7]

> One provision of the law permits a former Communist, who has not belonged to the Communist Party for ten years, to be naturalized. Another provision requires the deportation of any person who has ever at any time belonged to the Communist Party. And it works out that when a man who at any time in his past belonged to the Communist Party admits to past membership, in the process of filling out his naturalization form, he is at once served with an order of deportation. The naturalization provision is a trap to catch candidates for deportation.
>
> In scores of places in this Act, a visa can be denied or an alien excluded or deported if "in the opinion of the consular officer" or "of the Attorney-General" an individual seems likely to commit some vaguely defined act some time in the future. These provisions require every consular officer and every immigration inspector to carry a crystal ball, and to read the inscrutable future.
>
> No proof is required. All doubts are resolved against the alien.

He maintained a steady criticism of the Republican Administration for not redeeming its promises upon immigration, saying in the spring of 1954: [8]

> President Eisenhower promised time and again that he would seek a revision of the iniquitous McCarran-Walter Act. What has he done to fulfill that promise? What has his party done to carry out that pledge? The answer is nothing. Almost less than nothing. There

are several bills before the Congress to revise the McCarran-Walter Act—one a comprehensive bill—the so-called Lehman-Celler Bill, with 31 Democratic sponsors—and the other a very limited bill—the so-called Javits-Ives Bill, with 8 Republican sponsors.

But the Judiciary Committees of the Senate and the House have made no move to schedule hearings on those bills. There is no intention on the part of the Republican leadership to hold hearings on these bills.

And he called attention in severe terms to failures of administration, as in the noted Corsi affair in 1955; Edward Corsi, former industrial commissioner of New York, having been appointed special assistant to the Secretary of State on immigration matters: [9]

> Mr. Corsi took the job at the request of the White House to try to unsnarl the red tape and to clean up the mess involving the Refugee Relief Program. Under this program, enacted in 1953, the United States was going to admit 209,000 escapees and refugees from Europe and elsewhere into the United States. Well, to date, almost two years later, about 1,000 escapees and refugees have been admitted, along with some relatives. The entire program has turned out to be a fraud and a failure.
>
> So the White House called in Mr. Corsi, who has a considerable reputation as an administrator, and who is known as a friend of immigration. Corsi's job was to break the administrative log jam. He was to see to it that as many refugees and escapees as possible were admitted into the United States in the remaining months during which the Refugee Relief Act is still in effect.
>
> But in Washington Mr. Corsi made a critical mistake. He took his job seriously. He pushed, he scolded, he insisted that the red tape be cut and that refugees be admitted into the United States. He even spoke out against the racist and discriminatory McCarran-Walter Act and urged its drastic amendment.
>
> In Congress, powerful elements committed to the discriminatory principles of the McCarran-Walter Act attacked Mr. Corsi. They went over his past with a fine-toothed comb. They made veiled allusions to vague organizations he had belonged to 20 or 30 years ago. The witch hunt was on.
>
> Secretary Dulles, Mr. Corsi's boss, reacted to the attack against his subordinate by beating an inglorious, shameless retreat. He announced publicly that Mr. Corsi was being investigated for security, and that anyway, Mr. Corsi was in Washington on a temporary 90-day appointment only.
>
> This was news to Mr. Corsi, who had come to Washington prepared to stay and see the refugee program through. Secretary Dulles had more news for Mr. Corsi. He announced subsequently that Mr. Corsi was no longer to be Special Assistant for immigration problems.

In short, he was fired. It was not a question of Mr. Corsi's loyalty, Secretary Dulles said, it was just that Mr. Corsi was such a poor administrator.

To the end Lehman refused to compromise. Some associates pleaded with him to accept a mean-spirited little advance in the Watkins-Keating bill of 1956, a Republican gesture which offered some minor reforms but left the old quota system intact. He flatly refused, telling the chamber: "I want the Senate to have a chance to consider and vote not only on proposals for minor steps forward, but also on proposals for the major changes that everybody knows are needed. . . . I think we ought to do our duty as we see it, and at least face the issue—not merely the fringes of the issue, but the central issue involved here." He had no patience for such views as those of Lyndon Johnson, who in urging him to run for reëlection in 1956 wrote of the failure of immigration reform, adding: "As you know, it has seemed to me that the way to handle this issue is to begin nibbling at it. If we nibble long enough, we will break its back."

· II ·

Even after McCarthy was discredited, the atmosphere which surrounded the question of internal security was full of fogs and miasmas. Here, too, as in dealing with immigration, liberals found public apathy clogging their efforts. The persistence of the Cold War, the increasing weight of the armaments burden, the dread of sudden attack, the frustrations met in dealing with uncommitted nations, kept tensions high. The Internal Security Act of 1950 permitted many dubious administrative policies. It excluded some foreign visitors of high repute, for example, on the ground that they might prove dangerous. The Un-American Activities Committee continued to hold hearings and subjected innocent citizens to public opprobrium simply by issuing subpoenas for their appearance. Various government officers still held the doctrine of guilt by association valid, and various functionaries in private life still thought loyalty oaths an effective way of screening out subversives. The Supreme Court showed a tendency to divide on security issues, some justices led by Felix Frankfurter emphasizing public safety while others led by Hugo Black emphasized individual rights.

Intolerance and fear no longer inspired such dangerous excesses as when McCarthy had tried to bludgeon Secretary of the Army Stevens into submission, when the Senate had cited Corliss Lamont for contempt, and when Attorney General Brownell had made his clumsy attempt to indict Owen Lattimore for perjury. But they lurked in the background. As John F.

Kennedy said, some suspicious men thought they found treason in the best churches and in the Supreme Court. "They equate the Democratic party with the welfare state, and welfare state with socialism, and socialism with Communism." Lehman in 1953 pointed to the link between anti-Communist vigilantism and anti-immigrant hysteria. In dealing with both phobias, he said, fear and passion rather than intelligent restraint dominated too many minds: "In both cases the good name of national security is invoked to justify shameful acts and practices."

He could take a sad satisfaction in 1954 in commenting on the fact that the Internal Security Act passed four years earlier over Truman's veto had proved unworkable.[10] Despite the lapse of those four years, despite the expenditure of hundreds of thousands on an elaborate government bureaucracy, despite administrative and court proceedings, members of the Communist party had not been registered yet. "Meanwhile, the potentialities for evil in that broad and sweeping statute, its incipient dangers, lie embedded in our laws like a time bomb aimed at labor unions, fraternal organizations, charitable foundations, and associations of every kind." Some of the law's most vicious provisions, its immigration clauses carried into the McCarran-Walter Immigration Act, had done unmeasured harm. "They have eaten deep into the prestige of the United States in the world abroad. Countless injustices have been or are being worked upon hundreds and thousands of individuals —all in the name of security." The powers of the two laws had been used to ruin hundreds of lives. Most of the victims were aliens, but the same powers could be turned against American citizens and American freedoms.

No new legislation of any importance relating to internal security was enacted during Eisenhower's eight years; the only issues of importance related to the interpretation and administration of existing laws. Lehman believed the best service he could render lay in raising a voice of protest over every clear instance of hectoring and petty tyrannizing in the name of loyalty. He made himself continuously troublesome on principle, a gadfly. He consorted with other stinging gadflies, like former Senator Harry P. Cain of Washington, who had been given a lame-duck appointment to the Subversive Activities Control Board and who became conspicuous in fighting the excesses of Attorney General Brownell's security program.

In the case of Sidney Hatkin, a statistician suspended by the Air Force Department, for example, Lehman and Cain joined hands, for it gave point to Cain's question in a New York speech of May 5, 1956, "Have we made more security risks than we have found?" [11]

The suspension of Hatkin, Lehman found, was based on four charges.

The first was that he had registered in the American Labor Party in 1937, when the ALP was backing La Guardia and before anti-Communist groups broke away and denounced it. The second was that he had joined a discount group, the Washington Bookshop, in 1940 or 1941. So had thousands of other innocent people, for this was half a dozen years before the government listed it as subversive; he had simply paid a dollar for a discount card. The third charge was that his wife had participated in a Win-the-Peace Rally held in 1946 in the Commerce Department auditorium, a rally which neither of them could remember. The final count was that he had belonged to the United Public Workers, a union which the C.I.O. expelled as Communist-led; he had actually quit it before the expulsion. On these grounds he was dropped from his job and virtually blacklisted; for when he sought a new position, employment agencies repeatedly told him that there was no sense in looking for a place until the security situation was cleared up. He could not even get a District license to sell real estate or insurance. One agency said: "You're a dead duck." And the government would not clear up his security!

After Cain's and Lehman's intervention, Hatkin received justice; but of the hundreds of similar cases most escaped notice. Brownell, who had ruled that existing law required automatic suspension of any man the moment he was accused, asked Congress for an amendment to permit retention of employees on nonsensitive work while their cases were pending. In Lehman's opinion just a decent new ruling would suffice; Brownell was timidly passing the buck to Congress.

A different type of hardship was presented in the case of William Landy, a graduating student at Kings Point Merchant Marine Academy, who was denied his naval reserve commission in 1955 because his mother had once been a member of the Communist Party. When Lehman heard of this he was shocked. He recalled that in a similar instance the Air Force had tried to deprive a lieutenant of his reserve commission on the basis of his father's alleged political associations but had been halted by public sentiment. He called for a fresh exertion of public opinion:

> There is a proverb about "the sins of the fathers," but I am astounded to see this rule applied by a branch of the United States Government. In America, under Anglo-Saxon principles of law, guilt is supposed to be personal, and each individual is judged on the basis of his own merits and demerits. To deny a reserve commission to a brilliant young man who has led his class at the Kings Point School, and is willing and eager to devote his life to the operation of our Merchant Marine—and to serve his country as a Naval Officer when his country should need him—is illogical, unjust, and unjustifiable.

. . . Whatever the past political affiliations of this lad's mother—and he says that her Communist ties were severed eight years ago—the son must not be held accountable.

Brownell, in a speech of 1953, had presented what Lehman termed a new essay in sensationalism, dragging out the never-verified charge that Harry Dexter White of the Treasury Department had been disloyal—the Attorney General called him a Soviet spy—and imputing to President Truman the grossest laxity in dealing with subversives. The imputation was later disavowed. Brownell saw fit in his speech to use a selected part of an FBI file to strengthen his attack on the Truman Administration, and this particularly outraged Lehman. These files, as informed men knew, were largely filled with unsworn material from confidential sources including gossip and hearsay. They had always been secret and inviolate. Brownell had set a dangerous precedent.

"Certainly," said Lehman, "if an attorney-general, whose duty it is to enforce exact justice, may for partisan purposes publicly disclose secret police files on one individual, and may moreover disclose such parts of those files as suit his purpose and withhold other parts, then no one in our country is safe from attack. . . . This makes a mockery of the name of justice." [12] Later, Scott McLeod used his position as State Department personnel officer to strengthen his party for the 1954 campaign. This brought from Lehman not only the presentation of an amendment to the Hatch Act but a fresh explosion of wrath. "I consider it unconscionable," he said in a press release, "that any employe, officer, or official of our government, one of whose primary functions is to investigate, determine or judge the loyalty or security of other employes of the government, should be permitted to participate in overt partisan, political activities."

By such utterances the New York Senator did something not only to halt breaches of the security of individual citizens in the name of national security but to create a climate of opinion that would keep Federal Dogberryism well within bounds.

· III ·

His best opportunity to strike a blow for the civil rights of the Negro came in the Democratic convention of 1956. By that year Lehman was an ardent admirer of Adlai E. Stevenson and indeed one of the first leaders to declare for him. They had exchanged letters, seen each other frequently, and formed a bond of affection. The Senator went to Chicago pledged to Stevenson while nearly all the rest of the state delegation were bound to

Harriman; even to the end, only a handful of New York votes were cast for Adlai. "I felt isolated," Lehman later recalled. He was not on the platform committee, as he felt from his 1952 experience that the strain of almost two weeks of continuous hearings and meetings would be too great. Emanuel Celler had assumed his place. He did, however, present a 2,000-word statement to the committee, in which he asserted that the civil rights plank of 1948 and the still stronger plank of 1952 had given the party an enhanced reputation for courage and honesty. The 1956 platform should be even better.

The time had come, he argued, when the franchise could no longer be denied any group on the basis of race, color, or creed. Upon no point did American representatives in the United Nations insist more strongly than upon free elections in East Germany and the satellite countries. Secretary of State Byrnes had performed a historic service by inserting in a number of treaties with the Soviet Union a stipulation for truly free elections in Italy, Bulgaria, Rumania, Hungary, and other lands; but what about free elections in Byrnes's South Carolina? We were hypocrites! "The substance of the matter is that millions of our people are disfranchised and kept disfranchised by a whole combination of circumstances and practices." The Negro people of the South were at last actively demanding their full and equal rights and thus putting to rest the myth that they were satisfied with segregation and second-class citizenship.

"We must pledge Federal action," he wrote, "enlarging on the civil rights statutes enacted after the Civil War, so as to give the Attorney-General ample authority to enforce penalties and to seek relief by injunction against intimidation or coercion, or threats of any of these things, which deprive citizens of their Constitutional rights. It usually does little good to secure a court conviction for conspiracy to deny, deprive, or coerce. By the time the trial is ended, the election is long, long over. The present statutes are inadequate, and have never been a deterrent."

Unfortunately, Celler failed to make the strong fight for which liberals had hoped. Lehman, quite realizing that the committee majority would vote against a stronger plank than four years earlier, had expected a minority report. The fact that none was filed made it difficult to bring the issue before the convention. Finally, working with Walter Reuther and leaders of Americans for Democratic Action, he persuaded a group of delegates to sign a petition for convention debate of the subject. Under a hostile ruling by Representative Clarence Cannon of Missouri, the tough old parliamentarian of the gathering, the majority received at least an hour, while five of the liberals had to divide ten minutes among them. It was said later that Lehman, carried away by his emotion, took far more than his share! He was anxious when the debate closed to get a roll call, but Cannon rejected his demand for one, ruling that he did not have enough supporters. "Had it come to a vote," said Lehman, "we might have won; in any event, it would have been close." [13]

He was disappointed all around; disappointed in Celler, in the committee, in Harry Truman, who originally advocated a drastic plank and then backed down, and in the plank itself, which was tepidly wishy-washy. He was profoundly disappointed by the outcome of the ensuing campaign. Stevenson, very tired after the long primary fight he had waged the previous winter and spring, made an admirable presentation of the issues but found it hard to say anything new. Insuperable advantages of prestige and position lay with Eisenhower, who in the last days of the contest was assisted by stormy events in Hungary and at the Suez Canal. When it was all over Lehman could only express his deep dejection. He wrote November 8 to Adlai Stevenson: [14]

> I can't tell you how sad Edith and I are at the result of the election. You made a wonderful fight, and all your friends and admirers may well take great pride in the manner in which you conducted yourself. I doubt whether there was ever a comparable situation in any campaign. You discussed the issues freely and frankly and constructively, while President Eisenhower ran exclusively on his personal popularity and refused to be drawn into a discussion of the issues.
>
> I don't know that anything would have materially changed the ultimate result, but, like you, I feel that a great surge of Eisenhower support came within the last two weeks as a result of the tragic foreign situation, for which the Administration was undoubtedly responsible but for which he personally was forced to bear very little of the blame. . . . I do hope that you are not too greatly discouraged and that you will continue to give your great leadership to the Democratic Party, and better still, to the entire nation if the President has sense enough to seek it.

To which Stevenson replied with a warm expression of gratitude:

> I suppose that I have had literally no greater satisfactions in my brief ascent and descent in the political firmament than your unswerving loyalty and encouragement.
>
> Well, I have been defeated, but I am not bruised. But I am profoundly alarmed by the massive ignorance of our people about our situation abroad, and the extent to which the Administration has successfully contributed to this delinquency. To ratify failure is bad enough, but the ignorance it discloses is more serious. I hope we can be more effective in the opposition in the future than we have in the past.

Hypocrisy stalked abroad in the Senate on the civil rights issue. A majority of members professed adherence to the principles that Truman had enunciated, that Lehman tried to write into the Democratic platforms, and that Eisenhower gave his voice but not his strong right arm; a compulsory program that would end poll taxes, intimidation of Negro voters, racial discrimination in employment and transportation, and other wrongs. A real majority was openly or secretly opposed and obstructive or evasive. Lehman made few friends in the chamber when he exposed the hypocrisy and no progress when he and other liberals tried to strengthen the cloture that would have made evasion and delay more difficult. He rejoiced as loudly over the Supreme Court's decision of 1954 outlawing school segregation as James Eastland of Mississippi lamented it, and he stood for enforcement of the decision as firmly as Eastland, a bitter apostle of white supremacy, stood for nullification. The tragic fact was that after the deaths of McCarran and Harley Kilgore, the seniority rule made this latter-day Bilbo chairman of the all-powerful Judiciary Committee.

· IV ·

On measure after measure which came before Congress in these years Lehman took positions which hardly endeared him to a majority of Senate members. He was consistently with labor in its anxiety for amendments to the Taft–Hartley Act. He disliked, not big business, but what he called giant business—he estimated in 1957 that the country had seventy-seven giant corporations with more than a billion dollars each in assets; and he made plain his feeling that the giants like du Pont and General Electric were not transferring the benefit of their economies to the consumer. Opposing to the last the grant to the four states of California, Texas, Louisiana, and Florida of control over the offshore oil deposits, he offered in 1953 his own bill giving authority to the Federal Government to lease submerged lands to private oil companies, thus making possible a uniform and integrated program of development. Denounced by Holland as "hundred percent nationalization," his proposal was voted down by sixty Senators.

He stood against the proposal of the Dixon-Yates utilities interests to build a steam-generating plant at West Memphis, Arkansas, which brought him into collision with senatorial conservatives, President Eisenhower, and Lewis L. Strauss, who all favored the plant. At the same time (1954) he took a position on the Cole-Hickenlooper bill, amending the Atomic Energy Act of 1946, which again offended the senatorial majority. The amendments would have given private interests certain privileges in the use of government-generated nuclear power not previously enjoyed. Lehman argued that although the government had already spent twelve billions for the development of nuclear energy, Hickenlooper's measure contained practically no safeguards of the public interest. "This bill," he declared, "in its fullest implications, far transcends the infamous give-away of the offshore oil bill. The power potential of the atomic power give-away transcends a million times the threatened give-away of the waterpower resources of the Niagara Falls development." The bill went through. Although sufficient public pressure was mobilized to compel the Administration to cancel the Dixon-Yates contract, opponents of the Cole-Hickenlooper measure could neither halt it nor materially alter it.

As Paul Douglas took the lists against the Fulbright-Harris natural gas bill early in 1956, a bill which largely destroyed Federal regulation of the "independent" natural gas producers, Lehman vigorously joined him. A handful of the so-called independents, really rich and powerful companies, controlled this important industry. An increase of only a few cents in the price of gas at the well-head would mean increased costs of hundreds of millions of dollars to the consuming public and corresponding profits of hundreds of millions to the producers. Yet the Senate passed the bill 53 to 38, and President Eisenhower regretfully vetoed it on February 17 only because Senator Francis Case of South Dakota revealed that a registered oil lobbyist had made an unsolicited contribution of $2,500 to his campaign fund. "Grabbing and greed can go on for just so long," declared Lehman, "but the breaking point is bound to come sometime." [15]

The barons of Petrolia had three major objectives, the miscalled tidelands oil, the grant of *laissez faire* to the natural gas interests, and the freezing of the 27.5 percent tax allowance for oil depletion. Aided by the fact that some barons and baronets sat in the Senate, totally untroubled by any conflict-of-interest squeamishness, they attained all three. Douglas, Lehman, and a few others made a valiant effort to get the depletion allowance reduced to fifteen percent but amid howls of fury had to retire vanquished. "The oil gang," as the authors of *The Truman Merry-Go-Round* put it, "has many political henchmen in Washington: rank and filers, leaders, jurists, and socialites." [16]

Even in foreign affairs, where a wide area of general agreement among parties and factions had been reached, Lehman did not avoid offense to many associates; he did not try. He never wavered in his championship of the Truman-Acheson policies. In the spring of 1950 and again in the fall of 1951 Acheson wrote him messages of thanks for his unwavering defense of the State Department and its head. Paul Hoffman thanked him with equal warmth in 1951 for his spirited advocacy of legislation asked by the Economic Cooperation Administration, and that same year Averell Harriman expressed appreciation of what he had done to clear up misunderstandings of Yalta. Britain had of course given up her mandate in Palestine in 1948, and Israel had at once been proclaimed as the first independent Jewish state in two thousand years. Lehman made himself a staunch defender of the little republic as it began its marvelous development and its "ingathering of the exiles." To some he seemed all too staunch; even fellow Jews regretted his failure to criticize the harsher Israeli policies toward the Arabs, and the State Department at no time approved of such demands as that American ports be denied Egyptian ships because Egypt closed the Suez to Israeli vessels. Much as he deplored the plight of the 600,000 Arabs who fled or were forced from homes and acres they had held for 1,300 years, his emotions were deeply enlisted on one side and one alone. This again made him seem to some a special pleader.

Secretary of Defense Wilson amused few and angered many when, discussing unemployment in 1954, he observed: "I've always liked bird dogs better than kennel-fed dogs myself; you know, ones who get out and hunt for food rather than sit on their fanny and yelp." A business tycoon's crassness could hardly go further. Lehman's instant telegram to Eisenhower was natural: "As a member of the Labor and Public Welfare Committee and as a Senator deeply concerned with the problem of unemployment in the United States—a problem to which our committee has given deep and troubled thought—I am deeply shocked by the remarks attributed to Secretary of Defense Charles E. Wilson making light of the unemployment problem and comparing the unemployed to 'kennel dogs' who 'just sit on their own haunches and yelp.' This statement, reflecting both lack of appreciation of the nature of the unemployment problem and a total lack of feeling for the hardships visited on those unfortunate unemployed, impels me to urge that you either cause Secretary Wilson to issue a prompt and full retraction, in apology for his unfortunate statement, or request his immediate resignation. We have in New York upward of a quarter million unemployed. They and all the people in New York State violently and strongly resent both the tone and implications of Secretary Wilson's remarks. Those remarks are an affront to New York as a great industrial state and to all the working people of the United States." A justifiable response; but many wondered if a more moderate telegram would not have been a better rebuke to what was, after all, a maladroit rather than malicious utterance.

For his unyielding independence, which to many colleagues seemed intransigence, Lehman paid a penalty. He was never admitted to the central group of the Senate which did most to manage its business, giving the in-siders ready privileges and indulgences and thwarting outsiders. A shrewd Washington observer, William S. White, has described in *The Citadel* just what membership of this inner circle meant. "I have seen one member, say a Lehman of New York," he writes, "confined by niggling and almost brutal Senate action to the most literal inhibitions of the least important of all the rules. And again I have seen a vital Senate roll call held off by all sorts of openly dawdling time-killing for hours . . . for the simple purpose of seeing that a delayed aircraft had opportunity to land at the Washington Airport so that a motorcycle escort could bring, say a Humphrey of Min-nesota, in to be recorded." For Humphrey would make concessions to his colleagues and address them tactfully; Lehman on any point he chose to call a matter of principle would make no adjustment and often spoke like a Harold Ickes. The New Yorker was hence frozen out of the dominant group, an alien; the Minnesotan, by the mysterious operation of rules of congeniality, was welcomed to it.

Ability, experience, even politics had nothing to do with admission to the central club. "Humphrey," as White put it, "simply got along better." Ful-bright, similarly, was on the inside, while Paul Douglas was definitely be-yond the gate.[17]

Once in the Eighty-fourth Congress, relates White, Lyndon Johnson was able to get more than a hundred bills passed, some of them controversial, in a little more than an hour. The most important reason for this was simply that "Lyndon wants it." Lehman in an equal period could have gotten every one of his ideas opposed. In this statement lies a definition of his strength and his weakness as public servant in the national parliament.

· V ·

By 1956 he felt that this public service, so far as Washington was con-cerned, was drawing to an end. The hour hand of the clock was inexorable; he was growing too old, he believed, to withstand the anxieties and fatigues of the Senate for another six years. The response of his friends to this an-nouncement was well summed up by a letter from one of the closest, Eleanor Roosevelt. She wrote him just after Christmas thanking him for a letter which had touched her.

"No one can look back with greater satisfaction than you can on a life of public service," she added. "You have won the admiration of all of us, and it is good to know that while you are leaving the Senate, you are not retiring and will be able to do the innumerable tasks I know you will be called upon to perform. The world needs you very much and in voicing my sadness that New York State is not going to have the benefit of your voice in the Senate, I do rejoice that we will have you here in the State and I may hope to see you more often."

So the early weeks of 1957 found the Lehmans home again, comfortably reinstalled in the dark brick-and-stone apartment house at 820 Park Avenue, looking eastward to lighter brick-and-stone apartment houses. Here, in the familiar study with its large windows to catch the morning sun, its silver-framed photographs of Lincoln, Franklin D. Roosevelt, and Adlai E. Stevenson, its inscribed cartoons by Rollin Kirby and Herblock, its flower painting by Mrs. Lehman, its desk, bookcases, and sofa, the Senator was home again with the familiar problems and causes: the Democratic organization, housing, the Jewish Theological Seminary, the ORT, civil rights, the Niagara power project, desegregation, public health, and many more. The Senator?—no, for he now quietly resumed his older and more distinguished title of Governor. His return had been signalized by a flurry of editorials, a flood of letters, a succession of dinners, and a cascade of testimonials, including some new medals and diplomas. If it was marked by a visible lessening of strain, it saw no diminution of industry or the spirit of self-sacrifice. He probably thought he could lay aside the sword and cudgel of Mr. Greatheart and become a quieter, more relaxed Valiant-for-Truth; if so, he was mistaken.

Chapter XIX

THE LAST GOOD FIGHT

F<small>EATS</small> of broil and battle, in Othello's phrase, were not ended when Lehman passed out of the Senate door. He had begun his public career by enlisting against Tammany in the effort that ended in Sulzer's humiliation; it was appropriate that he should close it by a new assault on the same citadel. "The Shame of New York" was the title the *Nation* gave a special issue of October 11, 1959, and "Monster of a City" the heading of its first section. The former governor labored with others to bring the monster under better control and erase the shame.

· I ·

"Yes, when I got back from Europe I found myself confronted by the *fait accompli* of the state convention. But I must go back a little bit. Most people think that my interest and the interest of some of my colleagues in the reform movement which we began was due entirely to pique that Tom Finletter did not receive the nomination for Senator. I was for Finletter. So were Mrs. Roosevelt and other people who have been involved in this reform movement. But I was very much concerned about the Democratic Party long before the convention. I was concerned, quite concerned, with the ever-growing power of De Sapio and two or three other bosses."

So Lehman spoke on October 7, 1959, recalling some of the events of the previous twelvemonth. He was then in the midst of a struggle to reconstitute the Democratic organization in New York, which occupied him more than three years, from midsummer 1958 to autumn 1961, with toil, anxiety—and, it must be added, a certain exhilaration.

A mere outline of this battle indicates its drama. In the summer of 1958 the three principal Democratic leaders—Governor Harriman, running for reëlection, Mayor Wagner, well into his second term, and Lehman on the sidelines—expected the party to choose a liberal ticket that fall and win decisively. The best candidate for Senator would be Thomas K. Finletter; a good second best would be Thomas E. Murray. Suddenly the Tammany boss, Carmine De Sapio, took an arrogant position. He insisted that Frank S. Hogan, for sixteen years district attorney of New York County, was the only man he would accept for the seat and rammed the candidacy down the throats of Harriman and Wagner. Public resentment over this display of boss tyranny was instant and deep. The revulsion set the scene for the astonishing election of Nelson Rockefeller as governor and Kenneth Keating as Senator. Already a reform group of young Democrats had lifted a flag of revolt against Tammany; their object was to eject old party hacks from leadership in the districts and replace them with energetic new men animated by the principles of Woodrow Wilson and Franklin D. Roosevelt. As Lehman, Eleanor Roosevelt, and Finletter now sprang to their aid, a larger contest began, aimed at nothing less than the overthrow of De Sapio. It rumbled through 1959, grew fiercer in the presidential campaign of 1960, and became a mortal combat in the mayoralty election of 1961.

Yet this over-simplified outline omits the deeper drama; for this can be approached only by some acquaintance with the background of New York affairs, the intricacies of party organization, the bitter antagonism between the machine and the reform element, the personal rivalries, and the social and economic interests affected by the contest.

· II ·

In New York City the collapse of Jimmy Walker's Administration had brought in twelve years of stormy, colorful, and generally constructive government under La Guardia, a good era; then, unhappily, Fiorello's retirement in 1945—to die of cancer—fetched back a darker period. Fusion had broken down, chiefly because Republican leaders thought that they might seize all the prizes alone. They were mistaken. William O'Dwyer, a Democrat who, as district attorney in Kings County, had won some well-headlined victories over Murder, Inc., a horrifying Brooklyn combine of racketeers, sluggers, and killers directed by Albert Anastasia, became mayor. It was later alleged that he was helped to his high office by no less a power than Frank Costello, regarded by some as the foremost criminal in the United States; at any rate, he met in Costello's apartment in 1942 several of the men who did most to get him nominated and seated three years later. Reëlected without difficulty, he soon ran into such portentous difficulties that he was glad to resign in 1950 to become ambassador to Mexico. He had brought the Tammany tiger back to City Hall. After the brief incompetent interlude of Vincent R. Impellitteri as mayor, an interlude that proved repugnant to practically everybody, the tiger began purring still more comfortably when De Sapio in 1953 shrewdly managed the nomination of young Robert Wagner.

"Here comes Bob Wagner in the pants of his father," De Sapio had sarcastically remarked several years earlier.[1] But in a pinch he was glad to use both the old Senator's fame and the son's political shrewdness.

De Sapio had taken control of Tammany on July 20, 1949, the first American of Italian descent to hold the grand sachemdom. Born in Greenwich Village when it was still mainly Irish, he had worked his way up from the job of stableboy in his father's haulage business. Brilliant, industrious, adroit, he became able to speak with equal facility in the cultivated accents of a Harvard lecturer and the New Yorkese of the Bowery. His rapid rise was creditable. Tall, handsome, well-groomed, he exhibited poise in any gathering. His personal honesty was never impugned, and he had the insight to realize that a new political age had dawned. Nobody wished any longer to go to ward picnics, nobody sold a vote for a dollar, and nobody wanted handouts of coal and potatoes. Once people in trouble had sought a machine lieutenant. "Now," as Wagner put it, "if you're locked up you go to Legal Aid. If you need food, you go to Welfare." With a flexibility never before seen in the Hall, De Sapio cultivated the liberal blocs that Al Smith and the New Deal had created; he mastered the arts of Madison Avenue, and he sometimes lectured acceptably on good government. Lehman in 1956 complimented him on his "outstanding leadership."[2] But Tammany itself had changed little, and De Sapio had some very questionable allies and associates. His knowledge of such gangsters as Costello and Frank Luchese had been investigated by the state crime commission, and the Kefauver Senate Committee, some two years after he became head of Tammany, asserted: "Costello's influence continues . . . strong in the councils of the Democratic Party of New York County."

When Lehman returned from Washington in 1957, he found that Mayor Wagner had made a sound record in his first three years in office. Partly by his own initiative, and partly by the help of such advisers as City Administrator Luther Gulick, he had met a swarm of problems resourcefully. He had strengthened the police department against the appalling onsets of crime and hoodlumism, had built schools and raised teachers' pay, had hacked some holes in the slums with public housing, and had raised the morale of city officers. Racketeering was kept under the surface if not exactly under control; the bloated city budget was somehow carried even if the taxpayers staggered. True, the Wagner Administration had gradually lost its momentum and seemed sliding into a limp passivity, but the story as a whole was good. Lehman also found that Averell Harriman had dealt capably with the tasks of the governorship. For a man of his colorless and chilly personality, he had even won a surprising amount of personal popularity. Few Americans possessed such a combination of governmental and business experience as Harriman, and such a liberal yet practical outlook, virtues that triumphed over all his handicap of outer frigidity.

All this was reassuring, for as Lehman well knew, city and state had reached a point where they simply could not afford even brief periods of misgovernment. At least a million of the people of the metropolis lived in slums; for all the efforts of the 24,000 police no man dared enter the parks at midnight alone; the traffic problem began to restrain citizens from gibing even at Los Angeles; Michael Quill as head of the Transport Workers Union periodically made management of the subways and buses a nightmare; some school buildings barely stood up; and the policy game or numbers racket converted the dimes of the poor into huge fortunes for the protected harpies who robbed them. As for the state, it winced under a score of unalleviated tensions; its railroads, its highway system, its canals, its prisons and asylums, its university system, its water power, its fair employment standards, all presented unsolved problems. In city and state alike the political system cried out for renovation; the boss, the machine, and the apathetically helpless citizen made up a glaring anachronism.

Before Lehman sailed for Europe in mid-July 1958 for a vacation and to address a World Brotherhood Seminar in Berne, he had several talks with Harriman and De Sapio about the fall elections. People assumed Harriman's continuance in the governor's mansion as a matter of course. For the Senate, Lehman and Harriman preferred Finletter, though both were willing to consider Murray. In the metropolis, Finletter was highly respected as a member of the Coudert Brothers law firm, a man active in helping organize the United Nations and Economic Cooperation Administration, and a former Secretary of the Air Force; though upstate he had little following, and his reserved, colorless personality would make it hard for him to win one. Wagner refused to accept a draft (which De Sapio was determined to halt), because in running for mayor he had firmly pledged himself to serve out his term if elected. Murray held important distinctions in engineering and public service, ultimately becoming head of the Atomic Energy Commission. While in Berne, Lehman had further telephone talks with Harriman, Finletter, and De Sapio, all of whom continued to predict a harmonious march to victory.

But what a change when Lehman came back on September 16! His political friends greeted him with expressions of anger and despair. Voters by tens of thousands were shifting to the Republican ticket. Liberals and independents were execrating De Sapio for the boldest exhibition of bossism since Charles Murphy's day. Press and public spoke of Harriman with pity and contempt. A political grave for the party yawned ahead.

The convention had met in Buffalo with Paul E. Fitzpatrick presiding. It at once became plain that Harriman, who should have been in control— for it had long been the rule that the governor of the state should be active head of his party, fixing its policies, determining its tone, and exercising supreme authority in choosing his associates when he ran for office—was powerless. As De Sapio laid down his edict that Hogan, who throughout sixteen years of attorneyship had never meddled with politics, and whose convictions were unknown, must be named for Senator, Harriman made no floor fight for either the liberal Finletter or Murray. He was a Hamlet, full of vacillation. When county leaders asked which of this pair he preferred, he was said to have replied: "Mayor Wagner will be out there on the platform, and he will give the sign." Wagner *was* there, rose, said a few perfunctory words, and sat down. Yet the mayor apparently showed more backbone than the governor—who, to be sure, was still rather naïve in politics. Rumors circulated of a closed session in which Wagner had shouted that De Sapio must not forget he was mayor of the city and De Sapio had retorted that Wagner must not forget that *he* controlled the board of estimate.

Behind-the-scenes details of events at Buffalo will always remain controversial, because afterwards even the principal actors were confused. What is certain is that the great body of Democratic voters would have preferred Finletter or Murray, that Harriman's will should have ruled, that De Sapio exhibited a domineering temper that would have impressed Cromwell or Bismarck, and that when delegates caught their trains home, half the party was looking for some new refuge. Lehman telegraphed from Switzerland, "shocked and deeply distressed." Why had Harriman not said, during the intense behind-the-scenes fight, "If I do not get the associate I want, I will not run"? People well recalled how when Boss Murphy had once tried to force the nomination of William Randolph Hearst for senator, Al Smith had unflinchingly opposed him although they were good friends and had finally laid down an ultimatum: "No! No! I will not run with Hearst!" They recalled how Governor Roosevelt had insisted on Lehman's nomination in 1932 against Curry and McCooey. And why had De Sapio demanded Hogan, anyhow? Was it personal friendship? Pressure of the hierarchy? Even a desire to get a too-efficient prosecutor out of office?

The election of Rockefeller by a plurality of more than half a million, and Keating of Rochester by a quite satisfactory margin, was the most dramatic overturn in the state since Grover Cleveland's victory over the Republicans in 1882 and Theodore Roosevelt's over the Democrats in 1898; and men at once began to think of Rockefeller as a presidential possibility. Not for a quarter century had the Republicans held both of the New York senatorial seats. The demand from all parts of the state for Democratic Party reorganization was naturally concentrated in the metropolis.

For ten years a reform movement had smoldered in the Ninth Assembly District, an area south and east of Central Park where middle-class professional people, largely Jewish, had become convinced that the old-fashioned machine leaders no longer responded to the needs of the people and that able young men were being denied a proper opportunity for advancement in government. The discontent found a directing center in the Lexington Democratic Club, which since 1949 had sought to draw the rebels together, giving women the same standing as men and reaching decisions only by full debate in open meetings. In April, 1953, while Lehman was busy in Washington, Lloyd K. Garrison, Mrs. Roosevelt, David Lilienthal, and Telford Taylor, with others, had organized a Democratic Citizens Committee.[3] Their followers were young, keen, and idealistic. After the Buffalo convention, Finletter, Garrison, and close friends naturally talked with many resentful people about the need for a revolt. The movement gathered strength, but Finletter took pains to avoid any leakage of news to the press; it would blunt the edge of the crusade, he feared.

Then in late November Lehman began conferring with the young leaders. He had of course supported the Harriman-Hogan ticket; he had in fact cabled from Europe urging the hesitant Liberal Party to nominate both men. Before long he was making speeches in their behalf. But he agreed with Garrison and such young men as Arnold Fein, Richard Brown, Irving Wolfson, Paul Bragdon, David Levy, and Jack Shea, practical, tough-minded fighters, that party reform was exigent. Newspapermen besieged him; and on January 22, 1959, he held a press conference at the Belmont Plaza Hotel at which he gave out a statement on behalf of himself, Mrs. Roosevelt, and Finletter. It declared:

> Because we feel that much can be done to improve the Democratic Party in New York, we have decided that our best course would be to sound a call to all Democrats, both within and outside the present Party

organization, to join in a city-wide and statewide effort (a) to promote the organization of all Democrats, (b) to advocate and advance
the principles of democracy within all the reaches of the Democratic
Party organization of New York, and (c) to seek to make the Party
organization a vehicle to advance the Party's political programs in
state and nation, rather than to serve the urge for personal power by
political professionals.

Believing the achievement of these purposes to be of the highest
national importance, we have undertaken to set up a New York Committee for Democratic Voters to work toward these goals.

The activities of this committee will be directed toward the following objectives:

1. To encourage the widest possible participation by all Democrats
in Party affairs and, in furtherance of this purpose, to propose legislative and other measures (a) to achieve democratization of the Party
at all local levels, and (b) to abolish the many existing artificial barriers that now hinder participation in our Party's affairs.

2. To assist in the development of outstanding Democratic candidates throughout New York State and to support them financially and
otherwise.

3. To study the affairs of the Party throughout the state and to
make recommendations to the voters, particularly Democrats, based
upon such studies.

4. To provide a responsible Democratic Opposition; and to take
all other action considered desirable to restore public confidence in
the New York Democratic Party. . . .[4]

This press conference strikingly changed the aspect of the contest. The
dignity of Lehman's position (of which he was always very conscious) gave
new weight to the reform crusade. Inadvertently, the statement had the
effect of unveiling the movement as something quite new, instead of a new
phase in an old, well-rooted effort; many people jumped to the conclusion
that it had been freshly invented by Lehman, Mrs. Roosevelt, and Finletter,
when actually it had a broader base. Though this may have added to the impact of the news, it was unfortunate and some of the workers of the previous
decade resented it. Most important of all, the press conference gave an unexpected shift to the objectives in view. Reporters bluntly asked Lehman, in
effect, "Will you try to unseat De Sapio?" With equal bluntness he replied:
"Yes, certainly." The *New York Times* quoted him: "We will oppose Mr.
De Sapio and hope voters of the state will take steps to remove him."

To some of the young leaders of the movement this was disconcerting.
They thought an attempt to eject De Sapio from the leadership of the New
York County organization tactically premature. It was important to do care-
ful preparatory work, they believed, and build up their strength by organiza-

tion from the bottom, before striding out to overthrow Goliath. Though a few liked the boldness of the announcement, neither Mrs. Roosevelt nor Finletter had been prepared to go so far.

Yet it was soon evident that Lehman's instinct had been right. His statement dramatized the conflict, lifted it to a higher level of importance, and infused a spirit of militancy into the reform forces. Tammany was instantly full of mingled wrath and apprehension. Its leaders made slashing public attacks on the reformers; they responded by defiant counterattacks.

• III •

While the *Times*, *Herald-Tribune*, and other papers gave the movement their blessing, they warned that its road would be rough; "the established machine is always hard to beat." [5] Averell Harriman had refused to take a stand; so had Wagner. The decision for or against the boss had been made in the party primaries—usually with only a small turnout marking paper ballots, sometimes lost or miscounted. Lehman remarked that both Harriman and Wagner would be welcome, but both continued to be hostile; and Representative Emanuel Celler announced that he would oppose a change, for although De Sapio had made a mistake in forcing Hogan on the party, "you don't oust a man for one mistake." Undiscouraged, the reformers issued a new statement just after Lincoln's Birthday in 1959 which made it clear that they objected to State Chairman Michael Prendergast only less than to De Sapio himself. Francis W. H. Adams, a former police commissioner of tough public spirit, had joined the group, and he, Lloyd K. Garrison, Finletter and Lehman made up a group whom the press always mentioned, to the chagrin of some of the younger and very hard-working but less prominent leaders. Adams was ardently championing John F. Kennedy for President, a fact which gave him some strength with Irish-Catholic voters.[6]

The summer primary battle came on amid a fusillade of statements and speeches on both sides. On a hot, steamy June night the reformers kicked off their campaign with an appearance in De Sapio's own Greenwich Village district, where a rebel group had nominated Charles E. McGuinness for district party leader against the boss himself. "No campaign in which I have participated," announced Mrs. Roosevelt, "has meant more to me than this present struggle to bring real democracy into the party in this state." Lehman, calling De Sapio an unbearable burden, assured his hearers that "the eyes of millions are upon you in Greenwich Village." [7] On June 29, another torrid, sticky night, Lehman wrote a speech for the rally at Bohemian National Hall on East 73rd Street, which was read by someone else. The vigor and sparkle of this speech, wrote an observer in the *Atlantic Monthly*, repaid the crowd for its discomfort.[8] Meanwhile, De Sapio fought back, sending out personal letters by thousands, picturing himself as a liberal Democrat, and proposing that the ballot be given to eighteen-year-olds.

When the primary election took place September 15, De Sapio kept his district leadership by a razor-thin margin over McGuinness; but his hold on the county organization was materially weakened. In the twenty primary contests in Manhattan, marked by the use of voting machines, the regulars won nine places, but the insurgents took seven, the four others in Harlem going to friends of the explosive Representative Adam Clayton Powell, Jr. A change of 600 ballots in some 9,000 would have elected McGuinness, who had the support of the influential local organ, *The Villager*, which for the first time in two decades took a political stand. The election in Queens gave that county a new leader, John T. Clancy, free from any obligation to De Sapio. Though the boss still held a majority in the Tammany executive committee, he had been badly shaken. George Backer, formerly of the *New York Post*, on the rebel side declared that the new movement was fully launched. "Its victories and near victories mean that in its next contest there should be and will be a complete victory," he said, "for those young men and women" who stood for progressive government. And William Fitts Ryan, a liberal district leader, went further, announcing: "The old line bosses are through."

Lehman and his associates might well feel satisfied with their advance. They read with satisfaction the editorial in the *Times*. Unquestionably, it remarked, the primary "resulted in a setback for Carmine De Sapio. Not only was he hard pressed in his own Greenwich Village area by an inexperienced newcomer to the political arena, but the outcome elsewhere was a blow to his prestige and power." Moreover, the returns disclosed a significant trend. "In many areas, Mr. De Sapio's home district among them, new records were set for voter participation in the primaries. This is all to the good."[9] The election interested the *London Economist*, which noted that the independent anti-Tammany vote in Greenwich Village had risen in two years, 1957–59, from 38 percent of the ballots cast to 46 percent, and that Adam Clayton Powell's district leaders, animated by resentment over a recent effort to unseat him, were anti-Tammany. It concluded that De Sapio's star was visibly dropping: "His influence at next year's Democratic convention is bound to decline as the grass roots (or rather the city pavements) sink from beneath his feet—a fact that has not escaped those whose eyes are on the 1960 presidential nomination."

Amid heckling and applause, De Sapio on September 22, 1959, was duly reëlected chairman of the county committee, but only after he had announced his own program to rehabilitate the party organization. All eyes were now turning toward the presidential campaign.

· IV ·

This campaign for two reasons interrupted the anti-Tammany struggle in New York: voters centered their attention on national affairs, and as the duel between Kennedy and Nixon grew desperate, a cry arose for "closing the party ranks" to defeat the Republicans. Still, in various ways De Sapio lost ground. From the days of Tilden to those of Truman, it had been obligatory for Democratic candidates (Al Smith excepted) to shun association with ill-famed Tammany. Nobody was astonished when in the early weeks of 1960 Mayor Wagner emerged as leader of the state organization in national politics, displacing De Sapio. Truman had told him that unless he did so the New York delegation at the national convention would have almost no influence; if it was tarred with "bossism" it would have the biggest vote and the littlest voice. "Instead of being the state's top Democratic boss," wrote the *New York Times* political reporter, "De Sapio is being reduced to just one of the five county leaders in New York City." [10] The reform group wanted more than this. In a conference with Wagner, it asked for the elimination of De Sapio as national committeeman, election of a larger proportion of convention delegates by direct vote in Congressional districts, and abandonment of the unit rule in casting the state's 114 votes. [11] At that time Kennedy supposedly held 56 votes.

Prendergast, De Sapio, and other state machine leaders vehemently refused to make the selection of national convention delegates more democratic, a sign, as Finletter said, of their feeling of insecurity. Lehman for his part declined to attend the annual state committee dinner. The breach between the two party factions widened, primarily because Lehman refused to yield an inch to various overtures for a compromise. "I am not shadow-boxing," he told reporters. If the voters did not make a fresh advance against the machine in the June primaries, he added, the presidential ticket would suffer in the fall. And as the primary approached, he made a minatory gesture toward Mayor Wagner, who was still much too neutral for his taste. He was not sure he would support Wagner for reëlection in 1961, he remarked; the mayor had lost ground in public esteem because he had yielded to too many Tammany pressures; he had not shown proper vigilance in preventing scandals or vigor in punishing them.

"I think the mayor must have known about the abuses in Title I, for·

example," he ominously continued, referring to gross irregularities in carrying out the Federal Housing Act for joining city-national action in slum clearance. "I certainly hope that he will grow during this year." [12]

Happily, the June primaries did show continued progress by the reformers. The most conspicuous contest concerned the nomination of a new successor to the much-respected Congressman, Sol Bloom, in the Twentieth District, which once included Columbia University. On Bloom's death in 1949 Franklin D. Roosevelt, Jr., had held the seat until he resigned it in 1954, a Tammany man taking his place. Now it was being sought by William Fitts Ryan, the anti-Tammany district leader. Other important contests involved nominations for a state senate seat on the West Side and two assembly seats on the East Side. Rival party clubs threw themselves into the contest with intense vigor. Some district leaderships were again at stake. Feeling ran high; if the reformers were defeated, the New York Committee for Democratic Voters movement might collapse; if they won, they could look forward to a greater success in the mayoralty election of 1961.

And on a narrow front they won decisively. "A smashing victory," crowed Irving Engel, the executive committee chairman of the Committee for Democratic Voters. "No doubt about it," said the more judicial Mayor Wagner, "it's a setback for Carmine De Sapio." Ryan won the nomination in the Twentieth Congressional District. The young reformer Mark Lane carried one of the East Side assembly districts; another reformer, a publishing house editor named Charles D. Lieber, won in another. Tammany lost the state senate district on the West Side. In a downtown section the Liberal Party nominated a municipal court justice over a Tammany candidate. The political reporter for the *Times* could well state, "The results constitute a major blow to Mr. De Sapio's political prestige." [13] No one had a better right to feel elated than Lehman, who at eighty-two had gone to every rally and meeting, however small, all over town, to call on the voters to turn De Sapio out. [14]

Some episodes of the ensuing presidential campaign that summer and fall had a highly dramatic quality. The Los Angeles convention was serious enough. Lehman, Mrs. Roosevelt, and Finletter were there, striving to the last for Adlai E. Stevenson's nomination. They hoped against hope that the unmistakable sentiment of the crowds in the streets outside, where many of Stevenson's adherents paraded in tears as the odds against him mounted, might carry the day. When on the night of July 13 the demonstration for Stevenson began, Lehman tried to seize the New York standard to join the march around the hall. Two Tammany stalwarts, cigars clenched in teeth, held it fast while he tussled with them. Then Wagner stepped in with a

shout: "I told Lehman he could have the standard; give it to him *now!*"—
and he bore it off in triumph. Millions of television watchers across the country would long retain as their most poignant impression of the convention the memory of the passionate and eloquent appeal for Stevenson made from the rostrum by Lehman and Mrs. Roosevelt, an appeal that obviously came from their hearts. But when Kennedy won, they reconciled themselves to the choice and offered him every assistance.

Some other aspects of the campaign, however, had a comic-opera character. Men found a wry amusement in seeing the Wagner group and the De Sapio–Prendergast group staying at the same luxury hotel in Los Angeles, the Ambassador, but jealously maneuvering for a superiority of party position and credit. Kennedy welcomed New York support from every quarter; but all summer the Wagner Democrats and De Sapio Democrats covertly glowered at each other, while Lehman and the reformers marched aloofly under a Citizens-for-Kennedy banner. The reform element, Lehman explained at a rally at the Waldorf on September 14, 1960, where he introduced Kennedy, was "now totally engaged in the urgent task . . . of electing Senator John F. Kennedy as the next President of the United States." Lehman made more than twenty addresses for the candidate, hardly mentioning reform. Yet Prendergast and De Sapio rebuffed the insurgents at every opportunity.

Just before Lehman addressed a rally at Union Square, David Dubinsky of the ILGWU spoke to De Sapio about the wisdom of having ex-President Truman attend the affair. "Good idea," returned De Sapio. "I'll call you back." He never called back, and Dubinsky put in six telephone calls to him without an answer. Later the union leader heard from the Biltmore Hotel that Truman had indicated that he could not speak at open-air rallies "for reasons of health." After the rally, Dubinsky saw a photograph of Truman speaking bareheaded outdoors to a Westchester crowd and telephoned him. "We had a wonderful meeting today," he said. "Too bad you decided not to come." Truman responded: "Nobody told me about it. I'd have been glad to come if anybody had mentioned it to me." Two days later, on November 5, Tammany sponsored a great rally in the Coliseum, and Kennedy insisted that Lehman and Mrs. Roosevelt be included among the speakers. Both were on the stage in full view of television, but neither was given an opportunity to say a word.

When Kennedy carried New York City by a plurality of 791,333 votes, more than double the plurality of 310,000 won by Harriman in the election of 1958, Democratic voters could reflect anew on the plain evidence that the issue of "bossism" had cost their ticket hundreds of thousands of votes in the campaign against Rockefeller. Immediately after Kennedy's victory, the internecine party warfare in state and city broke out afresh. Irving Engel told an enthusiastic crowd of 2,500 reformers at the Hotel Astor: "We must take up the cudgels again. . . . The present leadership is an albatross around the neck of the party." When Lehman was asked whether a heavy new battle would mark the municipal elections of 1961, he replied: "Oh, yes! It will not be easy." And that same evening Wagner told a *Times* reporter: "I like being mayor of New York." [15]

· V ·

The first great event of 1961 in metropolitan politics was the alignment of Mayor Wagner with the reform forces. He was slow to declare his independence of Tammany; he knew well that although De Sapio's power in Manhattan might be waning, that of Representative Charles A. Buckley in the Bronx and Councilman Joseph T. Sharkey in Brooklyn remained tremendous. He had to be prodded into action—and Lehman's speeches and statements were sharp goads to the oxlike mayor. His outright break with De Sapio was precipitated by the disputed succession to Hulan E. Jack, deposed borough president of Manhattan, who had accepted favors from a building contractor doing business with the city, the choice being made by the six Manhattan members of the city council. When they tied between a reformer and a Tammany man, Wagner—who had been holding conferences with Lehman—saw an opportunity to avenge himself for petty ignominies he had suffered in Los Angeles and to demonstrate to the public his authority and resourcefulness. He chose Edward R. Dudley, former ambassador to Liberia and friend of Powell, for the vacancy, and Dudley won four to two over the Tammany regular.[16] This was a resounding public notice that Wagner had chosen the side he expected to win.

District leaders at once saw that this was the beginning of De Sapio's end. One of them told the *Times* that he was leaving the sinking ship. "I like Carmine. He is one of the best leaders we ever had. But I don't like him so much that I want to go down the drain with him." [17] And on February 3 the mayor sealed his secession with a statement that the *Herald-Tribune* headlined: "WAGNER BIDS DE SAPIO QUIT." "The time has come," he said, "for the leader of the New York County Democratic organization to step aside in the interests of the Democratic Party and a vast majority of its members in this county." De Sapio's reply was emphatic: "A loud No." [18] Lehman was still warily noncommittal as to the coming city election, for, as he commented, Wagner had burned his bridges only "to a very considerable extent" and still had a few timbers to ignite. The former governor simply

said: "We're going to watch how all levels of city and state government conduct themselves between now and the primaries."

These new primaries on September 7, critically important in the nomination of mayorality candidates and others, were preceded by a series of
exciting political developments. De Sapio fought valiantly to maintain his
power. He challenged Wagner and Lehman to a public debate on county
leadership, and when they rejected the suggestion, he delivered a Lincoln's
Birthday television appeal garnished with every Madison Avenue technique.

He strode upon the stage a few seconds before his hour-long broadcast
began, seated himself at a modern desk before a law-library background, and
began speaking in an even, softly modulated voice; rising at times to stand or
sit on the arm of his chair. His public relations agent, Sydney Baron, hovered
nervously in the wings. The boss began by explaining the dark glasses
which were as familiar to New Yorkers as Roosevelt's cigarette holder. "I
do not wear them for purposes of concealment. I understand perfectly well
that in the sensitive business of politics, they are no asset to a political leader.
When I was fifteen years old, I was stricken with iritis, which can best be
described as an arthritic condition of the eyes. Light is very painful to
me. . . ." He analyzed the Buffalo convention, accusing Wagner of repudiat-
ing a preconvention promise to remain neutral, and attacking the Finletter
group for sabotaging the Harriman-Hogan ticket. He asked why Governor
Lehman was so critical of the system of judicial nominations when he had
acquiesced without objection to the elevation of his brother Irving by that
method. And why was Mayor Wagner so suddenly hostile?—was it to dis-
tract attention from his poor record and gain support for a third term?

President Kennedy meanwhile took a cautious hand in city politics when
he diverted Federal patronage from the joint offices of Michael Prendergast
and De Sapio in the Biltmore and gave Wagner and Representative Buckley
a larger share in job distribution. It seemed plain that the President wished
Prendergast replaced as state chairman by Peter J. Crotty of Buffalo, who
had a brief talk at the White House in March. Though Lehman had no liking
for this iron-fisted, conservative machine leader, he pleaded for consideration
of Crotty and for deferring any decision. While he was in Florida with a
bout of pneumonia a militant group among the young reformers, led by
James S. Lanigan, lurched ahead with a resolution of condemnation, which
heads of the New York Committee for Democratic Voters passed 46 to 24.
These militants wished to protect the purity of their organization at all costs,
and their chilliness toward any alliance with either Crotty or Wagner pre-
saged a factional division in the reform element. This was most unfortunate.
When Lehman returned, and addressed the general committee, he empha-

sized the value of responsibility and the importance of broadening the base of the reform movement. He urged a greater realism in such matters as the acceptance of Crotty. The recent vote, he intimated, could be viewed as a rebuke to the President, and any such gesture would retard attainment of the main objectives of reform.[19]

All along, Lehman saw clearly that only through a fighting alliance with Wagner—after certain pledges had been extracted from the mayor, of course —could a victory over Tammany be made certain in the fall elections. By late May he had come close to an outright endorsement of the man. "Whatever his attitude may have been previously," the governor said, "he is alive to the great problems of the city, and I believe that he has made up his mind and is determined to carry on the reforms necessary for improved government." [20] Reform Democrats of the West Side had presented a resolution to the general committee of the NYCDV denouncing Wagner for eight years of laxity and indecision; this he thought unwise. When the committee met on June 7 he told it flatly that a battle against the mayor in the primary would destroy the reform movement and after a three-hour debate achieved a clear-cut victory. By a vote of 50 to 26 it was agreed to take no position in respect to designating a Democratic candidate for mayor at that time.

After this the situation rapidly crystallized. In mid-June four of the five county leaders, De Sapio, Buckley, Sharkey, and McKinney of Richmond, met and agreed to act together in making the regular Democratic nomination for mayor.[21] This was soon followed by their choice of Arthur Levitt, state controller and sole survivor of the Democratic debacle of 1958. On June 22 Wagner announced his candidacy for reëlection, making clear his repudiation of the machine. Lehman at once hailed his action: "It is a refreshing turn in the political history of our city to have the public leader of the Democrats of the city provide the leadership rather than the bosses. . . . Speaking personally, I think I can wholeheartedly support the ticket as proposed by the mayor." [22] As soon as Levitt announced his acceptance, the governor spoke still more emphatically to a press conference in his apartment: "I see the primary election, and the general election which will follow, as an opportunity which New Yorkers have not had for many years —and may not have again for many years more—to free this city with one blow from the shackles of the boss system. . . . I see this prospect, in realistic and practical terms, through the renomination and reëlection of Mayor Robert F. Wagner." [23]

Not without stormy debate and some heartburning, the general committee of the reform organization a fortnight later voted 84 to 1 to support Wagner. The crucial primary campaign between Tammany and Reform, between the Levitt forces and the Wagner forces, thus opened. Running its six-weeks course through August and early September, it would decide the destiny of the city, for the Democrats held so heavy a preponderance of strength that their candidate was almost certain to win over any Republican or Independent. The fact that it would be a grim conflict grew clearer when the machine Goliath filed 283,304 designating signatures with the Board of Elections against 64,831 brought forward by the reform Davids.

Yet backers of Wagner were full of optimism. If one half of the 1,500,000 registered Democrats eligible to vote could be brought to the polls, they believed, they could win. They lacked the cohorts of block captains and "pullers" that Tammany could muster; but their array of impressive leaders could make an "appeal to the people" in the fashion dear to Lehman's heart. With the best part of the press on their side, and television and sound trucks to help, they could reach the whole electorate. They established headquarters at the Astor Hotel, with Fire Commissioner Edward F. Cavanagh, Jr., as manager, Julius C. C. Edelstein as deputy, and George Backer, J. Raymond Jones, Paul O'Dwyer, Stanley Lowell, and Joseph Rappaport among the workers. Thirty-nine district clubs backed the campaign. Jim Farley lent his influence.

• VI •

To countless New Yorkers the memorable feature of the campaign was the indefatigable activity of the former governor and Senator, now eighty-three. His prestige, his record, his spirit, were all-important. He argued on radio, on television, and in press statements. He clambered (with some trepidation) to the top of sound trucks. He joined Mayor Wagner in the type of walking tour that Paul Douglas used in Illinois cities and that Nelson Rockefeller had adopted in 1958, talking Spanish with Puerto Ricans, eating blintzes with the Jews and pizzas with the Italians; he and the mayor avoided food but strode the pavements with loudspeakers for votes. One scorching hot Sunday Lehman traveled from Coney Island along the boardwalk, chiefly afoot, to Brighton Beach and Manhattan Beach. It was a six-hour march, the governor in ankle-high shoes and shirt sleeves, his collar buttoned and his blue tie drawn tight. Mrs. Lehman had provided an electric cart for the party, but he disdained it. Night after night packed halls in different parts of the city would be electrified by the quiet entry of the governor, unjaded, unruffled, temperate, to mount the stage for a speech.

Yet the *New York Post* of September 5 missed the mark when it commented: "After the polls have been closed and the votes have been counted on Thursday night, one image of human gallantry will endure regardless of the outcome. It will be the unforgettable portrait of an 83-year-old man named Herbert Lehman trudging through the sun-scorched streets from one end of the city to the other with his earnest pleas for support of the Wagner ticket. It is a spectacle that must humiliate the tired young men and inspire thousands who had hitherto remained aloof from the battle." The fact was that Lehman found the battle stimulating, the exertion exhilarating. When the struggle was over, friends commented that he looked better than ever.

Not that all was harmony this summer on the reform side. A certain mutual incomprehension persisted between the militant young reformers and the older leaders even while they fought shoulder to shoulder. Some young leaders still believed that the emphasis on destroying De Sapio was overdone. They thought it obscured the real goal, which was to democratize and liberalize the Democratic organization; that is, to build up district organizations of liberal voters, manage the clubs so as to bring in members who would take a zealous interest in housing, juvenile delinquency, and general civic decency, and get the district leaders freely elected. They thought Lehman too intent on purgation, too forgetful of construction. In this difference of opinion, it was natural that to some of the young element he seemed dictatorial. This was partly because he presented his opinions in a blunt way —he was blunt, not subtle, in his mental attitudes; partly because some reform leaders resented Lehman's support of Wagner.

Lehman, for his part, sometimes thought the younger element both selfish and self-willed. He would say, in effect, a bit petulantly: "These young people don't want to take my advice; all they want is to use me." The fact was that the young folk rather touchingly went out of their way— bent over backward—to make their deference clear. They were full of gratitude for his aid, which they knew to be indispensable. It was also a fact that Lehman with advancing years had grown somewhat more inflexible and stubborn in his attitudes. The factionalism touched other leaders.

Nevertheless, fighting unity was preserved to the end, and as Primary Day approached, the ranks solidified. The bitter, bruising battle ended September 7 amid general uncertainty as to the outcome. Many observers thought that Wagner had the better chance; others predicted victory for Levitt because he had the county organizations behind him. The governing factor, shrewd judges believed, would be the size of the total vote; if it approached 800,000 Wagner would win, and if it was below 500,000 Levitt would be nominated. The keenest attention was centered on Greenwich Village, where De Sapio's position as leader was contested by Lanigan, the forty-three-year-old Harvard-educated lawyer. On the Republican side, Attorney General Louis J. Lefkowitz was unopposed for the mayoral nomination.

It was a Tammany Waterloo that ensued. A total of 743,130 Democrats, the largest in the history of the primaries, went to the polls. They nominated Wagner by a plurality of 159,786. They routed the Tammany tiger in all boroughs, in thirteen of sixteen district leadership contests, and in eight of eleven races for the council. Especially impressive and astonishing was Lanigan's defeat of De Sapio in the Village, 6,165 to 4,745. Wagner instantly assumed a position in the state party that had not been attained by anyone since the years in which Al Smith, Roosevelt, and Lehman had held the governorship. His election as mayor over Lefkowitz and the independent candidate, City Controller Lawrence E. Gerosa, was taken as a certainty—and it so proved. A shower of congratulatory telegrams from all over the nation covered his desk. Mrs. Roosevelt expressed exuberant pleasure. "I am delighted," she exclaimed: "Wonderful!" Everyone agreed that De Sapio must now go, and he was shortly replaced as head of the county organization by Wagner's campaign manager, Cavanagh.

The man who as a boy had seen his father return home from a torchlight parade for Grover Cleveland, inveterate enemy of Tammany; who, as a young businessman, had enlisted with Sulzer against Boss Murphy; who, as lieutenant governor, had pleaded with his wife to "keep me a little vindictive" over Boss Curry's mean attempt to force him out of the state; who as governor constantly feared some Tammany stab in the back, had special reason to feel happy. The victory was astounding. No one at first had believed it even possible; now it proved crushing. Talking with James A. Wechsler of the *Post*, on election night, he recalled that many political writers had contended that the reform movement could never get off the ground, "and for a while it looked as if they were right." His eyes, however, were on the future. Wagner had the greatest opportunity ever given a mayor. "It is so great an opportunity—I have told him this many times—that I wish I could have had it twenty or thirty years ago, when I was a little younger."

Thereupon he quite properly withdrew to the rear, leaving the new reform movement to the able young people who had launched it before he entered the battle, and who had the arduous but hopeful task of carrying it forward.

Chapter XX

MAN AND IDEAS

Looking back over this long career of public service, these forty-odd years of work, of worry, and of warfare, how can we assess the man and the principles which guided him? The task is complicated, but it has this simplifying element, that with Herbert H. Lehman the primary force of the man has lain not in his intellectual faculties, estimable as they have been, but in his character. He is a man of action; not a thinker, not a student, but a doer.

The signal traits which have made him influential have been courage, social idealism, and industry: quiet bulldog courage, constructive sympathy with the neglected and oppressed, and unremitting industry. These qualities gave distinction to his work as governor, head of UNRRA, and Senator. Born to wealth, he never allowed riches to limit his sympathies or bind him with fealty to privilege and class; he always regarded himself as one with the poor. Reared in a self-conscious, closely-knit minority, he was as completely an American as anyone in the country. Exempted, at a comparatively early age, from the task of making a living, he worked all the harder for objects of a more elevated order. He was highly ambitious, but unlike most of the ambitious men about him, he stoutly refused to traffic with expediency. A great deal might be said of his integrity, which was never questioned, of his kindliness, which flowed from an unfailing inner wellspring, and of his optimistic faith in his causes—above all, the great cause of democracy. The main levers with which he moved his world, however, were the three which we have named.

Industry is a common American trait, but not industry as heavy, sustained, and effective as Lehman's. As governor and Senator he showed the capacity to work sixteen hours a day. "Yes, I remember going to see him in Washington about some changes in national banking law," says a Californian. "The two facts I recall are, first, that he set the appointment in his office at 7:30 A.M., and second, that he understood the matter at once." It could not be said that he was a prodigiously rapid worker, that, as Dumont wrote of Mirabeau and Rosebery of Gladstone, he could accomplish in a day more than most men did in a week. But whatever the task, he set at it early, concentrated his powers upon it, marshaled his helpers with skill, and kept at it until it was accomplished. In the campaign to unseat De Sapio, he toiled as long and strenuously as his young associates. Throughout life he has by no means disdained recreation. He has loved outdoor exercise—golf, tennis, walking, swimming, and fishing; in recent years he has still caught tarpon and sailfish in Florida waters. Nobody has enjoyed a good play, an interesting book, a pleasant dinner more than he. But even in his pastimes he is busy.

His social conscience was a more important trait. Its origins doubtless lay in the training of his home and synagogue, reinforced a little by his schooling under Dr. Sachs; but above all in the precept and example of his father, Mayer Lehman. All accounts speak of Mayer as philanthropy and conscience incarnate, and he often took Herbert with him to this or that charitable organization, to Temple Emanu-El, or to Mount Sinai Hospital. The father had an Old World courtesy, a grave urbanity and sweetness of manner, which Herbert partly inherited, partly imitated; but above all, he set the example of an exquisite consideration for others and of a profound interest in the unfortunate. Herbert Lehman has recorded how he agonized, as a growing boy, over his inability to rise to the level of his parents' expectations. The Jewish circle in which he grew up was one of the most philanthropic in America, and he imbibed its spirit. The statesmanship in the organization of benevolence exhibited by Jacob H. Schiff, the practical goodness of Rabbi Gustav Gottheil of Temple Emanu-El, and the visions of the future cherished by Judah L. Magnes, three men whom young Lehman knew well, could not but leave an impress upon him. When in 1914 he became one of the founders of the Joint Distribution Committee, he was thrown into the full current of work for the alleviation of the greatest volume of suffering witnessed for centuries.

Equipped with this training, he readily responded to all the impulses of the urban movement in social and political reform which early in the century supplanted the older agrarian crusades. The country had become industrialized; parts of it were overcrowded; poverty, unemployment, the abuse of labor, the spread of slums, had become urgent problems; the protection of the unfortunate and neglected could no longer be left to charity and local effort. Under Theodore Roosevelt, Woodrow Wilson, and Franklin D. Roosevelt, national policy was altered at first gradually and cautiously, then swiftly and completely. The states sometimes led the way, as Wisconsin did in unemployment insurance, and progressive state leaders like

Al Smith furnished a new vision of government responsibility for social welfare. Later, under the New Deal, the states had to move step by step with the Federal lawmakers. No undertaking could have been more congenial to Lehman than the promotion or reinforcement of health, education, decent labor policies, workmen's compensation insurance, and the protection of the crippled, the widowed, and the aged. His experience in settlement-house work, the far-flung JDC activities, his own model-housing venture, and the concerns of a score of philanthropic organizations in which he was active were a preparation which his long business experience strengthened in practical ways. He originated no great new ideas, but he gave a lusty impulse to the best social thinking of the time.

In following his social conscience he was a highly practical man; as practical as Al Smith and more cautious than FDR. Harold F. Linder, working with George Rublee in London during the later 1930s to try to save some of Hitler's many victims, used on his returns to New York to consult with him. "I can recall on one of my trips back, probably in the early spring or late winter of 1939, having a long talk with him in his apartment in New York about the desirability of our attempts to work out something with the Germans on behalf of the refugees. His attitude at that time was clearly not that of a 'soft' philanthropist but rather that of a kind man of affairs who had a lot of practical experience in business and government. That he had the interests of the people we were trying to help in mind there could be no doubt; nevertheless, he wanted to be certain that we were not being led along a garden path by the representative of the Nazi Government." [1] His opponents called him many names, but they never called him visionary, for he bent a keen eye upon ways and means. For example, after the passage of the McCarran Immigration Act a committee was formed to educate the public upon its injustices—and to do some lobbying. When Spyros Skouras, the head, proved inactive, Lehman was asked to take his place. He agreed only on condition that the committee make a firm commitment to raise $60,000 or $70,000 a year for costs—a condition not met.

Both his conscience and industry were in fact those of a keen-minded man of affairs. Conscience led him, when governor, to dispose of every security that might be affected by his public acts. Conscience was behind his overwork. "Governor Smith told me once," said former Insurance Commissioner George S. Van Schaick, "that he didn't see how Governor Lehman, being as conscientious as he was, could ever live through the grueling work of the Executive Office and do it that way. . . . He said, 'He is going to kill himself making every question of maximum importance.' Well, it was just Governor Lehman's temperament. He was thorough and liked always

Herbert H. Lehman and Mrs. Lehman at the inauguration of the Children's Zoo
in Central Park, September 28, 1961.

New York Daily News

Herbert H. Lehman and Mrs. Lehman in the Governor's study, 1953

Ted Kell, *New York Herald-Tribune*

Adlai E. Stevenson addressing Liberal Party Luncheon March 29, 1958, in honor of Herbert H. Lehman's 80th birthday   Photo Alexander Archer

Herbert H. Lehman at Coney Island during Mayoralty Primary Campaign, September, 1961. Mayor Robert F. Wagner is to the right.

The New York Times

Herbert H. Lehman and Adlai E. Stevenson during the presidential campaign
of 1952
United Press International Newspictures

Herbert H. Lehman at the mass meeting at the Polo Grounds, New York City,
April 27, 1958, for the Tenth Anniversary of the State of Israel. *Left to right:*
Commander Julius C. C. Edelstein, Herbert H. Lehman, Mrs. Franklin D. Roose-
velt, General Moshe Dayan, Former Chief of Staff of the Israeli Army, and
Ambassador Abba Eban.
Photo Fred Brand

to know what he was talking about." [2] Conscientiousness was at the root of his bad habit of worrying, worrying about matters large and small. Conscience—not private conscience but social conscience—prompted the governor's laborious vigilance in assisting all public departments and institutions. All this was quietly done; he never advertised it. Dr. Thomas Parran, his health commissioner, has related how some disastrous flash floods in the Chenango–Susquehanna Valleys and the Finger Lakes Region drew the careful executive to the scene:

"I travelled with the Governor's party as he surveyed at first hand the situation in the flood areas. My most vivid recollection was that wherever we went there was a publicity person from the American Red Cross issuing news releases about what that organization was doing to aid its victims. As a matter of fact, the major aid came from the State Departments of Public Works, Health, Welfare, and especially the Relief Administration. From the health point of view we were able to mobilize medical officers, sanitary engineers, and nurses, not only from New York but on loan from other states, to deal with the potential problems of epidemics in the wake of the floods." [3]

Lehman would not have thought of publicizing his work or letting his department heads do so; it was in the line of duty.

His courage was not only a practical but very emphatically an aggressive type of courage. He considered his course, gave due weight to the fact that in any battle, as Daniel Webster said, "if there are blows to be given there are also blows to be taken," and then struck hard. He was oversensitive to personal blows, and never forgot some supposed aspersions of Robert Moses, John Foster Dulles, and Fiorello La Guardia upon his character which might better have been taken in a Pickwickian sense. But in a good cause he was anxious to meet the foe not in the gate but in front of it. He need not have written his letter attacking Roosevelt's plan for Supreme Court reorganization, for example; he had abundant reason for not writing it—his friendship with the President, which might be wrecked, his loyalty to the party, which would be hurt, the certainty that some people would think Judge Irving Lehman dictated it; but his duty seemed plain. He was among the first to open the attack on McCarthy. It was unnecessary for him to spring to Mrs. Roosevelt's defense with his sharp letter of rebuke to Spellman, which astonished everyone. His manners were courteous and his measures mild, but Joseph R. McCarthy, Pat McCarran, and De Sapio all knew that he was aggressive.

This does not mean that much of his courage was not of the defensive type. He was such a firm protector of the civil service merit system in New

York that he was sometimes called the "Civil Service Governor." To be sure, he did yield a few times to the demands of politicians, but this was partly because he believed that politically trained men gave better service in some jobs than men graduated *cum laude* from Harvard or Yale. His leadership brought about the passage in 1937 of the Feld–Hamilton Act providing a sound reclassification of state positions with uniform titles and a sound and uniform salary plan. By a bold and shrewd stroke he induced the State Civil Service Commission to amend its rules so that, in general, appointments should be made in the strict numerical order of standing on the eligible lists but with some latitude in filling highly responsible posts. His defense of civil service principles required backbone, particularly when the politician offering pressure was a friend like Jim Farley or Ed Flynn. And he had the courage to defend Thomas E. Dewey's interests in one critical hour.

This was when Dewey, after his service in breaking the so-called rackets, was elected district attorney of New York County. As H. Eliot Kaplan, executive director and counsel of the Civil Service Reform Association, writes, Dewey was confronted with the problem of reorganizing his office, for most of the positions were filled by Democrats obviously unsympathetic to a Republican head. When drastic steps were taken, a hail of criticism beat upon Dewey and Lehman as well. "The Governor was particularly criticized by many of his political advisers for permitting the State Civil Service Commission to grant Dewey a free hand by exempting many of the positions from civil service examinations. It was charged that this would permit Dewey to build up a political machine of his own in the District Attorney's office." Mr. Kaplan, at Lehman's request, served as intermediary between Dewey and the Commission and helped Dewey obtain the privilege of filling more offices in his own way from his own party. Democratic anger rose high. "Governor Lehman, however, resisted political pressures to embarrass the new District Attorney"—something few could easily have done. As Mr. Kaplan writes, he "was steadfast in his refusal to interfere in an orderly reorganization" [4] of Dewey's office—and it was long before the complaints ceased.

· I ·

In his public labors Lehman had handicaps as well as advantages. His tendency to worry over matters great and small seemed to indicate, as Al Smith and other friends thought, an inability to distinguish properly between minor and major responsibilities. This was probably an accurate judgment in his early career; later, with experience, he both worried less and brought a better sense of proportion to his many tasks. He was long a flat if not an otiose speaker, his phrasing more often tired than athletic and his delivery monotonous. It is only in his later speeches that we meet an occasional witty thrust or flashing epigram.

He was never a complex man, with the picturesqueness that complexity brings. He had none of the Sinaitic fervors of Woodrow Wilson, the subtleties of Franklin D. Roosevelt, or the sparkle of Adlai E. Stevenson. He has been simple in thought, in action, and above all in obedience to his own fundamental morality, like two men he especially admired, Grover Cleveland and Oscar Underwood. To the general public, though never to close friends, he seemed and still seems colorless—and colorlessness in a political leader is a handicap. Certainly he is not a man about whom colorful anecdotes have clustered. He has been the despair of reporters and memoirists.

It is hardly possible, for example, to make a good story out of one fact reflecting his sense of duty: his extreme punctuality. It has often been noted. "The thing that impresses me," writes Elmo Roper of their service on the board of the Henry Street Settlement, "is that he and Mrs. Lehman always show up for meetings." [5] For so busy a man the hour fixed, five P.M. on Monday afternoon, is inconvenient; but as Miss Hall, the head, testifies, his and his wife's attendance record is better than that of anybody else. Men who have to come from Forty-second Street may be late; the Lehmans are on time even if they come from Washington or Buffalo. When he was lieutenant governor, he was promptly on hand daily at one P.M. for the opening of the session of the state senate, though many members lounged in later. Just once he was a few minutes late and was wrathful to find Senator Fearon in his chair. "I think I have been as punctual as any lieutenant governor in recent years," he said. "It seems in view of the courtesies the presiding officer has shown this house in many ways that he could have been given five minutes delay."

Nor is it possible to make a good story out of his devotion to Mrs. Lehman and reliance on her poise and judgment, which parallel Disraeli's dependence on his wife. At public meetings, it was long ago noted, he will look carefully about the hall as he rises; his face will light up as he sees her, and he will give her a tiny wave of his hand; then he will begin to speak. In his public relations he is belligerent—for he finds a great deal to be belligerent about. In private relations he is all gentleness and generosity.

"I came to realize that he was essentially a shy man," declares Dr. Parran, "who gave his confidence rather sparingly; but when he did give his confidence to someone, it was wholehearted and without reservation." Those taken into his confidence realize that, far from being colorless, he is a man of deep intensity of feeling. His emotions have been all the stronger for running deep. His feelings were hotly enlisted in gaining a place in the Anglo-Saxon, Gentile world of Williams College; in seeing Wilson elected and reëlected; in urging American participation in the First World War. When he fell in love he was madly in love. At the Democratic Convention of 1924, where he was so fervently engaged for Smith and against McAdoo, the long suicidal drag did more than stun him. "I was *heartbroken*," he has said—and he meant just that. So his intensity of feeling on critical matters continued down to the toppling of Tammany Hall. But his reticence and seeming imperturbability have masked all this, so that he is still to many "colorless."

He was long handicapped also by his awkwardness, a trait which became the source of a few stories that he has enjoyed as much as anybody. Nobody is more inclined to laugh at himself. He likes to tell of a dinner which President Roosevelt gave at the White House in 1933 or 1934 in his and Mrs. Lehman's honor. Fingerbowls were placed before them all. Then came the dessert. Lehman, engrossed in the talk, was ladling a great helping of ice cream into his fingerbowl when Roosevelt burst into gleeful laughter: "Just look at what Herbie is doing!" He likes to tell also of a trial involving some client of J. Spencer Turner in which, as a young officer in the firm, Lehman was a witness. Max Steuer cross-examined him, and his rapier queries soon left Lehman helpless and bleeding. After giving a plain statement of facts he could only stammer: "I have forgotten that"; "I guess you're right"; "My memory there is a blank." When he came down from the stand he whispered to the firm's attorney, "Sorry I did so badly." "Yes, you were terrible," agreed the lawyer. But the jury brought in a verdict for the firm and the foreman later explained: "It was all because of Herbert Lehman's testimony. He made such an exhibition of himself that we saw he was completely honest in what he did say!"

The journalist Hickman Powell, attempting a "profile" of Lehman for the *New Yorker* in 1936, was daunted by the governor's lack of saliency— of palette contrasts. He took refuge in personal detail—Lehman always wore a stiff collar, a pearl stickpin, a vest with two or three pencils and a fountain pen in the pockets, and a coat which he doffed on hot days to turn back his starched cuffs; he was always plowing through a vast heap of papers; and though he did little smoking, he usually carried an unlighted pipe or cigar in his mouth. The best story the writer could dig up was of a spring day when Mrs. Lehman ("whom he calls E-e-e-e in a sort of squeal") had telephoned him just after the legislature adjourned, leaving a thousand bills in its wake. "Oh, E-e-e-e!" Powell reported the governor crying into the telephone. "I bet you can't guess what I'm doing. I'm signing bills with Charlie Poletti, and planning the beer board with Sam Rosenman, and dictating letters, and having my hair cut, and talking to you—all at the same time!" [6]

As the author of the profile stated, the governor then delivered colorless speeches in a colorless way. "He reads from a mimeographed copy, with his head down; his horn-rimmed spectacles usually slide down his nose with agonizing slowness until they are about to drop; then he pushes them back. When, occasionally, he interrupts his reading with a gesture, the emphasis is likely to be an instant too late, as if it were an afterthought. . . ." But his plain business aspect somehow paid. The Republicans had nominated two colorful opponents against Lehman in 1932 and 1934, Wild Bill Donovan and the still wilder Bob Moses. "Mr. Lehman was dull in his campaign against Donovan, and his election was a triumph. He was still duller in 1934, and, running far ahead of the national New Deal candidates, carried the State by 808,000, the greatest plurality ever known in an off year. The talk today is that the Republicans are looking for a drab candidate who can trade monotony for monotony. . . ."

Sometimes his awkwardness, which could be engaging, paid unexpected dividends. He has always had a bad memory for names and faces. It was part of his duty year in and year out to make appeals for many causes. At one fund-raising dinner the chairman announced a donation from a man whom Lehman knew to be very rich. Turning to the person on his right, Lehman exclaimed: "Really a poor gift—a very poor gift." It was the man just named!—who at once rose and declared, "In honor of Governor Lehman, I wish to add a special gift." [7] Even through his awkwardness shone the essential goodness of the man, and even in his social errors people could see his unfailing consideration for others. Himself highly sensitive, he never forgot the sensibilities of others.

Arthur Corscadden, an Albany youth who worked in Governor Smith's office and continued under Roosevelt and Lehman, sent a long and affectionate letter on Lehman's seventieth birthday in 1948. Others would recall the big events, he wrote, "but I choose to think of you by the smaller, more intimate incidents." [8] He remembered that at Al Smith's last inauguration, Smith told him to escort Lehman to the platform and to get him there without fail. But the trapdoor to the stage was bolted, and a burly state trooper barred the way with an edict that nobody could go up. As Corscadden and the trooper wrangled, Lehman kept interposing for peace: "Please don't get into any argument on my account, young man; I will be glad to go back to the governor's office and wait until after the ceremony to see the governor."

Corscadden recalled also an occasion in New York when the governor, holding a conference with an important group, interrupted it to go out himself and explain to a caller why he must wait; and then, espying two casual tourists who had come to look at the Lehman paintings, he hurried over to them, introduced himself, and spent five minutes talking of the art. Corscadden related another instance of personal courtesy on the night in 1933 that the financiers of New York gathered anxiously at 820 Park Avenue to debate a bank holiday.

Residents in the Henry Street neighborhood long remembered a far more important incident early in Lehman's governorship. Five youths who had often been in the settlement house tried to hold up a store; one of them secretly carried a revolver, and when the storekeeper resisted, he shot him dead. All five, under the harsh law on the statute books, were convicted of murder. The area was prostrated with grief. Parents, other relatives, and friends crowded a train to Albany for a hearing before the governor. He sat gravely sympathetic as their spokesman made his plea. Unfortunately, the young man stumbled confusedly in his argument. "Just take your time," said Lehman; "do not hurry. I shall stay all afternoon for this case if you like." [9] Mrs. Lehman, as usual in such hearings, sat in the rear of the room, for the governor wanted her advice. The hearing lasted so long that she finally left. "She has to go home and make supper," one of the East Side women hazarded. In the end, a mitigation of sentence for three of the youths was arranged. What was more important, the governor obtained a change in the law which permitted a jury in such cases to make a recommendation of mercy, whereupon a life sentence might be substituted for execution.

Lehman's public appearances in 1928, Corscadden wrote the governor, were depressing to his friends. "I was on the campaign trip that year and listened to you make practically the same speech, night after night. Frankly, Governor, you were terrible. You appeared timid, your delivery was poor, and you had no idea at all on which lines to place particular emphasis. . . . The best I can say about your speeches was that you kept them short." Yet in the deeper earnestness of his later years he could speak with power; conviction not merely gave him force but lifted his argument to a higher level. He illustrated Lord Morley's saying that "great thoughts spring from the heart." He even achieved, on rare occasions, an epigrammatic phrase. Thus at the quarter-century anniversary dinner of the New York Federation of Jewish Philanthropies, which he had helped found, he said of his brother Arthur, long-time president: "He *lived Federation,* and I like to think that he did much, out of his wisdom and devotion, to *make Federation live.*" Some of his later speeches were dull, but it would be difficult to find a more moving address than that on "Discrimination: A Factor in the World Crisis," which he delivered to the World Brotherhood Seminar in Berne on August 18, 1958—a magnificent indictment of racial discrimination and prejudice.

His almost unbroken seriousness had one unfortunate consequence in the fact that throughout his public career people spoke of his lack of a sense of humor. Here a little discrimination is necessary. Mark Twain was once asked whether women had a sense of humor. He replied by pointing to his wife, who was crossing the lawn. "Now," he said, "I don't suppose that woman ever said a humorous thing in her life. But she always sees the point of my jokes." It is doubtful if Lehman ever coined a joke in his life; it would have been impossible for him to invent a comic situation or write a funny skit. But some of his most characteristic photographs, to close friends, show his features crinkled with infectious mirth; he always had a rich and ready laugh.

Early in his governorship Assemblyman Irwin Steingut, who liked the track, spoke up jovially at a meeting of legislative leaders discussing the large state deficit. "I know an absolutely sure winner at five to one at the Saratoga races next Saturday," he said, "If the governor will authorize the state treasurer to give me one million dollars to bet, I will turn it into five millions and bring us out of our troubles." All eyes turned to Lehman. With absolute gravity, he replied: "I do not believe that this would be a judicious employment of the state's financial resources." The following week Steingut told the same group: "My horse won easily last Saturday. If the governor had let me use a million of state funds, we would have five millions in hand today!" To which Lehman, with imperturbable countenance, replied in the gravest voice: "I do not believe that this would have been a judicious employment of the state's financial resources." And some of the legislators thought he had never seen the joke.

An equal difference of opinion existed on the question of his vanity or humility, and it involved a similar issue of semantics. Humility and modesty are different traits, and he had the first without the second. His invaluable aide, Dr. Thomas Parran, relates that Herbert and Edith Lehman once had a talk with him (probably in the late 1940s) in which they said that they had frequently discussed what they might do when he retired from public life. "Specifically he asked me if I thought they might make a contribution to medical science by taking jobs in a research laboratory. He explained that neither of them had any special training; but was there any merit in the notion? I told them that I thought there were many other directions and opportunities for human service in which they could make larger contributions." [10] This was humility; he was ready to serve anywhere if assured it was truly useful service. Dr. Frederick Brown Harris, chaplain of the Senate, once asked a prominent public relations man for labor why he had so high an opinion of Lehman and got the answer: "As a public servant he was so dedicated, humble, unassuming." [11] David Dressler has sketched the contrast between Governors Dewey and Lehman as they used to come into the Albany station: Dewey with self-conscious gait, pouter-pigeon chest, and dapper garb, flanked by two state troopers; and Lehman, unattended, for he sent the bodyguard ahead with the baggage, plainly dressed, an unlighted pipe in his mouth, lost in the crowd.[12]

He was unassuming in the way that shirt-sleeved FDR was unassuming, humble in the sense that Lincoln was humble; but he has a strong sense of dignity and his sensitiveness to criticism was one facet of his keen desire for a proper amount of honor. After all, as Aristotle said, honor is the only coin in which public servants are likely to be paid for their toils and sacrifices. Late in life he walked out of a party dinner in New York because he was not placed upon the dais; he felt at once, when he entered, that hostile politicians had arranged a deliberate slight by placing him—governor for ten years, Senator, long head of the party—in a corner. "Well, this is pretty cool," he remarked and quietly left. In this instance the dignity of his offices as well as his personal self-respect was involved. Friends perceived his touch of vanity, but they also perceived that as compared with John Adams, for example, he never exhibited it in overweening degree, and it was never tinged by jealousy. He might be petulant when hurt, but he was totally without malice.

This was part of his essential goodness. Senator Richard Neuberger, paying tribute to him in 1958 for his courage, unselfishness, and kindliness, added that although his judgment sometimes proved superior to that of colleagues, he never said, "I told you so." He called a conference of liberal senators in his office in January, 1955, to thresh out civil rights legislation; and he alone of the group wished to wage a stubborn fight then and there to alter Rule XXII, which permitted unlimited debate. Support failed. "Gentlemen," he said, "you are making a very serious mistake." Many times later Neuberger heard Douglas, Murray, Humphrey, and others admit he had been right. "The significant thing was that Lehman himself never rubbed it in. . . . It would not have been in character for him to do so. This was never a man to inflict personal hurt." [13] Like Lincoln, he would not willingly plant a thorn in another man's pillow. When he ran for lieutenant governor in 1930 politicians urged him to deal some shrewd blows at his opponent Caleb Baumes. "No," he said, "I don't want to hurt the poor old man's feelings." When Lehman was operated upon for cataract in 1962, better dinners were brought him from home than the ones the hospital provided; but Mrs. Lehman stayed to eat the hospital dinner that the staff might not feel aggrieved.

• II •

He was often called cautious, and in his early public years, while still much the businessman, doubtless deserved the adjective. Later, when certain causes enlisted his full devotion, he was conspicuously bold. When the Fund for the Republic was under raking fire from the Hearst press, the American Legion, the Catholic War Veterans, and like groups, he took special pleasure in joining its board. He said, Elmo Roper writes, "that he would not under normal circumstances take on any more responsibilities; that he was doing so only because we were under serious attack, and that what we stood for mustn't be allowed to perish for want of any support he might give it." [14] He is also a trustee of the Institute for Advanced Study in Princeton. In that post he distinguished himself for decisive utterance, as when he condemned all of three alternative sketches for a library as ugly and when he declared emphatically for placing contemporaneous history in the curriculum. But Robert Oppenheimer, whom the Atomic Energy Commission had denied access to restricted information as a security risk, defines his boldest action: "I know that after my hearings in 1954, the Senator played a clear, courageous, and decisive part in insisting that I continue as Director of the Institute. Of course, I have never known just what he did; I know only that it was effective." [15] Again and again, in the Senate he rushed into debate when friends tried to restrain him.

Perhaps the truth about his boldness and his caution is that, like other men, he possessed both traits and tried to accommodate them to the occasion. One of his closest friends in the Senate said that at times there he was "nervous as a cat" and sometimes "pugnacious as a bulldog"; sometimes he was impulsive and sometimes he would spend endless hours having his staff brief him on a coming issue. In short, he had as many human contradictions as other normal men.

One of these natural contradictions appeared in his belligerent espousal of peace. Internationalism in all its aspects, including the United Nations, foreign aid, the Hague Tribunal, mutual assistance, cultural interchanges, and tariff reductions, found a constant champion in Lehman, who was ready to fight for them. After the calamitous defeat of the West in China, the triumph of Mao Tse-tung and Communism, and the retreat of Chiang Kai-shek to Formosa, the White Paper which the State Department issued on August 5, 1949, with subsequent events, inspired Lehman to write an apprehensive letter to Secretary Acheson. They agreed that a new policy toward the Chinese people would have to be shaped and that it would have to be posited on a high moral plane. Lehman expressed fear that cynical and resentful groups in America might encourage Chiang to embark on perilous adventures, even to an invasion of the mainland, and embroil America.[16] He wrote:

"The first principle of the American people in foreign policy today is a search for peace, justice, and the well-being of all peoples. It is not to maintain a particular battleline along the Asia coast or to resist by force those ideologies which are not reconcilable with ours. . . . We must not invite war in order to avoid it. We must not practise evil in order to halt it. There is a slower and harder but surer way."

Then came the Korean War, the initial American victories, and the final deadlock as Chinese "volunteers" fought the United Nations forces. The situation which Lehman had feared developed. When General MacArthur wrote Representative Joe Martin on March 20, 1951, that the Chiang Kai-shek forces on Formosa should be thrown into the war "to meet force with maximum counter-force" and that they must win—"there is no substitute for victory"—Senators Taft, Knowland, and McCarthy energetically backed him. Truman did not and ordered MacArthur home. His declaration that "Our aim is to avoid the spread of the conflict" met Lehman's views precisely. Both men believed that they must limit the conflict to Korea to prevent a third world war and avoid jeopardizing the security of the United States and the free world generally. The UN forces could halt the Communist invaders, argued Truman, and thus discourage Red aggression everywhere; "a peaceful settlement may then be possible."

But Republican supporters of MacArthur were intransigent. A caucus in Martin's office discussed the impeachment of the President. Walter Lippmann declared in his syndicated column: "General MacArthur deliberately narrowed the choice [of alternatives] and meant to force a showdown with the President of the United States on the issue of a general war in the Far East." [17] Thereupon Lehman penned another statement. He declared, after MacArthur's appearance before Congress on April 19, that the General's position was a threat to world peace and expressed the hope that the foreign policy debate "will be brief and without partisan rancor."

Next day the Senate Recording Room witnessed a spirited scene. Homer Capehart, Hubert Humphrey, and Lehman met to record their views on MacArthur for a radio program called "Meet Your Congress." The Indiana Senator upheld the General's proposal for unilateral and drastic military action against Red China; Lehman and Humphrey condemned it as dangerous to the American people and their allies. Capehart, losing his temper, accused the two of Communist sympathies and a desire to see Mao prevail. The moment the broadcast ended, Humphrey strode across the room and addressed Capehart with solemn anger: "I deeply resent this type of vilification, character assassination, and malicious unfounded statement; I want no more of it!" The fat, short-winded Capehart seized Humphrey's arm, raising his own fist as if to strike. Lehman hastily stepped in to separate them, and a general tussle ensued. Fortunately it broke up without blows—though not without a general loss of dignity.

Upon one of Lehman's traits all observers were agreed: his determination to meet every duty. "He was a 24-hour-day man," said his assistant Julius C. C. Edelstein. Many members popped in and out of the Senate, as Paul Douglas put it, to make a speech or a headline; Lehman stuck to the hard drudgery of following bills and seeing that, if possible, deserving measures got some consideration. "Herbert and I happen to be members of the same two committees," added Douglas in 1956.[18] "I sometimes miss a meeting—he never does."

Richard Neuberger recalled the hot July evening in 1956 when a tired Senate was debating the Hells Canyon hydroelectric development. At ten o'clock Welker of Idaho was attacking the plan for a Federal dam. Neuberger looked about to see all the interested Senators there: Magnuson and Jackson of Washington, Dworshak of Idaho, Watkins of Utah, Mansfield of Montana, and a few others; it was *their* fight on one side or another—their states were involved. "Then I turned to the rear of the chamber. An elderly man sat there in solitary exhaustion, at that weary hour of the evening, Lehman of New York, representing a state 3,000 miles from Hells Canyon. At the age of 78, he was gray and tired. His eye twitched with fatigue." Neuberger inquired: "What are you doing on the floor, Herbert? You're the only Senator here who isn't from the Northwest." And Lehman replied: "I thought you and Wayne and Scoop Jackson might need me, so I decided not to go home."

As these pages show, his character changed over the decades. The crisp businessman of the gubernatorial years became possessed as he grew older by a greater humanitarian fervor. He cared about fewer objects, but he cared more deeply, fought more implacably, and spoke more sharply. The experience with UNRRA taught him the extent of human deprivation and anguish in the modern world. It sharpened his condemnation of the ambitions and hatreds which had poisoned international relations, his detestation of social abuses at home, and his contempt for the callousness of so many people in all countries—not least America—toward human need. He entered the Senate a more dedicated man. What he saw there of demagogy, ignorance, partisanship, and preference for private over public interest (for the Senate has seldom sunk lower than in the McCarthy-McCarran years) angered him. More passion entered his nature, more fire marked his speech. Newspapermen noted his attacks on McCarthy, his scorn for the oil-and-gas Senators, and his broadsword duel with De Sapio, as evidences that a leader of fiercer convictions and enthusiasms had emerged.

He paid a price for this in the greater intolerance of his later years; he made more opponents and felt more loneliness. But the deepening of his nature was on the whole a gain, for it expressed itself in many ways. "As I grow older," he said once with great feeling, "I grow more religious." It was a gain, too, in that it erased all vestiges of his whilom colorlessness and awkwardness.

A man might be able, hard-working, courageous, even noblehearted and yet be thoroughly disliked. It is certain that Lehman made inveterate critics even among good men; Robert Moses sometimes spoke harshly of him, and Robert Taft was no admirer. To the world in general, however, it was his lovable quality which was most memorable. This, for a man born to riches and a natural fighter, was remarkable. It might be said that there was little poetry in his nature, no transcendental vision, and no distinguished force of mind; but he had something far better. "He is kindliness personified," said Paul Douglas; "not only to mankind in the abstract, but to mankind in particular." He was duty personified, and grace of spirit, and magnanimity. For the abused and oppressed he was always ready to give battle, setting an example of fairness and sincerity as he did so. One representative of the abused, Thurgood Marshall, spoke of him as a living rebuke to cynicism. "In Washington he hears the cries of the persecuted in far-off localities here and overseas, and . . . he concludes rightly, as a sensitive custodian of the true greatness of our America, that neither his party nor his country can compromise with inequality and evil."

As a lovable man he had opportunity in his later years to find out how widely he was beloved. It would be misleading to say that in 1958 he celebrated his eightieth birthday. The city and state caught the anniversary away from his family and did the celebrating for him.[19] Dinner followed dinner, reception followed reception, in a festival that outlasted the spring. Some would longest remember the luncheon at the Astor tendered by the Liberal Party and Trade Union Council, where 1,500 crowded in to hear toasts from the mayor, labor leaders, Senators, and judges, with Adlai E. Stevenson opening and Carl Sandburg concluding the ceremonies. Some would best remember smaller gatherings. He himself would doubtless always feel a vivid pleasure in recalling the dinner dance in the beautiful Starlight Room of the Waldorf-Astoria attended by all his closer friends on March 28, an evening which reached its climax when suddenly, in the middle of the thronged hall, the dancing floor was cleared, the orchestra opened, and there alone, waltzing together under a brilliant spotlight, were Herbert and Edith Lehman.

The later years, busy as ever, have been filled with even more varied activities than when Lehman held public office, many of them laborious, but fortunately many also pleasurable. At the invitation of Ben-Gurion, he had visited Israel in 1949, with ample time to see the agricultural settlements in which he took a special interest, the various Hadassah activities, the government offices, and the Chaim Weizmann Institute. He and Mrs. Lehman had taken a refugee steamer from Marseilles, the *Negbah*, full of Jewish immigrants; a little vessel of 5,000 tons, but well appointed. Recalling that when they were in the executive mansion in Albany they had always kept a stock of lollipops for the neighborhood children who liked to run in, by a sudden inspiration they carried two large canisters of candies aboard. Lehman filled his pockets when he went on deck, and by the second day he was "Uncle Lollipop" to all the youngsters in the vessel. Since this trip he has maintained a close interest in the Weizmann Institute, the Hebrew University, and the Technion in Haifa. He became chairman of the board of overseers of the Jewish Theological Seminary. He has had time to resume his early interest in the Henry Street Settlement, where he and Mrs. Lehman erected a building, "Pete's House," in memory of the son lost in the war. A list of the organizations to which he belonged and contributed, made up by Carolin Flexner on October 30, 1945, had numbered 275, ranging from historical societies and civic bodies to Protestant, Jewish, and Catholic philanthropies; [20] and the number hardly shrunk in the ensuing years.

His sentiment for Israel has the depth that has become characteristic of him. As we have said, some of his fellow Jews thought that it was uncritical, although he emphatically reprobated Irgun and Stern Gang crimes and told Ben-Gurion to his face that he was flagrantly wrong in suggesting that American Jews had a duty to join the in-gathering of the race. He had refused to the last to become a Zionist, but once the new nation was born he accepted the *fait accompli* and supported its growth. His feeling has been not in the least chauvinistic, despite his natural pride in the brilliant accomplishments of the young republic; it is much like the feeling that Einstein confessed. He feels pride, too, in the heroism of his race, its fortitude under centuries of abuse, its unflagging idealism, and its superb contributions to the culture of the world. It is a feeling which, much earlier, an Englishwoman of genius had expressed better than he could voice it: [21]

> The pride which identifies us with a great historic body [wrote George Eliot] is a humanizing, elevating habit of mind, inspiring sacrifices of individual comfort, gain, or other selfish ambition, for the sake of that ideal whole; and no man swayed by such a sentiment can become completely abject. That a Jew of Smyrna, where a whip is carried by passengers ready to flog off the too officious specimens of his race, can still be proud to say, "I am a Jew," is surely a fact to awaken admiration in a mind capable of understanding what we may call the ideal forces in human history. And again, a varied, impartial observation of the Jews in different countries tends to the impression that they have a predominant kindliness which must have been deeply ingrained in the constitution of their race to have outlasted the ages of persecution and oppression. The concentration of their joys in domestic life has kept up in them the capacity of tenderness; the pity for the fatherless and the widow, the care for the women and the little ones, blent intimately with their religion, is a well of mercy that cannot long or widely be pent up by exclusiveness. And the kindliness of the Jew overflows the line of division between him and the Gentile. On the whole, one of the most remarkable phenomena in the history of this scattered people, made for ages "a scorn and a hissing," is, that after being subjected to this process, which might have been expected to be in every sense deteriorating and vitiating, they have come out of it (in any estimate which allows for numerical proportion) rivalling the nations of all European countries in healthiness and beauty of physique, in practical ability, in scientific and artistic aptitude, and in some forms of ethical value. A significant indication of their natural rank is seen in the fact that at this moment (1879) the leader of the Liberal party in Germany is a Jew, the leader of the Republican party in France is a Jew, and the head of the Conservative ministry in England is a Jew.

That his people had at last their own land, which they could make a theater for all the talents they had exhibited throughout the world, was a source of heartfelt gratification to Lehman.

It was fitting that as a simple man, who from young manhood had been warmly attached to children, he found special pleasure in his later years in the creation, with his wife, of a simple if ingenious attraction for youngsters of his city. "Today," announced a program printed for September 28, 1961, "Governor and Mrs. Herbert H. Lehman welcome the children of the City of New York to a new Central Park Zoo scaled to their size and dedicated solely to their interests in the hope that many generations of children will en-joy, and benefit from, their social concern with the penguins and ponies, the bunnies and lambs, the ducks and the piglets in their fanciful homes." The execution of the plan was as happy as the idea. The zoo was built about a pond which geese and ducks shared with the penguins. Any rapt child could step from the mouth of the jolly whale in front of the Ark (a neat aquarium housed inside its belly) to tour a storybook castle, a water mill, the domicile of the Three Little Pigs, Hansel and Gretel's Gingerbread House, and Mac-Donald's Barn—not to mention Mouseville and Flying-Bird-Cage. At every step youngsters could pet the ponies, the sheep, the pigs, and cows or help feed the raccoons, the monkeys, the rabbits, and the talking crow. (Animals and birds did duty in relays lest they become overtired.) It was an acre of enchantment, entered through gates which Paul Manship had fittingly adorned with bronze birds, animals, and a dancing shepherd boy.

The zoo, its idea suggested by Robert Moses, owed much to the architects, Aymar and Edward Embury, and Park Commissioner Newbold Morris, but most of all to the solicitude with which the Lehmans had watched over its construction. Its popularity delighted everybody. A year later over a million people had already visited it. The rule that grownups could enter only when accompanied by a youngster had to be modified to allow admission on Mondays to the childless adults who clamored for a sight. For a long time the Lehmans, when in town, visited the place daily. They had moments when the satisfactions of this creation seemed more immediate than all the achievements of city affairs, of the governorship, of UNRRA, and of the senatorial years.

A quietly touching expression of general gratitude, indeed, was visible to the observant in these years. Throughout the city no figure was better known than Lehman's or evoked a more spontaneous manifestation of popular respect. When he alighted from his car in lower-Manhattan elderly Jewish watchers could be seen pausing and murmuring cheerfully to each other, "He looks strong," or solicitously, "He doesn't look so well today." Most New Yorkers had ceased to wear headgear except in the bleakest weather, but as he walked slowly along the street what hats there were came off in a gesture that had hardly been seen since Peter Cooper's day. At public meetings it was noted that people—especially the older people—would lean out as he passed down the aisle and touch his sleeve, as if they thought that his garment would shed some virtue. If he went to the theater the intermission between acts would bring one or several strangers to his seat: "I just wanted to say, Mr. Lehman, how much I admire you." He ran a daily gamut of such tokens of appreciation and deference; and in Al Smith's phrase, they were "from the heart."

Appendices

TEXT OF LETTER TO PRESIDENT EISENHOWER BY SENATE LIBERALS ON TIDELANDS OIL

(From the Lehman Files)

UNITED STATES SENATE

April 17, 1953

THE PRESIDENT

THE WHITE HOUSE

Dear Mr. President:

The undersigned Members of the Senate are opposed to the passage of S.J. Res. 13, the proposed legislation to give to three states at the expense of the other forty-five the natural resources in oil and other minerals in the submerged lands of the marginal seas.

We do not believe a single valid reason exists for such a gift, nor for giving away the Federal revenues collected since the time the Supreme Court decided that the rights in the submerged lands of the marginal sea belong, in fact and in law, to the United States and not to the states.

What gives us concern, however, is the fact that S.J. Res. 13 is generally regarded as an administration measure, and is being supported by the administration leaders in the Senate. In the light of this circumstance, we have concluded that it is our duty to call your attention to the fact that S.J. Res. 13, if enacted in its present form, would be highly detrimental to the interests of the United States, not only according to our views but according to statements made by or in behalf of members of your own Cabinet.

The official spokesman for the State Department testified before the Senate Committee on Interior and Insular Affairs that any legislation by Congress attempting to extend or approve any state boundary beyond the three-mile limit claimed by the United States as the extent of its territorial sovereignty would seriously embarrass and obstruct the United States in its foreign relations.

S.J. Res. 13 purports to recognize state boundaries in the sea far beyond those of the United States, itself. The matter of state boundaries in the sea has never before been of any great national concern because the Supreme Court has made it clear that the international domain, despite any state boundary, begins at the low-water mark. If, however, your administration now proposes to give coastal states the title to submerged lands of the sea within state boundaries, then it becomes of vital concern to all of us to know exactly where those boundaries are.

S.J. Res. 13 proposes to give every coastal state a seaward boundary:

1. At a line three geographical miles distant from the coast line; or

2. At the line as it existed when the state became a member of the Union; or

3. At a line as "heretofore or hereafter" approved by Congress.

The State Department has publicly enunciated compelling reasons why no state should be given a boundary line in the sea extending more than three miles from the low-water mark. The three different sets of "boundaries" described in S.J. Res. 13 not only involve violations of the national policy first promulgated by Secretary of State Thomas Jefferson, but also create discriminations between the states and violate the policy of admitting all states to the Union on an equal footing. Of course, the effort to convey to the states property rights in the submerged lands goes directly against the advice publicly given by your Attorney General.

We are being told by Senate supporters of S.J. Res. 13 that this Bill sets up state sovereignty within a three-mile belt for every coastal state, except Florida and Texas, where the belt will be 10½ miles. But, in fact, S.J. Res 13 does not say that. It is far less definite. But even if S.J. Res 13 were specific on this matter, the extension of the boundaries of Florida and Texas to 10½ miles beyond the low-water mark would violate the boundaries of the United States, and cause complications with other nations, particularly Mexico; even at the present moment citizens of Florida and Texas are claiming fishing rights up to three miles off the Mexican coast, and are insisting that the State Department protect their claims.

Neither Florida nor Texas has established any right to a boundary of 10½ miles. They have only claims, most of them of recent origin. Unilateral claims are not proof of anything. Texas has enacted legislation claiming boundaries to the outer edge of the Continental Shelf, thus making two sets of claims. So have other states. Louisiana, for example, claims a boundary line 27 miles at sea, and is still collecting revenues from mineral resources in that area.

We respectfully ask why your congressional leadership is pressing for the enactment of provisions strongly opposed by leaders of the Executive Branch of your Administration. We would like to know, for instance, whether Congress has, in fact, "heretofore" approved any boundaries in the sea greater than three miles for any state, and, if so, what state and what boundary? There should be an official search of all court decisions and all statutes enacted down through the years to determine these facts.

We respectfully suggest that the people of the country should be told what the attitude of your Administration will be if S.J. Res. 13 is passed, with respect to these extended boundary lines in the open sea for Florida, Texas, California, Louisiana, and other coastal states which may claim more than three miles. Will your Administration oppose any such claims, or will it endeavor to give some states wider boundaries in the sea than others—boundaries greater than those ever claimed by the United States?

Respectfully yours,

CLINTON P. ANDERSON	HARLEY M. KILGORE
JAMES E. MURRAY	LISTER HILL
ESTES KEFAUVER	THOMAS C. HENNINGS, JR.
MICHAEL J. MANSFIELD	MIKE MONRONEY
PAUL H. DOUGLAS	WAYNE MORSE
J. WILLIAM FULBRIGHT	HERBERT H. LEHMAN
W. STUART SYMINGTON	HENRY M. JACKSON
MATTHEW M. NEELY	ALBERT GORE
THEODORE FRANCIS GREEN	CHARLES W. TOBEY
WILLIAM LANGER	JOHN O. PASTORE
JOHN J. SPARKMAN	DENNIS CHAVEZ
GUY M. GILLETTE	WARREN G. MAGNUSON
	HUBERT H. HUMPHREY

Appendix II

TOTAL SHIPMENTS OF UNRRA

BY RECIPIENT COUNTRIES AND COMMODITY DIVISIONS

(Gross Long Tons)

		(1)	(2)	(3)
LINE NO.		COMMODITY PROGRAMS	TOTAL	FOOD
1				
2		GRAND TOTAL ALL COMMODITY PROGRAMS	24,106,891	9,131,030
3				
4		SUB-TOTAL FOR COUNTRY PROGRAMS	23,938,493	9,109,086
5				
6		ALBANIA	130,048	70,199
7		AUSTRIA	1,114,461	623,568
8		BYELORUSSIAN S.S.R.	141,853	101,396
9		CHINA	2,360,915	1,091,617
10		CZECHOSLOVAKIA	1,619,627	767,211
11		DODECANESE ISLANDS	33,122	10,109
12		ETHIOPIA	1,551	11
13		FINLAND	5,623	1,681
14		GREECE	2,830,138	1,536,710
15		HUNGARY	19,127	18,140
16		ITALY	10,225,450	2,165,004
17		KOREA	6,424	
18		PHILIPPINES	47,160	42,306
19		POLAND	2,241,889	1,164,883
20		SAN MARINO	260	197
21		UKRAINIAN S.S.R.	467,049	315,748
22		YUGOSLAVIA	2,693,796	1,200,306
23				
24		SUB-TOTAL FOR SPECIAL PROGRAMS	168,398	21,944
25				
26		DISPLACED PERSONS, CHINA	8,633	8,170
27		DISPLACED PERSONS, GERMANY	12,453	5,046
28		DRIVES — CONTR. CLOTHING AND FOOD	94,963	6,415
29		MERRA AND NO. AFRICAN CAMPS	47,891	405
30		N.W. EUROPE EMERGENCY PROGRAM	4,458	1,908
31				
32				
33				

a/ Less than 1 ton.

(Reproduced from Volume 3, p. 429, George Woodbridge, *UNRRA, The History of the United Nations Relief and Rehabilitation Administration, New York, 1950*)

(4) CLOTHING, TEXTILES ND FOOTWEAR	(5) MEDICAL AND SANITATION	(6) AGRICULTURAL REHABILITATION	(7) INDUSTRIAL REHABILITATION	(8) TAKE-OVERS FROM MILITARY	LINE NO.
					1
626,293	134,537	2,314,363	11,290,558	610,110	2
					3
535,807	133,797	2,313,957	11,282,686	563,160	4
					5
2,727	2,019	19,857	32,571	2,675	6
4,165	1,619	168,780	132,790	183,539	7
5,784	646	8,050	25,977		8
169,339	41,024	395,014	663,921		9
44,048	11,901	410,593	385,874		10
194	9	682	4,358	17,770	11
a/	631	831	78		12
407	36	2,785	714		13
28,485	8,628	363,176	664,428	228,711	14
274	471		242		15
92,203	10,672	172,211	7,785,060	300	16
251	98	487	5,588		17
560	310	3,527	457		18
82,084	33,826	495,052	466,044		19
	48		15		20
16,225	1,037	38,069	95,970		21
89,061	20,822	234,843	1,018,599	130,165	22
					23
90,486	740	406	7,872	46,950	24
					25
412	50		1		26
1,034	389	406	5,578		27
88,548					28
170	21		345	46,950	29
322	280		1,948		30
					31
					32
					33

Manuscript Sources

The principal manuscript sources for any biographical work upon Herbert H. Lehman are his personal papers, now housed in the New York Public Library, the papers of UNRRA in the Library of the United Nations, and the personal memoir dictated by Mr. Lehman for the Oral History Office of Columbia University.

(1) The Lehman papers in the New York Public Library consist of 41 filing cabinets, to which others will later be added. Of these 41 cabinets, 34 contain 5 drawers, and 7 contain 4 drawers, 3 of these 7 being filled with materials pertaining to Lillian D. Wald. The 198 drawers include letters sent and letters received, drafts of bills, speech files, reports compiled by Mr. Lehman's staff on all the important subjects he considered while Senator, records of voting, interviews, press releases, and memoranda. They cover the whole of his public career from his election as lieutenant-governor until the present day. All documents of significance have been preserved, though the files show one unfortunate gap; near the termination of his governorship Mr. Lehman destroyed a part of the general personal correspondence which he had conducted in Albany.

(2) The UNRRA materials are almost dismayingly copious. Dr. Grace Fox, who, on September 6, 1943, was appointed historian of UNRRA, and Dr. George Woodbridge, who, on September 1, 1946, was named Chief Archivist and Historian, took very seriously the work of preserving the records of the great international organization. Dr. Fox's functions were defined as primarily "to prepare a chronological account of the development, origin and authorization and administrative structure" of UNRRA, and "to keep a library of such records as may be of historical value at a later date." Dr. Woodbridge oversaw the preparation of a series of monographs on the work of individual administrative units, written sometimes by historians, but in general by the executive or operating officials. These monographs were prepared under conditions of complete freedom, the authors being encouraged to express personal views even when they did not coincide with those of the higher officials of UNRRA. The monographs thus contain a great deal of material that does not appear in the official three-volume history by Dr. George Woodbridge and others, entitled "The History of the United Nations Relief and Rehabilitation Administration," published by the Columbia University Press in 1950.

The records of the Director General of UNRRA, in the years 1943–1948, fill boxes Nos. 100–182 inclusive, as kept in the United Nations Library. The records of the Office of the General Council fill boxes 200–665 inclusive; the records of the Office of the Historian fill boxes 700–804 inclusive, and the records of the Secretariat boxes 850–876 inclusive. The files of the Field Operations Branch are comprised in boxes 1150–1158; those of the Program Director in boxes 1175–1201, and those of the Office of Public Information in boxes 1500–1512. The Bureau of Administration is represented by an imposing mass of materials kept in boxes 2000–7251—a total of more than 286 feet of records. The Bureau of Supply is represented by boxes 10,000–13,086; the Bureau of Areas by boxes 20,000–20,104; and the Bureau of Services by boxes 21,000–22,431. The Historical Staff of UNRRA prepared careful finding aids which were deposited in the Library with the files. These have been guarded and extended by the Library staff of the United Nations. This storehouse of material contains material for new monographs of great interest in the history of Europe and Asia just following the Second World War. Indeed, these records throw light upon the post-war activities of all of the forty-eight nations which were ultimately concerned in the support and administration of UNRRA.

All these records are subject to the restrictions of the Librarian of the United Nations, based upon an agreement between UNRRA and the United Nations September 27, 1948. They are available for use at the discretion of the Secretary-General, if he is satisfied that the particular use requested will involve no improper employment of the information.

(3) The Oral History Memoir dictated by Mr. Lehman covers in detail all parts of his life including his service as lieutenant-governor, Governor, Director of UNRRA, and Senator. It is supplemented by a brief Oral History Memoir dictated by Mrs. Edith Lehman. These are deposited in the Library of Columbia University, and may be used only subject to restrictions imposed by Mr. and Mrs. Lehman and by Columbia University. They are not at present open to general inspection.

A comprehensive file of press clippings on Mr. Lehman's career, bound in uniform volumes, is kept in his study at 820 Park Avenue.

Acknowledgments

The writing of this volume would have been impossible without the assistance of many men and women. The author is deeply grateful to all those who have given him generously of their time. Imperfect as the following roster is, it partially indicates the debt owed to helpers and advisers.

Besides several whose aid is noted in the text, the author is especially grateful to Dr. Joseph Rappaport, who has been a skilled and indefatigable assistant in research; to Commander Julius C. C. Edelstein, Executive Assistant to the Mayor of New York, closely associated with Mr. Lehman during his senatorship; and to Dr. Wayne Andrews of Charles Scribner's Sons, whose patient assistance in seeing the book through the press has been invaluable.

Among scholars who have taken time to aid him he is particularly indebted to Professor Bernard Bellush of City College in New York; Mrs. Jewel Bellush of Hunter College; Professor Eric Goldman of Princeton University; Professor Moses Rischin of the University of California in Los Angeles; and Dean Harold Syrett of Queen College. He owes much to certain faculty members of the Jewish Theological Seminary in New York, notably Chancellor Louis Finkelstein and Dr. Simon Greenberg. Mr. Irwin M. Herrman of the American Council for Judaism has kindly sent valuable materials.

The Staffs of the United Nations Library, New York Public Library, and Columbia University Library have been consistently helpful. The author owes much to Sir Robert G. A. Jackson and Mr. Hugh Jackson for their careful scrutiny of the chapters on UNRRA, and to Colonel Alfred Katzin of the United Nations Secretariat for information. The Honorable Eric H. Biddle has supplied useful counsel on international affairs. The Honorable Adlai E. Stevenson has consented to the use of part of a letter to Mr. Lehman, and has given other help.

Among the men officially associated with Mr. Lehman during his governorship, Dr. Thomas Parran, Mr. George S. Van Schaick, Mr. Lithgow Osborne, and former Governor Charles Poletti have contributed information and advice. Mrs. Poletti has written a memorandum of illuminating personal reminiscences. Judge Edward Weinfeld and the Honorable Robert H. Moses have assisted in more ways than one. Among other prominent New Yorkers who have been generous in aid are Miss Helen Hall, head of the Henry Street Settlement; Mr. Samuel D. Leidesdorf, Mr. Alan M. Stroock, Mr. Aaron Rabinowitz, Mr. Abraham Kazan, Mr. Carlos Israels, Mr. Lawrence Arnstein, Mr. Robert N. Benjamin, Mr. Myer Alterman, Mr. Theodore Kheel, Mr. David Dubinsky, Mr. and Mrs. Frank Altschul, and Mr. William S. Bernard, co-director of the American Council for Nationalities Service. Mr. Everett R. Clinchy of the Council on World Tensions contributed a memorandum on Mr. Lehman's work for that body. The Honorable James J. Wadsworth and the Honorable Thomas C. Desmond have kindly supplied both facts and interpretations on legislative work during Mr. Lehman's governorship. The aid of Robert Oppenheimer, of President Sarah Gibbs Blanding of Vassar College, of Professor Lindsay Rogers at Columbia University, and of Dr. Louis Starr, head of the Oral History Office at Columbia, has earned the author's cordial thanks. He is very appreciative of the unfailing cooperation of his secretary, Mrs. Lillian Bean.

Finally, it is important to thank the members of Congress who have contributed reminiscences of Mr. Lehman during his seven years in the Senate. The full list is too long for inclusion, but special note must be made of the kindness of Senator Maurine Neuberger of Oregon, and Senator William Benton.

Footnotes

CHAPTER I: *When Cotton Seemed King*

1. Jacob Rader Marcus, *Memoirs of American Jews, 1775–1865* (Philadelphia, 1955), presents first-hand accounts, in letters, diaries, and memoirs, of some sixty important Jewish families, many of them Southern.

2. According to the careful office-compiled booklet, *A Centennial: Lehman Brothers, 1850–1950* (New York, 1950), Emanuel arrived in America in 1847, being then twenty years old. The same source states that Mayer came in 1850. Governor T. H. Watts of Alabama wrote in Dec. 1864 that Mayer "has been here fifteen years."

3. The Works Progress Administration volume *Alabama, A Guide to the Deep South* (New York, 1941) 231–235, describes prominent buildings in Montgomery in this period.

4. Minnie Clare Boyd, *Alabama in the Fifties* (New York, 1931), Chapter Two, describes the cotton trade in Montgomery County; Frederick Law Olmsted, *Journey in the Seaboard Slave States,* (New York, 1856), 191, treats the Alabama River trade.

5. See Boyd, *op. cit.,* 187, for the yellow fever epidemic of 1854. Factories in Montgomery are listed in the 1860 Census volume on *Manufactures,* Alabama, Table 9.

6. A careful genealogical table is in the Lehman Papers. See also the pamphlet, *In Memoriam, Mayer Lehman* (New York, 1897), with its reprinted obituary notices.

7. This story was related by a business associate, J. F. Maury, at a memorial meeting of the New York Cotton Exchange after the death of Emanuel Lehman. See *In Memoriam: Emanuel Lehman* (New York, 1907), 28–31.

8. "Uncle Ben" was Harriet Newgass's only brother; Herbert H. Lehman to Archibald A. Marx, August 24, 1950. Lehman Papers. For his speculative traits see Herbert H. Lehman, Oral History Memoir, Columbia University Library. I. W. Hellman wrote a short history, *Wells Fargo Bank and Union Trust Co.: A Century at the Golden Gate* (The Newcomen Society in North America; New York, 1952).

9. *A Centennial: Lehman Brothers, 1850–1950,* p. 13, describes the price-raising agreement.

10. Gov. T. H. Watts to Jefferson Davis, *Official Records of the War of the Rebellion,* Series II, Vol. VIII, 1222–1224.

11. See *Official Records,* Series II, Vol. VIII, 166, 1224.

12. James Grant Wilson, *Under the Old Flag,* (New York, 1912), II, 249–252.

13. John T. Trowbridge, *The Desolated States* (New York, 1866), 382.

14. *Ibid.,* 421–422.

15. The New Orleans house was first called Lehman, Abraham & Co., then Lehman, Newgass, and then Lehman, Stern. Lehman Papers.

16. For Parsons's statement see *Annual Cyclopaedia,* 1865, pp. 12, 18; for the general destitution, *Annual Cyclopaedia,* 1866, p. 12.

17. Mary Powell Crane, *The Life of James R. Powell and Early History of Alabama and Birmingham* (Brooklyn, 1930), 169–171.

CHAPTER II: *Contrast of Two Brothers*

1. Herbert H. Lehman has supplemented his full Oral History Memoir in the Columbia University Library by many reminiscent conversations with and letters to the author.

2. The author has spent some time at Kildare, now owned in part by a friend, Ralph Friedman.

3. The best accounts of Dr. Gottheil are by Dr. David de Sola Pool in the *Dictionary of American Biography*, Vol. VII, and by F. H. Vizetelly in the *Jewish Encyclopaedia*, Vol. VI.

4. Oscar S. Straus's autobiographical work, *Under Four Administrations: From Cleveland to Taft* (New York, 1922), says little of the family background, but it is fully treated in Jacob Rader Marcus, ed., *Memoirs of American Jews*, II, 287–319.

5. The detailed article by Geoffrey T. Hellman, "Sorting out the Seligmans," in *The New Yorker*, October 30, 1954, throws much light not only on the Seligmans but other powerful Jewish families. The author often heard A. P. Loveman (father of Amy Loveman) recall his early mercantile days in Alabama.

6. This flame makes *Reminiscences by Isaac M. Wise*, edited by David Philipson (Cincinnati, 1901), an eloquent book; but it has an acid flavor. The atheism prevalent among German Jews, the anti-Semitism common in some areas of American life, and the low esteem for Judaism and Judaic studies even among Jewish friends pained Wise. When he saw Millard Fillmore in the White House, the press headlined the event, "First Jew to Call on an American President."

7. Nathan Glazer, *American Judaism* (Chicago, 1957), 41, 42.

8. See the sketches of the school by Hans Zinsser in *As I Knew Him* (New York, 1940), and by Walter Binger in Marquis Childs and James Reston, eds., *Walter Lippmann and His Times* (New York, 1959), 21ff.

9. This episode is treated in the *New York Herald* and *New York Tribune*, April 27, 1880.

10. M. E. Ravage, *An American in the Making: The Life Story of an Immigrant* (New York, 1917), 66.

11. Lillian D. Wald has told her own story graphically in *The House on Henry Street* (New York, 1915) and *Windows on Henry Street* (New York, 1934).

12. Carlton J. H. Hayes, *A Political and Cultural History of Modern Europe* (New York, 1936), II, 646, 647.

13. The United Hebrew Charities asserted in 1900 that the tenements and sweatshops produced "unspeakable evils" in depressed vitality, poverty, and physical and moral sickness; Charles S. Bernheimer, ed., *The Russian Jew in the United States* (Philadelphia, 1905), 118. Yet Mary K. Simkovich testifies, on the basis of long East Side experience, that "life in the tenement can and does often exhibit the loftiest character and the finest human relationships"; Theodore Friedman and Robert Gordis, eds., *Jewish Life in America* (New York, 1955), 154.

14. "A Decisive Pattern in American Jewish History," in The American Jewish Archives, *Essays in American Jewish History*, (Cincinnati, 1958), 42.

15. Moses Rischin, *The Promised City: New York Jews 1870–1914* (Cambridge, Mass., 1962), 95–103.

CHAPTER III: *From College to Countinghouse*

1. Oral History Memoir, supplemented by conversations with Herbert H. Lehman.

2. The Rev. Calvin Durfee, *History of Williams College* (Boston, 1860), *passim*, recaptures the early atmosphere of the institution.

3. Leverett Wilson Spring, *A History of Williams College* (Boston, 1917) covers athletics and clubs; see especially Ch. VIII, "The New Williams," 243–276. The Lehman Papers include a large scrapbook of college records and mementos.

4. On Carter and his faculty see E. Herbert Botsford, *Fifty Years at Williams, Book II, Franklin Carter, Administrator, Builder* (Pittsfield, 1930).

5. Mayer Lehman left about $5,000,000, of which Herbert's share was about $400,000.

6. Of the many books on the cotton business, T. M. Young's *The American Cotton Industry* (New York, 1903), by an experienced Englishman, gives an especially expert view of the New England industry, pp. 1–53, and the Southern industry, pp. 54–106, with careful conclusions in four later chapters. This was Lehman's own period in the business.

7. The Lehman Papers contain fragmentary records of the Southern States Land & Timber Company.

8. *A Centennial: Lehman Brothers 1850–1950*, pp. 18–25, briefly covers these developments.

9. *Ibid.*, 26–38. The author has talked with Monroe C. Gutman and Robert Lehman of the firm. Lehman states in his oral reminiscences: "The firm took its relationship with the companies, with the public, very seriously. When we sold stock to the public, we always felt a great moral responsibility and followed the companies very closely, and if they got into any difficulties, we tried our best to help them work out their difficulties, and we were very successful in doing that. That was the kind of work that I did very largely." Pp. 56, 57.

10. Lawrence Arnstein to the author, January, 1962. Mrs. Lehman has deposited brief recollections with her husband's Oral History Memoir. Her chief interest was in painting (inspired by a talented aunt in San Francisco) and music; but she did some social work as well. She explains that Mt. Sinai Hospital at the time of her engagement had no women's social service department. The president and vice-president, noting the ability with which she conducted a bazaar, asked her to become head of a lay social-service committee, afterward called the Women's Board. She studied the work at Massachusetts General Hospital and at Bellevue. "Then we started in a big way up at Mt. Sinai. We had quite a group of volunteers who worked with the professional workers. And it took quite a bit of persuading, because at that time the doctors weren't too keen on it." For patients who feared that the home was deteriorating, that the children were not getting milk, that garbage was accumulating, the volunteer force would sally forth, take care of all needs, and bring back reassurance. Oral History Memoir, pp. 14–16.

11. Mrs. Henry Gale to the author, June 3, 1962.

12. Oral History Memoir, p. 15.

CHAPTER IV: *World War and Aftermath*

1. This was I. W. Hellman, Jr., who had been president of the Union Trust Company and whose father I. W. Hellman had helped organize the Nevada Bank, both of San Francisco. The two institutions merged in 1905 to form the Wells Fargo Nevada National Bank. Both I. W. Hellman, Sr. and his son died in 1920. I. W. Hellman III in 1944 became president of Wells Fargo Bank & Trust Company. See his previously cited brochure on the history of that institution, pp. 24–30.

2. A War Service Scrapbook kept by Lehman preserves much of his wartime correspondence, all curtly official. Lehman Papers.

3. On this naval work see Report of the Chief of the Bureau of Supplies and Accounts (McGowan) in *Annual Report, Secretary of the Navy*, 1918. Admiral McGowan on June 5, 1917, wrote Henry Morgenthau, Sr., thanking him for his part in bringing Herbert H. Lehman into the service. When you introduced him, wrote the admiral, "I was certain that he was exactly the type and kind of man that we wanted to assist in handling the many important problems that are confronting us"; and he "has more than fulfilled my expectations." Lehman Papers.

4. Lehman's War Service Scrapbook contains papers showing he was appointed captain in the ordnance section September 10, 1917; ordered to report for duty September 29; appointed major January 1, 1918; appointed head of equipment section in pro-

curement division, February 2, 1918; and appointed acting executive officer, procurement division, June 24, 1918. For the nature of his work see the Report of the Chief of Ordnance in *Annual Report, Secretary of War*, 1919, I, 1051, 1052.

5. Early in 1918 a Purchasing Service was organized in the Army General Staff Corps; General Orders No. 5, War Department. In April this was combined with a Storage and Traffic Service created earlier, under the name given in the text. See *Annual Report, Secretary of War*, 1919, II, *passim*.

6. Franklin Jerome Lunding, *Sharing a Business* (New York, 1931), 19-24, describes the origins and growth of the Jewel Tea Company, founded in 1899 by Vernon Skiff. He was joined in 1901 by Frank P. Ross.

7. *A Centennial: Lehman Brothers, 1850-1950*, p. 37.

8. Monroe C. Gutman to the author, December 12, 1961.

9. As Lehman says in his Oral History Memoir, business methods were changing. "In those days particularly we scrutinized the management very, very carefully in any company whose securities we offered to the public. . . . We were able to do this in those days because the tempo of business was much slower than it is now. A company like Lehman Brothers did three or four of these businesses a year, and it was all they needed, because profits of course were vastly bigger than they are today. Now, of course, a big firm, any one of possibly ten firms downtown, may be the manager or participant in maybe a hundred different undertakings, and it is not possible for a firm to study each one of them, and they certainly do not feel the moral obligation that was the case." Pp. 53, 54.

10. The merger of Studebaker with the Everitt-Metzger-Flanders Company took place when EMF made such a poor car that the public translated the initials into "Every Mechanical Fault." Lehman, chosen a director, played a part in selecting A. R. Erskine, a man of ability, imagination, and courage, as controller; and by the time he became president Studebaker had developed a good machine. At directors' meetings Lehman saw much of Paul Hoffman, who left the successful Los Angeles agency to enter the South Bend offices, and he became a warm admirer of Hoffman's brains and vision.

11. A. R. Erskine, *History of the Studebaker Corporation*, 31-50, describes the role of Lehman Brothers in organizing and helping operate the company 1911-1914. *Who's Who in America 1926-27* lists Herbert H. Lehman's directorships.

12. Lehman emphasizes the conscientiousness of his scrutiny. "We studied their statements. . . . We visited their plants. We were very successful in setting up what we thought a sound capital structure. I did a great deal of travelling. Everybody was kept very busy in those days. I think I was qualified to do that largely because of my training in a commercial business. Very few bankers at that time . . . had any commercial training. They didn't know the problems that confront any manufacturing concern." Oral History Memoir, pp. 96, 97.

13. Monroe C. Gutman to the author, December 12, 1961.

14. The Joint Distribution Committee in its full documentary work, *Reports Received by the Joint Distribution Committee of Funds for Jewish War Sufferers*, (New York, 1916), 9, 10, lists the sums sent abroad from January 20, 1915 to August 15, 1916, Russia heading the list with $1,800,000, German Poland standing next with $1,454,500, and Austria-Hungary coming third with $1,065,000. Later reports contain additional data.

15. This work is described in Herbert Agar, *The Saving Remnant: An Account of Jewish Survival*, covering work through the Second World War (New York, 1960), *passim*; Joseph C. Hyman, *Twenty-Five Years of American Aid to Jews Overseas* (New York, 1939), *passim*; successive volumes of the *American Jewish Year*

Book; and *The American Joint Distribution Committee in Russia* (New York, 1924). Mr. James N. Rosenberg has supplied helpful information to the author.

16. Hyman, *op. cit.,* 16–18.

17. This was the Riga Agreement of August, 1921; see *The American Joint Distribution Committee in Russia, passim,* for details.

18. Lehman published in the *New York Times,* August 26, 1923, a full press statement reviewing JDC work in aiding cooperative loan associations. This reviewed expenditures of $65,000,000 in relief funds. He wrote: "During the last eighteen months 353 individual loan associations have been set up and these have a membership of 144,896, all heads of families. This means that we reach more than 650,000 persons, all sufferers from the war." The work extended through Austria, Poland, Russia, Rumania, and the Baltic states.

19. Conditions improved and then worsened. Lehman wrote William Fox early in 1926: "We thought a year or two ago that our task was ended, but unfortunately the situation in eastern and southeastern Europe is worse today than it ever has been since the armistice. Hundreds of thousands of men and women are ruined and without either resources or means of employment." *New York Times,* March 14, 1926. He himself gave very large sums, and the town of Ponoviezh in Lithuania named its main street for him; *New York Times,* July 8, 1923.

20. Hyman, *op. cit.,* 30–33. See also the graphic record in Evelyn Morrissey, *Jewish Workers and Farmers in the Crimea and Ukraine* (New York, 1937).

21. Speech to Relief Conference, Ten Eyck Hotel, December 9; *New York Times,* December 10, 1928.

CHAPTER V: *From Sulzer to Alfred E. Smith*

1. J. A. Friedman, *The Impeachment of Governor William Sulzer* (New York, 1939) offers a brief biographical study. See also *Public Papers of Governor William Sulzer* (Albany, 1913), *passim.*

2. Lehman, in fact, pointed out the desirability of a volume of speeches; Herbert H. Lehman to Sulzer, June 24, 1912. Lehman Papers. See *New York Times,* October 8, 1913, for his cash gift.

3. An analysis of the Blauvelt bill and other direct primary measures may be found in The Citizens Union, *Report of the Committee on Legislation* (New York, 1913), 13–18. *The Public Papers of Governor William Sulzer,* 105, 106, give his proposals. Outlines, but not full reports of the debate, appear in *Senate Journal,* I, II, and *Assembly Journal,* I–IV (Albany, 1913).

4. Oral History Memoir. Lehman appeared as a defense witness to establish the fact that Sulzer came by part of his money honestly; Friedman, *op. cit.,* 210, 211.

5. Morris Hillquit, *Loose Leaves from a Busy Life* (New York, 1934) is an engaging book; see especially pp. 1–30.

6. "The Rise of the Tailors," *McClure's Magazine,* December, 1904.

7. Ray Stannard Baker, *An American Chronicle,* (New York, 1945).

8. See Louis Levine, *The Women's Garment Workers: A History of the International Ladies' Garment Workers Union* (New York, 1924); Joel Seidman, *The Needle Trades* (New York, 1942); Benjamin Stolberg, *Tailor's Progress* (New York, 1944), especially Chapters III–VI.

9. John Dickinson–Morris Kolchin, *Report of an Investigation* (New York, 1925), 1off. This contains a careful summary of the hearings. The huge bibliography of the subject is summarized by Seidman, *op. cit.,* 321–332.

10. Dickinson-Kolchin, *op. cit.,* 46ff.

11. Dickinson-Kolchin, 94ff.; Levine, *op. cit.*, 422–424.
12. *Justice* (ILGWU) July 18, 1924; Levine, *The Women's Garment Workers*, 424–426. For the signing of the agreement between labor and manufacturers, and the end of the strike, see *New York Times*, July 17, 18, 1924.
13. For enforcement difficulties see Dwight Edwards Robinson, *Collective Bargaining and Market Control in the New York Coat and Suit Industry* (New York, 1949), 71ff.
14. For the period of Communist control see Seidman, *op. cit.*, 158–166; Stolberg, *op. cit.*, 108–155.
15. *New York Times*, October 23, 1924.
16. *New York Post*, October 6, 1926.

CHAPTER VI: *The Rise of Franklin D. Roosevelt*

1. Jesse H. Jones to Lehman, July 12, 1928. Lehman Papers.
2. Alfred E. Smith, *Up to Now: An Autobiography* (New York, 1929), 398.
3. Henry M. Pringle, *Alfred E. Smith* (New York, 1937), Chs. VI and VII. See also Oscar Handlin, *Al Smith and his America* (Boston, 1958), a book of little over 200 pages, to be read entire.
4. Oral History Memoir. Smith defends his Oklahoma City speech and describes the situation there which made his friends fear personal violence, in *Up to Now*, 395–398. When he telephoned Mrs. Moskowitz in New York after the meeting, she demanded, "Where are you?" "Back at the hotel," he replied. "Thank God for that!" she exclaimed.
5. H.H.L. to Raskob, April 30, 1929, December 30, 1929, June 11, 1932. Lehman Papers.
6. Joel Seidman, *The Needle Trades*, 166–168.
7. Lehman had done what he could to assist in restoring the ILGWU. In 1928–1930 he loaned it a total of $50,000 to help get it on its feet; H.H.L. to George Gordon Battle, February 12, 1929; Lieutenant Governor's Official File. The author has used materials from the MS doctoral dissertation of Jewel Bellush entitled *Selected Case Studies of the Legislative Leadership of Governor Herbert H. Lehman* (Columbia University, 1959).
8. Roosevelt issued a statement in appointing Lehman as chairman: "In an industry broken up by so many small units, strong and comprehensive organizations of both employers and workers are of the highest importance." This was the nub of the matter. *U.S. Monthly Labor Review*, XXIX (September, 1929), 525; *Public Papers of Franklin D. Roosevelt*, 1929, pp. 581, 582.
9. Oral History Memoir; cf. Al Smith on his own experiences, *Up to Now*, 306ff.
10. The leadership in the prison reform movement was definitely Roosevelt's, but Lehman seconded him ably. See Bernard Bellush, *Franklin D. Roosevelt as Governor of New York* (New York, 1955), Ch. III, and Frank Freidel, *Franklin D. Roosevelt: The Triumph* (Boston, 1956), pp. 123–131.
11. Oral History Memoir. See his statement in *New York Times*, November 4, 1931, and Jewel Bellush, "Roosevelt's Good Right Arm," *New York History*, Vol. 41 (October, 1960), pp. 433, 434.
12. *Public Papers of Franklin D. Roosevelt, 1930*, I, 446ff.
13. Roosevelt to Lehman, May 14, 1930; Lehman Papers.
14. The treatment of the City Trust Company case in Alfred B. Rollins, Jr., *Roosevelt and Howe* (New York, 1962), pp. 284, 285, reflects more credit on Lehman and Moses than on Roosevelt.
15. Mrs. Rose G. Weiss to Carolin A. Flexner, October 10, 1930; Lehman Papers.

CHAPTER VII: *Helm of the State*

1. Seabury staggered voters when he proved that Sheriff Farley, with a legitimate income of $87,000 for seven years, had banked $360,000. "I had a little tin box," explained Farley; "a wonderful box" holding earlier savings. Charles Garrett, *The La Guardia Years: Machine and Reform Politics in New York City* (New Brunswick, N.J., 1931), 73–78; William B. and John B. Northrop, *The Insolence of Office: The Story of the Seabury Investigations* (New York, 1932), 5ff. The *Hearings* before the Joint Legislative Committee July, 1931–December, 1932 were published (New York, 1931–32).

2. The *New York Times*, October 22, 1931, gave it an appreciative editorial.

3. Editorial August 5, 1932.

4. Elliott Roosevelt and J. P. Lash, *F.D.R., His Personal Letters* (Four vols., New York, 1947–50), I, 300, 301.

5. Oral History Memoir. James A. Farley, *Behind the Ballots* (New York, 1938), 172–177, gives a version different only in details. He emphasizes Lehman's tension, writing that he had "the most intensely serious mental attitude of any man I have ever met." As a peacemaker after Curry's surrender, Farley told Curry he might select the candidate for lieutenant governor; and Curry perversely chose a conservative Utica lawyer, William M. Bray, at odds with Smith, Roosevelt, and all liberal ideas; see his obituary, *New York Times*, January 18, 1961.

6. *American Year Book* (New York, 1934), 229, 230.

7. Frank Altschul, an intent observer, emphasizes the acrimony of the debate as the bankers vainly tried to force Governor Lehman to act without their prior appeal; conversation with author, December 11, 1961.

8. Oral History Memoir, Columbia University. Files of the *New York Times* and *Herald-Tribune* cover the banking crisis and (below) the history of the liquor-control legislation fully.

9. Jewel Bellush, *Selected Case Studies of the Legislative Leadership of Governor Herbert H. Lehman* (unpublished doctoral dissertation, Columbia University, 1959), pp. 103–166 covers the milk difficulties thoroughly. Files of the *Rural New Yorker* for 1933 are valuable for its defense of the milk strikers, who were denounced by the N.Y. *Herald-Tribune* (August 8, 1933) for "rebellion."

10. State of New York, *Public Papers of Governor Herbert H. Lehman, 1933,* pp. 631ff., contain full documentary materials on the New York City financial crisis. In an address in the Bronx on November 1, 1934, he reviewed it in detail, *idem*, 1934, pp. 823–825. Hereinafter referred to as *Public Papers*.

11. At this point occurred one of the first sharp exchanges between Lehman and La Guardia. Its nature is explained by a telegram from the governor to the mayor October 16, 1933: "Your letter asking for an opportunity to discuss with me certain phases of the city finance plan was delivered at my home this afternoon and reached me just before I started for Albany on the four o'clock train. I would have been glad to receive you in New York but I was unable to postpone my departure for Albany on such short notice. The proposed legislation to be submitted to the legislature at the extraordinary session which convenes on Wednesday was drafted to make possible the carrying out of an agreement for the financing of New York City and for unemployment relief entered into by the city and the bankers on September 28th. The complete plan was published in the press on September 28th nearly three weeks ago. I have understood that you were in accord with the plan by which a default by the city will be avoided and relief for the unemployed assured. If however you had objections to the plan it is unfortunate that in the period between its publication and this late date you did not take the matter up either with those

drafting the legislation or with me. I have been in New York continuously since the plan was announced and would have been only too glad to have received you. In spite of this I shall be glad to receive you in Albany tomorrow Tuesday October 17th if you desire to confer with me providing however that before you come the purpose of your visit may be made public by me."

12. President Roosevelt on November 26, 1933 sent Lehman an admonition to the same effect. Lehman Papers.

13. Herbert H. Lehman to Lillian Wald, January 11, 1934. Lehman Papers.

CHAPTER VIII: *Battles Front and Rear*

1. H.H.L. to Mrs. O'Brien, April 30, 1940, and to Irving Lehman April 27, 1940. Lehman Papers. Lehman, at the end of the 1934 session, vetoed a bill giving the widows of four supreme court justices the salaries their husbands would have received if they had lived until the end of their terms. Such bills had always been approved in the past. He commented: "It isn't fair to do this in the case of men who earn $20,000 a year, and not to do it in the case of the fellow who earns $1800." See Albany *Evening News*, May 29, 1934, for a specimen of the widespread editorial approval.

2. *Public Papers, 1936*, p. 929.

3. Lehman appointed Poletti as counsel August 29, 1933; the *Knickerbocker Press* of August 30 published a good account of him.

4. *New York Times*, January 19, 1935.

5. Milton Mackaye, *The Tin Box Parade; A Handbook for Larceny* (New York, 1934), 303, 304.

6. To John Haynes Holmes, April 19, 1930; Frank Freidel, *Franklin D. Roosevelt* (Boston, 1952–60), III, 118.

7. *Public Papers, 1934*, 790, 791.

8. *New York Times*, June 20, 21, 22, 1934. The special session cost $65,000.

9. Bills to reform or end malpractices in utility submetering, accounting, and depreciation demands, and to give the Public Service Commission control over interlocking companies, remained unpassed in 1940; *Public Papers, 1940*, p. 26ff.

10. As the Brooklyn *Times* of January 23, 1935, pointed out, in a just reapportionment the Republicans would lose four or five Congressmen upstate and an equal number of state senators, the metropolis acquiring as many. Brooklyn, the Bronx, and Queens would gain, but Manhattan could well lose three seats both in Congress and the state senate.

11. The N.Y. *World-Telegram*, May 21, 1936, observed: "One of the best pieces of non-political advice ever given the people of this state is Gov. Lehman's recommendation to transfer to the Court of Appeals the reapportioning function which the Legislature has shamefully refused to exercise. It took the courage of right-minded fairness and common sense, not politics, to urge that."

12. *New York Times*, April 18, 1935.

13. See the article by Paul Fredrix, *New York Times*, March 5, 1933.

14. *Public Papers, 1934*, pp. 89–91, covers the drafting of the legislation; *idem, 1935*, pp. 324–328, the passage.

15. Arthur M. Schlesinger, Jr., *The Age of Roosevelt: The Coming of the New Deal* (Boston, 1959), 308–315.

16. *Public Papers, 1936*, pp. 302ff.

17. Lehman's radio appeal of May 7 is reported verbatim in the *New York Times* of May 8. The plea was moderate in tone. According to the *Times*, Ives, Fearon, and other leaders had so arranged the legislative schedule that the Republican members could not get home for the weekend; for they feared that pressure by "folks back home" might make some change their minds.

18. Four Republicans (one from Brooklyn and three from Erie County) had joined the Democrats. "Not in the memory of the oldest observers at the capitol has there been such a nip and tuck battle," wrote W. A. Warn in the Albany *Knickerbocker Press* of May 13, 1936.

CHAPTER IX: *Malice Domestic and Foreign Levy*

1. The *New York Sun*, a very conservative Republican organ, opposed Moses in 1934 because he was "a money-spender with the Napoleonic urge to destroy and construct without regard to cost." The *Sun* preferred Lehman on the ground that although he too made the money fly, he was not dictatorial and got a better return; September 29, 1934.
2. Frankfurter to H.H.L., December 27, 1934. Lehman Papers.
3. The *New York Herald-Tribune*, December 9, 1935, has a full account of the crime and its sequels; Russell Owen wrote another good account in the *New York Times*, November 17, 1935.
4. The *New York Times*, September 30–October 3, 1935, presented a fairly thorough coverage of the conference.
5. Lehman in a radio speech of February 23 printed in full in many newspapers was able to say that his sixty-point anticrime program had been generally acclaimed by the press, business organizations, churches, and civic bodies. Hundreds of citizens had written him commendatory letters. But credit, he said, should go to a group of jurists headed by Chief Judge Frederick Crane, to the law revision commission under Dean Charles Burdick of the Cornell Law School, and to the commission on the administration of justice under Senator John Buckley.
6. The editorial comment of the Albany *Knickerbocker Press*, May 15, 1936, was judicious: "The crime program submitted by the Governor contained a majority of meritorious bills and a minority of improper, poorly drawn, or vicious proposals. For the legislature to have swallowed this whole would have been disastrous. Fortunately, the Assembly dissected the program, passed some worthy bills, revamped some others, and rejected some more of the worst, the whole having a salutary effect."
7. Elliott Roosevelt and J. P. Lash, eds., *F.D.R., His Personal Letters*, I, 596, 597; *Public Papers*, 1936, p. 818.
8. *New York Times*, January 7, February 2, 3, 4, 6, April 28, March 2–11, June 3, 1937.
9. James MacGregor Burns, *Roosevelt: The Lion and the Fox* (New York, 1956), 309.
10. Oral History Memoir, Columbia University.
11. Carolin A. Flexner to H.H.L., July 20, 1937. Lehman Papers.
12. Oral History Memoir; conversations of H.H.L. with the author.

CHAPTER X: *Into War*

1. A good brief outline of this financial squabble appears in the *New International Yearbook*, 1939, 1940, article New York State; details may be traced in *Public Papers, 1939–1941*. The N.Y. *Nation*, January 13, 1940 remarked: "With a minimum of rhetoric, Lehman of New York continues to press forward with a progressive program that should be a model to other governors. In his quiet and methodical way this ex-banker has achieved far more than was accomplished by either Smith or Roosevelt in liberal legislation." It reviewed his proposals for state development of waterpower, for improving public control of utilities, for making it easier to oust corrupt judges and municipal officers, for speeding up public housing, and for broadening the rights of the Negro.
2. H.H.L. to Irving Lehman (two letters) July 28, 1939. Lehman Papers.

3. H.H.L. to President Roosevelt, January 10, 1939; Roosevelt to H.H.L., January 11. Lehman Papers.
4. Various men, including Judge Edward Weinfeld, told the author this story.
5. Edward J. Flynn, *You're the Boss: My Story of a Life in Practical Politics* (New York, 1947), 156.
6. Burns, *Roosevelt: The Lion and the Fox*, 427, 428.
7. Oral History Memoir.
8. Oral History Memoir.
9. H.H.L. to President Roosevelt, November 7, 1940. Lehman Papers.
10. *Public Papers of Governor Herbert H. Lehman, 1941*, p. 136.
11. *Ibid.*, 12ff.
12. *Ibid.*, pp. 66off., 722–724.
13. *Ibid.*, 66off.; Oral History Memoir.
14. *Ibid.*, 1942, p. 690.
15. *New York Times*, October 28, 1941.
16. *Public Papers, 1941*, 708–710.

CHAPTER XI: *UNRRA: The Organization of World Relief*

1. As early as May 11, 1942, Roosevelt had written to Lehman of "war work after the first of January." Lehman Papers.
2. In June, 1942, the American and British governments had created the Combined Production and Resources Board, and the Combined Food Board, which were to prove important to any international relief effort. See Robert E. Sherwood, *Roosevelt and Hopkins, An Intimate History* (New York, 1948), p. 578.
3. In the autumn of 1940 Churchill's ministry had established an interdepartmental committee under Leith-Ross to mitigate the embarrassments of overseas food producers and to prepare in advance for the earliest possible relief "of the plundered countries whose resources are being so ruthlessly drained." George Woodbridge, *UNRRA: The History of the United Nations Relief and Rehabilitation Administration* (New York, 1950; three volumes) I, 7–9.
4. A *Report of Proceedings* was published (London, 1941).
5. Hoover to H.H.L., November 25, 1942. Lehman Papers. The lunch was December 3. The Lehman Papers contain a full photostat set of letters exchanged by Hoover and Cordell Hull in 1941, setting forth their divergent views. Hoover was chairman of the Committee on Food for the Small Democracies. In his long letter to Lehman he quoted a Belgian publication: "The whole question is whether the United Nations are fighting to liberate oppressed peoples or to liberate a vast cemetery."
6. *House of Commons Debates*, CCCLXIV, 55.
7. Oral History Memoir, Columbia University Library.
8. Eliot Janeway, *Struggle for Survival* (New Haven, 1951) and Luther H. Gulick, *Administrative Reflections from World War II* (New York, 1948) describe this struggle.
9. Oral History Memoir, Columbia University Library.
10. Lehman and others so state, but Hugh Jackson, who joined Lehman's staff at this time, doubts the lot-drawing; Jackson to the author, February, 1962.
11. Speech File, March 30, 1943, Lehman Papers.
12. Text of speech, May 31, 1943, in Lehman Papers.
13. A careful diary of this trip, kept by Hugh Jackson, is in the Lehman Papers.
14. Though Leith-Ross was very English in appearance, manners, and speech, he struck Hugh Jackson as much like Lehman in temperament and outlook. One of the two fathers of UNRRA and later Deputy Director until May, 1945, he did other Allied war work of importance. See Woodbridge, *UNRRA,* I and II, *passim.* A full collec-

tion of UNRRA records and correspondence is in the United Nations Library, New York.

15. Arthur H. Vandenberg, Jr., and A. H. Morris, eds., *The Private Papers of Senator Vandenberg* (Boston, 1952), 66–74.
16. Dean Acheson, *Sketches from Life of Men I Have Known* (New York, 1961) 124–126.
17. Woodbridge, *UNRRA*, I, 24–32, describes the Atlantic City meeting.
18. Woodbridge, *UNRRA*, I, 81–143. It should be noted that contributions to UNRRA from nongovernmental sources amounted to about $210,000,000, the American people alone giving the equivalent of almost a dollar apiece. Roosevelt appointed Henry J. Kaiser as national chairman of the clothing drive. New Zealand, despite her heavy war strain since 1939, was exceptionally generous.
19. Wide publicity was given Lehman's appointment, plans, and work not only by UNRRA itself, as its records in the United Nations Library show, but by the Office of War Information; see its papers in the National Archives. Woodbridge, *UNRRA*, I, 280–300, describes the immense volume of public information issued. Films describing UNRRA operations were issued by the United States Army, the United Kingdom Ministry of Information, and the National Film Board of Canada.

CHAPTER XII: *The Race Against Human Ruin*

1. Of Yugoslavia, Greece, and the Balkans generally Churchill wrote President Roosevelt October 23, 1943: "We British have about eight separate missions under General Wilson's control working with partisans and patriot bands scattered over these immense mountainous regions, 900 miles by about 300 miles in extent." *Closing the Ring* (Boston, 1951), 466, 467.
2. Chart in Churchill, *Closing the Ring*, 9.
3. *Ibid.*, 224.
4. Woodbridge, *UNRRA*, I, 325.
5. *Journal, Second Council Session*, September 15–27, 1944, pp. 14–58.
6. *New York Times*, November 10, 1944. Woodbridge, I, 347; Argentina made a special gift of 100,000 tons of wheat to Italy early in 1944. *Ibid.*, 130.
7. Charles de Gaulle, *War Memoirs: Unity, 1942–1944* (New York, 1961), 258ff., 330ff.
8. Lehman, MS Diary, November–December, *passim*.
9. Lehman, *Ibid.*, November 20, 1944.
10. *Ibid.*, November 26, 1944.
11. *Ibid.*, November 26, 1944.
12. *Ibid.*, November 29, 1944; notes on meeting with General Gale.
13. *Ibid.*, December 3, 1944.
14. *Ibid.*, December 8, 1944.
15. *Ibid.*, December 12, 1944.

CHAPTER XIII: *Dawn Over the Shambles*

1. Fritz Sauckel, chief Nazi official for utilization of labor, declared in *Trial of the Major War Criminals*, Nuremberg, 1947, Vol. 19, p. 403: "Out of 5,000,000 foreign workers who arrived in Germany, not even 200,000 came voluntarily." George L. Warren, from first-hand experience, ably treats the war refugee problem in *Encyclopaedia Britannica*, 1959, XVI, 59, 60.
2. Hoess, commandant of Auschwitz from May 1, 1940, to December 1, 1943, estimated that in this camp alone 2,500,000 prisoners were in that time exterminated, and 500,000 more died from disease and starvation. Adolph Eichmann estimated that Hitler's policy resulted in the death of six million Jews, of whom two million died

in the extermination institutions. *Trial of the Major German War Prisoners*, Vol. 19, *passim*. Much of this evidence is summarized in Eugene C. Gerhart, *America's Advocate, Robert H. Jackson* (Indianapolis, 1958).

3. The health work of UNRRA is treated in its *Epidemiological Information Bulletin*, February, 1945. This declared, p. 108ff: "So far, diphtheria has turned out to be the leading epidemic disease on the European continent, both as a cause of morbidity and mortality. It is estimated that there were at least one million cases in 1943 outside the USSR. . . . Scarlet fever has spread almost as much as diphtheria. . . . The 'new' disease of the war has been epidemic jaundice (infectious hepatitis)." Polio epidemics appeared in Scandinavia, Holland, central France, and Switzerland; and syphilis increased from threefold to ninefold in some countries, wiping out the gains of twenty years.

4. He kept a careful diary himself, supplemented by letters home; the ensuing pages are founded mainly on these materials.

5. Woodbridge, *UNRRA*, I, 42–3.

6. Woodbridge, *UNRRA*, I, 108.

7. Oral History Memoir, Columbia University Library. The *Washington Post* and *New York Times* of November 23 gave careful reports of Eisenhower's plea. He opposed proposals that the army take over the job. "I would object most seriously," he said. "The Army is not a relief organization." In these five days of hearings, Representatives Vorys of Ohio and Jonkman of Michigan questioned Lehman with such sharp hostility that he became nettled. He replied with a denunciation of the "bitter, carping criticism" of petty opponents and an impassioned defense of UNRRA. Acheson pronounced the agency "one of the foundation blocks of our whole effort to secure a functioning international organization" and declared that the cooperation of forty-four nations which Lehman had organized was "to me an enormous achievement." Assistant Secretary Clayton was equally vigorous. Eisenhower mentioned, with special praise, the recent addition of Sir Frederick Morgan and Sir Humfrey Gale, who had played such important parts in the war effort, to the staff. President William Green of the American Federation of Labor, Mgr. John Boland of the National Catholic Welfare Conference, and representatives of the World Council of Churches made earnest plans for the energetic continuance of UNRRA. *New York Times, New York Herald-Tribune*, November 21–26, 1945.

8. Woodbridge, *UNRRA*, I, 357; II, 371.

9. The term was later extended to the Fifth Council meeting; Woodbridge, *UNRRA*, II, 487.

10. Mrs. Edith Nourse Rogers, a minority member of the House Foreign Affairs Committee, suggested in August, 1945, that the whole UNRRA effort be turned over to the International Red Cross. Representative Clarence J. Brown of Ohio suggested that the United States withdraw relief from any country that curbed its press; he was a newspaper publisher. Senator Overton of Louisiana blew up UNRRA for sending no sweet potatoes to countries whose people did not like them; Louisiana had a sweet potato surplus. But the Fort Wayne *News* really rang the bell (August 30, 1945), terming UNRRA "a clique of professional social workers . . . playing fast and loose with American tax money. Its payroll is padded with any number of persons with no understanding of what they are trying to do. . . . A small well-knit staff of practical, hardheaded Americans who would put more emphasis on common sense and less on social theories, could do the job far better and at a fraction of the cost." Lehman effectively answered such voices in a Thanksgiving Day broadcast over CBS, published in full in the *Washington Post*, November 23, 1945.

CHAPTER XIV: *Final Rewards—and Frustrations*

1. A wealth of UNRRA photographs are preserved in the United Nations Library.
2. Woodbridge, *UNRRA*, I, 244.
3. This figure comprehends resources used as well as cash spent; Woodbridge, III, 499.
4. *Epidemiological Information Bulletin*, II, No. 23 (December 15, 1946, final issue), p. 970. Dr. Sawyer here relates how the Health Division of UNRRA undertook the International Sanitary Conventions of 1944 beginning January 15, 1945, and met emergency duties in Europe and the Orient under war conditions until it transferred its responsibilities on December 1, 1946 to the interim commission of the World Health Organization. In these two years, aided by huge shipments of food, clothing, housing, and fuel, the Health Division did a work without which pestilence and famine over wide areas "would have dwarfed the sad aftermath of World War I." Of the 1,363 professional medical personnel of UNRRA (physicians, sanitary engineers, nurses, dentists) doing international service, the United States furnished 263, the United Kingdom 206, Belgium 104, and France 101.
5. Colonel Alfred Katzin, of UNRRA and later the United Nations, told the author December 10, 1961, that by far the greater number of European refugees "moved themselves" (with various aids) home, but that the "residual tragedy" was overwhelming.
6. New York, 1959, *passim*. Additional light on UNRRA assistance and Soviet recalcitrance is thrown by Ferenc Nagy, *The Struggle Behind the Iron Curtain* (New York, 1948), Konstantin Fotitch, *The War We Lost* (New York, 1948), and Leslie Roberts, *Home from the Cold Wars* (Boston, 1948). But these volumes are primarily political.
7. Operations in China, Korea, and the Philippines are fully if dryly treated in Woodbridge, II, 371–453.
8. *The Rape of Poland* (New York, 1948), 215, 216.
9. Lord Reading, son of the former Rufus Isaacs, who was made a marquess after serving as viceroy of India, spoke in the House of Lords of "UNRRA the Unready" and "The Muscle-Bound Colossus"; *London Times*, December 15, 1944. But most British opinion was highly favorable.
10. Bess Furman in the *New York Times*, September 9, 10, 1945, gave six main reasons why UNRRA leaders, chafing to move, had been delayed, the two chief being that they could not go in while the enemy held fast and that after the enemy was practically subdued, the military said, "Just enough relief to prevent such unrest and disease as would hamper military operations." Miss Furman added: "UNRRA is scouring the world for the supplies to do the job, and with the war ended looks on military surpluses as a good bet."
11. An Army-UNRRA Mission headed by Major General Donald Connolly, of the Army-Navy Liquidation Commission, was in Europe looking for surplus stocks with authority to buy $150,000,000 worth at once and more as UNRRA funds were augmented; Bess Furman in *New York Times*, September 10, 1945; Woodbridge, *UNRRA*, I, 392. Francis B. Sayre of the UNRRA staff reported late in the year that in a tour of India, the Middle East, and South Africa, he had rounded up $47,000,000 worth of surpluses and other relief supplies; *New York Herald-Tribune*, December 21, 1945.
12. Entitled *Herbert H. Lehman, Director General UNRRA, 1943–1946, Tributes and Other Relevant Documents* (Stamford, Connecticut, no date). Lehman's brother-in-law Frank Altschul, owner and director of the Press, used it to publish a number of beautiful volumes.

CHAPTER XV: *In the Post-War Reaction*

1. The demand for change, as Lehman notes in his Oral History Memoir, was world-wide, Churchill had been forced out of power in July, 1945, and Mackenzie King was about to give way in Canada to Louis S. St. Laurent.
2. His most important statements are in *New York Times*, June 21, October 7, 1946. The quotation here is from his United Jewish Appeal address in Washington, February 23, 1947.
3. *New York Times*, July 25, 1946.
4. Truman stated in 1955 that he had read no part of the speech before its delivery; Wallace declared in 1956 that the two had read it page by page, each with a copy. At the moment Communism was making gains all over the world, and Churchill's "iron curtain" speech at Fulton, Missouri, had just gotten a very mixed reception. Byrnes, who agreed with Churchill, reviews the Wallace episode caustically in *All In One Lifetime* (New York, 1958), 370–380.
5. *New York Times*, October 22, 1946, *New York Herald-Tribune*, July 24, 1949.
6. Speech File, September 17, 1948. Lehman Papers.

CHAPTER XVI: *Angry New Senator*

1. *Washington Post*, January 5, 1950.
2. *Jewish Daily Forward*, January 15, 1950. It was also well known that he opposed Truman's health insurance proposals.
3. *New York Times*, January 5, 1950.
4. James F. Byrnes writes in *All In One Lifetime* (New York, 1958), 6, that "the art of legislating is the art of intelligent compromise" and that the tendency of some men to justify an independent course by saying they could never compromise when a principle was involved had little validity. "In my experience, there were really few bills in which a great principle was involved; the issues were usually matters of policy, not principle." This was a view that Lehman was unwilling to accept.
5. In the second volume of his *Memoirs*, entitled *Years of Trial and Hope* (New York, 1956), 262–315, 465–503, Harry S. Truman describes many of his domestic trials.
6. Some scarifying pages upon McCarran and Kerr may be found in Robert S. Allen and William V. Shannon, *The Truman Merry-Go-Round* (New York, 1950); see index for the numerous references. Allen was a press correspondent whom Lehman specially admired. But Lehman remembered it as much to Kerr's credit that he had stood up manfully day after day, following Truman's recall of General MacArthur, to defend the supremacy of the civilian authority over the military. See William S. White, *Citadel: The Story of the U.S. Senate* (New York, 1957), 118.
7. George Wharton Pepper, *In the Senate* (Philadelphia, 1930), Ch. II, "The Senate at Work."
8. September 24, 1950.
9. Each member was sent official records of votes and absences, and Lehman preserved some in his papers. See also Drew Pearson's syndicated press column dated July 2, 1950.
10. Allen and Shannon, *The Truman Merry-Go-Round*, 280, 281.
11. Oral History Memoir, Columbia University Library.
12. The first Special Committee on Un-American Activities under Representative John McCormack in the 1930s had made out a cautious list of tests for determining whether an activity or organization was un-American. If it was under foreign control, if it promoted racial and religious bigotry, and if it tried to establish a principle of dictatorship, it was to be banned. When Representative Martin Dies became head, the committee adopted a much broader test of un-American activity. Congress had

passed legislation in 1938–40 requiring groups subject to foreign control, or inimical to constitutional government, or laboring to overthrow the government by force, to register; the enforcement of these statutes being vested in the Department of Justice. In March, 1947, the Truman Administration had adopted a new loyalty program of broad scope, and by November, 1950, the Attorney General had published a list of 197 interdicted organizations. See Raymond Ogden, *The Dies Committee* (Washington, 1945), and John H. Schaar, *Loyalty in America* (Berkeley, 1957), pp. 150, 151.

13. The fullest source for Lehman's speeches and acts is, of course, the *Congressional Record*, Vols. 96–102 inclusive (1950–1956), well-indexed under his name.

14. Early in his senatorial career Lehman took up the effort to establish a code of fair procedure for Congressional investigating committees, in which Kefauver had been a pioneer; besides these two men, Douglas, Humphrey, Morse and others were involved in the attempt. Kefauver's first proposal was submitted to the Senate in August, 1951. McCarthy's misbehavior made the subject more urgent. In 1954 the men named decided that they should draw up a code on which all of them could agree and laid it before the Senate in May, without result. See Kefauver's speech on resubmitting the code May 17, 1955; *Congressional Record*, Vol. 101, Pt. 5, p. 6405.

15. See Eric F. Goldman, *The Crucial Decade: America 1945–1955* (New York, 1956), 163–165, 171, 172. United Nations casualties in the Korean War approached 500,000, half of them Korean, and perhaps a third American; Walter Langsam, *The World Since 1914* (New York, 1954), 772.

16. For Lehman's battle on Niagara power see *Congressional Record*, Vol. 97, Pts. 12–14.

17. Critical parts of the tidelands oil struggle are covered in *Congressional Record*, Vol. 98, Pt. 3.

18. *New York Post*, October 20, 1950.

CHAPTER XVII: *McCarthyism: A Still Angrier Senator*

1. *Years of Trial and Hope, 1946–1952*, p. 269.

2. The anti-McCarthy newspapers included in New York, the *Times, Herald-Tribune*, and *Post; Baltimore Sun, Washington Post, Louisville Courier-Journal, St. Louis Post-Dispatch, Milwaukee Journal*, and *Christian Science Monitor*. It was the *Courier-Journal* that spoke of McCarthy's "shifting fabric of innuendo, and just plain lies." Conspicuous among his defenders were the Chicago *Tribune* and Los Angeles *Times*, with three widely circulated columnists, George Sokolsky, Westbrook Pegler, and Fulton Lewis, Jr.

3. Jack Andersen and Ronald W. May give a thorough factual treatment to McCarthy down to the date of publication of their book *McCarthy: The Man, the Senator, the "ism"* (Boston, 1952). An appendix, 389–416, covers his relations to public opinion. Richard H. Rovere's brilliant study, *Senator Joe McCarthy* (New York, 1959), contains less detailed information but more interpretation and embodies the results of several interviews with McCarthy.

4. For a tart characterization of Capehart see Allen and Shannon, *Truman Merry-Go-Round*, 289, 290.

5. It should be noted that Catholic leaders who were at first disposed to support McCarthy as an ally in fighting the enemy of religion, Communism, changed front as he adopted immoral methods. The national meeting of Catholic bishops in the autumn of 1951 condemned the use of dishonesty and slander; *New York Times*, November 17, 1951. The able Catholic weekly *Commonweal* attacked him in issue after issue beginning early in 1951.

6. *Senator Joe McCarthy*, 20–23.

7. Oral History Memoir, Columbia University Library.
8. Rovere, *op. cit.*, 23.
9. For this statement and ensuing debates see *Congressional Record*, Vol. 96, Pt. 2
10. Andersen and May, *McCarthy*, 174ff.; Rovere, *op. cit.*, 133
11. *Congressional Record*, Vol. 96, Pt. 2, p. 1958.
12. *Idem*, p. 2133 (February 22, 1950).
13. McCarthy's charges against Jessup were particularly brutal and outrageous. He alleged that Jessup had associated with known Communists in the Institute of Pacific Relations, that he had advocated an end to atom bomb construction in 1946, that he had appeared as a character witness for Alger Hiss, and that he was affiliated with five Communist-front organizations. Lehman's devastating reply of July 21, 1950, is in *Congressional Record*, Vol. 96, Pt. 8, p. 10777.
14. For an effective treatment of the Lattimore case see Rovere, *op. cit.*, 151–153, 169.
15. Lehman said later of McCarthy: "He was the most insensitive man I ever knew. You couldn't insult him. I would assail him in the most scathing terms, and after the debate he would come up grinning, throw his arm around my shoulder, and inquire, 'How are you, Herb?' He seemed to have no sense of the fact that principles of right or wrong were involved. His activities were all part of a political game. If anyone got hurt, it was too bad; but it was part of the game." Oral History Memoir.
16. Acheson caustically remarks in his delightful *Sketches From Life of Men I Have Known* (New York, 1961), p. 54, that for a considerable time it was not clear who was going to furnish leadership, "Dulles and the State Department or Senator McCarthy and Messrs. Cohn and Schine." Cohn Correspondence, Lehman Papers.
17. *Congressional Record*, Vol. 98, Pt. 3, pp. 3944ff (April 10, 1952).
18. *Washington Post*, January 18, 1952.
19. *Congressional Record*, Vol. 98, Pt. 8, p. A639.
20. Speech File, Lehman Papers.
21. Robert J. Donovan, *Eisenhower: The Inside Story* (New York, 1956), 87ff.
22. The *New York Times* hailed the decision of the Circuit Court of Appeals which upheld Judge Weinfeld on August 14, 1956. The *Boston Herald*, August 20, was still more emphatic: "It was essentially the same decision that Judge Bailey Aldrich made in the Kamin case here, to the great irritation of Senator McCarthy. We applaud this decision, as we applauded earlier ones, because it safeguards due process of law from the erosion of Congressional abuse."

CHAPTER XVIII: *The Lonely Independent*

1. See 1960 Census statistics in *New York Times*, July 6, 1962.
2. The Statistical Office of the United Nations publishes accurate data from the latest available censuses throughout the world; see also articles on population in the principal yearbooks for 1960–1962.
3. For debate on the McCarran Bill see *Congressional Record*, Vol. 98, Pts. 4 and 5.
4. May 24–June 13, 1952. For Lehman's final important speech, in which he lashed out at Walter George, see *Congressional Record*, Vol. 98, Pt. 5 (May 22, 1952). The actual drafting of Lehman's proposed omnibus substitute for the McCarran-Walter Act was done by a team of legal experts from all over the country. They included Dean Jefferson B. Fordham of the University of Pennsylvania Law School; Philip B. Perlman, formerly Solicitor-General; the Hon. Benjamin V. Cohen; Carlos Israels of New York; attorneys Jack Wasserman, Richard Schifter, Reuben Lazarus, Joe Fanelli, Ann Petluck, William Males; and the Harvard legal research expert, Charles Schwartz. Lehman contributed to the travel expenses of this group, who generously spent much time for six months in commuting to Washington and working on the

draft of the Omnibus Bill. Senator Humphrey participated actively in the labor. The bill is still, years later, the model embodiment of an enlightened immigration policy.

5. In his *Years of Trial and Hope,* 1946-1952, p. 479, Truman calls the measure "inhuman."

6. Statement before the President's Commission on Immigration and Naturalization, New York, September 30, 1952; Speech File, Lehman Papers.

7. Debate with Francis Walter, April 23, 1953; Speech File, Lehman Papers.

8. Speech to Nationalities Division of Democratic National Committee, May, 6, 1954; Speech File, Lehman Papers.

9. Radio Report to Constituents, April 17, 1955; Speech File, Lehman Papers.

10. Address at Truman Library Dinner, New York, May 8, 1954; Speech File, Lehman Papers.

11. For Lehman's speech on the Hatkin case see *Congressional Record,* Vol. 102, Pt. 6, p. 7567; the *New York Times,* May 7, 1956, reviewed the case.

12. Speech at N.Y. Chapter, Friends' Committee on National Legislation, December 11, 1953; Speech File, Lehman Papers. Roger Baldwin of the American Civil Liberties Union, July 6, 1955, congratulated him on his numerous Senate speeches defending civil liberties and on the recent change in public opinion; "a lot of the credit for this return to sanity goes to you." Lehman Papers.

13. Lehman's address in support of the minority report on civil rights, August 15, 1956, is in his speech file.

14. Lehman Papers.

15. Lehman's part in the debate over the natural gas bill, which ran through January and February, 1956, may be found in the *Congressional Record,* Vol. 102, Pts. 1, 2, and 3. Eisenhower's veto declared of the lobbying: "I deem it to be so arrogant and so much in defiance of acceptable standards of propriety as to risk creating doubt among the American people concerning the integrity of governmental processes"; *New York Times,* February 18, 1956.

16. Pages 182, 183. For typical speeches by Lehman and Douglas demanding that the oil depreciation allowance be reduced from 27.5 percent to 15 percent, see *Congressional Record,* Vol. 100, Pt. 7 (June and July, 1954), pp. 9303, 9315, 9462.

17. White, *The Citadel,* Ch. 7, "The Senate and the Club," 81-94.

CHAPTER XIX: *The Last Good Fight*

1. In "The Shame of New York," N.Y. *Nation,* October 11, 1959.
2. *New York Daily News,* September 13, 1959.
3. Full account in *New York Post,* September 1, 1959. Lehman is a member of the Lexington Democratic Club, and spoke at its annual dinner in January, 1957.
4. *New York Times,* January 23, 1959.
5. *New York Herald-Tribune* editorial, January 24, 1959.
6. *New York Herald-Tribune,* February 16, 1959.
7. *New York Times,* June 12, 1959.
8. *Atlantic Monthly,* October, 1960.
9. *New York Times,* September 17, 1959.
10. *New York Times,* January 18, 1960.
11. *New York Post,* January 19, 1960.
12. *New York Times,* May 16, 1960.
13. June 8, 1960; cf. *New York Herald-Tribune,* June 8, 9.
14. *New York Herald-Tribune,* June 8, 1960.
15. *New York Post, New York Times,* November 9, 1960.
16. *New York Herald-Tribune, New York Daily News,* February 1, 1961.
17. *New York Times,* February 1, 1961.

18. *New York Herald-Tribune*, February 4, *New York Times*, February 6, 1961.
19. *New York Times, New York Post*, April 21, 1961. President Kennedy's involvement in New York City politics had no connection with the reform movement. He was opposed to Prendergast and De Sapio because he felt that they had given him and the party inadequate assistance in the presidential campaign. In view of the widespread dissatisfaction with Prendergast, Kennedy looked with favor upon his replacement by Peter Crotty, if this won approval in the organization and by leading Democrats of New York State. Crotty was originally a liberal-minded political leader who had attained a special position in Buffalo largely because he was the first man of stature there to come out for Harriman in 1954; but he had later become wedded to the ways of machine politics. Lehman made it plain in several statements that he neither supported nor opposed Crotty's candidacy.
20. Radio interview; *New York Daily News*, May 22, 1961.
21. *New York Herald-Tribune*, June 19, 1961.
22. *New York Times*, June 22, 1961.
23. *New York Times*, July 10, 1961.

CHAPTER XX: *Man and Ideas*

1. Harold F. Linder to A.N., December 6, 1961.
2. Reminiscences, Oral History Office, Columbia University Library.
3. Thomas Parran, M.D., to A.N., November, 1961; undated memorandum.
4. H. Eliot Kaplan to A.N. March 6, 1962.
5. Elmo Roper to A.N. December 6, 1961.
6. *The New Yorker*, May 2, May 9, 1936.
7. Samuel D. Leidesdorf to the author November 15, 1961.
8. March 27, 1948; Lehman Papers.
9. Miss Helen Hall (director Henry Street Settlement) to the author, October 27, 1961.
10. Dr. Thomas Parran to the author, September 12, 1961.
11. Memorandum for the author, 1961.
12. Oral History Memoir, Columbia University Library.
13. *The Progressive* (Wisconsin), June 1958. Lehman believed, as he wrote the *Washington Evening Star* of December 1, 1958, "Rule XXII as adopted in 1949 was drafted with only one purpose in mind, to perpetuate the power of Southern Senators to block civil rights legislation, even if such legislation was desired by a substantial majority of the Senate and of the country." Since 1938 almost all filibusters had been conducted against civil rights bills. Senators Douglas, Humphrey, Javits, Case, and others finally did join hands, as Lehman had desired, in a proposal to limit the filibuster by making a Senate vote possible after three periods of extended debate.
14. Elmo Roper to the author, December 6, 1961.
15. Robert Oppenheimer to the author, December 19, 1961.
16. Lehman to Acheson, January 4, 1950.
17. *Washington Post*, April 12, 1951.
18. Speech at Americans for Democratic Action Dinner, February 3, 1956, New York.
19. Barbara Ward's article in the *New York Times Magazine*, March 23, 1958, "Lehman at 80: Young Elder Statesman" was one of many published tributes.
20. Lehman Papers, CAF File "C."
21. *Impressions of Theophrastus Such*; the three statesmen referred to were Eduard Lasker, Jules Simon, and Disraeli.

Index

439